A New History of
Southern Africa

Second Edition

Neil Parsons

MACMILLAN

First published 1982
Reprinted 1983, 1984, 1985, 1989 (twice), 1990
Second edition 1993

Published by THE MACMILLAN PRESS LTD
London and Basingstoke
Associated companies and representatives in Accra,
Auckland, Delhi, Dublin, Gaborone, Hamburg, Harare,
Hong Kong, Kuala Lumpur, Lagos, Manzini, Melbourne,
Mexico City, Nairobi, New York, Singapore, Tokyo.

ISBN 0-333-57010-3

Printed in Hong Kong

For Ann Neo and Jane Semane

Contents

Acknowledgements

Full acknowledgements by the author are listed at the end of the Preface printed in the First Edition. The author wishes to acknowledge the further comments of numerous readers in schools and colleges, and of colleagues most of whom are listed as authors in the Bibliography at the end of this edition.

The author and publishers wish to acknowledge, with thanks, the following photographic sources.
Africana Museum pp140; 181
Argus Africa News Service p327
Associated Press p302 bottom right
BBC Hulton Picture Library pp139; 157; 175 top; 182
Bodleian Library, Oxford pp160 (621.11. r.7 p58); 74 (610. 9s.4 p132); 116 (S610. 9s.4 p51) and (S610. 95.4 p16); 133 (S610. 9s.4 p162; S610 9s.4 p 163; S610. 111r. 48 p372; S610 9s.4 p178); 184 (S624. 1 r22 p375)
British Library pp59; 62; 110
Botswana Information Services p289
Botswana National Archives pp254, 317, 286 to p289
Botswana National Museum p265
By courtesy The British Museum, Natural History p146
Alec Campbell p9
Cape Archives pp11; 12; 63; 65; 95 left; 100; 104; 106; 116 bottom centre; 116 bottom right; 117; 121; 138; 147 top; 147 bottom; 148; 155; 158; 161; 208; 220
The Christian Science Monitor p332
Duggin-Cronin Collection, McGregor Museum, Kimberley, South Africa pp36; 37; 51; 53; 70 bottom; 77; 119; 130
John Hillelson p315 photo Ian Berry
Illustrated London News pp42, 75; 109; 193; 198; 230
International Defence and Aid Fund pp150 left; 173; 187; 203; 216 bottom right; 218 bottom centre, 232; 249 top; 249 bottom; 257, 272 bottom; 278, 281 top; 294; 298; 300; 304; 311; 321 left

Keystone p321 right
Mansell Collection p81 top right, 156
National Archives, Zimbabwe pp29; 70 top 192
Popperfoto p298 bottom
Public Record Office p308
Royal Commonwealth Society pp18 top right; 43; 45; 66; 76; 85; 86; 128; 129; 144; 175 bottom; 207; 228; 286 bottom
The Star p324; 329; 330; 335; 339; 340
August Sycholt p214
Cover illustration: *Die Moord Op Piet Retief*, by permission of South Africa Picture Framing Co. (Pty) Ltd., Capetown, South Africa.

The publishers have made every effort to trace the copyright holders, but if they have inadvertently overlooked any, they will be pleased to make the necessary arrangements at the first opportunity.

The author and publisher would particularly like to acknowledge the assistance of the staff of the following for their help in locating illustrations.
Cape Archives, Capetown
International Defence and Aid Fund
McGregor Museum, Kimberley
National Archives, Zimbabwe
National Museum and Art Gallery, Gaborone
Rhodes House Library, Oxford
Royal Commonwealth Society, London

The author and publishers wish to thank the following who have kindly given permission for the use of copyright material.
Cambridge University Local Examinations Syndicate for questions from the Cambridge International School Certificate Examinations, 1975-1980.
Office of the President, Republic of Botswana, for an extract from a speech by Sir Seretse Khama.

Prefaces

Those who wish to create a future may not lose sight of the past. Therefore look into the past for all that is to be discovered there which is good and beautiful. Form your ideals accordingly, and try to realise those ideals in the future.   *Paul Kruger, 29 June 1904*

We were taught, sometimes in a very positive way, to despise ourselves and our ways of life. We were made to believe that we had no past to speak of, no history to boast of. The past, so far as we were concerned, was just a blank and nothing more. Only the present mattered and we had very little control over it . . .

It should now be our intention to try and retrieve what we can of our past. We should write our own history books, to prove that we did have a past; and that it was a past that was just as worth writing and learning about as any other. We must do this for the simple reason that a nation without a past is a lost nation, and a people without a past is a people without a soul.
Seretse Khama, 19 May 1970

Revised Preface to First Edition

Segregated peoples have segregated histories. The above quotations from Presidents Kruger and Khama show how different groups of people choose to remember — or are obliged to forget — different things about the past. Rulers choose to ignore, and even to suppress, the history and cultural identity of the ruled. British rulers ignored the history of Afrikaners; Afrikaner rulers ignored the history of Africans; and African rulers ignored the history of common families. Older men have traditionally ignored women and children, town dwellers have ignored country dwellers, and farmers have ignored hunter-gatherers.

The segregation of history in colonial Africa began to break down with a new scholarly approach to the history of Africa in the 1960s, which spread southwards in the 1970s. This book was written to present such academic 'new history' in popular form for students of history in southern Africa, and for students of southern Africa elsewhere in the world. The book outlines the history of southern Africa from the later Stone Age to the present day, and focuses on events south of the Limpopo river and north of the Orange river. It uses the findings of academic research to present a narrative which differs from previously published textbooks. It treats the region's past as part of the history of the African continent.

A few readers may want to sit down and read this book from cover to cover. But many will read and re-read the parts that interest them, and will only skim the rest. Special attention has therefore been given to pictures with full captions, which illustrate major themes of the book. There are also references to further reading and an index featuring the main geographical areas, at the end of the book. It is hoped that this book will help push the teaching and examination of history away from the 'cramming' of facts. The details of history in this book are intended to be used by students as evidence to argue a particular interpretation of the past, and for imaginative reconstruction in drama or other classroom projects.

Above all the reader is urged not to accept what this book says as the final word on southern African history. History is constantly re-interpreted and rewritten as our perspectives change because of our present-day experience and the discovery of new knowledge.

Queen Elizabeth House, Oxford
March 1980

Preface to Second Edition

Fifteen years have passed since I started to write this book. It was written mostly at the University of Swaziland, after previous teaching in Botswana and Zambia. It was originally conceived to meet the needs of students leaving secondary school and entering college or university in the independent states of southern Africa. But I was also inspired by the need of student refugees, passing through Swaziland, for knowledge and grounding in the history which had been denied them in South Africa. My approach to the subject was then further developed by a burst of lecturing to university students in the U.S.A., who wanted deeper understanding of southern Africa than appeared in the media.

The First Edition caught the new wave of historical research in southern Africa. The Second Edition now charts some of the tide that followed that wave. It has a new first chapter and a new last chapter. Chapter 1 takes into account developing historical knowledge of the Iron Age. Chapter 21 brings the story of southern Africa up to date from 1968, where the previous edition left off.

Only minor revisions have been made to Chapters 2–20, though major revisions may be necessary in a future edition — following the evidence and conclusions offered by current research. Some of the most exciting current historical research is on the wars of the later 18th and early 19th century. This has made me change the order of Chapters 4–6, restoring the sequence of the original manuscript, to emphasise that European colonization and trade preceded and affected the Mfecane/Difaqane wars. But it is not yet possible to write a radically different narrative within these three chapters.

As before, the most detailed and comprehensive part of the book — which some readers have also found 'most absorbing' — remains its coverage of later 19th century conquest and resistance.

Institute of Commonwealth Studies, London
June 1992

Note to Teachers

This book is designed for students taking final secondary examinations and for students in introductory college or university courses.

The questions set at the end of each chapter, retained from the First Edition, meet the requirements of the Cambridge International Schools Certificate syllabus No. 2160, and of equivalent East and West African Schools Certificates. The exercises appended to the questions are more generally aimed at secondary students, to stimulate interest and reflection. They are in line with curricular approaches emphasising 'critical thought and questioning of inequality and oppression', as in the Cambridge syllabus No. 2166 taken by students in Zimbabwe. The latter syllabus includes 'source-based' and 'stimulus' exercises to direct students to the use of evidence in history — using quotations from documents, statistics or diagrams, pictures and maps, for student comment and analysis.

Three examples of source-based exercises are given on pages 4, 140, and 224 of this edition. The questions asked on each source are of two types: (i) testing the student's basic knowledge and understanding of the source itself; and (ii) assessing the student's powers of analysis, evaluation and empathy — including the background and context of the source. Teachers are encouraged to construct their own exercises using sources and stimulus materials. Picture captions in this book suggest some lines of questioning.

PART I

THE PEOPLING OF SOUTHERN AFRICA

Introduction

The history of southern Africa before European penetration into the interior has been the subject of much new research by archaeologists and historians since the 1960s. The period is open to much more research and reinterpretation, but its general outline in the later Stone Age and Iron Age is now clear enough to be recounted in the following chapters. This part of the book ends with the Mfecane/Difaqane wars of the 1820s and 1830s, which tore apart and reconstructed the two thousand year civilization known to archaeologists as the African Iron Age. That crisis highlights five major themes in the first part of this book:

Geographical environment   Archaeologists and many historians see people as having developed stages of technology and culture appropriate for different environments of climate and vegetation. Each stage of technology and culture might therefore last for thousands of years before it was faced with a crisis of survival in the environment. Such crises were basically natural, such as a drought which might remove the animals that people were hunting. But crises also became increasingly man-made as man's control of the environment led to 'overpopulation' — i.e. greater population than the technology and culture of the time could produce food and shelter to support.

Southern Africa has been through a number of climatic changes in the last 50,000 years — both hotter/drier and colder/wetter than today. At times the Kalahari and Karoo scrublands have been much larger, and at other times moist forestlands have expanded and the Kalahari has seen rivers flowing into a great Makgadikgadi lake. The present ocean shore-line of the southern continent is only three thousand years old. Before that, when the climate was colder the sea-level was lower because of the amount of water frozen into ice in the Antarctic and Arctic oceans. When the sea-level was 140 metres lower 20,000 years ago, there was a coastal plain up to 160 kilometres south of the present south coast — though much narrower on the east and west coasts. All these climatic changes were important for people who lived as hunters and gatherers, because new vegetation meant new wild animals and edible plants for which new weapons and tools might be needed. Vegetation might also change because of the grazing habits of animals, or because of fires caused by people or lightning.

The coming of the Iron Age, with its crop cultivation and livestock grazing, made people more independent of the environment for food. But natural crises became even more disastrous with increased human population, when they destroyed crops and livestock and reduced people to hunting and gathering. The crises had to be met with by new forms of political and economic organization in settled Iron Age societies.

Ethnic identities   Historians are faced with problems over how to identify ethnic groups in the past. Ethnic identities rise and fall, are broken up and disappear, or re-appear in a different form

1

SOUTHERN AFRICA: VEGETATION AND MAJOR RIVERS
Marking land over 1,000 metres above sea level.

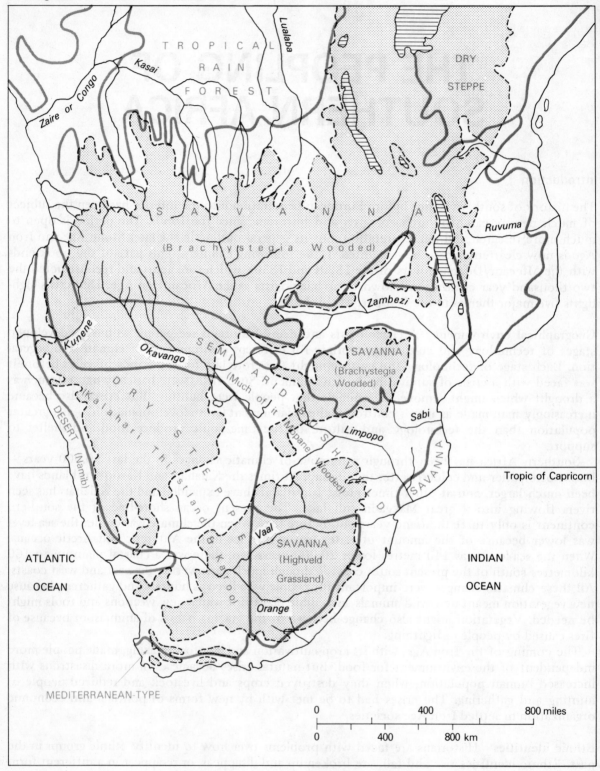

under the same name. For example, 'Zulu' means a small clan in the 18th century, a large kingdom in the 19th century, and a major language group or all black inhabitants of Natal in the 20th century. The histories and even the names of subordinate groups before the Mfecane/ Difaqane have often been forgotten, because history in oral tradition and written records is usually created and preserved by ruling groups. Ethnic groups also rarely have definite boundaries between them, and are even scattered among each other. Chiefdoms and families often included members of a number of ethnic groups, and the laws of male succession which determined a person's ethnic identity were not always followed — especially at times of crisis. The historian's search for ancient ethnic identities is also complicated by archaeologists and historical-linguists, who invent names for the 'cultures' and 'proto-languages' for which they discover evidence in the past. Archaeologists name their 'cultures' (or 'industries') after the site at which a type of pottery or other physical remains were first found. Historical-linguists deduce the form of ancient languages by comparing modern languages, and often name them as 'proto' or early forms of modern languages — hence 'proto-Shona', etc.

Development of states   At what stage of political development can we talk of 'states' being formed — in the sense of a defined population and territory under the control of a single government? African historians generally write of two kinds of pre-colonial state — the chiefdom and the kingdom. The chiefdom was a small state ruled by a hereditary lineage of chiefs: the chief was senior to, but dependent on, the headmen of different clans within the chiefdom. The kingdom was a much larger state, consisting of a number of chiefdoms under a paramount ruler or king, who was often also chief priest-doctor for the whole nation. Such sizeable states, which we may call kingdoms, apparently first appeared in southern Africa around the middle Limpopo valley by the 13th century. But it is misleading to think of all other societies as completely 'stateless'. Even among Khoisan hunter-gatherers there were family elders with governing powers, while Khoisan herders recognized the hereditary head of a senior clan to be a sort of chief. We have no direct knowledge of the kind of chiefdom found in the early Iron Age, except that the compactness of their villages suggests a common form of government.

What caused states to develop? Historians point to the rise of individuals as rulers skilled in warfare or in judgement when rising population led to warfare and disputes. But historians also explain the rise of states more generally as the rise of a ruling class to power in order to control the increasing wealth of production and trade. Thus we find states growing in areas of gold export, and on the ownership and control of cattle.

Rise of social class   Classes in pre-capitalist society were much less distinct and self-conscious than in modern capitalist society. But there were divisions in pre-capitalist society between groups of richer and poorer people who kept somewhat apart from each other. The division of labour into specialized roles began at family level between children and adults, females and males. Such specialization was extended when families lived together under common rule, and especially when there was a surplus of wealth which enabled a ruling class to live off local resources worked by the labour of commoners. This division between a chiefly ruling class and commoners was most obvious in states based on gold export or cattle ownership — where there was an economic surplus beyond what was needed for basic food and shelter. But even then members of chiefly families often engaged in forms of agricultural labour. Only in some of the military-based states that emerged with the Mfecane wars was there ever a large class of people, young men of military age, who did not engage in food production at all, but instead acted as raiders on the resources produced by other people.

Growth of overseas trade   Did the gradual growth of trade with Asian and then European sea traders have good or bad effects on the welfare of African societies? Some historians have suggested that the production of goods for export, such as gold and ivory, stimulated a general growth and specialization of production of goods for local use as well. This in turn helped to create states and to bring a higher standard of living – more food, more tools, more luxuries and more time for cultural activities. Other historians have objected that overseas trade and any rise in local production would only have benefited the overseas traders and the local ruling class. Overseas traders bought costly African goods, such as gold mined and carried by a considerable amount of labour, in exchange for cheap foreign goods, such as liquor and beads, which were quickly consumed and had no value in assisting local production. Only the local ruling class consumed these imported goods, while exploiting the commoners for labour and even selling them as slaves.

Keywords

Stone Age and *Iron Age; climate, vegetation* and *wildlife; technology* and *culture; 'overpopulation'; ethnic group; genealogies* and *lineages; state, chiefdom* and *kingdom; social class; economic specialization* and *surplus; production, trade* and *consumption; rulers* and *commoners; Khoisan* and *Bantu languages; hunter-<u>gatherer</u>, herder* and *farmer.*

Note-taking

Each chapter is divided under a number of main headings and numerous sub-headings at the beginning of paragraphs. These are guides for selective reading and note-taking. The simplest form of note-taking would be to copy down all the headings. But you should go on to note down points of further interest, and you may not always agree with what the printed headings consider important in the text.

Source-based exercise

'The following persons were publicly engaged to be married, as stated in this Evening's Resolution, 6th July, 1658: – Jan Zacharias of Amsterdam, bachelor and freeman, 27 years old, to be married to Maria, spinster, born at Bengal, 20 years old, ex-female slave of the sick comforter Pieter van der Stael, bought into freedom by the bridegroom, as shown by legal transfer. As Maria not only understands Dutch perfectly, but speaks the language plainly, and has a fair knowledge of Christ according to the reformed religion, the fair request of the young people was granted. The first notice to be published next Sunday; after the 3rd banns the marriage is to be performed in the Council Chamber. – Signed by J. van Riebeeck, R. de Man, J. van Harwarden and Abbr. Gabbema, Secretary.' [H. C. V. Leibbrandt (transl. & ed.) *Precis of the Archives of the Cape of Good Hope January, 1656-December, 1858, Riebeeck's Journal, & c.* Cape Town: W. A. Richards & Sons, Government Printers, 1897, p. 141.]

(a) Where and when was the marriage to take place, and what were the nationalities of the bride and bridegroom?
(b) From which parts of Africa and Asia were slaves brought to the Cape of Good Hope, and how were they employed?
(c) Compare the cultural and 'racial' aspects of this marriage with marriages at the Cape in (i) 1800, and (ii) 1950.
(d) Imagine you are Maria. How might she have felt about the marriage?

[There is no right or wrong answer to question (d); credit can only be given for disciplined and realistic use of imagination.]

4

Chapter 1

From the Later Stone Age to the Iron Age

Introduction

Our knowledge of the Stone Age and the Early Iron Age comes mostly from the work of archaeologists.

The *Later Stone Age* developed when people began to make microliths (miniature stone tools), rather than the larger blade-tools which they had made in the Middle Stone Age. We can date this from about 40,000 years ago in the area of southern Zaïre and Zambia, and from about 20,000 years ago in Zimbabwe and along the southern coast of South Africa.*

The *Early Iron Age* began for southern Africa around 2,000 years ago. Comparatively small numbers of people from the north brought with them knowledge of iron-making and the use of iron tools. Iron Age farming communities developed in the areas with better rainfall as far south-east as the Ciskei. Eventually, even people who lived by hunting and gathering in desert areas were using iron for their arrow-heads and other tools. By maybe 150 or 250 years ago the art of making microliths had disappeared from southern Africa.

*Archaeological remains up to 40,000 years old can be dated in special laboratories by the radio-carbon dating process. The laboratories measure the amounts of two types of carbon in former living matter, such as wood, bone and shell. The amount of ordinary carbon (known as Carbon-12) remains constant with age. It is compared with the amount of radio-active carbon (Carbon-14) which reduces itself by half every 5,568 years. Radio-carbon dating laboratories give us a carbon-date, with a margin of error, such as 900 AD ± 50. That means sometime between 850 and 950, in the later 9th or early 10th century.

We are still living in a sort of Iron Age, as our basic tools and machines are made of iron and steel. But our iron and steel tools are manufactured by great centres of industry rather than by small craftworkers.

All the main developments of the Stone Age probably originated in Africa. The earliest evidence of Early Stone Age core-tools and the earliest evidence of Middle Stone Age blade-tools are from Africa. Africa also probably saw the earliest development of Later Stone Age microliths, maybe 100,000 years ago. But the Iron Age seems to have originated in western Asia and then spread to Africa.

1 Later Stone Age Hunter-Gatherers

The Later Stone Age people of southern Africa spoke Khoisan languages, and lived by hunting or fishing and gathering wild foods (*veldkos*). Our knowledge of these people comes from excavation and study of their settlements (archaeology) — and also from study of the language (linguistics) and the study of the culture (anthropology) of recent Khoisan-speaking people.

Khoisan languages   The term Khoisan is used by linguists to include the languages of both the people who call themselves *Khoi* ('person'), and the languages of the peoples who are called *San* ('other people') by the Khoi.*

*The plural of *Khoi* is *Khoin*, and the singular of *San* is *Sa*. The *Khoi* people at the Cape called themselves *Khoikhoi*, while other Khoi people in the north called themselves *Khoc*, *Khwe*, *Kxoe*, etc.

STONE AGE TOOLS

How stone tools were made. Stone Age tools were made from rock with a high silica content, which splits along the lines of shock waves when it is hammered. You can see these shock waves yourself if you hammer a thick piece of glass, like a bottle bottom. Glass is almost pure silica.

Four basic types of stone tool. A core-tool is the name given to a piece of rock from which flakes had been chipped. A flake-tool is the name given to a flake from a core, from which smaller flakes had been chipped. A blade-tool is the name given to a flake with parallel sharp sides, twice as long as its width. A microlith (micro-tool) is the name given to a very small flake, often no bigger than a postage stamp. Core-tools and flake-tools were used throughout the Stone Age; blade-tools were first used in the middle Stone

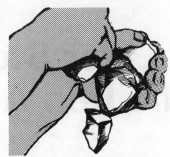

One stone used as a hammer against another for rough shaping of a tool

A piece of wood or bone being used as a chisel for fine shaping of a tool

Age; and microliths were first used in the later Stone Age.

How stone tools were used. Core-tools were usually large and heavy, being held in the palm of the hand. They were used for chopping and digging. Flake-tools were small enough to be held in the hand as a bulky knife with a cutting edge — or could be hafted

onto a wooden handle or spear with grass twine and vegetable glues. Microliths were used as barbs on the heads of wooden arrows or harpoons, as small blades for carving bone and wood into sewing needles, for cutting grass twine, and as small scrapers for preparing animal skins for clothing.

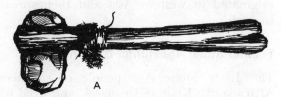

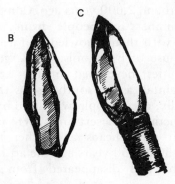

Recent Australian Stone Age tools (A & C) illustrate how African Stone Age tools could have been hafted with twine and glue onto handles. The flake-tool marked B is a Middle Stone Age tool found in the Transvaal.

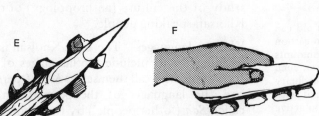

Later Stone Age microliths hafted with vegetable glue as barbs into a wooden arrow head (E), as razors in a wood or bone knife handle (F), and as a crescent-shaped adze head in a lump of vegetable glue attached to a bone handle (G).

Khoisan languages have numerous 'click' sounds (implosive consonants) — and are still spoken as far north as the Kwadi of southern Angola, and the Hadza and Sandawe of northern Tanzania. Linguists and archaeologists think that Khoisan languages were spoken during the Later Stone Age, up to perhaps 10,000 years ago, on the eastern grasslands as far north as southern Sudan and Ethiopia.

The earliest non-Khoisan language group to spread among the Khoisan-speaking peoples of eastern Africa were speakers of Central Sudanic languages. These Central Sudanic-speakers were hunter-gatherers, originating from the Sudanic grasslands north-west of Uganda up to 7–10,000 years ago.

Central Sudanic people were later followed southwards by speakers of other language groups. Eastern Sudanic (Nilotic) and Cushitic speakers ventured as far south as northern Tanzania. Then, within the last thousand years BC, Eastern Bantu-speakers from the Lake Victoria region followed Central Sudanic-speakers even further southwards.

By 500 BC (1,500 years ago) Central Sudanic speakers had possibly reached as far south as Zambia, where they were overtaken by the southward spread of both Western and Eastern Bantu-speakers.

Khoisan racial types People in Africa south of the Sahara consisted of Khoisanoid and Negroid racial types, closely related together within the African family of the human race. Khoisanoid peoples on the grasslands of eastern and southern Africa could almost be called 'yellow Negroes', while Negroid peoples in the forestlands of western coastal Africa could be called 'black Khoisan'.

The earliest skeletons of modern humans found in Africa south of the Sahara are of Khoisanoid racial type — as far north as Sudan, and as old as 120,000 years in Swaziland. The earliest Negroid skeleton, so far discovered by archaeologists, is only 6,000 years old (4000 BC).

Skeletons do not last long in the wet and acidic soils of the West African forests. But the much greater age of Khoisanoid skeletons suggests that Negroid people descended from

Khoisanoid people who migrated from the eastern grasslands to the western forests of Africa, where they developed darker skins over many generations.

The spread of Negroid people to areas outside western coastal Africa may have occurred 4000–3000 BC. They migrated eastwards and southwards through the forestlands and on to the grasslands, marrying with but reproducing faster than their Khoisanoid relatives already living there.

The descendants of Khoisan-speaking people today in southern Africa range from shorter and lighter-skinned people in remote desert areas, to taller and darker-skinned people around rivers and marshlands.

Origins of microlithic technology Hunter-gatherers developed microliths by progressively reducing the size of their blade-tools during the Middle Stone Age. This development in technology was probably a response to environmental change. As the climate grew wetter, areas of dense woodland spread over

KNOWN DISTRIBUTION OF LATER STONE AGE HUNTER-GATHERERS IN THE 18th-19th CENTURIES

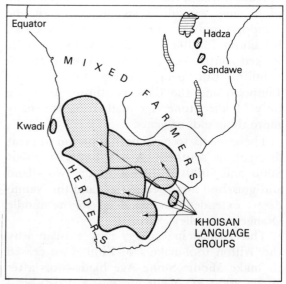

Smaller groups, usually known as Twa, survived along rivers and marshes in south-central Africa. Distribution of hunter-gatherers overlapped with that of mixed farmers and herders.

grasslands on the highlands of eastern Africa.

From maybe 40,000 BC the hunter-gatherers of the new woodlands north of the Zambezi and south of Lake Victoria needed to use light-weight bows and arrows, rather than the heavy spears previously used on the grasslands. Harpoons were needed to catch fish in the fast-slowing rivers. People therefore began to make microliths as barbs for the pointed heads of their arrows and harpoons, and as knives or scrapers for making clothing and utensils out of grass twine and animal skins.

Archaeologists distinguish between three main traditions of Later Stone Age culture in Africa south of the equator — the *Tshitolan* tradition in the forests of Zaïre, the *Nachiku-fuan* tradition in the woodlands of southern Zaïre and Zambia, and the *Wilton* tradition on the grasslands of eastern and southern Africa.

Nachikufuan people made and used many grind-stones for crushing the nuts and seeds of the woodlands, while Wilton people used digging sticks — weighted by a stone ring — for rooting out underground plants and tasty termites on the grasslands.

Spread of Wilton tradition Wilton technology of making microliths spread north of the Limpopo, and also to the southern Cape coast, by about 20,000 BC. Cape Wilton people looked south over wide coastal plains full of wildlife. But people living between the Limpopo and the Cape continued to make only Middle Stone Age blade-tools for many more thousands of years.

There seems to have been a period of great drought in southern Africa between about 8000 and 4000 BC. Areas of dry woodland and grassland increased in size, and the Namib desert extended far inland up to the middle Orange river valley.

This change in ecology may explain why the Wilton tool-makers of Zimbabwe ceased to make Middle Stone Age blade-tools after about 8000 BC, while increasing their use of weighted digging-sticks.

The warming of the climate also made the coastal plains of the south coast begin to dis-

appear, as the melting icebergs of Antarctica raised the level of the southern seas. Cape Wilton people, with their lightweight bows-and-arrows, though without weighted digging-sticks, began to look to the hunting lands of the north.

The Wilton tradition of Zimbabwe, with its digging-sticks as well as microliths, spread as far as the central Transvaal by 6500 BC. Wilton people were living along the Magaliesberg hills in small scattered groups.

The Cape Wilton tradition spread north after about 5000 BC, as far as the highveld grasslands of the Orange Free State and Transvaal. There it combined with the northern Wilton tradition in what archaeologists have called the *Smithfield* culture.

By 3600 BC Cape Wilton hunter-gatherers had also re-occupied the middle Orange river valley, which had been an unpopulated desert for 5,000 years.

Hunter-gatherer economy and culture By about 1300 BC — at least at the Cape — the Wilton tradition had reached a stage of technological development, in its tools, that survived until AD 1700 or 1800. But there have been great changes in the life style of Khoisan-speaking people over the past 2,000 years, and especially the last 200 or 300 years. We must be cautious in reconstructing the economy and culture of the Later Stone Age from recent evidence of Khoisan hunter-gatherers.

Gathering food The diet of hunter-gatherers included more vegetables and fruit than meat. People lived more by gathering wild plants, and trapping small animals, than by hunting larger wildlife. Most food gathering was done by women. They regularly left the camp to pick plants, or to dig up roots and tubers with digging-sticks — as well as to gather firewood for cooking. Small children and girls assisted their mothers.

Men assisted in digging up termite nests, collecting caterpillars and honey, gathering plants and leaves for medicine or poison. Men and boys made traps from grass twine and sticks to catch birds and edible rodents or reptiles.

Khoisan hunter-gatherers   Sarwa or 'Bushmen' boys in Botswana making fire by use of friction. One stick is drilled, by rubbing backwards and forwards between the palms, into another stick, until a flame is produced at the point of friction.

Hunting   Hunting might take days or even weeks away from home. Most hunting was by men using bows-and-arrows to kill wild buck and antelopes, among which the eland was the most prized for its meat. Animals as big as giraffe could be hunted with poison-tipped arrows. (People made sure the poison had drained out of the meat before eating it.)

In some areas, people used heavy spears to hunt elephants. In other areas, hippos might be killed by a heavily-weighted spear dropped from a tree. Hunters were often assisted by domesticated dogs. The long-nosed yellow (or black) type of dog, still familiar in rural areas today, originally came from the north, but was being kept by hunter-gatherers at the Cape by 1000 BC.

People near rivers and marshes lived by fishing, using harpoons (spears with barbed heads), trapping fish in dammed pools and gathering freshwater shell-fish. Similarly along the sea coasts, people collected shell-fish from rock pools, as well as trapping sea fish. These *strandlopers* or 'beach-combers' have left enormous piles of empty shells along the coasts of southern Africa.

Social organization   Khoisan hunter-gatherer societies were organized around the relationship known as *hxaro* — meaning the exchange of goods between 'woman the gatherer' and 'man the hunter' within each family. But families were patriarchal — with older men, and to some extent older women, controlling young men and women.

Hunter-gatherers lived in small groups ('bands') of families. In semi-desert country, where people had to be always ready to move after herds of wildlife, each band might be as small as 25 people in all. In the wetter grasslands and woodlands, and along the south coast, where water and vegetation or seafood were more plentiful, a band might be as large as 100 people. Smaller bands might also live together in a larger band in semi-permanent camps at some times of the year.

Each band had a territory, which it marked out with camp-sites. A camp consisted of small huts of grass or skins stretched over a frame of branches and twigs. Camps might by moved five or six times a year, returning to the same site every few years. In hilly country, camps might return to the same site in winter every year, at places where people could spy herds of game from a far distance.

Art and religion   There are many thousands of rock paintings and engravings surviving in hilly regions of southern Africa. Most of these are 'naturalistic' art portraying wild animals or humans, while others are 'schematic' art consisting of geometric patterns. Over the past few years, archaeologists have begun to offer detailed explanations of this rock art.

Nearly all the rock art which survives today, is probably less than 2,000 or 3,000 years old, as the weather washes it away. The oldest dated rock art in southern Africa is in Apollo-11 cave in the Huns mountains of Namibia, just north of the lower Orange river. It was buried in the Middle Stone Age when part of the cave collapsed, and it has been dated around 24,000 BC. However, it is of a different style to Later Stone Age rock art.

Some 'naturalistic' rock art records events, such as fights and battles between people, and even the coming of ships and waggons in the last few hundred years. Some 'schematic' art, mainly engravings, is probably a kind of map, recording the whereabouts of water-holes and camps. But most rock art is probably concerned with religion and magic.

Rock art of animals may have given hunters magical powers over the animals they hunted. But many paintings and engravings portray animals that were not common or were rarely hunted. There are also many similarities between the pictures and magical stories that are still told today, especially about medical practices and rain-making.

Many of the rock art sites were probably kept for secret ceremonies. Healers and rain-doctors, whom anthropologists sometimes call *shamans**, used the sites to prepare them-

Shaman: Russian and modern Greek word for a traditional healer.

selves for healing ceremonies and rain-making.

Painting new pictures on the rock, with animal grease and coloured pigments, might help healers to become 'entranced' or 'possessed' by animal-spirits — when they danced around the camp-fire that night. Paintings of beasts such as rhino and eland, which had grown strong from eating grass, may have given strength for rain-making.

Some archaeologists argue that the *shamans* needed to paint and engrave pictures, in order to hang on to power over their land, after stock-herders and crop-farmers had begun to challenge the land rights of hunter-gatherers. Hunter-gatherer *shamans* were sometimes paid by herders and farmers to bring rain.

But we cannot assume that all rock art was 'Bushman art' made by Khoisan hunter-gatherers. Some schematic rock art north of the Zambezi was certainly made during the secret boys' initiation schools of Iron Age farming peoples.

DISTRIBUTION AND ORIGINS OF DOMESTIC LIVESTOCK

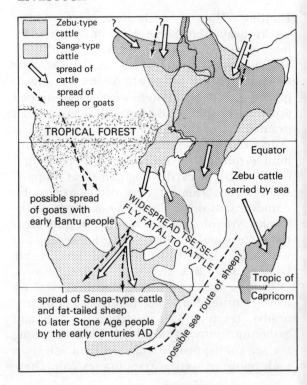

POSSIBLE ORIGINS OF LATER STONE AGE
HERDING

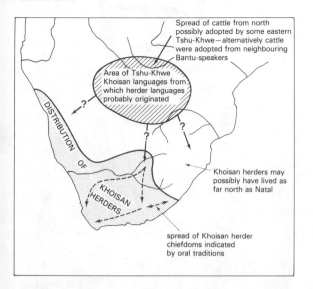

Spread of cattle from north
possibly adopted by some eastern
Tshu-Khwe—alternatively cattle
were adopted from neighbouring
Bantu-speakers

Area of Tshu-Khwe
Khoisan languages from
which herder languages
probably originated

DISTRIBUTION OF KHOISAN HERDERS

Khoisan herders may
possibly have lived as
far north as Natal

spread of Khoisan herder
chiefdoms indicated
by oral traditions

2 Later Stone Age Livestock Herders

During the last few hundred years of the **BC** era, some Khoisan-speaking people in southern Africa began to herd sheep and cattle, and to make a kind of clay pottery. Remains of such Later Stone Age pottery, found near Windhoek, have been carbon-dated to the 3rd–2nd century BC (around 205 BC). Remains of sheep bones and this pottery, found near the Cape of Good Hope, have been dated in the 1st century BC (around 70 BC).

Origins of livestock herding   In western Asia, sheep were domesticated around 9000 **BC** and cattle around 6500–6000 **BC**. Archaeologists debate whether sheep and cattle were being domesticated in eastern and northern Africa at the same time or even earlier. Shells found with clay pottery, which is associated with

Khoisan herders with their livestock   Scene of a Kora village on the Orange river, by the artist Samuel Daniell (1801). Note the dome-shaped housing, made of woven grass mats on a curved wooden frame. Pots of water or milk hang for cooling on a stand by the front door.

sheep and cattle herders, have been carbon-dated around 6470 BC in Kenya. But more research is needed to confirm this dating for the pottery.

By around 7470 BC the local Wilton tradition of Kenya and Uganda, and the marshlands of the Sudanic belt, had been replaced by a Later Stone Age tradition of people hunting and fishing with bone-headed harpoons. But there is no certain evidence of sheep and cattle herding until the Kenya-Capsian culture of the Late Stone Age, which lasted from about 4000 to about 1000 BC. Kenya-Capsian people made stone bowls, which were probably used for cooking milk and meat.

How then were sheep and cattle, and the making of clay pottery, brought through southern Africa as far south as the Cape?

Archaeological evidence Fat-tailed sheep and heavy Sanga-type cattle came to the grass-lands of southern Africa from the grass-lands of East Africa. They must have been herded along the highlands between Lakes Tanganyika and Malawi (across what is now the Tanzania-Zambia border).

The Tanganyika-Malawi highlands were infested by *tsetse*-fly, whose bite is fatal to livestock. But at certain times of extreme drought, when the woodlands dried up, the highest land became free of *tsetse*-fly. This would have allowed sheep and cattle along the highlands of north-eastern Zambia through to the south.

There is evidence of changing climate around 3000 BC in northern Botswana. The Okavango delta and the Makgadikgadi pans were fed by the rains of central Angola and western Zimbabwe. They had become lakes as their water levels rose in the humid period after 4000 BC. But by 3000 BC they were beginning to dry up again, first into marsh-lands and then into rich grassland in the period between 3000 and 500 BC. This grass-land would have been excellent pasture for large robust cattle until it dried up again. Pastures recovered with higher lake levels between 500 BC and AD 1000, when the herding of cattle was also taken to the south

Khoisan herder woman 'Hottentot' woman sketched by Samuel Daniell. She wears a fur cloak, necklaces made from ostrich eggshell beads, and earrings. The reed container hanging from a necklace may have contained medicine or snuff.

as far as the Cape of Good Hope.

A few stone bowls of the Kenya-Capsian type have been found north of Windhoek, south-west of Gaborone, and near Kimberley. None of the sites have been carbon-dated, but could they be evidence of who brought sheep and cattle south?

Linguistic evidence Linguists have shown that the Khoisan words for sheep (*gu*, or *ku*) and cattle (*goma*, or *koma*) are originally from the Central Sudanic language group of eastern Africa. This suggests that Central Sudanic herders might have brought sheep and cattle to Khoisan hunter-gatherers living north of the Okavango and Makgadikgadi lakes. The linguist Christopher Ehret suggests that this happened around 500 BC.

12

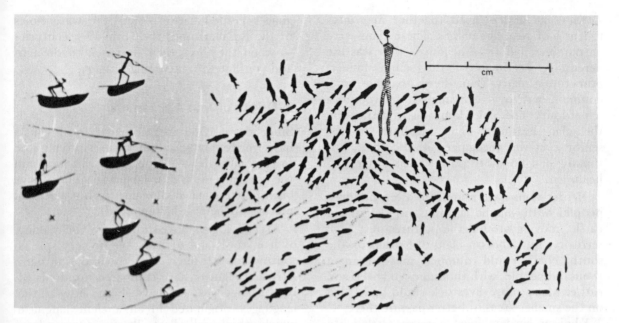

Fishermen in canoes — copy of a rock painting from the Mpongweni mountains in south western Lesotho. (Each fisherman is about 1.5cm high.) The earliest recorded date for a piece of rock art is about 25,000 BC for a slab of rock buried beneath material which could be carbon-dated at 'Apollo 11' cave in Namibia just north of the Orange River.

How were rock paintings made? Ladders, consisting of tree stems with lopped off branches, must have been used for painting on high walls. Pigments consisted of ground and powdered iron ores — red haematite, yellow limonite, and black specularite — or coloured muds, with bird droppings used for white. The pigments were probably mixed with egg or grease to make them into more permanent paints. A Khoisan artist, killed by whites in the 19th century, was found to be wearing a leather belt which held antelope horns in which different paints had been mixed.

Another linguist, E. O. Westphal, has shown that all Khoi herders' languages, as far south as the Cape of Good Hope, were derived from the Khoi or Khoe (Tshu-Khwe) languages spoken around the ancient Okavango and Makgadikgadi lakes. Khoi herders from northern Botswana would have taken sheep and cattle southwards to Namibia and the Cape.

Oral evidence These views are supported by oral traditions of the Nama and Khoikhoi of the Cape, who trace their chiefdoms back to Kora of the Kimberley and Orange Free State areas.* Nama traditions indicate origins up

*'Korana' and 'Namaqua' are the plural forms of Kora and Nama. Other Khoisan languages use the plural suffix '—ra'. Plural forms are not used in this book with the exceptions of Inqua, Griqua, and Damara — better known and understood than I, Gri and Dama.

the Orange (Gariep) river among early Kora. Khoikhoi on the coast trace their chiefs back to the Inqua of the Cape Folded mountains. Though Inqua traditions suggest origins in Ciskei/Transkei, some historians suggest earlier Kora origins.

Herder economy and culture Khoisan herders organised their lives around the pasturing and protection of livestock. They drank the milk of their sheep and cattle; and killed their sheep more often than their cattle for meat. Milk was kept in large and heavy pointed-base clay pots, hung from a branch, and was drunk after souring. The fat from sheep's tails was also stored in pots.

Livestock were the first form of substantial wealth. It was a form of property that could reproduce itself faster than it was consumed. Some families in Khoisan herder society therefore grew richer than others.

Khoisan herders lived together in groups ('clans') of related families. These clans were patriarchies, led by a headman who was the hereditary headman of the senior family. Sometimes many clans lived together in a common territory in a small state we call a 'chiefdom'. The chiefdom was governed by the clan headmen. The headman of the senior clan was recognized as the chief, but usually had no more power than other clan headmen.

Herder clans each numbered a few hundred people, with maybe a thousand sheep and cattle, moving around the pastures of a large territory. But Khoisan clans of herders on the south coast could number more than a thousand people, with thousands of sheep and cattle. Many more livestock could be herded on the smaller areas of better pasture there.

Khoisan herders lived a more settled life than hunter-gatherers, though they moved around their territory through the year to find the best winter and summer grazing for their livestock. Their houses were stronger than those of hunter-gatherers. Their dome-shaped (or bee-hive) houses consisted of a strong wooden frame, covered by woven grass matting and maybe animal skins. These houses could be carried away on the backs of oxen. Oxen were used for riding: the rider sat on the ox's back, controlling it with a stick in the beast's nostrils.

Khoisan herders and hunter-gatherers often lived together. Hunter-gatherers might become herders by first becoming the servants of livestock owners, and then by owning livestock themselves. This helps to explain how a small number of Khoi-speaking herders, from the far north, could convert a large number of hunter-gatherers at the Cape to herding livestock and speaking their northern language.

Khoisan herders continued to hunt and gather, as well as to herd and make pottery. Some might become purely hunter-gatherers again if they lost their livestock in drought or conflict, or when they moved to places unsuitable for livestock. This may explain why *strandlopers* on the south coast spoke Khoi instead of San languages.

People speaking San as well as Khoi languages herded cattle around the water-holes of the Kalahari until the 18th–19th centuries — when they lost their livestock to drought and conflict with incoming farmers.

3 Origins of Iron Age Farming

Since about 1960 archaeologists and linguists have made many advances in studying the origins and spread of Iron Age civilization and the speaking of Bantu languages. There have been debates and disagreements, but a general picture of the past has emerged.

Archaeologists have shown how the making of iron tools and of Iron Age pottery spread southwards through eastern and southern Africa. Linguists have compared hundreds of Bantu languages, and have shown how all the languages originated in an ancient language which they call Proto-Bantu. Comparison with non-Bantu languages in Africa shows that the Proto-Bantu language must have been spoken in the area of modern Cameroun, on the eastern side of Nigeria.

Origin of Bantu languages   More than 400 different Bantu languages are spoken today in Africa. The languages are classified as a single language-group because every one of them has a noun root similar to -*ntu* for 'person' and a prefix like *ba-* (*e.g. aba-, vha-, ova, wa-,* or *a-*) for that class of noun. All of the Bantu languages of Africa are about as closely related to each other as the Germanic languages of Europe including English and Afrikaans-Dutch.

Linguists place the Bantu language-group within the 'Niger-Congo' language family. It is closely related to other language-groups in that family in Cameroun and east-central Nigeria. Linguists have suggested how the original Proto-Bantu language in that area, spread eastwards and southwards. It developed new dialects which in time became separate languages, and which themselves in turn spread and developed new dialects which became separate languages. And so on, until after a few thousand years, up to half the continent had been covered by Bantu languages.

Bantu languages developed into two main

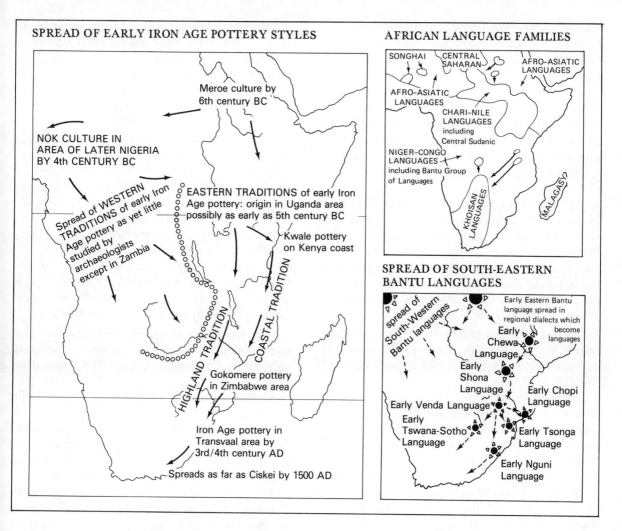

SPREAD OF EARLY IRON AGE POTTERY STYLES

Meroe culture by 6th century BC

NOK CULTURE IN AREA OF LATER NIGERIA BY 4th CENTURY BC

Spread of WESTERN TRADITIONS of early Iron Age pottery as yet little studied by archaeologists except in Zambia

EASTERN TRADITIONS of early Iron Age pottery: origin in Uganda area possibly as early as 5th century BC

Kwale pottery on Kenya coast

COASTAL TRADITION

HIGHLAND TRADITION

Gokomere pottery in Zimbabwe area

Iron Age pottery in Transvaal area by 3rd/4th century AD

Spreads as far as Ciskei by 1500 AD

AFRICAN LANGUAGE FAMILIES

SONGHAI

CENTRAL SAHARAN

AFRO-ASIATIC LANGUAGES

AFRO-ASIATIC LANGUAGES

CHARI-NILE LANGUAGES including Central Sudanic

NIGER-CONGO LANGUAGES including Bantu Group of Languages

KHOISAN LANGUAGES

MALAGASY

SPREAD OF SOUTH-EASTERN BANTU LANGUAGES

spread of South-Western Bantu languages

Early Eastern Bantu language spread in regional dialects which become languages

Early Chewa Language

Early Shona Language

Early Chopi Language

Early Venda Language

Early Tswana-Sotho Language

Early Tsonga Language

Early Nguni Language

---

sub-groups. The sub-group of *Western Bantu* languages covers the tropical forests between Cameroun and Zaïre, and extends over the Angolan and western Zambian grasslands south of the forests. The sub-group of *Eastern Bantu* covers the eastern grasslands of Africa, from around Lake Victoria extending south of the Limpopo. (The South-Eastern Bantu languages, including Shona, Venda, Chopi, Tsonga, Sotho-Tswana, and Nguni are therefore a 'sub-sub-group'.)

Most linguists now believe that Western and Eastern Bantu languages split from the original Proto-Bantu in the Cameroun area. Eastern Bantu languages spread eastwards along the Sudanic grasslands to the area of Lake Victoria in East Africa. Western Bantu languages spread southwards into the forest-

lands of the Congo-Zaïre basin.

Eastern and Western Bantu languages met again around in eastern and southern Zaïre and interacted together in their spread further southwards. This view of linguists, as we shall see, fits in well with archaeological evidence for the spread of the Iron Age.

Linguistic evidence shows that the original Proto-Bantu people were Late Stone Age farmers cultivating crops with wooden hoes — without knowing about metals. They kept goats and dogs, and also made clay pottery.

Archaeological evidence shows that Late Stone Age farmers further west, on the coast of modern Ghana, were harvesting oil palm seeds and making clay pottery from about 4000 BC. They were also making the polished stone-tools that are called 'Neolithic' by

15

archaeologists. We know that Late Stone Age farming in Cameroun was similar to the Ghana coast, but we have no dates for it anything like as early.

The adoption of Neolithic farming by Late Stone Age people explains the population growth of Negroid farmers in West Africa during the last few thousand years BC. It also explains the expansion of people of Bantu-speaking Negroid farmers southwards and eastwards.

By 900 BC archaeologists believe Neolithic farmers were cultivating oil-palm seeds on the west coast as far south as the mouth of the Congo-Zaïre river. Archaeologists have found the remains of their pottery and polished stone tools. This shows that the expansion of the Proto-Bantu southwards in West-Central Africa was before the Iron Age.

Origins of Iron Age technology The Iron Age began around the 7th century BC, at about the same time, in East Africa as in North and West Africa.*

In West Africa there is evidence of iron making in the Termit massif mountains northwest of Lake Chad from about 678 BC. Iron making had reached Nok in Nigeria — not far from the original Proto-Bantu area — by around 590 BC.

By around 300 BC the Neolithic farmers on the west coast on the mouth of the Congo-Zaïre river were beginning to use iron tools. By around 175 BC they were making the kind of pottery that is called 'Western Stream' (see below).

In East Africa, iron making had certainly begun around Lake Victoria in East Africa by about 685 BC. Some archaeologists argue that it began in Rwanda, south-west of Lake Victoria, as far back as around 1230 BC.

These early dates in West and East Africa suggest that iron-making may have been invented in Africa independently from its origins in western Asia. Alternatively, know-ledge spread across the Red Sea to the Sudanic Belt at the same time as, or even before, it reached Ancient Egypt.

Spread of Iron Age farming Archaeologists trace the spread of the Iron Age by identifying and dating types of pottery found in excavations. People showed their common culture by making pottery of similar shape and patterning over many generations.

In publications of 1973–77 the archaeologist David Phillipson** outlined the spread of the Iron Age, using analysis of different pottery styles and more than 400 carbon-dates from archaeological research in East Africa, Zambia and Zimbabwe. Phillipson showed that eastern African pottery styles of the Early Iron Age originated from the style known as *Urewe*, in the Uganda area near Lake Victoria in the last few centuries BC.

The Urewe tradition of the Early Iron Age then spread southwards, in what Phillipson called the *Eastern Stream* of the Early Iron Age.

Phillipson identified two traditions of the Eastern Stream moving southwards — the *Highland tradition* moving through inland Tanzania into Malawi and eastern Zambia, and the *Coastal tradition* moving from the Kenya coast down to the coast of Mozambique.

Phillipson also identified, in western Zambia, the southern end of a *Western Stream* of the Early Iron Age. This he assumed to have come from Angola and the Congo-Zaïre basin, and originally from the Proto-Bantu homeland in the Cameroun area.

Phillipson's ideas have been revised by new archaeological studies in South Africa, Botswana and the mouth of the Congo-Zaïre river. This research shows that most of the earliest Early Age sites south of the Limpopo have pottery of the Western Stream, not the Eastern Stream. Archaeologists are still debating, but we can outline a general picture of how the Iron Age came to southern Africa.*

---

*Smelting and forging of iron originated in the area of modern Turkey-Syria-Iraq, about 1700 BC. But the new technology was kept secret for a thousand years, and only reached Egypt in the 7th century BC.
**See C23 Phillipson in Bibliography, pp. 337–42.

*Some archaeologists refer to the Eastern Stream as the Urewe tradition, and its Coastal and Highland traditions as its Kwale and Nkope branches. Similarly, the Western Stream may be referred to as the Kalundu tradition. The Urewe and Kalundu traditions may be together called the Chifumbaze Complex.

4 Western and Eastern Streams of the Early Iron Age

Western Stream of the Early Iron Age Neolithic farmers, speaking Western Bantu languages, had spread as far as the mouth of the Congo-Zaïre river by 900 BC, and by 300 BC had adopted Iron Age technology. They herded goats and cultivated oil palms, and smelted and forged iron tools. Similar people spread southwards over the Angola highlands into the area of western Zambia. *Situmpa* pottery of the Early Iron Age was being made on the upper Zambezi maybe as early as 4th–3rd centuries BC.

In the area of the upper Zambezi the Western Stream of early Iron Age farmers met with Khoisan-speakers herders of cattle and sheep. There was a long period of interaction lasting centuries in the area of south-western Zambia and south-eastern Angola.

The name 'goat-people', given by Khoisan herders to Bantu-speaking farmers, may date from this period. The farmers obtained cattle and sheep from the Khoisan herders by trading the metal goods that they made. Farmers, with their better food supply of crops and their need for labour to grow them, grew in population faster than the Khoisan herders.

Khoisan responses to the Western Stream Some Khoisan-speaking people, especially women obtained through marriage payments in metal goods, probably joined the new Bantu-speaking communities around the upper Zambezi. Other Khoisan-speaking herders may have been forced to pay tribute to their farming neighbours by hunting or herding for them.

Some Khoisan herders south of the Zambezi continued to live independently but adopted elements of Early Iron Age culture. This can be seen in western Zimbabwe in the *Bambata culture*, named after a cave site dated about 190 BC near Bulawayo. Bambata pottery is a rough type of Western Stream pottery. The pottery was made by herders from about the 2nd century BC; and as late as the 4th century AD as far west as the Tsodilo hills near the northern Namibia-Botswana border.

Other Khoisan herders may have chosen to preserve their independence by moving away to fresh pastures in the south. Tshu-Khwe migrations, from the Okavango-Makgadikgadi region as far south as the Cape of Good Hope, may have preceded Western Stream settlement around the upper Zambezi. Alternatively, they may have been caused by it.

As Western Stream/Western Bantu-speaking societies gained wealth in livestock, they began to adopt Khoisan herder ideas of valuing cattle as the main store of wealth — as well as cattle-based Khoisan ideas of kinship and marriage. Such changes probably began in the upper Zambezi area, and they grew stronger when Western Stream people migrated further in the Khoisan-dominated south.

Eastern Stream Early Iron Age farmers, speaking Eastern Bantu languages, spread slowly from the Lake Victoria region into Kenya and northern Tanzania, from about the 7th century BC.

The *Kwale culture* of the Eastern Stream on the Kenya coast spread south as the Stream's Coastal tradition. By around AD 70 it may have reached the southern end of the Mozambique coast. (This carbon-date at Matola near Maputo, from a site excavated in 1976, has been challenged: the next known carbon-date at Matola is around AD 230.)

By about AD 270, pottery of the Coastal tradition was being made by people in the north-eastern valleys of the Transvaal. Similar sites have also been found along the Natal coast as far south as Durban, dated around the 3rd–4th centuries AD. Farmers, without livestock, were living by fishing and collecting shell-fish as well as by millet farming.

The Highland tradition of the Eastern Stream spread south over the plateaux down to Lake Malawi (Nyasa). These farmers kept many small Zebu-type cattle as well as cultivating millet and sorghum. But they encountered *tsetse*-infested areas through which they could not take their cattle. Zebu-type cattle are therefore today still restricted to East Africa and a few *tsetse*-free areas west of Lake Malawi. Eastern Stream people who went further south than Malawi had to acquire the

An iron smith at work   He is using goatskin
bellows, pumped with handles, to heat already
smelted iron so that he can then hammer it into
shape. Note the spearhead by the fire, which may
have been brought for repair.

Iron smelting   Two different types of iron
smelting furnaces, surviving until recently in the
area of Zambia. The furnaces were built of
puddled ant-hill clay, up to the height of a man.
Iron ore was smelted between layers of burning
charcoal. The furnaces were ventilated by jets of
hot air that came from blast pipes, usually around
the base of the furnace, sometimes assisted by
bellows. Temperatures over 1800 centigrade might
be reached, and African iron was in fact a mild
form of steel — an alloy of iron with the carbon of
the charcoal. The swordmakers of India therefore
imported iron from eastern Africa to make their
best swords: the iron was hammered thin and
folded many times to make a flexible but durable
blade.

Sanga-type cattle kept by Khoisan herders and Western Stream farmers.

The *Nkope culture*, on the south-western side of Lake Malawi, is a good example of the Highland tradition of the Eastern Stream. Nkope people had no livestock but hunted and fished, grew crops and smelted iron. The language of the people of the Nkope culture was probably an early form of Chewa (Nganja).

The Eastern Stream spread further across the Zambezi to the *Gokomere/Ziwa culture* of the northern Zimbabwe highlands. Gokomere/Ziwa sites date from at least AD 180, and possibly as early as 20 BC. These people grew millet and pumpkins, and hunted for meat. They began to herd a few sheep, and later cattle — probably acquired from Bambata people in the west.

Western Stream people spread from the upper Zambezi across eastern Botswana into the western Transvaal and western Natal, long before evidence of the Eastern Stream can be found in those areas. It is possible that Western Stream farmers were pushed southwards by Eastern Stream farmers settling to the east of them in Zambia and Zimbabwe.

The culture of Western Stream farmers south of the Zambezi and Limpopo became even more mixed with that of Khoisan herders. Though the farmers made Western Stream pottery, their houses were dome-shaped wooden frames covered by matting and clay — more like those of Khoisan herders than the square framed houses of Western Stream farmers north of the Zambezi. Some anthropologists also suggest that skeletons of Western Stream farmers are more Khoisanoid than Negroid in racial type.

A Western Stream site in Botswana, an iron-smelting furnace in the Tswapong hills near Palapye, has been dated from about AD 180. In South Africa, a site in East Griqualand, just south of Lesotho, has been dated as early as around AD 360.

The best known Western Stream site in South Africa is a village at Broederstroom (Pelindaba) near Pretoria in the Transvaal, dated from around AD 350 and lasting to around AD 600. Forty-eight small dome-shaped houses were excavated at Broederstroom, near remains of iron-smelting furnaces and forges. No seed remains have been found to tell us what crops they were cultivating. Their main livestock at first was goats, but later they had increasing numbers of cattle.

The Broederstroom people were developing trade with the east coast, as Indian Ocean seashells have been found in their graves. There is also evidence of people at Broederstroom having their two upper front teeth chipped or removed, like some groups of people do in southern Angola.

On the slopes of the northern Natal midlands, between the escarpment and the coast, Western Stream sites dating from the 7th century have been excavated along the Thukela (Tugela) river. These farmers herded mostly goats and sheep, and were also making many iron tools.

5 Early Iron Age Development

Early Iron Age villages grew in size and wealth — herds of cattle, locally-produced minerals, and goods imported from the sea coast. In the later part of the Early Iron Age, around 700–1100, some cultures began to develop into small states or chiefdoms with wealthy rulers.

Trade with the Indian Ocean increased around the time Muslim traders began to settle on the Tanzania coast in the 8th century, sending their ships southwards on annual trading trips.

Lydenburg culture   Around the 5th–6th century there was remarkable cultural development in Western Stream sites around Lydenburg (Marambane), near the Drakensberg escarpment of the eastern Transvaal.

The Lydenburg people made clay sculptures of human heads, hollow like pots, which have been dated around 540. Shiny black specularite (*sebilo*) has been rubbed into their hair and eyebrows. Archaeologists think that these sculptures may have been used in adolescent initiation schools. Small clay animals like those made in Later Iron Age schools have also been found.

Clay pottery in the shape of a human head, found at Lydenburg in the eastern Transvaal and carbon-dated 5th – 6th century AD. The head stands 38 centimetres high, and is hollow with slits for eyes.

The people of the Lydenburg culture seem to have been organized into a small state, with age-regiments schooled for communal labour, hunting and war. The state may have made its wealth from mining and exporting minerals to the Matola people on the coastal lowlands. Matola people were trading with ships on the Indian Ocean, maybe from as far as India and Persia.

Specularite and other iron ores were being mined from about 400 onwards in the Drakensberg south of Lydenburg, at Ngwenya in western Swaziland. Salt was being manufactured in the Drakensberg north of Lydenburg from about the same time.

Eiland tradition   The Lydenburg culture developed and began to slowly spread southwards, northwards and westwards, from the 7th–8th centuries onwards. People began to herd larger numbers of cattle, as well as goats and sheep. Archaeologists call this development of the Lydenburg culture the Eiland tradition.

The Eiland tradition can be seen near Molepolole in south-eastern Botswana by about AD 673, and on the Thukela river in northern Natal in the 9th century. The site of Eiland, a salt-producing area of the northeastern Transvaal, is dated around 950.

These extensions of the Eiland tradition can be identified with Later Iron Age ethnic groups. The pottery at Molepolole is basically that of Khalagari or Kgalagadi (Western Sotho-Tswana) people, while Thukela pottery is basically Fokeng (Southern Sotho-Tswana) and Lydenburg and Eiland cultures are Early Pedi (Eastern Sotho-Tswana).

Toutswe culture   By the 8th century there was remarkable development in east-central Botswana of an Early Iron Age culture of mixed Eastern and Western Stream origins, similar to the *Zhizo culture* in western Zimbabwe.

Major sites of this Toutswe culture have been dated between about 710 and 1305. The large capital town on Toutswe hill (north of Palapye) flourished between about 960 and 1200. Archaeologists have identified three or four such hilltop towns of 1,000 to 1,500 houses, 17 hilltop villages of 120 to 200 houses, and hundreds of small settlements on the plains. Each one was built around a large cattle kraal.

Toutswe people were receiving trade or tribute in cattle and hunting products from the northern Kalahari. The main wealth of Toutswe rulers was great numbers of large

Sanga-type cattle. The rulers controlled this wealth, by collecting cattle in central town kraals and then distributing them to village kraals. There was some trade through the Limpopo valley with the Indian Ocean, but no evidence that Toutswe rulers became rich in such goods.

People of the northern Kalahari The Kalahari was slowly drying up, pushing cattle out to better-watered pastures. Tshu-Khwe herder culture continued along the Boteti river west of the Makgadikgadi pans. But increasing numbers of Bantu-speaking farmers settled among them, until the herders eventually abandoned speaking their Khoi language in the 18th–19th centuries.

At Divuyu in the Tsodilo hills, west of the Okavango, Western Stream iron-smelters with sheep but no cattle were living alongside Khoisan herders and hunter-gatherers from about 550. They were importing sea-shells from the Atlantic coast, copper ornaments probably from Namibia, and fish from the Okavango. From about 730 they had cattle as well as sheep, and were importing sea-shells from the Indian Ocean.

Around 850 the *Divuyu culture* was replaced by a new culture with pottery which can be identified with later Yei and Mbukushu people. Most of these Early Yei-Mbukushu lived further north, as farmers and fishing folk around the present Caprivi Strip.

Early Iron Age mining Some Early Iron Age people began to mine and smelt other metals besides iron. People of the (Western Stream) *Chondwe culture*, on the copperbelt of the Zambia-Zaïre borderlands, began to mine copper in the 4th–5th century and were cutting deep trenches into copper-bearing rock by about 1000.

Copper mining in north-eastern Zimbabwe dates from about the 7th century, around Chinoyi (Sinoia). Copper miners and smiths from the copper mines in Zambia appear to have come and mixed their pottery style with local Eastern Stream (Highland stream) people to form the new *Chinoyi culture*.

Copper mining at Phalaborwa in the north-

MINING AND TRADE IN METALS DURING THE IRON AGE

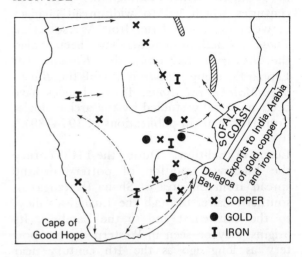

Exports to India, Arabia

SOFALA COAST

Exports of gold, copper and iron

Delagoa Bay

Cape of Good Hope

× COPPER
● GOLD
I IRON

east Transvaal dates from about the 8th century. Archaeologists have shown how local Western Stream pottery developed into a new culture, which they call *Kgopolwe*, at a time of extensive mining in the 950–1350 period.

The history of gold production is less well known. Archaeologists believe that the earliest gold producers collected alluvial gold from rivers, and later used copper mining techniques to mine it.

Gold exports from the central Mozambique coast around Sofala began about the 7th century — and may be linked to the Chinoyi culture on the northern Zimbabwe plateau. Gold exports from the southern Zimbabwe plateau down the Shashe and Limpopo rivers, through the port of Inhambane, probably began after about 950. The gold was carried by Muslim ships from the east coast to India, Arabia and Persia.

6 Later Iron Age Origins

Around the 11th–13th centuries there was a significant change in the styles of pottery made in most Iron Age societies in southern Africa. Early Iron Age pottery tends to have thick walls of red or yellow clay, with heavily incised patterns. Later Iron Age pottery tends to be of thinner grey clay, with neater patterning, and often painted or polished in red or black.

There were three great cultural movements in southern Africa during the 11th–13th centuries which led to widespread changes between Early and Later Iron Age societies. These cultural movements have been called the *Luangwa tradition*, the *Kutama* (or Leopard's Kopje) *tradition*, and the *Blackburn/Moloko traditions*. These changes have been most fully studied by the archaeologist Tom Huffman (in publications of 1974–89).*

Luangwa tradition   During the 11th century the Luangwa tradition of pottery making spread from the area of Shaba (Katanga) in southern Zaïre, through the Luangwa valley, to the east coast and to the Zambezi. Its origins may be seen in Western Stream pottery as long ago as the 4th century near later Lubumbashi.

The best known site of the Western Stream culture that gave rise to the Luangwa tradition is at Sanga, near Lake Kisale, in the north of Shaba. Here, dated from about 720, archaeologists have found a graveyard with thousands of skeletons. The bodies were in pots, up to six in one grave, buried with copper and iron objects. These objects included many small H-shaped copper crosses and bells (without clappers) made of copper, as well as copper wire or iron wire necklaces and ear-rings, iron hoe-heads and spear-heads and axe-heads.

The Luangwa tradition spread eastwards and southwards in the 11th century. Eastwards, the Luangwa probably took 'Forest Pattern' (see below) ideas of settlement, and matrilineal ideas of kinship across Lake Malawi to the shores of the Indian Ocean. (This accounts for the 'matrilineal belt' across eastern Africa, with patrilineal societies to the north and south of it.)

The progress of the Luangwa tradition southwards can be seen in new pottery cultures in northern Zimbabwe from about 1100, notably the *Musengezi culture*. Musengezi people were buried in graveyards, sometimes in caves, together with pottery and metal objects.

*See T. N. Huffman 'Ceramics, settlements and Late Iron Age migration', *African Archaeological Review* (Cambridge), vol. 7 (1989), pp. 155–82.

Another, though later, Luangwa tradition culture was at *Ingombe Ilede* in the middle Zambezi valley, dated in the 14th–15th centuries. Here archaeologists have studied a graveyard of people buried with pottery, copper crosses and bells, gold beads and gold foil, tools for making copper and iron wire, and locally woven bark and cotton cloth, as well as imported sea-shells, thousands of glass beads and fine cotton cloth from India.

The Luangwa tradition was connected with copper smithing and mining from the start, and later with gold production and trading with the Indian Ocean. It also brought along, as we shall see, new ideas of kings being sacred and all-powerful.

The Luangwa tradition was to contribute to the growth of the Great Zimbabwe culture, and especially to the culture of the Munhumutapa kingdom. But the basic origins of Great Zimbabwe lay to the south, in the Kutama tradition.

Kutama tradition   The Kutama tradition is sometimes also called the Leopard's Kopje (Ntabazingwe) tradition by archaeologists. This new tradition of pottery making spread into southern Zimbabwe around the 11th century, to absorb and replace the Zhizo and Gokomere/Ziwa cultures of the Early Iron Age on the Zimbabwe plateau.

The origins of the Kutama tradition south of the Limpopo, in the northern Transvaal area, are still somewhat mysterious. More research is needed on the northern part of the Transvaal.

The earliest well-known site of the Kutama tradition is found in the *Bambadyanalo culture*, dated from about 970. It was located around Mapungubwe hill in the Limpopo valley, near the point where the South Africa, Zimbabwe and Botswana borders meet.

The people of the Bambadyanalo culture were related to both the Early Iron Age people of the Toutswe culture to the west and Zhizo people of the north. The Bambadyanalo people lived and died around concentrations of cattle, but they made their wealth from elephant hunting. They were carving and exporting ivory to the Indian Ocean. They also seem to have had initiation schools and age-regiments like Eiland tradition people, as archaeologists have found small clay figures of cattle such as were made in those schools.

The Bambadyanalo culture developed into what archaeologists call the *Mapungubwe culture*, which can be dated by carbon-dates around 1110 and 1380. Mapungubwe hill was the centre of a gold-exporting state (see chapter 2).

The Kutama tradition spread to the north, around later Bulawayo, where its *Mambo culture* is named by archaeologists after Ntaba-zika-Mambo hill. Mambo people collected alluvial gold from rivers, and also began to mine for gold. This gold was exported, together with ivory, to the Indian Ocean at first through Mapungubwe and later through Great Zimbabwe. Mambo people also built their houses on stone foundations, surrounding their houses with stone walls.

Origin of Great Zimbabwe   The Kutama tradition reached south-central Zimbabwe by about 1050, in the form of what archaeologists call the *Gumanye culture*. It was Gumanye people who first developed the trading and political centre which we call Great Zimbabwe, where they began the building of stone walls. The Gumanye culture was the first part of what archaeologists call the *Great Zimbabwe tradition* of pottery making and culture.

Blackburn/Moloko traditions   The third great cultural movement in the 11th–13th century period was of two closely related new pottery traditions known as *Blackburn* and *Moloko*. These two pottery traditions are particularly important, as they can be clearly associated with the later Nguni and the Tswana (Central Sotho-Tswana) respectively.

The Blackburn tradition is named after a site near Richards Bay on the northern Natal coast. (Some books also called Blackburn pottery NC-2, i.e. Natal Coastal type 2). This type of pottery originated from the Transvaal. When and how is not known, except that it was closely related to Moloko pottery. During the 11th–12th century this tradition can be

seen moving southwards through Natal into the Transkei area. (See above for Blackburn's association with early Nguni.)

The Moloko tradition is named after a type of pottery that first appeared in the Phalaborwa copper-mining area, alongside Kgopolwe pottery, in the northern-eastern Transvaal, in the 12th–13th centuries. It is not clear where the style originated from, as it has been found in both the central Transvaal and south-eastern Botswana around the same time. But its development is obviously associated with the rise of early Tswana rulers, whose oral traditions indicate origins in the central/western Transvaal in the 13th–15th centuries. (See Chapter 3.)

The origins of the closely related Blackburn and Moloko traditions are as yet unknown and disputed. Some archaeologists look for indigenous origins in the Eiland tradition of the Transvaal and northern Natal. Others look to the southern Mozambique lowlands, or even as far north as Lake Malawi.

7 Later Iron Age Development

Advances in archaeological research during the 1970s–80s have given a firm foundation for the study of Later Iron Age peoples and states over the last 500 years or more. Such history follows in the next chapters. But much work remains to be done by archaeologists, linguists, historians and other scholars and scientists on the cultures of the Later Iron Age.

Later Iron Age social organization   Following the work of the anthropologist Adam Kuper*, archaeologists refer to the 'Central Cattle Pattern' of Later Iron Age settlement south of the Zambezi.

People lived in circular houses and circular compounds, located around their cattle kraals. Men were buried (crouched on their right sides, facing south-west) under the cattle kraals, women (crouched on their left sides, facing north-east) under household areas, and infants (in water pots) under house areas.

*A. Kuper *Wives for Cattle: Bridewealth and Marriage in Southern Africa* London: Routledge & Kegan Paul, 1982.

Such societies were centred around the ownership of cattle as the main source of wealth. Cattle were the main political resource accumulated by rulers and distributed to loyal subjects.

The societies were also patrilineal like those of Khoisan-speakers of southern Africa, and Bantu-speakers in East Africa. This meant that inheritance of property and status (and family names) passed down the father's blood line, from father to son.

We can see this 'Central Cattle Pattern' in the Western Stream south of the Zambezi and then in the Eiland tradition, as well as in the Kutama and Blackburn/Moloko traditions. As already suggested, it most likely originated in the interaction of Western Stream and Khoisan herder societies.

North of the Zambezi and in west-central Africa — though not in East Africa — most Later Iron States were organized along the lines of what Huffman has called the 'Forest Pattern' of settlement. People lived in rectangular houses along straight streets. They buried their dead with pottery and often with wealth in metal goods, in graveyards outside their villages.

Oral tradition tells us about the importance of metal-working, and of metal goods used as currency and wealth, in 'Forest Pattern' societies. Men also made clay pots, while women made them in 'Central Cattle Pattern' societies.

'Forest Pattern' societies were matrilineal. Inheritance and family names and inheritance of property passed down the mother's blood line, from maternal-uncle to nephew. But older men dominated families and chiefdoms, so 'Forest Pattern' societies were patriarchies similar to 'Central Cattle Pattern' societies.

Marriage payments ('dowries') were also different in matrilineal and patrilineal societies. In matrilineal societies the husband gave 'bride service', in the form of labour while living with and working for the wife's parents. In patrilineal societies the husband's family gave 'bride wealth' (lobola), in the form of cattle passed over to the wife's parents while the wife lived with and worked for the husband's family.

Matrilineal and patrilineal elements were sometimes mixed in Later Iron Age societies. We can see this, for example, in the special role still given to the maternal-uncle (malome) in 'Central Cattle Pattern' societies.

Types of Later Iron Age state We may distinguish between cattle-based confederations, divine kinships, trading states and military despotisms as different kinds of state in the Later Iron Age.

Cattle-based confederations were groups of chiefdoms organized on the 'Central Cattle Pattern' with the senior chief as king. The king and chiefs accumulated and 'loaned' out cattle to loyal followers on the system known as mafisa* (or 'cattle-feudalism').

Divine kingships were states in which the king was venerated as a god, as a descendant of God, or as a priest secretly linked to the gods.

Trading states were stimulated by competition for control of trade and of production of goods for trade — carried to the Indian Ocean or Atlantic coasts.

Military despotisms, strictly ruled by kings and chiefs who gained status as battle leaders, were to emerge in the 17th–18th centuries.

We can see most Later Iron Age states as some kind of mixture of these types. There were elements of divine kingship when kings acted as chief priests in leading the annual planting and harvesting ceremonies, or acted as chief rain-doctors in procuring rain.

Age-regiments There were both political and religious elements in the age-regiment system. Age-regiments united men and women of the same age but different ethnic origins into the state, with a form of common 'national' loyalty to each other and to state leaders. The regiments were available to the state for collective tribute and tax, communal labour

---

*Mafisa refers to cattle which are lent or loaned. The cattle-loaner gave allegiance and tribute to the cattle-owner, in return for being allowed to herd and use the cattle. 'When milking a mafisa cow', says the proverb, 'always look over your shoulder at the gate' — just in case the owner comes to claim the cow or its milk.

and hunting, and for raiding and war.

Each age-regiment, male or female, was bound together by going to the same initiation school — learning and sharing the same secrets of initiation for life, notably the experience of male circumcision.

The origin of male circumcision is not known, though the rites were similar in East Africa. Were young boys circumcised in the initiation schools of the Lydenburg culture? '
officers overthrew the fascist government in
Later Iron Age production: crafts and mining
As the Iron Age societies of southern Africa grew bigger in size and more complex, so more individuals could specialize and make their living as craft-workers.

Both women and men became herbalists and healers. Some women became midwives and specialist potters. Some men became rain-makers, smiths, leather tailors, weavers of cotton or bark cloth, and mining engineers. Mine labourers had to be slim to enter narrow shafts, and so were often women and older children. Most of these crafts or specialized jobs were 'dry season professions': everyone was called by the needs of agriculture during the wet season.

Mines and metal-working   Hundreds of Iron Age mines and smelting sites have been located on the Zimbabwe and Transvaal plateaux by archaeologists.

At Phalaborwa, archaeologists have discovered 31 shafts and a large open pit along 400 metres of copper vein. Burnt wood at the bottom of shafts shows that the ore was cracked by fire — the hot rock being suddenly cooled by water, before it was broken from the shaft walls with stone-headed hammers.

Gold mines in Zimbabwe and in the eastern Transvaal were mined by similar techniques to copper mines.* One tin mine in the western Transvaal has been carbon-dated to the 15th–16th centuries. There were probably other tin

*The archaeologist Revil Mason points out that no ancient gold mines have been discovered on the Witwatersrand. Modern mining on the Witwatersrand began in the 1880s next to an ancient *iron* mine in Struben's valley west of Johannesburg.

mines in the Transvaal and Swaziland. Other minerals mined include asbestos (mixed with clay for fire-proof pottery) in the Transvaal and Botswana, and possibly zinc in Zimbabwe (mixed with copper to make the alloy called brass).

Later Iron Age trade   Trade goods were relayed over long distances by inter-village trade. There were also professional traders, such as the *vashambadzi* or *vashavi* of the Shona. These traded with Muslim traders, mostly Swahili rather than Arabic-speaking, on the sea coast.

Arabs, and later on Europeans, were known as *wazungu* by the Swahili, while the Arabs called non-Muslims 'kaffirs', meaning heathen. In the south, the traders known as *balckane* (age-mates or comrades) in Setswana, matched themselves with a comrade trader in a distant village.

Cowrie and conus shells from the islands of the Indian Ocean were imported and valued as a form of currency for trade. Trade goods such as ostrich egg-shell beads and beads made of iron or copper, as well as imported glass beads, might be used as a form of currency. Copper, iron, salt and tobacco were often traded in standard shapes and sizes, which could also be used as currency.

Pack-oxen were used for transport in *tsetse*-free areas. Elsewhere goods were carried on the backs or heads of porters, in dug-out wooden canoes, and small sailing *dhows* up rivers like the Zambezi.

Later Iron Age religion and ideas   Ideas of divine kingship strengthened the political control of rulers over their people. Royal ancestors became the objects of religious worship. The health and strength of the nation was equated with the health and strength of the ruler, who presided over national ceremonies — including rain-making, planting and harvest festivals, initiation schools, marriage celebrations, and doctoring of widespread disease or misfortune.

People also respected and worshipped the nature spirits of the land and water around them — who might include the spirits of previous 'owners' of the land, such as the spirits of long dead hunter-gatherers.

Belief in a single God higher than other spirits seems to have been common — an ultimate ancestor figure as with *Nkulunkulu* among Nguni people, or the greatest nature spirit of all as with *Modimo* among Sotho-Tswana. However, the High God rarely intervened directly in the affairs of people, except in the Ngwali (*Mwari*) cult of the Venda and Shona.

People maintained contact with the spirit world by rituals for birth, death and marriage, and whenever they ate or drank. The divining tablets ('bones') of diviners also spoke for the spirits. Some inspired individuals, both men and women, became mediums or prophets through whom spirits spoke.

Religion explained the laws of nature and morality, of sickness and health. It was brought to people by rituals and words, as well as by dancing and music.

There was also scientific knowledge based on observation and deduction. This was evident in techniques of agriculture and metallurgy. Today we have also begun to appreciate the sophistication of 'Iron Age' African cosmology of the stars, chronology of the seasons, and arithmetic based on digital (ten-fingered) counting.

Questions

1   Outline the main stages of the later Stone Age in different parts of southern Africa. Illustrate your answer with a chart and map.

2   What do you know about the way of life of the San and Khoikhoi before the arrival of Dutch colonists at the Cape in 1652? [Cambridge International School Certificate, 1980]

3   How did livestock-keeping and agriculture make people live a more settled life?

4   How was the growth of states in the later Iron Age related to trade and religion?

Activities

1   Find out about and draw a date-chart of the early, middle, and later Stone Age (called the *lower, middle* and *upper Palaeolithic* in some books) in Africa and elsewhere.

2   Imagine yourself as the mother of a Khoisan hunter-gatherer family in the later Stone Age. Describe your everyday life.

3   Make parallel lists of words in a number of Bantu languages and dialects for common actions and objects — e.g. sleep, eat, water, sky, hand, hair, axe, spoon. What do you find in common between them?

4   Search out and describe examples of 'traditional' pottery, noting their shape, thickness, colour, patterning, and probable method of construction. What were the pots used for?

See Bibliography, pp. 337–42: B32 Readers Digest; C3 Denbow; C8 Garlake; C9 Hall; C11 Humphreys; C12 Inskeep; C13 Johnson; C14 Lewis-Williams; C16 Malherbe; C23 Phillipson; C33 Woodhouse; J5 AAR; J8 Azania; J10 Digging Stick: J14 JAH; J21 SAAB.

Chapter 2

Later Iron Age: Eastern Region

Trade in metals and hunting-products extended from southern Africa overseas during the Iron Age, when ships from Asia and later from Europe came to barter on the east coast. Powerful states emerged near trade routes to the coast, as their rulers profited from trading or from control of mining and hunting.

Kalanga trader, shaded by his tortoise-shell hat, carries a battle-axe, spears, cloth and a gourd full of quills. The quills could have contained gold dust or beads.

African states and foreign traders competed among themselves and with each other. The gold exports of the Zimbabwean plateau to the coast, which lasted for over a thousand years, linked 'Azania' into the world economy.

1 Early Trade on the East Coast

'Azania' was the name given to the east coast of Africa in a shipping guide to the Indian Ocean, titled *The Periplus of the Erythrean Sea,* first published in Greek in the 2nd century AD. The Greek word Azania was taken from the Persian name 'Zanji-bar', meaning the coast of the *zanj* (black) people. The Persian word still survives in the name of Zanzibar island.

Persians and Arabians traded along the Azania coast, from Mogadishu south to Inhambane Bay in southern Mozambique, from the first few centuries AD. Archaeologists have found evidence of this trade, in the form of beads and sea-shells, as far south as the western Transvaal near Pretoria as early as the 5th-6th centuries AD. Sea traders bought ivory, rhinoceros horn, tortoise shell, and other rare luxuries, for which they sold glass beads, shells and glazed pottery, and even cattle and iron weapons in areas where these were not otherwise available. African goods were then traded across the Indian Ocean as far as China and the Mediterranean.

Madagascar and the islands   Asian immigrants from the East Indies (probably south Borneo)

27

settled the great island of Madagascar in the first few centuries AD. These 'Malagasy' or other Asians brought the first bananas, coconuts and yams to Africa. (One historian suggests they were sailors on Indian ships.) They also probably brought the xylophone (*marimba*), which spread from Asia to Africa and Europe. Meanwhile the Comoros and other islands between Madagascar and Azania were populated by people speaking a mixture of Persian or Arabic, Bantu (kiSwahili and chiShona), and Malagasy languages.

Muslim trade   Arabia and Persia were converted to Islam, the Muslim religion, in the 7th century AD. Trade prospered, towns expanded, and agricultural plantations were set up in the Arabian-Persian Gulf. Azanian slaves were imported for plantation labour, and were even re-exported as far as China. But continuous slave revolts and agricultural decline reduced the number of slaves imported into Arabia and Persia from the 9th century (until the 18th-19th centuries). Muslim traders began to settle in coastal ports around the Indian Ocean, where they mixed and married with local people and converted them to Islam. The Malagasy, the early Swahili, and some Shona traders in the Zambezi valley, adopted Muslim religion and customs. *Ndarama* meaning 'gold', *mari* meaning 'money', *boma* meaning 'fort', and *shava* meaning 'to buy', are examples of Persian and Arabic words that were adopted into the kiSwahili and chiShona languages.

Sofala gold trade   By the 11th century Muslim trading posts had been set up on the coast between the Zambezi and Inhambane Bay, known as 'Sofala' — the chiShona word for a sandy coastline. Ships came to trade for gold-dust and ivory with the Shona people known to Muslims as the 'Waq-Waq'. Gold was much in demand for currency in Arabia. The soft ivory of Africa was prized by the carvers of India and China. Its mild steel was valued by Indian sword-makers. Gold production and export from the Zimbabwean plateau to the coast probably reached its height between the 12th and 15th centuries,

and may have totalled more than two hundred million grammes.

Muslim traders came to bargain with Shona traders at trade-fairs or *bazaars* held occasionally at river or coastal trading ports. By the 15th century the main trading ports being used by Muslim traders for the gold trade were on the Zambezi. The marshes between Inhambane Bay and the Limpopo mouth were known as the 'copper rivers' because of copper exports brought from around Phalaborwa in the interior.

Kilwa   The shipping route from Sofala northwards to Arabia and Persia was controlled by the Swahili city-state of Kilwa, which prospered in the 13th-14th centuries. The African geographer Ibn Battuta, who visited Kilwa in the year 1331, thought it 'one of the most beautiful and well-constructed towns in the world'.

2 Ancient Zimbabwe States

Our knowledge of the people of the Zimbabwean plateau before about 1500 comes almost exclusively from archaeological findings. Later Iron Age pottery spread over the south and western part of the plateau from the 9th-10th centuries onwards. This new pottery may have been spread by people from south of the Limpopo, who built the earliest stone walled settlements in southern Africa. These people built clay-walled houses on rock platforms, surrounded by walls of stone blocks, without mortar or cement.

On the north and eastern part of the Zimbabwean plateau a number of later Iron Age pottery-groups replaced the local Early Iron Age from around the 12th-14th centuries. These new pottery types may have been brought from southern Zaire. Oral tradition suggests that early Luba migrants from southern Zaire brought new ideas about kingship being sacred and priest-like.

Origin of Zimbabwe states   The city-state of Great Zimbabwe in the 13th-15th centuries probably originated from political and economic developments further south around the middle Limpopo valley. Archaeologists have found evidence of earlier hilltop villages or towns in east-central Botswana and at Mapungubwe on the Limpopo, and may find more sites in the northern Transvaal. Villages on hilltops around the Motloutse and Lotsane headwaters in east-central Botswana, dated between the 8th and 13th centuries, have deep deposits of cattle dung from old cattle kraals. Good grazing during wetter than usual centuries would have increased both the cattle and human population of the area. Rulers might have risen to power by bringing cattle and people together in villages, and loaning out cattle to leading subjects on a *mafisa* system.

But by the 13th century east-central Botswana was depopulated. Drought and over-grazing may have reduced cattle numbers and driven people northwards to the more fertile Zimbabwean plateau.

Mapungubwe Archaeologists have found numerous gold ornaments at Mapungubwe, a hilltop village on the south bank of the Limpopo river near the Shashe confluence. The end of its occupation has been carbon-dated around the 14th century. The village was probably the base of traders or rulers who benefited from trade carrying gold from the Shashe headwaters (including Tati) through the Limpopo valley towards the Sofala coast. We know that export of gold and ivory first flourished on the southern part of the Sofala coast in the 11th century.

Great Zimbabwe The styles of pottery and building at Great Zimbabwe developed from

The Great Enclosure area of Great Zimbabwe   Note size of walls compared with people on the left. The Great Enclosure was possibly the residence of the city's rulers, after they moved from the hilltop. Two sets of massive stone walls were built around a cattle kraal and large houses — made of traditional thatch and plastered clay floors and walling. The wards of royal relatives or rich traders outside the Great Enclosure, enclosed by lesser stone walls, can also be seen in this photograph. Beyond these wards there were hundreds of tightly packed thatch and clay houses in which poor subjects lived. (The nearest modern equivalent to the city is a rural town in Botswana consisting of numerous traditional houses.) Today, only the stone walls of Great Zimbabwe remain.

the local culture of the area — part of the local later Iron Age tradition that had spread from around the Limpopo valley. People living with their cattle in a hilltop village grew rich and powerful in the 13th century by controlling the small valley beneath them, through which gold was exported to the Sofala coast. These people built more and more elaborate clay and stone-walled buildings on the hilltop. They then moved down into the valley to found a city of up to ten thousand people.

A large number of elaborate stone walls at Great Zimbabwe, built without mortar up to nine metres high, enclosed richer family wards (homesteads and cattle kraals) of the city. Together with evidence of manufacture of gold ornaments, they show that the rulers of the city employed skilled craftsmen and large numbers of workers. The rulers must therefore have also controlled the agricultural surplus of a wide area to feed the city.

Who were the rulers of Great Zimbabwe? Archaeology and oral traditions indicate that the rulers were ancestors of the later Torwa dynasty of rulers at Khami in the west. (There is no good evidence that the rulers were ancestors of the later Munhumutapa dynasty in the north, as some historians have assumed.) Archaeology indicates that the rulers of Great Zimbabwe had considerable wealth and political power over people. They may also have had religious power. The famous conical tower in the valley's great enclosure, and bird sculptures in the hill cattle kraal, may have been symbols of royal ancestors or fallen heroes whose memory was worshipped.

Decline of Great Zimbabwe Archaeology shows that the city of Great Zimbabwe was almost completely abandoned during the 15th century, when housing in the valley was burnt down. Why was the city abandoned? The most likely reason was famine and water shortage brought on by over-population and over-grazing in a period of drought. It is quite normal in southern African history for towns and villages to be abandoned for such reasons after a few decades. (Only Capetown can rival Great Zimbabwe in lasting for centuries.) The amount of wealth invested in buildings at Great Zimbabwe would have delayed the decision to move until the problems became even worse.

Other reasons for the city being abandoned might have included internal revolt, external attack, and decline in trade. The gold trade to the Sofala coast shifted north from the Sabi-Lundi valleys towards the Zambezi — just as it had previously shifted from the Shashe-Limpopo valleys, which led to the decline of Mapungubwe.

Archaeologists have found many smaller *zimbabwes* to the north of Great Zimbabwe, which may have been or become independent of Great Zimbabwe. Archaeologists have also found the remains of a rich trading village at Ingombe Ilede near the confluence of the Kafue and Zambezi rivers, carbon-dated around the 15th century. Ingombe Ilede probably exported gold from the Zimbabwean plateau to Muslim traders in the lower Zambezi valley.

Kingdom of Butwa The Torwa dynasty, founded by the rulers who abandoned Great Zimbabwe, ruled the kingdom known as 'Butwa' on the western Zimbabwean plateau between the 15th and 17th centuries. The kingdom was based first at the stone walled town of Khami, and then at Danangombe (Dhlodhlo). Excavations at Danangombe have revealed numerous gold objects, including much gold leaf (for covering wooden head-rests, etc.) and even gold thread for weaving. The kingdom stretched as far west as the gold-fields of the upper Shashe, and possibly to the salt-pans of the Makgadikgadi. The language of Butwa was almost certainly the dialect of chiShona later known as tjiKalanga. But little is yet known of the political history of the Torwa dynasty, or of the archaeology of the Butwa kingdom.

Munhumutapa kingdom A new kingdom rose to power on the north-eastern Zimbabwean plateau in the later 15th century —

1498	*First Portuguese ship* (captained by Vasco da Gama) arrived on Sofala coast, opening Indian Ocean to ships from the North Atlantic coast of Europe. The ship was then taken from Malindi (Kenya) to India by a Muslim pilot.
1505-07	*Major ports of Azania* including Kilwa and Mombasa taken. Portuguese then conquered ports in India, Ceylon and the East Indies. From 1510 all Portuguese in the Indian Ocean were subject to a governor at Goa on the west coast of India.
1511-29	*Involvement in Zambezi politics* — taking from Muslims the port of Angoche and sending gunmen to assist Munhumutapa Chikuyo in a civil war with southerners.
1530-52	*Expulsion of Muslims from the Zambezi* — Portuguese captured Sena, Tete and Quelimane and built fortress on small coastal island called *Mozambique* (Msambiji) to control shipping in the Madagascar-Mozambique channel.
1560-72	*Competition with Muslims for trade* and influence with the Munhumutapa (Nogomo, ruled 1560-89). Culminated in Portuguese invasion and massacre of Muslims to avenge murder of Portuguese envoy.
1575-1629	*Three Portuguese-Munhumutapa treaties* Munhumutapa Nogomo ceded land along Zambezi south bank to the Portuguese king (1575), later divided into *prazos* (plantations) ruled by settler chiefs known as *prazeros*. After Gatsi Rusere (ruled 1596-1627) ceded more gold and silver mines by treaty (1609), the Portuguese no longer regarded the Munhumutapa as an independent ruler, refusing to pay tribute. Finally in 1629 Munhumutapa Mavura agreed to pay regular tribute to the Portuguese king.
1629-90	*Munhumutapa as Portuguese subject* The Munhumutapa continued to rule his own people, but Portuguese settlers were exempt from his laws and traded without paying him tribute.

Later 17th century *Decline of Portugal* The Portuguese lost control of much Indian Ocean trade to the Dutch in the mid-17th century. By 1698 Muslims had recaptured the coast north of Mozambique. The French and British became stronger powers than the Portuguese in the Indian Ocean by the early 18th century. But Portuguese ships from Mozambique port continued to trade south with Inhambane and Delagoa Bay. Meanwhile *prazeros* on the Zambezi became semi-independent of Portuguese control, using local slaves as hunters and soldiers for their private armies.

the kingdom of Munhumutapa.* The king was treated as a god like the priest-kings of the Luba and Lunda (in Zaire), surrounded by many aristocratic officials at court. At the same time, there was close contact with Muslim traders in the Zambezi ports over trade in gold and imported goods such as cloth. The Munhumutapa kingdom flourished for a century until the reign of Chikuyo (about 1494-1530), during which the kingdom was troubled by civil wars. In one of these wars, a chief called Changamire declared the independence of his area in the south. A later war of 1628-29 gave the Portuguese their first chance to intervene in the Munhumutapa kingdom.

*Munhumutapa (also spelt 'Monomotapa') was the praise-name taken by its first ruler, and was subsequently adopted as a title by later rulers. Some historians have mistakenly modernized the title into 'Mwene Mutapa' or 'Mwana Mutapa'.

3 Changamire Kingdom and Rozvi Confederacy

The greatest Mambo of the Changamire kingdom was Dombo, who came to power in the 1670s. Around 1680 he led his army, known as the Rozvi ('destroyers'), westwards to the kingdom of Butwa where he conquered the Torwa dynasty. He then marched back eastwards to attack the Portuguese nearer the coast, whom he defeated at the battle of Maungwe in 1684. Dombo's army, armed with bows and arrows as well as spears, clubs and battle-axes, surrounded the enemy with the chest-and-horns battle formation later made famous by the Zulu. In 1693 and 1695 Dombo again attacked the Portuguese at their trade-fairs in the Zambezi valley, to reduce their control of gold mining and trade on the north-eastern Zimbabwean plateau.

Dombo's new Rozvi kingdom over Butwa This now controlled the gold production and export of the whole Zimbabwean plateau. Dombo diverted the gold trade from passing through the Munhumutapa state as previously, to run direct to Zumbo upstream from Tete on the Zambezi. The Rozvi dynasty descended from Dombo took the former Torwa capital of Danangombe as its own capital. The old Torwa rulers married into the new ruling families of the Rozvi, and became Rozvi chiefs under the Rozvi king, who was titled the Mambo. The Rozvi themselves adopted the local tjiKalanga dialect and no longer spoke their original chiZezuru dialect of chiShona.

But the Mambos of the Rozvi who ruled after Dombo were less powerful individuals than him, and were forced to share power with other Rozvi chiefs. For reasons not yet known the capital was moved to Manyanga (TabazikaMambo). The later Rozvi kingdom is usually called the 'Rozvi confederacy' by historians because it was a union of semi-independent chiefdoms, whose unity became looser in the 18th century. For example the chiefdom of Mengwe in the south-west became more and more independent. It extended its power over Pedi and Tswana groups migrating from the south to join it in the upper Shashe area.

4 Chopi/Tonga and Tsonga States

Around the 15th century Shona migrants from the Zimbabwean plateau migrated to the river marshes and sandy plains north of the mouth of the Limpopo. They were probably attracted to the coast by the trade route which was carrying gold down the Limpopo valley to Muslim sea traders on the coast south of Inhambane Bay.

The Wutonga kingdom The Shona migrants brought new ideas of kingship with them and founded a new kingdom known as Wutonga. They settled among the local people of the area, whom we may call early Chopi/Tonga* since their descendants were later known as the vaTonga and vaChopi. The immigrants mixed themselves thoroughly with the local people and became part of the southern Chopi/Tonga, while the northern Chopi/Tonga remained independent.

The history of Wutonga still has to be more thoroughly researched. What we do know is that the last powerful king of Wutonga was a man called Gwambe, who ruled in the middle of the 16th century. Under Gwambe the state prospered, selling ivory, copper, beeswax and slaves to a Portuguese ship which came annually from Sofala. After the reign of Gwambe, the kingdom broke up into large local chiefdoms, but the southern Chopi/Tonga of Wutonga continued to follow many Shona customs.

Origin of the Chopi During the 17th and 18th centuries there was migration into Chopi/Tonga country of many Tsonga from the south, and Pedi (northern Tswana/Sotho) from the east, who married into Chopi/Tonga families. Again it seems that the migrants were attracted by the wealth of trade between the Limpopo valley and Inhambane Bay. Portuguese sea traders had replaced Muslims on the coast, and the export of copper and tin from the northern Transvaal area had replaced the export of gold from the Zimbabwean plateau.

The northern Chopi/Tonga lived in small

*The Chopi/Tonga should not be confused with other people of the same or similar name — their southern neighbours the Tsonga, or the Zambezi Tonga and Malawi Tonga.

village chiefdoms, unlike the large chiefdoms of Wutonga. Many of them adopted the language and customs of their new Tsonga rulers and forgot their own. On the other hand the southern Chopi/Tonga of old Wutonga — because they already had stronger governments — accepted the Tsonga and Pedi migrants as new subjects rather than as new rulers. The southern Chopi/Tonga now began to call themselves 'vaChopi' to distinguish themselves from their northern relatives who had discarded the old language and culture.

Spread of northern Tsonga The Tsonga peoples spoke a language distinct from their Chopi/Tonga and Nguni neighbours, and lived in large numbers on the sandy plains of the lower Limpopo valley around Delagoa Bay. During the 17th and 18th centuries there were continuous Tsonga migrations northwards into Chopi/Tonga country. This migration may have been the result of a population boom following the introduction of maize, brought by Portuguese traders from South America, as an extra crop which increased food supplies.

The northward migrations gave rise to the Hlengwe, Tswa and other groups of northern Tsonga. But the resistance of Chopi/Tonga and Shona chiefdoms led to wars which supplied captives to be sold as slaves to ships at Inhambane Bay. The Portuguese at Mozambique island sent at least one ship to Inhambane every year to trade, and from 1731 there was a permanent Portuguese trading post at Inhambane.

Ronga (southern Tsonga) chiefdoms The Tsonga who remained south of the Limpopo were known as the Ronga and were organized in numerous chiefdoms. By the 16th century the most senior Ronga chiefdom at Delagoa Bay was the Mfumo chiefdom at the mouth of the Mbuluzi river. To the north of Mfumo lay the chiefdom of Manhica; to the south lay the chiefdom of Tembe; to the south-east lay the chiefdom of Nyaka.

Portuguese trade at Delagoa Bay Sea trade at Delagoa Bay was opened after the visit in the 1540s of a Portuguese official named Lourenco Marques, who reported favourably on the prospects for trade. Previous to that date there had been little direct coastal trade, either Muslim or Portuguese. After that date the Ronga chiefdoms traded with an annual Portuguese ship from Sofala or Mozambique island. The Ronga chiefdoms on the north side of the bay competed with each other in sending trade expeditions to mining areas in the northern Drakensberg such as Phalaborwa. The chiefdoms south of the bay competed to obtain ivory by hunting or tribute in elephant-hunting lands that stretched as far south as St Lucia Bay in present Natal. Competition became violent, and numerous small wars were fought from the 16th until the 18th century with the Ronga weapons of large bows and arrows. In the late 16th century war between the Mfumo and Tembe chiefdoms forced the Portuguese to abandon their trading post in Mfumo country for new seasonal trading posts among the Manhica and Nyaka. Captives from these wars were sold as slaves to foreign ships.

The Nyaka kingdom Three large Ronga states arose in succession to each other on the southern side of Delagoa Bay between the 16th and 18th centuries — first the kingdom of the Nyaka, followed by the kingdoms of the Tembe and the Maputo. The Nyaka kingdom expanded its control during the 16th century over an area as far south as St Lucia Bay. Ronga and Nguni people living in the area were raided for ivory and cattle, or paid them in tribute to the Nyaka king. The ivory was sold to the Portuguese, while the cattle built up the wealth of the Nyaka rulers.

The Tembe kingdom This kingdom rose to power by waging war against other Ronga in the 17th century at the expense of the Nyaka kingdom, which declined into being a subject chiefdom. At its height the Tembe ruled as many as twenty-seven regional chiefdoms, of both Ronga and Nguni origin. The Swazi royal historian J.S.M. Matsebula records that traditionalist Swazi still sometimes call themselves 'bakaTembe', thus recalling the days when their Dlamini ancestors were under Tembe rule.

European rivalries for Ronga trade, and raids by European pirates based in Madagascar, excited continual rivalries between Ronga chiefdoms and therefore helped supply war captives as slaves to European traders. Rivalries within Ronga chiefdoms led to competing chiefs and lineages and new Ronga chiefdoms emerged, while Ronga chiefdoms further inland, such as the Kosi (Kosse), rose to new importance in supplying slaves. The Mfumo were defeated in their attempt to bring other northern Ronga together into a larger king-dom. War between the Ronga and inland chiefdoms of the Pedi stopped the Pedi from coming directly to the coast to trade.

In the mid-18th century the Tembe king-dom became embroiled in civil war and lost control of Nguni subject chiefdoms, which migrated south-westwards to become fully independent. The Tembe royal lineage itself split into senior and junior chiefdoms at war with each other. Eventually, in 1794, one of these junior chiefdoms, the Maputo, took over control of the Tembe kingdom.

The Maputo kingdom This kingdom on the southern side of Delagoa Bay was smaller in area, and ruled fewer chiefdoms, than the old Tembe kingdom. But the Maputo sold large amounts of ivory at Delagoa Bay to ships of many European nationalities, in exchange for glass beads and brass ornaments. The ivory came from expeditions armed with firearms sent southwards to hunt or trade with in-dependent chiefdoms in the Natal area. Euro-pean sea traders did not go inland, but Dela-goa Bay trade-goods were exchanged from chiefdom to chiefdom as far south as the Xhosa. During the 18th century the northern Nguni chiefdoms of the Mthethwa and Ndwandwe rose in power and competed in order to control the ivory trade from the Natal area to the Maputo kingdom.

5 Northern and Central Nguni Chiefdoms

There appear to have been no large centralized states among the Nguni before the end of the

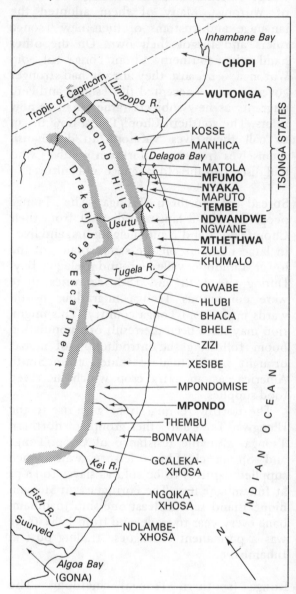

CHOPI, TSONGA AND NGUNI STATES

18th century, but only a great number of clans scattered in very small village home-steads. The early history of the Nguni is therefore a complex web of conflicting oral traditions from numerous chiefdoms. Only among the Nguni of the south are there clear traditions of the origin of chiefdoms.

Nguni origins Some historians have suggested that the Nguni people originated from three broad groupings of clans, and recent archeology has supported such a view (see Chapter 1).

The first grouping of clans, possibly Lala, were Eastern Stream (Coastal tradition) farmers, who came from southern Mozambique — by the 3rd–4th centuries AD. This grouping would also presumably include Western Stream farmers with Khoisan herder connections, who came from the Transvaal highveld — by the 7th century AD.

The second grouping, called Mbo, were Eiland tradition migrants from the Transvaal highveld around the 9th century.

The third grouping, 'pure' Nguni or Koni, were Blackburn tradition (NC-2) farmers also from the Transvaal highveld (closely related to early Tswana with Moloko tradition pottery), from the 11th–12th century.

Clans of both the Lala and Mbo groupings in the north are also noted for their *tekela* dialects, meaning that they pronounce the 'nz' or 'z' of the central and southern Nguni dialects as 't'. Thus the people known to the Zulu and the world as Swazi in fact call themselves 'Swati'.

Northern Nguni traditional origins Oral traditions of the Dlamini, Hlubi and Swazi trace back their ancestry to the Langeni group of Mbo people who lived maybe four hundred years ago. Oral tradition records the names of twenty-five Mbo leaders before the founder of the Langeni, named Dlamini I; and the Swazi royal lineage can be traced back in succession to Dlamini I fourteen generations before Sobhuza II. Given that the length of the average Swazi royal generation from father to son has been 26 years, that would put Dlamini I as having lived at some time around the first half of the 16th century. We know from tradition that Dlamini I lived on the flat marshlands of the Pongola, just inside the present borders of Mozambique. During the 17-18th centuries the Langeni certainly formed part of the Tembe kingdom of the Ronga, and they may also therefore have been part of the previous Nyaka kingdom of the 16th-17th centuries.

The Langeni of the north continually split into new clans which migrated southwards into present Natal to set up new states over the existing Nguni population. The new Ngwaneni clan was followed by the Dlamini and Ndwandwe, and the last remaining Langeni clan in the north was the Langa, from which the Hlubi and Swazi are descended. Chief Langa was succeeded by his son Hlubi (around 1720-30), who decided to lead the Langa clan southwards. Oral tradition tells us that the Langa had lost land during the Tembe civil wars and had to look for new land. Hlubi led the Langa southward along the Lebombo hills to settle south of the Pongola river as subjects of the Ndwandwe. The Langa then split into two clans — one under Hlubi and the other under his brother Dlamini III. When Dlamini III died he was succeeded around 1750-70 by his son Ngwane, whose clan was thereafter known as the 'amaNgwane' (later Swazi).

Rise of Ndwandwe power Both the Hlubi and the Ngwane clans paid tribute to the Ndwandwe chieftaincy, which became a powerful kingship during the reign of Zwide who began to rule around the 1790s. The Ndwandwe took tribute from the numerous small clans living in the area of northern Natal and southern Swaziland. The decline of the power of the Tembe kingdom, and its replacement by the smaller Maputo kingdom after 1794, removed Ronga control of northern Natal ivory-hunting and opened the way for the rise of the Ndwandwe kingdom. Zwide seized control of numerous local clans, such as the Khumalo, the Buthelezi, and the Ngwaneni, by ruthless attacks and capture of their large herds of cattle, which he treated as his own property. On Zwide's behalf the Hlubi and Ngwane conquered Pedi or Sotho clans in the northern valleys, known to the Nguni as 'uSutu' (i.e. Sotho-land), as well as Nguni already in the north remembered in Swazi tradition as *emakhandzambili* ('those found ahead').

Central Nguni origins Pre-Mfecane oral traditions in the area of central and southern Natal have been largely lost, because old chieftaincies have since been destroyed. Surviving oral traditions usually relate to chiefdoms that later became powerful, such as the Mthethwa and Zulu. The Mthethwa trace their origin to an ancestor chief called Nyambose, apparently with Tsonga connections, who may have lived around 1600. The Zulu trace their origins to the Zantsi clans which spread over the coastal area of central Natal in the 17th and 18th centuries from Babanango mountain west of present Ulundi. One of these Zantsi clans split into the Qwabe clan and the Zulu clan, which settled on the Mhlatuze river.

Contacts across the Drakensberg Nguni and Sotho peoples traded goods and exchanged ideas across the Drakensberg (uKahlamba) escarpment. From the Sotho the Ngwane probably adopted ideas about royal marriage and the political importance of the queen-mother, while the Ndwandwe and Mthethwa may have adopted the idea of using age-regiments in war. In the other direction there were Nguni migrations back across the escarpment into Tswana/Sotho country from about the 16th century onwards. These migrations appear to have come from the area around the Tugela headwaters, where the number of stone-walled ruins found by archaeologists suggests a fast growing population in close contact with other builders of stone walls in the west. The Zizi clans migrated into the area of present Lesotho, where they were the first Iron Age groups to settle. The Nguni clans which migrated north-westwards onto the highveld were known by such general names as 'Koni' and 'Tebele' among the Tswana/Sotho.

6 Southern Nguni Chiefdoms

All pre-Mfecane southern Nguni chiefdoms — apart from the Bomvana — may be traced to the Zwedi clan living north of the Mzimkhulu river before 1500. The southern Nguni appear to have spread southwards in two or three stages. First, before 1500, they became well established in the coastal area between the Mzimkhulu and Mzimvubu rivers. Then after

1500 the Mpondo, as the senior Zwedi clan, remained in the area while junior clans spread southwards across the Mzimvubu and inland towards the escarpment. Finally during the later 17th century the group of central Nguni called the Bomvana migrated to Mpondo country seeking refuge from war in the north, while a junior section of the Mpondo known as the Mpondomise also moved southwards.

Khoisan hunter-gatherer and herder contacts The inland area was inhabited by small groups

Early 20th century photographs portray aspects of ancient Nguni life that survived the Mfecane wars. **Left:** *Old Zulu man playing an 'ugubu'.* He holds the calabash resinator against his left breast and strikes the metal string of the instrument with his right hand. His left hand pinches or 'stops' the string to produce a higher or lower pitch.

Above: *Xhosa adolescents at initiation school* Boys were circumcised at the beginning of school, and then remained in camp for a number of months, learning the laws and customs of adult society. In this early 20th century photograph the initiates (*abakweta*) are being painted with white chalkstone and dressed in palm leaf skirts and headdresses. Initiation schools and circumcision died out among central and northern Nguni peoples during the wars of the early 19th century.

of Khoisan hunter-gatherers, whose rock paintings tell us of fights between them and Nguni or Khoisan herders. As the numbers of cattle increased, less land remained for hunting. Eventually the Khoisan hunters withdrew to the open grassland beneath the escarpment (later Griqualand East), fighting off the advances of Nguni, Griqua and European farmers who took over the land in the 19th century.

Khoisan herders south of the Mzimvubu herded their cattle in the grasslands that lay between the thickly-forested river valleys, and southern Nguni clans settled among them. Despite different languages and cultures, Khoisan herders and Nguni farmers had much in common. They were both organized in chiefdoms, and thought of their cattle as their wealth. Both made pottery, though of different types, and made sleeping-mats and baskets from reeds and grass. Both wore leather and furs for clothing, and feathers and ostrich eggshell beads for decoration. But southern Nguni chiefdoms, farming more and more land and raising bigger families, grew faster in population than Khoisan herder chiefdoms. Junior sons of the ruling dynasties of the southern Nguni went further and further south and west to found their own chiefdoms.

Thembu and Xhosa origins The early history of the Thembu clans is little known. In particular, the original relationship of the Thembu with the Mpondo and Xhosa is not clear. The Thembu appear to have settled south of the Mzimvubu in the 16th century, and by the reign of their tenth chief in the mid-17th century were settled around the Mbashe river.

The original Xhosa clan probably broke away from the Mpondo around 1600, and was led by its chiefs beyond Thembu country to the Kei river, where it settled in close contact with Khoisan herders. Then in the mid-17th century junior Xhosa chiefdoms began to break away and migrate further south and west — some going as far west as beyond the Great Fish (Nxaba) river.

The Gona (Gonaqua) clan was founded by a Khoisan herder chief, son of a Xhosa mother, in the early 1700s between the Kei and Keiskamma rivers. The chiefdom grew in size over scattered Khoisan and immigrant Xhosa, and then began to break up. By the end of the 18th century the Gona clan were all subjects of other chiefdoms. Some Gona joined the new Xhosa chiefdom of the Gqunukwebe, who migrated as far west as the 'Bushmans' river by the 1760s, where they at first paid tribute to a local Khoisan herder chiefdom.

The senior Xhosa chiefdom around the Kei river was respected and given tribute but not much feared by other Xhosa chiefdoms. The senior chief did not have enough military power to make himself king of a large centralized state, and the population was scattered in small villages over a very large area. The senior chiefdom itself was split when Rarabe, brother of the chief Gcaleka, challenged his brother's rule and was driven off to the south. Oral tradition records that Rarabe considered himself equal to Gcaleka because his mother had been made 'right-hand-wife' equal to Gcaleka's mother as 'great-wife' — one being daughter of the senior Mpondo chief and the other of the senior Thembu chief.

Questions

1 How important was the impact of sea trade for the Zimbabwean plateau before 1700? (Refer also to Chapter 6.)
2 Why did the Portuguese gain power within the Munhumutapa kingdom?
3 Write what you know of the Rozvi kingdom. [Cambridge International School Certificate, 1976]
4 Outline the distribution and lifestyle of Nguni peoples before the rise of Zwide.

Activities

1 Write an imaginative account of the removal of the kingdom of Great Zimbabwe to Khami.
2 Draw a date-chart of events on the Zimbabwean plateau and on the Mozambique coast. Divide the chart into two or more separate columns for different geographical areas.
3 What is the myth of origin of your own clan or of any clan known to you? Can the myth be accepted as literal truth?

See Bibliography, pp. 337–42: B6 Duminy & Guest; B20 Matsebula; B22 Mazikana; B33 Roberts; B37 Tlou & Campbell; C1 Axelson; C2 Beach; C6–7 Garlake; C9 Hall; C20 Mudenge; C22 Peires; C25 Randles; C27 Saunders & Derricourt; C28 Sutton; C29 Thompson; C31 van Waarden; D14 Peires; J8 Azania; J28 ZimHist.

Chapter 3

Later Iron Age in the West

Southern Africa during the later Iron Age was criss-crossed in all directions by trade in goods and ideas and by small migrations of people. Even the Kalahari and Karoo thirstlands were not complete blocks to travel, though few except hunter-gatherers could live there. People with cattle could move along river courses, digging in their sandy beds for water, and along known routes between wells and pans after rains had filled them. But most recorded history concerns the people of the plateaux between the Orange and Limpopo rivers. The ruins of thousands of stone-walled settlements, made of blocks piled without mortar between them, dating from between about the 16th and 19th centuries, are evidence of dense population on the Transvaal and Orange Free State highveld before European penetration.

1 Venda and Pedi States of the Soutpansberg and Bushveld

Relatively few Venda or Pedi oral traditions before the 19th century have been collected and analyzed, and archaeology has been limited to the northern Drakensberg escarpment. But the little evidence that has been published shows that Venda settlement was probably more extensive before the 17th century than today, and Pedi settlement was certainly less extensive.

Venda states Venda settlement was concentrated around the Soutpansberg mountains, but also extended into the bushveld north of

STONE-WALLED SETTLEMENTS
Marking areas of stone ruins, sites of major Iron Age towns or mines and routes of Iron Age traders.

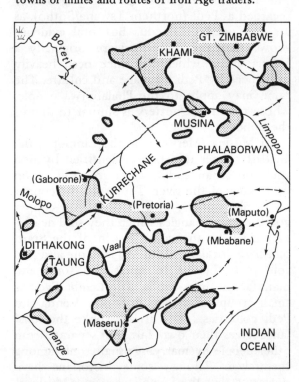

Areas of stone-walling show up clearly on modern aerial photographs of southern Africa. Most ruins south of the Limpopo are associated with Tswana-Sotho-Pedi traditions. Sites on the middle Limpopo are associated with Venda tradition. At the Vaal-Orange confluence ruins are associated with Kora herders. The area of stone-walling on the south-eastern side of the Drakensberg is associated with the Nguni-speaking Zizi, Bhele and Hlubi — most were expelled during the Mfecane wars to form the basis of the later Mfengu people far to the south.

39

the Limpopo and as far south as the Great Letaba river. Most recorded Venda tradition, however, is that of rulers who originated from north of the Limpopo apparently around the 17th-18th centuries. The history of early Venda groups before the coming of these northern rulers remains obscure.

Copper and iron mining Archaeologists have shown that copper was mined at Phalaborwa between about the 10th and the 19th centuries by people making basically the same sort of pottery during all that time. The people lived on nearby hills, cooler and freer from tsetse-fly than the hot bushveld plains, and terraced the hills to build gardens and house platforms. The Phalaborwa people are today generally regarded as Pedi (northern Tswana/Sotho), as are the nearby Lobedu. But oral evidence shows that the Lobedu were originally a Venda group which has since been heavily influenced by Pedi language and culture. The same may apply to the Phalaborwa people, whose traditional pottery is similar to that of the Lobedu.

At Musina (Messina) on the Limpopo, the ancient copper miners are identified by oral tradition as an early Venda group living on both sides of the river. They sold the copper to Lemba traders, who made it into copper goods such as bangles which they sold nearby or carried to the coast. South of the Soutpansberg, local Venda mined iron ore and also sold it to Lemba to smelt and forge and manufacture iron goods. The Lemba lived as small groups of traders in Shona, Venda and Pedi countries. They always spoke the local language as their own, but kept separate from other people by marrying usually only among themselves. Though some historians have suggested that the Lemba were once Muslims, converted by Arabian and Persian sea traders, their apparent Muslim customs of male circumcision and not eating pork are not unique but are also found among neighbouring peoples.

Lobedu history Clans of Rozvi origin spread among eastern Venda and some neighbouring Pedi to found new chiefly dynasties around the 17th century. Lobedu oral tradition tells how the original Lobedu people received new rulers from the north, fleeing from a civil war in the Rozvi kingdom, bringing with them a daughter of the Rozvi king. The new rulers introduced male circumcision (referred to in oral tradition as 'fire'), and some Lobedu fled north to the Soutpansberg rather than submit to circumcision. After the death of their last male chief around 1800 the Lobedu were ruled by a dynasty of 'rain-queens', each known by the title Mudjaji. As Pedi migrants arrived in the country, they paid tribute to the Mudjaji for making rain. In time, as the Lobedu chiefdoms included more people of Pedi origin, the Lobedu became more Pedi than Venda in language.

Singo chiefdoms of the Soutpansberg Meanwhile the early Venda of the Soutpansberg gradually came under the rule of the Singo dynasty of rulers. The Singo came originally from the north, across the Limpopo, but whether they were originally northern Venda or Shona is not known. All that seems certain is that the original Singo capital in the Soutpansberg was Dzata, a stone-walled town whose ruins still stand. Like the Rozvi kingdom, the Dzata kingdom eventually split up into a confederacy of chiefdoms under different Singo lineages.

Each Singo chiefdom had its own stone-walled village as capital. The Singo were an aristocracy who lived somewhat apart from the common people; the Singo usually married among themselves, saying that a Singo who married a commoner would die. Commoners, being uncircumcised, were not admitted to Singo religious ceremonies held in ancestral graveyards. But the Singo also paid respect to the commoners as the original owners of the land. The commoners continued to live in their own chiefdoms, though their chiefs were reduced to being headmen within Singo chiefdoms. Commoner chiefs remained in charge of annual planting and harvest ceremonies — biting the first pumpkin of the harvest before the Singo, and giving thanks for good years to their ancestor spirits living in mountain lakes and pools.

Pedi states Oral tradition suggests that most of the early Pedi lived around the northern Drakensberg escarpment until some migrated eastward and westward in the 17th-18th centuries. Archaeology shows that the northern Drakensberg saw the growth of a dense agricultural population during the later Iron Age. People lived in small villages on hillsides next to their agricultural lands. They terraced their fields by piling long lines of stones along the contours of the hillsides, so that soil was not washed away by the rains. But erosion around streams and pathways became a serious problem, which may explain why some Pedi began to migrate eastward and westward in the 17th-18th centuries.

Eastward and westward migrations The eastward Pedi migrations were absorbed into Tsonga and Chopi chiefdoms of the coastal area. The westward Pedi migrations settled around the hills of the western bushveld as far as the Tswapong hills of Botswana.

East-central Botswana between the Shoshong hills and the Shashe river had been sparsely populated since the 13th century. By 1700 its Iron Age population was probably limited to a small number of Pedi in the east and Khalagari in the south, as well as Kalanga in the north, under the nominal sovereignty of the Rozvi kingdom. The bushveld of the Limpopo valley and north-western Transvaal was similarly sparsely populated. Khoisan hunter-gatherers lived on the plains, while hills were occupied by Iron Age people who herded cattle and hoed crops above the tsetse-infested bush, bringing their cattle to water on the plains only at night when the tsetse slept. The types of stone walls found on these Iron Age hill sites suggest that many of the people were Rozvi subjects or Venda, but some were certainly Pedi. The Mamabolo, a Pedi clan in the central bushveld, record that their chiefly dynasty came from the Venda probably before the great westward Pedi migrations.

Many of the Pedi migrant clans paid tribute to the Rozvi, who claimed control of the bushveld as far south as the Shoshong hills in Botswana. The Birwa clans of the Pedi record that they left their original homeland around the northern Drakensberg and travelled across the Limpopo to pay tribute to the Rozvi Mambo. The Mambo recognized a chief among them who then married into the Mambo's family, and the Birwa became divided into two clans which scattered southwards.

Tswapong chiefdoms of Botswana The Tswapong hills, rich in iron deposits, attracted iron-workers and traders from all directions. The Pedi-speaking people of the hills, known as the baTswapong, came under the leadership of a Pedi migrant from the east in the early 18th century. A clan of Kalanga origin, skilled in iron-working, came from the north to settle and adopted seTswapong language and customs and forgot their old tjiKalanga ones. Birwa and other groups of Pedi came from the east.

Oral tradition records that the baTswapong were famous for their hoes, axes, spearheads and musical instruments, made from strong steel. Traders came from long distances to buy Tswapong iron goods. But trading for profit could too easily become raiding for tribute. Some time in the earlier part of the 18th century a clan of Transvaal-Nguni origin — successful cattle traders — settled in the area south of the Tswapong hills on a mountain above the dense tsetse-infested bush of the Limpopo river. They raided and conquered the baTswapong, though baTswapong chiefs remained the spirit-lords of the Tswapong hills. A junior Transvaal-Nguni clan, the Seleka, took political power over the area in the later 18th century. The Seleka chiefs were famous rain-makers, inheriting a round piece of skin from the forehead of their original chief to be soaked in water when rain was wanted.

Pedi kingdom of Leulu mountains Meanwhile migrants of Tswana origin from the southern bushveld settled among the main Pedi groups of the northern Drakensberg. Probably the migrants were attracted by the riches of trade with the coast resulting from mineral production in the northern Drakens-

Tswana village kgotla (court or forum) on the Vaal (Tikwe) river in the mid 19th century Note that the men are preparing karosses or sniffing snuff while they talk and listen to music. The main figure in the foreground, presumably the young chief, is sewing. Another man is rubbing down the inside of an animal skin.

berg. One such Tswana (Kgatla) migrant named Thobele founded a chiefdom around the Steelpoort (Thubatse) river valley during the later 17th century, which was to become the powerful Pedi kingdom of the 18th century. Thobele and his successors built up the Pedi kingdom in the Leulu mountains by using wealth in cattle and military might to bring local clans into tribute and chiefly inter-marriage. First the Pedi of the mountains were conquered, and then the Pedi of sur-rounding areas. The Pedi kingdom controlled trade from the interior in ivory, cattle and furs, as well as local production of copper, gold and iron. Tsonga traders came from the Inhambane coast or sometimes from Delagoa Bay to exchange goods for European or Asian brass, glass beads, and cloth.

The Pedi kingdom was, like other southern African states before the Mfecane/Difaqane, really a confederacy of chiefdoms paying tribute to a royal chiefdom. The king used his military power to discipline the chiefdoms, and all young men and women within the central part of the kingdom were members of national age-regiments. But the king did not keep a permanent army, and did not break up the subject chiefdoms or impose his own rela-tives as their chiefs. There was no definite frontier between Pedi and Sotho clans on the north-eastern highveld, but the power of the Pedi kingdom probably did not extend further south than the Little Usutu river in modern Swaziland. When the Ngwane attacked

Tswana village near the Orange (Ntshu) river, from a sketch by Samuel Daniell in 1801   Note the clay granary on the right, houses with a thatched roof standing on poles, and the ostrich feather umbrellas shading people from the sun.

and conquered the Pedi or Sotho of the Little Usutu in the early 19th century there was no counter-attack from the Pedi kingdom.

2 Tswana States of the Northern Highveld to 1770

Oral traditions trace back the ruling lineages of Tswana states to the Witwatersrand area sometime around the 13th-15th centuries, and archaeology indicates that the later Iron Age began there some time between the 11th and 13th centuries. From about the 16th century onwards there is abundant archaeological evidence of stone-walled villages and later, by the mid-18th century, of large towns on the northern Witwatersrand, spread-ing to east, west and south. Historical evidence suggests that Tswana states developed on the basis of royal control of cattle through the *mafisa* system, and on the profits of mining, manufacture, and trade.

The Tswana states around the Witwatersrand and Khalagari in the south, as well as Kalanga ing of towns set in the middle of their agricultural lands, with cattle posts scattered over a wider area. The territory of such 'city-states' overlapped with each other and contained chiefdoms under their own traditional headmen living in the town or in a separate village. Junior relatives, usually brothers in the royal family, might break away to found their own chiefdoms over other Tswana, or over Sotho, Pedi and Kgalagari further south, east and west.

Dithakong, 1812 'At length the most gratifying sight which my journey had yet afforded, presented itself; and part of the *Town* of *Litakun* [Dithakong] now appeared before me. As we advanced nearer, and gained higher ground, the multitude of houses which continued rising into view as far as I could see, excited astonishment . . . . . In our way we passed through many *clusters of houses;* between which there were most frequently large stretches of unoccupied ground . . . . . . The houses were all built in the neatest manner imaginable. . Such a town may be considered as a *collection of little villages,* each under the superintendance of its own chieftain.' (W.J. Burchell, *Travels in the Interior of Southern Africa.* London, 1822)

Tswana origins All Tswana ruling lineages are traced to one of three founding ancestors, named Morolong, Masilo, and Mokgatla. Morolong appears to have lived in the western Witwatersrand area around the 13th-14th centuries; Masilo appears to have lived in the northern Witwatersrand area around the 14th-15th centuries; Mokgatla appears to have lived in the north-eastern Witwatersrand area around the 15th-16th centuries. The reasons for their rise to power can only be guessed at. But historians have suggested that the family of Morolong were iron-smiths. We may also note that the family of Masilo lived between grassland and bushveld suitable for extensive cattle grazing, while the family of Mokgatla lived around likely trade-routes across the bushveld to the escarpment and the coast.

The early baRolong — followers of Morolong — moved west towards the Kalahari by about 1500, possibly pushed by the rise of the lineage of Masilo. Further evidence of the spreading power of the lineage of Masilo may be seen in the traditions of some baKgatla lineages, which do not trace themselves back to Mokgatla at all but to the Masilo lineage. This may be explained if migrants of the Masilo lineage brought Tswana ideas of chieftainship to the baKgatla and married into the lineage of Mokgatla.

Oral traditions of subsequent descent from Morolong, Masilo, and Mokgatla often disagree as to exactly who was father or brother, son of a senior wife, etc. One explanation for such disagreements is that chiefdoms when possible claim seniority over related chiefdoms, and do this by consciously or unconsciously changing their traditions of origin. For example there is now a common tradition in Botswana of Masilo having had three grandsons named Kwena, Ngwato and Ngwaketse. But this tradition may well reflect the political alliance of the baKwena, baNgwato and baNgwaketse in the 19th century, rather than being an accurate historical record of the 15th-16th centuries.

44

Karechuenya, 1820   The Hurutshe capital of Karechuenya (Ka-re-tshwenyega), in the hills north of later Zeerust, excited admiration among European visitors:

'The town stands on the very summit of a mountain, on every side of which access is extremely difficult . . . One path only presented itself to the waggon . . . Their cattle-folds were built chiefly of stone; and their habitations . . . commodious . . . the walls are usually decorated . . . in a style that shows the germ of genius'. (Stephen Kay, *Travels and Researches*, London 1833) 'Sinosee's house was neatly finished; it was circular like all the others, having not only the wall plastered both within and without, but likewise the inside of the roof. The wall was painted yellow and ornamented with figures of shields, elephants, cameleopards [giraffes], etc. It was also adorned with a neat cornice or border painted of a red colour.

In some houses there were figures, etc carved or moulded in hard clay, and painted with different colours . . . . They are indeed an ingenious people . . . . . Every part of their houses and yards is kept very clean. They smelt both iron and copper. The rain-maker took us to see one furnace, in which they smelted the iron. It was built of clay, almost equal in hardness to stone.' (John Campbell, *Travels in South Africa*. London 1822)

Hurutshe and Kwena origins   The lineage of Masilo was split into two new lineages in the late 15th or early 16th century by a chieftainship dispute. The rightful chief was a woman called Mohurutshe, granddaughter of Masilo, but a majority of elders chose to follow her brother Kwena as chief, and Mohurutshe fled to the baRolong. But future Kwena chiefs continued to respect Hurutshe chiefs, and would not plant their crops or bite the first pumpkin of the harvest before the senior Hurutshe chief had done so. After Mohurutshe's death in exile, her two sons returned to the bushveld north-west of the Witwaters-rand. There they also quarrelled: oral tradition tells us it was over the ownership of a pet baboon. The winner, named Motebejane, built his capital on a mountain called Tshwenyane about twenty-five kilometres north-east of modern Zeerust. The loser, named Motebele, fled to the south-east and then returned with Nguni mercenary soldiers, who unsuccessfully laid seige to Tshwenyane. Defeated a second time, Motebele fled west and then north to the Limpopo valley where he became chief of the Ganawa group of Pedi. This may have occurred in the middle of the 16th century. The *Hurutshe* kingdom (or confederacy)

45

had a strong base at Tshwenyane, with its own wells and fields around the mountain top, for control over surrounding peoples. The town grew in size, with households of metal-workers and carvers of the local soap-stone (for smoking-pipes). By the later 17th century the town had been extended into a new suburb, known as Karechuenya (or Kurrechane), between the two peaks of the mountain. But the Hurutshe lineage split into two competing lineages in the middle or later 17th century, when the rightful chief was defeated in battle by his brother Menwe, after a dispute over cattle ownership ear-marks. Menwe took over the capital town now located at Karechuenya. Under Menwe's son and grandson in the later 17th and early 18th centuries, the Hurutshe kingdom stretched as far as modern Rustenburg and the Pilanesberg hills.

Chiefdoms of the *Kwena* lineage were scattered in the southern bushveld along the Odi river from the Pretoria area as far north as its confluence with the Marico river. Splits in the lineage of the later 17th and early 18th centuries gave rise to three new lineages, which continued to call themselves baKwena, and to one new lineage which took the name of its ancestor Ngwaketse instead.

Fokeng and Transvaal-Nguni origins It seems most likely that the *Fokeng* were the original group of Tswana/Sotho living south of the Witwatersrand, who were pushed south by Tswana expansion, and acquired chiefs of the lineage of Masilo and of the lineage of Kwena in the process. Few baFokeng remained north of the Vaal (Lekwa) river; most migrated to the southern highveld around the 15th-16th centuries. But it has also been suggested that the Fokeng were originally Nguni rather than Tswana/Sotho.

Nguni migrants crossed the central Drakensberg, as we have seen in Chapter 2, from about the 16th century onwards. The main 'Transvaal-Nguni' chiefdoms of the Ndzundza and Manala on the eastern highveld continued to practise Nguni languages and culture, while other Nguni groups split off from them and settled as far west and north-west as Ramotswa

and Tswapong in Botswana. They settled among Tswana and Pedi as mercenaries or mine-workers, and became metal-workers, traders and rain-makers. In time they adopted Tswana or Pedi language and culture, but kept their separate identity as independent chiefdoms.

There is no agreement as to how these Transvaal-Nguni became known among the Tswana/Sotho as 'maTebele', from which they adopted the word into their own language as 'amaNdebele'. Some people suggest it was because the Nguni made their name among the Tswana/Sotho as the mercenaries who came to the aid of Motebele, the son of Mohurutshe who failed to gain the Hurutshe chieftainship. Other people suggest that the word means 'those who sink' (i.e. out of sight), because they fought behind much bigger shields than the Tswana/Sotho. Both suggestions stress that the Transvaal-Nguni initially gained fame as soldiers.

Tlokwa and Kgatla origins The founders of the *Tlokwa* lineage broke away from the lineage of Mokgatla around the late 16th century, first travelling west and then south across the Witwatersrand. Here they were attacked by a group of Kora, which tells us that later Stone Age herders were living north of the Vaal as late as around 1600. The Tlokwa then settled in the area of Tlokwe (Potchefstroom), from which they took their name as baTlokwa. From Tlokwe, various Tlokwa chiefdoms split off to settle in the north, south and east during the 17th-18th centuries. Eventually, in the mid-18th century, the main body of Tlokwa migrated north to the Pilanesberg hills, probably driven there by bad drought.

The original *baKgatla* of the north-eastern Witwatersrand split into two new lineages under Mogale and Tabane by the early 17th century. The lineage of Tabane remained in the original homeland until it split into three under quarrelling brothers around the mid-17th century — the most junior brother being Thobele who migrated east to found the Pedi kingdom of the Leulu mountains. Meanwhile the lineage of Mogale migrated westwards and itself split between followers of a woman chief and of her brother around the mid-17th century. The brother, Kgafela, fled into exile even further west, where by the mid-18th century the Kgafela-Kgatla had become strong enough to conquer other chiefdoms and set up a new state in the Pilanesberg hills. Kgafela-Kgatla oral tradition records that they first made their enemies poor by planting tsetse-fly on their cattle, and then invited their enemies to herd *mafisa* cattle for them as subjects.

3 Tswana/Sotho States of the Kalahari and Southern Highveld

From about the 16th century onwards Tswana chiefdoms spread westwards into the fringes of the Kalahari, while smaller groups of Tswana spread southwards across the Vaal (Lekwa) river to found the Sotho chiefdoms of the southern highveld.

Growth of the Rolong kingdom During the reigns of the chiefs who followed Morolong

TSWANA/SOTHO STATES

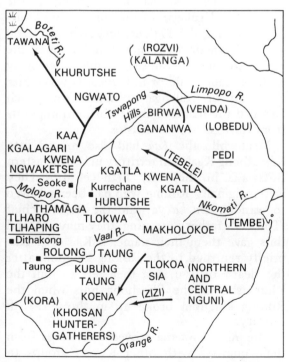

himself the Rolong lived around the western Witwatersrand, probably in close contact with the Kgalagari of the desert areas. The Rolong then moved to the area around Mafikeng about the early 16th century, and kept their capital in the area until the later 17th century. They may have had good political reasons for such a move because of conflict with the Kwena and alliance with the Hurutshe. There were also economic reasons for settling on the north-western corner of the highveld dominating the Kalahari fringes, which was fair hunting and herding land with iron ore deposits. Trade was opened with the Kora and other Khoisan in the south, and even with Bantu-speaking herders far to the north-west in northern Namibia.

The most powerful and famous rulers of the Rolong were Thibela and his son Tau, who reigned in the 17th-18th centuries. They may justly be called kings and their state a kingdom. The kingdom covered much of what later became the northern Cape province and the south-western Transvaal. Its capital, south of later Vryburg, though actually founded by Thibela, became known as Taung — the place of Tau. Its subjects included groups of Kora, Kgalagari and Hurutshe origin. The Rolong built extensive towns with stone walling, including Taung itself and the town in the west later known as Dithakong. It was probably also the Rolong who opened up iron and specularite mines south of Dithakong.

The power of the Rolong kingdom extended hundreds of kilometres north-west through the Kalahari. Herero oral tradition records that they were defeated in battle around the 17th century in the Okahandja district of Namibia by a Tswana chief called Kativine — this could possibly have been Thibela or one of his generals. Other evidence of the Rolong crossing the Kalahari can be seen in stone-walled ruins found in the Kalahari. The wells and iron mines of the Kgwebe hills south of Lake Ngami are said to have been originally dug by the Rolong, while stone cattle enclosures two hundred kilometres to the west, near ancient copper mines, were built on a similar pattern to Dithakong. (European writers later roman-

47

ticized such ruins into 'the lost city of the Kalahari'.) Apart from iron and copper, most of the trade across the Kalahari was probably in cattle; the large long-horned cattle of Namibia were much desired among the Tswana.

King Tau himself is remembered in Rolong oral tradition as a ruthless military leader like Shaka. During his reign numbers of Rolong were driven away by his ruthlessness to settle among Kora on the lower Vaal river. Because of worsening drought these people took to eating fish from the river, and were therefore called baTlhaping – 'fish people'. Tau's attempts to control these people brought him into conflict with the Kora who had previously controlled the area. As early as the 1660s, Kora who came to Capetown to trade had told the Dutch commander there of the 'Bri-qua', who were black people under a great king called Eijra living in houses made of stone and clay. The Bri-qua (meaning 'goat people') were at war with the Kora over the copper trade, and were trading with other black people in the north.

War with Tlhaping rebels, including Tau's own brother, brought about the death of Tau some time in the period 1720-40. The Tlhaping were joined by Kora allies after Tau had killed a Kora chief, whose brother Matsatedi (Taaibosch) then ambushed Tau with bows and poisoned arrows. The king subsequently died from wounds received in the battle.

After Tau's death the kingdom retreated back to the area of Mafikeng. After the death of Tau's successor, Ratlou, and of Ratlou's son in a smallpox epidemic, the kingdom became a loose confederation of chiefdoms descended from four sons of Tau – Ratlou, Seleka, Tshidi and Rapulana.

The scattered *Tlhaping* people became independent of Rolong rule with the death of Tau in the early 18th century. A ruling lineage emerged among the Tlhaping from the descendants of a famous Rolong hunter. This lineage achieved effective power in the mid-18th century by marrying the daughters of important Kora families in the area, and by controlling the increasing volume of trade with the Cape Colony in the south and with Tswana states in the north-east. By the late 18th century the Tlhaping state had become an impressive Tswana kingdom based on a large capital town.

Conquest of the Kgalagari Virtually nothing is known about Kgalagari history before their conquest by Tswana chiefdoms. The Kgalagari clans around south-eastern Botswana became part of the Rolong kingdom, taking the Kgwatheng lineage of Rolong headmen as their rulers. Later the widespread territory of the Kgwatheng-Kgalagari was conquered by the chiefdoms of the Tswana who came from the east in the 18th century – the Khurutshe, Kaa, Kgabo-Kwena, and Ngwaketse. A possible reason for these Tswana conquests may have been the demand for ivory and furs to supply an increasing trade in hunting goods with the coast. Kgalagari karosses (tailored furs) are known to have reached even China.

The *Khurutshe* originated around the 16th century as a group of Hurutshe loyal to Motebele, the son of Mohurutshe, when he was finally defeated by his brother in battle and retired first to near Lobatse in south-eastern Botswana. Motebele abandoned his people there after a quarrel, and they subsequently joined other Tswana in conquering the Kgwatheng-Kgalagari of the hills around Molepolole during the 17th century. Around 1700 some of them went north to conquer the Kgalagari of the Shoshong hills, previously under Kalanga rule or influence. It was either Kgalagari or Kalanga pronunciation which changed the name of these northern migrants from Hurutshe to Khurutshe.

Meanwhile the *Kaa* had also moved into Kgwatheng-Kgalagari territory in south-eastern Botswana in the early 17th century. They were originally Rolong who had been allowed to wander. '*Ba ka ya*' said the Rolong chief (Thibela's father), meaning 'they may go', and thus gave them their name, baKaa. The Kaa briefly returned to the Rolong kingdom after the death of Tau, and then left to join the Khurutshe in the Shoshong hills when the Rolong kingdom broke up in the mid-18th century.

The *Kgabo-Kwena* moved westwards from their quarrels with other Kwena groups to conquer the Kgwatheng-Kgalagari of the hills around Molepolole soon after 1700, and were joined by the Ngwaketse. Together they occupied the area around modern Molepolole, Gaborone and Mochudi. At this stage the Kgabo-Kwena and Ngwaketse probably still paid tribute to the Hurutshe kingdom at Kurrechane in the east.

Origins of Sotho chiefdoms Archaeological studies show that the highveld south of the Vaal was not settled by Iron Age people until the 15th century. The earliest type of stone-walled settlement was limited to an area just south of the Vaal around the hill of Ntsuana-tsatsi near modern Frankfort. This first type of settlement then developed into a second type around the 16th-17th century which spread broadly across the highveld as far south as the borders of modern Lesotho and as far north as the source of the Vaal river around modern Bethal. Meanwhile also around the 16th-17th century a third type of stone-walled settlement spread across the Vaal from the direction of modern Klerksdorp in the north-west.

The archaeological evidence appears to fit other historical evidence remarkably well. The first type of settlement must have been the early Fokeng clans who record their origins at Ntsuanatsatsi in oral tradition. The widespread second type of settlement must have been the spread of Fokeng and Tlokoa (Tlokwa) and other clans, joined by more Koena (Kwena) clans from the north, who founded the numerous small chiefdoms of the Sotho on the highveld. The third type of settlement must have been the Kubung and possibly others, who trace their origins to the Rolong around Thabeng (Klerksdorp) across the Vaal. The archaeological evidence shows that all three types of settlement, despite their different origins north of the Vaal, were all part of a common culture. This fits the historical evidence of Iron Age people south of the Vaal, despite their 'Tswana' origins, coming to feel themselves part of a new 'Sotho' ethnic identity — including Fokeng, Tlokoa, Koena, Kubung, Taung and Zizi.

Fokeng clans appear to have been pushed southwards by Kwena expansion over the Witwatersrand in the 15th-16th centuries, and then made Ntsuanatsatsi their base for further expansion. *Tlokoa* clans scattered from their original home at Tlokwe (Potchefstroom), north of the Vaal, as far west as Natal, in the 17th-18th centuries. Some Fokeng clans settled around Ntsuanatsatsi and others spread as far south as the western Caledon (Mohokare) valley. *Koena* clans, claiming clearer and more recent descent from the Kwena chiefs of the Witwatersrand than the Fokeng, arrived in the Ntsuanatsatsi area possibly in the 17th century and pushed the expansion of Sotho settlement further south along the fertile Caledon valley. There were numerous marriages between these Sotho clans; Moshoeshoe was himself Koena but his mother and three of his four chief wives were Fokeng. There was also intermarriage with Khoisan hunter-gatherers as the previous owners of the land, and Sotho language was influenced by Khoisan words and click-sounds. However, there was at least one case where a Sotho chief was rejected by his people for being too light-skinned, i.e. for being too much of inferior Khoisan origin.

The *Kubung* originated as Rolong who spread from Thabeng (Klerksdorp) across the Vaal to Bodibeng (Kroonstad). They almost certainly intermarried with the Kora, who were living in the area. Kora influence may explain why some early Sotho houses, built entirely of stone slabs, were dome-shaped like the reed house built by the Kora. A practical reason for building houses in this shape was protection from man-eating lions.

The *Taung* appear to have originated as Hurutshe followers of Motebele, the son of Mohurutshe, who migrated southwards after his defeat by his brother around the 16th century. They adopted the lion (*tau*) as 'totem' and crossed the Vaal in the 17th century, apparently after the Kubung, to settle east and south of the Kubung. From there they began to take over Kubung or Kora land and people.

Finally, we have already seen in Chapter 2 that the *Zizi* clans of Nguni origin crossed the Drakensberg into the Lesotho lowlands before the arrival of Sotho clans in the area. This is confirmed by the fact that stone-walled settlements of the same type spread from the Tugela headwaters in Natal across the Drakensberg to the Caledon headwaters.

4 Tswana-Sotho States in Crisis, c. 1770-1820

In the later 18th and early 19th centuries there was an increasing number of wars between Tswana states, while certain Sotho chiefdoms began to build larger states on the southern highveld. Two general reasons may be suggested why competition between the Tswana states turned to warfare — shortage of agricultural land or pasture, and a growing volume of trade between states and with the east and south coasts.

Chiefs established themselves as battle leaders with an increasing hunger for the cattle and pasture land of other chiefdoms. Tswana raiders reached as far as central Namibia and western Zambia. Royal demand for imported luxury goods, including glass or porcelain beads, brought the first European wagon traders from the south coast to the major kingdoms of the Hurutshe, Tlhaping, and Ngwaketse in the first two decades of the 19th century. A young Hurutshe prince confessed to a European traveller in 1820 that 'had he plenty of beads, he should cover his whole body with them, and wrap them round his throat till they touched his chin'. But the growth of local production, particularly of copper ornaments, karosses and ivory, appears to have kept pace with the growth of foreign trade. Not all of this production was exported. Tswana aristocrats wore numerous locally-made copper rings and beads on their arms or legs and in their ear lobes. Iron of course was used to manufacture hoe heads for agriculture, as well as axes, spears and knives. The grain surplus was stored in covered pits or enormous baskets raised above the ground.

Tswana wars c. 1770-1820 Why should disputes over cattle and pasture, and possibly over crop lands, have become so frequent among Tswana chiefdoms in the later 18th

CLIMATIC CHANGE
Evidence (from tree-ring dating) suggests that rainfall in areas receiving Indian Ocean rains declined from a high level around 1600 until the later 18th century, when the rains increased to a high level around 1790. The rainfall then began to drop dramatically into a bad drought, known as the *madlatule* in Natal, in the years immediately around 1800. Thereafter the previous high level of rainfall returned temporarily around 1815.

century? The answer may be found in the pattern of rainfall and drought affecting the whole eastern half of southern Africa.

A long period of plentiful rains in the Tswana area of highveld and bushveld would have increased the amount of suitable land for livestock and cultivation, particularly in the drier western areas. The increase in food supply would have promoted the growth of both cattle and human population. The already most fertile areas around the Witwatersrand would have been under the heaviest pressure of 'overpopulation', resulting in disputes over livestock, land, and subject people between states. Previously dry lands in the west might become more attractive for settlement. But then when drought finally came between 1790-1810 it would have hit all the more disastrously on overpopulated old lands and recently populated new lands alike.

Ngwaketse kingdom During the 18th century the power of the Hurutshe kingdom was challenged in the west by the growth of the Ngwaketse kingdom in the area of south-east Botswana. The Ngwaketse chiefdom broke away from the Kgabo-Kwena in the Molepolole hills and rapidly grew in strength during the reign of Moleta (c. 1770-90), who finally conquered the southern Kgwatheng-Kgalagadi of the Kanye/Lobatse area. Moleta then turned to stave off the Tlhaping kingdom which had previously taken tribute in hunting goods from the southern Kgwatheng.

At the battle of Phata-ea-Barwa, just south of Lobatse, Moleta's Ngwaketse fell upon the invading Tlhaping and Kora mercenaries and expelled them southwards again (c. 1780).

The Ngwaketse state became a powerful independent kingdom under Moleta in his stone-walled capital of Seoke (now in ruins near Lobatse). It produced ivory and furs from its extensive hunting lands and copper from its mines near Kanye, and traded westwards with the Hurutshe and southwards with the Tlhaping. Moleta's son Makaba II (ruled c. 1790-1824) moved the capital to Kanye hill in the west, on which he built a town fortified with stone walls. Here he established his reputation as a great warrior king by fighting off the invasion of Kora and Griqua gunmen from the far south, led by Jan Bloem, in 1798-9.

By the 1790s the Hurutshe and Ngwaketse kingdoms were engaged in continuous warring against each other. They allied with other Tswana chiefdoms and spread warfare across the western Witwatersrand area. From the south there were interventions of Tlhaping, Kora and Rolong. The last surviving son of Tau, Makgetla, was killed in battle with the Hurutshe (c. 1805). With his death the breakup of the Rolong kingdom into competing chiefdoms was complete, as Makgetla had been the last chief recognized as senior by all the Rolong chiefdoms.

Tswana conquest of central and northern Botswana   The Kaa seized the Shoshong hills of east-central Botswana from their Khurutshe rulers during the famine and drought of about the 1760s. When news of the Kaa triumph reached a large party of Khurutshe hunters in the north, they became cattle raiders across the Zambezi, reaching as far north as the Luyana kingdom.

Meanwhile in the south a junior clan of the Kgabo-Kwena called the Ngwato broke away in a civil war around 1770. The pretext for the dispute between the Kwena and the Ngwato was a quarrel over women, hence their battle on the Ngotwane river is sometimes called 'the battle of the skirts'. The

Pedi woman resting on a sleeping mat, her head against a wooden rest.   An early 20th century photograph.

Ngwato were defeated and fled north to the Shoshong hills. For the next twenty years or so the Ngwato paid tribute to the Kaa, until a quarrel between two sons of the Ngwato chief Mathiba split his people in two.

Tawana, the favourite son of Mathiba, was defeated by Khama I, the more senior son of Mathiba, during the 1790s. Tawana then took his followers on a great journey northwards to a new homeland on the Boteti and then in Ngamiland. Mathiba soon quarrelled with Tawana and returned home to the Shoshong hills where, rejected by both his sons, he drank poison, covered himself with a kaross, and died in despair. Back in the Shoshong hills Kaa and Ngwato chiefdoms clashed for control around the year 1800. The Kaa finally drove the Ngwato, who had been weakened by another chieftainship dispute, northwards out of the Shoshong hills.

Under the rule of Kgari (c. 1817-27), a powerful Ngwato state emerged around Serowe to control the trade routes between the Boteti river, Shoshong hills and Tswapong hills. Kgari is remembered as a great ruler who 'hammered' the Boteti and Tswapong peoples into submission. From the Boteti people, who included Khoisan spearmen skilled in elephant hunting, Kgari took tribute in ivory; from the

Tswapong people he took tribute in iron hoe-heads. From all subjects he took tribute in cattle and sheep. Kgari built up the power of the kingship by appointing powerful commoner headmen (i.e. indunas), who held large herds of *mafisa* cattle and had jurisdiction over all Ngwato clans and subject chiefdoms on his behalf. In this way the king had loyal subjects more powerful than his royal relatives who might otherwise seize power.

Meanwhile there were similar developments in the new state set up by Tawana in Ngami-land. By 1800 he had settled in the iron-rich Kgwebe hills, south of Lake Ngami, where Tawana was killed in a battle with his own son Moremi I about 1820. Moremi, like his cousin Kgari of the Ngwato, appointed powerful indunas to control his royal relatives.

Western Tswana wars c. 1805-20   After 1805 the previously strongest Tswana kingdom of the Hurutshe at Kurrechane was weakened by a succession dispute. To the north-east the Kgafela-Kgatla were also split by succession disputes around 1805. Meanwhile the Ngwaketse kingdom to the west under Makaba II and the Tlhaping kingdom to the south under Molehabangwe were at the peak of their strength, trading or raiding as far north-west as the Herero in Namibia, and down the newly opened wagon route to the Cape. Europeans who arrived at the Tlhaping capital, Dithakong, were amazed to find that it was a city as big as or bigger than Capetown, which then had a population of 15,000.

In 1808 the Tlhaping, Hurutshe and Kwena formed an alliance against the Ngwaketse, and attacked Makaba's capital at Kanye. After a major battle they were beaten off. The Ngwaketse followed up their victory by raiding the Kwena in the Molepolole hills for cattle, but a Kgafela-Kgatla army led by Pilane came to the aid of the Kwena. Pilane established himself as the strong man of his people despite a succession of weak and unpopular chiefs above him. The Kgatla later claimed that the Kwena had promised Pilane ownership of the Mochudi hills as a reward for his services.

Hurutshe decline   The last powerful Hurutshe king, Sebogodi, was killed in about 1815 when attacking a group of subjects who were trying to assert their independence by refusing to surrender the tribute of breast-meat from wild game due to the Hurutshe king. Hurutshe oral tradition records that Sebogodi was warned not to make the attack by the spirit of his great ancestor, Thobega, who spoke through his spirit-wife, a priestess who lived in a cave in the side of Kurrechane mountain. Because Sebogodi disobeyed her, she deserted the mountain and left her curse on the city that it would soon be utterly destroyed. After Sebogodi's death, the regent who ruled on behalf of Sebogodi's young son dreamed that Thobega had died and had left the people for ever.

By 1820 warfare was so widespread among the western Tswana that hardly a chiefdom had not seen its chief recently killed in battle. Allies of one year became the enemies of the next. Unpopular leaders were assassinated or, like the Tlokwa chief at the battle of Boswela-Kgosi (1819), were deliberately exposed to certain death in battle by their own people.

Rise of Sotho chiefdoms   By the early 19th century there were at least two Sotho chiefs on the highveld south of the Vaal attempting to unite the scattered chiefdoms into a large state.

Moletsane, chief of the northern Taung people, attempted to build his kingdom by military means, and became a major figure in the Difaqane wars of the 1820s. Mohlomi, chief of the Monaheng, in the western Caledon valley around present Marquard, attempted to build his kingdom by more peaceful means. His power was based on his being a rain-doctor and a wise judge of disputes between his people; a hater of witchcraft; a chief who paid lobola (*bohali*) for his poor subjects to marry with; and a man who married many wives to make their fathers his allies. However, Mohlomi died in about 1815 before he had succeeded in building up a large state.

Southern Sotho oral tradition tells us how the lessons taught by Mohlomi were learnt by

Venda mbila (xylophone), played by one or two players. The sounding board consists of calabashes closed by thick cobweb. The hammers in this photograph have modern rubber heads.

a young man called Leqoqo, born around 1786, the son of Mokhachane, chief of the Mokoteli. Leqoqo first built up herds of cattle, for using to recruit subjects by the *mafisa* system and for paying *bohali,* by raiding small numbers from other chiefdoms. He took the praise-name 'Moshoeshoe' (Mo-shwe-shwe), an

onomatopoeia meaning 'the shaver', after he had stealthily taken a particular chief's cattle as if he had shaved off the old man's beard.

5 States of the Okavango and Upper Zambezi

The marshlands of numerous rivers between the Okavango swamps and the upper Zambezi cut through an area of northern Kalahari which is otherwise dry and extremely sandy. The later Stone Age and early Iron Age population of the area consisted of groups of fishermen isolated from each other by large stretches of thirstland. Not until the 17th-18th centuries were the baTeti (reed people) of the Boteti and the baNoka (river people) of the Okavango organized in chiefdoms. The original Noka and Teti were later Stone Age rather than Iron Age fishermen, using basket fish-traps and stone or bone-headed harpoons. Khoisan hunter-gatherers of the thirstland

IRON AGE PEOPLES OF SOUTH-WEST CENTRAL AFRICA

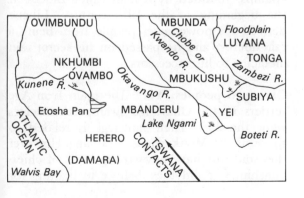

53

areas, covering parts of modern Angola and Zambia as well as Namibia and Botswana, continued to practise later Stone Age technology up to the 19th-20th centuries.

Luyana kingdom On the upper Zambezi the Luyana (or Luyi) kingdom became a powerful state during the 18th century, though it had been founded a century earlier. The Luyana were the people of a large flood-plain, who fished its waters during the flood season and pastured their cattle on its grasses during the dry season. They traded fish and cattle with surrounding peoples for wood, ironware and honey or wax.

Under the rule of a line of priest-kings, the Luyana developed an aristocratic state which controlled the labour of slaves who built village mounds, fish dams and drainage canals on the flood-plain. By the later 18th century the kingdom was involved in much trade with the Angola/Zaire region and in slave-raiding wars with its neighbours in southern and central Zambia. Khurutshe raiders from Botswana were turned back, but Mbunda mercenaries from Angola became rebellious. (They said: '*Na yange nji mwene*', meaning 'I am my own master'.) By the 1830s the Luyana kingdom was deep in civil war between aristocrats and mercenaries over succession to the kingship. Its twelfth *Litunga* (king), Mubukwanu, inherited a disunited kingdom on the eve of the Kololo invasion.

Okavango peoples: Subiya The first Iron Age people to penetrate the Okavango swamps in wooden canoes were Tonga people from the middle Zambezi valley. The Subiya chiefdom of the Tonga south of the Chobe river was founded around the early 18th century. The Subiya chiefdom spread its control over fishermen along the flood channel between the Chobe and Okavango swamps. The Subiya became well known for their skill in medicine, as expert carvers in wood and as makers of beautiful pottery.

Okavango peoples: Mbukushu Other Iron Age groups entered the Okavango swamps from the north-west. The Mbukushu were

> A curse on you flood.
> I can see you have come, again,
> to chase me away.
> But my cattle won't suffer.
> I am taking them away
> to the forests where they
> can find good grazing.
>
> Now, my cattle, see where
> I have brought you
> to enjoy green pastures.
> But be careful not
> to pass through the bowels
> of the hungry forest lion.
>
> (Song of a Lozi or Luyana herdsman)

living on the upper Zambezi around the Katima Mulilo rapids when they came under attack by the Luyana in the later 17th century. Some Mbukushu became Luyana subjects; others fled west to the Kwando (upper Chobe) river. These Mbukushu on the Kwando were raided many times in the mid-18th century by the Luyana in search of slave labour for canals and mounds on the upper Zambezi flood-plain. Mbukushu who remained on the Kwando became Luyana subjects. Others fled in small groups westwards towards the Angola plateau or south-westwards to the Okavango.

The Mbukushu were careful river-edge cultivators, using their iron hoes to grow millet successfully on the otherwise infertile Kalahari sands. The main Okavango chiefdom of the Mbukushu was just north of the swamps, founded by a man called Libebe at the beginning of the 19th century. Libebe derived his power over people from being a rain-doctor, and he passed on his secret rain medicine to his successors.

Okavango peoples: Yei The main Iron Age settlers in the Okavango swamps themselves were the Yei. Their language is related to those of the Mbukushu and Luyana. However they did not have any strong ideas of chieftainship, nor did they believe in fighting for power over their neighbours. David Livingstone called them Africa's pacifists.

Yei traditions tell of originally living in the Kwando swamps as subjects of the Subiya in the south and of the Mbukushu in the north. But the flight of the Mbukushu to the Kwando from Luyana raids in the late 17th — early 18th centuries forced the Yei to fish further south. They followed the rivers and marshes in their canoes, through the Okavango swamps where they intermarried with the Noka, until some reached Lake Ngami in the south by the end of the 18th century. Scattered over the whole area of the Okavango swamps, the Yei could boast: 'We are like the flies that float on a milk pail.'

6 States of the Namibia Plateau

Like the Zambezi-Okavango area, the area around and between the Kunene and Kuvelai rivers (cut in half by the present Namibia-Angola border) consists of numerous rivers set in dry countryside. But the rivers are smaller and rainfall even lower, so that the Kuvelai unlike the Okavango is a network of seasonal flood-plains rather than a permanently wet swamp.

The Nkhumbi and Ovambo of the Kunene-Kuvelai area were related by language to the Ovimbundu of the north and to the Herero/Mbandu of the south. The Nkhumbi lived around the flood-plain of the Kunene river, while the Ovambo were scattered across the Kuvelai delta. The Nkhumbi lived in a single kingdom, which some historians believe also ruled the Ovambo up to the 18th century. The Ovambo lived in many chiefdoms, some large and some small, of which the Kwanyama chiefdom had become the most powerful by the 19th century. The Kwanyama controlled the import of iron ore from the north to ironsmiths in all Ovambo chiefdoms. Two other chiefdoms also became important through trade — the Ndonga chiefdom controlled the import of copper ore from the mines around Tsumeb in the south, while the Njandjera traded Ovambo-made metal goods for salt with the Herero of the south.

Ovambo iron-smiths travelled eastwards along the Okavango (Kubango) river to smelt and forge iron and sell it to local people such as the Mbukushu. But from the 18th century onwards the main trade and source of profit was in selling ivory and slaves northwards to the Ovimbundu, in exchange for cloth and liquor. As in other African societies engaged in the slave trade, the aristocracy of the Nkhumbi kingdom and Ovambo chiefdoms sold off the labour power of their communities in exchange for quickly consumed personal luxuries. (By contrast the Luyana used the labour power of slaves to make their flood-plain more productive in growing food.)

Mbandu peoples: Mbanderu and Herero origins South of the Okavango and Kunene there were few suitable soils and insufficient rainfall for Iron Age crop farming — except by irrigation around isolated springs. The Iron Age people of the plateau of northern Namibia, originally called the Mbandu, were therefore nomadic cattle herders rather than crop farmers with fixed homes. The origin of the Mbandu probably lies in a long period of exchange and intermarriage between Iron Age people and Khoisan herders.

Mbandu oral tradition records their defeat in the 17th century by a Rolong army of the Tswana, who had originally come to trade cattle. The Mbandu then quarrelled with the Rolong over cattle, but the Rolong were too strong to be resisted and most of the Mbandu decided to abandon their cattle to the Rolong. Those Mbandu who left and migrated north-westwards to the Kaokoveld area west of Etosha Pan became known as the Herero, meaning 'the deciders'. The Mbandu who stayed where they had been living, around present-day Omaruru, became known as the Mbanderu.

The Mbanderu retained trading contacts with Lake Ngami, where first the Rolong and later the Tawana group of Tswana had settlements. The Herero gained in wealth and military strength as an independent nation during the 18th century. They fought with the Ovambo over control of the Tsumeb copper mines and with the Nama over cattle in the south. But it was not until about 1820, according to Herero tradition, that they were strong enough to defeat Tswana raiders (probably Tlhaping) who came to seek tribute. The battle was at Etemba, near Omaruru, two hundred kilometres from the Atlantic Ocean.

The indigenous later Stone Age people of the Kaokoveld were a northern group of Damara called the Tjimba. The Tjimba became part of the Herero nation, working as huntsmen, herdsmen and metalworkers for the cattle-owning aristocracy. As a result, people to the north and south saw the Herero more as a continuation of the later Stone Age population than as a new nation. The Ovambo called all Herero 'Tjimba' and the Nama called all Herero 'Damara'.

Damara The main group of Damara in Namibia are often referred to as 'Berg-dama' (meaning mountain-Damara) because they lived in and around the Aub mountains inland from Walvis Bay. The Berg-dama were hunter-gatherers who kept no cattle, who served the Nama as iron and copper-workers and spoke the Nama language, yet who had their own customs and a religion based on holy fire. Did they once speak a Khoisan language like other hunter-gatherers in southern Africa? Some words used by the Berg-dama seem to be neither Khoisan nor Bantu in origin, and unlike Khoisan hunters they are very dark-skinned. All this leads some historians to suggest that the Damara were descendants of migrants who brought the earliest knowledge of iron-making from east to west central Africa, and who may possibly have spoken a Central Sudanic language.

Questions

1 Describe and give reasons for the distribution of Bantu peoples in Africa south of the Limpopo before 1800. [Cambridge International School Certificate, 1976]
2 Why did sizeable states develop earlier on the plateau between the Orange and Limpopo rivers than in the coastal zone south of the Pongola?
3 What was the crisis that beset Tswana Sotho states in the fifty years before Difaqane?
4 Discuss the importance of thirstland and marshland environments for the development of states around the Kalahari basin.

Activities

1 Discover the whereabouts and mark on a map the stone-walled ruins and other later Iron Age sites in your district or any district known to you.
2 Draw a map of the mineral resources (excluding diamonds) of the Orange-Limpopo plateau, and mark major later Iron Age settlements and trade routes on it.
3 Construct a 'family tree' of the relations between founding ancestors of Tswana Sotho groups as recorded in oral tradition. (Note where relationships are uncertain or disputed.)

See Bibliography, pp. 337–42: B21 Maylam; B33 Roberts; B37 Tlou & Campbell; C9 Hall; C10 Hamilton; C15 Maggs; C17–18 Mason; C19 Miller; C29 Thompson; C30 van Waarden; C31 Wilmsen; J9 BNR; P 21 SAAB.

Chapter 4

European Colonization on the Coast (to 1800)

From the 1590s onwards the Dutch from the Netherlands, and to a lesser extent the English and French, began to compete with the Portuguese for the rich Indian Ocean trade in Asian spices (pepper, mace, nutmeg, cloves, cinnamon), calico and silks, and African gold or copper, ivory and slaves. The Dutch, sailing round the southern end of Africa, soon replaced the Portuguese as the main sea trading power in West Africa and around the Indian Ocean. In the 17th and early 18th centuries the Netherlands became Europe's richest trading nation, until it was superseded by Britain in the later 18th and 19th centuries.

European powers tried to control trade between the Atlantic and Indian Oceans by building forts on the coasts of Africa and Madagascar. The Dutch fort at the Cape of Good Hope grew into a thriving colony, with European settlers and African or Asian slaves. These immigrants developed a distinctive culture, which was 'Africanized' in the 17th–18th centuries as it spread to neighbouring peoples in the interior.

1 Dutch Trading at the Cape of Good Hope

European ships started calling at the Cape of Good Hope to pick up fresh water and food supplies around the year 1600. The most powerful African chiefdom in the area was that of the Cocho (Cochoqua) Khoisan herders, who lived inland north-east of Table Mountain. The Cocho were trading with their senior relatives of the Chaimo chiefdom to the east, who were trading with the most senior Khoisan herder chiefdom — the Inqua — in the southern Karoo. To the north-west the Cocho traded with the Chairi-griqua of the Cape west coast, who in turn traded with the Nama of the lower Orange river. Junior sections of the Cocho chiefdom lived nearer the coast around the Cape of Good Hope — including the Goringhai-khona on the shore of Table Bay, who collected shellfish for food and sold them to sailors from ships which anchored in the bay.

The Africans traded sheep, cattle, ivory, ostrich feathers and shells with Europeans in exchange for beads and metals, liquor and *bhang* (marijuana) from India, some of which were traded inland to the Nama or Inqua who traded copper beads, goats and ivory southwards. Most of the European visitors trading at the Cape in the first half of the 17th century were English. As early as 1614 a young Khoisan leader from the Cape of Good Hope was taken back to England to learn the English language and European trading practices. When the Dutch led by Jan van Riebeeck landed at Table Bay in 1652, they found that the leader of the Goringhai-khona who greeted them on the beach, whom they called Herry, spoke to them in English.

The Netherlands East India Company, founded in 1602 to have a monopoly of all Dutch trade in the Indian Ocean, decided to set up a small permanent station at the Cape of Good Hope in the mid-17th century. The company had its overseas headquarters at Jakarta on the island of Java in the East

Indies, and sailed two or three fleets of its ships every year between Java and the Netherlands around southern Africa. These ships needed fresh water supplies, so in 1652 the company placed its station at the point where a stream ran into the north-facing Table Bay, where ships could anchor in shelter from the storms around the Cape of Good Hope sixty kilometres further south. The new station, under commander van Riebeeck, served the company's fleets with water, vegetables and meat, and had a small hospital for sick sailors, and a small fort for protection.

Khoisan-Dutch relations The Khoisan were at first happy to sell sheep and cattle to the Dutch at Table Bay, though they complained that the Dutch paid less than the English used to. Quarrels began when the Dutch moved out of the trading station and started herding livestock and growing crops in ranches and farms on Khoisan land.

In 1659-60 the first war broke out between local Africans and European settlers at the Cape, when the Dutch attacked the Khoisan herders for giving refuge to escaped West African slaves from the new Dutch farms. The local Khoisan, led by Herry and Doman, attacked Dutch farms on rainy days when the firearms of the Dutch became too wet to fire. But Herry and Doman were captured and imprisoned on Robben Island in Table Bay — the first people to be detained there. In 1664 the Dutch tried to show new friendship with the local people by great celebrations for the Christian marriage of Herry's niece to a senior Company officer. But the Khoisan complained that the Dutch were taking more and more land from the Khoisan for settlement. If we came to your country, Khoisan leaders asked Dutch settlers, would you allow us to do the same thing?

Origin of Cape Colony The village which the Dutch called 'Kaap Stadt' (Capetown) became an important port, supplying passing ships with fresh water and vegetables, bread flour, and salted mutton or beef. Soon more land was needed for farms and ranches than could be found between Table Mountain and Table Bay. But the powerful Chocho chiefdom of Khoisan herders on the other side of the mountain stood in the way of Dutch expansion inland. So, in a war between 1672 and 1677, the Dutch fought the Chocho under chief Gonnema, seized their sheep and cattle, and took their land.

Capetown grew from a trading station into the beginnings of a *colony* — a state with a population of settlers, slaves and 'natives', who had to be governed, a territory with frontiers to be protected against enemies. In 1691 the Netherlands East India Company recognized this by promoting the military commander of the Cape of Good Hope to the rank of colonial governor. Dutch farms and ranches continually pushed the frontiers of the Cape Colony further north and east. Khoisan herders and hunters in the new frontier areas, like the Chocho before them, lost their livestock and land.

2 Colonial Life at the Cape

The Netherlands East India Company developed the Cape Colony as 'the tavern to two seas' between the Indian and Atlantic Oceans. Company ships on their way from Asia or Europe were supplied with cheap and plentiful food and drink. The Company also sold provisions at high prices to ships of other European nations, particularly the French and English. In the 18th century up to 1779 when the average number of Dutch ships every year was 55, there were often more foreign ships in port than Dutch ones.

Settlers and slaves The ever-growing demand of ships for food and drink was supplied by extending agricultural production over the mountain from Capetown. After the defeat of the Chocho in 1677, the Dutch took their land for farming. The land was colonized with white settlers and developed for the production of wheat and wine grapes by Simon van der Stel, the commander of the Cape from 1679, who became the first governor of the colony (1691-99).

Simon van der Stel and his son Willem, who succeeded him as governor (1699-1707),

An English map of Africa south of the equator, dated 1729-35, illustrating tne extent of European knowledge and ignorance. Known details of coastal regions are extended to cover the unknown interior. Hence Monomotapa near the east coast, including the town of Zimbaoe (Zimbabwe), is marked where the Kalahari should lie.

developed the colony for the greater profit of the Company and themselves. They founded the village of Stellenbosch (Stels' bush) as the centre of a new inland district in 1682 and, together with other Company officials, took large estates in the district for themselves as private wheat farms and vineyards. Slaves from other parts of Africa and from Asia were imported to labour on the land. European settlers were imported to settle in Capetown or to manage production as *boers* (small farmers) on private farms given to them by the Company.

Slaves were regularly imported from 1658 onwards, and were either kept by the Com-

pany or sold off to private owners. The Company forbade enslavement of the indigenous peoples of the Cape and Java colonies, so slaves were bought elsewhere in Africa and Asia. The first slaves were West African: thereafter most slaves were Malagasy imported from Madagascar, or Malays from the East Indies, and Indians from the Bay of Bengal.

Most European settlers were imported between 1685 and 1700. Male settlers not employed by the Company were known as *burghers* (citizens). Though all settlers arrived from the Netherlands, and most were Dutch Calvinists, many were German Lutherans or French Calvinist refugees. The van der Stels insisted that they all learnt to speak the Dutch language and obeyed the laws of the Company.

Company monopolies Dutch East India Company profits were based on monopoly control of all trade and on collecting rents and taxes. The Company sold its trade monopolies within the Cape Colony to rich burghers who held the monopoly concession for all trade in meat, or wheat flour, or wine, or tobacco, etc. All burghers could only buy and sell that commodity through the concession holder. Monopolies could only be avoided by smuggling goods to and from ships, or by bribing Company officials.

By the beginning of the 18th century the Cape Colony was producing more meat, wheat and wine than visiting ships were buying, and both concession holders and burghers began to complain when their incomes fell. The concession holders complained of the high bribes taken by the governor; the other burghers complained of the private farms owned by the governor and officials which freely sold their products to passing ships. In 1707 the Company acted to solve the political crisis between the settlers and its officials. It removed Willem van der Stel as governor and forbade officials to own private estates. It stopped assisting immigration of settlers from the Netherlands in order to limit the growth of settler political power, though a few settlers continued to come privately. And it began to export wheat and wine to Java, thus finding a market for surplus production at the Cape.

Economic prosperity From 1707 until the 1770s, agricultural production and trade progressively increased, and the burghers of the Cape Colony were generally prosperous and politically quiet. The colony shared in the rising prosperity of northern Europe and of its trade with India and the East Indies. The demand for meat grew steadily after the meat trade monopoly was relaxed in 1743. The crews of Dutch ships alone in the mid-18th century ate up to 8,500 sheep annually. Greater quantities at higher prices were sold to foreigners, especially during the Anglo-French wars in India (1744-1748 and 1756-1763) when so many foreign ships called at Capetown. Meanwhile the demand of visiting ships for Cape wheat and wine was much less predictable, as ships could more easily keep them in store from Europe. But trade was very profitable when such products were in poor supply or too expensive in Europe.

Population By 1710 almost two thousand Dutch settlers and officials and more than two thousand slaves lived in the Cape Colony – nearly all within a hundred kilometres of Capetown. By 1800 there were about 22,000 Dutch and more than 25,000 slaves in the colony, some living as far as a thousand kilometres from Capetown. The numbers of Khoisan are not known, but the *Oxford History of South Africa* suggests that a Khoisan population of 200,000 south of the Orange River in the 17th century was reduced by nine-tenths to around 20,000 by the end of the 18th century. The major cause of this population decrease was probably smallpox epidemics which spread from ships in Capetown, beginning in 1713. Other causes include death by war or famine, marriage into the Cape coloured population, and emigration across the Orange.

Agricultural production and slavery Most of the Dutch and slave population, together with Khoisan servants, continued to live in the farming area of the south-western Cape within a hundred kilometres of Capetown. Successful burghers grew rich as estate owners and slave-owners, from wheat production on the fertile black soil called the Swartland; from wine production on the sunny but well-watered hillsides around Stellenbosch, Paarl and Franschoek; or from fattening up sheep and cattle trekked from the interior. Unsuccessful burgher farmers became employees of rich relatives or left to become townsmen and frontiersmen.

Slavery was the basis of Cape agricultural production. Slaves worked in the fields and vineyards and in burgher households, under the control of landless burghers or company soldiers employed by the landowners. Slaves might be given a 'dop' of brandy and a piece of tobacco to keep them docile when not working. Dutch law gave slave-owners all rights of ownership over slaves except killing them. Khoisan servants were employed as herdsmen on sheep and cattle ranches. They were also not paid except in food and housing and brandy or tobacco, but were seen in Dutch law until 1775 as free people without the citizenship rights of burghers.

Culture and race   At first the Dutch settlers thought of themselves as superior people because of their culture, especially their language, customs and religion. But as more Khoisan and coloured people adopted Dutch culture the settlers came to believe that Europeans were born into a superior race. They did not want to share their wealth or their burgher rights with a mass of non-Europeans.

The ruling European minority of the Cape population remained largely European in race because European women (with very few exceptions) married European men, while most European men officially married European women even if they also had non-European unofficial wives or lovers. Few new European settlers came to the Cape in the 18th century, but the local European population expanded rapidly because of the very high fertility of European women — each one had an average of six surviving children. In fact many people accepted as Europeans had had non-European ancestors in Asia (like Simon van der Stel), or in Africa; most of these were women born of a coloured or Khoisan mother by a European father.

The Cape Coloured population originated in interbreeding, including a few official marriages, between Asian or African slaves (mostly Malagasy and Malay), European settlers or sailors, and the remaining Khoisan population of the Cape. The slave population continued to grow because all coloured children with a slave parent automatically became slaves. A burgher father could declare his coloured child legitimate, but this rarely happened except to some coloured women, because all legitimate male children could inherit their father's property. Instead such coloured children might become privileged slaves in their father's household or even slave-bosses! There were a few official marriages (i.e. in church) between European men and non-European women during the 18th century. The most notable was when the architect of the main Capetown church married an African woman in the building that he had designed, but such marriages were exceptional. It is estimated that one out of every ten European men in the 18th century lived as man and wife with a non-European woman without a church marriage, and others had non-European women as lovers or polygamous wives in addition to a European wife.

The number of coloured people released from slavery, by the gift of their master or by buying their freedom, was small. But in time a free coloured population developed in Capetown, many of them Malay by culture and Muslim by religion, working as craftsmen and beginning to compete with Europeans in business. In the countryside of the south-western Cape the coloured population consisted largely of Malagasy slaves, while in the frontier districts the coloured population developed from much larger numbers of Khoisan and fewer imported slaves. The Khoisan remained free in theory, but any attempts to avoid labour on Boer farms were increasingly resisted by farm owners, and children of slaves by Khoisan mothers became slaves like their fathers.

Later 18th century political developments So long as trade was profitable and land and labour were freely available, the burghers were politically content with Company rule. Governor Tulbagh (1751-71) was well thought of for giving the burghers clearer legal powers over their slaves (1754). But profits began to fall in the trade depression of the 1770s. Richer burghers agitated against company monopolies and political control, calling themselves 'Patriots' in imitation of burghers calling for democracy in the Netherlands and British colonists in North America. However, trade prosperity returned to the Cape in the 1780s until the 1790s, when wars in Europe led to increased Company taxes for defence. So the burghers did not object strongly when the British captured Cape Colony from the Dutch in 1795. Twice as many ships as before now called at Capetown, and a British army stationed at the Cape was a ready market for wheat, meat, wine and other local products.

3 Cape Frontier Expansion and Frontier Wars

The demand for livestock and hunting products pushed the frontier of Cape Colony eastwards across the interior parallel with the south coast. The burghers who trekked beyond the frontier farms to trade and hunt with Khoisan herders were known as *trekboers*. They traded iron tools and copper ornaments, liquor and tobacco, for Khoisan sheep, cattle and goats, and hunted for furs, feathers and ivory. Trekboers took pieces of land on the frontier between older farms and independent Khoisan country, on which to herd their livestock. Sometimes they had Khoisan permission to stay, sometimes they were squatters without Khoisan permission. But they now regarded themselves as true Boers owning their own farms, and the Netherlands East India Company regarded the land as part of the Cape Colony, 'loaning' it to the white colonist in return for a small

annual rent. Thus the frontier was extended by new, very large (up to three thousand hectares) unfenced 'loan farms', and the African inhabitants became squatters with no right to live on their old land.

Khoisan herders lost their sheep, cattle and goats in trade, and their land to new Boer farms. Either they became servants in the colony to earn the milk, meat, fat and skins they had once owned, or they became independent hunters outside the colony. Khoisan hunter-gatherers on the other hand had little to trade and hunted the livestock on Boer farms. The Company made war on them by forming commandos, troops of mounted and armed horsemen, to attack and destroy hunter-gatherers and take their land and children for servants. From 1715 the Company allowed burghers to form commandos under commandants elected from among themselves.

The second period of frontier expansion in the 18th century arose with the high demand and high prices for meat in the Capetown of the 1740s. By that time the frontier had reached across the Gouri (Gouritz) river north of Mossel Bay. During the 1740s the number of frontier 'loan farms' increased and came under the new colonial district of Swellendam. From 1743 onwards the Company gave each farmer sixty hectares within each 'loan farm'

A panorama of Table Bay, originally published in 1675, with a Khoisan herder family and the Dutch castle as inset illustrations.

DELAGOA BAY AND OTHER COASTAL SETTLEMENTS

1595-97	Dutch and English ships began trading in the Mozambique channel along the Madagascar coasts and at Delagoa Bay; also calling at Cape of Good Hope.
1642-74	French trading station (Fort Dauphine) in south-east Madagascar; English fort at Tulear on south-west coast 1644-45.
1652	Dutch founded fort at Cape of Good Hope, trading with Khoisan for cattle.
1684-1724	European and Arab pirates raiding and slaving in the Indian Ocean around northern Madagascar and the Comoros.
1690	Dutch ships began trading along Namibia coast for cattle and slaves.
1721-30	Dutch fort at Delagoa Bay; local wars producing slaves for Cape Colony, but disappointing trade in ivory, copper, gold and tin. After 1730 regular Dutch and occasional Portuguese, English and French ships continued to trade at Bay.
1731	Permanent Portuguese trading station founded at Inhambane north of Delagoa Bay.
1777-82	Austrian-Italian fort on Nyaka island, trading with Maputo kingdom on south side of Delagoa Bay. Captured by Portuguese.
1780s-90s	Increasing numbers of European and North American whaling ships calling along Namibia coast (Walvis or Whalefish Bay), at Cape Town and Delagoa Bay for water, meat and grain.
1786	British failed to establish colony at Voltas Bay (south of Orange river mouth), deciding instead to found Sierra Leone (1787) for ex-slaves and Australia (1788) for convicts.
1796-1803	Portuguese expelled from Delagoa Bay by French. Returned to found new fort called Lourenço Marques — where Mfumo allies supplied slaves from north-east and ivory from south.

as freehold, while he continued to rent the rest of the farm from the Company, which could, in theory, remove it at any time. Trekboers now extended trade further eastwards into the lands of the Inqua group of Khoisan herders in the southern Karoo, who were themselves trading northwards to the Orange river and eastwards beyond the Suurveld.

The third period of frontier expansion in the 18th century was pushed by continuing high demand and high prices for meat at the Cape from the late 1760s to the 1780s. The eastern border line claimed by the Cape Colony was advanced four times in seventeen years from the Gamtoos river in 1770 to the Tarka and Baviaans rivers in 1786.

During this period new products were brought by wagon from the frontier zone to Capetown in increasing quantity. Butter was carried from the Swellendam district to be salted for preservation and exported to the Dutch and French colonies of the Indian Ocean. Timber for building was carried overland from the Knysna forests instead of being imported from overseas. Large blocks of soap — made from sheep's fat boiled with ash from the *canna* bush common in the Karoo — were transported from the Karoo to Capetown by frontier Boers on a sixty-day wagon journey.

Frontier Boers prospered in the southern Karoo because it was good country for grazing sheep. The fat-tailed Khoisan type of sheep, with long legs and nimble mouth, survived in dry country by moving fast and picking out the sweet grass from among bitter shrubs. In the 1770s each Boer farm on the southern Karoo plains had between a thousand and three thousand sheep, and farms in the escarpment up to three or four thousand sheep.

Labour: origins of 'apprenticeship' Few slaves were kept by Boers outside the south-western Cape, so they obtained labour for their sheep farms from local Africans who became servants in exchange for, food and shelter. Young Khoisan boys and girls were brought up in Boer households as servants known as 'apprentices', bound to their masters by law until they were adults. Apprenticeship was therefore a form of temporary slavery. From 1775 the laws of Cape Colony declared that all young Africans captured in war should remain 'apprentices' from the age of eighteen months to twenty-five years old. In practice 'apprentices' usually continued as servants after they became adults, though some escaped to become independent hunters and raiders.

From the southern Karoo trekboers and Boer 'loan farms' expanded northwards and eastwards along the old Inqua trade-routes. But northward expansion across the escarpment mountains was stopped between the 1770s and 1790s by the bitter northern Karoo ('Bushmanland') wars between Khoisan and the Cape Colony, when Khoisan raiders pushed Boers back into the southern Karoo. Boer commandos hunted down Khoisan and killed them in thousands like wild game and took their orphaned children as 'apprentices'.

Conflict on the Suurveld Boers continued to expand eastwards into the Suurveld ('sour' grass country), an area of grazing equally good for cattle and game. Trekboers traded with the scattered Khoisan and Xhosa population living there and began to settle in the western Suurveld – the land of the Hoengei and the Gqunukwebe. Both chiefdoms had mixed Khoisan and Xhosa population, the Hoengei chief being Khoisan and the Gqunukwebe chief, who at first paid him tribute, being a Xhosa immigrant. Other Xhosa families migrated into Hoengei land in this period of the later 18th century to become independent herders and hunters in the Suurveld. The most senior chief of the western Xhosa, Rarabe, remained east of the Fish river, respected but not feared by small chiefs on the Xhosa western frontier. Rarabe was more concerned with his eastern frontier where he fought with the Thembu.

Trekboers in the Suurveld traded iron (for local forging into spear-heads), cloth, tobacco, beads, and liquor in exchange for ivory and cattle, and by the 1770s were claiming 'loan farms' in the Suurveld for cattle herding. In 1775 the eastern border of the Cape Colony was declared to include the western half of the Suurveld. Boers now looked jealously even further east at the large herds of cattle owned by African groups. Boers and Africans therefore clashed several times between 1779 and 1812 in a series of Suurveld wars, also known to historians as the first four Cape-Nguni frontier wars. The Suurveld wars began as Boer cattle raids, capturing land and driving small African chiefdoms eastwards. Then African chiefdoms took the initiative and drove Boer families westwards back across the Suurveld.

1st Cape-Nguni war, 1779-81 The Suurveld wars consisted of endless small cattle raids, in which some Boers even joined Africans against other Boers. Boers often provoked Africans into war because their government rewarded them for commando service with captured cattle, labour and land. The most notorious case during the first war of 1779-81 was when Adriaan van Jaarsveld, a commando commandant, threw tobacco before a group of Xhosa, and then had his men shoot anyone who picked it up from the ground.

In order to control Boers on the northern Karoo and Suurveld frontiers the Netherlands East India Company founded a fourth district of the colony in 1784 based at the village of Graaff-Reinet just south of the escarpment. Only the government *landdrost* (district magistrate) could call the burghers out on commando service. Each burgher had to provide a horse and a man (himself or a servant) to ride the horse, while the company provided firearms and ammunition. The rule of the *landdrost*, however, depended on councillors drawn from the richest and most powerful burghers. Furthermore, the burghers elected their own commando commandant from among themselves, and after 1804 elected their own officers for each sub-district called *veld-kornets*.

British navy ships at anchor in Table Bay in the early 19th century.   Britain captured the Cape in 1795; returned it to the Netherlands in 1802; and recaptured it again in 1806. It was confirmed in British possession by the European peace treaty of 1814.

2nd Cape-Nguni War, 1789-93   Around 1782 Rarabe was succeeded as senior western Xhosa chief by his son Ndlambe, who acted as regent until Rarabe's grandson Ngqika (Ndlambe's nephew) was old enough to rule. Ndlambe tried to bring under his rule the Xhosa and Gona in the Suurveld previously defeated by the Boers, and this resulted in a second Suurveld war in 1789-93. After two years the Company tried to stop the war because of its expense, but local Boers kept the war going by allying with Ndlambe against the Gqunukwebe until peace was eventually achieved by the Graaff-Reinet *landdrost,* Honoratus Maynier, in 1793.

Graaff-Reinet and Swellendam 'republics', 1795-96   Many of the frontier Boers blamed Maynier for their being chased out of the Suurveld. They took the opportunity of war in Europe and weak Company control in 1795 to drive Maynier back to Capetown. The rebels called themselves 'Patriots' and declared the districts of Graaff-Reinet and Swellendam to be independent 'republics'. Meanwhile the British captured Capetown during 1795 and took over Cape Colony from the Dutch. The British stopped ammunition supplies to the frontier and both 'republics' surrendered in 1796.

In 1796 Ngqika took the chieftainship of the Rarabe-Xhosa away from his uncle Ndlambe after a short civil war. Ndlambe decided to settle in the Suurveld to be inde-
pendent from Ngqika. There were few Boers in the Suurveld; only one third of the 148 Boer families who had settled in the Suurveld in the 1770s-80s had returned to their 'farms' by 1798. So Ndlambe competed with the Gqunukwebe chief rather than with the Boers to rule the people of the Suurveld.

Graaff-Reinet Boer 'rebellion', 1799   In 1799 the British arrested Adriaan van Jaarsveld, as Graaff-Reinet commando commandant who had been president of its 'republic'. Local Boers rose in rebellion to release him, and planned to ally with the Xhosa of Ngqika against the British. However, Ngqika refused to join them because the British had recognized him as senior chief over his uncle Ndlambe. The Boer rising was quickly defeated by the British. The people of the Suurveld now seized their chance to revenge themselves on the Boers who had taken their cattle and land in the previous twenty years. Khoisan servants, given arms by the British to fight their Boer masters, refused to surrender the arms when the Boers were defeated, and were led by Ndlambe in burning Boer houses and taking over their farms.

4 Trekkers Beyond the Frontier

People of mixed African and Dutch culture trekked far beyond the Cape frontiers to set up independent states in the interior during the 18th century. Earlier trekkers included

Nama ivory traders returning to their home on the northern Cape frontier – a 19th century engraving. Note the oxen used for riding and for carrying ivory, followed by a man carrying a gun.

the Kora and Orlam; later trekkers included the Griqua and Trekboers.

The Kora (Korana) were people from Khoisan chiefdoms around the south-western Cape, who escaped from Dutch rule by trekking northwards (from the later 17th century onwards) up the western trade-route to the western Orange (Gariep) river. There they settled as neighbours of Nama herders and groups of Khoisan hunter-gatherers, while groups of Tswana/Sotho lived not far to the north-east. The Kora used firearms to raid sheep and cattle from their neighbours – Nama herders in Namibia and the Tlhaping kingdom of the southern Tswana. Other Khoisan and slaves from the south-western Cape escaped eastwards to the Inqua and Gona groups of Khoisan herders. Ruyter, an escaped slave, became chief of the Hoengei group of Gona in the Suurveld in the mid-18th century.

The Orlam were mixed groups of Khoisan and escaped slaves from the Cape, who followed the Kora northwards in the late 18th century.

Some of these Khoisan had been attacked by the Dutch on the northern Cape frontiers; others had been made poor by trading away all their cattle and sheep for food, drink and tobacco that were quickly consumed. The leaders of the Orlam trekkers, often escaped workers from the wine and wheat estates of the colony, took the name Orlam, meaning 'wise guys', from the Malay language spoken among slaves at the Cape. Orlam trekkers spread far north into Namibia, raiding the Kora as well as the Nama for sheep and cattle. The most famous group of Orlam was led by Jager Afrikaner, an escaped Khoisan farm worker from the Cape, and therefore called themselves 'Afrikaners'.

The Griqua were groups of Orlam and other trekkers who migrated up the Orange river sometime around the 1770s, having been cut off from the Cape Colony by the northern Karoo wars. They took their name from the old Chairi-griqua group of Khoisan herders in the western Cape. The Griqua were led by Barend Barends and Adam Kok, and were joined on the Orange by more Khoisan and coloured (Dutch-Malay, etc.) trekkers escaping from the colony. The Griqua settled in the area where the Orange and Vaal rivers meet, later known as Griqualand West. Unlike earlier trekkers who were only herders, the Griqua were also the first Dutch-speaking farmers north of the Orange river. Like the Dutch Boers of the colony, the Griqua grew melons, pumpkins, maize and beans along the river banks, as well as herding sheep and cattle. They were Christians who spoke Dutch in their homes and used many imported European goods.

Trekboers were Dutch Boers who remained burghers (i.e. citizens) of the Cape Colony even when they trekked far beyond the frontier to hunt and trade. They lived in their wagons, or settled for the summer in one place to grow crops, and then moved on in winter. As we have already seen, trekboers often settled on the Cape frontier when they were older and had a family by a Dutch wife, to start a 'loan farm'. From the later 1790s there was constant trade between the Griqua on the Orange river and the Boers south of the escarpment mountains. Trekboers and Griqua traded and lived together, and went hunting and raiding further north on to the highveld.

Origins of Afrikaans culture The trekkers beyond the frontier mixed Dutch and African customs, clothing and speech in a new South African way of life. They lived in wagons, or reed and thatch houses with mud floors, herding sheep and cattle, growing a few crops, wearing home-made clothes of European type, carrying firearms and riding horses to trade and raid. Their Khoisan-type sheep, goats and cattle have become known as Afrikaner (or Africander) breeds. Their *veld-skoen*, *biltong*, and *rooi-bos* originated in traditional African shoes, hung meat and herb tea. The South African dialect of Dutch,

known as the *Taal*, which grew into the Afrikaans language, borrowed words and phrases from Portuguese, Malay, Khoisan, and Bantu languages. Coloured and white trekkers were united by common culture but divided by consciousness of shades of colour.

Questions

1   What kind of society did the Dutch establish in the Cape between 1652 and 1800? What contact did they have with other people in the area? [Cambridge International School Certificate, 1979]
2   Describe the relationship of the Dutch with the San and Khoikhoi before 1800. [Cambridge International School Certificate, 1978]
3   How important were European settlements at Delagoa Bay and the Cape of Good Hope before 1795 for the history of African peoples inland?
4   Outline the origins of 'coloured' communities within Cape Colony and on its frontiers. How appropriate is it to call them 'African' or 'Afrikaner'?

Activities

1   Write short accounts of the landing of a ship at the Cape of Good Hope in the 17th century from the points of view of (a) a Khoisan herder, and (b) a Dutch Company official.
2   Write an imaginative account of life *either* (a) on a Boer sheep farm in the escarpment mountains, *or* (b) among Orlam bandits along the Orange (Gariep) river.
3   Draw a map marking migrations from the Cape into the interior between about 1700 and 1850. (Refer also to Chapter 7.)

See Bibliography, pp. 337–42: B4 Cameron; B5 Davenport; B13 James & Simons; B16 Lamar & Thompson; B32 Readers Digest; B42 Wilson & Thompson; C4 Elphick; C5 Elphick & Giliomee; C10 Hamilton; C16 Malherbe; C19 Miller; C26 Ross; C27 Saunders & Derricourt; C29 Thompson; C31 Wilmsen; C32 Worden.

Chapter 5

Mfecane Wars in the East

In the 1820s–30s, southern Africa was torn apart by violent wars that were called *Mfecane* by the Xhosa and *Difaqane* by southern Sotho on the highveld. The literal meaning of the words seems to have been 'crushing', or grinding between stones like grain.

Some historians see the Mfecane as having begun with revolutionary political and military changes among the northern Nguni. This 'revolution' reached its local peak with the growth of a Zulu empire, and also spread as far as the Transkei and Tanzania.

Other historians see the Mfecane/Difaqane as the climax of the small wars of the 18th century, covered in previous chapters. Increased trading and raiding from the east and south coasts for ivory, cattle and labour, brought to the boil the competition of states in the interior for hunting, cattle, people and land.

1 The Origins of the Mfecane

At the end of the 18th century two chiefdoms rose to power over the northern and central Nguni and became important kingdoms. To the north there was the Ndwandwe kingdom ruled by Zwide, and to the south there was the Mthethwa kingdom ruled by Dingiswayo. Both kingdoms remained powerful until 1818-19, when the Mthethwa were defeated by the Ndwandwe and the Ndwandwe were defeated by the Zulu. Out of the ruins of the Mthethwa kingdom arose the Zulu kingdom of Shaka. Out of the ruins of the Ndwandwe kingdom arose the Ngwane (Swazi) kingdom and the Ngoni kingdoms

that scattered far to the north.

Why did the Ndwandwe and Mthethwa become so powerful at the end of the 18th century? First, one should remember that the old Tembe kingdom broke up in civil war during the 1790s. The new Maputo kingdom that took power at Delagoa Bay was weaker and smaller, and no longer controlled elephant hunting as far south as St Lucia Bay, as the Tembe kingdom had. But at the same time demand for ivory by ships calling at Delagoa Bay was increasing, and elephant hunting was spreading further southwards to satisfy that demand. Chiefs like Zwide and Dingiswayo could increase their power and wealth by controlling elephant hunting and the local ivory trade — distributing their profit in imported cloth and beads and metal to gain the loyalty of subjects. A chief who employed a body of armed hunters could easily convert them into soldiers to control traders and chiefdoms in his hunting lands. Dingiswayo therefore put to death people who tried to avoid his chiefly monopoly over trade and hunting.

It is also likely that rising population led to competition between chiefdoms for grazing and cultivation lands, which in turn led to fighting and conquest. Improved food supplies probably accelerated population growth in the Natal area during most of the 18th century. There were good rainy seasons, especially in the 1760-90 period. Maize, originally South American, was introduced from Delagoa Bay and was planted in addition to the traditional crop of sorghum, and could double the size of the annual grain harvest in good years. But maize needs good rains to grow well, and after 1790 the annual rains declined and the harvests decreased in the great *madlatule* drought that was most severe in the period 1800-10. Some of the people who benefited most from the good rains would have suffered most from the drought. The Ndwandwe and Mthethwa chiefdoms both lived on the edge of great river valleys, where hills suitable for farming gave way to expanses of bush-covered lowlands. The lowlands were full of wild animals for hunting, including elephants, and provided good winter pasture for cattle, although malaria and tsetsefly made it unhealthy for man and beast during summer. But drought reduced harvests on the hills and winter pasture in the lowlands, and might have turned Ndwandwe and Mthethwa hunters into raiders of their neighbours' crops and cattle.

Before the Ndwandwe and Mthethwa rise to power there had been no large centralized states among the Nguni. Previously when one chiefdom had grown too large it had split into new small chiefdoms under competing relatives of the old chief; when one chiefdom had defeated another it had not absorbed it but had returned home instead. But the Ndwandwe and Mthethwa chiefdoms used wars to conquer other chiefdoms and make them part of a new larger nation. The subject chiefs continued to rule their own people, but young men and women became members of national age-regiments instead of each chiefdom having its own initiation school, and the old custom of male circumcision disappeared altogether. This new type of Nguni state seems to have developed first among the Ndwandwe, and the idea may possibly be traced to Ndwandwe origins as subjects of the Ronga kingdom (see Chapter 2).

Ndwandwe kingdom The growth of the Ndwandwe state had begun before the mid-18th century when their Hlubi and Ngwane (Swazi) relatives had settled with them around the Pongola valley. The Ndwandwe chief Yaka and his son Zwide, who had succeeded him by the 1790s, conquered local Nguni chiefdoms, including the Khumalo and Ngwaneni. Zwide is remembered as being much more ruthless than Dingiswayo of the Mthethwa. He attacked chiefs who disobeyed him and killed them, rather than fining them a number of cattle like Dingiswayo.

Zwide surrounded himself with doctors and made people fear him as a magician. He gathered the nation together for great annual ceremonies, of which the most important was the 'first fruits' harvest ceremony called *incwala* — probably of Ronga origin. In a week of *incwala* ritual the king was doctored as the national leader, first in public with songs and dances until he bit the first gourd of the harvest, and then in private with medicines to strengthen and purify himself and the nation.

Zwide's ruthlessness can be seen in his relations with the Ngwane. Around 1816 the new Ngwane chief Sobhuza I tried to renew an old claim to use crop lands near the Pongola. Zwide reacted by sending an army which attacked and burnt down Sobhuza's capital on the southern border of present Swaziland.

Mthethwa kingdom Dingiswayo was born in about 1770 among the Mthethwa on the Mfolozi river inland from Richard's Bay. He was the son of the chief but he quarrelled with his father and fled abroad in the 1790s, probably travelling as far north as Delagoa Bay. One famous tradition tells us that when he arrived back home he was riding a horse and carrying a gun, but the story may be a later invention, and certainly he did not continue to ride a horse or carry a gun as king.

Dingiswayo returned home around the year 1800 when his father died, and seized the Mthethwa chieftainship from his brother. He began to conquer neighbouring chiefdoms, and organized regular trade with Delagoa Bay — caravans of people marching with ivory on their heads. The Maputo kingdom at Delagoa Bay became Dingiswayo's ally, united against the Ndwandwe and the Tembe as their common rivals. Maputo soldiers armed with firearms helped Dingiswayo conquer and incorporate the powerful Qwabe chiefdom

Annual incwala ceremony Zwide and later northern Nguni rulers used the ceremony as a unifying national event, held every year during the rains. The king reviews his army, dancing his praises. The king is also doctored in secret, so that he and the nation are strengthened for another year. The ceremony was of southern Tsonga (Ronga) origin before it was adopted by Zwide and other northern Nguni former subjects of Tsonga states. (This picture was sketched by a European missionary, Croonenberghs, who visited the Ndebele capital in 1880. He depicts himself sketching at the bottom of the picture.)

that challenged the Mthethwa on the Mfolozi. These firearms may also explain why Zwide's Ndwandwe kingdom failed to block the trade route along the coastal flats between the Maputo and Mthethwa kingdoms.

Ndwandwe-Mthethwa war The two kingdoms met in battle at Mbuzi hill near Zwide's capital in the Pongola valley during the winter of 1818. Both armies had adopted the 'chest-and-horns' battle formation, earlier used by the Rozvi and possibly by the Ronga. The 'chest' was a large body of soldiers who attacked the enemy in force, while the 'horns' closed round the enemy on either side. Some say Dingiswayo was made mad by Zwide's magic during the battle. He wandered away from his army, was captured, and put to death by Zwide. His skull was then displayed on the doorway of the powerful Ndwandwe queen-mother (*ndlovukatı*), the mother of Zwide.

The Mthethwa kingdom, built upon the

Shangane head-ring maker, photographed in the early 20th century, using an old metal helmet as a mould. The head-ring (izicoco or sidhlodhlo) was worn by married men among the Nguni as a sign of maturity. It was made on a circular frame of palm leaf from the wax of certain grubs, dyed black, and was then sewn into the man's hair.

personal power of Dingiswayo, fell apart on the death of the king. But one of Dingiswayo's chiefs, Shaka, immediately began to build up a new kingdom based on his own chiefdom of the Zulu. He killed the new Mthethwa chief and brought all the former Mthethwa subjects under his rule.

Ndwandwe-Zulu war Before Shaka could become too powerful, Zwide sent an army south to attack the Zulu kingdom. An Ndwandwe army surrounded the smaller army of the Zulu on Gqokoli hill just south of the Mfolozi. Every time the Ndwandwe attacked, the Zulu protected themselves with their large shields from the spears thrown at them. The Zulu then used their short-handled stabbing spears to drive the Ndwandwe away. Zwide was furious at this defeat and led his whole army against the Zulu at the end of 1818. Some sources say that Zwide had re-equipped his army with stabbing spears. Shaka first retreated southwards, drawing the Ndwandwe further and further from their home base until they were exhausted and without food in unfamiliar territory. The Zulu then attacked the Ndwandwe in small guerrilla groups, and Zwide turned the Ndwandwe army homewards. Then, on the Mhlatuze river, Shaka attacked the tired and starving Ndwandwe with a full army. The Ndwandwe were roundly defeated. Most survivors fled northwards with Zwide to attack the Ngwaneni of Matiwane, and then settled with Zwide in the upper Nkomati valley on the present Swaziland-Transvaal frontier. Here Zwide's generals Zwangendaba and Soshangane quarrelled with Zwide and marched down the Nkomati to attack the Ronga around Delagoa Bay.

The Ndwandwe-Mthethwa and Ndwandwe-Zulu wars of 1818-19 set off the chain of wars across southern Africa known as the Mfecane and Difaqane. The Ngwaneni of Matiwane, attacked by the fleeing Ndwandwe, themselves attacked the Hlubi, who refused to give back Ngwaneni cattle previously sent for safe-keeping. The Hlubi crossed the Drakensberg to raid the Sotho in 1821, and thus began the Difaqane wars on the highveld.

Meanwhile Zwide's former generals Zwangendaba and Soshangane founded the Ngoni and Shangane nations and spread the wars to the far north, while Shaka waged endless war to bring the people of the Natal area into his Zulu nation.

2 Shaka and the Zulu Nation

Shaka was born in about 1787. He was the son of the chief of the small Zulu clan on the Mhlatuze river, but his father disowned him and he became a soldier in Dingiswayo's army

The conventional picture of Shaka is a fanciful artist's impression, published in 1836, based on sketches by a British naval officer who visited Shaka in 1824.
The spear is incorrect: it should be a short stabbing-spear. The shield and the plume on his head are extravagantly long. But the picture conveys the great height and royal bearing that struck visitors to Shaka's royal court of KwaBulawayo.

— so brave that he was known as 'Dingiswayo's heio' When Shaka's father died in about 1816, Dingiswayo made Shaka chief of the Zulu clan within the Mthethwa kingdom. Shaka was permitted by Dingiswayo to lead his own Zulu regiments as a royal general within the Mthethwa forces.

Shaka drilled his regiments in the tactics of close hand-to-hand fighting, made possible by adopting the short-handled, large-headed stabbing spear (often called an assagai — a Portuguese word derived from Arabic). The traditional battle weapons carried by a soldier had been a bundle of long-handled throwing spears to be thrown at a distance, and a battle-axe and a small shield for close fighting. But Shaka gave his soldiers large shields which fitted together to protect a close rank of soldiers from chin to legs from flying spears. Soldiers were forbidden to wear sandals in battle as they made running clumsy and slow, and carried just one stabbing spear so that they could run fast to tackle the enemy in close fighting. A Zulu soldier would be executed if he lost or left his stabbing spear on the battlefield. Punishment of cowardice or incompetence among soldiers was extremely harsh. But Shaka gained the loyalty and devotion of his men by making sure they were well fed and cared for before and after battle. Soldiers were given young boys to carry their sleeping mats and to cook their food. The abundance of captured cattle created a taste for good beef among Shaka's troops that could only be satisfied by capturing more cattle from more enemies. Shaka created regiments of smart, disciplined, loyal men which formed the basis of the Zulu army of later years.

Growth of the Zulu state   Shaka may have deliberately betrayed Dingiswayo, as his regiment arrived late for the battle in which Dingiswayo was captured by Zwide. But Shaka soon defeated Zwide at Mhlatuze river, on terrain chosen by Shaka, in his original home area. This victory opened the way for the unlimited expansion of the Zulu kingdom. New regiments from the youth of conquered chiefdoms were added to the original Zulu

regiments to form a permanent army. Soldiers did not return to their homesteads for the agricultural season, nor were they allowed to marry and have a family until they were too old to fight. Each regiment lived close together in the same military town, and one regiment was distinguished from another by the uniform of different coloured ox-hide shields. The women must have been hard pressed to grow sufficient surplus crops to feed such a large military population — itself economically unproductive.

With this military might, Shaka conquered and brought into the Zulu kingdom most of the Nguni between the ocean and the escarpment, south of the Pongola and north of the Tugela river. Chiefs no longer had separate chiefdoms paying tribute to the king as they had had under Dingiswayo. Instead they became *indunas,* meaning royal representatives, who could be replaced or moved to another area at the will of the king. Indunas of outlying districts had no control over members of serving regiments in the military towns, only over the old and very young who still lived in the homesteads. The Zulu kingdom became a highly centralized state with all power concentrated in the hands of the king.

Mzilikazi breaks away   At least one induna may have been allowed to have his own regiments as Shaka had done under Dingiswayo — Mzilikazi, born about 1795, hereditary chief of the Khumalo. The Khumalo had once been subject to the Ndwandwe kingdom and Mzilikazi's mother was a daughter of Zwide. But Zwide killed Mzilikazi's father on suspicion of having conspired with Dingiswayo, and Mzilikazi had no reason to love his grandfather. Mzilikazi took his Khumalo soldiers to join Shaka and fought on the Zulu side in the battle of Mhlatuze river.

Mzilikazi built up his power and wealth by raiding Sotho cattle on the highveld, but without surrendering the captured cattle to Shaka. So in 1821 Shaka sent an army to punish Mzilikazi. The Khumalo were defeated but not destroyed. Mzilikazi and the survivors fled north onto the highveld and began a long career as a nation on the march.

Zulu conquests to south and north To the south of the kingdom, regiments regularly raided the Nguni living between the Tugela and uMzimkhulu rivers, and raided the Mpondo of Faku beyond the uMzimkhulu every one or two years. By the time of his death Shaka was planning to raid as far south as the frontier of Cape Colony, east of the Fish river. To the north-east of the kingdom Shaka, like Dingiswayo, took control of the ivory trade to Delagoa Bay, after Zwide had briefly controlled it in 1818-19. The Maputo who traded with Europeans at the bay were excellent blacksmiths making spearheads, and were therefore not raided by Shaka but were treated as allies giving tribute. But in 1824 English traders first visited Shaka, and the king began to prefer English goods to Portuguese ones. The Zulu now traded less with Delagoa Bay, and more with Port Natal on the coast of Zulu country, later called Durban. A Xhosa man named Jacob became Shaka's trusted interpreter in dealing with these English traders.

Final defeat of the Ndwandwe To the north of the Zulu, the Ndwandwe under Zwide recovered some of their former strength in the upper Nkomati valley during 1819-26. They raided southern parts of the Pedi kingdom, but remained at peace with their Ngwane neighbours under Sobhuza I as allies. In about 1824 an Ndwandwe army ventured as far south as the Pongola river, and a Zulu army failed to stop it. But in 1825 the Ndwandwe were weakened by the death of Zwide and by the disputes of his sons over who should succeed him as king. Then in the following year Zwide's son Sikunyana decided to test Ndwandwe strength against the Zulu and marched south with an army of over twenty thousand, but was defeated by a much larger Zulu army under Shaka — assisted by a few English traders with noisy firearms. Many of the Ndwandwe were killed; the survivors fled to swell the ranks of Ndebele, Shangane, Ngoni, and Ngwane nations in the north.

Shaka's political achievement So long as his armies were fighting, Shaka had complete loyalty and discipline among his subjects, and the Nguni clans of the Natal area came to think of themselves as part of a larger Zulu nation. Like Zwide, Shaka stressed annual national ceremonies to hold the nation together. The symbol of the nation was the *inkhata,* a ring of woven grass a metre in diameter and cased in a python skin. The *inkhata* was constantly strengthened with more grass containing the bodily fluids, hair, nail-clippings and other strengthening medicines of each Zulu king and of all his indunas. By the time it was captured, destroyed and burnt by the British in 1879, the *inkhata,* and therefore the nation, had grown to a great size: the python skin had stretched to some thirty centimetres thick.

Shaka's downfall Shaka's harsh one-man rule, based on continual conquest and capture of cattle, and upon the killing of those who

NGONI DISPERSAL

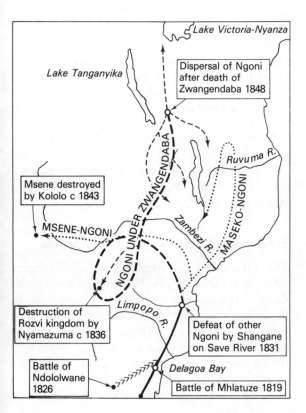

73

Mgungundlovu, capital of Shaka's successor Dingane, built in 1829 The town was laid out like Shaka's towns of Gibixhegu and KwaBulawayo, as a great ring of reed fences and houses around an open parade ground. Serving regiments of young men and women, housed in separate quarters, lived in these towns and were continually drilled to obey orders.

disagreed with him, was a political system that ate away at its own foundations. New lands to be conquered were always further and further away, while the soldiers who had been on military service for so many years began to look forward to marrying and settling down. Shaka justified the killing of political opponents as the execution of witches plotting to disease the king and therefore the nation. But the more people that Shaka executed, the more there were relatives and friends of those executed who might become discontented with Shaka's rule — and so Shaka had to execute yet more opponents, and thereby created more discontent.

Having nearly died from an assassination attempt, Shaka became obsessed with fear of death. After the death of his mother in 1827 Shaka became mentally ill, executing subject after subject who flouted his orders in any way. Stories are told that he tried to avoid becoming a father by killing his wives when they became pregnant, and that he even believed that hair-darkening oil, sold to him by English traders, was a magic medicine to stop him becoming grey-haired and old. On September 22nd, 1828, Shaka's two brothers

Dingane and Mhlangane, together with the induna in charge of Shaka's household, assassinated him.

Dingane comes to power The assassination of Shaka occured while the main Zulu army was away in the north attacking the Ngoni of Soshangane on the north side of Delagoa Bay. Dingane and Mhlangane became joint kings of the Zulu, but soon quarrelled. Dingane killed Mhlangane before Mhlangane could kill him. When the Zulu army arrived back home, after a not very successful campaign, there was common relief that Shaka the hard taskmaster was dead. Their general, Mdlaka, was indeed put to death by Dingane — not for objecting to the killing of Shaka, but for objecting to the killing of Mhlangane.

Dingane set up his capital at eMgungundhlovu, near the later Zulu capital of Ulundi. It was he who had to face the threat of whites and coloureds with their firearms, horses and wagons, come to take away parts of his land. Jacob the court interpreter warned Dingane of the great desire among whites living in Cape Colony for settlement in 'Natal'. As early as 1831 Dingane sent a Zulu regiment to attack English traders at Port Natal as a warning against white settlement plans of which he had heard rumours. And three years later, a Boer expedition under Piet Uys arrived in Dingane's country from Cape Colony to spy out the land for settlement, avoiding any meeting with Dingane himself. Meanwhile the Zulu state under Dingane had re-established its power as far north as Delagoa Bay by attacking the Portuguese at Lourenço Marques in 1833.

3 Mfecane Spreads North of the Pongola

The Mfecane wars were spread by refugees who, defeated by the Ndwandwe or by the Zulu, became new nations on the march, organized on the military system of the Ndwandwe or Zulu. These Mfecane nations moved across the land as an army for up to ten or twenty years, spreading the 'crushings' of Mfecane far and wide. Captured crops were burnt if unwanted and cattle were seized if uneaten; captured men were often killed and their women and children taken into the new nations. Refugees from attack either formed new Mfecane nations on the march or fled to remote deserts and mountains.

Ngwane (later Swazi) state The Ngwane under Sobhuza I (Somhlolo) were driven northwards by the Ndwandwe, who attacked them every time they settled down. On their way north the Ngwane attacked the Maseko clan of Nguni in the Great Usutu valley, causing them to become another Mfecane nation of marauding refugees. The Ngwane were then expelled northwards, conquering Pedi (or Sotho) clans on the way. They finally settled in the upper Nkomati valley, beyond range of Ndwandwe attack while Zwide was at war with Dingiswayo and Shaka in the south (1818-19).

When Zwide fled from defeat in 1819, he took his people to Ngwane country around the upper Nkomati and Sobhuza withdrew south-eastwards. The Ndwandwe were now too weak to follow and attack the Ngwane, and Sobhuza and Zwide became allies with the marriage of Zwide's daughter Thandile as great wife to Sobhuza. So around 1820 Sobhuza began a more peaceful process of state-building, fixing his capital in the Little Usutu valley. From this centre Sobhuza brought into regular tribute the Pedi of the neighbouring highveld and Tsonga in the low-veld, as well as small Nguni chiefdoms in the middleveld country around the Little Usutu valley. He thus founded the state known as kaNgwane, or later as 'Swaziland'.

One can see Ndwandwe influence on the politics of the emerging Ngwane nation in the use of the *incwala* as a national unifying ceremony — stressed strongly by Sobhuza's son Mswati as the son of a Ndwandwe princess. The strong political role of the queen-mother among the Ngwane as a check on the power of the king also seems to have been of Ndwandwe origin. The responsibility of the Ngwane king to a national council of elders (*libandla*) may have been adopted from the Pedi. Pedi or Ronga influence on the Ngwane may also be seen in the siSwati language, in

MFENGU ORIGINS

The Mfengu (Fingo) people originated as refugees from the Mfecane/Difaqane wars, who settled among the Xhosa in the 1820s-30s. **Mfengu** means beggar or scavenger in iziXhosa. Many Mfengu were Zizi, Bhele and Hlubi who fled from areas conquered by the Zulu kingdom. Some were Ngwaneni and Hlubi led by Matiwane, who were defeated by the British in 1828 after crossing the Drakensberg from Lesotho into the Transkei area. Because they were reduced to begging, the Mfengu became servants of the Gcaleka-Xhosa and neighbouring peoples.

In 1836 the Mfengu were invited by the British to cross the border into Cape Colony, where they would settle as friendly peasant farmers on conquered Xhosa land. 17,000 Mfengu with 22,000 cattle then crossed the Kei river. The Mfengu supplied crops and labour to colonial markets, and offered themselves as troops in times of war. Many were converted to Christianity and to Western ways of costume and culture. **Above:** Mfengu woman, sketched at Port Elizabeth in 1850 by Thomas Baines. She wears a traditional fur cloak but here her headdress is made of imported European cloth.

royal marriages by cousins of the same clan, forbidden among all other Nguni, and even in hair-styles.

Ngoni origins The Ndwandwe survivors who deserted Zwide after the Ndwandwe defeat by the Zulu in 1818-19 may all be called 'Ngoni', either another name for the Ngwandwe or the name given to Nguni north of the Zambezi. Soshangane and Zwangendaba, former generals of Zwide, began raiding around Delagoa Bay in 1819-20, after leaving Zwide in the upper Nkomati valley. The Tembe were conquered and the Nyaka driven onto their island in the bay, but the Maputo were spared because they bought ivory from the Ngoni and paid them with spearheads and overseas goods. By mid-1821 the Ngoni invaders were attacking and conquering chiefdoms north of the bay, reaching as far as Inhambane by 1822.

Meanwhile more Ngoni were breaking away from Zwide. After being expelled from the area of central Swaziland by the Ngwane, the Maseko had joined Zwide but then broke away under the leadership of Nxaba, chief of the Msene clan. Together the Maseko and Msene first joined Mzilikazi in attacking the Pedi (1822-23) and then marched to join other Ngoni on the coast around Inhambane.

In 1823 Shaka sent a Zulu army which took control from the Ngoni of trade through Maputo country. But on the north side of Delagoa Bay the Ngoni of Soshangane continued to trade with the Portuguese through the Mfumo chiefdom. They sold Ronga captives to the Portuguese as slaves, who were shipped to the sugar plantations of Brazil or to Reunion island east of Madagascar.

In 1826 the numbers of Ngoni were further increased by Ndwandwe refugees from their final defeat by Shaka (other Ndwandwe stayed in the Nkomati valley under Sobhuza or joined Mzilikazi). Zwangendaba and Nxaba continued to raid the Tsonga and Chopi north of Soshangane. Then in 1828 the last Zulu army sent out by Shaka attacked the Ngoni of Soshangane and, though not defeated, Soshangane decided to withdraw his raiders northwards.

Shangane state Soshangane went to live with Zwangendaba and Nxaba around the Save river mouth. The Ngoni leaders soon quarrelled with each other and in 1831 there was a war in which Soshangane was the

Shangane troops arriving at Shapanga, on the lower Zambezi river, to collect annual tribute (curva) from local Portuguese settlers in the 1860s. Soldiers chant and rhythmically beat their shields, while two soldiers in the foreground salute a leader who carries a gun.

victor. Zwangendaba and Nxaba fled inland with their followers. Soshangane established a nation that spoke the local Tsonga language rather than Ngoni, and called his kingdom 'Gaza-nkulu'* in honour of his grandfather, Gaza. As well as the baNgoni raiders who had stayed with Soshangane, the nation included people known as baShangane (Soshangane's people) — mostly Tsonga but also Chopi and the former Manyika group of Shona. Portuguese trading posts in the area recognized the sovereignty of Soshangane by paying him annual tribute.

4 Ngoni Invasion of the Zimbabwean Plateau

The Rozvi kingdom under the Changamire lineage of Mambos (kings) had grown weak since the days of the great Dombo and had become a loose confederacy of chiefdoms. The Mambo had lost military, political and religious power, succession to the position was disputed, and drought and war had further weakened the confederacy by the time the Ngoni invaded around 1832.

The Rozvi army, which the Mambo had used to raid and collect cattle tribute from his Kalanga subjects, had come increasingly under the control of the Mambo's general and tax-collector with the hereditary title of Tumbare. Tumbare — originally a pre-Rozvi Torwa chief in the area — lived north-east of present Bulawayo. The Mambo's power was mostly restricted to the area around the capital at Manyanga. Continuous civil wars since the late 18th century encouraged regional chiefs within the Rozvi confederacy to think of themselves almost as Mambos in their own areas. These regional chiefs included Mavudzi, the hereditary high priest and rain-doctor to the Mambo, who had turned against the Mambo Gomboremvura by 1800. It appears that national religious unity was thereby destroyed, and each regional chief could have his own priest and shrine for the worship of Mwari (God). Tradition tells us that the Mambo ceased to believe in Mwari — which

Early 20th century photograph of an old Shangane warrior in traditional dress. He is now forbidden to carry an assagai by Portuguese colonial law.

probably means the Mwari of Mavudzi!

The civil wars resulted in a split of the Changamire lineage in two houses, supporting different successors to Gomboremvura. Meanwhile new enemies began to advance from the south and eat up territory formerly ruled by the Rozvi — the Hlengwe group of Tsonga, the Mhari group of independent Shona, and the unsuccessful Difaqane raid of Kgari's Ngwato, defeated in the Matopo hills (1827).

Around 1832 the Rozvi confederacy faced the invasion of Mfecane raiders — Zwange-

nkulu: grandfather (literally, 'great one').

ndaba's Ngoni — coming from the north-east. But Zwangendaba had first to attack Tumbare, whose hill guarded the centre of the confederacy, and Zwangendaba was beaten off, retreating north across the Zambezi in 1835. Zwangendaba left behind a number of Ngoni raiders, including a remarkable woman general named Nyamazuma. She attacked the Rozvi and succeeded in killing the Mambo Chirisamhuru II, son of Gomboremvura, at Manyanga around the year 1836. One tradition says that Chirisamhuru was skinned alive; another tradition says that his heart was cut out to prove that Mambos were not double-hearted; and yet another tradition says he jumped to his death off a cliff. Manyanga hill became known as Mambo hill (Ntaba-zikaMambo) by the Ngoni and Ndebele in memory of the last ruling Mambo of the Rozvi.

5 Ndebele Invasion of the Zimbabwean Plateau

Early in 1838 the Zimbabwean plateau was invaded by the Ndebele of Mzilikazi, who had spent the 1837-38 rainy season in the Tswapong hills of Botswana. (The history of the Ndebele between 1821 and 1837 is covered in Chapters 5 and 7.) Mzilikazi himself determined to follow the Kololo army of Sebetwane towards Lake Ngami, while he sent the main body of the Ndebele under the command of Kaliphi Gundwane to the Zimbabwean plateau, which some Ndebele already knew from long-distance raiding.

The main body of the Ndebele marched under Kaliphi, driving large herds of cattle, across the Motloutse and Shashe rivers to the Zimbabwean plateau, where they settled around Tumbare's hill. When, after two summers, Mzilikazi had still not arrived, Kaliphi decided to install Mzilikazi's son Nkulumane as king. Mzilikazi had meanwhile followed the Kololo from the direction of Lake Ngami to the Chobe and Zambezi rivers. He heard of Kaliphi's plans as he was preparing to cross the Zambezi. Mzilikazi rushed south to confront Kaliphi, leaving his men to cross the river and attack the Kololo.

Mzilikazi takes control Ndebele traditions disagree about what exactly happened when Mzilikazi returned to the main body of the Ndebele. Kaliphi and his main supporters were undoubtedly killed, hence Tumbare's hill became known as Ntaba-yezinduna — indunas' hill. Nkulumane disappeared and Mzilikazi never talked about him again. He was either killed or fled abroad. Most likely he was murdered in secret, though after Mzilikazi's death a man from Zululand claimed to be Nkulumane and therefore the true heir.

The Ndebele found the country under the control of Ngoni raiders who had destroyed the main Rozvi settlements, their most important leader being Nyamazuma, whom Mzilikazi determined to marry. So Nyamazuma became his queen and her soldiers joined the Ndebele army.

The new Ndebele kingdom covered the western part of the former Rozvi kingdom. Many of the local Kalanga people and families of Rozvi chiefs had fled into the hills, but they returned when Mzilikazi showed that he was more peaceable than the Ngoni. The Ndebele had brought many cattle with them, and Mzilikazi gave out cattle to Kalanga and Rozvi chiefs on the *maziza* (mafisa) system in return for loyalty. The subject people, whom the Ndebele rudely referred to as 'ama-Hole' or dogs surrendered grain as annual tribute and their young men to join the Ndebele regiments. Mzilikazi followed the Zulu in placing military towns round the centre of his kingdom and gave them Zulu names, including Gibixegu and Bulawayo. He drew his main indunas from the Ndebele of Nguni origin, and the nation was divided into three castes who were not allowed to intermarry so long as Mzilikazi ruled — an upper caste of Nguni origin, a middle caste of Tswana/Sotho origin, and a lower caste of Shona (mostly Kalanga) origin.

6 Ngoni Dispersal North of the Zambezi

After his defeat by Soshangane in 1831, Zwangendaba took his Jere-Ngoni through the area of Munhumutapa where they were defeated in battle by Nxaba's Msene-Ngoni, also fleeing from Soshangane. In desperation Zwangendaba marched onto the Zimbabwean plateau to attack the Rozvi, but was defeated. Persistent as ever, he turned away to plunder the north-east of the plateau for cattle and grain. Finally, in 1835, he decided to cross the Zambezi. Around November 19th-20th, 1835, Zwangendaba's army, including Tsonga and Shona soldiers, crossed the Zambezi river near the Luangwa confluence. The precise date is known because there was an eclipse of the sun. Ngoni tradition records that there was darkness during daylight while they crossed the river in canoes.

Zwangendaba led his Jere-Ngoni northwards until they reached the area of south-western Tanzania. There he settled at the capital he called Mapupo ('dreams') and died in 1848. The Jere-Ngoni then split into five new Ngoni nations – the Tuta-Ngoni in south-eastern Tanzania; the Mpezeni-Ngoni where present-day Zambian, Malawian and Mozambican borders meet; the Mombera-Ngoni in northern Malawi; and the Chiwere-Ngoni in central Malawi.

The Maseko-Ngoni and Msene-Ngoni split from each other after being defeated by Soshangane in 1831. The Maseko-Ngoni crossed the Zambezi near its mouth and settled between Lake Malawi and the Indian Ocean in south-eastern Tanzania, later fleeing to southern Malawi. The Msene-Ngoni, on the other hand, were led by Nxaba towards the old Munhumutapa state, where as we have seen, Nxaba defeated Zwangendaba. During the 1830s the Msene raided along the northern Zimbabwean plateau, moving north of the Zambezi after the Ndebele arrived on the Zimbabwean plateau. The Msene attacked the Kololo kingdom but were driven westwards into the desert, where the Kololo cut them off from water and food supplies so that they had to eat even their sandals and shields before the Kololo destroyed them (around 1843-45).

Conclusion All the Ngoni groups lived by raiding for cattle and grain, destroying villages and breaking up old states. The wars that they spread in eastern Africa gave slave-traders a plentiful supply of captives to buy and export as slaves. Yet the new Ngoni nations were mostly made up of foreign captives and took over the territory and population of old states. In time, even the rulers who were of pure Nguni descent adopted the local language and culture and forgot their own. The Shangane-Ngoni became Tsonga, the Mpezeni-Ngoni became Chewa, etc. But their historical traditions, family names and military organization reminded the Ngoni nations of their origins in the Mfecane of southern Africa.

Questions

1 What were the causes of the Mfecane, and what were its effects on the distribution of African peoples *south* of the Limpopo? (You may illustrate your answer with a sketch map.) [Cambridge International School Certificate, 1977]
2 How were the Mfecane states of Zwide and Dingiswayo different from previous kingdoms and chiefdoms elsewhere in southern Africa?
3 Describe the rise of the Zulu nation. What were the effects of the military and political changes made by Shaka? [Cambridge International School Certificate, 1976]

Activities

1 Find out about and try to visit sites connected with the Mfecane/Difaqane wars in your district.
2 Debate in the classroom whether the Mfecane/Difaqane wars were a great disaster or a great advance in African history.
3 Write an account of the life of an *udibi* in Shaka's army. (An *udibi*, later translated into chiShona as *mujiba*, was a young adolescent boy who acted as mat-carrier and cook for three soldiers.)

For references to Bibliography, see p. 89.

Chapter 6

Difaqane Wars in the West

The Difaqane wars west of the Drakensberg are usually said to have begun in 1821–22, with the invasions of Hlubi, Khumalo and Ngwaneni fleeing from the Mfecane wars east of the escarpment. As has been seen in Chapter 3, the area of the Transvaal had been suffering constant minor warfare since about the 1770s. But the Difaqane wars beginning in 1821-22 were more disastrous than the previous warfare, which had been limited to cattle raiding between neighbouring peoples. The Difaqane saw new military nations being formed by refugees from previous attacks, who marched hundreds of kilometres to devastate faraway lands and peoples before settling down to form more peaceful states.

The Difaqane among the Tswana/Sotho saw the development of a new type of centralized political state. The old Tswana kings, with a few exceptions such as Tau of the Rolong, were respected for their seniority in the royal lineage rather than as dynamic leaders in battle or in diplomacy with foreign states. The new kings had to be successful in battle and subtle in negotiation, as well as rich in cattle or trade goods, in order to attract the loyalty of new subjects. The king led his regiments in war, and appointed talented commoners as well as his royal relatives as his officers (indunas) and chiefs.

The history of the Difaqane is extremely complex because of the number of chiefdoms attacking and being attacked by each other. The different oral traditions recording these attacks are inevitably confused. The account of the Difaqane wars in this chapter may

therefore differ from other published accounts, and will no doubt need to be revised by more historical research.

1 Difaqane South of the Vaal River

Tlokoa of Mma-Ntatisi The first people attacked by Mpangazita's Hlubi when they crossed the Drakensberg in 1821-22 were the Tlokoa of Mma-Ntatisi in the area between present Harrismith and Warden. Mma-Ntatisi was a remarkable woman, regent since the death of her husband for her young son Sikonyela. She led her people westwards where she attacked the Patsa and other Fokeng, but was herself attacked again by Mpangazita's Hlubi. Both armies then marched separately south to the Caledon valley.

At Butha-Buthe Mma-Ntatisi attacked young Moshoeshoe and his Mokoteli people, and took most of their cattle, but failed to capture the mountain fortress in 'the battle of the pots'. The Tlokoa soon fought with the Hlubi again, and tricked them into fleeing by lining up women with hoes and sleeping mats to look like men with spears and shields! Mma-Ntatisi and Sikonyela then marched south through present south-western Lesotho, raiding the Zizi people, until they reached the Orange (Senqu) river. However they could not cross the fords towards Cape Colony because the river was in flood.

Around 1824 Mma-Ntatisi and Sikonyela returned north, besieged Moshoeshoe on Butha-Buthe mountain for two months, and

Moletsane of the Taung, sketched in later life when wearing Western dress.

Moshoeshoe of the Mokoteli, in 1833   An engraving based on sketches and descriptions by French missionaries.

Myth of Mma-Ntatisi   Mma-Ntatisi never led her Tlokoa army very far to the west or north. But her name became a word of terror and respect over the whole highveld. All Tswana-Sotho raiders might be called booMma-Ntatisi by their neighbours, or 'Mantatees' by the English missionaries who lived among them. (White farmers in Cape Colony similarly called all Sotho migrant workers 'Makatese'.) Rumour had it that Mma-Ntatisi herself was an ugly one-eyed giant, who suckled her troops at her breast. In fact she is known to have been a good-looking woman. No portrait is known, but an 1827 portrait of one of her Tlokoa women (left) gives us an idea of what she might have looked like. In 1824 her Tlokoa settled on Marabeng mountain where her son Sikonyela — portrayed here in 1834 (far left) took power.

then decided to find their own flat-topped mountain to settle on permanently. They chose Marabeng mountain on the north side of the Caledon river, around which they built stone walls. Here Sikonyela began to rule for himself, and his mother fell from power, and was in later years described as 'a very drunken old lady'.

Ngwaneni of Matiwane* The Hlubi of Mpangazita were followed across the Drakensberg by the Khumalo of Mzilikazi who turned north, and then by the Ngwaneni of Matiwane who turned south. The Ngwaneni fled to the highveld in 1822 after being raided by the Zulu — first attacking the Taung of Moletsane on the Vaal river and then the Hlakwana of Nkharahanye in the Caledon valley. Matiwane and his Ngwaneni settled in the Caledon valley, raiding and collecting tribute from Moshoeshoe and other Sotho chiefs, and twice defeated the Hlubi of Mpangazita in battle (about 1824-25). Mpangazita himself was killed and the Hlubi were dispersed, some joining the victorious Ngwaneni, others fleeing northwards to join the Khumalo of Mzilikazi.

Mokoteli of Moshoeshoe Moshoeshoe moved stealthily with his Mokoteli followers from Butha-Buthe to a better mountain fortress in the eastern Caledon valley, avoiding the Tlokoa to the west and being attacked by cannibals. These cannibals, known as *makhwata* ('lean ones'), had been driven to man-eating by widespread famine, and captured and ate Moshoeshoe's own grandfather.

From his capital on Thaba Bosiu mountain Moshoeshoe began to build up his Sotho kingdom as a rival to the Sotho kingdom of Sikonyela on Marabeng mountain. Some people he defeated in battle, but with others he used the lessons of peaceful state-building that he had learnt from Mohlomi. So instead

*Otherwise *Ngwane* of Matiwane: 'Ngwaneni' is an alternative name used here to distinguish them from the Ngwane of Sobhuza (later Swazi).

of killing the *makhwata* who surrendered to him, Moshoeshoe said that they were the living graves of his grandfather and gave them cattle to start a new life with a new source of meat. Moshoeshoe ensured peace with more powerful enemies by paying tribute to both Matiwane of the Ngwaneni and to Shaka of the Zulu. He then complained to Shaka that Matiwane was too greedy in taking cattle due to Shaka, so Shaka sent an army to punish Matiwane for his presumption!

Demise of the Ngwaneni Matiwane's Ngwaneni were twice attacked by Mzilikazi's Ndebele in 1826-27, and unsuccessfully attacked Moshoeshoe for acting too independently in 1827. Matiwane decided to lead his people across the Drakensberg passes into Mpondo country, near the Cape Colony.

The British in Cape Colony mistook the advent of the Ngwaneni for a threatened Zulu invasion and sent a strong army to attack the Ngwaneni at the beginning of 1828. The Ngwaneni were thoroughly defeated and broken up by a British force, including Xhosa and Thembu soldiers, on the Umtata river at the battle of Mbholompo. Most of the Ngwaneni (including former Hlubi) survivors settled among the Xhosa and Thembu as refugees, known locally as 'amaMfengu' ('Fingo'), meaning beggars. Matiwane himself escaped to live first under Moshoeshoe and then under Dingane, who killed him, and his few remaining followers fled to Swaziland.

Rival Sotho kingdoms Freed from the Ngwaneni threat, Moshoeshoe began to build up his cattle herds. The cattle were loaned out to subject chiefdoms on the *mafisa* system, to be kept so long as the subject chief gave allegiance and tribute to the king. In 1829 Moshoeshoe obtained large numbers of cattle for the first time by following the route used by Matiwane to raid the Thembu on the other side of the Drakensberg. In March 1831 Moshoeshoe's growing Sotho kingdom was attacked by an Ndebele army, but the Ndebele failed to capture Thaba Bosiu after two attacks, and Moshoeshoe made peace with them by sending them cattle. The

Ndebele returned home and never attacked the Sotho again. Moshoeshoe's 'victory' over the Ndebele gave him great prestige, and more and more Sotho came to pay him allegiance.

From about 1831 onwards times became more peaceful for the Sotho. But two kingdoms in the Caledon valley competed for the allegiance of the Sotho and might some day clash — the Tlokoa kingdom under Sikonyela in the west, and the Mokoteli kingdom under Moshoeshoe in the east. New troubles soon came with the invasion of horsemen with firearms — Kora, Griqua and Boers from the west and then from the south.

2 Difaqane North of the Vaal River

The Tswana/Sotho peoples of the Witwatersrand and bushveld areas north of the Vaal river were hit hard first by Difaqane invaders from the south and then by the Ndebele of Mzilikazi from the east.

Phuting of Tshwane and Ratsebe When the Khumalo of Mzilikazi fled across the Drakensberg onto the highveld in 1821-22, they attacked the Phuting in the south-eastern corner of the present Transvaal and passed northwards, while the Phuting organized themselves as a Difaqane raiding force. In 1822, led by Tshwane and his son Ratsebe, the Phuting marched westwards down the Vaal valley to attack the Seleka-Rolong at Thabeng*. They. then turned to the north-western Witwatersrand to attack the Kgatla, Kwena and Tlhako, turning west through the bushveld to the Marico valley where they attacked the city of Karechuenya, capital of the Hurutshe kingdom. The city was destroyed. Diutlwileng, the Hurutshe regent, fled with survivors further west, followed by the Phuting who then attacked the Ngwaketse kingdom in southern Botswana.

The Ngwaketse under Makaba II proved too strong for the Phuting, who were beaten off in a battle at the Ngwaketse capital of

---

*West of present Klerksdorp and now called Buisfontein, after Coenrad de Buys who stayed there about 1818-20.

Tlhorong. So the Phuting turned south to attack other groups of Rolong on the Molopo river. On hearing news of the Phuting advance these Rolong decided to flee to their relatives further south. This is how a Tshidi-Rolong historian has described their flight in the early winter of 1823:

> Early in the cold morning pack-oxen were loaded with food-stuffs and houseware. Frightened women, children and old men filled the road; cattle, sheep and goats were collected and driven at a quick pace by boys and young men, while fighting men formed a rearguard of the retreating multitude.

The Phuting followed them to Khunwana, the Rratlou-Rolong capital, which they destroyed, together with the nearby capital of the Thamaga people — who then disappear from history as an independent group (May or June 1823).

Phuting-Hlakwana alliance The Phuting were being tracked by the Hlakwana raiders of Nkharahanye. After being attacked by the Ngwaneni of Matiwane in the later part of 1822, the Hlakwana had been slow to organize themselves into a Difaqane army. The man who emerged as the Hlakwana chief, Nkharahanye, married a daughter of the Phuting chief Tshwane. Then the Hlakwana followed the Phuting like vultures, cleaning up the bones of the victims of the Phuting. So when the Phuting decided to attack the rich Tlhaping kingdom at Dithakong and Kuruman, the Hlakwana made moves to join them there. Meanwhile a third Difaqane army, the Patsa-Fokeng under Sebetwane, was marching towards Tlhaping country from the east.

Origin of the Kololo The Patsa-Fokeng were attacked by invaders in 1822. The invaders were probably the Tlokoa of Mma-Ntatisi, though Mfumo raiders from the coast have also been suggested.

The Patsa fled to Fokeng relatives hunting game on the Vet (Tikwe) river. Sebetwane became their chief, after his elder brother was killed by a lion. 'My masters, you see that the world is collapsing', he told his people, 'We

83

shall be eaten up one by one. Our fathers taught us *khotso ke nala* (peace means prosperity), but today there is no peace, no prosperity. Let us march . . . to find some land where we can live in peace!'

The Patsa-Fokeng marched westward to Dithakong and arrived before the Phuting from the north-east. The six thousand inhabitants of Dithakong had fled to the west before the Patsa-Fokeng arrived. The Phuting then found the Patsa-Fokeng at Dithakong, and expelled them. But Sebetwane captured a young widow of the Kolo clan from the Phuting and fell in love with her. She became his chief wife (mother of his heir) and in her honour Sebetwane named his nation the 'Kololo' after the name of her clan.

Battle of Dithakong, 1823   The Phuting now decided to march from Dithakong to Kuruman, the new Tlhaping capital to which king Mothibi had moved from Dithakong six years before. But in late June 1823 the joint army of the Phuting and the Hlakwana was attacked and defeated by the joint army of the Tlhaping and Griqua in a great battle outside Dithakong. It is said that there were tens of thousands of Phuting and Hlakwana, armed with spears and battle-axes and oval shields, against only one thousand Tlhaping and one hundred Griqua. But the Tlhaping had bows and arrows, which could shoot a longer distance than spears could be thrown, and the Griqua had the newest and most terrifying weapons of all — guns and horses. The flint-lock muskets were heavy and could not be fired accurately for more than a hundred metres, but they inflicted terrible bloody wounds on the tightly packed enemy and the Griqua had horses to make a quick escape after the muskets were fired. During seven hours of battle both Tshwane of the Phuting and Nkharahanye of the Hlakwana were killed, and the Difaqane invaders retreated into Dithakong in chaos and burnt the town down.

The battle of Dithakong, fought on 26th June, 1823, was a most important battle because it showed the power of the horse and gun for the first time in the interior of southern Africa. The victory gave prestige to the coloured and white people known as *Masetedi* ('bright faces') who owned guns and horses, and to the Christian missionaries and British agents who seemed to have power over the Masetedi. It had been the missionary Robert Moffat at Kuruman who had brought the Griqua to the aid of the Tlhaping, and the Griqua were accompanied by a British official (sent to them from the Cape Colony in 1822). Sebetwane, Mzilikazi, and other chiefs on the highveld never forgot the lesson of Dithakong — that a few men with guns and horses could destroy an army of thousands, but they might be controlled by friendship with British missionaries or officials.

Aftermath of the battle   The Hlakwana were chased to the Vaal river, which was in flood: many Hlakwana women and children were drowned trying to cross it. Survivors scattered and the Hlakwana disappear from the record as a Difaqane nation. The Phuting under Ratsebe marched all the way back to their original homeland to attack the south-west of the Witwatersrand, but found it occupied by the Ndebele, who defeated them (1823-24). Phuting survivors led by Ramabusetsa then raided the Kgatla, Kwena and Tlhako north of the Magaliesberg, while other Phuting under Ratsebe crossed the Vaal into the southern highveld. The Kololo under Sebetwane did not fight at Dithakong, but withdrew north-east to the western Witwatersrand where they joined the Taung of Moletsane.

Taung of Moletsane   The Taung, having been attacked by the Ngwaneni near the Vaal about 1822, eventually became organized as a military nation under Moletsane, who led the Taung northwards in mid-1823.

During 1823-24 Moletsane and Sebetwane joined together in raiding people north and west of the Witwatersrand. After conquering six Kwena towns they attacked the Hurutshe at Mosega (south of Zeerust) to which the Hurutshe had moved since the destruction of Karechuenya by the Phuting earlier in 1823. The Hurutshe record their defeat at the battle of Lokolontwane outside Mosega and the

BATTLE OF DITHAKONG, 1823

'Waterboer, the chief, commenced firing, and levelled one of their warriors to the ground; several more instantly shared the same fate ... Though they beheld with astonishment the dead, and the stricken warriors writhing in the dust, they looked with lion-like fierceness at the horsemen, and yelled vengeance ... Soon after the battle commenced, the Bechuanas came up, and united in playing on the enemy with poisoned arrows, but they were soon driven back ... The undulating country around was covered with warriors, all in motion, so that it was difficult to say who were enemies or who were friends. Clouds of dust were rising from the immense masses, who appeared flying with terror, or pursuing with fear. To the alarming confusion was added the bellowing of oxen, the vociferations of the yet unvanquished warriors, mingled with the groans of the dying, and the widows' piercing wail, and the cries from infant voices ... When both [Phuting and Hlakwana] parties were united, they set fire to all parts of the town, and appeared to be taking their departure, proceeding in an immense body towards the north. If their number may be calculated by the space of ground occupied by the entire body, it must have amounted to upwards of forty thousand. The Griquas pursued them about eight miles ... It seemed impossible for the men to yield. There were several instances of wounded men being surrounded by fifty Bechuanas, but it was not till life was almost extinct that a single one would allow himself to be conquered. I saw more than one instance of a man fighting boldly, with ten or twelve spears and arrows fixed in his body.' (Robert Moffat, *Missionary Labours and Scenes in Southern Africa.* London, 1842)

Tlhaping warriers, drawn by a European artist in 1824. They carry Tswana/Sotho type shields (probably drawn too wide here) and long throwing spears.

85

death of their regent Diutlwileng. Moletsane now proudly called himself *Mophati a phatega tsa Lefhurutshe,* the spoiler of Hurutshe country.

After attacking the Ngwaketse, Moletsane and Sebetwane parted. From April until August 1824 the Taung laid waste the area between the Molopo and Vaal rivers where traditions remember them as the 'Makgare' after their most famous warrior called Mokgare. Griqua horsemen helped the Rolong to turn back the Taung in a battle on the Molopo river in August 1824, remembered as 'the battle of the chiefs' because Moletsane's father and the main Rolong general were killed.

The Taung withdrew to the Vaal river, where in 1825-26 they were attacked by Griqua and Kora bandits and Rolong. The attack was beaten off, and the bandits became allies of the Taung against the Ndebele of Mzilikazi. Almost continuous fighting between the Taung and Ndebele caused the Taung to withdraw southwards across the Vaal in 1827, while the Ndebele withdrew northwards across the Witwatersrand. Moletsane settled in the former Taung homeland around later Kroonstad. He launched his last major raid with Kora bandits of the Bloem family against the Ndebele in 1828. After the Ndebele retaliated in 1829 the Taung ceased to be a major military power on the highveld, and Moletsane fled to Moshoeshoe.

Kololo conquest of western Tswana The first Ndebele raid on the western Witwatersrand, in about 1823-24, probably caused the Taung to abandon the area. The Kololo moved only a short distance through the bushveld around the Pilanesberg hills, where they attacked Tlhako, Kwena and Kgatla chiefdoms. The Kgafela-Kgatla chief Motlotle, much hated by his people, fled through bush country across the Marico river, where he was killed by Kgatla and Kgalagari. So when the Ndebele attacked the Kololo for the second time in 1826, Sebetwane led his Kololo in the path of Motlotle westwards.

The Kololo settled in the hills around pre-

An old Kololo soldier, photographed in 1908.   This man was born in about 1840, and escaped to Ngamiland after the fall of the Kololo kingdom in 1864.

sent Molepolole in Botswana. Here they collected tribute from the local Kwena, and fought the Ngwaketse at the battle of Losabanyana, north-west of Kanye, and killed their great king Makaba though some say Makaba was trampled underfoot by his own people. Sebetwane himself was seriously wounded in the chest — the wound which broke open twenty-five years later and caused his death. Before he could recover, Ngwaketse survivors counter-attacked with the support

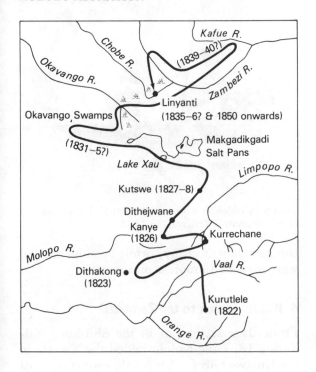

of horsemen and muskets from the south, burning the Kololo capital in the Molepolole hills to the ground (August 1826). After lasting out the 1826-27 summer in either the Molepolole or Mochudi hills, Sebetwane led his people to the Shoshong hills in the north where he had previously raided in pursuit of refugees.

3 Ndebele Conquests North of the Vaal River

After Mzilikazi's Khumalo attacked the Phuting in 1822, they passed northwards, avoiding the valleys where Zwide and Sobhuza were living, to the Steelpoort (Thubatse) river. Here Mzilikazi temporarily joined forces with Nxaba, the leader of the Msene and Maseko-Ngoni, and settled among Ndzundza 'Tebele' (Transvaal-Nguni) at a place which Mzilikazi called Ekupumeleni ('the resting place'). The size of the Khumalo nation was swollen by these Ndzundza and by other 'maTebele', so that the Khumalo nation itself eventually became known as the Tebele or Ndebele.

Ndebele-Pedi war, 1822-23 While living on the Steelpoort river the Ndebele of Mzilikazi were attacked by Makopole, one of the sons of the great Pedi king Thulare. Thulare had recently died, and the Pedi kingdom was split by civil war between nine sons. Makopole at first defeated Mzilikazi, but Mzilikazi and Nxaba then conquered the whole area of the old Pedi kingdom, killing five of the nine sons of Thulare in battle. But one son, Sekwati, fled north to the Soutpansberg mountains, where the Birwa and Venda gave him refuge for four years. Pedi oral tradition claims that an Ndebele army followed Sekwati, to find him living on top of a mountain. Sekwati's followers threw rocks and spears down at the Ndebele, and laughed and sang: 'The evil beast sleeps; it is tired; its roars trouble us no more.'

South of the Witwatersrand, 1823-27 Mzilikazi decided to move again in about 1823 — possibly this was because he had fought with Nxaba, and feared attack by the Ngoni from Mozambique. Drought in the bushveld may also have made his cattle thin. Mzilikazi led his nation south-west to the southern Witwatersrand around the Heidelberg hills — the land of the Khudu, a Sotho group, who then fled to the Rolong in the west. Here the Ndebele beat off an attack by Phuting under Ramabusetsa fleeing from their defeat at Dithakong.

North of the Witwatersrand, 1827-32 In about 1827 Mzilikazi was forced to move northwards by the constant attacks of Kora or Griqua bandits and the Taung of Moletsane. The Ndebele entered the country north of the Witwatersrand through the Magaliesberg hills at the site of the present Hartbeespoort dam. Here they were attacked by the Mogopa-Kwena of old chief More, said to have been so toothless that he sipped minced lung and liver like gravy. At the battle of Kutatu (present Silikaatsnek), the Mogopa-Kwena were defeated, and after two more battles their nation was destroyed. More and his sons were killed, and all their cattle were taken by the Ndebele. Ramabusetsa of the Phuting, who had raided

87

DIFAQANE AND DEPOPULATION

European travellers in the later 1820s noticed that wide areas of highveld grassland had been cleared of population. For example, there were the stone-walled ruins of many large Tswana towns in the area between the places which we today call Pretoria and Rustenburg. The missionary Robert Moffat wrote of this area as having 'become the habitation of wild beasts and venomous reptiles, where lions roam at large, so inured to gorge on human flesh that they are now a terror to the traveller.'

The Ndebele had moved people out of a wide area around the centre of their state in the south-west-central Transvaal, as a security measure against sudden attack. People were either incorporated into the Ndebele state at the centre, or were expelled to live far away.

Tswana chiefdoms moved back to cultivate their lost lands when the Ndebele were expelled from the Transvaal in 1837–38.

The Transvaal Boers in the 19th century regarded themselves as replacing the Ndebele as conquerors of the land and rulers of its 'native' inhabitants. But after the Natives' Land Act of 1913, the myth of 'empty land' was developed to justify 'native reserves' being restricted to a 'horse-shoe' of South Africa's borderlands — arguing that the **Mfecane/Difaqane** wars had exterminated the native people of the Orange Free State and southern-central Transvaal.

Charge by Ndebele troops   An artist's impression drawn in central Transvaal in 1835.

the permanent army, while young women were married to more senior men.

4 Kololo March to the Zambezi

From their settlement in the Shoshong hills during 1827 the Kololo raided the Ngwato in the Kutswe hills further north, capturing most of their cattle and either taking or destroying their harvest. So the Ngwato chief Kgari decided to make good his losses as another Difaqane army on the march, to capture the grain and cattle of the Kalanga on the Zimbabwean plateau. But Kgari's army was ambushed by the Kalanga in the Matopo hills, and Kgari and many of his brothers and half his soldiers were killed.

Kololo invasion of east-central Botswana The Ngwato survivors in the Kutswe hills were attacked by the full force of the Kololo in 1827-28. After spending the 1827-28 summer around the Kutswe hills, Sebetwane followed those Ngwato who had fled to the Boteti river in the north-west. The thousands of Kololo probably only reached the Boteti with great difficulty, travelling across the dry thirstland in small groups over a long period of time. There was drought and wells were few along the way. But Sebetwane appears to have been well pleased with a country of such large and long-horned cattle, and stayed on the Boteti for some years. Sebetwane made his capital near Lake Xau, where the Boteti river fills

and ruled the bushveld north of the Magaliesberg since 1824, wisely decided to join Mzilikazi rather than fight him. He became one of Mzilikazi's generals until around 1830 when he fled to join Sebetwane in the far north-west.

Between 1827 and 1832 the Ndebele lived on the Apies river, just north of present Pretoria, in three military towns. The military power of the nation was strengthened by Ndwandwe survivors fleeing from their final defeat by Shaka in 1826, and the nation grew in size and riches by conquering local people, and by raiding far and wide — even as far as present Lesotho, Botswana and Zimbabwe. Young men from conquered groups became soldiers in the regiments of

Tswana-Sotho and Ndebele soldiers in hand to hand combat   The man on the left has already thrown his spears, and swings with a battle-axe: his small shield of the southern Tswana or Sotho type is suitable for warding off axe blows. The man on the right thrusts with his short stabbing-spear (assagai): his large Nguni type shield is of no use in close fighting, and is only good for deflecting flying spears or clubs.

the great Makgadikgadi salt pans. He was joined by the Phuting chief Ramabusetsa, fleeing from Mzilikazi, who had attacked the Shoshong and Kutswe hills on his way in about 1831.

Invasion of Ngamiland and Chobe   Between about 1831 and 1835 the search for large long-horned cattle took the Kololo further and further west. Sebetwane first conquered the Tawana kingdom around Lake Ngami, and then led his army westwards along the trade route into the desert to attack the Herero enemies of the Tawana who had such fine cattle. Inside Namibia the Kololo were stopped by a surprise attack of bows and arrows — possibly by the Mbanderu. A small son of Sebetwane was killed by an arrow, and the Kololo turned back to Ngamiland. Perhaps the bows and arrows reminded Sebetwane of the battle of Dithakong and the threat of finding horsemen with guns in the

far west. A tradition says that he was marching towards the Atlantic to buy guns from traders at Walvis Bay.

This time Sebetwane followed in the tracks of Tawana refugees to a place in the Chobe swamps that Sebetwane re-named Dinyanti, meaning 'the reeds'. At Dinyanti Sebetwane ruled both the Tawana and the local Subiya fishermen. It was a Subiya dispute with the Leya that took Sebetwane down the Chobe to the great waterfalls on the Zambezi called Shongwe-na-Mutitima ('the boiling pot') by the Leya, which Sebetwane re-named Mosi-oa-Tunya ('the smoke that thunders').

5 Kololo North of the Zambezi

Sebetwane led the Kololo onto the Tonga plateau of southern Zambia during 1839-40, while Mzilikazi's Ndebele drew closer to the Zambezi from the south. The Kololo defeated many Tonga chiefdoms on the plateau, and crossed the flood-plain of the Kafue river to Ila country. The Ila were defeated after a three-day battle and Sebetwane finally arrived not far from modern Lusaka, where he captured the priestess-chief of the Sala people.

Tradition records that in Sala country a Kololo prophet warned Sebetwane from going further east: 'There I behold a fire, avoid it; it may burn you.' (This may have referred to Afro-Portuguese and Swahili slave-traders.) He then pointed Sebetwane to the west, to a land of fine red cattle. 'But when your soldiers have captured the red cattle, do not kill their owners: they will be your nation.' The Kololo turned back onto the Tonga plateau, where they defeated the Ndebele army sent by Mzilikazi at a hill near modern Kalomo. As all the Kololo, including the women, joined in the fighting, it became known as the battle of the women's mountain (Thaba ya Basadi).

Invasion of the upper Zambezi When the Kololo arrived on the upper Zambezi the Luyana kingdom was in a state of civil war. Sebetwane was helped by Luyana rebels in defeating king Mubukwanu, and Sebetwane thereafter had strong support among some of the Luyana. Mubukwanu died in exile, but his heir Sipopa and other young Luyana royalty were educated as privileged members of the Kololo nation. Royalty in Kololo society were not cut off from the people as god-like figures as they had been in the Luyana kingdom. Sebetwane mixed with the common people and controlled them by the force of his personality and not by public cruelty.

Sebetwane made his capital at the southern end of the Luyana flood-plain. But he was threatened by further Mfecane/Difaqane invasion, and trade was opened up in the south with Griqua who brought British goods from the Cape, as well as with Ovimbundu who brought Portuguese goods from Angola. So Sebetwane spent much time round the Chobe-Zambezi southern frontier of the kingdom. Meanwhile the Msene-Ngoni inva-

sion of about 1843-45 and the Ndebele invasions of 1845 and 1850 were craftily defeated by catching and destroying them in the hostile environments of desert, river and marsh.

Return to the Chobe swamps In 1850 Sebetwane decided to move his capital back to Dinyanti in the Chobe swamps, where the tsetse-fly belt stopped wagons from Ngamiland and the Cape going any further. The capital in the swamps was safe from Ndebele attack, but malaria poisoned the health of older Kololo born on the malaria-free highveld south of the Vaal river. Sebetwane died at Dinyanti on July 7th, 1851 from his old battle wound, made worse by malarial fever and too much dagga (marijuana) smoking, according to the missionary Dr Livingstone who had just arrived there to visit him.

Questions

1 Write briefly on the parts played in the history of Africa by (a) Mzilikazi of the Ndebele; and (b) Sebetwane of the Kololo. [Cambridge International School Certificate, 1977] (Refer also to Chapter 9.)

2 Discuss the role of horses and guns in the Difaqane wars before 1836. (See also Chapter 7.)

3 Were the Rozvi and Luyana states ripe for conquest?

Activities

1 Draw a series of maps illustrating the migration route of Sebetwane's Kololo. Annotate the maps with notes and approximate dates.

2 Imagine that you are an eye-witness of a battle fought by Mzilikazi's Ndebele, e.g. against the Mogopa-Kwena of More in the Magaliesberg hills.

For references of Chapters 5 and 6 see Bibliography, pp. 337–42: n.b. C10 Hamilton and C21 Omer-Cooper; also B6 Duminy & Guest; B17 Lye & Murray; B20 Matsebula; B21 Maylam; B39 Roberts; B37 Tlou & Campbell; B42 Wilson & Thompson; C2 Beach; C9 Hall; C12 Inskeep; C15 Maggs; C22 Peires; C27 Saunders & Derricourt; D10 Langworthy; D13 Marks & Trapido; D14 Peires; D17 Sanders; D18 Saunders; D19 Thomson.

PART II

CONQUEST AND RESISTANCE

Introduction

European powers conquered and divided southern Africa amongst themselves in the 19th century, but historians disagree as to which events were most important in European penetration of the interior. Some historians point to the struggle between British capitalists and Boer states over control of Witwatersrand gold production at the end of the century. Other historians point to the 'mineral revolution' of diamond mining at Kimberley in the 1870s, which led to military confrontation and defeat of the most powerful African states by British imperial forces. Other historians look back to the migration of Boer hunter-herders into the interior in the 1840s, and their founding of states claiming control of the highveld grasslands. Other historians look as far back as the Cape Colony in the 18th century, as setting the pattern of white supremacy and black enslavement that was later spread into the interior. Which set of events was the most important? The answer depends on which major themes of 19th century history we consider most important:

European imperialism   The economic and political expansion of European, particularly British, power over the rest of the world may be outlined in three phases. First there was *mercantile-imperialism* when emerging capitalist industry in Britain sought to obtain monopoly of overseas trade by colonization – such as the capture of Cape Colony from the Netherlands and its territorial expansion eastwards. Second there was the *'imperialism of free trade'*, after British industry became the most developed in the world and could sell goods more cheaply and plentifully than any foreign competitor. Britain therefore had no need for expensive colonies to protect its trade. This period lasted from about the 1840s to the 1870s. Third there was *capitalist-imperialism* when European capitalism moved directly into southern Africa to invest in production of minerals. Colonies again became necessary to monopolize such production and protect it from foreign competition.

Horse-and-gun technology   New tools, weapons and machines, which were produced during the industrial revolution in Europe, obviously gave an advantage to Europeans from overseas in Africa – and to whichever Africans could obtain them. The wagons, horses and guns associated with mercantile-imperialism made possible the Boer treks into the interior, and African states which adopted them therefore sought friendly relations with the British as suppliers. By the 1870s, with 'free trade' at its height, African states were so well armed that the British were obliged to fight wars of disarmament in order for capitalist-imperialism to move into the interior. Only the Boer states succeeded in adopting the more advanced technology of railways and machine-guns associated with capitalist-imperialism, and were therefore disarmed at great cost by the British in 1899-1902.

Trading-based and military-based kingdoms   The period of 'imperialism of free trade' saw the

91

rise of trading-based kingdoms in the interior of southern Africa. These kingdoms originated as mountain or desert-edge refuges from Mfecane/Difaqane, and stood on the trade routes of the interior supplying hunting goods, crops or labour to British traders. Military-based kingdoms founded during the Mfecane/Difaqane had less reason to trade with the British or to adopt aspects of European technology and culture, because they were already strong. But military-based kingdoms also saw advantages in trade, just as trading-based kingdoms saw advantages in military force once they were strong enough.

European missionary influence   Many historians have only looked at Christian missionaries from Europe as good or bad influences on European imperialism and settler politics in Africa. But the missionaries saw themselves as coming to change customs and ways of thinking for a new civilization that would consist of much more than simply religious belief in Christianity. Why did missionaries succeed or not succeed among different peoples at different times? Trading-based states welcomed missionaries as trading agents and interpreters who were willing to teach the mysteries of European technology. Indigenous churches developed under state rather than missionary control. But the period of capitalist-imperialism saw the rising prestige of missionaries as British diplomatic agents in the far interior, and increased missionary control of indigenous churches.

Boer states in the interior   The mass immigration of Boer hunter-herders into the interior of southern Africa can be seen as a breakaway from European mercantile-imperialism at the Cape, which came to be tolerated by the British during the period of 'free trade'. It can also be seen as setting up new African states in the interior, based on kinship (between whites) and tribute (from blacks) like other interior chiefdoms which combined into new states. The Orange Free State may be seen as a trading-based state still closely connected with the Cape by economics and culture. The Transvaal may be seen as a military-based state, with small areas under true colonization and large areas under tribute and raiding until capitalist production on the Rand made it into a state more along European lines. Yet the Boer states kept the legal system and land tenure of earlier mercantile capitalism, which made them more adaptable to advanced industrial capitalism than other African states.

It is possible to find 19th century roots for characteristics of 20th century southern Africa, notably racial segregation. Historians have found early forms of discrimination against Africans because of their race (rather than because of their culture) in industrial employment at Kimberley and in Natal land tenure during the 19th century. But we should beware of assuming that anything in the past was exactly the same as similar things later or today. We should not exaggerate white supremacy in 19th century southern Africa, or date it too early. Most people living in southern Africa would probably have considered the Zulu kingdom to be the greatest power in the region until its defeat by the British in 1879. That defeat tipped the balance of power from black states to white states in southern Africa, but not until the 1890s was white or British power unstoppable.

Keywords

capitalism and *imperialism; mercantile-capitalism* (i.e. early capitalism, usually abbreviated as 'mercantilism') and *industrial-capitalism* (i.e. mature capitalism, the usual meaning of the word 'capitalism' today); *mercantile-imperialism, the 'imperialism of free trade'*, and *capitalist-imperialism* (the usual meaning of the word 'imperialism' today); *monopoly* and (economic) *competition; disarmament; missionaries* and *diplomatic agents; racial discrimination* and *racial segregation.*

Chapter 7

The Boer Trek, or Afrikaner Difaqane

European traders and settlers spread across the escarpment into the interior during the period of the Mfecane and Difaqane wars. Cape Colony had become a British colony, being captured from the Dutch in 1795, then handed back in the peace of 1803, and captured again in 1806. Britain emerged from its industrial revolution and the European wars of 1793-1815 as the world's first industrial-capitalist power. At first Britain only saw the Cape as a naval base on the trade route round Africa to India. But after Britain decided not to hand back Cape Colony to the Dutch in the peace of 1814-15 it began to develop the colony for trade and settlement, like Canada and Australia. British industry converted itself from production of war materials to goods like textiles and cutlery, and sought ever-expanding trade markets overseas. British trade spread by wagon into the interior and by ship along the coast of southern Africa, while British settlement began at Capetown and spread to the eastern frontier districts.

The Boer migration or invasion into the interior, sometimes called the 'Great Trek' (i.e. the great haul), was both a reaction to the British take-over of Cape Colony and a response to the opportunities in the interior opened up by the *Mfecane/Difaqane* wars. The trekkers set out to capture hunting, cattle and labour, as well as land. The historian Colin Webb has called the Boer Trek a 'White Difaqane'.

'Afrikaner Difaqane' might be more accurate, as the trek across the Orange began with Orlam or coloured Afrikaners in the west. The Boers also had numerous Afrikaans-speaking Khoisan or coloured servants, as well as African allies who fought beside the Boers against common enemies.

1 The Eastern Frontier 1800-1820

The 3rd Cape-Nguni frontier war of 1799-1803 was the last of the Cape-Khoisan wars. By 1799 there were no independent Khoisan in the Cape Colony; all were servants living on settler farms. Their leader, Klaas Stuurman, first demanded that the British give them land and free their children from Boer enslavement ('apprenticeship'); and then when the British refused he led an army of 700 Khoisan with 300 horses and 150 firearms to regain Khoisan independence in alliance with the Xhosa of Ndlambe. Together the Khoisan and Xhosa drove a Boer commando of 300 and a British army of 200 out of the Suurveld, burning farmhouses and taking over Boer farms.

The *landdrost* Maynier and the British authorities quickly acted to promise the Khoisan better treatment as workers (1800). Some Khoisan returned to work on Boer farms, but Boers had been driven out of much of the Suurveld, and the Xhosa of Ndlambe continued to raid and conquer the area. Khoisan leaders like Stuurman withdrew to land independent of the colony, but again allied with Ndlambe in 1801-02. When peace returned in early 1803, Boers complained they had lost fifty thousand sheep and fifty thousand cattle since 1799.

Batavian rule, 1803-06 The Netherlands became a republic known as 'Batavia' after a French-type democratic revolution before it took back Cape Colony in 1803. Historians dispute just how different Batavian rule was from previous Dutch and British rule. The Netherlands East India Company and its monopolies had been abolished, as the Batavian rulers proclaimed their belief in freedom and democracy. But free trade and political representation were limited to burghers. Slaves remained slaves, and new laws which talked of rights for servants in fact favoured masters by backing their rights over servants with law courts and police.

The Batavian government exploited Khoisan and Xhosa quarrels over captured cattle and sheep in the Suurveld by recruiting the Khoisan as allies. Klaas Stuurman was given a farm on the Gamtoos river and Batavian master/servant laws promised fair treatment for Khoisan servants by giving them written contracts registered with the *landdrost*.

Second British occupation (1806) The British carried on with many Batavian policies. They kept Dutch as an official language and used the Roman-Dutch law code in the courts. They tried to control chief Ndlambe in the Suurveld by allying with Ngqika beyond the Fish river as the senior Rarabe-Xhosa chief. The British also continued to make master/servant laws, the so-called 'Hottentot Code', to control Khoisan farm workers.

Labour laws By a proclamation of 1809, all Khoisan had to be registered as workers on a particular white farm. Unregistered Khoisan, classified as 'vagrants', were to be arrested and given to a farm owner. A proclamation of 1812 tied the children of Khoisan servants between the ages of eight and eighteen as 'apprentices' to the master of their parents. The anti-vagrancy and apprenticeship laws were in effect pass-laws as people had to carry proof of employment if they wished to travel — a wooden or metal pass issued by their master and worn around the neck on a string.

Khoisan could only avoid this bondage by fleeing from the colony or by settling on a farm owned by Christian missionaries.

Xhosa reoccupation of the Suurveld Between 1807 and 1811, the remaining Boers of the Suurveld were either driven out or became the subjects of Ndlambe or the Gqunukwebe chief Cungwa. The British administration of the Cape Colony began to fear a Xhosa expansion further west. 'Unless a sufficient force is immediately sent,' wrote a British officer on the frontier, 'I shall not be surprised to see the Kaffer [Xhosa] Nation extend itself within a short distance of Cape Town.' British troops failed to stop the Xhosa of Ndlambe and Cungwa: Ndlambe, standing near the Sunday river, stamped his foot on the ground and told a British officer: 'This country is mine, I won it in war and shall maintain it.'

4th Cape-Nguni War, 1812 A new British military governor, General Cradock, decided on immediate action against the Xhosa

---

THE BLACK CIRCUIT AND SLAGTER'S NEK REBELLION

After the Batavian administration had encouraged ideas of burgher democracy, British military rule of the Cape Colony seemed doubly oppressive to many Dutch settlers. An annual circuit court travelled around country districts, hearing burgher cases, and enforcing court decisions with Khoisan troops under British officers. The circuit court of 1812 heard numerous complaints brought by Khoisan servants against their Dutch masters, and became known as the 'Black Circuit'. In 1815 frontier Boers rose in revolt after the shooting of a Boer resisting arrest under a court order. The revolt failed because the rebels twice failed to persuade Ngqika to aid them. The rebels then surrendered, and five were publicly hanged at Slagter's Nek. In the prosperous years that followed for frontier Boers the rebellion was soon forgotten, but its memory was revived over sixty years later as part of a tradition of anti-British bitterness.

above: *Hintsa, senior chief of the eastern Xhosa, died in 1835.* From a sketch by a British official.

left: *Ngqika, senior chief of the western Xhosa (died 1829)* 'His fine, tall, well-proportioned form, at the perfect age of six-and-twenty; his open, benevolent, confiding countenance; the simplicity yet dignity of his deportment; the striking readiness of his judgement and of his answers; his frankness and the rational views he took of things; — all these properties combined.' (H. Lichtenstein, *Travels in Southern Africa.* London, 1812)

advance which threatened to cut meat supplies from the eastern colony to the Cape. An army of British, Griqua and Boer troops under Colonel Graham marched into the Suurveld and expelled its African population (estimated at 22,000) eastwards across the Fish river in the first three months of 1812. Graham then built a line of forts, between new villages called Cradock and Grahamstown, to stop people returning across the river. Cradock gave farms to white settlers around the frontier forts on 'quit-rent', i.e. rent paid to government annually for a lease of fifteen years or more. But as British troops were withdrawn to meet the threat of a French invasion of Capetown later in 1812, some Xhosa began to recross the Fish river until the European wars ended and British troops returned in 1815.

While living east of the Fish river Ndlambe was forced to accept the rule of Ngqika, an ally of the British. But in 1818 Ndlambe was inspired by a prophet named Makana, also known as Nxele ('the left handed'), to rise against Ngqika and defeat him at the battle of Amalinde. After the British invaded to assist Ngqika, and withdrew taking ten thousand cattle, Ndlambe and Makana defeated Ngqika once more, and turned to attack the Cape Colony:

> To chase the white men from the earth
> And drive them to the sea.
> The sea that cast them up at first . . .
> Howls . . . To swallow them again.*

5th Cape-Nguni War, 1818-19   Makhanda led the march across the Fish as a crusade to expel the whites who had taken the Suurveld. In April 1819 Makhanda and ten thousand Xhosa soldiers attacked Grahamstown but failed to capture it; three months later the white counter-attack drove them as far back as the Kei river with great bloodshed. Makhanda surrendered rather than see his people destroyed, and Xhosa elders begged the British to see the justice of their attack against the oppression of Ngqika and the Boers who had stolen their cattle and land. But the conquering British forces took thirty thousand cattle and cleared all Xhosa from the land between the Fish and Keiskamma rivers, henceforward to be 'neutral territory' kept empty by British patrols. The British saw trade with the Xhosa as a profitable alternative to war and encouraged them to trade in hunting goods and livestock with Fort Willshire on the Keiskamma. By 1824 there was so much trade at Fort Willshire that three market-days were being held every week.

2 The Northern Frontier 1801-1825

European adventurers began to visit the Khoisan and coloured communities of the Orange river in the later 18th century. The river, actually known as Gariep to the Nama and Senqu to the Sotho, was given the name 'Orange' in 1779 by a Scottish visitor employed by the Dutch East India Company in honour of the Dutch princes of the house of Orange. The first major attack by trekboers from the Cape Colony on the Orange river was in 1786, on the Kora living in the dense bush of the Gariep islands. One of these

*These are the words of the white settler poet Thomas Pringle, but may well reflect Xhosa opinion that he actually heard spoken.

MAKHANDA

There is no known portrait of the prophet Makhanda. But his memory was kept alive among the Xhosa by a strong tradition of hope for regained freedom. Makhanda had apparently believed that the God of blacks, Dalidupu, was angry with his people for bowing before the inferior God of the alien whites, Tixo. Makhanda prophesied that Dalidupu would raise up the spirits of dead men and cattle to help in a holy war against the followers of Tixo. After he was captured by the British in 1819, Makhanda was detained on Robben Island in Table Bay. On Christmas day of that year he led a mass escape of prisoners by boat. Close to the mainland shore the boat was overturned in the surf. All swam to safety except Makhanda, who was last seen clinging to a rock and encouraging the others in his deep bass voice.

---

trekboers, a German known by the Dutch name Jan Bloem, settled down as a leader of Kora and Griqua bandits, who raided with firearms as far north as the Ngwaketse kingdom in 1798 or 1799. An escaped convict from the Cape, a man of Polish-Greek origin called Stephanos, arrived with a Bible and declared himself as prophet to the Kora people. He fled after committing a murder to join the Orlam bandits of Jager Afrikaner.

Perhaps the greatest adventurer was Coenrad de Buys, a trekboer who fled after the Graaff-Reinet rising of 1799 to the Rarabe-Xhosa of Ngqika. There he lived as the husband of Ngqika's mother until 1814, when he migrated north with a small army of Xhosa family and followers. They crossed the Orange, staying with Griqua and Seleka-Rolong, and hunted and traded as far north as the Limpopo valley. Buys is probably the man remembered in Tswana tradition as Kgowe, 'the peeled one', with red flesh looking as if his real skin had peeled off. Kgowe's name has since been given to all Europeans — the *maKgowa*. Buys died in about 1823 in the Tswapong hills of eastern Botswana, leaving a son with the Ngwato. His other sons settled and married among the Birwa. Moving into the Soutpansberg mountains, the Buys clan hunted elephants and traded for firearms and gunpowder with Tsonga traders from Inhambane or Delagoa Bay.

Rise of trekker power north of the Orange Kora, Griqua and Boer trekkers, who traded and raided with horses and guns, became known as 'Masetedi'* among their Tswana neighbours to the north. The most important group of trekkers in the Orange region were the Griqua who lived under their chiefs Berend Berends and Adam Kok along a line of waterholes west of the Vaal-Orange confluence. In 1801 the British sent envoys to open up cattle trade with the Griqua and the Tlhaping kingdom of the southern Tswana at Dithakong. The expedition left behind Christian missionaries. Two missionaries with the Tlhaping soon became fulltime traders instead. The missionary left with the Griqua, William Anderson, became a very influential religious and political figure in Griqualand between 1801 and 1820.

Griqua republic Anderson's settlement at the Klaarwater waterhole came to be known as Griquatown as it grew into the centre of what was soon described as a 'republic under the patriarchal government of the missionaries'. In 1813 the Griqua republic was given a written constitution of laws and law courts. In 1820 it gained a single chief or president, and during the next four years a council was formed to advise him. Anderson's London Missionary Society (LMS) even arranged for the republic to have its own silver coins. When Anderson retired in 1820 he was replaced as missionary by Robert Moffat, who moved north to live with the Tlhaping in 1821 but remained in close contact with Griqualand.

Like later Boer 'republics', the Griqua colony near the Orange river was not a centralized state, despite its constitution, but was really a loose alliance of chiefdoms under powerful clan leaders. Adam Kok II and

*Masetedi: possibly 'bright faces' in seTswana; alternatively followers of Matsatedi, the Kora chief known in Afrikaans as Taaibosch.

Berend Berends moved away from Anderson's influence at Griquatown in 1814 to live at other waterholes named Campbell and Danielskuil. More Griqua left Griquatown in 1820, when Moffat managed to get the Griqua church leader — Waterboer — elected as president of the republic. All the Griqua combined under Waterboer in 1823 to assist the Tlhaping, at Moffat's request, in fighting Difaqane raiders at the battle of Dithakong. But dissention soon returned, resulting in Adam Kok abandoning Campbell and trekking eastwards with the majority of his people to settle at the London Missionary station of Philippolis in 1825. *Bergenaar* ('mountain men') Griqua bandits living in the Langeberg hills even raided Griquatown itself in 1828.

After the victory of Dithakong in 1823, Griqua became increasingly bold as bandits and traders in the north. *Bergenaar* Griqua combined with Kora, including the Bloem clan from the Riet river, and with Tswana allies in hunting and raiding on the highveld. Berend Berends in particular ran profitable wagon expeditions for ivory in the western Transvaal area. Finally in 1831 Berends abandoned Danielskuil to conquer that area from the Ndebele of Mzilikazi, but was heavily defeated and retired in humiliation to the Caledon valley on the south-eastern highveld.

Wagon trade and Christian missionaries Adam Kok's new Griqua settlement at Philippolis opened up trade and missionary contacts between the eastern Cape Colony and the interior. Clothing, firearms and wagons from the Cape were exchanged for ivory, feathers and cattle from Griquatown and Kuruman. From 1827 Sotho from the upper Caledon valley came to Philippolis to trade sorghum or maize carried on the backs of pack-oxen. Trekboers began to settle around Philippolis and brought increasing numbers of sheep from the escarpment mountains to graze north of the Orange during the drought of the late 1820s and early 1830s. The border of the Cape Colony was advanced to this part of the Orange river in 1824, and the frontier village of Colesberg was founded in 1830.

With the rising power of the 'Masetedi' on the southern highveld came the rising prestige of the Christian missionaries who appeared to control them. After the battle of Dithakong, Moshoeshoe was one of the first to go to Griquatown to pay tribute to Waterboer in 1824. Mzilikazi sent envoys to fetch Moffat from Kuruman in 1829 to obtain his personal friendship. Even Sobhuza I sent an envoy to Kuruman in 1833-34 to bring back a missionary to kaNgwane (the future Swaziland).

As the Difaqane began to die down on the southern highveld after 1831, new settlements were established under missionary influence. In 1833 four chiefdoms moved from the drought-ridden west and settled around new Wesleyan mission stations in the western Caledon valley — the 'Wesleyan alliance' of Seleka-Rolong, Griqua under Barends, Kora under Taaibosch (Matsatedi), and 'Newlander' *bergenaars*. Also in 1833 Moshoeshoe received his first French missionaries from the Paris mission, which also started stations at Bethuli and Beersheba where the roads from the Cape Colony crossed the Orange and lower Caledon rivers. The river crossings formerly used in the iron trade between Sotho and Xhosa, by 'Maketese' labour migrants and the invasions of Matiwane and Moshoeshoe in the 1820s, were now opened up in the mid-1830s to Boer wagoners and sheep-trekkers in search of new pastures up the Caledon valley.

3 Origins of the Boer Trek

Eastern frontier economy The eastern frontier districts of Cape Colony began to prosper in the 1820s with the development of coastal shipping from Capetown, which had begun with the carrying of salted beef by the Korsten shipping company in 1812. The settlement of British immigrants in the Albany district in 1820 had increased demand for imported consumer goods, which resulted in increased bulk and lower costs of shipping. And the growth of towns — including Port Elizabeth, Grahamstown, Graaff-Reinet, Cradock and Colesberg — further increased consumer demand for these imported goods. British exports of manufactured goods were vigorously expanding throughout the world, and the new rich classes of Britain and elsewhere were demanding luxury imports from abroad. Rising prices in the world market for ivory, horns, skins and ostrich feathers, pushed hunter-traders from the Cape Colony further east and north along the frontier trade routes. Feather prices rose with the rising fashion for wearing feathers among ladies in Europe. Ivory was in demand for cutlery handles, billiard balls and piano keys; exports from the Cape rose from a mere £3 worth in 1813 to £16,500 worth in 1825. Great profits were made by white traders exchanging cheap glass or porcelain beads for ivory sold by black hunters, but in 1825-27 Xhosa coming to Fort Willshire began to demand more expensive beads and the ivory price given to them rose from 4 to 67 shillings per pound.

The eastern frontier economy stayed prosperous while wheat and wine production in the south-western Cape suffered from an early 1820s world trade depression, resulting in further migration from Capetown to the eastern districts. Eastern frontier farmers prospered from new export of tallow as well as increasing trade in salted beef at the Cape (for beef-eating Englishmen rather than mutton-eating Dutchmen). Soap production on frontier farms had become unprofitable when the colony began to import cheap manufactured soap from England. The sheep's tail fat, formerly used for soap, was then made into tallow candles instead and transported (without cracking up) by improved wagon roads and shipping from Port Elizabeth. But frontier sheep farmers over-stocked their ranches with too many sheep, so that from the late 1820s they had to use winter pastures north of the Orange river in drought and even normal years.

Consumer demand for firearms, wagons and spare parts, and for tea, coffee, rice, sugar, brandy, linen and Sunday-best clothing, together with improved wagon roads and regular market days in the new villages, stimulated the rise in numbers of professional traders, moving from farm to farm in their wagons. They were known in Dutch as *smous,* a word originally meaning a Jewish peddlar in the days of Dutch rule but now also given to immigrant Scots and English and German traders. Historians have pointed out that there could have been no Boer Trek without *smouses* keeping the trekkers in contact with coastal ports. The power of the horse and gun in the interior depended on the buying of imported firearms and gunpowder, and the selling of ivory to pay for them.

Causes of the Boer Trek   We have seen that Boer sheep farmers had already begun to expand across the Orange during the drought of the 1820s-30s. But the immediate causes of the Great Trek were grievances against British rule which accumulated between about 1828 and 1838. By 1834 a few Boers in the eastern Cape Colony began to discuss and agitate among themselves how to resist British rule, and their ideas were spread among Boers who served in commandos during the 1834-35 eastern frontier war.

The most important colonist to join the Boer emigration, Piet Retief, issued a *Manifesto of the Emigrant Farmers* in February 1837 which listed Boer grievances for the English language newspaper in Grahamstown. He complained about the threat to peace by (Khoisan) 'vagrants'; the abolition of slavery by the British; frontier raiding by the Xhosa; and about Christian missionary influence on British policy. We have few records of what other Boers thought. But we may sum up Boer grievances as five issues of British policy — labour laws, land policy, frontier expansion, general colonial administration, and the threat to property rights.

Labour policy   The *50th Ordinance* issued by the governor of Cape Colony in 1828 abolished the 'Hottentot Code', the anti-vagrancy and apprenticeship pass-laws of 1809-23 which forced all Khoisan to work for Boer or English masters. The 50th Ordinance was a triumph for the liberals like Dr John Philip who influenced the British government to follow their belief in a free market for labour under capitalism. The result was that some Khoisan went to work for the more capitalist farmers, usually new English settlers, who paid higher wages. Other Khoisan also refused to work for the low wages (usually just food and shelter and no cash) offered on Boer farms and became unemployed, travelling around (as 'vagrants') in search of work or food. The British also started a settlement scheme on the Kat river (Ciskei) in 1829 for Khoisan peasant farmers, which drew labour away from Boer farms. The Cape government started to re-introduce anti-vagrancy laws in 1834, because of the farm labour shortage, but stopped because of liberal missionary pressures on the British government in London.

Also in 1834 the Cape Colony heard that the British parliament had voted at the end of 1833 to abolish slavery throughout the British empire. Parliament had acted in the liberal belief that free trade and free labour were essential to the growth of capitalism, which was the inevitable future of the world. Slaves in Cape Colony now became 'apprentices' for four (or sometimes six) years, tied to their masters till complete freedom was to take effect in 1838 (or 1840).

The richer Boers in the eastern colony, like Piet Retief, owned slaves on their farms or in their new town houses and hired them out to poorer Boers to use. Slaves had become more valuable as farms in the east turned to field cultivation of wheat, grapes or tobacco like those of the west, and with the growth of local towns. Abolition of slavery, and the way in which it was done, became sources of grievance among slave-owning frontier Boers. By the time British government compensation for slave-owners reached them in the frontier districts from London and Capetown, unscrupulous lawyers and agents had reduced the money (by charging handling fees) to less than one-fifth of the slaves' market value.

Farm land policy   The colonial administration wanted frontier loan-farms to become quit-rent or freehold farms, as such security of tenure would encourage capital investment in agriculture. British settlers with capital were importing expensive merino sheep, heavily wooled unlike the hairy indigenous

Imaginative engraving of Hintsa being persuaded to surrender by the athletic colonel (later governor) Harry Smith. After Hintsa surrendered, he was treacherously shot.

sheep, and grazed them in great numbers to produce wool for export to Britain. In 1832 the rumour went round that poorer Boers would lose their loan farms. Such fears helped push Boers into trekking northwards, which ironically left many loan-farms to be taken up by agricultural capitalists.

Frontier policy   The British tried to restrict Boer expansion into Xhosa country to the east and into Griqua country in the north-east. British troops attempted to police the eastern frontier, while Boer and Xhosa raiders, like Maqoma son of Ngqika, tried to avoid them. Between 1829 and 1833 the British pushed Maqoma back and forth between the Kat river and the future Lovedale area so much that he complained, 'When shall I and my people be able to get rest?' Meanwhile the drought made increasing numbers of Boers seek pasture for their cattle in Xhosa country during 1833-34. The result was the *6th Cape-Nguni Frontier War* which began in December 1834, with Maqoma leading a Ngqika-Xhosa army (on behalf of his brother

Sandile, chief since 1829) to attack settler farms as far west as the Fish valley. British and Boers counter-attacked as far east as the Kei, where they shot the Gcaleka-Xhosa para-mount chief Hintsa dead and made his son Sarili (Kreli) chief in his place. Maqoma was sent to Robben Island.

In May 1835 the new British governor, Benjamin D'Urban, annexed the land between the Kei and Keiskamma rivers as British territory called Queen Adelaide Province (later Ciskei), and promised farms to Boer settlers at the same time as promising reserves to Xhosa if they laid down their arms. But the Colonial Office in London believed that Boers had incited war in order to have the use of a British army to conquer the eastern Xhosa. So at the end of 1836 the British withdrew from the Kei-Keiskamma area, making treaties of friendship with local Xhosa chiefs as indepen-dent allies. There was a great outcry of pro-test from the would-be settlers, who had expected to gain land and labour as rewards for fighting the war.

On the northern frontier, Boer movement

100

was restricted by British treaties of friendship with Waterboer in 1834 and with Mzilikazi (signed by Ndebele envoys in Capetown) in March 1836, and by friendly contacts with Moshoeshoe and Adam Kok II by the British envoy Dr Andrew Smith in 1835-36. In 1836 the British parliament passed the *Cape of Good Hope Punishment Act,* which made Cape courts responsible for British subjects, including Boers, as far north as 25 degrees south latitude — a line just north of present Pretoria. This was in fact the first step towards removing the sovereignty of African states in the interior, but the Boers saw it as a direct challenge to their northward trekking. The act, however, proved to be a dead letter: only two British magistrates were appointed outside the colony — one at Griquatown, the other at Port Natal (Durban).

Colonial administration   The old system of administration, based on burgher councils which advised the government and elected officials, was replaced during the first few decades of British rule. *Landdrosts, veldkornets* and commando commandants, previously responsible to and even elected by burghers, were replaced by British officials strictly responsible to the governor at Capetown or to his lieutenant-governor at Grahamstown appointed in 1836. Dutch language and customs in government were replaced by English ones, though Roman-Dutch law and the use of the Netherlands language remained official policy. The question of Boers rejecting English culture at this time has perhaps been exaggerated by historians, being confused with Boer rejection of 'Anglicization' seventy years later. But there seems to have been a general belief that the good old burgher democracy had been replaced by British despotism.

Threat to Boer property   The great migration of the Boers, or Afrikaner Difaqane, had causes in Africa but must also be seen as part of world history. The migration was made possible by the growth of trade and gun power in the interior, which were offshoots of capitalist development in Europe. And the

Boer fears of black 'vagrants' attacking them were not unlike the fears of conservatives in Europe around the same time that the liberalism of equal rights for all might lead to the communism of equal property of all. What drove the Boers into the interior was the fear that capitalist reforms would open the floodgates for revolution in which landless blacks would take over white farms. Nor was the Boer Trek the only long distance migration of European settlers across a continent during the 1830s-40s. Europeans were trekking in wagons to expand the United States westwards; the Russian empire was expanding eastwards over Asia; and European settlers were beginning to spread into the interiors of South America and Australasia.

4 Boer Trekkers Cross the Orange

The Boers of the eastern Cape Colony concluded that revolt against British military might was hopeless. But if migration into the interior beyond British rule was the answer, where could they migrate to? During 1834-35, three parties of Boer hunters set off to scout out the lands of the interior for future settlement and farming — avoiding the main 'missionaries' road' through Griquatown and Kuruman to the headwaters of the Limpopo, where the 'Central Africa Expedition' under Dr Andrew Smith was making friends with local chiefs and kings on behalf of the British government.

Scouting the land   One Boer scouting party, under Andries Pretorius, followed the Orlam into Namibia. A second party, led by Scholtz, took the new road to Wesleyan alliance settlements in the western Caledon valley and then crossed the eastern highveld, avoiding the Ndebele kingdom to the west, to meet up with the Buys clan in the Soutpansberg mountains. A third scouting party, under Piet Uys, followed a previous journey of Dr Andrew Smith along the trading paths from Xhosa country across numerous rivers to the fertile hills of Zulu country (Natal).

When the scouting parties returned to Cape Colony they reported at semi-secret meetings on conditions in the north. The most fertile land for crops seemed to be Natal. The best land for grazing seemed to be the southern and eastern highveld. The best wagon route to Natal was through the highveld and over the central Drakensberg. The Soutpansberg in the far north was excellent for elephant hunting in the Limpopo valley, and the ivory could be exported through the Portuguese ports of Inhambane or Lourenço Marques.

Trichardt trek During 1835 two groups of elephant hunters, under Louis Trichardt and Jan van Rensburg, migrated northwards across the Orange river to settle in the Soutpansberg mountains. Before reaching their destination, van Rensburg decided to find the road to Inhambane. He and his party were then killed by Shangane in the lower Limpopo valley. Trichardt stayed with the Buys clan, awaiting the arrival of more settlers who never arrived, and in 1837-38 took the road to Lourenço Marques, guided by English-speaking Tsonga traders of the chiefdom of Mfumo.

Potgieter trek Hendrik Potgieter and Sarel Cilliers led larger groups of Boers across the Orange at the end of 1835, when rumours circulated that the British would abandon Kei-Keiskamma territory. They eventually settled north of Thaba Nchu in the country of the Taung chief Makwana in mid-1836, on friendly terms with the Wesleyan alliance, especially the Rolong under Moroka and the Griqua under Piet Davids. All of these chiefdoms, together with the nearby Tlokoa under Sikonyela, possessed some horses and firearms, and were counted among the 'Masetedi' enemies of the Ndebele north of the Vaal River.

5 Trekker-Ndebele Wars

Trekker and Zulu attacks on the Ndebele, 1825-34 The Ndebele had been frequently attacked by 'Masetedi' hunter-raiders under Jan Bloem in support of the Taung of Moletsane between 1825 and 1828, after which a large Ndebele army crossed the Vaal in 1829 and destroyed the Taung nation around Bodibeng (Kroonstad). Moletsane fled to become a sub-chief under Moshoeshoe, and the Taung who remained in their old homeland came under the chieftainship of Makwana. Mzilikazi thought that he had solved the problem of 'Masetedi' raiders in 1829 by making friends with the missionary Robert Moffat at Kuruman, having been advised to do so by the first two European traders to visit him around present Pretoria. In future the wagon road from Kuruman was the only route by which Mzilikazi would allow the entry of trekker hunters and traders into his country.

The Griqua of Berend Berends came up the Kuruman road to trade in ivory with Mzilikazi in 1829. They were invited by the Kgatla and other Tswana to liberate the country from Ndebele rule with their firearms. Berends suffered from the delusion, according to Moffat, that he was destined to sweep Mzilikazi from the land. So while the main Ndebele army was occupied in the south attacking the Taung and southern Sotho, Berend Berends led an invasion of 1,600 Griqua and Tswana (with 600 horses and many wagons) into Ndebele country in mid-1831. All but 400 of Berends' men were killed in an Ndebele counter-attack in a battle on the Kgetleng (Elands) river, and Berends fled to the Caledon valley — where he joined the Wesleyan alliance and was succeeded by Piet Davids.

While the Ndebele followed up their 1831 victory by attacking the Tswana in the west, a Zulu army invaded their country, sent by Dingane to finish off Mzilikazi after the losses of the Griqua war. The Zulu invasion was defeated in a pitched battle around present Ga-Rankuwa just west of Pretoria. Mzilikazi decided to retreat from the threat of further invasion. The Ndebele settled around the Marico headwaters in early 1832, taking over the land formerly controlled by the Hurutshe kingdom, and placing military towns at its main centres — including Tswenyane mountain where the city of Karechuenya once stood, and Mosega which guarded the road to Kuruman.

In 1834 the Ndebele were attacked by the

Kora of Jan Bloem and Griqua of Piet Davids. The Ndebele beat off the attack and captured wagons, horses and Davids' niece Gertrude.

Arrival of Maritz trekkers In 1836 new groups of 'Masetedi' began to cross the Vaal river from the south without taking the official Kuruman road or receiving the permission of Mzilikazi. They were hunters from the Potgieter-Cilliers Boer settlement in Taung country. Moffat records that Mzilikazi heard that they were poaching his game and mistreating his subjects, so Ndebele troops were sent to expel them as bandits. An army under general Kaliphi attacked the main Boer camp (*laager*: square or circle of wagons tied together) at the hill later called Vegkop, and captured all their livestock. The Potgieter-Cilliers trekkers were rescued by Seleka-Rolong who brought oxen to draw them back to the Rolong capital of Thaba Nchu, where a large group of trekkers had recently arrived under Gert Maritz. Maritz was a prosperous businessman, a wagon-maker from Graaff-Reinet, who had brought many trekkers from

Mzilikazi sitting in his wagon, listening to praise-singers The wagon was captured from the Bloem-Davids attackers of 1834. This water colour was painted by Charles Bell, a member of Dr Andrew Smith's 'Central Africa Expedition', which visited Mzilikazi early in 1835. Mzilikazi sent an induna back with Andrew Smith to make a treaty of friendship with the British at Capetown (March 1836). Mzilikazi was also persuaded by Robert Moffat to accept American Congregationalist missionaries in his country.

that district. In December 1836 a mass meeting of male Boers elected Potgieter as military commandant, and Maritz as both president of their *volksraad* (people's assembly) and *landdrost* of their court.

1837 Potgieter-Davids attack Potgieter determined to revenge himself on the Ndebele to recover sheep, cattle and horses, in alliance with other enemies of the Ndebele. Potgieter and Piet Davids commanded a carefully planned attack, led by a Rolong guide, which approached the Ndebele kingdom at speed along the unguarded Kuruman road with a mounted commando of Boers, Griqua, Kora, Rolong and Tlokoa. They fell upon Mosega at the crack of dawn on January 17th, 1837, firing on the town from horseback, appearing to the people of Mosega in the dim light like ostriches spitting lightning. In fact there were only old men, women and children at Mosega because the army under Kaliphi was away in the north, and the town was soon burnt to the ground and the inhabitants killed. Newly arrived American missionaries abandoned their station at Mosega and went with Potgieter and Davids.

Arrival of Retief trekkers The new Boer community was not a united nation but an alliance of family households under competing chiefs. Potgieter and Maritz quarrelled over sharing out captured livestock and then over who should be the trekkers' minister of religion. These quarrels were temporarily solved by the arrival of Piet Retief, the leading burgher of the eastern frontier districts, who had been dismissed from his post as commando commandant of Albany district and now decided to join the trekkers north of the Orange.

Retief was both the richest and the most experienced in political and military matters of all the trekkers. He brought with him the largest single group of Boer trekkers to leave the colony, and the Boers already in the north greeted him as their natural leader. He was elected both head commandant and governor of the whole community, while his friend Maritz was elected president of the *volksraad* and Potgieter was left without an official position. In June of 1837 a constitution was drawn up at Winburg — the main Boer camp in Makwana's country — under which officials swore allegiance to 'The Free Province of New Holland in South-East Africa'. The Boers thought of themselves as Hollanders freed from British rule, and determined to invite the king of the Netherlands to accept them back as subjects when they reached Natal.

Ndebele decide to migrate northwards Meanwhile Dingane sent a second Zulu expedition to attack the Ndebele. It was beaten off, but the Ndebele suffered severe losses and were then victims of further attacks from Griqua and even from Hurutshe and Ngwaketse raids on their frontier cattle posts. Mzilikazi decided to migrate northwards, like Sebetwane before him, after the 1837-38 harvest. While Mzilikazi temporarily settled at eGabeni further down the Marico river, an advance party of the Ndebele army was sent north under Kaliphi to scout out land for future settlement.

While Retief went on ahead to Natal to negotiate a Boer settlement with Dingane, Potgieter arranged with Maritz and Uys that the main Boer forces should attack and expel the weakened Ndebele of Mzilikazi. Potgieter knew that the Ndebele were suffering constant cattle raids and may also have known of Mzilikazi's plans to migrate northwards after the harvest.

Trekker expulsion of Ndebele Potgieter, Maritz and Uys parked their wagons around present Klerksdorp and dashed north with 330 mounted Boers and 50 unmounted Rolong to attack the Ndebele. The commando found Mosega still burnt and deserted, and attacked an Ndebele camp ('Mezeg') still sleeping. In a nine-day running battle, between November 4th and 12th, 1837, the commando attacked and burned Ndebele camps further and further north down the Marico river, driving the Ndebele before them. After Mzilikazi's capital of eGabeni was captured, the Ndebele decided to trek north while there was still time to plant their crops.

Piet Retief, commandant and governor of 'The Free Province of New Holland in South-East Africa', 1837-38 Retief was formerly commandant of the Albany (Grahamstown) district of the Cape Colony. But he quarrelled with the lieutenant governor of the eastern Cape, appointed in 1836, in the columns of the Grahamstown newspaper. After deciding to leave the colony, Retief published his 'Manifesto of the Emigrant Farmers' in the same newspaper in February 1837.

On November 12th the Boers stopped their advance on top of the Dwarsberg hills, looking down on the Ndebele streaming down the Marico through the Sikwane gorge in the distance.*

6 Trekker-Zulu Wars

Piet Uys had returned to the Cape Colony in 1835 without having even met the Zulu king

*The modern Botswana-Transvaal border from Sikwane (Deerdepoort) towards Gaborone seems to mark the frontier of the Boer invasion on 12th November, 1837.

Dingane, Zulu king 1828-40   Sketched by a British military officer.

avoided service on the Zulu expedition which attacked the Ndebele on the Marico later in the year by sending their firearms instead. Durban whites complained loudly about Dingane restricting their hunting and the British appointment of Gardiner as their magistrate under the terms of the Cape of Good Hope Punishment Act. So when Piet Retief and his Boers arrived at Durban in October 1837, local whites saw them as allies against both Zulu and British control.

Retief trekkers in 'Natal'   Retief first recruited the support of the Durban traders, essential for supplies to an inland Boer colony, and then went on to Dingane's capital of eMgungundlovu in November. Dingane refused to listen to Retief's plea for land to settle because Boers from the Drakensberg had been raiding his cattle. Retief assured Dingane that the raiders were not Boers but Tlokoa of Sikonyela — who also rode horses and carried firearms. Retief returned to the Drakensberg promising to bring back Dingane's missing cattle. (It is possible that Dingane ordered a minor chief on his frontier to kill Retief at this stage but, if so, the attempt failed.)

Back in the Caledon valley, Retief tricked Sikonyela into entering a Wesleyan mission so Retief could ask permission for the trekkers to pass through his country. When permission was given Retief gave Sikonyela presents in return, placing a pair of what were called bangles for great rulers on the chief's wrists. The bangles were in fact handcuffs, which snapped shut. Retief refused to unlock them until Sikonyela surrendered seven hundred cattle, three hundred of which were for Dingane, the rest being kept by Retief and his men.

Execution of Retief trekkers   When Retief returned to eMgungundlovu in February 1838 he openly boasted of both the defeat of the Ndebele and of the tricking of Sikonyela. A British missionary staying at eMgungundlovu later recalled that, when Retief arrived, his men rode round the town firing their weapons in the air in order to scare the people.

Dingane to ask permission for a Boer settlement in Natal. In fact Dingane was already in dispute with English traders at Port Natal over plans for white settlement. When Dingane first heard rumours of a large number of Englishmen coming to settle in his kingdom in 1831, he had attacked Port Natal as a deterrent. In 1835 Dingane appointed the missionary A. F. Gardiner as chief of Port Natal, under Zulu sovereignty, but Gardiner treated the appointment as a concession of land ownership. Gardiner tried to persuade governor D'Urban at Capetown to make the 'concession' a British colony, and Port Natal whites even renamed their town Durban in honour of the governor. But the British declined to take up the offer. Dingane, on the other hand, showed his sovereignty over the Durban whites by forcing them as Zulu subjects to join an expedition against the Ngwane in present Swaziland (1836). Whites only

Andries Pretorius, elected Boer commandant in 1838 to lead Boer revenge on Dingane.

there, Weenen, meaning 'weeping'.) When Durban whites rashly started to raid local Zulu for cattle, women and children, an army was sent in retaliation to burn down the port while whites sheltered on ships in the bay. During April 1838 a commando under Potgieter and Uys was defeated by a Zulu army at the battle of Ethaleni during which Uys was killed. Potgieter retreated back onto the highveld with what became known as the *vlug kommando,* 'the commando that fled'. Boers remaining in Natal retreated into one large camp and laid claim to deserted Durban.

Pretorius assumes Boer leadership Potgieter refused to return to face the Zulu. Maritz sent for reinforcements to the frontier districts of Cape Colony but died before he could lead them. The reinforcements arrived in November 1838 under a rich Graaff-Reinet farmer, Andries Pretorius, who was elected commandant and began to train a commando

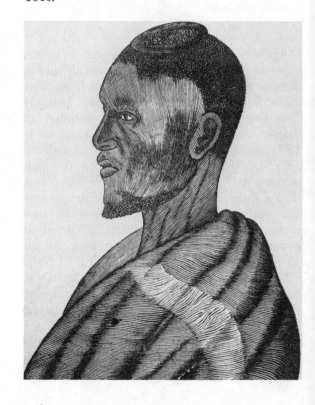

Mpande, brother of Shaka and Dingane, who was assisted to power by the Boers in the civil war of 1840.

Dingane therefore decided to eliminate the Boer threat by killing Retief and his men — seventy Boers and thirty Khoisan or coloured servants. Popular tradition adds that the Boers had aroused suspicion as witches by creeping round the town in the dark. It seems that Dingane persuaded them to believe that he was giving them a land concession. Then, on February 6th, Retief's men were dragged to the execution hill and executed as witches, wooden stakes being driven up into their bodies. The few British in eMgungundlovu at the time were left untouched, and may even have encouraged Dingane by denouncing the Boers as rebels against the British monarch.

Zulu troops followed up the killing of Retief's party with dawn attacks on Boers camped along the Tugela river. Over five hundred people were killed, of whom half were Khoisan or coloured servants and a third were Boer children, and 10,000 cattle were captured. (Boer horror at the attacks can be seen in the name of the village later founded of Boers, Khoisan and coloureds to attack the Zulu, who were joined by local African allies and a few Durban English on the march. Pretorius, with Cilliers as his veld preacher, whipped the commando up to a fever-pitch of confidence to fight a holy war against the heathen. According to Cilliers' later memoirs, they all swore a common oath or 'covenant' to keep the day holy forever on which God gave them victory, and they renewed the oath every night.

Blood river battle On Sunday 16th December, 1838, a Zulu army attacked Pretorius's army in its heavily fortified weekend camp on the Ncome river. The camp was protected by steep banks and a ditch in which thousands of Zulu soldiers were trapped by gunfire and massacred, staining the water red with their blood. At the end of the battle perhaps three thousand dead Zulu lay 'heaped like pumpkins on a rich soil' while nobody had been killed in Pretorius's army.*

It was not the main Zulu army that was defeated at 'Blood river', but the Zulu now understood the power of gunmen on horses making rapid sorties from an armed wagon camp. When Pretorius' army reached eMgungundlovu they found it deserted; Dingane had fled to the north. The bodies of Retief's party were found on the execution hill. Tradition claims that a concession from Dingane, dated February 4th, was discovered still intact on Retief's body. It conceded the land from the Umzimvubu river to the Tugela, and from the Drakensberg mountains to the ocean. Pretorius' army then retreated to this promised land in the south, and Dingane soon returned to rebuild eMgungundlovu.

7 Orlam-Afrikaners in Namibia

Groups of Orlam from the Orange river migrated through Nama country as far as central Namibia in the first half of the nineteenth century. The Nama immediately north

*The battle was similar to the American battle of New Orleans in 1814, in which British troops were massacred when caught in ditches around an American fort.

JAGER AFRIKANER AND HIS GROUP OF ORLAM BANDITS ATTACKED THE LONDON MISSION STATION OF WARMBAD, NORTH OF THE ORANGE RIVER, IN 1811

'Finding it abandoned, his followers commenced a rigid search for any articles which might have been concealed for safety in the earth, and were but too successful . . . one of the chieftain's attendants strayed into the burial ground . . . Stepping over what he supposed a newly closed grave, he heard, to his surprise, soft notes of music vibrate beneath. He stood motionless, gazing over his shoulder, with mouth and eyes dilated, hesitating whether to stand still, and see the dead arise, which he had heard the missionaries preach about, or take to his heels . . . The chief, fearless of the living or the dead, was not to be scared even by the supposed spectre of the tomb, arose, and ordered his men to follow him to the spot. One jumped and another jumped, and at each succeeding leap, succeeding notes of the softest music vibrated on the ear from beneath. Recourse was had instantly to exhumation. The mysterious musician was soon brought to light. It proved to be Mrs Albrecht's piano-forte, which she had taken with her from London . . . it had been buried in a soil where, from the entire absence of moisture, it might, but for this circumstance, have remained unscathed.'
Robert Moffat, who wrote this account, adds that the piano was broken up and divided among the Afrikaner bandits.

---

of the Orange lived in small scattered groups, but the Nama further north were organized in a strong alliance dating from the previous century known as the 'Red Nation' (*Awakhoi*), its senior chief between 1800 and 1835 being a formidable woman named Games. The most important group of Orlam were the Afrikaners under Jager Afrikaner who lived as bandits in the Orange river islands, raiding the Nama and Kora for sheep and importing firearms from the Cape. (Hence the Nama called the Orlam the *Gu-nu*, meaning 'sheep-stealers'.)

An attempt was made to convert the Nama

to Christianity, and the Orlam to more peaceful trading, by British missionaries who founded the London mission station at Warmbad just north of the Orange in 1807. But four years later the mission was completely destroyed by the Orlam-Afrikaners; it was rebuilt first at Pella and then moved to Bethanie (1815). Orlam who attached themselves to the mission then divided into two groups — the larger group under the leadership of Amraal ('Admiral') Lamberts.

It was the missionary Robert Moffat who in 1818, before going to the Griqua and Tswana, finally succeeded in converting Jager Afrikaner to Christianity. Thereafter Jager learnt to read and encouraged education, while the Orlam-Afrikaners engaged less in raiding and more in hunting and trading. But after Jager's death in 1823 his youngest son Jonker broke away from his uncles and brothers to resume a bandit career like his father. Jonker Afrikaner's men became known as the *Aich-ai* ('warlike people') among the Nama, and in the early 1830s Queen Games sent for them as mercenaries to drive out a Herero invasion from her country.

Orlam-Herero relations The Herero had extended their cattle grazing further and further south during the drought of the early 1830s. They drove Damara groups along the Swakop river into the Auas mountains from the places which the Herero named Okahandja and Otijimbinwe. Now the Herero grazed their cattle on the sheep pastures of the Nama 'Red Nation' almost as far south as Bethanie. Queen Games summoned Jonker Afrikaner and his men, who used firearms to chase the Herero beyond the Auas mountains until they reached Okahandja in about 1835. Then Jonker settled down as chief of a mixed population of Orlam-Afrikaners, Nama and Damara, in the country between the 'Red Nation' and the Herero, finally settling in about 1840 at the hot and cold springs of the Ai-gams valley which he renamed 'Windhoek'. (It reminded him of Winterhoek near Tulbach in Cape Colony where his father had once been a slave.) Here the Orlam-Afrikaners grew tobacco and pumpkins on irrigated land.

Jonker obtained permission to settle at Windhoek from Tjamauha the Herero chief at Okahandja, in order to show his independence of the Nama 'Red Nation' which had previously employed him against the Herero.

Conclusion The Afrikaners in east and west had succeeded in establishing themselves in the interior, demonstrating the power of horse and gun in brief offensive wars against Ndebele, Zulu and Herero. But they had yet to fight defensive warfare against an attacking force superior in numbers or weapons.

Questions

1 Write briefly on *three* of the following: (a) the Black Circuit; (b) Chief Ngqika of the Xhosa; (c) the 1820 settlers; (d) the 50th Ordinance; (e) the emancipation of slaves and its effects on South Africa. [Cambridge International School Certificate, 1976]

2 What were the main causes of the Great Trek? How far did they arise from basic differences of attitude held by the Boers and British towards other races in South Africa? [Cambridge International School Certificate, 1980]

3 Why did Mzilikazi's Ndebele abandon their territory in the Marico (Madikwe) valley?

4 What attracted Boer trekkers to Zulu country, and how did they succeed in colonizing southern parts of it as the republic of Natal ('Natalia')? (Refer also to Chapter 8.)

Activities

1 Draw up a date chart of Cape frontier wars, with notes on their participants, battles and where they were fought. (Refer also to Chapters 6 and 9.)

2 Imagine that Mzilikazi and Potgieter met and argued about who should rule north of the Vaal (Lekwa) river. What would they have said to each other?

For references to Bibliography see p. 124.

Chapter 8

The Rise of New Colonies (c. 1838–1868)

The years between the end of the Mfecane and the coming of aggressive European imperialism saw the rise of a new network of African states and European colonies in southern Africa. In the interior of the continent the Afrikaner states were both colonies of European settlement and part of the network of African kingdoms and chiefdoms. Colonies under imperial control from Europe were restricted to the coast. The only large colony was the Cape Colony on the south coast; the Portuguese trading settlements of the east coast and the British colony of Natal were of little importance in African affairs before 1870. During this period the difference between the interests of the 'imperial factor' based in Britain and of the 'colonial factor' of local settlers emerged in Cape politics. The Cape parliament representing settlers confronted the policies of the British high commissioner representing the Colonial Office in London.

For the British, the period between the 1830s and the 1870s was the period of 'free trade'. Britain, as the world's most advanced industrial power, could sell manufactured goods more cheaply and in greater quantity than any competitor. Liberal capitalists believed that peace and freedom in the world meant profit for all, and pressed the British government into the liberal-imperialism which some historians have called the 'imperialism of free trade'. They argued that there was no need to extend British rule over the interior because the benefits of trade would convert Africans into allies. British

military power should only be used to impose peace and freedom on the interior. Once Africans were free, argued the liberal imperialists, they would be converted to Western culture by the example of traders and missionaries.

White or black traders and missionaries based in Cape Colony were an increasingly common sight in the interior of southern Africa from the 1830s onwards, living in their wagons and moving from state to state. By the 1870s the main trade routes carried considerable traffic of wagons and livestock herds being driven to market, and trading stores and mission stations stood on the edge of interior capital towns or at the centre of their own new villages. Trade expanded to feed the expanding overseas markets of Europe and the USA. The Cape exported its wool and hunting products from the interior in exchange for imports of ironware, clothing, firearms, and luxury consumer goods. Wool exports rose from £178,000 worth in 1846 to over £2 million in 1866. Elephants and other wildlife in the interior were rapidly exterminated by hunter-traders with newly improved firearms. In 1860 just one such trader and his employees shot a total of 61 elephants, 30 buffaloes, 23 rhinos, 11 giraffes, and numerous antelopes and smaller game.

1 Boers in Natal and Orange-Vaal Country, 1838-46

Six thousand Boer trekkers settled in Natal after the victory at Blood river, and adopted a

1857 map of David Livingstone's recent travels illustrates European knowledge of the interior of southern Africa at the time. Livingstone followed major trade routes.

new constitution in 1839. A *volksraad* of twenty-four elected men, passing laws and sitting in judgement, soon clashed with Andries Pretorius, the commandant-general, over the powers of government. The clash between burgher democracy and chieftainship was to be a constant theme of Afrikaner history in the interior.

Trekker land and labour policy The Republic of Natal (or Natalia) was divided into districts with military commandants and *landdrosts* on the old pattern of the Cape Colony before the British. The capital was named Pietermaritzburg in honour of Piet Retief and Gert Maritz, and the state claimed boundaries on the Buffels and Tugela rivers in the north and the Mzimkhulu river in the south. Each family took one or two 3,000 morgen farms of grazing land. There were also many disputes between burghers over the ownership of land and of blacks captured on farm areas and made into 'apprentices'. Each burgher would register his land claim, naming the streams and hills of its boundaries. The local *landdrost* would then give him a certifi-

Ivory and fur sale at Grahamstown market in 1850   The occasion was the arrival of the trader David Hume from one of his regular expeditions into western Tswana country. Note the ivory of over fifty elephants. Wool from the district is also being sold in the background. Engraved from a painting by Thomas Baines.

cate of ownership, though it might be many decades before the farm was occupied. In later years commissions of inspection, made up of local farmers, became necessary to settle disputes and demarcate farms, after which a title-deed was issued and quit-rent was due to be paid to the government. Even then the title-deed might be bought and sold many times before occupation. African claims to own and occupy land were ignored when possible; Boer claims to land and the use of its inhabitants as labour were backed by force if necessary.

Zulu-trekker relations   After Dingane rebuilt his capital at eMgungundlovu, British traders at Durban made their peace with him in 1839 but the Boers of Natal remained intransigent. When Dingane's brother Mpande broke away from Dingane's rule at the end of 1839 he took 17,000 men south of the Tugela. The Boers of Natal therefore regarded Mpande as their subject, though Mpande regarded himself as an ally. Together they plotted war, first demanding 19,000 cattle and then 40,000 cattle from Dingane as tribute. When Dingane tried to negotiate, his envoys were

executed. Civil war broke out among the Zulu in early 1840, and Dingane was defeated in the battle of Makonko hills by Mpande's army. Dingane fled north and was killed by Nyawo allies of the Ngwane near the present Swaziland border. A Boer commando which accompanied Mpande's army took 60,000 cattle and many 'apprentices' as payment, while Pretorius claimed that Mpande, now king, remained a tributary of the Natal Republic.

Origin of 'native reserves'   The Natal *volksraad* made labour laws of the type that Boers had wanted in the Cape Colony. Every male African had to carry a pass in the form of a metal or wooden plate strung round his neck, else he would be arrested for vagrancy and given to a burgher as a labourer. But the labour shortage rapidly became a labour surplus as more former inhabitants of the area, driven out by the Zulu, now returned home. So the *volksraad* resolved to expel 'surplus' Africans southwards into a 'native reserve', and claimed Mpondo territory for this. Meanwhile farms were extended south-eastwards towards the Drakensberg by expelling the Bhaca and Khoisan hunter-raiders.

British annexation of Natal Faku of the Mpondo appealed for British aid, while British missionaries pressed for the annexation of Natal to stop Boer slave-raiding. The Boers had been allowed to take control of Durban but the arrival of American and Netherlands ships aroused British fears of losing naval control of the coast. A Boer war with the Mpondo might even spread to the Cape frontier. The British therefore sent a small force to aid Faku and to capture Durban. The Boers besieged the British in Durban, but a British trader (Dick King) rode 900 kilometres on horseback in ten days to fetch reinforcements from Grahamstown. The Boers then surrendered (1842).

Natal was formally annexed by the British in 1843. Mpande was induced to concede sovereignty over the St Lucia Bay coastline to Britain as a gesture of friendship, and Natal's southern border was fixed along the uMzimkhulu by treaty with the Mpondo. The Natal *volksraad* continued to meet at Pietermaritzburg until 1845, but Boers had already begun leaving Natal in large numbers for independence on the highveld. By 1848, when Pretorius left, there were few Boers in Natal. The so-called Klip River Republic declared in 1846 on land given by Mpande north of the Tugela was annexed to Natal in 1848.

Boers in Orange-Vaal country The Boers established the right to settle on the highveld, at least in their own law, by a series of treaties of friendship with African states in 1837 — Makwana's Taung, Moroka's Rolong, Piet Davids' Griqua, Sikonyela's Tlokoa, and others. No such treaties, however, were made with the two major African states on the southern highveld — Adam Kok's Griqua and Moshoeshoe's Sotho. And it is doubtful if any of the African rulers expected more than temporary Boer settlement in their country.

Griqua of Philippolis Most of the Boer trekkers passed through the Philippolis state during the six year dispute over succession to its presidency which followed the death of Adam Kok II in 1835. The traffic of trekkers and traders was considerable enough by 1838 for Griqua to start the first hotel north of the Orange. But the lack of strong government until 1841, when Adam Kok III succeeded, enabled some Griqua to ignore their law forbidding land sales to foreigners. This was to have serious consequences when Boers claimed Griqualand as their own.

Sotho of Moshoeshoe Moshoeshoe's country was largely to the east of the Boer migration. Moshoeshoe declined to send troops to help the Boers attack the Ndebele in 1837, but permitted individual Boers to stay among his subjects in the western Caledon valley. These Boers did not travel onwards as expected and began to build clay houses like the Sotho, instead of living in reed houses or in their wagons as previously. As early as 1839 Moshoeshoe was warning these Boers that they were guests living on his land. But they began to claim that Moshoeshoe had given them their farms as private property, and that they were now outside his authority.

Competing Boer groups on the highveld After the failure of his April 1838 attack on the Zulu, Potgieter determined to build up his personal power over other Boers on the highveld by obtaining personal control of land to be redistributed among loyal followers. Potgieter first 'bought' all the land between the Vaal and Vet rivers, including the village of Winburg, from the Taung chief Makwana for the price of forty-nine cattle in June 1838. (In fact the 'sale' was only a settlement tribute, *pefho*, which did not affect Makwana's sovereignty at all.) But the Boers of Winburg refused to accept Potgieter's authority. So Potgieter withdrew north of the Vaal and in October 1839 laid claim by right of conquest to all the land once ruled by Mzilikazi. The document making this claim was witnessed by Potgieter's main African ally, Matlaba of the Rapulana-Rolong, and included the areas of five chiefs, including the Kgatla chief Pilane and the Po chief Mogale, after whom Boers named the Pilanesberg and Magaliesberg hills. Potgieter's capital just north of the Vaal river became known as *Pot-chef-stroom*, i.e. 'chief Pot(gieter)'s stream', and Matlaba settled nearby as the headman of Potgieter's labourers. Other Boer followers settled in the Magaliesberg at Mogale's village, later known as Rustenburg.

Potchefstroom had a burgher council (*raad*) subordinate to the Natal *volksraad*, which declared itself independent in 1844. But Boers living south of the Vaal around Winburg, led by Jan Mocke, refused to recognize the authority of Potgieter and the Potchefstroom *raad*. So the Boers of the highveld were divided into three effectively independent groups — the Potchefstroom colony, the Winburg colony, and trekboers around the southern Caledon river. These trekboers, led by Michiel Oberholzer, paid tribute to the sovereignties of Adam Kok and Moshoeshoe and declared themselves loyal to British rule in the Cape Colony. But the Winburgers attempted to ignore the sovereignties of Adam Kok and Moshoeshoe, and proclaimed the highveld north of the Orange to be under their independent control in 1842. 'It is written in the Bible,' a Winburger told an African chief, 'that men with white faces and long hair ought never to be governed by a black man with crinkly hair.'

British intervention   The British responded to the Winburger initiative by recognizing the sovereignties of Adam Kok and Moshoeshoe by treaties at the end of 1843. Adam Kok claimed sovereignty as far north as the Modder (Qhaba) river, while Moshoeshoe claimed sovereignty in traditional manner over people rather than land — including the Taung as far north as Winburg. The Winburger claims, however, were reinforced by the arrival from Natal in 1844-45 of numerous Boers hungry for land.

Eventually war broke out between Griqua and Winburgers around Philippolis. A British army marched northwards, beat the Winburgers at Swartkoppies and expelled them further north (1845).

The British decided to maintain peace beyond the Cape border by a *treaty-state system*, supervized by a British agent, and allowing limited land for white settlement. New treaties of 1845-46 with Adam Kok III and Moshoeshoe recognized land between the Riet and Modder rivers as 'alienable' Griqua territory, which could be sold off to Boers as farms, while Moshoeshoe conceded a triangle of land between the Orange and Caledon rivers as 'alienable' territory. The British agent, Henry Warden, was placed in the Riet-Modder territory at Bloemfontein — which took its name from Jan Bloem's Kora. In 1846 Warden helped beat off a Winburger attack on the Griqua, and many Winburgers retreated north to Potchefstroom.

2 Boer Colonies of the Transvaal (1844-51)

There was conflict between traditions of chieftainship and burgher democracy in the Boer colonies north of the Vaal right from the start. Potgieter had withdrawn from Winburg to Potchefstroom to assert his personal authority over other settler families, and the same struggle pushed him onwards to found the later colonies of Ohrigstad and of the Soutpansberg. Each Boer colony elected its military commandant and its *veld-kornets* in charge of distributing land and labour captured in war. But officials saw themselves as chiefs personally owed allegiance by other Boers. Officials were not paid in cash, but accumulated personal wealth in land and labour and sought to pass on their positions as well as their wealth to their children. Each Boer farm owner regarded himself as chief of his poorer relatives and of Africans living on his farm. Burgher democracy in the form of elections and settler representation in government was only possible when conditions were peaceful enough. So long as there was war, Boer chieftainship prospered.

Potchefstroom-Magaliesberg colony   The farms claimed by Boers were often little more than private wildlife areas marked by a few beacons of piled stones. But farms in the productive Magaliesberg area might consist of a square house of clay walls and thatched roof, next to a vegetable and tobacco garden fed by an irrigation channel. African peasants who were allowed to stay on the farm cultivated their own plots but gave crops and labour as tribute to the farm owner. Ox-drawn ploughing, irrigation, and new crops such as maize and tobacco, enabled agriculture to become more productive and to support a larger population. At the same time these changes demanded more labour. Ploughing with oxen increased the area under cultivation and the area needed for fallow much more than previous hoe cultivation. The digging of irrigation channels needed virtual slave labour, and maize and tobacco increased the need for labour in manuring, weeding and reaping over a longer period of the year.

Tribute labour was at first willingly supplied by Tswana of the Potchefstroom-Magaliesberg area who saw the Boers as their liberators from Ndebele rule. But, for example, the Po of Mogale began to complain when forced to dig irrigation channels on what had been their own land. The Tswana began to say 'that Mosilikatze [Mzilikazi] was cruel to his enemies, and kind to those he conquered; but that the Boers destroyed their enemies, and made slaves of their friends'.

More Boer settlers arrived from Winburg and Natal in the 1845-48 period. The Potchefstroom-Magaliesberg colony or republic was extended into new districts as Boer settlers followed African allies back to their pre-Difaqane homelands — Klerksdorp and Makwasi among groups of Rolong west of Potchefstroom; Marico and Mosega among groups of Hurutshe west of the Magaliesberg; and the Apies river colony among Mogopa-Kwena and others north of the Magaliesberg. These Africans soon found that they were regarded as subjects and farm-workers of the Boers. After initially being given cattle in return for labour, the Mogopa-Kwena were forced to labour without payment. The Mogopa-Kwena chief, Mmamogale, was whipped by a Boer and fled for safety around 1845 to Moshoeshoe in Lesotho. He was followed by Mogale of the Po around 1847, after it was discovered that he was smuggling arms to the Laka enemies of the Potgieter Boers in the north.

Ohrigstad colony Potgieter founded a new Boer colony in 1845 in a valley leading from the eastern highveld towards the sea at Delagoa Bay. The capital village was named Ohrigstad in honour of the head of a Netherlands trading company, which undertook to supply the highveld Boers with vital goods in exchange for ivory. Potgieter obtained permission for the settlement from both the Pedi king, Sekwati, and the Portuguese commander at Delagoa Bay, and the colony proved attractive to Boer settlers leaving Natal and seeking similar grazing for sheep and cattle. The settlers formed themselves into a *volksraad* at Ohrigstad and challenged the paramountcy of Potgieter by making a treaty with the Ngwane (Swazi) regent, Somcube, in 1846. This gave them the right to settle the same area as Potgieter claimed to 'own' by treaty with the Pedi. Rather than risk civil war with the superior forces of the Ohrigstad *volksraad,* Potgieter abandoned the colony in 1848 and trekked northwards.

Soutpansberg colony Potgieter founded his third Boer colony near the Buys people south of the Soutpansberg mountains. The Potgieter family combined with the Buys family and a Portuguese trader named Albasini in supplying ivory and slaves to Delagoa Bay, hunting and raiding as far north as the Ndebele kingdom on the Zimbabwean plateau. But Potgieter's colony met resistance from the Laka of Mapela and Mankopane (Makapan) living in the Waterberg mountains. Mankopane, a young man still in his early twenties, was trying to build up a mountain kingdom like those of Sekwati and Moshoeshoe, by attracting refugees and marrying wives of many chiefdoms, including the Po and Mogopa-Kwena.

Attempts to disarm Transvaal Africans Transvaal Boers realized that their power as a white minority over a black majority rested on their monopoly of firearms. African rulers such as Sekwati and Mankopane also realized this, and did their best to collect firearms to use against Boers and other enemies. (Only the Zulu, Swazi and Shangane had armies large and well disciplined enough to do battle with the Boers without using firearms.) So the Transvaal Boers attacked the smaller African states which attempted to acquire firearms. The Ohrigstaders frequently attacked the Kopa under Maleo and the Ndzundza under Mabhogo, who threatened the Boers' road from Lydenburg to the Magaliesberg, but refrained from attacking the altogether too powerful Pedi kingdom.

Meanwhile the Potchefstroom-Magaliesberg Boers wanted to disarm Tswana states which were blocking the westward expansion of Boer hunting and farming. The situation was complicated by British missionaries and traders along the 'missionaries' road' stretching north from Kuruman. Missionaries like David Livingstone had taken up residence in the Marico area; had given muskets to chiefs as payment for the right to settle; had attracted traders who sold muskets; and had been expected by their hosts to service and repair muskets. All this was exaggerated by rumour: a large cooking pot lent by Livingstone to Sechele of the Kgabo-Kwena was believed to be the gift of a cannon, and rumour added five hundred muskets.

Boers threatened to raid the Kwena of Sechele and the (Mmanaana-) Kgatla of Mosielele, groups of Hurutshe and Rolong, and the Tlhaping kingdom of Mahura. But they were held back by the fear of Tswana firepower and of British interference to protect their traders and missionaries.

3 Rise and Fall of British Treaty-State System, 1838-53

The Colonial Office in London was gradually converted to ideas of the 'imperialism of free trade' from previous mercantile-imperialist ideas of colonial expansion. The governor of Cape Colony came to be more of a judge upholding the rule of law, than a general upholding the rule of force, to open up areas to British trade. From 1846 onwards the governor was also appointed as 'high commissioner' to represent Britain in 'South Africa' outside the Cape Colony.

British administration in London and Capetown became more bureaucratic, making decisions by written rules and regulations like lawyers rather than by intuition and initiative like soldiers. Increasingly there were more administrators, better paid and less corrupt. But there was not complete reform. Letters between London and Capetown took months by sea, and were often lost or left for months before answering. Not until the 1870s could London and Capetown even begin to correspond efficiently for mutual decision-making, when for the first time there were regular mailships taking less than a month each way and a cable carrying telegram messages under the ocean (via the Azores islands).

Origins of the treaty-state system The 'imperialism of free trade' flourished in the British interest during times of peace but was threatened in times of war. The trade itself helped to spread war in the interior by the sale of firearms, horses and wagons to Boers and Africans. Constant threats of war in the interior threatened to disturb the peace of the British colonies. The Great Trek removed many of the Boer settlers who had been pressing for land-grabbing wars on the eastern Cape frontier, but the new Boer states in the interior were a threat to the peace of frontier states that lay between the Boers and the British. British imperial troops were therefore prepared to enforce peace in the interior by conquest. However, the imperial government was reluctant to administer conquered areas for long, turning them over instead to Cape Colony or abandoning them altogether.

Britain tried to avoid the necessity for military intervention in the interior during the later 1830s and early 1840s by adopting the treaty-state system advocated by the missionary John Philip. Independent African states were tied by treaties of friendship with Britain to keep the peace beyond colonial frontiers, and a resident British missionary usually acted as intermediary between the two governments. The treaty-state system was adopted with the various Griqua states, the Sotho of Moshoeshoe, and the states of Ciskei and Pondoland.

The Cape frontier wars of the 19th century were fought in rugged and thickly wooded valleys running down towards the sea. British troops and Xhosa guerillas fought by sudden attacks in the woods and hand-to-hand combat, with the British trying to drive the enemy into the open where cavalry could attack. Note the widespread use of firearms by the Xhosa in this illustration of an ambush. They carry muskets and gunpowder horns. The muskets were loaded with ammunition pushed down the muzzle by a rod — as can be seen on the right in this picture. The ammunition was then fired by a charge of gunpowder sparked by a flint attached to the trigger.

left: Sandile, son of Ngqika, who ruled the Rarabe-Xhosa 1840-78, after the regency of his brother Maqoma.

right: Sarili (Kreli), son of Hintsa, who ruled the Gcaleka-Xhosa 1835-92.

An English settler view of the reason for Cape frontier wars   Note that the sheep is an expensive imported merino-type, valued for its wool production rather than for its meat. White hunger for more pasture for more woolled sheep helped push the frontier eastwards.

War of the Axe, 1846-47 The treaty-state system began to break down across the Keiskamma in the mid-1840s when white settlers demanded more land over the border. Farm values had risen with the increasing prosperity of wool farming, and more land meant profit from either its sale or wool production. The Ngqika-Xhosa chief, Sandile, realizing that Xhosa sheep raids across the Keiskamma would give settlers the pretext for war, welcomed a new line of British forts along the Keiskamma — including Fort Hare — built in 1844 to stop Xhosa raids. But governor Maitland at Capetown used the occasion of the murder of a Khoisan policeman, by a group of Xhosa recovering a man arrested for stealing an axe, as the pretext for declaring war. The *7th Cape-Nguni war*, otherwise known as the 'War of the Axe', lasted from 1846 to 1847. British invaders across the Keiskamma were swept back by an allied army of Ngqika-Xhosa, Gcaleka-Xhosa and Thembu, which was then broken into small guerrilla groups by British horse soldiers and slowly pushed back eastwards.

Annexation of Ciskei The British tried to restore a treaty-state system by declaring Sarili of the Gcaleka-Xhosa to be paramount chief over Sandile of the Ngqika-Xhosa. But a new governor, Harry Smith, was determined to be an old-style military governor and rushed to the eastern frontier to abolish the treaty-state system. He annexed various areas to Cape Colony and proclaimed the Kei-Keiskamma territory to be the new colony of 'British Kaffraria' — later called Ciskei (1847).

Orange River Sovereignty, 1848 Harry Smith rushed northwards to settle disputes in Orange-Vaal country and decided impulsively to annex the whole area as the 'Orange River Sovereignty' (1848). Smith then crossed the Drakensberg and annexed the small Klip River Republic to Natal. (Its Boers migrated northwards to territory claimed by conquest at the battle of Blood river, which became the Utrecht Republic in 1854.) Returning home across the highveld, Smith found that Pretorius had raised the remaining Winburgers in revolt against British rule. At the battle of Boomplats (1848) Smith defeated Pretorius and expelled him across the Vaal.

8th Cape-Nguni war, 1850-53 War soon returned to the Ciskei despite its being a British colony. Historians have explained the renew-

*Maqoma (1798-1873), pictured **left** with his wives, and Harry Smith (1787-1860), pictured **right** — the two most remarkable military commanders of the Cape frontier wars.* Maqoma came to prominence as regent for his younger brother Sandile in 1829-40, distinguishing himself as the Xhosa general in the 6th war of 1834-35. He was twice detained by the British on Robben Island, where he died in 1873. Harry Smith first confronted Maqoma in the 6th war as a colonel, and returned as governor of Cape Colony for the 7th war. Smith then forced Sandile to kiss his feet and placed his heel on Maqoma's neck. Announcing the new colony of British Kaffraria (Ciskei) in 1847, Harry Smith assembled local chiefs together and exploded a gunpowder wagon full of paper before them, crying, 'There go the treaties! Do you hear? No more treaties!'

ed war as the result of oppression by British magistrates who ruled the area, ignorant of Xhosa law and custom, after it had been divided into white settler farms and black reserves. The people of the Ciskei rose against the British after Harry Smith deposed Sandile from his chieftainship in 1850. Sandile's war-doctor, Mlanjeni, preached that victory was inevitable with his medicines and the right sacrifices to the ancestors. The Xhosa and emigrant Thembu 'rebels' were joined by Khoisan peasants from mission settlements and African policemen who had deserted from the British. The British were joined by their old Mfengu allies and by small groups of Khoisan and of Ndlambe-Xhosa. The civil war then threatened to spread beyond the colony. The Zulu king Mpande offered to aid the British, while the Sotho of Moshoeshoe, with the Gcaleka-Xhosa and the Mpondo, considered whether to join Sandile. The war reached a climax when Mfengu troops under British command invaded Gcaleka-Xhosa country and set off bitter fighting between Gcaleka and local Mfengu who had settled among them.

4 Cape Colony, Natal and Ciskei, 1854-68

From 1854 the Cape Colony was given 'representative' parliamentary government by the British in return for carrying the costs of administration through increased taxes. The executive of government remained in the hands of officials appointed by the Colonial Office in London, but a parliament of elected representatives discussed policies and passed laws, including the annual budget based on taxes. The vote was given to tax-payers who met income and property qualifications, on the principle of political representation in return for paying tax. Any adult male resident of the colony could vote if he earned £50 a year or owned a house worth £25.* The franchise was therefore 'colour blind', though few Africans earned enough cash or owned saleable buildings.

*Very roughly equivalent to an income of more than R 15,000 a year and a house worth over R 7,500 by the early 1990s.

Cape economy Trade and agricultural production in the Cape Colony, stimulated by demand in Britain, grew steadily in the 1850s but was temporarily interrupted by depressions and droughts in the 1860s. Small traders and producers prospered, particularly in the eastern Cape, while capitalists more closely linked to Britain moved in to take up a large share of the market. Thus between 1856 and 1863 the number of small Cape banks rose from seventeen to twenty-eight, but were joined by two large 'imperial banks' from London (one of which was the Standard Bank). Cape government expenditure on roads and telegraphs, prisons, white schooling and white immigration rose accordingly. The population of Cape Colony (excluding Ciskei) stood at 181,000 Europeans and an estimated 315,000 Africans (including coloureds) by 1865.

The eastern Cape prospered from wool production and from trade into the interior. Between 1857 and 1866 its exports of wool and other goods rose from £1.1 million worth to £1.8 million. Port Elizabeth — 'the Liverpool of the Cape' — expanded in size, as did market towns on the roads to the interior. Large capitalist firms such as Mosenthal Brothers started to take over the export trade in wool, ivory and skins. Meanwhile the western Cape economy suffered from rapid decline of wine production after 1859 when Britain, its main export market, opened up free trade with France which produced better and cheaper wines. Cape wine exports dropped from 3.5 million litres in 1859 to as low as 360,000 litres by 1874, and wine producers looked to other markets such as 'Cape Smoke' brandy for the interior trade. However a new source of exports for the western Cape was opened in 1852 by copper mines near the Orange river, of which Okiep was being described as the 'richest copper mine in the world' in the 1870s when it produced 5,000 tons of copper ore every year.

Natal: 'tribalism' under Shepstone After 1856 Natal — an area only between the Tugela and Mzimkhulu rivers — was administered as a separate colony from the Cape. Its government failed to settle large numbers of whites on the land, which was therefore bought up by large commercial companies instead. In 1863 Natal's white population numbered less than 14,000 compared with a black population of over 150,000.

From 1849 onwards Natal began to reject the Cape 'native policy' of legal equality between whites and 'civilized' blacks in favour of the Boer policy of permanent inequality between whites and blacks. Theophilus Shepstone acted as Natal's 'diplomatic agent to the native tribes' from 1853 to 1875. He recruited the allegiance of African chiefs by a policy of 'tribalism', which became the model for other colonies. All Africans were placed under the law and custom of tribal chiefs in the reserves even after they moved into white-owned areas. Shepstone replaced uncooperative chiefs and invented chiefdoms where they did not previously exist. Tribalism was a divide-and-rule policy to keep the white minority dominant over the black majority.

Capitalists recognized the potential of Natal for sugar and possibly cotton to meet the rising demands of Europe. Large sugar plantations were set up in the humid coastal area, and from 1860 onwards indentured labourers were imported from India and were tied by contract to work for an employer at low wages for five years. Even an increase in 'hut tax' from 7 to 11 shillings did not push local Africans into working on the plantations as regularly and therefore as cheaply as the indentured Indians. Africans were, however, compelled by government to build roads to serve the plantations.

Most Natal whites nevertheless continued to live off black rents rather than agricultural production. Of the 3 million hectares out of 4.3 million hectares in white ownership by 1866, only 16,000 hectares were cultivated under white management. Black peasant 'squatters' on the rest of white-owned land were charged between 5 and 28 shillings annual rent per family. As elsewhere, people classified as 'squatters' without rights to the land in colonial law might see themselves as the legal owners of the land, even if forced to pay tribute to its white chief.

Ciskei settlement Cape 'native policy' was developed further by George Grey, who became governor of Cape Colony and the

The unmarried daughter of a Gcaleka-Xhosa chief, photographed in the early 20th century, possibly dressed as Nongqause would have been.
Nongqause's vision was of men and cattle rising up from the reeds after they had been purified of witchcraft. Her uncle Mhlakaza, doctor to Sarili, then began to preach that the Xhosa people should purify themselves — by killing all cattle, destroying all grain, and planting no crops. After that, the ancestors of people and cattle would rise from the dead; the old would become young again; plentiful food and imported Western goods would appear; and a great wind would sweep all whites and unbelieving blacks into the sea.

News of Mhlakaza's preaching spread among a despairing people like wildfire. Those who were doubtful at first were persuaded that there was no other way in which lost freedom would be regained. Some commentators have since then suggested that such a self-destructive prophecy must have been spread by the enemies of the Xhosa. But there is no clear historical evidence for this.

Ciskei ('Kaffraria') in 1854. Grey looked forward to the 'civilization' of blacks by schooling and cash employment. He foresaw an eventual Cape society divided — like England — into classes rather than into races. He started with the Ciskei, which he began to break up into a checkerboard of small white farms and small black reserves. These communally-owned reserves would eventually disappear as Africans became 'civilized' and converted them into individual small-holdings. In Grey's words, Africans would become 'a part of ourselves with a common faith and common interests, useful servants, consumers of our goods, contributors to our revenue'.

But Grey's checkerboard plan, by breaking up and scattering the chiefdoms of the Ciskei, increased the fears of people on both sides of the Kei for their future. White settlers prepared for war; black people, losing their faith in old political leaders, turned to religious leaders who offered victory by a miracle. Rumours even circulated that the Russians, who were beating the British in the Crimean War (1854-56) on the Black Sea, would liberate the Ciskei.

Great Xhosa cattle-killing In October 1856 the word went out among the Xhosa for everyone to slaughter their cattle so that, following the prophesy of Nongqause, a great wind might sweep the whites into the sea. Up to 200,000 cattle were killed in the area as far west as the Fish river and as far east as Thembu country, and no crops were planted when the summer rains came. By February 1857 there was widespread famine; maybe 20,000 people died of starvation in the Ciskei, while 30,000 migrated onto white farms to seek work for food.

The great cattle-killing was an enormous disaster. There was no organized resistance to colonial rule in the Ciskei for another twenty years. Grey's checkerboard plan became much easier to implement. Sandile's reserve was reduced; other reserves were even abolished. German men who had been mercenaries in the Crimean War, and Irish women to be their wives, were imported to take up new white farms.

In 1866 the Ciskei became part of Cape Colony. For the first time the Cape had electoral districts where the electorate was, at least potentially, mostly black. However, as qualified Mfengu found in 1866, local whites tried to stop blacks registering as voters in any significant number.

5 Orange River Sovereignty and Free State (1848-68)

The Orange River Sovereignty (1848-54) The commissioner Henry Warden (1848-52) attempted to control Boers and Africans by dividing them into numerous districts. Warden ignored the 'Napier line' boundary agreed with Moshoeshoe in 1843, and imposed a 'Warden line' making the four small states of the Wesleyan alliance independent from Moshoeshoe. But Boer and African groups began to invade each other's territories, and Moshoeshoe proved himself to be the strongest power when he defeated Warden at Viervoet (Kononyana) in 1851.

Warden was removed by the British in 1852 and his successors, assistant commissioners Hogge and Owen, began to withdraw Britain's failed sovereignty north of the Orange. Britain in future would rely on the Boers to police the troubled northern frontier of Cape Colony. Hogge and Owen signed the *Sand River Convention* with Boers north of the Vaal (see below), abandoned the 'Warden line' which protected the Wesleyan alliance from Boer settlement as well as from Moshoeshoe, and encouraged Boers to settle in the western Caledon valley. Meanwhile governor Cathcart of Cape Colony (1852-54) marched north to deter Moshoeshoe from raiding the new Boer farms. Finally the Orange River Sovereignty was abolished when the British signed the *Bloemfontein Convention* with local Boers in 1854, which abandoned all treaties with African rulers north of the Orange except Adam Kok.

The Orange Free State, founded in 1854, was in effect a treaty-state for the British because it combined the traditions of a Boer

left: *Adam Kok 111 (ruled 1837-75)*   right: *Philippolis: founded 1826; abandoned by the Griqua 1863.*

republic with strong English influence. It had the usual Boer commandant-general and *volksraad,* but it also had a strong president and a constitution based on that of the United States of America. Its economy was based on sheep and cattle raising, and wheat farming. It traded with Transvaal Boers for tobacco and dried fruit, with Africans on the Caledon for maize, and with the Cape Colony for all other goods, including wagons, fire-arms and coffee. Continual wagon traffic with the interior resulted in its villages being largely English-speaking, and even the Bloem-fontein newspaper, *The Friend of the Sovereignty,* continued to be published in English.

The first president of the Orange Free State, Josias Hoffman (1854-5), was soon deposed in an armed coup by burghers alarmed at his friendly relations with African states. Hoffman had entertained Moshoeshoe at a public banquet in Bloemfontein and had given him gunpowder. He had also recognized the rights of the Griqua chief Nicholas Waterboer to land claimed by the Free State east of the Vaal. The second president, Jacobus Boshof (1855-59), was at first forced by the British to come to terms with Moshoeshoe and with Adam Kok III, accept-ing Moshoeshoe's independence and a

'Vetberg line' between Griqua states in the west (1855). But continuing clashes between Boer settlers and African states to east and west made war inevitable, while other Boers ate away at Adam Kok's sovereignty by buying up Griqua farms south of the Riet river.

1st Sotho-Boer War, 1858 Boshof declared war on Moshoeshoe in 1858, but Free State commandos which reached Thaba Bosiu were broken up by Sotho forces and returned home. Free State and Transvaal forces were more successful in raiding the independent Tlhaping chiefdoms in the west, and this prompted the Transvaal leader Marthinus Pretorius to begin interfering in Free State politics. But the British high commissioner, George Grey, persuaded the Free State government to make peace with Moshoeshoe at the 1st Treaty of Aliwal North before it collapsed from intrigue.

Undefeated, the Sotho of Moshoeshoe under his brother Posholi began to reoccupy the land west of the 'Warden line' but within the former 'Napier line'.

George Grey and Marthinus Pretorius Grey recognized that the treaty-state system, even when limited to Boers and denied to Africans, had once again proved a failure in keeping frontier peace. So he proposed a *South African federation* of self-governing white states — including Cape Colony, Natal and the Orange Free State — to be responsible for peace in the interior. Grey's federation scheme (1858-59) failed however to persuade the British government, which refused to resume 'sovereignty in any shape or form' over the Free State. So the Orange Free State looked to a strong man instead of to the British, and chose Marthinus Pretorius as its president in 1860; he also acted as Transvaal president for the first seven months. Pretorius saw it as his task to establish legal title to all the land claimed by the Orange Free State, even disputing the claim of the Transvaal to land around the Vaal source. He bought up mission station lands in the south and west, and most importantly the remaining land owned by the Griqua of Adam Kok III around Philippolis.

In 1863 Marthinus Pretorius abandoned the presidency of the Orange Free State to regain the presidency of the Transvaal, which he saw as a greater or easier prize. J. H. Brand was elected the fourth president of the Free State (1864-88), and turned to the problem of Moshoeshoe's claims to the western Caledon valley which Pretorius had failed to solve to Boer satisfaction.

Griqua trek from Philippolis In 1863 Adam Kok III led the wagons of his people on a remarkable trek across the south-western corner of modern Lesotho to a new homeland in the foothills known as 'Nomansland', which then became known as Griqualand-East. Declining to pay tribute to Moshoeshoe's son Nehemiah, Griqualand-East became a treaty-state of the British in the Transkei region.

6 Transvaal Boers and the South African Republic 1852-68

The unification of the Boer colonies north of the Vaal into one state took ten years after the first combined meeting of *volksraad* representatives in 1849 at Deerdepoort

(modern Mamelodi east of Pretoria). The representatives referred to themselves as the South African Republic, but its disunity was recognized when the united *volksraad* appointed no less than four commandant-generals — Hendrik Potgieter for Soutpansberg, Andries Pretorius for Potchefstroom/Magaliesberg, Willem Joubert for Lydenburg, and Jacob Enslin for Marico.

Andries Pretorius seized the opportunity to assert himself as leader of all the Transvaal Boers in 1852 by negotiating alone with the British assistant commissioners Hogge and Owen at the Sand river, after failing to convene a united *volksraad* of the SAR to authorize the negotiations. In return for Pretorius' guarantee of free trade for British commerce, the British recognized the independence of Boers north of the Vaal, renounced all friendship with African states north of the Vaal, and prohibited the sale of firearms or ammunition to Africans by traders from British colonies. The Sand River Convention was never formally confirmed as a binding treaty by the British government, nor did it recognize the South African Republic as a state. But it opened the way for Transvaal Boer expansion at the expense of neighbouring African states without fear of British intervention.

BOER SETTLEMENT BEYOND THE VAAL
1830s-50s
Marking major African kingdoms and wagon routes.

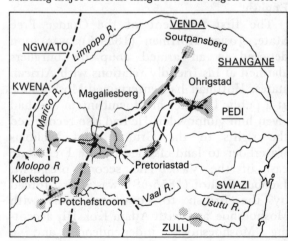

Marico war   A month after the Sand River Convention, the Marico commandant began to demand tribute labour from Tswana chiefdoms on the important 'missionaries' road' to the interior, which had been previously protected from Boer attack by the presence of British arms traders and missionaries. Tswana chiefs took refuge with Sechele, ruler of the Kwena, who had moved away from the Boers five years earlier to found a refugee kingdom at Dimawe (west of later Gaborone). Sechele, who had well-armed troops, refused to surrender the refugees to the Marico commando: they would have to cut open his bowels, he said, before a refugee chief would drop out. The Marico commando with its own Tswana allies attacked Dimawe, destroyed the nearby mission station of David Livingstone on the Kolobeng river, and then raided the Ngwaketse and other neighbouring Tswana in 1852. Sechele travelled to Bloemfontein and Capetown, and even tried to take ship for England, but British officials washed their hands of any responsibility.

Soutpansberg war   Hendrik Potgieter's Soutpansberg Boers lived by more or less continual hunting and raiding expeditions. Potgieter turned on his previous ally Sekwati, the Pedi king in the Leulu mountains, in 1852 in order to secure the trade route for ivory and slaves to Delagoa Bay. When Hendrik Potgieter died in 1854 his post as commandant was inherited by his son Piet, who led a major attack on Mokopane's Laka in the same year. After Piet Potgieter was killed by a Laka bullet, his commando blockaded a cave in which about three thousand Laka men, women and children were sheltering. They were all starved to death or were shot dead when trying to escape. (A new settlement nearby was then named Potgietersrust in memory of Piet.)

Lydenburg-African relations   After years of strained relations the Lydenburg Boers came to terms with the Swazi of Mswati in 1855 and with the Pedi of Sekwati in 1857, by agreeing not to interfere in their affairs in

---

SLAVERY AND SLAVE TRADING

The missionary David Livingstone proclaimed the facts of Boer slavery to the world, when he denounced the 'bloody slave raid' of Transvaal Boers on the Kwena kingdom of Sechele in 1852. But the accusation of Boer 'apprenticeship' being a form of slavery had already been used ten years earlier to justify British annexation of Natal from the Boers. It was the Orange Free State, rather than the British, which took the lead in accusing eastern Transvaal Boers of slave trading in the later 1850s. There was evidence of Boers selling slaves to each other by selling the written forms of indenture by which children were 'apprenticed'. Such apprentices were sometimes bought as war captives from the Swazi and other African peoples in the Delagoa Bay hinterland. But apprenticeship was in theory temporary, until the slave became a full adult. It was like the domestic slavery practised by other African peoples, rather than like the plantation slavery practised in the Americas and in the islands of the Indian Ocean. The Boer farmer saw himself as chief-father of his black subjects, rather than as owner-manager of black labour.

Northern Transvaal Boers, on the other hand, were engaged in supplying slaves and ivory to Delagoa Bay for export overseas, especially after 1859 when the Portuguese slave-trader Joao Albasini became 'native commissioner' for the Potgieter clan in the Soutpansberg.

Slave trading at Delagoa Bay and Inhambane became risky but very profitable when British anti-slavery warships began to patrol the Mozambique-Madagascar channel, limiting the supply of slaves overseas. Slaving ships sailed secretly to the mouth of the Nkomati river in Delagoa Bay, and sent small boats over thirty kilometres upstream into the interior to buy slaves. In 1859 an American whaling ship, having failed to catch any whales in the ocean, loaded 740 slaves in Delagoa Bay instead. The slaves were sold for an enormous profit at Rio de Janeiro in Brazil — each American crewman received eighteen hundred Spanish dollars. The last slave ship reported in Delagoa Bay was in 1875, when an Arab dhow was caught there by the British navy, taking slaves to Zanzibar.

return for free access to Delagoa Bay. Mswati had raided Lydenburg in 1853 and 1855 until he killed a rival brother supported by the Boers. The Lydenburg-Swazi peace treaty of 1855 in effect recognized Swazi power through the lowveld northwards to the Limpopo, while the Lydenburg-Pedi treaty of 1857 recognized the Steelpoort (Thubatse) river as the border between them.

Unification of the Transvaal, 1855-59 Both Andries Pretorius and Hendrik Potgieter died in 1853, being succeeded as commandants of their respective colonies by their sons Marthinus and Piet. Piet was then succeeded by Stephanus Schoeman in 1854, who took Piet's widow as his own wife. Marthinus Pretorius continued his father's efforts to bring the Boer colonies of the Transvaal together into a united state. In 1855 he was elected 'provisional president' of the South African Republic (SAR) by his own western Transvaalers, and in 1856 he donated a capital site on the Apies river — Pretoriustad, later called Pretoria — for meetings of the united *volksraad.* Pretorius succeeded in winning over Schoeman after bitter quarrelling which nearly resulted in war. Western and northern Transvaalers then agreed to a constitution along Free State lines at Rustenburg, which made Pretorius president and Schoeman commandant-general (1858). This constitution was then reluctantly agreed to in 1859 by eastern Transvaalers who had previously boycotted negotiations.

The situation was complicated by religious rivalries. Pretorius had obtained burgher support in the west by pressing that their new Dutch reformed church founded in 1853, called the NHK (*Nederduitse Hervormde Kerk*), should become the state church of the republic. But northern and eastern Transvaalers held to their membership of the old Dutch reformed church controlled from Cape Colony, the NGK (*Nederduitse Gereformeerde Kerk*); and a group of western Transvaalers who objected to the liberal theology of the NHK — though not to its internal democracy — broke away in 1859 to form a third church called the AGK (*Afgeskeie Gereformeerde Kerk*) or 'Dopper' church.

Transvaal civil war, 1862-63 Marthinus Pretorius was elected president of the Orange Free State as well in 1860, as a first step towards uniting the two republics under his leadership. The SAR *volksraad,* swayed by eastern burgher democrats, first deposed Pretorius in 1860 — leaving Schoeman as acting president — and then elected one Willem van Rensburg as provisional president in 1862. Schoeman rebelled with the encouragement of Pretorius, but van Rensburg had the support of Paul Kruger as his commandant — a rich and powerful western Transvaaler who had broken from Pretorius with the 'Doppers'. After van Rensburg defeated Schoeman in the war of 1862-63 he was elected full president. Pretorius therefore resigned from the Free State presidency to return and oppose van Rensburg.

The Transvaal civil war encouraged African states on the frontiers of Boer colonies, and on the roads between them, to reassert their independence by refusing to pay tribute to the SAR. Marthinus Pretorius was therefore re-elected president in 1864, with the support of Kruger and others, as a strong man to reconquer resisting Africans. The chiefs Maleo and Mabhogo, who controlled the Lydenburg-Pretoria road, were reduced to tribute once more by a Boer commando in 1864. But other eastern chiefdoms had transferred their allegiance to the Pedi or Swazi kingdoms, who were too strong for the Boers to consider attacking and conquering.

SAR abandons Soutpansberg The Soutpansberg colony took on more powerful African enemies than it could handle. Its good fortune in intervening in Shangane politics encouraged it to embroil itself in Venda politics. The Soutpansbergers had successfully supported Mzila against Mawewe as successor to the great Soshangane in 1858-61. But Soutpansberger attempts to oppose Makhado as successor to Ravele (Ramabulana) of the Venda in 1864-67 proved disastrous. Venda troops destroyed Boer settlements, and a Boer commando led by Kruger in 1867 not only failed to defeat the Venda but retreated southwards taking most Boer settlers with it. Other local chiefs, including Mokopane, rose against Boer rule and the SAR abandoned its Soutpansberg district. Boer settlers who remained paid tribute to African chiefs instead, and the Shangane king Mzila began to claim tribute from the chiefdoms.

The Swazi at the height of their power under Mswati, having laid siege to Lourenco Marques and expelled the Shangane northwards in 1863-64, were treated as important allies by the Boers, who used Swazi mercenaries against Maleo, Mabhogo and Makhado. Meanwhile Boer settlers from the Lydenburg and Utrecht colonies pushed their winter grazing deeper into Swazi-ruled territory, and the SAR took the opportunity of Mswati's death in 1865 to press reduced borders on the Swazi regency in the following year.

7 Orlam-Afrikaners of Windhoek c. 1840-70

The Orlam-Afrikaner bandits under Jonker Afrikaner, who had settled at Windhoek around 1840, raided far and wide for cattle and ivory and subjected local peoples to their rule. By 1842 even the Herero accepted the Afrikaner presence at Windhoek. Indeed, one of the four main Herero chiefs, Tjamuaha at Okahandja, not only accepted Jonker Afrikaner's sovereignty but also sent his son Maherero to Windhoek to lead Herero mercenaries fighting for the Afrikaners.

Herero-Afrikaner relations Maherero was brutally treated as Jonker's personal servant. The story is told that when Maherero killed a lion single-handed with a spear, he was tied to a wagon wheel and left for days as punishment for killing game reserved for Afrikaners. Though Jonker Afrikaner called Tjamuaha his brother and Maherero his son, both bore bitter resentment towards Afrikaner rule.

Windhoek became an important centre of population, attracting Orlam and Nama as well as Herero, and white missionaries and traders from the south. German missionaries of the Rhenish Missionary Society, to which the London mission had abandoned its

Namibian station, arrived at Windhoek in 1842. Traders came in increasing numbers overland from the Cape Colony to buy raided sheep and cattle in exchange for firearms, ammunition and brandy. Windhoek began to distill its own type of liquor from honey and berries — later known as *kgadi* among the Tswana when the secrets of its manufacture crossed the Kalahari. Jonker opened up fuller trade between the interior and the coast by constructing a wagon road from Windhoek to Walvis Bay in 1843-44.

The Afrikaners resumed constant war with the Herero of the north between 1846 and 1850. Their allies, the Orlam under Amraal at Gobabis, hunted, traded and raided eastwards as far as Lake Ngami to which Amraal took forty-seven wagons before 1851. European traders then followed in the tracks of Amraal from Gobabis to Ngamiland, and opened up trade with the missionaries' road in Botswana. Jonker Afrikaner's wars were briefly halted in 1850-51 by Francis Galton, a British traveller who ordered him to make peace in the name of the British high commissioner at Capetown. Despite British attempts to ban the sale of firearms and ammunition north of the Orange river, the arms trade increased because of the number of Europeans in the area, which was becoming known as 'South West Africa'.

Angra Pequena and Walvis Bay There was a rush of prospectors from the Cape to open up copper mines in the lower Orange valley during the early 1850s, and a small port was founded at Angra Pequena (later Luderitz) on the coast north of the Orange to serve the mines. More traders also settled further north at Walvis Bay, which had opened as a port in 1845. In order to have peace for copper mining, the Orlam-Afrikaners and the Nama 'Red Nation' even agreed to a common border around Rehoboth. But by 1860 richer copper ores had been exhausted and mines north of the Orange closed down. European traders continued to prosper by giving low prices for hunting produce or livestock and taking high prices for imported goods. As one European remarked, 'It is only right that the traders should suck the Namas dry so that they can be forced to work.' Herero captives or slaves were therefore sent southwards to the copper mines of the Cape Colony to earn cash for their Orlam or Nama masters.

By 1857 the whole of Hereroland and all its cattle had been captured by the Orlam-Afrikaners who then began raiding into Ovamboland further north, where people grew extensive crops around the flood-plains as well as raising fine cattle. But these raids brought back lung-sickness (*pleuro-pneumonia*), the dreadful cattle disease sweeping from central Africa which wiped out great numbers of cattle.

Succession of Maherero Both Jonker Afrikaner and the Herero chief Tjamuaha died at Okahandja in 1861, within a few hundred metres and a few months of each other. Maherero then succeeded to his father's office as the priest-chief who kept the holy fire of the whole Herero nation continually burning in his courtyard. Maherero used his religious position to unite the Herero into one kingdom. Maherero took numerous wives from other Herero chiefdoms. He finally succeeded in being elected king in 1863, after war had been declared on the Orlam-Afrikaners.

Maherero began a seven-year struggle for Herero freedom from Orlam-Afrikaner rule in 1863, killing Jonker's successor Christian Afrikaner in a battle later that year. The Herero and Mbanderu under the Orlam of Amraal at Gobabis then joined the rising. However the Nama 'Red Nation' under Oasib joined the remaining Orlam-Afrikaners against Maherero. Oasib was then forced to a peace in 1866 by Maherero with the aid of the Swartbooi Nama from Rehoboth, but the Orlam-Afrikaners fought on under Jan Jonker Afrikaner as their new chief. Maherero was encouraged to carry on fighting by Ovambo chiefs in the north and by European traders. An attack by Jan Jonker Afrikaner on Walvis Bay prompted the British (who had annexed the offshore Guano islands in 1861-62) to send a warship as a warning against his attacking Europeans. Yet both the British and German governments, to whom local Europeans had appealed, declined to colonize the area.

After worsening drought and determined attacks by Maherero on Jan Jonker, peace was made between Herero and Orlam-Afrikaners at Okahandja in 1870. Maherero was confirmed as owner of the land, but Windhoek was leased to Jan Jonker 'on feudal tenure' which the Herero understood to be temporary.

Questions

1 Describe the four main stages of the Great Trek and its results during the period 1836 to 1852. [Cambridge International School Certificate, 1979]
2 Describe the relations between the Xhosa and white settlers and successive governments at the Cape to 1848. [Cambridge International School Certificate, 1975]
3 Why did the British fail to keep a treaty-state system going in the interior?
4 How did the Orlam-Afrikaners succeed in establishing and maintaining their power at Windhoek?

Activities

1 What evidence is there for conflicting traditions of individual chieftainship and burgher democracy among the Boers? Act out a *volksraad* debate in the classroom.
2 Compare British attitudes to Boer independence in 1852-54 with British attitudes to Rhodesian UDI in 1965. (See also Chapter 20.)
3 How would the Boers have justified their rule of areas in the interior? Debate this in the classroom.

For references of Chapters 7 and 8 see Bibliography, pp. 337–42: B4 Cameron; B5 Davenport; B6 Duminy & Guest; B9 Frederickson; B13 James & Simons; B16 Lamar & Thompson; B32 Readers Digest; B38 Tsotsi; B42 Wilson & Thompson; C16 Malherbe; C26 Ross; C27 Saunders & Derricourt; C31 Worden; D6 Gray; D11 Lau; D12 Majeke; D14–15 Peires; D16 Ross; D18 Saunders; J7 AN & N.

Chapter 9

The Rise of New Kingdoms
(c. 1838–1868)

While British colonies spread along the coastal belt, and the two Boer republics expanded on the grasslands of the interior, a number of African kingdoms consolidated their power elsewhere in southern Africa. By the end of the 1860s there were few groups of people south of the Limpopo still independent of a larger African, Boer or British state.

African kingdoms after the Mfecane/Difaqane tended to be one of two types, based either on military power or on wealth from trading. Military-based states were usually modelled on the Zulu kingdom, with a well-disciplined large army and a strong king given absolute powers of life and death over his subjects. Such states tended to reject Western technology and culture in the form of fire-arms and missionaries, because traditional defences and beliefs had been so successful for them. Trading-based states on the other hand usually originated in places of refuge from military states, and were ruled by skilful kings who recruited allegiance by persuasion rather than compulsion. Such states generally welcomed Westernization in the form of wagons and ploughs, as well as firearms and missionaries, so long as the rulers' power and wealth were not threatened by, for instance, abolition of male polygamy and abolition of marriage payments in cattle.

The major trade routes from the British colonies ran through the trading-based states of the interior. The rise of these new states, often in alliance with each other and with the British, provoked opposition from the already established military-based states. Military-based states by their very nature competed with each other and rarely combined in effective alliances against Boer or British intruders.

1 The Sotho Kingdom of Moshoeshoe

Moshoeshoe stubbornly resisted attempts to incorporate his kingdom into the Orange River Sovereignty or Free State, while continuing to expand his rule over the Caledon (Mohokare) valley. By 1836 Moshoeshoe ruled about 25,000 people around his capital on Thaba Bosiu mountain. Moshoeshoe consolidated control of the eastern Caledon valley by placing his elder sons Letsie and Molapo together with his new Paris missionaries around Morija (1833), while his brothers Mohale and Posholi placed themselves even further south and west. Moshoeshoe began to assert control of the western Caledon valley in 1838 by placing Moletsane and a Paris missionary between Moshoeshoe's rivals Moroka at Thaba Nchu and Sikonyela at Marabeng. By such 'placing' of subordinate chiefs and missionaries in outlying areas, and by finally defeating Sikonyela in 1853, Moshoeshoe came to control a large territory that bore little relation to the borders agreed upon between British and Boers on their inaccurate maps.

Christian mission work At first, like missionaries among other Tswana/Sotho, the Paris missionaries among the Sotho were treated merely as middlemen in negotiations with British traders and officials. But by 1839, missionaries began to make converts to Christianity with Moshoeshoe's encouragement. Moshoeshoe saw Christian education as the way in which his children and other young relatives could understand and use Western technology for the future advantage of the state. He had told the missionaries: 'It is enough for me to see your clothing, your arms, and the rolling houses in which you travel, to understand how much strength and intelligence you have.' The evangelical morality of the missionaries also appealed to Moshoeshoe personally as he hated strong drink and belief in witchcraft because they confused otherwise reasonable minds. But Moshoeshoe refused to abandon polygamy, which linked him and his close relatives by marriage to the subject chiefdoms and thereby held the state together. Even though he granted divorces to two of his wives who became Christians he insisted they still 'prepare food for me and for the strangers who come to visit me'.

Moshoeshoe's brothers Mohale and Posholi led traditionalist opposition to Christianity. Other members of the ruling Koena (Mokoteli) group, especially women and young men, were strongly pro-Christian and by 1848 there were a thousand church members. Moshoeshoe did not admit conversion to Christianity until just before his death in 1868. He had always been of two minds, wanting to rule a Christian nation but without having to go through the disruptions of conversion:

'Would to God that this religion were a drink! I would make you all swallow it . . . You still know nothing and you hold me back.'

Sotho-British relations Moshoeshoe's relationship with the British was also contradictory. He respected them but only gained their respect by defeating them. When Moshoeshoe defeated the British under Cathcart at the battle of Berea in 1852 he sued for peace before the British could bring in reinforcements:

'I entreat peace from you, — you have chastised, — let it be enough I pray you; and let me be no longer considered an

Moshoeshoe (with top hat, seated in the middle) and some of his advisers, dressed to meet the second son of the English queen who came north on a hunting trip from Cape Colony in 1860. Moshoeshoe's brother Mopeli has a hand on his shoulder.

enemy of the Queen.'

Moshoeshoe's trust in the British backfired on him in 1858 at the 1st Treaty of Aliwal North when the British settled the 1st Sotho-Boer war to the advantage of the Free State losers rather than the Sotho victors. The British also freely supplied the Free State with arms in the 1850s and 1860s, while officially banning their sale to baSotho in common with other Africans north of the Orange. But the British connection proved its value in 1868-69 when the British intervened to stop the 2nd Sotho-Boer war (see below).

Sotho economic prosperity threatened LeSotho under Moshoeshoe was at the height of its power and wealth in the 1850s and 1860s. Moshoeshoe saw himself as protector and supplier of firearms to Sotho groups threatened by Boers, which included the Pedi of Sekwati and Laka of Mankopane. Encouraged by trade in grain and cattle with the Cape Colony and elsewhere, Sotho peasants became productive farmers of wheat and maize for export. As early as 1838 Moshoeshoe

THE MISSIONARY MOVEMENT

Bird's eye view of Kuruman, 1835   Note the village in the background, the church on the left, and the gardens in the foreground. The gardens are irrigated by a water channel visible in the bottom left of the picture where someone is crossing a small bridge over it.

The movement of British Christian missionaries into Africa was an offshoot of the evangelical revival in late 18th and early 19th century Britain. Evangelicalism itself was a religious answer to the godless faith in material progress promoted by Britain's industrial revolution. It combined Christian ideas of individual salvation with liberal capitalist ideas of freedom and inevitable progress.

Missionaries therefore came to Africa convinced of the righteousness of their culture as well as of their beliefs. But there were differences among them. Many settled down like other white settlers, and even gave up evangelism for trading. A few married into the African communities that they wished to convert. Some believed in destroying, some believed in adapting, and many believed in ignoring non-Christian cultures.

During the first half of the 19th century the main Christian mission in southern Africa was the London Missionary Society. Its local head from 1820 onwards was John Philip (1775-1851), a political activist pressing for liberal reforms and African legal rights in Cape Colony. Other famous missionaries of the London society provide a contrast with Philip. Robert Moffat (1795-1883) was a political conservative, who made his mission at Kuruman from 1821 onwards the main centre of evangelism north of the Orange river. He masterminded the translation and printing of the whole Bible into seTswana at his Kuruman printing press, in the belief that literacy was the basis of conversion. The events of the Difaqane encouraged Moffat to feel that Africans were godless and otherwise hopeless people in need of firm missionary guidance. His son-in-law David Livingstone (1813-73), on the other hand, had more respect for African culture and looked forward to independent African Christian nations, though he came to believe that small settler colonies of model British Christians would aid the process.

The certainties of Christianity may have appealed to Africans whose world had been broken apart by widespread wars. It was seen as the religion of a new and obviously wonderful technology and way of life. Missionaries in the interior were both the agents of European power and the interpreters of the outside world for African states. These two roles came into increasing conflict, as European penetration of the interior became stronger and as African states became more dependent on missionary advice.

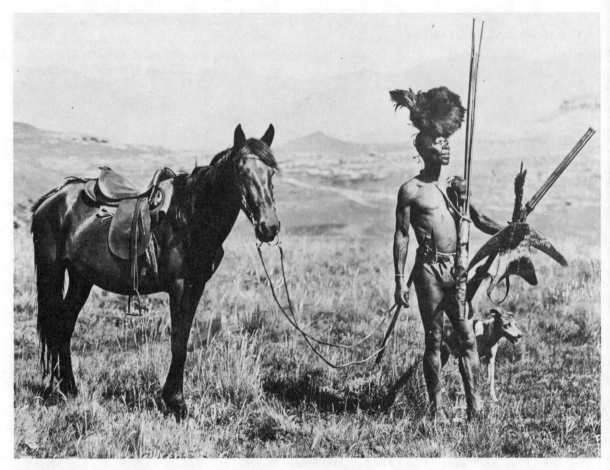

A Sotho soldier posing with his pony, dog, gun, spears and shield for an early 20th century photograph.

had enough grain stored at Thaba Bosiu to last seven years. There was widespread purchase of imported capital goods – ox-drawn ploughs to increase the area under cultivation, wagons to transport crops to market, horses for quick communication over the mountains, and smuggled firearms which gave leSotho a formidable army of armed horsemen.

By the mid-1860s competition had become intense between baSotho and Boers for the fertile land of the western Caledon valley. Sotho cattle-herders seeking land for pasture and grain cultivation expelled Boer sheepherders who had begun to farm fruit by irrigation. From 1862 Moshoeshoe appealed for a British resident agent to live at Thaba Bosiu to conduct relations with the Boers on his western lands, but the British refused, having recognized most of the western Caledon

valley as Free State territory in 1858. Fights between groups of Boers and baSotho resulted in the 2nd Sotho-Boer war of 1865-69. The extensive maize and wheat fields of the baSotho were burnt to the ground by Boer raiders, so that the baSotho soon suffered from famine. By 1866 Moshoeshoe's independent-minded son Molapo, who had been placed as a chief in the north-western Caledon valley, was sueing for peace. Moshoeshoe then signed the Treaty of Thaba Bosiu with the Orange Free State as a truce in which to plant and harvest the 1866-67 crop. When the war resumed, however, Boer attacks were even more disastrous.

British colonization of Basutoland The British high commissioner, Philip Wodehouse, recognized the unfairness of the Anglo-Boer treaties which prevented the supply of fire-arms to leSotho: 'I have strictly observed these very unequal treaties, and while with-holding supplies from the Basutos, have permitted the Free State to purchase all they needed.' Meanwhile, as Moshoeshoe grew older, disputes began to emerge among his sons and relatives. The fear of Orange Free State bankruptcy from the war and of leSotho anarchy made the British answer Moshoeshoe's pleas for protection in 1868. They declared leSotho as the British colony of Basutoland and brought the war to a conclusion at the 2nd Treaty of Aliwal North. Under this humiliating treaty, Basutoland lost the whole western Caledon valley, referred to by the Boers as the 'conquered territory'.

Moshoeshoe died in 1870, an enigma to the last. He had announced his conversion to Christianity, but died before he could be baptized by his French Protestant missionaries and while new Catholic missionaries, also French, were attempting to convert him to their faith.

2 Southern Tswana Chiefdoms of the Road to the North

Though abandoned by the Anglo-Boer treaties of 1852-54, the independent Griqua and Tswana states west of the Boer republics became increasingly important trading partners and potential allies of the British as the volume of trade between Cape Colony and the interior increased.

Griqualand-West After Adam Kok III sold Philippolis to the Orange Free State in 1861, Nicholas Waterboer (ruled 1852-78) was left in sole charge of Griqua territory north of the Orange — the area that became known as Griqualand-West. Waterboer's sovereignty west of the Vaal was undisputed, but the Orange Free State claimed much of the land within the Vaal-Orange confluence because it had once belonged to Adam Kok. The land was valued for its good watering for cattle (and, after 1867-69, for diamonds), and Waterboer's claims were pressed by a white businessman named David Arnot who made his fortune by selling ranches in Griqua country to whites from Cape Colony.

Southern Tswana-Boer relations The Tlhaping kingdom broke up into a loose confederation of chiefdoms on the death of its last king, Mothibi, in 1845. The largest chiefdom, based in the capital town of Taung, was ruled by Mothibi's brother Mahura (1845-69), and extended as far as the mission station of Kuruman. Two smaller chiefdoms lay to the south and were ruled by Mothibi's senior son Gasebone (1845-58) and by a junior son who adopted the Dutch name Jantje (1845-81). Two more chiefdoms were not ruled by members of Mothibi's family — the Maidi-Tlhaping living close to Taung, and the Tlharo ruled by Toto (born 1808; died 1901) in the Langeberg mountains of the west. Tlhaping country stretched as far east as the Makwasi river.

Groups of Rolong re-settled in their old pre-Difaqane homeland on the Makwasi river, near the Boer colony of Potchefstroom during the 1840s. The Tsidi-Rolong under Montshiwa (ruled 1849-96) and Rratlou-Rolong under Gontse (ruled 1840-53) were privileged as so-called 'burgher chiefs' for their services to the Boers since leaving Thaba Nchu in the south. However they refused to send troops to aid the Boers against Sechele in 1852 and were attacked and scattered westwards with their cattle. Montshiwa took his people to the Ngwaketse to the north-west, and the Rratlou took refuge with the Tlhaping of Mahura and Gasebone. Boers then threatened to attack Mahura and Gasebone for sheltering 'cattle-thieves', and began to settle across the Makwasi, taking Tlhaping cattle as their own. Mahura and Gasebone appealed in vain for Nicholas Waterboer to mediate with the Boers.

Attempts to control missionaries' road The missionaries' road became increasingly impor-tant to British hunter-traders as well as to missionaries in the 1850s. It was extended into three northern branches — through Ngamiland to Walvis Bay; across the Zambezi to the Kololo kingdom; and direct to the Ndebele kingdom on the Zimbabwean plateau. The Transvaal Boers therefore tried to block the road before the London missionaries at Kuruman could set up proposed new stations in the Ndebele and Kololo kingdoms. In 1858 Pretorius and Kruger attacked and killed Gasebone (whose body they decapitated) and raided Mahura. When Mahura demanded the return of women and children stolen by the Boers, Kruger demanded eight hundred cattle and many more horses and guns than Mahura owned as a pretext for attacking and conquering Mahura's country. The South African Republic announced that it would beat Mahura so thoroughly 'that a future history of the Batlapis [Tlhaping] will be unnecessary'. It particularly looked forward to capturing the fertile mission station at Kuruman.

The Boer threats produced strong protest among Cape businessmen with interior trading interests. As the Port Elizabeth *Telegraph* put it, 'The high road of the interior must not be given up to the white savages of the Transvaal!' David Livingstone's best-selling memoirs, published in 1857, also awakened interest in the economic potential of central Africa accessible by wagon along the missionaries' road. The British government warned the Transvaal that an attack on the Tlhaping would cancel the Sand River Convention, which would then allow the British to sell arms to the Transvaal's African enemies. Marthinus Pretorius therefore abandoned plans for westward expansion until 1867-68.

3 Allied Kingdoms of the Northern Tswana

The 1852 Boer attack on the Kwena of Sechele at Dimawe prompted an alliance of emerging Tswana kingdoms which was eventually to result in a unified boTswana — including the Kwena, the Ngwaketse, the Rolong of Montshiwa, and even the Ngwato of Sekgoma (who threatened to kill Boer hunters as retaliation for the Dimawe raid). The alliance, which had roots in pre-Difaqane history, was reinforced by trade along the missionaries' road, by royal inter-marriage,

and by the continuing Boer threat.

The Ngwaketse had been scattered across the Kalahari by Ndebele attacks, but had begun to come together under two rival chiefs by the time they were raided by the Boers in 1852 following the raid on Dimawe. From 1853 the two chiefs, Gaseitsiwe and Senthufe, lived together at the kingdom's old capital of Kanye, until Gaseitsiwe defeated Senthufe in battle. Gaseitsiwe then ruled a reunited kingdom at Kanye from 1857 till 1889. Kanye became an important stop on the trade route between Kuruman and Sechele's capital, and accepted an African teacher of the London Missionary Society in 1850. The Rolong of Montshiwa who had fled to Gaseitsiwe in 1852 remained within the Ngwaketse kingdom at Mosaneng until 1870.

Kwena under Sechele Sechele built the (Kgabo-)Kwena chiefdom into a sizeable state during the later 1840s and early 1850s by attracting the allegiance of refugee Tswana chiefdoms and defying the attempts of the Marico Boers to rule him. By trading with wagoners from the south he armed his people with guns and attracted a missionary of the London society, David Livingstone, to settle with him (1846). Though he remained a church member for only three years before he was expelled for defying the church's ban on polygamy, Sechele was the most important Christian among the Tswana between the 1840s and the 1870s. He even became the first missionary to preach Christianity in Matabeleland some years before Robert Moffat.

After resisting the Boer attack on Dimawe in 1852, Sechele found no help from British officials in the Cape, and discovered that he had been abandoned by the London Missionary Society. He therefore came to terms with the Transvaal by asking president Pretorius for a missionary. But by the time a German missionary of the Hanover (Hermansburg) society arrived in 1858, the British were beginning to restore their influence along the missionaries' road and the Boer states were weakened by internal disputes. The Hanover missionaries withdrew back to the Transvaal in 1863-64 after London missionaries had

above left: *Mosielele of the Mmanaana-Kgatla, at Moshupa in 1865.*

above right: *European hunter-trader* buying food and fuel from children at Molepolole, the Kwena capital in Botswana, 1865.

left: *Sechele of the Kwena (ruled 1829-92), at Molepolole in 1865.*

'The first thing that struck us was a fine new house, beautifully built and thatched — and with great taste . . . Two gents from Natal (traders) have a mason with them — this is the man who has done it, and he is about to build a second . . . it seems the two houses are to cost Sechele £500 in feathers, ivory and karosses! Three large rooms I think this one has.' (Bessie Moffat at Molepolole, writing to her sister Jean, July 1866).

below: *Moshupa, on the wagon road between Kanye and Molepolole, in 1865. Note the wagons parked in the distance.*

returned to Sechele's capital. The Ngotwane river became accepted as the dividing line between Kwena and Transvaal sovereignties.

Besides attracting refugees to swell the size of his kingdom, Sechele tried to extend his influence over the neighbouring Ngwato and Ngwaketse kingdoms. Sechele made it his 'life long endeavour', in the words of the missionary John Mackenzie, 'to secure some of the treasures of ivory and ostrich feathers and furs which are brought from extensive [Ngwato] hunting grounds, extending north-wards to the Zambese.' Sechele was less successful in influencing the Ngwaketse of Gaseitsiwe to the south, who controlled the hunting routes into the Kalahari.

The Ngwato under Sekgoma proved their

Khama (1835-1923) heir to Sekgoma of the Ngwato, in 1865 Khama was converted to Christianity by an African preacher named Kgobadi, and became a church member in 1860. Khama clashed with his father and led a Christian party in the Ngwato civil wars between 1866 and 1875. After a brief and unsuccessful rule in 1872-73, he finally wrested power from his father in 1875 and then ruled continuously until 1923.

independence by executing Mzilikazi's tribute collectors in 1844 without Ndebele retaliation and by expelling the rival Kaa chiefdom from the Shoshong hills in 1849. By the early 1850s Sekgoma had extended his power north across the Tswapong hills towards country ruled by the Ndebele kingdom of Mzilikazi. Sechele of the Kwena therefore tried to control the growing Ngwato kingdom by an alliance with Mzilikazi. He induced Mzilikazi to release from captivity a man named Macheng, who had a stronger claim to the Ngwato kingship than Sekgoma but had been captured by the Ndebele fifteen years earlier. Macheng entered Shoshong in triumph and was proclaimed king, causing Sekgoma to flee — to Sechele (1857).

Macheng proved to be a monarch too much along Ndebele lines. He used the *mafisa* cattle held by headmen for feeding Ndebele mercenaries and entertaining visitors, and expected absolute obedience from chiefs and headmen without previously consulting them. Also Sechele found Macheng to be too faithful to his former master Mzilikazi. So, after two years' rule, Sechele deposed Macheng with a Kwena army and reinstated Sekgoma in 1859. Macheng, fearful of Mzilikazi, fled to refuge with Sechele! Sekgoma's eldest sons, Khama and Kgamane, had meanwhile been converted to Christianity, and brought back with them a branch of Sechele's state church — the Hanover mission — which opened at Shoshong in 1860.

Khama as rival to Sekgoma Khama first made his name as a leader among the Ngwato by leading his regiment, reinforced with horses and firearms, to repel a Ndebele invasion in a battle outside Shoshong in 1863. (This was the first and the last Ndebele raid on the Ngwato after the 1840s.) The Ngwato followed up their success by raiding Ndebele cattle posts along the Shashe river. When Sechele sent a Kwena force to discipline the Ngwato in the following year the attack was easily beaten off.

Distress from drought, smallpox and measles, and cattle lung-sickness, helped recruit important members into the spiritual security of the Shoshong church at the time when the London Missionary Society took it over in 1863-64. Like other African rulers who encouraged Christianity without adopting it themselves, Sekgoma found himself faced with a strong Christian party within the ruling class. The Christian party, led by Khama and Kgamane, adopted Western dress, literacy, and marriage customs and was in friendly contact with the traders who smuggled arms along the missionaries' road.

The conflict between Sekgoma and his Christian sons came into the open in 1865 when they opposed the circumcision of a new age-regiment. The conflict then became civil war in 1866. Sekgoma invited Macheng back as an ally against the Christians, and was surprised when Macheng favoured the Christians and deposed him. Sekgoma fled south, this time not to Sechele but to a small rival Kwena chief.

Shoshong as trading centre   Macheng's reign of 1866-72 coincided with the rise of Shoshong to replace Sechele's capital as the greatest trading centre of the hunting trade in the interior. Shoshong was soon connected to the Transvaal by a new road, and thence with Bloemfontein and Port Elizabeth or Pretoria and Durban — shorter and cheaper routes than the old road through Kuruman to Capetown. All this was encouraged by president Pretorius who wanted to expand the South African Republic westwards into the Kalahari. During Macheng's second reign, Shoshong was probably the second largest city in southern Africa after Capetown, with a population of 30,000 in the dry season after harvest and before planting.

4 Tawana, Kololo/Lozi and Ndebele Kingdoms

From Shoshong the trade routes reached north-west to the Tawana kingdom in Ngamiland, north to the Kololo and Lozi kingdoms of the upper Zambezi, and north-east to the Ndebele kingdom (Matabeleland).

The Tawana   Around 1840 Tawana leaders escaped from Kololo rule in the Chobe swamps and gathered at Toteng on Lake Ngami to elect young Letsholathebe, Moremi's son, as their chief. Letsholathebe (ruled 1840-84) then began to build a Tawana kingdom by extending his power over Yei fishermen in the Okavango swamps, Shageng-Kgalagari cattle herders in the Kgwebe hills, and Khoisan hunter-gatherers in the surrounding thirstlands. Attacks by both the Ndebele (1842 and 1863) and the Kololo (1860) on Letsholathebe's kingdom proved ineffective as the raiders were exhausted and confused by Tawana knowledge of rivers, swamps and reed beds.

Relations with Ngwato and Orlam distant neighbours were more cordial because Toteng was linked to Shoshong and Walvis Bay by wagon trade routes. Wagoners found that ivory at Toteng was extremely cheap by coastal standards, as it had previously only been exportable by porters or pack-oxen over hundreds of kilometres of thirstland. Ngwato kings tried to profit from the trade by asserting their seniority over Tawana kings in much the same way as Sechele of the Kwena did over the Ngwato.

Kololo and Lozi states   Sebetwane was succeeded by his son Sekeletu, who wrested the right to rule from his sister Mamochisane (previously her father's main deputy) and ruled from 1851 to 1863. Sekeletu proved unpopular with non-Kololo subjects, trusting only Kololo advisers and marrying only Kololo women. He was a leper and hid away from his people, not daring to travel round the kingdom and visit subject chiefs like his father had. When he died, civil war broke out at the capital, Dinyanti, and the Toka and Luyana subject peoples revolted in the east and north. A Kololo general, Mpololo, proclaimed himself king and marched north, where he ordered that all Luyana chiefs' sons should be executed. This was the signal for a general rising to massacre the Kololo led by the Luyana general Njekwa. Only Kololo women and children were spared. Some Kololo men managed to escape, but the Kololo kingdom was finished (1864).

Njekwa restored the Luyana kingship by installing Sipopa, the son of the last ruling king, as the new king. But the Luyana rulers had been heavily influenced by Kololo education. Sipopa and other chiefs' sons had been favourites at Sebetwane's court, but had escaped from Sekeletu to regain their independence in the north-east. Sipopa (ruled 1864-76) therefore governed a Luyana state reformed by Kololo culture. The rulers spoke a dialect of siKololo in which they called themselves the maLozi — their Luyana way of pronouncing the name 'maRotse', given them by the Kololo. The language helped them to incorporate more easily the Toka and Subiya, previously subject to the Kololo in the Lozi nation.

Sipopa ruled like a traditional Luyana king through a prime minister, Njekwa. But he also followed Sebetwane's example in using a female relative — first his sister and then his daughter — as his most important deputy, known as the Mulena Mukwae, in ruling the southern part of his kingdom. The new Lozi kingdom looked south towards Botswana for its trade and diplomatic relations, using its Tswana/Sotho language for communication, unlike the old Luyana kingdom which had looked to the areas of Angola or Zaire for trade and diplomacy.

Ndebele state   The visits of Robert Moffat to Mzilikazi between 1854 and 1859 opened the Ndebele kingdom on the Zimbabwean plateau to British hunter-traders, just as Moffat's visit to Mzilikazi in 1829 had opened the Ndebele kingdom on the Transvaal plateau. Mzilikazi was influenced by his need for British firearms and ammunition, superior to the cheap Portuguese weapons being imported in increasing numbers by his Shona enemies in the east. So he was disappointed when British traders, constrained by the Sand River Convention and by anxious Tswana states in the south, proved unwilling to sell arms. The missionaries sent by Moffat to settle at Mzilikazi's capital, Inyati, in 1859-60 were an even greater disappointment when they refused to repair firearms and make bullets in the manner of older London missionaries

on first arriving in Tswana states. They were too useful as interpreters and contacts with the south to be expelled, but Mzilikazi refused to allow them to make any converts and moved his capital away from them to Mhlahlandela in 1860-61.

The Ndebele kingdom was built upon the ruins of the Rozvi confederacy, and depended on the Kalanga subject people for its basic prosperity. Kalanga youths were taken into the Ndebele regiments, often in return for *maziza* royal cattle loaned to Rozvi chiefs of the area. The Kalanga gave regular tribute in grain and animal skins. The Ndebele also became more and more dependent on trade with the Kalanga for grain since this was needed first for beer supplies to the enlarged army and then because of famine in the early 1860s. The Ndebele were hard-hit by drought in 1860-61, followed by lung-sickness (brought by ox-wagons from Namibia via Shoshong) and by smallpox and measles, the latter being fatal to malnourished children.

Mzilikazi was a sick man for most of the 1860s. By 1863 he was so desperate to regain lost grain, cattle and youths that he launched a series of not too successful military expeditions, against the Tawana in Ngamiland and the Ngwato at Shoshong, and against his Kalanga subjects in the west as well as other Shona in the east. The Kalanga of the upper Shashe had found grain trade more profitable with the Tswana and other wagoners than with the Ndebele. Mzilikazi destroyed the Talaote chiefdom as an example to others. However, Kalanga of the upper Shashe continued to trade southwards and to assert independence from the Ndebele and friendship for the Ngwato. The Shona to the east of the Ndebele kingdom proved to be stronger than expected. Mzilikazi thought that any strong resistance there had been solved in 1857 with the surrender of the leading Rozvi chief Chirumanzi. But the two claimants to the Rozvi paramountcy, Tohwechipi and Mutinhima, settled their differences to resist Mzilikazi from 1863 to 1866. Eventually Tohwechipi was captured and became a subject chief in charge of Mzilikazi's *maziza* cattle, and the eastern Rozvi resumed peaceful trading.

In his dying years Mzilikazi grew fearful of Tswana and even Zulu attacks on his kingdom and more desperate for firearms. White hunter-traders who supplied the Ndebele with firearms and ammunition were permitted for the first time to hunt in the east of his territory as far as the Umfuli river. Two Transvaal citizens, Henry Hartley and (former US citizen) Adam Renders, then discovered the riches of Zimbabwe previously unrealized by whites. Renders settled in the Mugabe chiefdom near the ruins of Great Zimbabwe, while Hartley brought in a German geologist called Carl Mauch to confirm the value of gold-bearing reefs exposed by Shona mines around the Umfuli river. Hartley and Mauch also inspected abandoned gold mines around the Tati river near Shashe on the road to Shoshong. It was their announcement at Potchefstroom in December 1867 of their discoveries in the north that began southern Africa's first gold rush in 1868-69.

5 Shangane, Pedi and Swazi Kingdoms

While the Tswana and other states of the west were linked together by wagon roads, the states of the east on either side of the Drakensberg mountain spine did not stand on major highways. They were more isolated from each other and self-sufficient, connected with the outside world by a network of foot-paths down which goods were carried on the heads or backs of porters. Their trade with the outside world was therefore limited, and tended to be with the middlemen of Portuguese or Muslim merchants on the east coast in ivory and slaves, rather than with British merchants from the south coast.

Shangane kingdom   Portuguese coastal settlements along the Mozambique coast were few and far between, and were sometimes reduced to giving tribute to the Shangane. Soshangane, who had settled at Chaimite in hills near the Save river, attacked and defeated the Portuguese at Inhambane in 1834 and Sofala in 1836. He also destroyed trading posts in the former Manyika kingdom. The Portuguese at

Tete and Sena along the Zambezi paid annual tribute to Soshangane for up to twenty years after being raided in 1844. Most of the *prazo* estates south of the Zambezi were abandoned, and the few *prazeros* who remained became slave-raiding chiefs in well-fortified villages, with proud titles and grand uniforms given them by the Portuguese authorities.

Soshangane − known to the Portuguese as 'Manicusse' − died in about 1858 and was succeeded by his son Mawewe who moved the capital southwards to the mouth of the Limpopo river. Mawewe was deposed three years later by his brother Mzila (ruled 1861-85), who had recruited Soutpansberg Boers and the Madolo (Matola) chiefdom of the Ronga at Delagoa Bay to his side. Mawewe turned to the Swazi, who took control of the coastal area between the Tembe and Limpopo rivers until the 1870s, beseiging the Portuguese in Lourenço Marques fort in 1863-64. Mzila therefore withdrew the Shangane capital back to the north side of the Save river in 1864.

Pedi kingdom   Sekwati, the last surviving son of the Pedi king before the Ndebele invasion, arrived back in the Leulu mountains from northern exile around 1826. Sekwati first defeated a Koni chief called Marangang, who was founding his own kingdom in the mountains. Oral tradition records that Sekwati sent a beautiful woman to lure Marangang into an ambush. Sekwati then rebuilt the Pedi kingdom of his father by defeating other local chiefdoms and giving them *mafisa* cattle to keep them loyal.

Sekwati (ruled about 1826-61) set his capital on a rocky mountain named Phiring, where he beat off Swazi and Zulu raids in the 1840s. Sekwati made peace with the Zulu in the same manner as Moshoeshoe, by sending cattle after them as tribute. Zulu-Pedi friendship against common Swazi and Boer enemies was to last until the 1870s.

Pedi-Boer relations   Hendrik Potgieter was granted the use of land to the east of the Pedi kingdom by Sekwati in 1845, but the African inhabitants of the Ohrigstad/Lydenburg Boer colony continued to recognize the sovereignty of Sekwati. The Lydenburg *volksraad,* which wanted peaceful grazing for its increasing herds of sheep and cattle, was cautious about expanding into Pedi territory. But Potgieter had no such caution and attacked the Pedi kingdom with his Soutpansberg Boers in 1852 in order to capture firearms imported from Moshoeshoe or the Portuguese. Potgieter's Boers besieged Sekwati on Phiring mountain, cutting it off from water supplies until Sekwati's son Sekhukhune broke through the Boer lines at night with a party of young women to bring back water. When the Boers eventually withdrew, Sekwati decided to move his capital to another mountain with a well on top called Mosego. Pedi tradition records that by this time Sekwati was so fat and old that he had to be carried up the mountain in an ox-skin sling by relays of young men.

In his last years Sekwati came under Transvaal Boer influence and was persuaded to accept German missionaries of the Berlin society, loyal to the Transvaal, who had failed to establish a mission in Swaziland. Other Berlin missionaries settled with chiefs Maleo and Mabhogo who had been resisting Transvaal rule.

Sekhukhune (ruled 1861-81) seized power on the death of Sekwati, expelling his elder brother Mampuru to Swaziland. Sekhukhune determined to reduce Transvaal influence and expelled the Berlin missionaries, who had refused to supply or repair guns, in 1864. The missionaries, led by Merensky, withdrew with a Christian party of Pedi under Sekhukhune's brother Dinkoanyane to a site named Botshabelo (i.e. refuge) near present-day Middleburg. Sekhukhune became more reconciled to the Christian party when Dinkoanyane supported him against Mampuru. But Sekhukhune continued to be at enmity with the Boers and Swazi, who launched unsuccessful attacks on him in 1867 and 1869. The Pedi kingdom built up large stockpiles of weapons smuggled from Delagoa Bay and Cape Colony in preparation for inevitable full-scale war with the Transvaal and the Swazi kingdom.

Sekhukhune, Pedi king (1861-79)

Swazi kingdom Sobhuza I (ruled 1815-39) of the Ngwane – later Swazi – was slowly drawn into an alliance with Boers by his desire for firearms and their mutual hostility towards the Zulu. In the 1820s Sobhuza had used Portuguese mercenaries with firearms to conquer the powerful Magagula clan, but the Zulu blocked access to the Portuguese at Delagoa Bay and Sobhuza looked inland to British missionaries. Envoys sent to Moffat at Kuruman in 1833-34 made contact with Wesleyan missionaries and the Wesleyan alliance of African states on the southern highveld, which in turn led to contacts with Boer trekkers. Thus when the Boers beat the Zulu at Blood river in 1838 Sobhuza sent a message of congratulation. The Swazi were then invaluable allies of the Boers in the Zulu-Swazi-Boer wars that followed, during which Sobhuza died (1838-39). The *1st Swazi-Boer treaty* of friendship was agreed in 1840

Reputed portrait of Mswati, Swazi king (1840-68), sitting in the centre among his chiefs.

between the Natal *volksraad* and the regency that followed Sobhuza.

Mswati, son of Sobhuza, was considered too young to rule alone until 1845. He soon established himself as the greatest of Ngwane kings, giving his name to the nation as the people of Mswati, — emaSwati or (in isiZulu) amaSwazi. Mswati was at first strongly influenced by regents — his mother Thandile and his brother Somcuba. Thandile, a daughter of Zwide, organized the state along Ndwandwe lines: the king as leader of annual ceremonies, notably *incwala*; royal villages in outlying areas under royal wives; subject youths pressed into the army and constant raiding abroad; and the queen-mother (*ndlovukati*) as the most powerful figure next to the king. Somcuba on the other hand was responsible for the *2nd Swazi-Boer treaty* with the Ohrigstad *volksraad* (1846) which gave the Boers the country previously claimed personally by Potgieter as a gift from Sekwati.

After suffering Zulu invasions and quarrelling with Somcuba and the Boers, Mswati attempted to ally with Soshangane and with Shepstone, the effective British ruler of Natal. But Soshangane and Shepstone stood back while the Zulu invaded Swaziland again in 1852. Shepstone concluded: 'the Amaswazi are destroyed as a tribe.' But Mswati recovered sufficiently to attack Lydenburg and killed Somcuba in 1853. This led to peace under a *3rd Swazi-Boer treaty* of 1855, which was an anti-Zulu alliance. Though Mswati soon withdrew the offer of a ten-mile-wide strip along the Pongola river for Boer patrols against the Zulu, that clause in the treaty became the basis of later Transvaal territorial claims.

Mswati, who moved his capital north from Ezulwini to Hhohho in 1847, became the master of the lowveld bush country between Swaziland and the Limpopo up to his death in 1865. He took advantage of civil wars among the Shangane and Transvaal Boers in the early 1860s to raid for cattle and ivory as far north as the Shona peoples and as far west as the source of the Vaal river. The Swazi also, as we have seen, besieged Lourenço Marques in 1863-64, and remained the dominant power in the area of Delagoa Bay – despite Zulu threats – until the late 1860s. Captured Tsonga people in the lowveld became slaves (*bugcili*) who were either incorporated into Swazi families or sold to Boers as 'apprentices' and to Portuguese for export overseas. Mswati ensured that subject chiefs could not become rich and independent-minded by marrying his sisters to them and demanding continuous *lobola* payments in cattle.

The death of Mswati, leaving no clear heir, led to two or three years of uncertainty before the regency – consisting of Mswati's prime minister Sandile Zwane, Thandile, and others – could firmly establish itself in power behind a new king, Ludvonga. Ronga chiefdoms around Delagoa Bay and the Zulu took advantage of Swazi weakness and expanded across the Pongola river. The Transvaal Boers, using the Zulu threat as cause for a renewed

alliance with the Swazi, pressed their claims for winter pasturage deep inside Swazi territory on the Drakensberg and in the Nkomati valley.

6 Zulu Kingdom and Transkei States

The Zulu kingdom enjoyed its longest period of peace and stability during the reign of Mpande (1840-72). Having used Boer aid to seize the kingship in 1840, Mpande paid them tribute until 1843. But he was no puppet-king. When the British annexed Natal in 1843 they recognized Mpande's independence north of the Tugela river. In return Mpande forbade raids across Natal into Mpondo country. Though Zulu armies were sent north during the 1840s to attack the Pedi, Swazi and Shangane, raids abroad became less frequent under Mpande.

Mpande continued to show friendship towards Boers who paid tribute to settle in his country – the Klip river settlement granted in 1846 and the Utrecht settlement granted in 1847-48. Mpande appears not to have objected to their annexation to Natal (Klip river, 1848) and to the Transvaal (Utrecht, 1859). Zulu relations with the Transvaal did not sour until 1861 when Marthinus Pretorius forced the treaty of Waaihoek on Mpande. The treaty – originally made between Pretorius and Mpande's son Cetshwayo – pushed the Utrecht district of the Transvaal southward down the Buffels river to point like a dagger at the heart of Zululand. Mpande turned to the British in Natal under Shepstone as allies against the Boers. Meanwhile the Zulu gained a valuable ally at Delagoa Bay in the Mabudu chiefdom and began to reassert their power in the north following the death of Mswati in 1865.

Rise of Cetshwayo Zulu tradition records that Mpande deliberately encouraged rivalry between his two eldest sons, Mbuyazi and Cetshwayo, so that they would not combine to depose him (as he had deposed his own brothers Shaka and Dingane). Mbuyazi's followers, known as the isiGqoza, fought with Cetshwayo's followers, the uSuthu, and were

Mpande, the Zulu king (1840-72), reviewing his troops.

BASUTOLAND AND TRANSKEI 1840s-60s

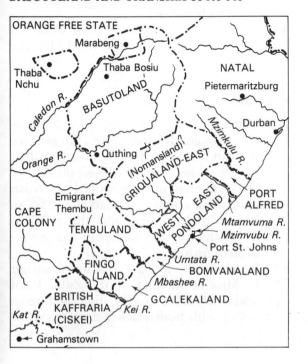

Smith to annex it in 1850, 'Pondoland' was an independent treaty-state, tied by formal treaty with Britain to keep order in the Transkei. Not until 1866, when Natal annexed a northern part of the kingdom, did it begin to forfeit its formal independence.

The independence of the Orange Free State and its aggressive expansion into Sotho country gave rise to British fears of its annexing a corridor of land down the Mzimvubu river to Port St John's. The British responded by trying to set up the sparsely populated territory between the seaward slopes of the Drakensberg, known as 'Nomansland', as a treaty-state under a recognized ruler. After Lehana, the son of Sikonyela, failed to re-establish the Tlokoa kingdom in the area because of raids by Moshoeshoe's son Nehemiah, the British encouraged the Griqua of Adam Kok III to settle there. Hence Nomansland became the treaty-state of 'Griqualand-East' (1863).

A third treaty-state, 'Fingoland', was set up in 1865 as part of an attempt by the British to divide the whole Transkei area neatly into treaty-states and dependent chiefdoms, in order to ensure the peaceful supply of labour and peasant produce to neighbouring colonies. Fingoland was settled with Mfengu peasant farmers, adapted to Western customs and loyal to the British, who themselves employed local Xhosa labour. The remaining territory between the treaty-states was then divided — at least on maps — into tribal reserves of dependent chiefdoms. The Gcaleka-Xhosa under Sarili were allowed back into their coastal homeland, 'Galekaland', from which they had been expelled by the British after the great cattle-killing. Thembu and Bomvana were allotted 'Tembuland' and 'Bomvanaland', while Thembu who migrated north-westwards in the late 1860s were recognized in 'Emigrant Thembuland'.

utterly defeated at Ndonda-kusuka on the Tugela river in 1856. Shepstone then threw his support behind Cetshwayo as the winner, and Cetshwayo responded by appointing an Englishman, John Dunn, as his induna for relations with Natal. Eventually, after the treaty of Waaihoek had embittered Zulu relations with the Boers, Shepstone — with an eye to the future for British influence — arrived at Dingane's court to proclaim the blessing of the British queen for the succession of Cetshwayo to the Zulu kingship.

Transkei states The British recognized the Mpondo kingdom under Faku (ruled 1824-67) as the only substantial state in the independent area that lay across the Kei between the Drakensberg and the ocean. Port St John's, a small settlement of English traders on the Mpondo coast, was the only significant stop for coastal trading ships between Cape Colony and Natal. Wesleyan missionaries were influential at Faku's capital Quakeni (Palmerton). So from 1844, despite a brief attempt by high commissioner Harry

7 Conclusion

The Mfecane/Difaqane and Boer Trek changed the political face of southern Africa with new kingdoms and colonies. Everywhere

141

there were small groups of people being forced by circumstance into accepting the sovereignty of expanding states. Colonies and kingdoms grew in population and territory until they inevitably clashed in competition. The period of imperialism from the end of the 1870s was to see these states begin to eliminate each other.

Questions

1 Give short accounts of the work and importance of *three* of the following: (a) Dingane; (b) Zwide; (c) MmaNthatisi; (d) Waterboer; (e) Mswati. [Cambridge International School Certificate, 1978]
2 Describe the career and show the importance of Moshoeshoe I of Lesotho. [Cambridge International School Certificate, 1976]
3 Discuss the importance before 1870 of the 'missionaries' road' from Kuruman through Shoshong.
4 Compare the histories of the Pedi and Swazi kingdoms between the 1830s and the 1870s.

Activities

1 Debate in the classroom why Moshoeshoe, Khama III and other 19th century African rulers were so opposed to their people taking strong alcoholic drink.
2 Draw a map of pre-colonial Christian mission stations — marking African states, trade routes, and the religious denomination and European nationality of the missions.
3 Imagine that you are a political adviser to Mpande as king of the Zulu. What advice would you give him on foreign policy with both black and white states?

See Bibliography, pp. 337–42: B4 Cameron; B6 Duminy & Guest; B17 Lye & Murray; B20 Matsebula; B21 Maylam; B22 Mazikana; B32 Readers Digest; B42 Wilson & Thompson; C2 Beach; C20 Mudenge; C22 Peires; C27 Saunders & Derricourt; D1 Beach; D2 Bergh & Bergh; D3 Bonner; D4 Comaroff & Comaroff; D5 Delius; D9 Hodgson; D10 Langworthy; D14–15 Peires; D16 Ross; D17 Sanders; D18 Saunders; D19 Thompson; E1 Beach; E2 Beinart; J16 JNZH; J18 Mohlomi.

Source-based exercise

Look at the illustrations and text on page 131 as well as the following passage:
'We found Sechelli in high good humour. He supplied us with abundance of beef, corn, milk and tamanies, the last a kind of large bean growing on a creeping plant with an edible root resembling a yam and called *morama*. When roasted the bean is a very good substitute for cocoa. We remained here over Sunday, when Sechelli, who had been reading the first portion of the translation of the Old Testament, gave Mr. Moffat a text (concerning polygamy) and asked him to preach on it.' (James Chapman, June 1854)

(a) What kinds of goods did European hunter-traders buy and sell in trade with the Tswana kingdoms?
(b) Show on a sketch map how wagon routes linked the world economy with the interior of southern Africa.
(c) How did relations with British hunter-traders build up the economic prosperity and political power of Sechele?
(d) Discuss Sechele's relations with Christian missionaries.

Chapter 10

Mining Development and the Scramble for Africa (1868–1886)

European penetration of the interior gained a new character at the end of the 1860s. Up till then Europeans who had ventured into the interior had had to adapt to the existing pattern of African states and economies. The Boer colonies in the interior had become in effect African states, though culturally linked to the coast and Europe. However, European capitalism had rapidly grown overseas and developed a great appetite for raw materials, particularly gold and diamonds, from southern Africa. Instead of simply trading with African states as before, European capitalists began to move in to take over land and minerals for production using advanced technology and local unskilled labour. The African states that already owned the resources and controlled the labour were reluctant to lose control of land and labour. The European imperialists on the other hand became more and more involved in African politics to secure or extend their investments. The clash of African and European interests eventually led to wars of conquest, or treaties of 'protection', which robbed African states of their sovereignty.

1 The New Imperialism and the Scramble

Just as mercantile-imperialism had been re-placed in the 1830s-40s, so the 'imperialism of free trade' gave way in the 1870s-80s to capitalist-imperialism which revived colonial expansion. Britain as the world's only mature industrial power was beginning to export surplus capital to invest overseas. Other European nations and the USA were in the middle of their own industrial revolutions and were looking abroad for markets for their manufactured goods. Capitalist countries challenged British dominance of free trade, first by protecting themselves from cheaper British goods by high customs duties, and secondly by expanding their protected national markets through conquering their neighbours or seizing overseas colonies. Britain responded with its own aggressive nationalism during the Conservative party government of 1874-80. The very word 'imperialism' entered the English language at that time.

Surplus capital — the profits from Britain's industrialization — was invested in overseas development projects such as railways and mining. These would expand the market for British exports or provide raw materials for British consumption. North America and other areas of European settlement were the major areas of British overseas investment apart from India. British capitalists began investing money in Cape Colony banks in the early 1860s, speculating on the hope that local companies would borrow it at high interest rates to expand wool production and interior trade. So much money came in and moved from bank to bank in search of greater profit, without sufficient development projects to use it, that twenty-eight of the thirty-one banks collapsed in bankruptcy during the Cape bank crisis of 1863-65 when investors suddenly withdrew their deposits. Only the two London-based 'imperial' banks and one Cape-based local bank survived.

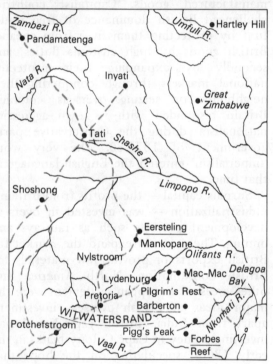

Tati mining village in 1870 — southern Africa's first European gold rush settlement. Note the stone walling dating from previous African mining, much of which was demolished to build new walls and houses. A wagon is crossing the Tati river at the extreme right.

'About this time quite a little village had arisen on the north bank of the Tati river. As nearly as I can ascertain, the following were the [9] companies at work: — No. 1, Dr. Coverly's party; No. 2, Rocky, Dalton and James, with three small stampers worked by the Limpopo Co.'s steam engine . . .No. 9, London and Limpopo Mining and Trading Co. The company of 35 Australians, sent up from Durban, went about 32 miles up the river and located themselves on "Todd's Creek." Several of the shafts were 50 feet deep; but, though 150 tons of quartz, some of it apparently rich [in gold], had been got out, the crushing machines . . . did not succeed [in extracting gold] .' (Thomas Baines *The Gold Regions of South Eastern Africa* London & Port Elizabeth, 1877).

GOLDFIELDS KNOWN TO EUROPEANS
1860s-80s (underlined)

There was a depression in British world trade during the 1870s after the collapse of a boom in American railroad construction. But British capitalists noted that trade and profits did not decline in India and Australia, which were colonies under British rule, unlike the USA. Some British capitalists therefore began to think of colonizing Africa as a 'nearer India' which would remain profitable even during world trade depressions; and the discovery of gold and diamonds made southern Africa the most attractive part of the continent for British investment. Gold and other precious metals were needed in increasing quantity for currency as world trade expanded, while diamonds were valued as indestructible reservoirs of wealth by individuals recently grown rich in Europe and America.

When the world economy recovered in the early 1880s, France and Germany and a private company owned by the Belgian king took the lead in colonizing Africa. Britain and Portugal, the already established colonial powers, responded by claiming enormous hinterlands for their coastal colonies. The continent was carved up between the European powers in what *The Times* newspaper of London called 'the scramble for Africa'. In southern Africa settler capitalists and politicians pressed for the annexation of new colonies in the interior, while the Colonial Office in London favoured the cheaper alternative of treaty-states known as 'protectorates'.

2 Early Gold Rushes 1868-73

Southern Africa's first gold rush followed the announcement of the discoveries of gold at Tati and Umfuli north of the Limpopo. Prospectors and miners from Europe and Australasia began to stream northward during 1868-69 up the missionaries' road to open up old mines at Tati, which lay in the frontier zone between the Ngwato and Ndebele kingdoms.

Tati gold mining The richest ores were soon worked out and the smaller companies, without the machinery to crush poorer ores or to pump water out of deeper shafts, were forced to abandon mining. By 1870 only the London and Limpopo Company survived, with the first steam engine ever imported into the interior. It obtained a concession to mine from the new Ndebele king, Lobengula. But the company abandoned the concession area in about 1874, and mining was not resumed until 1880 when a new company founded the village of Francistown, named after its director Daniel Francis, next to its main mine. After the collapse of mining in 1874 Tati remained a trading centre for Matabeleland and for the Zambezi along the new Pandamatenga road. It was effectively independent of

both Ndebele and Ngwato sovereignties, and served as a buffer-zone to keep the kingdoms from clashing.

The South African Republic failed to obtain Tati in 1868 by persuading Mzilikazi of the Ndebele and Macheng of the Ngwato either to grant the land or to go to war with each other so that the Boers could intervene. Macheng was persuaded by his British missionary to offer Tati to Britain. President Pretorius of the SAR quickly proclaimed Mzilikazi and Macheng to be his subjects and placed a *landdrost* at Nylstroom in the north-west Transvaal to rule their territories. He also claimed a two-mile strip of land through Swaziland along the Pongola and Maputo rivers to Delagoa Bay. But Pretorius' April 1868 proclamation was unenforceable in east or west, was discounted by the British and Portuguese, and never took effect.

Early Transvaal gold mining Gold prospecting and mining soon spread from Tati to the Transvaal around Mankopane's town on the Soutpansberg road (1869). With the first crushing of gold ore there in 1871, the place became known as Eersteling (first crushing), and Marabastad mine village was founded nearby in 1872. The largest gold mines of this period were in the eastern Transvaal at the villages of Mac-Mac (named after the prospector MacLachlan) and Pilgrim's Rest between Pedi and Swazi territories. These mines could be reached on foot from Delagoa Bay. Mining was stopped by the Pedi-Boer war in the later 1870s, and when it was resumed in the early 1880s it was concentrated around Barberton (founded 1882) deeper inside Swazi territory.

3 Diamond Rush and Kimberley Mines 1867-85

The gold rushes were overshadowed by the great diamond rush to the lower Vaal area. The first diamond found at Hopetown in 1867 was followed by large quantities around Klipdrift (Barkly West) on the north bank of the Vaal in 1868. The area was claimed by both Boer republics, by the Griqua chief Nicholas Waterboer, and by the Tlhaping

NDEBELE SUCCESSION CRISIS

Mzilikazi died in September 1868 without naming a successor. The regents then chose Mzilikazi's son Lobengula as king. But a leading general objected that Lobengula was only the son of a Swazi rather than a truly royal Zulu mother. Lobengula's installation was delayed while a search was made for Mzilikazi's son Nkulumane, who had been missing since 1840 and might be with his mother's people, the Zulu. Theophilus Shepstone, the effective ruler of Natal, sent his gardener north to claim the throne as Nkulumane. But this man was refused entry into the Ndebele kingdom, and Lobengula was installed in February 1870. (Shepstone's secretary, Rider Haggard, later wrote a novel based on the story, titled *King Solomon's Mines*.)

Lobengula first had to crush the revolt of his Zwangendaba regiment, and then he faced an attempt by Shepstone's gardener to raise an army in the south. Lobengula therefore secured himself in power by recruiting the allegiance of his Rozvi and Kalanga headmen, previously oppressed by Mzilikazi, and allowing them freer use of the *maziza* cattle. He secured himself from southern or eastern attack by friendlier relations with the new Ngwato king, Khama III, and by sending tribute to the Shangane king, Mzila.

The original caption by the painter Thomas Baines reads: 'The installation of NoBengula into the Supreme Chieftainship of Matabili land about 18 months after the death of his father Umselegasi or Mosilekatse. The young king exercising his first act of sovereignty by sacrificing cattle to the manes of his father, to the Molimo or great spirit and for other causes at Inthlathlalangela Monday Feby 22 – 1870 –'

chiefs. The white 'diggers'* of Klipdrift formed their own government in 1870 under a local trader named Stafford Parker, who had lived in the area for twelve years and claimed to represent the true Kora owners of the land.

Territorial disputes over diamond fields The Tlhaping chief Mahura blocked the Klipdrift-

*Calling themselves 'diggers' in the Australian fashion, though they employed Africans to do the actual digging.

Potchefstroom road to prove his claims as far east as the Makwasi river, and Pretorius counter-claimed as far west as Kuruman in his April 1868 proclamation. Boundary negotiations between Transvaal, Tlhaping, Kora and Rolong chiefs proved fruitless until the British intervened by laying down the 'Keate line' along the Makwasi river between the Transvaal and independent African chiefdoms (1871). The British then grabbed the diamond fields for themselves later in the year, by annexing all land claimed by

Nicholas Waterboer as the new British colony of 'Griqualand-West'. The Orange Free State, which had boycotted the negotiations, protested hotly until diamonds were discovered within its own undisputed territory at Koffiefontein and Jagersfontein.

Griqualand-West The colony included 'wet diggings' along the Vaal river around Klipdrift and newly discovered 'dry diggings' some distance south of the Vaal. Four diamond pipes were discovered there in a six-kilometre radius, each being the throat of an extinct volcano full of diamonds. The biggest pipe was named Kimberley in honour of the British colonial minister of the time, and a township of 30,000 people in tents and shacks rapidly developed next to it. Another pipe was known as De Beers' after the Boer brothers who had owned the farm there. The four pipes were divided into a total of 3,600 small square claim-holdings, each owned by an individual 'digger'. By November 1871 the small hill on top of the Kimberley pipe had been dug out and the mine was already twenty metres deep into yellow ground, rapid-

Nicholas Waterboer (ruled 1852-78) The British used his claim to the diamond area to found their Griqualand-West colony.

Wet diggings on the Vaal river Black labourers dug up and washed the river bed gravel, sifting out larger pieces of gravel, using chutes and simple machinery. The white claim holders, seen here with their families, then sorted out diamonds from the finer gravel.

Dry diggings at Kimberley   The Kimberley mine became a hive of activity within a few months of its opening. Thousands of men burrowed deeper and deeper into the yellow ground, after removing the small hill that stood on the diamond pipe. The area was divided into hundreds of small square claims. At first, as this picture shows, lines of claims were separated by roadways. Then the roadways themselves became claims, and the exposed diamond pipe became the 'Big Hole', each claim being linked to the side of the hole by expensive hauling machinery and a cobweb of wires. On the left of this picture note the white 'digger' kicking black workers, while behind them there are three whites and a black conducting business over a diamond.

ly approaching deeper blue ground which was feared to be diamondless.

Feverish digging was promoted by the high price of diamonds during the 1870-73 world trade boom. Rough-living, hard-drinking whites, often with anti-black prejudices imported from overseas, were in cut-throat competition for wealth and insisted on being absolute masters of black labour. White claim-holders from Europe, America or Australasia ganged up against a minority of Kora, Griqua, Tlhaping, Malay, Indian and Chinese claim-holders. African claim-holders were obvious suspects in cases of IDB (illicit diamond buying), because they were of similar language and culture as workers. Workers hid diamonds from their employers and sold them illegally

to other claim-holders at more profit than their regular wages. Whites viciously attacked African or Asian claim-holders in 1872 riots as scapegoats for IDB accusations. The British authorities responded by cancelling non-European claims at three of the four mines.

White 'digger' representatives ran the government of Griqualand-West, and rioted for joy, burning down liquor saloons, when the Cape parliament refused to annex Griqualand-West to Cape Colony in 1872. The British 'imperial factor' then tried to take control, but the lieutenant-governor Richard Southey (1873-75) was eventually driven out by the 'diggers' for arming black policemen to deal with rebellious whites. Southey's successor was downgraded from lieutenant-governor to administrator in order to save on imperial expense, but his job proved easier as white 'diggers' were bankrupted by the mid-1870s world trade depression.

Labour, food and fuel supplies The Kimberley mines needed labour, food and fuel. Labour came on foot, food came by wagon from as far as Port Elizabeth, while firewood was collected locally in wagons over a wide area. Labourers flocked to Kimberley from all parts of southern Africa at the rate of two or even three thousand a month by 1874. Many came from the Ciskei/Transkei and Basutoland, where people also responded to the opportunity to sell food to migrants and to wagoners for sale in the growing towns. Mfengu peasants in Fingoland exported five hundred wagonfuls of sorghum or maize in 1873, and by 1875 the annual trade between Fingoland and the Cape Colony was worth £150,000. Mfengu peasants invested in ploughs and wagons to increase and transport their crops, or in sheep to produce wool while world prices were high. Where the Mfengu led, neighbouring Xhosa, Thembu and others followed. In Basutoland the annual foreign trade equalled Fingoland's. People expelled across the Caledon river by the Boers since 1869 crowded out the fertile foothills, and pressed the Sotho into increasing agricultural production as well as labour migration. Basutoland supplied both labour and grain to Kimberley along the south bank of the Orange to avoid the hostile Orange Free State. Its prosperity can be seen in the 1875 census, which counted 2,700 ploughs, 300 wagons and 35,000 horses in the territory, plus numerous sheep and cattle.

The British encouraged labour migration to Kimberley from deep in the interior by relaxing their ban on the sale of firearms to Africans beyond colonial frontiers. Modern rifles as well as old-fashioned muskets were in great demand by African states for military and hunting reasons. Distant rulers sent parties of men, often from subject or 'slave' groups, to the mines to earn a gun each. Large numbers of Pedi and smaller numbers of Zulu or Shangane walked across the Boer republics braving robbers and labour taxes to smuggle back firearms. The slave-trader Albasini in the Soutpansberg mountains converted from selling lowveld Tsonga to Delagoa Bay to sending them as labourers to Kimberley.

The supply of labour across the Transvaal was stopped by Pedi-Boer hostilities in the mid-1870s. Competition between claim-holders for scarce labour pushed unskilled workers' wages up from 10 to 25 or 30 shillings a week.* The British authorities of Griqualand-West therefore looked north instead, where labourers from as far as the Zambezi had started to come to Kimberley after the Tati mines closed down. A British agent was sent north in 1876-77 to recruit labour along the missionaries' road as far as the Ndebele kingdom. Northern Tswana states sent their men, including Khoisan servants, southwards to earn firearms for hunting deeper into the desert and tsetse-infested valleys. Zambezi-Tonga and Shona were also sent by their Lozi and Ndebele rulers, or came independently to earn firearms to fight the Lozi and Ndebele. Some workers preferred to remain at Kimberley rather than return home to their old servile positions. Shangane (Tsonga) workers in particular were prepared to stay on the mines for two or three years, rather than trying to return home for the annual agricultural season like many other workers.

Boers and Africans who lived around the diamond mines competed for agricultural and firewood land or for transport contracts and positions as wagon-drivers. Local Tlhaping usually only worked on the mines long enough to earn the cash to buy ploughs and wagons. In 1874 a trader was selling a hundred ploughs to Tlhaping peasants along the Harts river who were supplying Kimberley with grain. In 1875 he sold two hundred ploughs. By 1876 he was selling one a day. Cash earning promoted the use of European

*Very roughly equivalent to a rise from R 600 to R 1,500 or R 1,800 a month by the early 1990s. Such figures even exceeded wages for manual labour in Britain in the 1870s–80s.

ORIGIN OF CLOSED LABOUR COMPOUNDS

White and black miners at Kimberley came out on strike in 1884, because they were stripped naked and searched in all body openings for hidden diamonds every time they left work. Mine security had become stricter with the growth of monopoly companies, and the Kimberley law courts treated IDB (illicit dia-mond buying) as worse than murder. White miners won better treatment by striking in 1884. But black miners were from 1885 in future restricted to closed compounds — the first 'concentration camps'. Workers were locked up in the new compounds, without their families, for between three and six months, surrounded by metal and wire fencing.

When De Beers introduced the closed compound in 1885, the black miners went on strike against being imprisoned in it. But the company had prepared itself by recruiting fresh workers from interior chiefs, and the strikers were all sacked and replaced within a week.

A worker caught smuggling diamonds Workers who left the closed compounds, after months of internment, were kept naked in solitary confinement — with their hands locked in a sort of boxing glove — until they had excreted all that they had swallowed in the compound. This man appears to have swallowed no less than seven large diamonds, seen on his right glove, and is obviously discomfited by the experience of being caught.

De Beers compound at Kimberley in the 1890s   Note the watch-tower, the wire netting covering vast areas (to stop diamonds being thrown out), the communal bath (right), and the electric lamps to light the compound at night. The city of Kimberley can be seen in the distance. 'Here in the vast oblong compound,' wrote a visiting British historian in 1895,' one sees Zulus from Natal, Fingos, Pondos, Tembus, Basutos, Bechuanas. Gungunhana's subjects from the Portuguese territories, some few Matabili and Makalaka, and plenty of Zambesi boys from the tribes on both sides of that great river.' There were 2,600 workers in the compound at the time from as far north as Lake Tanganyika.

We have few records of what life was like inside the compound. But it was not a prison, as the miners earned relatively good wages. Some earned extra income as barbers, tailors and sellers of cooked meat.

consumer goods, particularly clothing. By the later 1870s traditional clothing was rare among the southern Tswana, and shields and spears were no longer in use.

Claim amalgamation and rise of mining capitalists As mining went deeper from yellow into blue ground at Kimberley, the costs and dangers of mining increased but so did the quantity of diamonds. Capital was needed for elevator cars on wires to carry men down to each claim and to carry earth back upwards to the edge of the mine for sifting. Capital was needed for steam-engine pumps to stop claims being flooded by underground water seepage or rainfall, and claims had to be worked together to stop them falling in on each other. Claim-holders without capital suffered from the falling price of diamonds after 1875, which was a result of both economic depression and over-production. So amalgamation between claim-holdings became necessary for both financial and technical reasons. In 1874 the one-owner-two-claims restriction was lifted so that a 'digger' could own up to ten claims. By 1877 the Kimberley mine had been amalgamated into 408 claim-holdings, up to seventy metres deep and employing three to four thousand labourers at a time in the 'big hole'. The small 'digger' had been eliminated, and the population of Kimberley township had been reduced from 30,000 to 17,000.

Two types of businessman moved in to take control of diamond mining. One type was the diamond buyer in the town, who set prices given to claim-owners and sold the stones overseas. The most famous of these diamond buyers was 'Barney' Barnato, who first made his fortune and trading capital from IDB. The other type of businessman was the pumping contractor at the mine, who owned a steam pump and hired out his services to claim-holders. The most famous of these pumping contractors was Cecil Rhodes, who probably first made his fortune by bribing officials to give pumping contracts. Both these types of businessmen, with technical knowledge and ready capital behind them, were in a good position to move in and take over unsuccessful claim-holders.

Small claim-holders who went bankrupt during the 1873-79 depression were doing so at the very same time as more European capital was beginning to come into Africa through the banks to seek profitable investment. Claims were amalgamated into companies with British, French or German capital and shareholders overseas. Cecil Rhodes founded his De Beers Ltd in 1880 after amalgamating his claims with those of other major claim-holders in the De Beers mine.

Competition became fierce between companies on the diamond fields during 1882-87, driving the price of diamonds down as they over-produced for the limited demand of the world market. Rhodes and other capitalists like Barnato began to realize that the only way to keep diamond prices high was for a monopoly of producers to control the market — keeping diamonds rare enough to be valuable but plentiful enough to be profitable. By 1885 the original 3,588 claims of the four mines around Kimberley had been reduced to 98. By 1888 Rhodes and Barnato, heading the two largest companies, were battling for control of the largest mine — the Kimberley 'big hole', which now had deep underground shafts. Rhodes' De Beers Ltd won with the capital support of the great European banking house of Rothschild. By 1890 complete monopoly was achieved over the four mines when Barnato combined his interests with Rhodes in a company called *De Beers Consolidated Mines*. The new company reigned supreme, while defeated diamond company owners like J. B. Robinson moved into the new Witwatersrand gold fields.

White workers as a 'labour aristocracy'
Meanwhile white 'diggers' either left or became workers employed by the mine companies. Many became skilled technicians as mining became more technical with machinery and underground shafts. They maintained their tradition of militancy in demanding high wages and a promotion bar to prevent Africans rising to join them as technicians or foremen over unskilled workers. White workers were therefore an aristocracy of labour maintained in their privileged position by a job colour-bar.

4 The South African Republic 1868-77

President Pretorius' 1868 proclamation of the Transvaal's borders, from the Kalahari to the ocean and beyond the Limpopo, mapped out the territorial ambitions of the South African

Republic for the rest of the 19th century. The republic had in fact barely recovered from civil war, and its government was small and inefficient, its sovereignty limited to the southern and western half of the Transvaal area. To the north the Venda chiefdoms and to the east the Pedi and Swazi kingdoms were independent of any Boer control, while to the west scattered Tswana chiefdoms resisted Transvaal claims to authority.

To the south a dispute between the Transvaal and the Orange Free State over land south of the upper Vaal (Lekwa) was settled in the Transvaal's favour by the arbitration of Keate, the lieutenant-governor of Natal (1870). But Keate's arbitration of the lower Vaal dispute of the following year was not so favourable: the southern part of the 'Keate line' cut the Transvaal off from the diamond fields by a large margin. The protests of his burghers forced Marthinus Pretorius to resign, and the new president Thomas Burgers (1872-77) simply refused to accept the 'Keate line' at all. (For map see p. 163.)

Attempts to modernize under Burgers The Transvaal *volksraad* chose Burgers, a modern-minded clergyman of the NGK church in the Cape, in the hope that he would improve the finances and administration of the state. Under Marthinus Pretorius there had been virtually no central administration at Pretoria, and no effective means of national taxation. The local officials, consisting of full-time *landdrosts* and part-time *veld-kornets,* had usually been paid with state land given them as farms. Government debts to foreign trading companies and bankers had also been paid with land. Even the national paper currency introduced in 1865 was backed by the security of state farms, rather than by gold or silver bank deposits as in European states. Pretorius' government had suffered from two attempts to set up a national bank by foreign businessmen – one a Netherlander in 1853 and the other a Scotsman in 1865. Both attempts failed and left large areas of state land in the hands of foreign creditors. The Transvaal rapidly became short of state land, and could only increase its land holdings through war. But war increased government debts because firearms and ammunition had to be imported and paid for by the state, and the burghers who fought had also to be rewarded with captured land.

Burgers' development schemes The discovery of gold opened up the possibility of the Transvaal becoming a modern state along European lines. Officials could now be paid in cash from state taxes on gold production. President Burgers drew up grandiose plans for railways, telegraphs and schools, and set off for Europe to raise development loans from European banks. But Burgers arrived in Europe in 1875, in the middle of economic depression when gold sales had slumped, and failed to raise the loans. Instead he had to resort to a loan on unfavourable terms from the Cape Commercial Bank.

Transvaal tax collection became more efficient at the same time as economic depression made burghers less able to pay in cash. Widespread tax defaulting led to state confiscation of farms and to burghers abandoning farms which gave them no income and could not be sold for cash. Richer burghers such as the Kruger and Joubert families were able to buy up large amounts of land very cheaply. On the other hand the Transvaal government approached bankruptcy as its expenditure exceeded its income while its land sales and land security for foreign bank loans brought in so little cash.

The rise of a class of large landowners among the Boers helped intensify the land hunger and warlike nature of the South African Republic. *Landdrosts* and *veldkornets* had the first choice of land acquired in war and the pick of old farms which came up for sale or were confiscated by the state. There was land hunger, but there was hardly a land shortage in the Transvaal as under 35,000 whites had up to 10 million hectares to divide between themselves. Land had little value in cash terms before the 1880s, but it gave a burgher prestige as the owner of cattle and chief of people who lived on it. Burghers loaned out their cattle to poorer landless burghers to herd on much the same *mafisa* relationship as African chiefs. The typical Transvaal burgher owned a number of farms, all unfenced and often many kilometres apart. The burgher and his family would move from farm to farm with the seasons, taking cattle or sheep to fresh pastures and cultivating little else besides vegetables or fruit and tobacco, while African peasants farmed the land for grain crops paid to the landowner as rent. Meanwhile landless burghers, or those who wanted more and better land, would press for commando service in war for the reward of new farms.

Westward and northward expansion The Transvaal tried to continue westward expansion by claiming all Tlhaping, Rolong and Kora country as its own in 1874, but the British insisted on the 'Keate line' and wrote friendly letters to the threatened chiefs. British policy, however, changed when president Burgers visited London in 1875 and was welcomed as an ally. The Transvaal was again allowed a free hand with its African neighbours and annexed Tlhaping country as far west as the Harts river without interference (1875).

Further north the Transvaal government did not stop the migration through Tswana country of Boer 'thirstland trekkers' bound for Herero country in Namibia (1876-77). These trekkers were landless burghers from the Rustenburg district who had followed the old trekboer life of hunting and herding which was fast disappearing in the Transvaal as the land passed into private ownership. As members of the 'Dopper' (AGK) church, who held that all necessary wisdom was contained in the Bible, they quarrelled with Burgers' attempt to modernize the Transvaal with secular ideas of development from Europe. Meanwhile the area of the northern Transvaal around the gold mining at Eersteling was allowed to slip out of Boer control once again by 1875, when white miners and prospectors resumed paying tribute to chiefs Mokopane, Mankopane and Mmamobolo.

Eastward expansion Burgers' development plans for a railway linking the gold fields of the eastern Transvaal to Delagoa Bay had to contend with both the Swazi and Pedi kingdoms. The Swazi under Ludvonga (ruled 1865-74) became reluctant allies of the Transvaal, periodically threatened by the visit of Boer commandos to their country, after being disastrously defeated by the Pedi and by lowveld Tsonga during 1869. White prospectors and Transvaal officials tried to exploit this new weakness when seeking mineral concessions and road and railway rights to cross Swaziland to Delagoa Bay in 1871. But only a few Boers already known to the Swazi succeeded in obtaining permission to graze sheep on the highveld, because as a missionary remarked:

'[The Swazi] are suspicious of every stranger, and fancy that he can have no other motive than to obtain their cattle or their land.'

After Mbandzeni (ruled 1874-89) had been installed as king, president Burgers tried to force him to accept a Transvaal 'protectorate' whereby Swaziland would lose sovereignty in foreign affairs. But the Boer commandos sent to the Swazi capital fought among themselves and returned home in disarray. Mbandzeni was still obliged to ally closely with the Transvaal because of a Pedi-Zulu alliance against them both after another Swazi attack on the Pedi in 1874.

Pedi-Boer war The continued independence of the powerful Pedi kingdom was a threat to Transvaal control of its Lydenburg goldfields and of the planned railway. The kingdom had built up its supplies of firearms and had defeated the Swazi allies of the Transvaal. People fled to Sekhukhune for protection from being forced to work on Boer farms supplying the new gold fields. Sekhukhune ignored the Steelpoort river as a boundary and sent his Christian brother Dinkoanyane to settle near Lydenburg in 1873. So when Pedi forces threatened the villages of Mac-Mac and Lydenburg in 1876, the Transvaal declared war.

A joint Boer and Swazi army attacked and captured Dinkoanyane's mountain fortress, and advanced on Sekhukhune's capital in the

153

Leulu mountains. When it came under heavy fire from well-defended Pedi gunmen, and news reached the Boers of their farms being attacked and burnt by other Pedi forces, the army broke up and retreated home (August 1876). The victorious Sekhukhune was only forced to make peace in February 1877 by a few determined Boers, camped on his frontier, who threatened to burn down the Pedi harvest.

5 White Confederation and Transvaal Annexation (1868-77)

British government policy British officials considered annexing the goldfields or the Boer republics. But the Liberal party government in Britain of 1868-74 (under Gladstone as prime minister) was committed to reducing the responsibility of the 'imperial factor' for colonies. It amalgamated Basutoland into Cape Colony in 1871, and only annexed Griqualand-West in the expectation that Cape Colony would take it over almost immediately. Cape Colony itself was given 'responsible' government in 1872, which meant that in future ministers drawn from and answerable to parliament were in charge of the executive. The Liberals ended previous British reliance on the Boer republics to police the African states beyond British colonial frontiers. Friendly relations were opened up with kingdoms and chiefdoms supplying labour or hunting produce to British markets. The trade and labour supply route to the north was secured for free trade by the 'Keate line' of 1871. The ban on selling firearms and ammunition to Africans, introduced in 1852-54, was relaxed. In the four and a half years before 1875, up to 400,000 firearms are believed to have been paid out or sold to Africans on the diamond fields.

The Conservatives under Disraeli, who replaced the Liberals as the British government between 1874 and 1880, were less reluctant colonialists than the Liberals. They pressed the idea of a *South African confederation* of white states, including the Boer republics but dominated by Cape Colony, to secure British trade and labour supplies in the sub-continent. The Liberal policy of securing British interests by friendship with African states was dropped. Even the lieutenant-governor of Griqualand-West was berated for daring to criticize white people, the Transvaal Boers, in a letter to a black ruler, Montshiwa.

White settler reactions The Conservative government gave the Orange Free State £90,000 compensation for loss of the diamond fields, and welcomed the Transvaal president Burgers in London. But British plans to persuade Burgers into accepting South African confederation were frustrated by the award of Delagoa Bay to Portugal by president MacMahon of France in arbitration of a dispute between Portugal and Britain. Burgers grasped the chance to build a railway to a non-British port which would avoid the Transvaal's previous dependence on Natal and Cape Colony. Tsetse-fly had prevented ox-wagon traffic to the bay, but the MacMahon award would give overseas bankers the legal security to lend capital for building a railway.

Burgers was only partly successful in raising capital in Belgium and elsewhere during his European trip of 1875, and blamed British interference. Meanwhile settler politicians in Cape Colony began to resist the idea of South African confederation, as they also did incorporation of Griqualand-West, for fear of the expense. Only the colony of Natal, dominated by the political influence of the Shepstone family and by the economic interests of large land-owning companies, shared the Conservative enthusiasm for South African confederation. Durban was the Transvaal's nearest port; it was threatened by the proposed Delagoa Bay railway. On the other hand Natal stood to gain from building its own railway to the Transvaal, as long as the railway was not cut off by the independent Zulu kingdom.

Settler delegates at a conference in London in early 1876 made it clear that a confederation of white states could only be achieved by first disarming all black states. This was the lesson that settlers drew from the Langalibalele affair of 1873-74 in Natal.

Langalibalele (1818-89) was the chief of Hlubi who were settled in the Drakensberg foothills. His people, who acquired many firearms by working at Kimberley, came to be seen as a threat to the neighbouring white farms. They were ordered to surrender their arms by the Natal government in 1873, but refused, and fled towards Basutoland for refuge. Natal troops waylaid them at the top of a Drakensberg pass (near Giant's Castle), and brought Langalibalele back in chains. Shepstone had him tried in a special court for murder, treason and rebellion, and sentenced him to detention for life on Robben Island. Bishop Colenso, the great champion of African interests in Natal, protested and sailed to London to publicize the injustice. However, the notoriety of the case convinced the Conservative government in Britain that it was necessary to disarm blacks in southern Africa — before confederation of white states could be successful.

Transvaal becomes a British colony The defeat and bankruptcy of the Transvaal government by the Pedi kingdom gave the British their chance to achieve the first step towards confederation by annexing the Transvaal. British 'diggers' in the Lydenburg gold mines, threatened by the Pedi, petitioned for British annexation, while the Cape Commercial Bank sought to recover its loans to the Transvaal government. The British government drew up laws enabling it to annex the Transvaal, and handed the problem to Theophilus Shepstone, who was appointed special commissioner to annex the Transvaal, and Bartle Frere, the new high commissioner in Capetown (1877-80).

Shepstone relied on the threat of Zulu invasion in support of the Pedi to persuade the Transvaalers to accept British annexation. The Zulu were particularly incensed over the fact that Boers were moving in to occupy the Blood river territory, claimed by the Transvaal under an 1861 treaty (see p. 163). In January 1877 Shepstone arrived in the Transvaal with twenty-four mounted policemen and eight officials, and was welcomed by the bankrupt officials and English-speaking townsmen of Pretoria. In April the Transvaal was declared a British colony under Shepstone as administrator (1877-79). Burgers retired to the Cape, while Kruger, Joubert and Marthinus Pretorius retired to their farms.

6 British Conquest and Disarmament of African States 1877-86

With the Transvaal under British rule, the British 'imperial factor' proceeded with the task of black disarmament that must precede white confederation. The Pedi kingdom had to be conquered for the Transvaal. Frontier chiefdoms around Griqualand-West and the Transkei had to be subdued before Cape Colony would agree to annex the territories. The British found their opportunity during the drought of 1876-79 when chiefdoms and colonists began to compete violently for pasture and water supplies. Finally there were the problems of how the most powerful kingdoms in southern Africa, the Zulu under Cetshwayo (ruled 1872-84) and the Sotho under Letsie I (1870-91), were to fit into the proposed confederation.

Pedi military revival Sekhukhune was prepared to make peace with the British, but not to surrender his sovereignty over chiefdoms previously subject to the Transvaal. When the British began settling English-speaking white farmers along the Steelpoort border, Pedi troops expelled them with Boer encouragement. A British force invaded the Pedi kingdom in October 1878, but soon retreated because of drought and horse-sickness, and the offensive could not be resumed until after the Anglo-Zulu war.

Griqua-Tlhaping rising Meanwhile the Griqualand-West colonial government had deprived Africans of their land by a court decision of 1876, which awarded much land to Boers from the Orange Free State. As an observer remarked, the court very much favoured 'Boer squatters on land, i.e. that if a white man squats on land it belongs to him, but if a native lives on land, even on which his forefathers before him have lived, he has no rights to that land.' The Griqua were deprived of their former country and became landless workers on white farms. The Tlhaping of Jantjie were expelled from the colony, and the Tlhaping of Botlhasitse were threatened by British troops at the beginning of 1878.

This was the signal for Griqua, Tlhaping and Khoisan at Danielskuil within the colony to rise and attack white farms. Attacks on white settlers became widespread inside and outside the colony, and whites north of the colony fled to Kuruman mission station for protection. A British force relieved them and attacked the Tlhaping bandits of Jantjie and Botlhasitse, who retreated elsewhere and then surrendered.

The Cape eastern frontier became the responsibility of the new Cape Colony government rather than the 'imperial factor' after 1872. The Cape Colony placed diplomatic agents in all the Transkei states except Pondoland to act as magistrates and advisers, gradually assuming powers of administration for the Cape Colony. 'Government is a wolf,' complained chief Manthanzima of the emigrant

British artist's impression of a Zulu army charge, 1879 Note the use of firearms as well as traditional weapons.

Thembu. 'One by one my rights are stolen from me in the dark.'

A 9th Cape-Nguni war (1877-78) was sparked off by the governor of Cape Colony summoning the Transkei chief Sarili to complain of his Gcaleka-Xhosa ill-treating Mfengu who were friendly to the colony. Sarili, mindful of his own father's treacherous murder by the British in similar circumstances (1835), refused to cross the Kei. The Cape therefore sent its army across the Kei, which soon retreated in disarray before Xhosa and

Thembu resistance. Imperial troops were then sent in to rescue the Cape forces and enforced disarmament on the Transkei states (except for Pondoland). The Ngqika-Xhosa chief Sandile who rebelled in the Ciskei was hunted down and killed despite trying to surrender.

Anglo-Zulu war Bartle Frere as high commissioner and Shepstone as its administrator believed that the Zulu rather than the Pedi were the strongest military challenge to the Transvaal. The drought had driven Zulu cattle to pasture on the Buffels and Pongola river headwaters claimed by the Transvaal, and that could be the start of a deeper invasion. Because the Transvaal was the key to South African confederation, the supposed Zulu threat to the Transvaal came to be seen as

Britain's biggest problem in southern Africa. It was even feared that white confederation might produce its own reaction in a black confederation led by Cetshwayo. In fact, though Cetshwayo was in friendly contact with the Pedi and Sotho kingdoms, there is no evidence that they considered invading the white colonies.

The British invaded Zululand from Natal in January 1879, with Transvaal and Swazi forces standing guard in the north. At the battle of Isandhlwana the British army was decisively defeated later in that same month. When reinforcements arrived from overseas the British invaded Zululand once again in July 1879. Meanwhile Cetshwayo had not attempted to invade Natal but had been fighting a defensive campaign against remain-

Cetshwayo, Zulu king (1872-84), in exile at Capetown.

ing British troops. Zulu troops, often starving from the drought and famine, could not be maintained in the field in any large numbers. The British general Chelmsford forced a decisive battle on the Zulu before his replacement, General Wolseley, could take command. Chelmsford marched on Ulundi, the Zulu capital, captured it and forced Cetshwayo to flee northwards.

Wolseley arrived in Zululand in August 1879 and offered peace to the Zulu if they laid down their arms. The offer was accepted gladly by a starving people anxious to plant their crops. Cetshwayo was captured and exiled to Capetown. Wolseley then followed the advice of the Shepstone family in dismembering the Zulu kingdom into thirteen chiefdoms, independent from each other and without a monarchy to unite them. Three of the thirteen chiefdoms were in effect treaty-states, being placed under proven British allies (including John Dunn) as rulers, and Natal colonial officials attempted to supervise the thirteen states along Transkei lines.

Conquest of the Pedi Wolseley arrived in Pretoria in September 1879 and ordered Sekhukhune to surrender his sovereignty to the Transvaal colony. When the Pedi refused, Wolseley despatched a British expedition consisting mostly of Swazi soldiers which quickly overwhelmed the Pedi capital at the end of November. Sekhukhune was captured and led captive into Pretoria.

Confederation fails The crippling expense of the Anglo-Zulu war killed the idea of white confederation and nipped in the bud the new imperialism of Disraeli's Conservatives. Confederation, after all, had been an imperial plan to get the white states to carry the costs of colonialism. Yet it had only succeeded in increasing the costs incurred by the imperial government. The Conservative government in Britain was swept out of office by Gladstone's Liberals in 1880 elections, on the promises of reducing expenditure and restoring peace and justice abroad. But imperialist fervour did not die so quickly in Cape Colony. Ngqika-Xhosa territory in the Ciskei

Capture of Sekhukhune's stronghold by British and Swazi troops.

was sold off as white farms. Cape military forces were expanded to enforce total disarmament on the Transkei, from which the treaty-states of Griqualand-East and Fingoland were annexed to Cape Colony in 1879.

Basutoland Gun war Cape rule resulted in the so-called Moorosi rebellion of 1878-79 in south-west Basutoland. The local magistrate arrested a son of the aged Moorosi, chief of the Phuti, in 1878. The Phuti then sacked the magistrate's camp and freed prisoners. During 1879 the Phuti were attacked by Cape troops, who finally stormed Moorosi's mountain and found him dead with a bullet in his neck.

Cape authorities then doubled taxes in Basutoland to recoup the costs of the Moorosi war, and decided to enforce disarmament strictly on the mostly heavily armed black nation in southern Africa. In addition the Quthing district of Basutoland, Moorosi's former country, was to be opened to white settlement. The deadline for disarmament was set for the end of May 1880. But the only rulers to obey the order were Letsie the 'paramount chief' and Jonathan Molapo, who believed that collaboration was to the best advantage of the baSotho. (Letsie had petitioned for, and been refused, Sotho representation in the Cape parliament.) Their people were then attacked by the people of other chiefs, including those of Lerotholi, Masopha, Joel Molapo, and Lesoana.

Cape troops, supported by Jonathan while Letsie hung back, invaded Basutoland to crush the resistance in September 1880. Hampered by torrential rains which broke the drought, the Cape government spent £4.8 million on the 'Gun war', but failed to subdue or disarm the majority of baSotho. The only major battle, at Kalabani, was lost by Cape forces to Lerotholi. Peace returned in April 1881 after the new high commissioner Hercules Robinson (1881-89) intervened on behalf of the imperial government in a war between two groups of British subjects. Instead of disarmament there was to be a tax of £1 on every gun, and there was to be no white settlement. Basutoland returned uneasily to Cape rule; the victors saw no reason to pay tax or to obey the magistrates of the vanquished.

Transkei rebellion Armed resistance to Cape rule spread to parts of the Transkei. Having disarmed their friends first in Fingoland and Emigrant Tembuland, the Cape government then tried to disarm the rest of the Transkei, and threatened annexation and white settlement. Sotho and Tlokoa in Griqualand-East rose against Cape rule at the end of September 1880. They were followed by emigrant Thembu and Mpondomise chiefdoms, which sank previous rivalries to form a united resistance. But the Transkei 'rebellion' did not

spread to the Gcaleka-Xhosa so decisively defeated in 1878 or to independent Pondoland. By April 1881 the 'rebellion' was over at a cost of £1.25 million to the Cape Colony.

Zulu civil war Most of the thirteen new

Moorosi, Phuti chief, leader of the 1878-79 rebellion against the rule of Letsie and Cape Colony.

Letsie, paramount chief or king of Basutoland (ruled 1870-91)

159

Zulu chiefs appointed by the British allowed previous chiefs to continue in power, but three — Zibhedhu, John Dunn and Hamu — insisted on absolute control over their chiefdoms. Royalists seeking the restoration of Cetshwayo began to organize opposition to these three chiefs, reviving the name of Cetshwayo's party, uSuthu, for their party.

The new Liberal government in Britain entertained Cetshwayo in London and released him to return home in 1883. But the colonial authorities of Natal arranged that only central Zululand around Ulundi should be under Cetshwayo; the north was to be independent under Zibhedhu, and the south was to be attached to Natal as the Zulu Native Reserve. On hearing this, the uSuthu attacked Zibhedhu in March 1883, but were defeated and a full civil war erupted.

Zibhedhu burnt down Ulundi and killed the royal indunas in a surprise attack. Cetshwayo died in early 1884, perhaps murdered, and was succeeded by his son Dinizulu. USuthu leaders then recruited Transvaal Boers for a successful counter-attack on Zibhedhu, after which the Boers demanded Zibhedhu's country as payment and the uSuthu appealed to the British to intervene. The British allowed the Boers to declare Zibhedhu's country as the 'New Republic' in 1886. In 1887 the British annexed uSuthu country as the new colony of 'Zululand', and incorporated it into Natal ten years later.

Basutoland becomes a separate colony The Cape government was hard pressed to maintain the peace of 1882 in Basutoland, as people refused to register their firearms and pay tax on them. General 'Chinese' Gordon, a famous British mercenary (later to die in Egyptian service at Khartoum) was given the task of pacifying Basutoland. He resigned after his first brief visit. Civil war erupted between the brothers Jonathan and Joel Molapo, while Masopha led passive resistance to colonial rule from his village near Thaba Bosiu.

Eventually the Cape government persuaded the British imperial government to take over Basutoland. Letsie and Lerotholi petitioned for a British protectorate; Joel Molapo and Masopha, impressed no doubt by the Warren expedition in Bechuanaland (see p. 165), accepted British rule without protest when it was announced in 1884. Basutoland became a separate British colony, often referred to as a 'protectorate' because of the nature of its colonization by request and not by conquest.

Transkei annexation Cape Colony was happy to lose largely barren Basutoland but hankered after the more fertile Transkei. In the words of a young Cape politician named Cecil Rhodes, what the colony needed was more land for more settlers, not more 'natives' to be expensively administered. So Gcalekaland and Tembuland were annexed to the Cape Colony in 1885 to bring its border as far as the Umtata river, leaving only Pondoland independent. The Mpondo kingdom had itself split into two paramountcies on the death of Faku in 1868: Faku's successors Mqikela (ruled 1868-86) and Sigcawu (ruled 1887-1905) effectively ruled only the eastern Mpondo. Cape Colony became increasingly involved in Pondoland politics in the 1880s because the British feared German or Russian support for the western Mpondo, who resisted the rule of the eastern kingship recognized by the British.

7 Transvaal Nationalism and Imperialism (1877-86)

Shepstone as first British administrator of the Transvaal (1877-79) put Transvaal government finances under the charge of a representative of the Cape Commercial Bank, the government's main creditor. The representative, J. C. A. Henderson, also set up a private land company buying farms cheap and selling them dear. The Cape Commercial Bank itself went bankrupt in 1881, and paid off some of its creditors by selling Transvaal state farms held as security for loans.

Afrikaner nationalism had its roots in resentment against British annexation of the Transvaal among Dutch-speaking white settlers in both the republics and Cape Colony. As one of their leaders put it, 'The annexation of the

AFRIKAANS CULTURE

Stephanus du Toit (died 1911)

Afrikaner cultural nationalism was based on developing a common language, a common religion, and a common history. Language and history were developed together in Stephanus du Toit's pioneer *Geskiedenis van Ons Land in die Taal van Ons Volk* (History of Our Land in the Dialect of Our People), published in 1877. 'Weep Afrikaners!' wrote du Toit in a typical passage from his book, '— Here lie your flesh and blood! — Martyred in the cruellest fashion!'

Previously half-forgotten events were given pride of place in the new Afrikaans history — the Dutch, German and French Calvinist roots of the nation; resistance to early British rule; and above all what was now called the *Groot Trek* ('great haul'), when people now honoured as *Voortrekkers* trekked to freedom in the interior. One of the survivors, Anna Steenkamp, published her memoirs on the trek (though ironically written in English). 'Dingaan's Day', the anniversary of the Blood river battle on December 16th, became the central national ceremony of the Afrikaner people. But Afrikaner nationalism was also inspired from overseas by nationalist and religious developments in Germany and the Netherlands.

Transvaal has filled the [Cape] Africanders, otherwise grovelling in the mud of materialism, with a national glow of sympathy for the brothers across the Vaal.'

Afrikaner nationalism as a cultural movement originated among teachers and ministers of religion in the south-western Cape Colony. Its leading figure was Stephanus du Toit, who took over the running of the magazine *Die Afrikaanse Patriot* in 1878, which he used for developing Afrikaans consciousness in language and history. Afrikaans religion was strengthened by the anti-liberal revival of Calvinism imported from the Netherlands. Burgers, who had accepted liberal theology, had led the Transvaal into disaster. Paul Kruger who rejected all liberalism now put himself forward as the 'Moses' who would lead his people to freedom.

Afrikaner nationalism as a political movement originated among landowners in the south-western Cape, organized by Jan Hofmeyr into the *Boeren Beschermings Vereeniging* (farmers' protection association) of 1878 to fight new taxes on wine exports by the Cape government. The *Afrikaner Bond* was then founded in 1880 to unite the cultural and political movements in one organization. The Bond, based in the Cape but with members as far north as the Transvaal, where Joubert was its local chairman, looked forward to a united South Africa, independent of Britain but protected from other European powers by the British navy.

1st Anglo-Boer war The victory in the British parliament of Gladstone's Liberals in April 1880 gave Transvaal Boers the hope that annexation would be reversed. Kruger and Joubert toured Cape Colony and helped defeat British plans for confederation presented to the Cape parliament in June. But as the British government then made no move to disannex the Transvaal, Kruger and Joubert with Marthinus Pretorius decided to raise armed rebellion — timed for the sacred national day of Blood river, December 16th. While many Boers gathered at Paardekraal (later Krugersdorp) to declare their independence, other Boers fired the first shots at Potchefstroom. British reinforcements from Natal were blocked by Boer forces in a Drakensberg pass. The British reinforcements were then disastrously defeated on the peak of Majuba mountain when trying to skirt the pass by a night march (February 1881).

Regained Transvaal independence The British, who had only 3,500 imperial troops in southern Africa, feared that continued war in the Transvaal would lead to Afrikaner rebellion in the Cape. The Transvaal's independence was therefore recognized, subject to the *Pretoria Convention* of August 1881. The convention conceded internal sovereignty to the Transvaal under a triumvirate of Pretorius, Kruger and Joubert (1881-83), but reserved powers of 'suzerainty' — meaning control of foreign relations with both European and African powers — for the British. Africans in the Rustenburg district then complained that the British had betrayed black Transvaalers who had loyally supported them against the Boers.

The Transvaal triumvirate chafed under the terms of the Pretoria Convention and sought complete independence. The Transvaal economy was strengthened by the world trade boom and the opening of the important Barberton goldfields in the eastern Transvaal. The Transvaal developed its own nationalism, and indeed its own imperialism beyond its borders. Afrikaner nationalism split up into separate colonial and republican movements. The Afrikaner Bond became a Cape parliamentary political party. Stephanus du Toit migrated north, becoming the Transvaal's first director of education and associating himself politically with Joubert.

Kruger was elected president of the republic in 1883 over Joubert as commandant-general. Kruger consolidated his power by negotiating fuller independence from the British by the *London Convention* of early 1884, which recognized the 'South African Republic' under its own president. The British resident commissioner at Pretoria who had overseen government affairs since 1881 was withdrawn. British 'suzerainty' over foreign relations was allowed to lapse, though not formally cancelled.

Land speculation and state monopolies Speculation in the buying of land by foreign capitalists, in the hope of finding precious minerals, began to boom in the early 1880s. Transvaal officials from the president downwards used their official positions to acquire farms and founded land companies to profit from land speculation. Fortunes were won and lost. Johannes Rissik as surveyor-general in charge of demarcating farms and young Louis Botha as a *veld-kornet* were among those who made their fortunes. But other Boer farm-owners were bankrupted in unwise or unfair land deals, and joined the ranks of landless *bywoners* (white squatters) living insecurely on the land of richer Boers.

The Transvaal government sold state monopoly concessions to private individuals and companies, which gave them exclusive rights to supply goods and services — such as 'the sole right to manufacture liquor from grain, potatoes, and other products growable in the Transvaal, excepting fruit trees and grapes, and the right to sell in bulk and bottle free of licence.' These monopolies enabled the government to tax the rising prosperity of the Transvaal without risking its own capital. But concessions were usually granted to friends of officials rather than skilled managers, and then were sold from hand to hand for speculative profit. The liquor monopoly concession, for example, was first granted to a friend of Kruger, who then sold it to a company which opened a distillery in 1883 on Hatherley farm outside Pretoria. The company was named *Die Eerste Fabrieke,* i.e. 'the first manufacturing' company in the Transvaal.

Renewed territorial expansion The Pretoria Convention of 1881 limited the Transvaal to generous borders. The Limpopo was recognized as the northern border, despite the effective independence of the Soutpansberg under African rule. Swaziland lost the Nkomati lowveld, necessary for a Transvaal railway to Delagoa Bay. The British rejected suggestions of a Pedi 'protectorate' and of a neutral zone between the Transvaal and Zululand, and included Pedi country and the Blood river territory in the Transvaal. The 'Keate line' in the south-west was finally abandoned in favour of a new 'Moysey line' further west.

Joubert as commandant-general made the conquest of African peoples within proclaimed Transvaal borders into his life's work. He first turned his attention to the Pedi, where the British had deposed Sekhukhune in 1879 to replace him by his brother Mampuru as 'paramount chief'. When Sekhukhune was allowed home he was killed by Mampuru in

TRANSVAAL BORDERS 1870s-80s

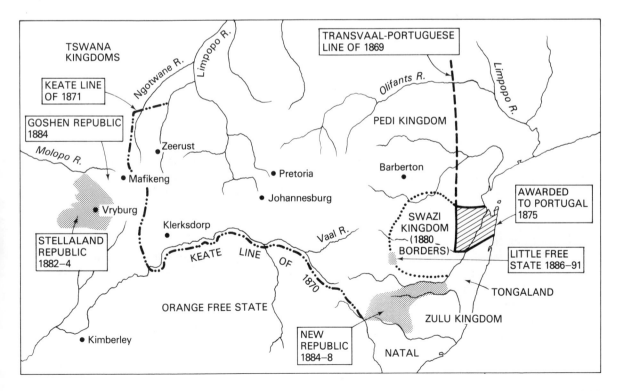

1882. Joubert then appointed Sekhukhune's son as Sekhukhune II, and Mampuru fled south to safety with Njabele the son of Mabhogo, the ambitious and independent chief of the Ndzundza. Joubert attacked with a force of two thousand Boers and defeated Njabele by dynamiting his followers out of their cave refuge after a siege of eight months (1883). The Ndzundza were divided up and given to Boer farms as 'apprentice' labour.

Mbandzeni's early concessions in Swaziland Joubert tried to increase Boer power in Swaziland by diplomatic rather than military means, since it lay outside the Transvaal's proclaimed borders. King Mbandzeni saw friendship with the Transvaal as a method of decreasing the power and influence of the former regents, led by Sandlane Zwane, who objected to concessions of grazing land given to Transvaal sheep-farmers in 1877 and 1881. But Mbandzeni ignored Pretoria Convention borders and attempted to tax gold miners in the Barberton goldfields in 1883, and claimed the right to grant mineral concessions inside Transvaal territory. Gold was not discovered within undisputed Swazi territory until 1884, when it was found by William Pigg and the Forbes brothers on the mountain peak and gold reef which still bear their names.

The 1884 London Convention gave the South African Republic a more or less free hand in Swaziland. Meanwhile Mbandzeni began to ignore the advice of his *libandla* (general council) in granting concessions to whites. Boer officials pressed him to grant a bewildering variety of land leases, which the officials then gave to their own supporters. Mbandzeni was also faced with increasing numbers of non-Boer whites who came to seek mining concessions.

After border clashes and further disputes with whites, Mbandzeni acquired a legal agent for dealing with white concessionaries — young Theophilus Shepstone, better known as 'Offy', the nearly bankrupt son of old Theophilus Shepstone. Offy's appointment was confirmed by the Swazi *libandla* in early 1887.

164

8 Britain Secures the Road to Central Africa 1877-86

The crushing of the Griqua-Tlhaping rising of 1877-78 weakened the most southerly Tswana states. People dispersed from the villages in which chiefs had tried to keep them. They settled down as peasant producers or firewood gatherers for the Kimberley market, became wagoners on the road to the north, or went to work for whites. Meanwhile whites settled on the land amongst them to be able to claim farms when Transvaal or British rule was extended to the area.

British plans for Bechuanaland British interest in extending power and influence as far north as the Zambezi was stimulated by the labour needs of Kimberley. An official labour recruiter travelled as far north as the Ndebele kingdom in search of labour during 1876-77. He found rulers unwilling to send men so long as war was threatened with Boers and white adventures in search of profit, and with other African states. The acting administrator of Griqualand-West therefore concluded that 'the surest means of securing an abundant supply of labour' would be a 'policy of assuming jurisdiction' over areas along the missionaries' road to the north. The idea of a 'protectorate' as far north as the Zambezi was taken up by the high commissioner Bartle Frere with the advice of John Mackenzie, an influential missionary pressing for an alliance between British imperialism and northern Tswana states. A protectorate would be supervized by British 'frontier agents', along the lines of the American Indian territories of the USA or of British India, until the area could be annexed for white settlement.

Cis-Molopo Bechuanaland The first stage towards such a protectorate was to set up a treaty-state system south of the Molopo river. British 'border police' were posted to Kuruman in 1878, and British agents were attached to Mankurwane (ruled 1869-92) as the most powerful Tlhaping chief and Montshiwa as the most powerful Rolong chief in 1879. But the border police were withdrawn after the Pretoria Convention of 1881. So the treaty-state system only survived unofficially with the two agents staying on as private advisers to Mankurwane and Montshiwa.

The Transvaal countered the British by setting up their own treaty-states in competition with Mankurwane and Montshiwa. Both Mankurwane and Montshiwa were attacked and defeated at the end of 1882 by Boer volunteers, while the British denied them the right to recruit counter-volunteers from Kimberley. The republic of 'Stellaland', named after a passing comet in the sky, was founded next to Mankurwane's country by Boer volunteers fighting for the Kora chief Massouw and for the Tlhaping chief Botlha-sitse. Another republic, given the biblical name of 'Goshen', was founded next to Montshiwa's country by Boer volunteers fighting for the Rolong chief Moswete. Stellaland rapidly expanded with the immigration of new whites to settle in its capital of Vryburg ('free-town') and to claim farms almost as far west as Kuruman. Goshen dwindled to little more than its small capital, Rooigrond, as Montshiwa recaptured the area.

Montshiwa recruited support from the Ngwaketse, Kwena, Kgatla and Ngwato states north of the Molopo, most of which had previously allied together against the Transvaal in 1852. Mackenzie campaigned in Britain for a protectorate over cis-Molopo Bechuanaland, recruiting the politician Joseph Chamberlain to his cause. Meanwhile Cecil Rhodes, the Kimberley millionaire now a Cape parliamentarian, was developing his own ideas for colonizing Bechuanaland as the 'Suez Canal' to open up central Africa.

The London Convention of 1884, which moved the Transvaal border further west, encouraged the Transvaal to complete the conquest of Mankurwane's and Montshiwa's lands as a prelude to annexing the two puppet republics. Mankurwane recruited black and white mercenaries, including bandits and British policemen, to fight his second war with Stellaland. The British government responded by declaring a British protectorate south of the Molopo in April 1884, and appointed Mackenzie as its deputy commissioner. He was told to recognize Stellaland farm titles, but to drive the Goshenites back into the Transvaal. Mackenzie raised the British flag at Vryburg, shouting 'God send us a united, peaceful and prosperous South Africa', but was replaced by Cecil Rhodes in August. Rhodes pacified the Stellalanders by promising all they wanted, but failed to stop the Goshenite war with Montshiwa and his allies. Montshiwa surrendered at the end of that month to Transvaal forces.

The British government responded to the April 1884 declaration of a German protectorate over southern Namibia with fears of a German-Boer territorial link-up through Bechuanaland. President Kruger of the Transvaal tried to annex Goshen in September. But British reaction was so angry that he withdrew. The British parliament voted to send a military expedition 'to remove the filibusters from Bechuanaland, to pacificate the territory, to reinstate the natives on their lands'.

Warren expedition Four thousand troops under General Charles Warren arrived in Bechuanaland in January 1885, and the Boer 'filibusters' melted away to become peaceful farmers or crossed into the Transvaal rather than fight. In March 1885 the British announced the extension of their protectorate over Bechuanaland to beyond the Molopo, to the longitude of the German protectorate and a latitude just north of the Limpopo including the Ngwaketse, Kwena and Ngwato states. Warren, who shared Mackenzie's liberal-imperialist ideas, constantly quarrelled with the high commissioner Hercules Robinson, who shared Rhodes' pro-settler views. Eventually Warren was dismissed and his expedition withdrawn in August 1885.

Having failed to persuade Cape Colony to take it over, the British divided their protectorate over Bechuanaland in two by a proclamation of September 30th, 1885. The part south of the Molopo known as *British Bechuanaland* became a separate British colony under the lawyer Sidney Shippard as

165

administrator at Vryburg. The part north of the Molopo known as the *Bechuanaland Protectorate* (later the Republic of Botswana) remained a protectorate also with Shippard as its commissioner.

British Bechuanaland   Shippard set up a land commission in 1886 to establish white farming areas and 'native reserves'. As a result most of the productive land east of Kuruman was alienated for white settlement. Stellaland titles to land were accepted by the British. Former Goshen Boers were able to buy farms along the Molopo cheap from British border policemen, who had been granted them as a reward for their services. A white township known (and incorrectly spelt) as 'Mafeking' was founded around the police camp next to the Rolong capital of Mafikeng. Montshiwa was still threatened by warlike whites, many of them former policemen, and even fled north to the Ngwato kingdom in 1886 before being persuaded to return.

9 Northern Tswana, Ndebele and Lozi States (c. 1869-86)

The 1852 Transvaal war with the Kwena of Sechele brought a number of smaller chiefdoms into the area of south-eastern Botswana from the Transvaal. Besides the Mmanaana-Kgatla of Mosielele and the Hurutshe of Mangope, the other chiefdoms that sought refuge with the Kwena included the Lete under chief Mokgosi (ruled c. 1820-86) and the Tlokwa under Matlapeng (ruled c. 1835-80). Matlapeng fled from the Transvaal after killing a Boer who had attempted to rape his wife.

Sechele, the Kwena king, remained the most powerful Tswana leader from the 1850s till the 1870s. But other northern Tswana states began to challenge his influence, and his subject chiefdoms began to move away into semi-independence. The Ngwato kings Sekgoma and Macheng, and the Ngwaketse king Gaseitsiwe, became strong enough to ignore Sechele's opinions. Mosielele took his Kgatla to Moshupa, and Mokgosi took his Lete to Ramotswa in the 1870s, setting up semi-independent towns in the Kwena-

Ngwaketse frontier zone, to play one power off on the other. Matlapeng withdrew his Tlokwa eastwards. They finally settled at Mosaweng, since called Gaborone, in 1884 during the reign of Matlapeng's son Gaborone (1880-1932).

Linchwe (ruled 1875–1924) of the Kgafela-Kgatla posed the greatest challenge to Sechele. Linchwe's father Kgamanyane had fled from the Transvaal to Kwena territory at Mochudi in 1869-70, after being publicly flogged on Kruger's orders for supplying insufficient labour to Boer farms. Linchwe, on becoming chief, determined to resist both Kwena and Transvaal claims for tribute, as there was no defined border between them. This resulted in sporadic guerrilla warfare between the Kgatla (supported by the Tlokwa) and Kwena from 1875 until 1881, when Montshiwa of the Rolong ended the war by recruiting both sides as his allies against the Goshen Boers.

Khama III finally seized the Ngwato kingship for the second time in 1875 and ruled, with a state church backing his power, until his death in 1923. Khama's first external challenge was the 'Dopper' Boers threatening to force their way across his country to Namibia in 1876-77. The situation was calmed by the British annexation of the Transvaal. But the 1881 Goshen challenge in the south brought Khama into the alliance of Sechele, Linchwe and Gaseitsiwe of the Ngwaketse with Montshiwa.

Bechuanaland Protectorate   Following its declaration by the British in March 1885, General Warren took the news to Gaseitsiwe, Sechele and Khama in their capitals. The news was received well by Gaseitsiwe and Khama, but angrily by Sechele. Khama offered border farms for white settlers of proven Christian character to pay for the costs of protectorate administration. Warren called it a 'magnificent offer'.

Neither British officials or Tswana kings were clear as to what a protectorate meant. But it was seen as a treaty relationship between equal partners. So when the 'magnificent offer' of land, by Gaseitsiwe and Sechele as well as Khama, was turned down by the British government, the kings feared annexation like Montshiwa's country and threatened to fight the British in that event.

The declaration of the Bechuanaland Protectorate opened the way for a stream of 'unsuccessful miners from California and Australia; fugitives from justice in England or other parts of Europe; men of decent birth who had come to grief, and men of low origin who were birds of prey by nature.' Khama was approached by Boer and British adventurers, and by German businessmen, seeking concessions or trying to incite war between the Ngwato and Ndebele kingdoms. 'It must be remembered,' wrote the British high commissioner in 1887, 'that the territory is not British soil. Khama is an independent chief, and he cannot be allowed, while retaining his sovereignty, to put us to the trouble and expense of policing his country. A protectorate involves no such obligations.'

Ndebele kingdom threatened The Ndebele kingdom maintained cordial relations with the Ngwato from the accession of Lobengula in 1870 until 1882, when Ndebele forces raided the Tawana allies of the Ngwato in Ngamiland. Cattle raids on Ngamiland in 1882 and 1884 followed on years of drought and loss of cattle in Ndebele country. The second raid was a disaster because the Ndebele were drawn into the swamps and massacred by Tawana rifle fire. Only 1,500 raiders returned out of an army of 4,000. News of the disaster encouraged white adventurers to plan to seize Lobengula's gold country. 'After witnessing the return of the impi from Lake Ngami, and hearing the reports concerning that campaign,' wrote one such adventurer, 'I am of the opinion that a force of 1,500 mounted men, well armed, could sweep the Matabele power out of the country.'

Lobengula realised that Khama's country was the key to any southern white invasion. So he wrote to Warren in June 1885, 'I have always lived in peace with Khama and shall continue to do so.' He wrote to Khama, saying: 'The white men are not your neighbours. I was your neighbour. You settle everything without consulting me,' (1887). Lobengula also attempted to ally with Lewanika of the Lozi against the threat of white invasion, but was cold-shouldered.

Lozi kingdom strengthened Lewanika (ruled 1878-84 and 1886-1916) seized power in a series of civil wars. He first came to power by deposing his own brother, but was then himself deposed by a rising of southern Lozi chiefs and Mbunda mercenaries. After two years of exile he seized back the kingship. 'Ours is a land of blood,' said the Lozi. 'Kings and chiefs follow one after another like shadows; they are never allowed to grow old.'

Lewanika determined to stay in power by removing his enemies and reforming the state. Families of opponents were drowned, and Mbunda mercenaries were executed or enslaved for supposed witchcraft. Powerful chiefs were reduced to royal servants, i.e. court (*Kuta*) officials dependent on his favour. Lewanika also revived the Luyana tradition of a priest-king only speaking to the people through a prime minister. Commoner chiefs were replaced by royal relatives. His sister became Mulena Mukwae in charge of the southern half of the kingdom, and his son, daughter and nephew became chiefs of the three other major districts. Lewanika restored land on the floodplain to Luyana aristocrats who had lost it under Kololo rule. The Toka and Ila of the south and east were raided for cattle and slaves. New mounds, dams and canals on the floodplain improved the supply of crops and fish for the king and aristocracy to redistribute to their followers or to sell to foreigners. Lewanika encouraged loyalty to a greater Lozi nation by keeping siKololo, known as siLozi, as the national language, and by reviving annual Luyana ceremonies.

10 Origins of German South West Africa 1870-86

Following the defeat of the Orlam-Afrikaners in 1870, the southern Herero under Maherero enjoyed ten years of peace. The grazing of Herero cattle spread southwards to new pastures around Windhoek and Rehoboth, and eastwards around Gobabis. The Orlam-Afrikaners of Windhoek began to look to the Nama nations of the south for an alliance against further loss of land to the Herero. Herero power also threatened the Amraal group of Orlam at Gobabis, where they made their living by taxing or raiding wagon traders on the road to Lake Ngami. Meanwhile Rehoboth was also occupied from the south in 1872 by 'Basters', an Afrikaans-speaking group of coloured people thereafter known as 'Rehobothers'.

Temporary British protectorate over Herero-land Maherero heard of Boer 'thirstland trekkers' from the Transvaal and of Griqua and white diamond prospectors crossing the Orange river to take land in the north. He therefore appealed to the British high commissioner in Capetown for aid. A British agent arrived at Walvis Bay in April 1876, and persuaded Maherero to accept a British 'protectorate' over Hereroland. The Orlam-Afrikaners and Rehobothers also accepted the offer, but no Nama except the Bondelswarts accepted it.

Two years later in 1878 the British annexed the vital port of Walvis Bay to Cape Colony, and proclaimed Hereroland to be a British protectorate. Boer 'thirstland trekkers' therefore migrated northwards, eventually crossing the Kunene river to become Portuguese subjects. But neither the British government nor the Cape parliament were prepared to spend money on protecting the Hereroland protectorate. So the protectorate was withdrawn in 1880 when Hereroland was invaded by Nama forces. German missionaries in Hereroland then protested to the German government at the British leaving them defenceless.

The 2nd Nama-Herero war of 1880-84 grew out of disputes over grazing land and cattle stealing. The Nama were joined by Orlam groups such as the Afrikaners and by the Rehobother 'Basters', but their invasion of Herero country was beaten back. The Orlam-Afrikaners were expelled from Windhoek, and

the Rehobothers sued for peace in 1882 and joined the Herero side against their previous allies. Maherero marched south and held the Rehoboth frontier until he was challenged by a remarkable new Nama leader — Hendrik Witbooi. Witbooi led a daring raid on the Herero capital of Okahandja in 1884, which forced Maherero to return northwards to defend it. After a short, inconclusive battle the two leaders agreed a truce in June 1884.

German colonization Following the 1880 missionary appeals, a German capitalist named Franz Luderitz drew up plans for German colonization of South West Africa. Luderitz began buying up coastland south of Walvis Bay in 1882, in payment for rifles sold to local chiefs. By the end of 1883 he had bought the important harbour of Angra Pequena, which he renamed Luderitz Bay after himself. The German government now took an active role, sending a gunboat to warn off a British gunboat in the bay.

Bismarck, the conservative chancellor of the German empire, was converted to

Hoisting of German flags at Angra Pequena (Luderitz Bay) on August 7th, 1884. German troops fire a volley with their rifles to salute the flags.

colonial adventures overseas after previously pouring scorn on them. He needed an issue to distract liberals and socialists in Germany from his internal policies, and to distract other Europeans, particularly the French, from the threat of German imperialism in Europe. It was Bismarck who hosted the so-called West African Conference at Berlin in late 1884 and early 1885, which divided up the map of Africa between the European powers.

In April 1884 Luderitz informed the British that his territories were now under German protection, and Bismarck authorized Luderitz to extend the protectorate inland. German agents began signing treaties of 'protection' with African rulers, and moved inland to exploit Herero-Nama rivalry during the truce of 1884-85. The Orlam-Afrikaners dismissed a German agent as a mere pedlar. But another German agent, H.E. Goering, was more successful in treaty-making with inland chiefs, arriving at Okahandja in October 1885 to sign a treaty with Maherero.

A few days later the Nama-Herero truce was broken, when Hendrik Witbooi led his people to seek a new home in the north and came to blows with Herero forces over a water-hole. Hendrik Witbooi was heavily defeated, and retired to the mountains to conduct bandit warfare against the Herero for the next five years. Goering failed to persuade Hendrik Witbooi to accept a German protectorate, although Germany had proclaimed its protectorate over Nama as well as Herero country in August 1884.

Even while he fought with him, Hendrik Witbooi wrote letters to Maherero full of his sense of prophecy and divine mission:

'You are to be protected and helped by the German Government but, my dear Captain, do you appreciate what you have done? . . . in the end you will have bitter remorse, you will have eternal remorse for this handing of your land and sovereignty over to the hands of white people . . . This giving of yourself into the hands of the whites will become a burden as if you were carrying the sun on your back.'

Questions

1 What were the effects of the discovery of diamonds and gold on the relations between the Boer Republics and the British? [Cambridge International School Certificate, 1975] (Refer also to Chapter 11)

2 What were the causes of, and what were the results of *two* of the following: (a) the Anglo-Zulu War of 1879; (b) the first Anglo-Boer War of 1880-81; (c) the Cape-Basuto War of 1880-81? [Cambridge International School Certificate, 1977]

3 Why did President Burgers' attempt to modernize the Transvaal fail?

4 Account for the rise of white settler political power in the Cape and Natal colonies before 1890.

5 What did the Tswana alliance led by Montshiwa in 1883 have in common with the one led by Sechele in 1852?

Activities

1 Write an imaginative description of everyday life in a diamond mining compound.

2 Discuss in the classroom to what extent whites were justified in fearing a black military alliance led by the Zulu in the later 1870s.

3 You are a British soldier in one of the battles with Africans or Boers in the 1870s-80s. Describe what you see and hear and feel.

4 The word 'imperialism' entered the English language in the 1870s-80s. What was so remarkable about the new imperialism of the time that the British needed a new word for it?

For Bibliography see references for Chapters 8 and 9 on pp. 124 and 140, and also pp. 337–42: B41 Walker; D7 Guy; D8 Herd; D13 Marks & Trapido; E2–3 Beinart; E6 Bundy; E8 Davenport; E9 Davidson; E11 Dreschler; E13 Guy; E20 Marks & Rathbone; E23 Newbury; E31 Schreuder; E30 Rotberg; E33 Turrell; E34 van Jaarsveld; E39 Welsh; E41 Worger.

Chapter 11

Colonial Conquest and African Resistance (1887 – 1898)

The map of Africa was partitioned between European powers in the 1880s, giving each other roughly defined 'spheres of influence' in different parts of the continent. It then remained for more precise borders to be drawn by treaties between individual European powers, after they had obtained rights to land by conquest or persuasion of African states. It is therefore not true that colonial borders always ignored African states. But colonial borders cut across already existing territories because Europeans chose to draw borders along the riverbeds, roads, watersheds and lines of longitude or latitude marked on their maps, rather than await the results of the long and costly process of finding out who lived where on the ground.

The second stage after conquest or persuasion of African states was administration and development of the colony by taxation of the people and alienation of land to white companies or settlers (i.e. taking communal land for private ownership). European powers collaborated closely with large capitalist companies interested in mining or plantations, and even contracted out responsibility for administration and development to them. The British South Africa Company was given a British royal charter in 1889, following previous British chartered companies for Nigeria and East Africa. The Liberal tradition of free enterprise without state intervention in Britain was replaced by a new Conservative tradition of the state intervening on behalf of large companies seeking to monopolize trade and production.

Even where a protectorate had been first established by persuasion, the second stage of taxation and land alienation usually had to be achieved by use of force. Where a colony had first been established by annexation without complete conquest, chiefly or popular resistance was all the stronger. Major armed risings of African peoples under their traditional rulers against colonial taxation and land alienation were wide-spread in the 1890s. Few of these risings were 'rebellions' in the true sense of the word, because few African states had previously surrendered their sovereignty to a colonial power either by treaty or conquest. Such risings have been dubbed *primary resistance* to colonial rule by African historians, because they sought to throw off colonialism before it could be properly imposed.

Resistance to colonialism did not only take the form of armed risings led by traditional leaders. Individuals and groups, who might have otherwise welcomed and collaborated with colonialism, protested at aspects of colonial rule such as land alienation or racial discrimination. They made their protests by diplomacy rather than by open revolt. Apparent collaborators with colonialism, such as Christian converts, often became the most effective resisters; and it is out of their *secondary resistance* to colonial rule that modern nationalist movements developed. On the other hand the closest collaborators with colonialism — black policemen and mercenaries — were often drawn from the ranks of defeated primary resisters.

1 The South African Republic and Growth of the Witwatersrand (1887-96)

The opening of the Witwatersrand* goldfields dramatically altered the political importance of the South African Republic (Transvaal). By 1895 the Witwatersrand was producing almost a quarter of the world's total gold supply, worth £8.6 million at then current prices. The steadily rising production of the Witwatersrand helped persuade all the major trading nations in the world to adopt gold, rather than silver or other irregularly produced metals, as their standard currency. One of the last major nations to convert to the gold standard was the United States, where the pro-silver Democratic candidate for the presidency was defeated in the 1896 election. All of this helped stimulate Witwatersrand development even more.

Origins of Witwatersrand mining The main gold reef along the Witwatersrand was discovered by an employee of Fred Struben. He had been attracted to the area by the presence of abandoned iron mines, worked by Africans in pre-colonial times and by Europeans since 1854. In two years of prospecting he discovered three or four veins of gold-bearing conglomerate rock, each one being one or two metres wide, running parallel together and projecting out of the ridges of the Witwatersrand hill range. In fact the main reef was more than 30 kilometres long. The conglomerate rock of the veins was known as *banket* (nougat) to local Boers, since it looked like candy with broken nuts in it: in fact the 'nuts' were gold-bearing pebbles. Struben set up a stamping mill in 1886 to crush and wash the gold out of the conglomerate rock. For every ton of rock crushed, he extracted up to an ounce of gold — a proportion of about 1:35,000 gold to tailings (waste).

The announcement of Struben's findings resulted in a rush of prospectors and companies to buy up farms along the Witwatersrand. The government of the South African Republic then proclaimed all the land between farms called Roodepoort and Vogelfontein to be a public goldfield (1886-87). This meant that the state left one-tenth of each farm to its owners, and sold off nine-tenths in small plots.

Origins of Johannesburg In the centre of the goldfield a public township was marked out next to a mining camp on land bought up by the government mining commissioner. It was named 'Johannes-burg' after the common first name of the three officials who laid out the roads, including the government surveyor Johannes Rissik. Each block of land between the rectangular network of roads was divided into stands for buildings, which were auctioned off in February 1887 at less than £10 each. (The reason why central Johannesburg has smaller blocks between streets by comparison with other cities is because officials wished to profit from more corner stands auctioned for a higher price.) Within a few months a city of buildings had begun to spring up at Johannesburg. Small buildings of corrugated-iron sheeting or sun-dried ('kimberley') brick were expanded with extra rooms and second storeys. In time an increasing number of houses, hotels, bars and shops were built of kiln-burnt brick to a few storeys high. The market square was soon filled with wagons selling a hundred wagonloads of foodstuffs a day.

Thousands of Europeans came to the Witwatersrand mostly from Kimberley but also from Barberton — as skilled workers, as managers of mines and businesses, or as lawless adventurers. Landless Boer *bywoners* found employment as unskilled workers in building construction and brick-making. Africans with · previous experience in Kimberley, many of them baSotho, took the more skilled labouring jobs in the mines like shaft sinking. Most of the unskilled labour in the mines was performed by Zulu workers, imported in large gangs walking from Natal, and often not paid until they returned home. Increasing numbers of 'Shangane' (Tsonga or

*Wit-waters-rand, i.e. 'white waters ridge' over which streams frothed white. Known as 'the Rand' for short.

Chopi) workers came from Portuguese East Africa as the gold mines in the eastern Transvaal, which had previously employed them, declined. Few of the local Tswana people of the Witwatersrand worked in the mines as they were employed as peasants or farm workers on Boer farms producing food-stuffs for the mines and Johannesburg. The city that grew up amongst rural Tswana and Boers was therefore an alien city from the start, full of alien whites and blacks.

Development of mining capitalism Mining capitalists from Kimberley moved in to buy up Witwatersrand mines and farms. Joseph Robinson, almost bankrupted at Kimberley, arrived in mid-1886 and bought up numerous farms very cheaply with money borrowed from Alfred Beit, Rhodes' partner. He became the richest man on the Witwatersrand by buying up much of Langlaagte farm in the centre of the main reef and land as far west as Randfontein. Unlike other mining capitalists, Joseph Robinson had great faith from the beginning that the main reef was not a nine-days' wonder and must stretch down hundreds of feet into the earth. Cecil Rhodes arrived on the Witwatersrand later in 1886, having missed the best bargains, and bought western Witwatersrand plots more cautiously. Barney Barnato did not arrive at Johannesburg from Kimberley until 1887, and spent money extravagantly on buying mines to compete with already established companies. Between 1887 and 1889 there was feverish speculation in buying and selling of Witwatersrand gold company shares by investors in London and overseas. New gold mines opened on the eastern Witwatersrand in 1887-88 included Germiston, Benoni and Nigel*. Coal mining around the government camp of Boksburg on the eastern Witwatersrand provided fuel conveniently and cheaply near the goldfields from early 1888.

*Named after its owner's birthplace in Scotland (Germiston); the biblical name of the previous farm (Benoni); and named after a Walter Scott novel (Nigel).

Deep-level mining Like Kimberley, the Witwatersrand saw the amalgamation of the large number of small mining companies as cost and technical difficulties grew. Deep-level mining became necessary, particularly on the western Witwatersrand. Also the declining quality of deeper ores (from 1:35,000 to 1:60,000 proportion of gold to waste) made increased scale of production necessary to maintain profits. Gold could not be extracted from low-grade ore simply by mechanical crushing and washing the gold out with water, but needed the (Forrest-McArthur) chemical reduction process using large quantities of cyanide. All of these needed imported capital and technical skills for mining or surface machinery and buildings.

In 1889 no less than forty-four mining companies were bankrupted in the collapse of the speculative boom caused by rising costs on the Witwatersrand. Mining was re-financed during 1890-92 by the 'group system' of large mining capitalists pooling their capital together in mining 'houses', of which the largest was Wernher & Beit to share the financial risks of individual mining companies. The Witwatersrand capitalists, popularly known as the 'Randlords', had overlapping interests in Transvaal monopoly concessions, in De Beers Consolidated Mines, and in the British South Africa Company dedicated to finding a 'second Rand' in the north. Much of their capital came from the merchant banks overseas, such as the Rothschilds of London and Paris; the rest of it came from overseas shareholders who eagerly speculated in buying and selling gold shares ever rising in price. Gold shares, known as 'kaffirs' on the London stock market, went through another speculative boom after the discovery by drilling in 1893 that the main reef was up to 750 metres deep. The so-called 'kaffir boom' on the London, Paris and Berlin markets eventually collapsed in October 1895, when shareholders in Barnato's companies panicked on learning of their mines' low productivity.

Black labour recruitment and wages The Witwatersrand chamber of mines, representing gold and coal mine owners, was

Gold miners at leisure, in the Robinson Deep Mine compound. Board games and music were virtually the only legal pastimes for the single male migrants in the compounds. Here miners play *umtshuba,* with pebbles in pockets in the ground. This ancient pan-African board game is otherwise known by many names, including *morabaraba, mancala, tsoro* or *tsolo.* The nearest English equivalent is called fox-and-geese.

founded in 1889. It was soon dominated by deep-level mine owners, seeking to reduce their high capital and labour costs to increase their rate of profit. One of the chamber's main tasks was 'the gradual reduction of native wages to a reasonable level'. But the reduction of black wages from 60 to under 45 shillings a month in 1889-90 resulted in a drop in the number of men recruited. So wages were raised again up to almost 64 shillings by 1895, helping to raise the numbers recruited from 14,000 in 1891 to 70,000 in 1896. The chamber of mines then began to reduce wages again, from about 61 shillings in 1896 to less than 50 shillings by 1899. There was widespread protest among African miners when the pay cuts began in October 1896, at the same time as liquor was prohibited to them. The police force was strengthened and pass laws were strictly enforced. The chamber of mines was assisted by famine, disease and war all over southern Africa, which pushed people to the mines to earn money for food. When the rinderpest cattle epidemic broke out, a white 'expert' on black labour recruitment rejoiced: 'The outbreak of rinderpest will drive the natives into the labour market.' The number of black workers on the Witwatersrand in fact rose from 70,000 in 1897 to 97,000 in 1899.

Perhaps two-thirds of men recruited to the Witwatersrand mines were 'Shangane' from

Mozambique, where the chamber of mines began regular recruitment through Portuguese officials in 1897 after the defeat of Ngungunyane. The mines preferred 'Shangane' to other black nationalities, because the men did not return home during the agricultural season. The reasons for this are debated by historians. 'Shangane' men had a limited role in agriculture because ox-ploughs could not be used on the sandy coastal plains and traditional hoe cultivation by women continued. Cash was needed to import food, because harvests were killed by drought or washed away by river floods, and for consumer goods and liquor made popular by Portuguese traders. But above all the new colonial rulers of Mozambique saw the taxation of labour migrants as the basis of colonial finance, and encouraged or enforced labour migration for that reason.

Early crime on the Witwatersrand Migrant labourers on their way to or from the Witwatersrand had to run the gauntlet of Boer officials and farmers demanding unofficial taxes, and robbers, black and white. White travellers were robbed at gunpoint, black travellers by robbers pretending to be policemen. By 1889 there was a gang of black robbers (*izigelekege*) living in the Klipriviersberg hills south of Johannesburg. After their first leader left to become a Bible preacher in the city, they were taken over by 22-year old Nongoloza who renamed them the 'Ninevites' or *Umkosi wezintaba* (regiment of the hills), He recruited secret members in the mine compounds and prisons. The prohibition of liquor sales to Africans on the Witwatersrand in 1896 opened a whole new field for organized crime. Drinking places for Africans, known as 'forts', were surrounded by metal walls and fitted with electric bells to warn of police raids. Policemen and government officials were bribed by the white 'liquor kings' to allow the 'forts' to operate.

2 Transvaal Imperialism and Swaziland (1886-98)

Westward expansion of the South African Republic had been blocked by British imperialism in the Bechuanalands in 1884-85. But the SAR kept to its imperialist ambitions northwards across the Limpopo and eastwards through Swaziland to the sea. And even within its proclaimed borders it still had to conquer the African peoples of the north.

Attempts to expand north of the Limpopo The SAR joined the rush of concession-seekers through Khama's country to the Ndebele kingdom by sending a hunter-trader named Piet Grobler to Bulawayo as its agent. Grobler induced Lobengula to sign a treaty of friendship with the SAR in 1887; Lobengula took it simply to be a renewal of his father's treaties with Transvaal leaders of 1853. The British responded by sending John (son of Robert) Moffat to induce Lobengula to sign a treaty renewing the first Anglo-Ndebele treaty of 1836, which stopped Lobengula from 'entering into any corres-

Workers and overseers at Hatherley distillery near Pretoria in 1885. The distillery was established in 1881 at *eertse fabrieke* (the first factory) in the SAR. It was extremely profitable, making its money by a monopoly of liquor sales to white and black miners, and the mining companies took large shares in the company from 1892. But heavy drinking led to high absenteeism on the mines, and in 1896 the gold companies succeeded in banning the sale of liquor to blacks on the Rand. As a result, illegal sales flourished, while Hatherley continued to supply the liquor.

above: *Piet Joubert*, commandant general of the South African Republic, and conqueror of the northern Transvaal. Pictured here (seated with hat on his left knee) with his staff in October 1899.

right: *Mmalebogo (Malaboch), Gananwa chief conquered by Joubert in 1894*. This drawing was probably made after his capture. Mmalebogo was jailed at Pretoria for six years until 1900.

The Gananwa resisted the Zoutpansberg and Pretoria commandoes and the Transvaal state artillery, who were reinforced by the Zeerust, Rustenburg and Middelburg commandoes.

'. . . all through the campaign the poor Malabochians were seldom, if ever the aggressors, their attitude being nothing more or less than a gentle protest against what they considered an unjust encroachment on their ancestral rights . . . I firmly believe that had Malaboch's life been guaranteed him from the first, both he and his people would have surrendered without having fired a shot' (Colin Rae, *Malaboch, or, Notes from my Diary of the Boer Campaign of 1894 against Chief Malaboch of Blaauwberg District Zoutpansberg, South African Republic* London & Cape Town, 1898, p. 63).

pondence or treaty with any foreign State or Power' except the British (1888). Grobler returned to Bulawayo in 1888, in collaboration with Cape businessmen anxious to obtain concessions from Lobengula. Khama sent troops to block the Baines' Drift road through the north-eastern corner of his country, and Grobler died of gunshot wounds after a skirmish. The Transvaal protested; the British gave Grobler's young wife a life pension; but Baines' Drift remained closed to Transvaal expansion.

Another attempt to expand the Transvaal north of the Limpopo occurred in 1890-91, when a party of Boers obtained a concession from a Nyai chief to set up a 'Republic of the North' between the Limpopo and the Zambezi. But British troops prevented the 'Banyailand' trekkers from crossing the Limpopo, and the trek party was disbanded.

Conquest of the northern Transvaal Strengthened by its gold revenues, the South African Republic imposed its sovereignty on the African peoples within its northern borders during the 1890s. Joubert placed a new 'native commissioner' among the lowveld Tsonga south-east of the Soutpansberg in 1889. White settlers followed to take up farms in the valleys, which proved fertile for citrus growing though fever-ridden with malaria. The land was also claimed by the Lobedu of queen Mudjaji, who were seeking winter pasture during the drought, and a small war resulted in 1890. Boer settlement west of the Soutpansberg followed the opening of regular wagon and coach traffic from Pretoria to Fort Tuli in 'Rhodesia' via Pietersburg (1890-91). Zeederberg Company coaches on the route, imported from America, were pulled by mules and even by a team of trained zebras. White wood-cutters moved in and chopped down huge areas of forest to supply the Witwatersrand with fuel.

The defeat of the Ndebele in 'Rhodesia' in 1893-94 and the SAR's new economic strength encouraged whites to be bolder in their treatment of independent Africans in the northern Transvaal. In 1894 taxes were demanded for the first time since 1881 from the Gananwa chief Mmalebogo (Malaboch) living in mountains on the road to Tuli. When the Gananwa refused, Joubert led an army against them. Mmalebogo retreated into a mountain fortress with some of his people, while most of them fled to Bechuanaland and elsewhere. Two thousand SAR troops besieged five hundred Gananwa, mostly women and children, for a month until they surrendered and were given to local Boer farmers for five years' forced labour. Joubert then crushed the tax revolt of the Tlou of Makgoba (Magoeba), east of Pietersburg, and forced queen Mudjaji of the Lobedu to pay him tribute (1894-95). Makgoba was caught and beheaded by Swazi mercenaries in the kloof (gorge) that still bears his name near Tzaneen.

Lastly Joubert turned to the task of subduing the Venda of Makhado, who had expelled the Boers from the Soutpansberg in 1867. Makhado had recently been succeeded by his son Mphephu after a dispute in which the SAR supported a rival brother (1895-96). Mphephu, a former migrant worker to Kimberley, continued his father's independence of Boer rule and encouraged other chiefdoms to resist SAR taxation. But Joubert led an army which captured Mphephu's capital. Mphephu escaped with ten thousand followers north across the Limpopo (1898), and a white settler village called Louis Trichardt was placed at the foot of his former mountain capital. The conquest of the northern Transvaal was apparently complete.

Swaziland concessions scramble Offy Shepstone as Mbandzeni's agent for concessions encouraged the king to become more and more reckless in granting them. Offy took half the king's income by agreement, and much more in practice; during the first half of 1888 Mbandzeni may have only received £150 in cash of his £15,000 annual income. Bribery and corruption were endemic among white and black residents of the royal capital eMbekelwini. Boer graziers competed with *uitlander* (non-Boer) mining prospectors for land, threatening violence but restrained by Mbandzeni's prime minister Sandlane, who told them the land was not theirs, only lent (*bolekele*) to them.

The South African Republic bought the monopoly concession for a railway across Swaziland in 1887, and three concessions covering the main economic functions of the Swaziland government in 1888-89 — the royal revenue monopoly (covering the right to collect all royal cash income), the customs

SWAZI CONCESSIONS

On March 29th, 1887, Boer sheep graziers led by Stoffel Towsen marched into Mbandzeni's court to complain about mineral concessions being given to *uitlanders* on their grazing lands. This is an extract from the minutes of the meeting:

The King: 'Are you owners of the country? Why are you talking about fighting us? Did you ever suppose we should call the Hlavela [regiment] up to eject white people? We will not fight white people. Do you mean to say that I have no more power to deal with my own country? If people are not to have concessions then the land and all rights given over it shall revert to me.'

Towsen: '. . . I am spokesman for others. I only came first lest it should be said that we all came at once, and [that] an impi came to you. There are [i.e. we are] many.'

The King: 'It comes to this; if people are not to have land, it must all revert to me. I shall send to the two Governments [i.e. Transvaal and Britain], and ask if by giving you grazing licences I have given up the right to deal with my own country.'

Towsen: 'If you call in a Government, your time is up. You are done, and you will never have the [royal] salute "Bayete!" again.' ('The deputation then left, muttering further threats.')

Mbandzeni then made Offy Shepstone, one of the sons of Theophilus Shepstone, his agent in dealings with white people, with powers to collect all royal income from concessions. When Mbandzeni fell sick, there was an even greater rush of *uitlander* speculators from the Rand to grab concessions before the king died. His prime minister, Sandlane Zwane, who tried to stop the concession giving, was executed. Offy was dismissed and replaced by an even more corrupt white agent, Alistair Miller, in January 1889.

By the time Mbandzeni died, in October 1889, Miller had sold 52 major new concessions on the king's behalf — including monopolies on dynamite, gunpowder, electricity, telegraphs (concessions all then sold to the Transvaal government), wool washing, tanning, tobacco manufacturing, cement making, oil drilling, gas manufacture, autioneering, pawnbroking, printing, photography.

monopoly (the right to collect all customs and excise dues), and the unallotted lands monopoly (covering all land south of the Nkomati not already sold). Swaziland therefore became an economic satellite and unofficial protectorate of the SAR. Meanwhile the British had blocked Swaziland's access to the sea in 1887 by declaring a protectorate over 'Tongaland' — including inland Nyawo and Mngometulu chiefdoms of coastal Tsonga subject to the Swazi, as well as the Tembe kingdom. For their part the Portuguese began settling the Lebombo hill chain with white farms in 1887-88, pushing the DuPont and MacNab bandit families into Swaziland, and casting envious eyes on the Swaziland lowveld coalfields.

Anglo-Boer Swaziland conventions The SAR and Britain intervened in the succession crisis that followed Mbandzeni's death in 1889 to impose a triumvirate which would rule Swaziland for five years; this consisted of SAR and British commissioners, and Offy Shepstone as representative of the Swazi nation! The triumvirate government bought a trader's store at Manzini near the royal capital for their headquarters, and the trader insisted on the colonial capital being named Bremersdorp after himself. The Anglo-Boer arrangement was formalized by the *1st Swaziland Convention* of 1890.

In return for abandoning its claims north of the Limpopo, the SAR was given a more or less free hand in Swaziland by the British in the *2nd Swaziland Convention* of 1893. Swaziland would become an SAR protectorate on condition that the Swazi regency agreed. But the Swazi regency, from which Offy had been ousted, was dominated by the mother of the appointed boy-king Bhunu (Ngwane V), a formidable politician by the name of Labotsibeni Mdluli. Labotsibeni not only refused to agree but she also sent a delegation to London to protest against the Convention. But the protest was in vain. Britain signed a *3rd Swaziland Convention* with the SAR in 1894 which recognized the SAR's protectorate without Swazi consent, so long as a railway was not built across it.

From 1895 an SAR special commissioner, Johannes Krogh (Nkoseluhlaza), took charge of Swaziland, imposing the high annual tax of £2 on every adult male and 10 shillings per wife in order to oblige Swazi to work in the labour-starved Witwatersrand mines. After the rinderpest epidemic killed many cattle in 1896-97, the Swazi came near to armed revolt in 1898. Krogh attempted to try the king for murder after the execution of a pro-Boer induna at eMbekelwini. Swaziland was suddenly filled with Boer commandos under Joubert, flushed with their final victory over the Venda. Bhunu fled to Natal but was persuaded to return for open trial on condition that he was not found guilty. The British then agreed to amend the 3rd Swaziland Convention to make the sovereignty of the king over his people subject to the SAR commissioner in every respect. In effect Swaziland had ceased to be a protectorate and had become an annexed colony, its king reduced to a paramount chief.

3 The Rise of the British South Africa Company (1887-93)

The search for a 'second Rand' in Zimbabwe was pushed forward by the speculation in Witwatersrand gold shares of 1887-89. Syndicates of prospectors were formed to obtain concessions from Khama and Lobengula. Khama was persuaded to grant his only mineral concession ever in 1887, over territory between the Motloutse and Shashe rivers. Lobengula, though prospectors tried to convince him of how well Mbandzeni was doing from concessions in Swaziland, at first only agreed to marginal concessions in the south. He reconfirmed his 1880 agreement with the Tati Concession Company, and granted a rival concession to Khama's over the Shashe-Motloutse territory to Transvaal-based capitalists.

Rhodes' scramble for Matabeleland Rhodes and Beit first attempted to obtain a concession from Lobengula at the end of 1887, but their envoy failed in his task. Rhodes realized that only the British 'imperial factor' could

gain Lobengula's confidence. He was already close friends with Robinson, the high commissioner, and Shippard, the commissioner for Bechuanaland. He played on their fears that English-speaking capitalists in South Africa might break away from Britain to join a republican confederation, if Britain did not satisfy their demands for colonial expansion. Rhodes and Beit committed their mining companies to colonial expansion as a form of capital investment, which could draw the money of investors overseas if given the approval of the 'imperial factor'.

John Moffat was appointed Shippard's assistant in late 1887 to be British agent to Khama and envoy to Lobengula. It was John Moffat who persuaded Lobengula, as the son of Mzilikazi, friend of Robert Moffat, to sign the Anglo-Ndebele treaty of early 1888 and to look upon Rhodes's partner Charles Rudd with favour later in the year. The so-called Rudd Concession was signed by Lobengula with Rudd on behalf of Rhodes, Beit and others in October 1888, a few days after Shippard himself had visited Bulawayo. The concession granted all mineral rights in the Ndebele kingdom, except for the Tati area, and added vague permission for the concessionaries 'to do all things that they may deem necessary'. Lobengula was assured in conversation that *not more than ten* white men would prospect or mine in his country; but this was deceitfully left out of the concession document written in English. In return Lobengula was promised a thousand rifles and a gunboat on the Zambezi as well as money payments.

Rhodes sailed to London at the end of 1888 with the Rudd concession, and tried to persuade the British government to grant a royal charter to his syndicate for a chartered company to administer and develop Lobengula's country. Lobengula than learnt of his deception by Rudd from the Gifford and Cawston syndicate, which had bought up Khama's Shashe-Motloutse concession in 1888. Lobengula renounced the Rudd concession in the main Bechuanaland newspaper and refused to accept the rifles sent to him as payment for the concession. He despatched two senior indunas as envoys to London to deny that he had ever signed away his country: 'a king gives a stranger an ox, not his whole herd or cattle.' But Gifford and Cawston withdrew their support and the British government ignored Lobengula's renunciation of the Rudd concession.

Foundation of British South Africa Company The Gifford and Cawston syndicate applied for its own royal charter over Bechuanaland in January 1889. The London-based syndicate had better business and political contacts in Britain, but Rhodes and Beit, based in South Africa, had much more capital. So the British government persuaded the two syndicates to combine their interests in Bechuanaland and Matabeleland into one chartered company. After delay caused by the Tati Concession Company not joining the new company, the 'British South Africa Company' was given its royal charter in October 1889 — to 'make treaties, promulgate laws, preserve the peace, maintain a police force and acquire new concessions' in the region of British influence from the Molopo river to 'the great lakes of Central Africa'. British troops, dressed in brightly-coloured costumes and heavy armour despite the summer heat, presented Lobengula with a copy of the BSAC charter in January 1890.

Rhodes' scramble for Barotseland Khama was persuaded that it was his duty as a British ally to support the BSAC, and he aided the company in obtaining the Lochner concession from Lewanika in Barotseland (Lozi country) in June 1890. Lewanika was persuaded that the mineral and trading concession given to Lochner of the Bechuanaland border police was in fact a treaty with the British government like Khama's agreement of 1885. (Lewanika was threatened by rebellion of some of his indunas and saw a British alliance as a way of checking them.) Lewanika was tricked by Lochner, as Lobengula had been by Rudd, by being given a copy of the concession different to the 'official' version. Lewanika's copy promised that a British resident agent would live with Lewanika, and

the BSAC would set up 'churches, schools and trading stations', and it would not 'interfere in any matter concerning the king's power or authority over any of his own subjects'.

Colonial occupation of Zimbabwe Some of Rhodes' advisers suggested that the BSAC should colonize Matabeleland by a rapid military invasion to crush the Ndebele kingdom. But Rhodes decided to begin white settlement around the gold mines of 'Mashonaland', and therefore to establish BSAC power on three sides including Bechuanaland and Barotseland before facing the problem of the Ndebele kingdom.

During 1890 a 'pioneer column' of two hundred white men, who had each been promised 15 gold claims and 1,250 hectares of land, was led forward to Mashonaland by five hundred Bechuanaland border police to the Shashe river, by two hundred and seventy Ngwato troops to the Lundi river, and by two hundred BSAC police to Harare which was named Fort Salisbury in honour of the British prime minister. Lobengula still refuted the Rudd concession, but also held back the young men of the Ndebele regiments who wished to expel the white intruders, realizing that that would give the British justification for war. 'You are driving me into the lion's mouth,' he told them.

Once it had established its main settlements, the BSAC proclaimed the independence of Mashonaland by denying that Lobengula had ever had sovereignty over its Shona peoples. In 1891 Lobengula granted a new concession to Lippert, a Transvaal-based Randlord and colleague of Offy Shepstone, to replace the Rudd concession, but the BSAC bought it up in early 1892. Lobengula then belatedly recognized the Rudd concession so that the BSAC could not discard its recognition of his sovereignty over Mashonaland. But the BSAC used Ndebele raids asserting Ndebele sovereignty over the area as the pretext for declaring war in September 1893.

Anglo-Ndebele war, 1893-94 Henry Loch, the high commissioner (1889-95) who had replaced Robinson, consented to the war

Great Zimbabwe was occupied by the Mugabe clan between the 1830s and 1890s. Chief Mugabe, carrying a ceremonial axe, is pictured with his headmen in 1891.

Destruction of archaeological evidence at Great Zimbabwe around 1900 The Mugabe clan was expelled when the site became a national monument. Untrained white enthusiasts then dug out the Great Enclosure down to bedrock level in the hope of finding evidence of exotic non-Africans who they believed must have built the city. All that they found they called 'native rubbish' — in other words they destroyed much evidence of the city's African origin. Note the depth of soil excavated round the nearest tree in the photograph, with men probably digging behind the tree. Every trained archaeologist who excavated later at Great Zimbabwe, from 1905 onwards, confirmed its African origins.

against the Ndebele, but had grown wary of Rhodes' ambitions. As the Colonial Office in London noted: 'The interest of the Company is to drive out Lobengula and possess his lands — ours is to keep him there with his claws clipped and his teeth drawn — to become a sort of second Khama.' Loch therefore insisted on a large imperial force, consisting of border police and a Ngwato army under Khama, to check BSAC ambitions in the war. But Dr Leander Jameson led BSAC horsemen — each promised a 2,500 hectare farm and 20 gold claims — in a 'flying column'. It moved so quickly into Matabeleland that it entered Bulawayo, finding it burnt and abandoned, when the imperial invasion from the south was only half way. The imperial forces had fought one large indecisive battle while Jameson's column had won two smaller battles decisively. The failure of the 'imperial factor' in the Anglo-Ndebele war of 1893-94 opened the way for the BSAC to take over imperial responsibilities elsewhere.

While the imperial forces withdrew southwards, BSAC troops followed Lobengula, who was fleeing to refuge among the Ngoni across the Zambezi. Lobengula offered to surrender to two BSAC policemen with a gift

Lobengula, Ndebele king 1870-94 (a clay tobacco pipe in his mouth) 'Did you ever see a chameleon catch a fly? The chameleon gets behind the fly and remains motionless for some time, then he advances very slowly and gently, first putting forward one leg and then another. At last, when well within reach, he darts his tongue and the fly disappears. England is the chameleon and I am that fly.'

of gold, but they stole the gold and suppressed the message. Another BSAC patrol was competely wiped out by an Ndebele patrol, the survivors being shot in the head to avoid capture. Lobengula, exhausted from his flight, died of smallpox early in 1894 and was entombed in a cave of the lower Shangani valley.

4 BSAC Attempt to Incorporate Bechuanaland (1890-99)

In June 1890 the Bechuanaland Protectorate was extended north from the twenty-second parallel to the Zambezi, and the British took jurisdiction over whites away from African states in the area. Then in August 1890 the British parliament passed its *Foreign Jurisdiction Act,* which gave itself the right to proclaim British sovereignty over any part of the world without previous treaty or agreement with the indigenous people. The high commissioner in Capetown then unilaterally claimed full British sovereignty over the Bechuanaland Protectorate and BSAC territory in June 1891. Shippard was appointed so-called 'resident commissioner' for the Bechuanaland Protectorate (though in fact still resident at Vryburg), and assistant commissioners were posted to Gaborone's town in the south and Khama's town of Palapye in the north. The protectorate in effect became a colony without formal annexation or changing its title, but it was considered too risky to inform Tswana rulers of the outright loss of their sovereignty. So Khama was soon complaining of the British:

'And now, without formal conclave or agreement, when I should have the opportunity of consulting my headmen, and putting all important matters fairly before my people, they proceed to place a ruler in my town, so that I myself, before I can buy a bag of gunpowder, have to go and obtain a permit. This is not fair or open-handed; it puts me in the wrong with my tribe, who say, "How then is Khama no longer chief in his country?" and I feel deeply that I am slighted and made small.'

Rhodes' bid for Bechuanaland Cecil Rhodes tried to persuade the British government to incorporate British Bechuanaland into the Cape Colony (of which he was prime minister), and to transfer the Bechuanaland Protectorate to BSAC administration. Clashes between BSAC police and Ngwato troops on the Bechuanaland frontier after the Anglo-Ndebele war suggested that Rhodes was seeking an excuse for a war to capture Khama's country. John Moffat, who had quarrelled with Rhodes over the unprovoked war with Lobengula, concluded that 'Khama is the next victim', and was dismissed from the protectorate administration by Shippard. The British government agreed to Rhodes' proposals for incorporation and transfer of the two Bechuanalands in early 1895. Henry Loch, the high commissioner, protested that Khama had always been 'a faithful friend and ally', and it would be a breach of faith by the British government to abandon Khama to a profit-making company. Loch resigned and was replaced by Rhodes' friend Hercules Robinson as high commissioner once again.

Tswana kings resist incorporation The Liberal government of 1892-95 in Britain was replaced by a Conservative government. Joseph Chamberlain, Britain's leading imperialist politician, became colonial minister. As soon as Chamberlain was appointed, the Ngwato of Khama addressed a petition to him against transfer to 'the injustice and oppression which the Chartered Company inflict upon the tribes who live in the north'. Petitions followed from the Kwena of Sebele (ruled 1892-1911), the Ngwaketse of Bathoen (ruled 1889-1910), and the Kgatla of Linchwe. Kings Khama, Sebele and Bathoen travelled to London, ignoring the threats and persuasions of Robinson and Rhodes in person, and found Chamberlain cool. (This was probably because Chamberlain knew that Rhodes needed Bechuanaland as a base for the planned Jameson Raid into the SAR.) The three kings then toured major British cities to drum up support from churches and chambers of commerce, and returned to negotiations with

Khama, Sebele and Bathoen in Glasgow, Scotland, October 1895 In Glasgow and other British cities they were greeted by the lord mayor and city officials, by church bodies, and by chambers of commerce. They were successful in persuading the British government to preserve their countries from Rhodesian rule. British South Africa Company officials in London cabled Cecil Rhodes in Capetown: 'Native chiefs with Lord Loch and Temperance carried England with them.' Rhodes replied: 'It is humiliating to be utterly beaten by these niggers.'

strong British public support behind them. In return for being recognized as powerful chiefs over large reserves under a continuing imperial protectorate, Khama, Sebele and Bathoen surrendered their eastern frontiers to the imperial government as a railway strip. Northern and western areas of the protectorate outside the three reserves were also to be handed over to BSAC administration.

Meanwhile the Lete and Rolong were tricked by Shippard into concessions of their sovereignty to the BSAC, on the pretence that the concessions were for temporary railway construction only. 'It's dirty work but somebody has got to do it,' remarked Shippard, remembered in seTswana history as *Morena-Maaka* ('Lord-Lies'). No attempt was made to obtain a concession from Linchwe of the Kgatla, as the threat of war with his 'ferocious Bechuana' was the pretext for the BSAC bringing troops needed for the Jameson Raid south from Matabeleland 'to protect railway construction'.

Confirmation of imperial rule The fall of the BSAC from British government favour because of the failure of the Jameson Raid ensured that the southern and eastern Bechuanaland Protectorate remained under imperial administration. But the BSAC pressed ahead with white settlement plans for the north-western area of Ngamiland.

Moremi II of the Tawana kingdom in Ngamiland had granted various mineral concessions before his death in 1891. His successor, Sekgoma Letsholathebe (ruled 1891-1906), was tricked into a much more extensive concession by a BSAC agent called Bosman, who presented himself as an envoy of the British queen (1893). The BSAC then started to colonize the Ghanzi area near the German border with Boer settlers from the Cape and Orange Free State. But the Bosman concession had to be abandoned after John Moffat proved that Bosman had obtained it by deceit. Hercules Robinson solved the problem of the Boer trek by declaring Ghanzi to be outside Sekgoma Letsholathebe's sovereignty. The BSAC then combined with the Moremi concession-holders to form the British West Charterland Company, which obtained a comprehensive mineral concession for the Tawana kingdom in 1896. Sekgoma Letsholathebe accepted the loss of Ghanzi and the new concession in return for the British promise of a large reserve like those of Khama, Sebele and Bathoen. But an expedition led by Frederick Lugard (of later Nigerian fame) failed to find payable minerals in Ngamiland, and BSAC plans for a West Charterland colony (i.e. Western Rhodesia) were abandoned.

The Bechuanaland Protectorate settled down to life as a British colony. The capital was moved from Vryburg to the police headquarters at Mafeking in 1895, though this was still twenty-five kilometres outside the protectorate! External borders (including Tati and Ngamiland) and internal borders between reserves were delineated by British officers, and defined by two proclamations of the high commissioner in 1899. A third proclamation introduced the collection of tax from all adult males at 10 shillings a year, and a fourth proclamation licensed recruiters of labour for Kimberley and the Rand. But chiefs were left with extensive powers in justice and administration, including collecting the colonial tax. Though they lost their sovereignty as kings, most historians argue that paramount chiefs under colonial 'protectorates' such as Barotseland and Bechuanaland in fact gained in power and wealth. They were no longer always forced to be responsible to councils of headmen or popular assemblies, and began to build up personal wealth derived from their chiefly privileges, such as free labour on house building and rights to unclaimed stray cattle.

5 Armed Resistance and the Making of the Rhodesias (1896-1900)

A great rinderpest epidemic originating in the Middle East spread to the Horn of Africa by 1889 and reached Barotseland in 1895. From there it was spread rapidly down the wagon routes into Bechuanaland, reaching Palapye and western Matabeleland by March 1896. As a natural disaster — killing off more than three-quarters of the cattle and wild buck in south-eastern Africa by the end of 1897 — it closely followed the human disaster of colonization by whites, and helped to spark off desperate African risings against colonial rule. After all it was ox-wagons mostly owned by whites which spread the disease; and even if it was not deliberately spread by whites to reduce Africans to poverty, it had that effect when whites shot African cattle indiscriminately to prevent the disease spreading.

Ndebele rising, 1896 The Ndebele rose against the British South Africa Company after hearing of the defeat of BSAC troops on the Jameson Raid. The company had left very few police in Matabeleland, assuming that the

Ndebele leaders at Bulawayo after peace had been made in 1896 The photograph includes both former enemies and allies of the BSA Company. The front row includes the leading elder indunas and spokesmen for the nation—Babyana with a very long staff at the extreme left and Somabulana squatting next to him. The most educated and Westernized spokesman, Karl Khumalo, stands centre-left in a blazer with his left hand on his hip. The leader of younger indunas, Dhliso, is kneeling on the far right of the photograph — wearing a hat and woollen sweater. Senior indunas who refused to join the rising were Faku — squatting next to Somabulana — and Gambo — standing third right from Karl Khumalo, wearing a striped waistcoat.

Somabulana had led the indunas who negotiated with Cecil Rhodes in the Motopo hills during August 1896. 'You came, you conquered,' Somabulana told Rhodes. 'The strongest takes the land. We accepted your rule. We lived under you. But not as dogs! If we are to be dogs it is better to be dead.' Younger indunas were even angrier. When Rhodes promised to give land to the Ndebele, one interjected sarcastically: 'You will give us land in our own country! That is good of you!' When Rhodes ordered the young man to put down the rifle he was holding, the young man replied: 'You will have to talk to me with my rifle in my hand. I find if I talk with my rifle in my hand the white man pays more attention to what I say. I am just a dog to be kicked.'

Ndebele had been utterly defeated in 1894. But the Ndebele had secretly appointed Lobengula's son Nyamanda as king. The old regiments and most subject chiefdoms rose against BSAC rule before all land and wealth was lost to white settlers and the rinderpest.

A land commission of 1894 had reserved central Matabeleland for white farms, and Ndebele chiefs were beginning to be pushed into badly-watered reserves on poor soils in outlying areas. Aristocratic Ndebele families who remained on white land were forced to labour like common people by white farmers and officials. But the greatest grievance was over cattle; the BSAC native affairs department devoted itself to cattle raiding on the excuse that it owned all cattle that had belonged to Lobengula and Lobengula had owned all cattle. Out of over 200,000 cattle only about 40,000 were left in African possession at the outbreak of rinderpest.

The Ndebele rising lasted from March 1896 until August 1896. Ndebele regiments attacked white farms and laid seige to Bulawayo, with the support of most of the subject chiefdoms. But one major Ndebele induna near Bulawayo, Gampu Sithole, and Kalanga chiefdoms under the paramountcy of Mengwe around the Shashe river, remained neutral or friendly to the BSAC. They helped keep the vital road from Bechuanaland open for reinforcements. The Ndebele rising was aided by the inspiration of the Mwari priests of the former paramouncies of the Rozvi confederacy now allied to the Ndebele.

BSAC troop reinforcements arrived from the south in May 1896 and began an offensive campaign. One white American adventurer even sought out and killed a friendly priest under the delusion that the priest was Mwari (God) himself! Meanwhile railway construction proceeded at speed from Gaborone directly across Khama's country — rather than along the Limpopo 'railway strip' — eventually reaching Bulawayo in 1897. Ndebele leaders sued for peace in August 1896. Rhodes, anxious to regain a good reputation after the failure of the Jameson Raid, negotiated with them himself in the Matopo hills. In the peace settlement Matabeleland — like Zululand in 1879 — was divided into twelve chiefdoms, in which Nyamanda was merely one of twelve chiefs. The Ndebele soon discovered that no land in central Matabeleland was returned to their ownership.

Separate Rhodesian colonies set up After the Zimbabwean risings had been crushed the 'imperial factor' insisted on greater supervision of the British South Africa Company, but without committing itself to the expense of administration. The name 'Rhodesia' was officially recognized for BSAC territory, and a resident commissioner was placed in Salisbury to represent the high commissioner at Capetown. The BSAC administrator of 'Southern Rhodesia' shared power with a legislative council including settler representatives, and BSAC administration in general was reorganized along the lines of Cape Colony.

The two colonies that eventually became Northern Rhodesia (Zambia) — 'North-Eastern Rhodesia' and 'North-Western Rhodesia' — were set up under BSAC administrators in 1899. The BSAC claim to North-Western Rhodesia was based on two new concessions by Lewanika in 1898 and 1900, which granted rights of administration over Ila and Tonga country outside Barotseland, and the right of the BSAC to sell Ila and Tonga

---

SHONA RISING 1896-97

Armed resistance to white rule on the Zimbabwean plateau spread from Ndebele country to north-eastern Shona chiefdoms. These chiefdoms had accepted the peaceful settlement of whites in the gold mining area around Harare (Salisbury) in 1890. But white settlers began to raid villages for labour, and white tax collectors raided villages for livestock or burnt down the houses of tax resisters. News of Ndebele success, and of advancing rinderpest and locusts, therefore prompted the north-east Shona to attack white settlers and police, foreign blacks and Shona Christians (June 1896). The central Shona around Fort Victoria, however, did not join the risings because they saw whites as allies against the Ndebele. South-eastern Shona were too concerned with the Portuguese war with Gaza to attack British colonists.

The risings were probably spread by doctors carrying anti-locust medicine, and were kept going by the spirit-mediums of the *mhondoro* ancestral cult. The spirit-medium Kaguvi, who was given the holy praise-name of 'Murenga', became the main inspirer of the risings. Hence the risings are remembered in chiShona as chiMurenga.

The BSA Company counter-attacked with two columns of armed men, which forced their way through to Salisbury from Beira and Bulawayo. But Shona resistance was strengthened when a leading chief, Makoni, was treacherously executed after surrendering. War resumed after the 1896-97 agricultural season, and did not end until December 1897 after Kaguvi and a woman leader named Nehanda had been captured. The two leaders were executed in April 1898. Their bodies were buried in a secret place, 'so that no natives could take away their bodies and claim that their spirits had descended to any other prophetess or witch-doctor'.

country to white settlers. The borders of North-Western Rhodesia were extended to include the Copperbelt in 1905, because BSAC claims to mineral rights under chiefly concessions in North-Eastern Rhodesia were legally much weaker than the 1900 concession from Lewanika.

6 Cape Colony and Basutoland, Natal, and Mozambique (1887-99)

Cecil Rhodes became prime minister of the Cape Colony in 1890, as well as being the leading director of De Beers, the Consolidated Gold Fields Company, and the British South Africa Company. So for six years he was the most powerful politician in southern Africa after president Kruger, as well as the most powerful capitalist. Rhodes was supported in the Cape parliament by Hofmeyr's Afrikaner Bond, which was attracted by his policies encouraging the development of agricultural capitalism. Rhodes' government promoted wine exports, set up a ministry of agriculture to aid meat and fruit production, and extended railway lines to carry agricultural produce to market – as well as opening up the northern Cape Colony for white settlement. Bond leaders like Stephanus du Toit (now returned home from the Transvaal) also became important shareholders in Rhodes' mining and development companies.

Rhodes proclaimed himself in favour of 'equal rights for every white man south of the Zambesi' to bring Afrikaners and English together for a new Cape-dominated confederation. Rhodes changed 'white' to 'civilized' when coloured voters – so important in constituencies around Capetown – protested. But the message was in effect the same, because the economic standards by which voters were considered 'civilized' were raised in order to cut down the number of non-white voters. A previous government had passed a *Voters' Registration Act* of 1887 which made registration more difficult. Then under Rhodes in 1892 the *Franchise and Ballot Act* tripled the landed property qualification for the vote from £25 to £75. The Acts were a response to the rising political consciousness of an increasing number of educated blacks in the eastern Cape. Though the number of coloured voters seems to have remained constant around thirty per cent of the total Cape electorate, the number of black voters dropped from over twenty-five per cent in the 1880s to about fifteen per cent in the 1890s.

Glen Grey and the Transkei The few white liberals in the Cape parliament came into conflict with Afrikaner Bondsmen over a 1892 parliamentary enquiry into an overcrowded reserve in the western Transkei named Glen Grey. Liberals like James Rose Innes proposed that Glen Grey be divided into 48-hectare farms owned by black families on freehold tenure, in order to give rise to a class of small black commercial farmers enjoying full political responsibility as parliamentary voters. People rendered landless would either be employed on the farms or migrate elsewhere. Afrikaner Bondsmen on the other hand wanted Glen Grey to be given up to larger white farmers and all blacks to be obliged to work for them by heavy taxation. Rhodes' compromise policy in the *Glen Grey Act* of 1894 was to grant freehold house-and-garden plots so small (3.5 hectares) that only a single peasant family could live on it. Inheritance of plots was to be by eldest sons only, so that younger sons would 'have to go to the Colony in search of labour'. Landless men had to pay an extra labour tax if they did not work abroad. As Rhodes said, 'Every black man cannot have three acres and a cow ... it must be brought home to them that in future nine-tenths of them will have to spend their lives in daily labour'. Rhodes summed up his policy as 'no liquor and no vote'. In exchange for representation of headmen in a local district council, all parliamentary representation for Glen Grey district was abolished and the sale of liquor to Africans was banned.

The final piece in the Transkei jigsaw, Pondoland, was annexed by Cape Colony in 1894, when the Mpondo were threatened with the latest Maxim machine gun used in

'His Last Ox. A scene on the Bulawayo Road.'   Risings and rumours of risings spread rapidly across southern Africa during the time of the 1896–97 rinderpest. South African newspapers were full of reports of war between whites and blacks — in Matabeleland and Mashonaland, in North-Eastern Rhodesia (with Mpezeni's Ngoni), in German South West Africa, in Portuguese East Africa, in the South African Republic (against the Venda), in the northern Cape Colony, in Basutoland, and in Griqualand-East. There was also unrest in Swaziland and among the Khoisan and Kora in the islands of the lower Orange River. False rumours told of unrest in the Bechuanaland Protectorate, and a large gang of Zulu migrant workers crossing the Natal border into the Transvaal was mistaken for an armed invasion by scared whites. There was also the threat of war between European powers and even between Britain and the USA. Imperialist expansion had produced a world-wide threat of war, and in southern Africa the prospect of war between Boers and British grew increasingly inevitable.

Matabeleland. Sigcawu was arrested for defying the new magistrates, but he was released after an appeal before the Cape supreme court.

British Bechuanaland was annexed to Cape Colony in 1895 at Rhodes's insistence. Tlhaping peasants and wagoners were soon given reason — according to a missionary living among them — to believe that the Cape Colony was 'plotting to take away their land, their cattle, their children even, and reduce them to servitude'. Houses, wagons and child births all had to be registered with the government and each wagon wheel was taxed to force Tlhaping wagoners out of business, while white settlers openly called for more

black land and more black labour. Then came the rinderpest, and Cape police took to shooting cattle in order to stop the southward spread of the disease.

Langeberg rising 1896-97 Southern Tlhaping under Phetlu and Galishiwe rose in revolt at Phokwane in December 1896, after their cattle were shot and the cattle of neighbouring white farms were spared. Phokwane was destroyed by Cape police. The people fled to the Langeberg mountains in the west. The police recruited white settlers eager for farms on captured land, and attacked and captured the lands of both hostile and friendly Africans. The Tlharo chief Toto and Luka Jantjie of the Tlhaping decided to join

Masopha, third son of Moshoeshoe's senior wife, with his standard bearer in traditional uniform.

was taken by government, and other Tlhaping and Tlharo lands were divided into new white farms.

In Basutoland paramount chief Lerotholi's son Makhaola confronted anti-rinderpest patrols crossing the border from Griqualand-East and Natal in 1896-97, which he saw as the advance guard of white settlers into eastern Basutoland. Makhaola was warned off by a show of force of the Basutoland colonial police, and retired to Mafeteng threatening all whites who came near. Two other potentially rebellious sons of Lerotholi, Letsie and Griffith, were brought into line by the Masopha civil war of 1897. Masopha, the hero of the Gun War, raised ten thousand men on Thaba Bosiu to protect his son fleeing from an Orange Free State jail. But the challenge to

Galishiwe and Phetlu in the mountains because 'whatever they did the Government would make rebels of them'.

Between February and August 1897 about four thousand men, women and children were besieged in the Langeberg mountains by two thousand colonial troops. The rebels controlled local wells, and the besiegers had to import water tanks on wagons which were punctured by rebel fire. Eventually the rebels gave way. Old Luka Jantjie was caught by a colonial ambush (and his severed head was taken by a colonial officer as a souvenir). Toto led the surrender of the survivors. Phetlu was subsequently executed; meanwhile Galishiwe was imprisoned on Robben Island. The rest of the 'rebels', including women and children, were given to southern Cape farmers as forced labour. The Phokwane reserve the Boers and British was also a challenge to royal power in the very heart of the country: Letsie and Griffith led attacks which made Masopha surrender in three weeks. The fortifications on Thaba Bosiu were dismantled and the mountain has been abandoned ever since.

In Griqualand-East a Griqua leader called Andries le Fleur used the rinderpest issue to gather support against white settlers under the slogan 'East Griqualand for the Griquas and the Natives'. Le Fleur was first arrested, then released, and plotted a large rising from a secret base. But he was arrested again and sentenced to fifteen years in prison.

Colonization of southern Mozambique The Portuguese succeeded in establishing colonial rule over the Tsonga and Chopi south of the Save river in the 1880s, after the decline of Swazi and Zulu power in the west and south. Then the death of the Shangane king Mzila north of the Save in 1884 gave the Portuguese the chance of extending their power to the Zambezi. Mzila's successor Ngungunyane at first agreed to a treaty of friendship with Portugal, which recognized his Gazankulu kingdom as a 'protected' state (1885). But he soon began to challenge the Portuguese over control of the coastal Chopi. Ngungunyane moved his capital to the lower Limpopo in 1888-89 in order to discipline the Chopi allies of the Portuguese nearby, who had sent him a defiant message describing the 'lion of Gaza' as a man with a fat belly.

Ngungunyane was approached from the west by the British South Africa Company and used the opportunity to renounce the 1885 Portuguese treaty and to accept a 'Treaty of Alliance between the said [Shangane] Nation and the Government of Her Britannic Majesty, Queen Victoria' (1890). Of course the BSAC treaty was nothing of the sort: it was in fact a concession. After the Anglo-Portuguese treaty of 1891 recognised the bulk of Gazankulu as Portuguese territory, the BSAC used the concession to incorporate Manyika country into Rhodesia. The Portuguese then formed a Mozambique Company along the lines of the

BSAC to obtain more territory by concessions from African rulers. (The BSAC failed to buy out the Mozambique Company in order to extend Rhodesian territory to the port of Beira.)

Ngungunyane negotiated with the Mozambique Company in 1893-95, while trying and failing to interest the British 'imperial factor' rather than the BSAC in a Gazankulu protectorate. Eventually war erupted with the Portuguese out of the Shangane conflict with the Chopi in 1895. Much to the surprise of the British, the Portuguese were able to defeat Gazankulu quickly with machine-guns and modern rifles. Ngungunyane was exiled to the Azores islands where he died. His people, despite an attempted rising in 1898, were taxed into regular labour migration to the Transvaal mines.

Questions

1　Compare the scramble for concessions in Swaziland with the scramble for concessions in Matabeleland.

2　Give the causes and results of the Ndebele and Shona risings of 1896-97. [Cambridge International School Certificate, 1980]

3　Why did some Africans collaborate with British imperialism in the 1890s while others resisted it? Give examples to illustrate your answer.

4　Discuss the importance of railway construction and tariffs in the politics of southern Africa before 1899. (Include a map in your answer and refer also to Chapter 12.)

Activities

1　Draw a map of southern Africa marking and dating colonial boundaries and wars of African resistance.

2　Discuss and compare the suppression of African peoples in the Transvaal and in Rhodesia in the 1890s.

For references to Bibliography see p. 222.

Chapter 12

The Triumph of European Imperialism (1895 – 1906)

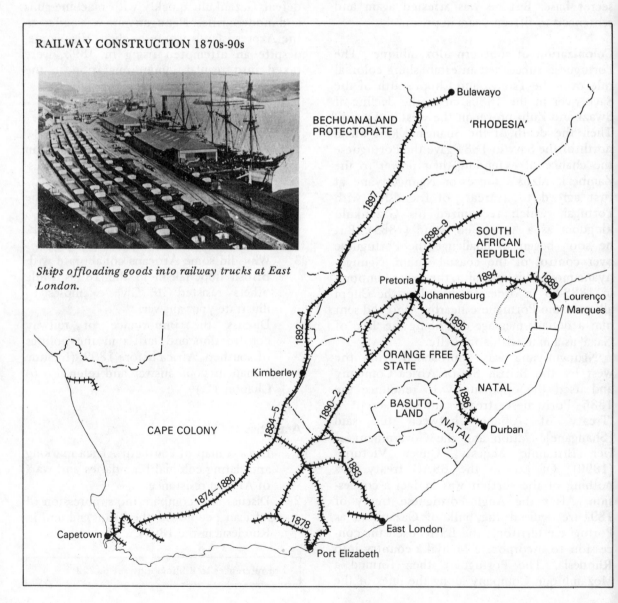

RAILWAY CONSTRUCTION 1870s-90s

Ships offloading goods into railway trucks at East London.

British imperialism reached the height of its industrial and military power over the world in the 1890s. Britain had an empire 'on which the sun never set' and rapidly expanded it into the interior of Africa with machine-guns followed by railways. But two new world powers were beginning to overtake Britain in industrial power and military might — Germany and the United States of America. These countries had been more successful in the 'secondary industrial revolution' of electricity and steel in the later 19th century than Britain, which had pioneered the 'primary industrial revolution' of steam and iron. Nevertheless Britain was still rapidly expanding its industrial production. Its greatest imperialist statesman, Joseph Chamberlain (colonial minister 1895-1903), had been a screw manufacturer who became mayor of Birmingham — the centre of Britain's secondary industrial revolution.

Germany began to challenge Britain and other European powers in Africa and then in Europe, while American imperialism was restricted to the western hemisphere. It was the backing of German capitalism which enabled the Boer republics in southern Africa to build up their strength against British imperialism, although Germany, Russia, France and the Netherlands eventually refused to provide the military support that the Boers hoped for in the South African War of 1899-1902.

1 The Jameson Raid and Origins of War 1895-99

The economic centre of 'South Africa' rapidly shifted from Kimberley to the Witwatersrand during the later 1880s. British colonies on the coast and Boer states in the interior then competed to capture the Rand's import-export trade by building railways from coastal ports. Railway development and railway freight tariffs became the focal issue of political rivalry between white states in the early 1890s.

Railway economics and railway politics   Railway construction was enormously expensive and capital costs could not be paid off for many years after completion. Construction was financed by a combination of private capital and state capital; railway companies were given land for sale along their lines, and overseas bank loans were guaranteed by the republican or colonial governments. Once built, railways had to run profitably to pay off their capital costs. But competing railway companies might force freight tariff charges lower and lower until one company went bankrupt. Here again the state might step in to protect its investment and use of the railway. Railway capitalists in turn became deeply involved in colonial and republican politics.

The Transvaal was already linked by wagon roads to railway lines on its borders from Capetown (1885) and Durban (1891). But Kruger's SAR government grabbed the chance of building the long-desired railway to Delagoa Bay which would give it economic and political independence from British colonies. German banks stepped in to finance the Netherlands South African Railway Company (founded 1884) in 1887, making it an effectively German company under Dutch management. The railway from Lourenço Marques reached the Nkomati valley on the Transvaal border in 1890. But British opposition would not allow it to climb up the Nkomati valley through Swaziland onto the highveld, and it was not completed to Pretoria until 1894 by a more difficult route. Meanwhile, the company had financial difficulties. It was obliged to build a link to connect the Rand with the Cape railways on the Orange Free State border in 1892 in return for capital aid from Cape Colony. Finally in 1895 the company completed a link from the Rand to the Natal railway on its border.

The Cape and Natal lines made enormous profits from Rand traffic; most of their £3.9 million freight charges in 1894-95 were on Rand traffic. But the Netherlands South Africa Railway Company decided to take the lion's share of traffic for the Lourenço Marques line. As its director overseas reminded its Transvaal manager, 'our origins are anti-English [and] our goal is to make the SAR

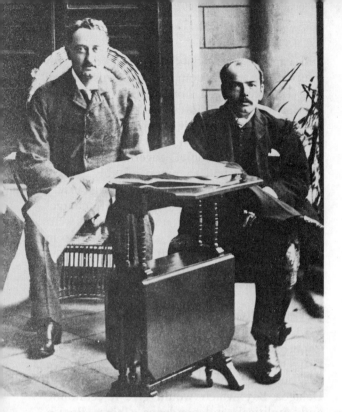

Cecil John Rhodes (1853-1902) and Leander Starr Jameson (1853-1917). Leading conspirators to take the Transvaal by force in 1895-96.

economically independent'. However as soon as the Lourenço Marques line was open, Cape railways reduced their freight charges from the Cape ports to the Vaal river to undercut the new line. The Netherlands company answered by tripling freight charges on its short line from the Vaal to the Rand. When the Cape railways failed to get those charges reduced, it organized a cheap wagon service over the sixty-five kilometres from the Vaal to the Rand.

President Kruger then threatened to close the Vaal drifts (fords) to ox-wagons carrying railway goods in August 1895, and the drifts were closed in November. The response to the closure by the new Conservative government in Britain was immediate and strong, and force was threatened. Kruger backed down and re-opened the Vaal drifts only seven days after he had closed them.

Capitalists plot revolution The railway tariff war and the Vaal drifts crisis, coming at the time of the 'kaffir boom' in gold market shares (see above), excited Rand capitalists with the prospect of overthrowing Kruger to set up their own government. The British high commissioner had already considered seizing the Transvaal when Kruger was re-elected in 1894. Now from about June 1895 Cecil Rhodes and allied capitalists planned to do so by a BSAC 'flying column' — like that used against Lobengula — linking up with a rebellion in Johannesburg. (Rhodes had now come to realize that the 'second Rand' he sought lay not in the north but in the deep levels beneath the existing Rand.)

Uitlanders (i.e. expatriate whites) on the Rand had been talking of rebellion since Kruger's re-election, because they were denied citizenship and local government rights except on strict conditions. Their demands for reform were backed by five of the ten large mining houses in the chamber of mines, notably by Wernher & Beit and Rhodes' Gold Fields Company. But the five other major mining houses, including Lewis & Marks and Joseph Robinson, backed Kruger's resistance to *uitlander* demands. Some historians have attempted to explain this as a split between anti-Kruger deep-level mining interests and pro-Kruger shallow-level interests. The division was not quite that simple in practice. But Rhodes himself later explained that it was the economics of deep-level mining that made the overthrow of Kruger necessary.

Rhodes and others argued that 'good government' in place of Kruger's corrupt and inefficient regime would save the mining companies at least six shillings on every ton of earth mined, making a total saving of £2.5 million a year. The costs of machinery and of supplies such as dynamite and chemicals were too high because of customs tariffs, railway freight charges and state monopolies. The costs of labour were too high because of government unhelpfulness in the recruitment and control of black labour, which needed to be expanded by tens of thousands, with reduced wages, in order to maximize production. The companies were mining hundreds of thousands of tons of ore, from which only tiny quanties of gold were extracted, so they thought in terms of costs per ton. Every penny saved on a ton was a penny towards increasing production by sinking deeper shafts, opening up larger networks of stopes underground, investing in better surface machinery. Every penny saved beyond a certain point was pure profit for the company.

Jameson Raid fails British South Africa Company envoys in London cabled Rhodes that the new colonial minister Chamberlain would give assistance 'provided he does not know officially of your plan'. Chamberlain then obtained a 'railway strip' along the Bechuanaland border from Khama, Sebele and Bathoen for use as the base for the raid on the Transvaal. But Kruger's re-opening of the Vaal drifts removed the need for direct involvement of the 'imperial factor', and the raid was left to private enterprise. By the time that Jameson had organized BSAC forces at the Pitsane railhead in Bechuanaland, the *uitlander* reform movement in Johannesburg had died down. Jameson's forces crossed the border on December 29th only to surrender near Krugersdorp on January 2nd, 1896, after *uitlander* forces had failed to join them from Johannesburg.

Rhodes resigned as prime minister of Cape Colony as the Afrikaner Bond withdrew its support for him. The British government pressured the SAR to be lenient with the Jameson raiders and *uitlander* rebels. Death sentences on the four leading rebels were commuted to fines of £25,000 each, paid for by Rhodes and Beit. The BSAC raiders were deported; the senior officers were sentenced to imprisonment by a court in Britain, but Jameson was excused jail on grounds of ill health.

Effects of the Jameson Raid The Jameson Raid caused a temporary international crisis for Britain when Germany threatened to ally with Russia and France in support of the South African Republic. There was even the possibility of an armed clash between German and British ships off Delagoa Bay. When Jameson was captured, the German *kaiser*

Jameson in Pretoria prison, before being deported to England, being sketched by an artist for an illustrated news magazine. Note that the South African Republic employed black as well as white jailers for white prisoners.

(emperor) sent a congratulatory telegram to Kruger that caused great offence to the British queen, who was his grandmother. Germany had considerable investments in the Transvaal. Besides the railway company, three of the five pro-Boer larger mining houses were predominantly German; the dynamite monopoly was held by a Swedish-German company (Nobel); and Germany supplied much of the electrical and chemical technology of the mines, as well as military weapons to the SAR government. There were 15,000 Germans living in the Transvaal.

The failure of the Jameson Raid convinced 'Pushful Joe' Chamberlain that the British 'imperial factor' would have to succeed where private enterprise had failed to take control of the Transvaal. Chamberlain replaced Rhodes' friend Hercules Robinson as high commissioner by a dynamic imperial bureaucrat called Alfred Milner (1897). Milner's task was to mastermind the joining of the two Boer republics to a British-ruled South African confederation, by persuasion if possible but by war if necessary. Chamberlain publicized continuing *uitlander* grievances over Transvaal injustices and the franchise question. In 1898 Britain and Germany came to terms over African questions, with Germany agreeing to British paramountcy over the south-east corner of the continent. This gave Chamberlain and Milner the chance to claim the British 'suzerainty' over Transvaal affairs that had lapsed since the 1884 London Convention.

Agitation was revived in Johannesburg by businessmen and through newspapers owned by Rhodes and other 'Randlords'. Kruger responded by stamping down on the inefficiency and corruption of which the Randlords complained. At the same time Kruger refused the franchise to *uitlanders,* except on strict conditions of application for citizenship, for fear of the Transvaal electorate being swamped out by disloyal anti-Boer voters. It was mistakenly believed that *uitlanders* out-numbered Afrikaners in the SAR, because only 35,000 men were registered as burghers in a white population of 288,750 (1898). (But Afrikaners, unlike *uitlanders,* had many children, and many poor Afrikaner males were not registered. In fact the total Afrikaner population in all states south of the Limpopo was maybe 434,552 against 324,015 *uitlanders.*)

Transvaal militarization Kruger's hardline policies were reinforced by his re-election as president in 1898 by an even greater majority of voters. Rising state revenues and an active policy of military armament gave the SAR confidence to resist British demands over the *uitlander* franchise. State income tripled between 1894 and 1895 to about £1.5 million, rising to £2 million in 1896. (The value of gold production rose from £8.6 million in 1895, to £16.2 million in 1898.) SAR military expenditure rose from £28,000 in 1894 to £496,000 in 1896. As a correspondent of *The Times* newspaper of London found when he visited Pretoria in 1896:

'One attempt had been made to take their country from them; they were thoroughly convinced that the attempt would be renewed at some future date; so the Boers were determined to be thoroughly on their guard a second time.'

During 1896 all SAR commandos were issued with German Mauser rifles, superior in fire power and quicker loading than British army rifles. Boers were sent to Europe for military training, and German instructors were imported to train an artillery brigade. As well as machine-guns, the SAR imported four French Creusot heavy field guns, known as 'Long Toms' because of their long barrels which could fire 42-kilogram shells up to ten kilometres. (The British army in South Africa only had light field-guns firing 3- or 6-kilogram

President Paul Kruger (1825-1904) and his new commandant-general Piet Cronje, who replaced Joubert on the latter's death in late 1899.

SOUTH AFRICAN WAR 1899-1902
1899
October: War declared; Mafeking, Ladysmith and Kimberley besieged by Boers.
November: Boers invaded Cape Colony; British began counter-offensive.
December: Boers defeated British at Stormberg, Magersfontein and Colenso.
1900
February: New British counter-offensive successful; Kimberley and Ladysmith relieved.
March: Bloemfontein captured.
May: Mafeking relieved and Johannesburg captured.
June: Pretoria captured.
August: Boers defeated at Bergendal.
September: President Kruger escaped to Lourenço Marques and exile in Holland; Transvaal declared a British colony. Boers turned to guerrilla warefare until British gained the upper hand in February 1902, leading to Peace of Vereeniging in *May 1902*.

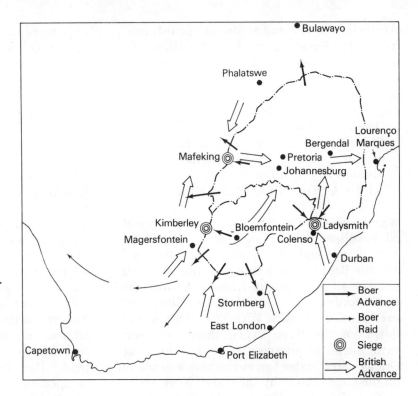

shells.) The SAR also spent considerable sums outside its military budget on building fortifications to defend Pretoria and Johannesburg.

The climax of confrontation between Milner and Kruger came at the Bloemfontein conference of June 1899. Milner had already decided that the conference should not succeed. He had sent a long telegram to Chamberlain, intended to sway the British press and public in favour of war, accusing the Transvaal of keeping British *uitlanders* 'permanently in the position of helots, constantly chafing under undoubted grievances' and of seeking to bring all of South Africa under an Afrikaner republic. Now at Bloemfontein Milner snubbed Kruger's improved offer of *uitlander* franchise after seven years' residence, by demanding the franchise for those who had already been resident for five years. Kruger cried out, 'It's my country you want!' and refused to concede. Further negotiations in August were a failure, and the British government found that Chamberlain and Milner had committed it to a war on

behalf of the Randlords against Kruger. Tens of thousands of *uitlanders* fled from Johannesburg, and African miners rioted in the compounds or fled to neighbouring British colonies.

2 The South African War (1899-1902)

The South African Republic and the Orange Free State, probably urged on by Germany, declared war on Britain on October 11th, 1899, before British reinforcements could arrive from overseas. The republics put 40,000 men into the field against half that number in the British colonies. British troops were already massing on the Natal-Transvaal frontier, to draw Boer forces away from the Orange river where British reinforcements would arrive by rail from the Cape ports to advance on Bloemfontein and the Rand. The Boer military plan, on the other hand, consisted of blocking the threatened invasion from Natal (possibly capturing Durban), and of capturing the Kimberley railway to invade deep into Cape Colony and arouse fellow

195

Afrikaners to rise and throw off British rule. Young Jan Smuts touched on this vision of a united Afrikaner nationalism or imperialism in his introduction to a pamphlet, *A Century of Wrong,* published as propaganda for the Boer cause in the Netherlands and Germany:

'Liberty will surely rise in South Africa like the sun out of the mists of the morning . . . Then from the Zambesi to Simon's Bay it will be —
AFRICA FOR THE AFRIKANER.'

War declared The two Boer republics opened hostilities on the night of October 11th and by the end of the month had besieged 18,000 British troops and possibly an equal number of Africans at Ladysmith over the Natal border, and at Mafeking and Kimberley over the Cape border. With 32,000 Boers tied down on the three sieges, there were few extra men for invading Cape Colony. But Orange Free States forces reached Stormberg on the Cape railway by the end of November.

The British offensive commenced in November. The only victory was by a small British force from Rhodesia at Deerdepoort north of Mafeking. The British army in the Cape was roundly defeated first at Stormberg, and then at Magersfontein when trying to reach Kimberley. The British army in Natal was more disastrously defeated at Colenso when trying to relieve Ladysmith. The British commander-in-chief Redvers Buller signalled Ladysmith to surrender once it had spent its ammunition (December 1899).

The three defeats and Buller's cowardly message caused an uproar of despair in Britain and delight on the continent of Europe. Buller was replaced as commander-in-chief by an ageing British hero named Frederick 'Bobs' Roberts, assisted by Horatio Kitchener the recent conqueror of the Sudan. 'Please understand,' explained Queen Victoria, 'that there is no one depressed in this house. We are not interested in the possibilities of defeat. They do not exist.' About 85,000 extra British troops were sent to South Africa, and thousands of horses were imported to make the forces mobile like the Boer commandos.

Meanwhile the Boer armies, commanded by

old Piet Joubert (SAR) and Piet Cronje (OFS), failed to take the initiative to advance and capture the British ports before overseas reinforcements arrived. The only battle in January 1900, at Spion Kop in Natal, was extremely bloody but indecisive. In February massive British counter-offensives with heavy artillery got underway, defeating Cronje at Paardeberg to relieve Kimberley, defeating other Boers at Crocodile Pools north of Mafeking, and defeating Joubert to relieve Ladysmith.

Boer forces began to retreat and British optimism was summed up in a popular song, 'We are marching to Pretoria'. Boer overtures for peace were swept aside as the British had the taste of victory in their mouths. Bloemfontein was captured in March 1900. But Roberts delayed further advance until new reinforcements — from Canada, Australia and New Zealand as well as Britain — were in the field. The British army from Natal also stopped its advance on the Drakensberg edge of the highveld. Meanwhile irregular OFS forces under Christiaan de Wet had begun guerrilla warfare near the Basutoland border. Then Roberts moved forward in massive strength in early May. Mafeking was relieved in the middle of the month and Johannesburg was occupied at the end of the month. On June 5th, 1900, Roberts took Pretoria. Roberts and his generals mistakenly assumed that the SAR was a modern European state, in which the capture of railways and towns, and above all the capture of the capital city, would automatically result in surrender of the government and armed forces. But Kruger retreated with government papers along the railway towards Lourenço Marques.

Louis Botha, the new SAR commandant-general after Joubert's death, did indeed begin negotiations with Roberts at the Hatherley distillery outside Pretoria. But the success of de Wet's forces in the Orange Free State stung Botha and his generals into renewed defiance. SAR forces massed with their four 'Long Toms' along the Drakensberg ridges of the eastern Transvaal, where the final open battle of the war took place at Bergendal in August 1900. The Boer forces were split in two and

SIEGE OF MAFEKING

Plan of Mafeking under siege
The shaded line marks Boer trenches; the thick line marks British outer defences; the broken lines mark British inner defences to protect the white town if the Rolong town is over-run.

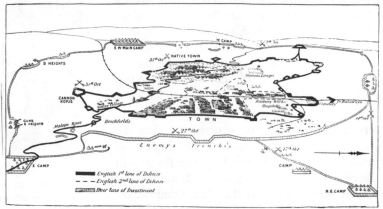

The trader Julius Weil anticipated the siege by stocking up well with food and drink for sale to British officers and men.
Christmas 1899 was celebrated with suckling pig, roast beef, mutton, hams, plum pudding and tarts, washed down with hock wine, ginger beer, and 'the beer that made Milwaukee famous'. Easter 1900 was celebrated with fun and games, including the fancy dress show by British officers pictured **right**.

Mafeking was not, however, merry for its African population under frequent fire from the Boer beseigers. The African diarist Sol Plaatje refers to refugee miners from the Rand, including Mpondo, Shangane, Lozi, 'Zambezian and South Central African Breeds', who were reduced to digging up dead dogs for food. Cattle raiding parties ventured beyond Boer lines and attacked Boer farms in the Transvaal. Other Africans were suspected of being Boer spies, and were executed on the orders of the British commander, Robert Baden-Powell (**above right**).

London crowds go wild at the news of the relief of Mafeking, adding a new word to the English language — 'to maffick', meaning 'to exult riotously', hence 'mafficking'.

chased to Lydenburg and Barberton, which were captured without any formal surrender by the SAR. The British regarded the war as being effectively over; while Kruger escaped to Portuguese territory, Roberts declared the Transvaal to be a British colony once again (September 1900).

Guerrilla war Roberts returned home to Britain in triumph, leaving Kitchener as commander-in-chief to mop up the Boers still at large with mounted police. Remnants of the SAR army followed the OFS example by melting into the landscape to become small highly mobile guerrilla units, harassing the British with surprise attacks. For almost two years guerrilla war continued in the countryside while the British controlled urban areas and main lines of communication. Two hundred thousand British troops were tied down by under sixty thousand Boer guerrillas. The British adopted their traditional scorched earth strategy, used against Xhosa and Shona guerrillas, of burning crops and housing to deny the guerrillas food and shelter. But the Boers were different from other guerrillas in two ways. Firstly the Boers were horsemen and therefore moved rapidly across the grasslands south of the Witwatersrand. Secondly the Boers were of European ancestry and British atrocities against them received wide publicity in Europe. That helped to limit British repression and to stimulate bitter nationalism among Afrikaners in the Cape as well as in the ex-republics.

British strategy Transvaal guerrilla commandos were pushed southwards by drought and famine in the bushveld north of Pretoria at the end of 1900. Kitchener responded early in the new year by clearing the northern Transvaal of remaining Boers, and dividing his mounted forces to chase guerrilla commandos in three operational zones — against Botha in the eastern Transvaal; against de Wet and James Hertzog in the Orange River Colony; and against de la Rey and Smuts in the western Transvaal. But so long as farming continued in the affected areas, a complete scorched earth strategy was impossible. So,

An armed African scout directs British troops
African assistance to the British army created much bitterness among Boers. President Kruger accused the British of using African allies at the battle of Deerdeport, on the Bechuanaland-Transvaal border, in November 1899. The British denied this at the time, but historians have proved Kruger correct. The British used over 50,000 Africans as wagoners, cattlemen, scouts, messengers, guards, personal servants and general labourers, and the Boer armies used them in similar roles. African peasants produced most of the food eaten by the armies. African lands in battle zones were laid waste. But those areas outside the battle zones, when not crowded with refugees, even prospered from high crop prices and labour wages during the war.

during the winter of mid-1901, Boer families and their black servants were removed from the land and put into rural compounds known as 'concentration camps' (i.e. protected villages).

Kitchener next extended the blockhouse system that had proved successful in defending the railways — small two-storey houses built of rocks and metal, each manned by seven British soldiers and four African night guards, linked together by telephone, and less than two kilometres apart. No horsemen could cross the railway without being noticed, and no wagons could cross without being shot at. Kitchener extended a network of blockhouses along barbed-wire fences from the railways across the operational zones. By early 1902 there were 10,000 blockhouses along 8,000 kilometres of fence. The open highveld was therefore divided up into geometric sections, which were first swept clean of civilians and then patrolled by mounted British troops.

African participation In hillier country, which could not be easily cleared and fenced, the British relied on African scouts and friendly villagers for intelligence on Boer movements. Africans who had fought for the Boers now declared their allegiance to the British. Boers in turn began to attack such black 'rebels'. In the northern Transvaal the Venda and Pedi kingdoms effectively regained their independence, and Boer farms elsewhere were abandoned or left in the charge of armed servants guarding Boer women and children. Only in the western Transvaal was there continuous warfare between an African group, the Kgatla of Linchwe, and local Boers. The Kgatla-Boer war begun when the Kgatla joined the British at the Deerdepoort battle in September 1899. The war continued as a series of cattle raids until mid-1902. Boer settlers abandoned large areas of farmland after Kgatla ambushed Boers south of Deerdepoort at Kayesput in March 1900.

In Basutoland the paramount chief Lerotholi held his people back from joining the war to regain the 'conquered territory' from the Orange Free State. But some chiefs did conduct their own cattle raids into the

Joel Molapo in 1896 (**seated left**)   Orange Free State Boers found him a useful ally against the rule of Lerotholi and the British in Basutoland during the South African War. In 1902 the British punished him with a year's jail sentence.

territory. Sotho patrols on the frontier stopped Boers escaping from the British siege at Wepener. The Boer guerrilla leader de Wet preferred to risk crossing British lines rather than enter Basutoland, though some Sotho chiefs were in friendly contact with Boers by 1901-02. But the British kept the baSotho neutral by their alliance with Lerotholi, and by good prices and steady demand for Sotho grain and Sotho horses.

Swaziland became effectively independent when the SAR abandoned its administration at the beginning of the war. King Bhunu, who had been won over to Kruger by a state visit to Pretoria before the war, died in December 1899. His mother Labotsibeni and brother Malunge took power as regents for Bhunu's son Nkhotfojeni (born 1899), later titled Sobhuza II. The regents allowed British raids across Swaziland to attack the Transvaal railways, and took the opportunity to appeal to the British queen to tear up the 3rd Swaziland Convention of 1894. However the British did not expel all Boers from Bremersdorp until 1901, and the village was burnt down in a Boer counter-attack soon afterwards.

Zululand within Natal remained quiet. But the Zulu of the Vryheid district inside the SAR actively assisted the British cause. Around 1900 they rebelled and attacked Swazi allies of the Boers on the Pongola river, and aroused great Boer bitterness by guiding British troops in night attacks on Boer guerrilla camps. A Zulu-Boer battle in the Vryheid district actually pushed Botha's Boers into finally surrendering in 1902 (see below).

Concentration camps 117,000 whites and 107,000 blacks were interned in concentration camps in the Orange River Colony and Transvaal. The camps rapidly became overcrowded and unhealthy with epidemics of enteric dysentery, measles and other diseases. By December 1901 the death rate had reached thirty-four per cent in white camps and forty-seven per cent in black camps. The British army — which itself lost many more men to dysentery and pneumonia than to the Boers — then began to improve sanitation and medical care in the camps, and the death rates fell. But a legend of bitterness was born among Afrikaners of British ill-treatment of their women and children in the camps – even to the claim that food had been deliberately poisoned.

'Bitter-enders' and 'hands-uppers' As the Afrikaner resistance to British conquest dwindled to about 9,000 men and their families, some Afrikaners joined the British forces. The war became more than ever a civil war between Afrikaners, between the 'bitter-enders' still fighting and the 'hands-uppers' who had surrendered. A small body of Boers under Smuts broke out of the western Transvaal in mid-1901 in a vain attempt to raise the long-awaited rebellion of Afrikaners in the Cape Colony. Smuts crossed the Orange and reached the western Cape, but he was chased north by British troops into the thirst-land, where he laid siege to Okiep copper mine.

In February 1902 Kitchener began systematic attempts to sweep the highveld plains clear, using large numbers of troops advancing in broad fronts across the open countryside – the technique of wildlife hunting with nets and lines of beaters on a massive scale. In February Botha withdrew his forces south into the Drakensberg foothills of the Vryheid district, while his second-in-command withdrew north to the mountains around Pilgrim's Rest. In March de Wet withdrew from the north-eastern Orange River Colony to join de la Rey in the hillier western Transvaal.

Peace negotiations between Boers and British began in March 1902. Cecil Rhodes died in the same month, and the train taking his body for burial in Rhodesia was delayed south of Mafeking by one of the war's last battles. The Zulu of Vryheid district entered the war with a vengeance, killing fifty-six Boers at Holkrantz, where Botha's forces had been reduced almost to rags and near to starvation. The forces of the South African Republic and the Orange Free State finally surrendered to the British at Vereeniging on May 31, 1900. The reason given for making peace was that the combination of scorched earth strategy, deaths in concentration camps, and attacks by armed Africans, would lead to the extermination of 'our whole nation'.

In return the British offered the ending of military rule, and later the resumption of self-government in the conquered colonies 'as soon as circumstances permit'. Meanwhile Boers might keep their rifles for protection against Africans, the Netherlands language could be used in schools and law courts, and the British would spend £3 million on post-war reconstruction in the colonies. The contentious question of extending the 'colour-blind' Cape parliamentary franchise to the two ex-republics – for which Britain had told Africans it was fighting the war – was shelved indefinitely by saying that the Transvaal and Orange Free State could decide for themselves after self-government. In other words the Boers were promised a free vote on whether more 'civilized' Africans should get the franchise – a choice which would also disenfranchise poor or uneducated whites, and which the Boers could confidently be expected to reject.

3 Post-War Reconstruction 1901-06

Resumption of gold production Botha had restrained wilder Boers from destroying mines before the British captured the Rand, but most mines had closed down and African wages were reduced to 20 shillings (£1) a month in 1900. When mines were re-opened wages were raised to only 31 shillings. By mid-1902 there were only 30,000 black miners, against the 100,000 needed to return to the level of pre-war production. By mid-1903 a raise of wages to 45 shillings raised the number of black miners to only 50,000. Africans had found alternative employment, were making a living from selling their crops, or had built up savings from earnings during the war. Africans did not feel obliged to return to the mines until employment and wages declined elsewhere with the onset of economic depression in 1904, until drought and stock disease destroyed peasant prosperity and land was lost to new white farms, or until regular taxation and policing of country districts made labour migration necessary. But the mining companies were determined to reduce the costs of labour. They succeeded in reducing working costs from 30 shillings per ton in 1900 to 17 shillings in 1914. They were not prepared to raise black wages higher than the 54 shillings a month that they offered in 1904.

Chinese labour on the Witwatersrand The gold companies investigated Mozambique and Nyasaland, North Africa and Italy for regular supplies of labour, and finally decided on importing indentured labour from China. The Witwatersrand Native Labour Association ('WENELA') of the chamber of mines organized recruitment from Mozambique after the British and Portuguese governments signed the so-called *Modus Vivendi* Agreement over labour in 1901. Up to 1910 Mozambique supplied about two-thirds of the black labour to the Rand. WENELA also competed with the Southern Rhodesian mines for 'Nyasa' labour. Many of them died of pneumonia on the Rand after completing the exhausting journey on foot, until the death rate reached a peak of 15.8 per cent (against 2.6 per cent for black South Africans) in 1906. This led to a Nyasaland government ban on recruiting.

More than 63,000 Chinese workers, mostly from northern China, were brought to the Rand mines in 1904-05. They were indentured to stay up to four years on very meagre wages before being repatriated home. Their miserable condition became a political issue in Britain during the parliamentary elections of 1906, when the Liberals accused the Conservative government of 'Chinese slavery' on the Rand. When the Liberals won the election they stopped the importation of Chinese labour into the Transvaal, and by 1910 virtually all Chinese had been repatriated to China. The Chinese 'experiment' was a success, supplying 35 per cent of unskilled labour on the mines and enabling production to climb from 1.7 million fine ounces of gold in 1902 to exceed the 1898 production figure in 1905 — at 4.7 million ounces worth £20

million. As the Chinese left, they were replaced with Africans from South Africa, and production figures continued to rise steadily.

Milner's reconstruction plan Milner ruled South Africa from Johannesburg between 1901 and 1905, supervising the reconstruction of the ex-republics' economy and administration with the assistance of young British university graduates, known as his 'kindergarten'.

Economic reconstruction was based on a £35 million loan, mostly raised from the mining companies, to the Transvaal and Orange River Colony governments — to be spent on railways, agriculture, social services and compensation for damage to property. Of this loan, £13.5 million was used as compensation to stock-holders of the Netherlands South African Railway Company when the Transvaal railways were taken over by government. A further £8 million was spent on public works, mostly on 2,000 extra kilometres of railway to serve agricultural districts (while the Cape extended its own railways by a similar distance). £3 million was given as compensation to Boer property owners as promised at the peace of Vereeniging; African claims were all reduced to a sixth of their value, and it is not clear if any were eventually paid out. Most of the remaining loan was spent on state aid to agriculture, with smaller amounts on 'native administration' and white education.

The main aim of economic reconstruction was to develop productive capitalist agriculture to feed the mines and towns with maize, meat, wheat and milk. The Transvaal and Orange Free State were surveyed for agricultural potential; scientific services for improved crops and livestock were set up; and the immigration of English-speaking capitalist farmers was awaited. But the immigrants did not come, a 1903-08 drought reduced agricultural yields, and government aid was used to capitalize Boer farmers. Farmers in the southern Transvaal and Orange River Colony became more commercially minded. They cleared poor *bywoner* (squatter) Boers off the land, and replaced them by productive black peasants as tenant share-croppers giving at least half their harvest to the farmer as rent. Landless Boers were resettled as cattle-ranchers in the western and northern Transvaal, cleared of tsetse-fly by rinderpest before the war; others went to settle as workers on the Rand; and some emigrated as far as Kenya.

The first aim of 'native administration' was to disarm Africans and keep them peaceful; the second aim was to ensure a regular labour supply to mines and white farms. By the time the war ended, the army and mounted police had persuaded nearly all Africans in the conquered areas to surrender their arms and register for taxation. The army even compiled a *History of the Native Tribes of the Transvaal* from oral traditions in an effort to understand and control the relations between chiefdoms. But the man placed in charge of the native affairs department, Godfrey Lagden the former Basutoland resident commissioner, openly despised African culture. He was chairman of the *South African Native Affairs Commission* of 1903-05. The commission toured all the colonies taking evidence on how to partition the land between white areas and black reserves, and at the same time to ensure black labour supply to white areas.

State education under Milner was intended to 'anglicize' Afrikaners with values of service to the British empire. English was the medium and Netherlands was a foreign language for teaching; Afrikaans was ignored. History was taught as the civilization of the world by the British. As Milner himself said of South African children, 'Everything that cramps and confines their views to South Africa only — makes for Afrikanerdom and further discord [i.e. between Boers and British]'. But state education in the ex-republics was almost entirely confined to whites. African education was left to African initiative, which proved to be considerable. In the years immediately following the South African War there was tremendous demand for education as the key to success in a new world. In fact there were more independent African schools — run by Ethiopianist churches or tribal governments — than white schools in the Transvaal.

Afrikaner nationalist reaction   The reaction of most Afrikaners to 'anglicization' in state schools was to place their children in independent schools — run by the so-called 'Christian-National' educational movement. Christian-National education originated as a separate school system for Calvinist children in the Netherlands, closely associated with the Anti-Revolutionary Party that came to power in 1901. In South Africa it meant that children should be taught their national religion and national history in their own language. (The major Afrikaans historical writings of Gustav Preller and others also date from this period.) The movement spread through all three Dutch reformed churches and took the old Transvaal capital of Potchefstroom as its base. Christian-National education appealed to poorer Afrikaners but did not receive support from aristocratic national leaders like Botha and Smuts.

Botha and Smuts founded a political party called *Vereeniging Het Volk* (people's party) in 1905, to revive the leadership of pre-war SAR landowners and officials for forthcoming elections. A similar party called *Orangia Unie* was founded in the Orange River Colony. Pro-Boer Randlords such as Joseph Robinson supported them, but most Randlords backed the Transvaal section of the Progressive Party led by Dr Jameson in the Cape. An important third party, the so-called Labour Party, was founded by Fred Creswell (in fact a small mine-owner) in order to attract the anti-capitalist vote of white workers on the Rand.

With the coming to power of the Liberal party in Britain during 1905-06, Milner's policy of anglicization was finally abandoned. Selborne the new high commissioner (1905-10) was instructed to conciliate Afrikaner politicians and to prepare the way for political union of the South African colonies. The Transvaal became self-governing in 1906, with Het Volk elected to power, while the Orange River Colony became self-governing as the Orange Free State again in 1907. The *uitlanders* in the Transvaal, though a majority of the voters, had been split along class lines of labour versus capital, while the Afrikaner

Unrepentant followers of Bambatha, after capture by Natal colonial troops. The original caption reads (from left to right): 'Mesini, one of Bambata's *indunas;* Nkomo, Bambata's chief *induna;* one of Sibindi's rebels; Cuyaganya, implicated in the mutilation of Sergeant Brown.'

vote had been united along national lines and therefore took the balance of power.

Cape Colony and Natal affairs The Afrikaner parliamentary triumph was completed in 1908 when Jameson was forced to resign as prime minister of Cape Colony. He was replaced by John X. Merriman with the support of the Cape's Afrikaner Bond. The only colony south of the Limpopo remaining under English white settler control, Natal, was discredited by its handling of the Zulu rising of 1906.

'Bambatha rebellion' When a new poll tax was imposed on Africans in Natal in 1905-06 whites anticipated trouble, and in doing so provoked more trouble. Though Dinizulu the uninstalled Zulu king (returned from exile in 1898) paid up, other chiefs tried to delay payment. In February 1906 two white policemen were killed on a farm south of Pietermaritzburg when they attacked tax resisters belonging to an independent African church. The killers of the white policemen were publicly executed. Natal colonial troops began to march through black reserves, burning and looting the fields and houses of tax resisters. Attempts by the Colonial Office in London to intervene were rejected by the Natal government as unwarranted interference. Bambatha, a minor Zulu chief near Greytown, became the symbol of Zulu resistance when he defied the tax-collectors and retired to fight a guerrilla campaign in the Nkudla mountains. Zulu patriots flocked to join him in the mountains. So Bambatha was ruthlessly hunted down and killed at the battle of Mome valley by Natal forces in June 1906.

Rumours of black rebellion spread far and wide. There were rumours that the baSotho would attack the Cape railways bringing troops reinforcements to Natal. There were rumours of Dinizulu sending envoys to the Swazi, Lobedu, Venda, Ngwato, and Kgatla asking their rulers to rise with him. In the western Transvaal, Boers reported stories of envoys from Witbooi in South West Africa inciting the Tswana to revolt. Rumours among blacks accused Botha and Smuts of inciting the Zulu to massacre the British, or of white settlers inciting revolt so that they could take the land and labour by conquest. Certainly some white Natal troops attacked friendly chiefdoms in order to incite them to join the rebellion.

By August 1906 the 'Bambatha rebellion' had been crushed. It had never become a general Zulu rising let alone a general black rising, because Dinizulu had not given it his approval. He was perversely rewarded for his loyalty. In 1907 he was arrested for sheltering tax resisters, and was sentenced after a long trial to four years imprisonment. The publicity surrounding the trial made Dinizulu a national hero among Africans in South Africa. The new Union government in 1910 therefore released him from prison as a gesture of reconciliation, but also exiled him from Natal in case he became the effective leader of the Zulu.

4 British South Africa Company Policy in the Rhodesias

The failure of a 'second Rand' to materialize north of the Limpopo resulted in a slump in the value of the BSAC and Rhodesian gold mining shares after the South African War. Between 1903 and 1911, therefore, the company restructured the economy of the Rhodesias. It withdrew its monopoly control over mining and agricultural developments, to rely instead on royalties and taxes from private capitalist production.

Southern Rhodesia The gold mines were relatively shallow and scattered along a number of small reefs. So the BSAC was hard-pressed to finance so many small mines. The mines were opened up to outside capital in 1903. Capitalists both big and small from the Rand moved in to set up mining companies, which sought to maximize output and minimize working costs. The black labour force was increased fivefold during 1903-11, and wages were drastically reduced. Black wages stood as high as 80 shillings a month in 1903. Wages had climbed from 5 shillings a month in 1896 largely because of the scarcity of local Shona labour, which found peasant farming more profitable. The mines now brought in large numbers of workers from Mozambique, Nyasaland and North-Eastern Rhodesia (eastern Zambia). They were prepared to accept much lower wages, because there was no other way to earn cash for colonial taxes at home, and because colonial police rounded them up and marched them to the border.

Partition of land into white areas and 'native reserves' began after the 1896-97 risings. (Small areas set aside for blacks within the white areas were known as 'native locations'.) Less than twenty per cent of Matabeleland and thirty-three per cent of Mashonaland were recognized as reserves. Nearly all the high lands and land near railways were declared white. But Africans only learnt they were living on white land when its owner began to demand rent — generally after 1898 in Matabeleland and after 1904 in Mashonaland. Most white farm owners lived off rent given in crops by peasant tenants, selling the crops on the open market, rather than investing capital and managing black labour themselves.

The BSAC encouraged the growth of capitalist agriculture to ensure plentiful and regular supplies of foodstuffs to the mines of Rhodesia and Katanga (Belgian Congo). In 1908 it launched its 'white agricultural policy'. The company brought in settler farmers owning at least £700 capital, provided them with financial credit and scientific advice, and further reduced the 'native reserves' for new farms. Blacks were not allowed to purchase farms: the first to apply and be turned down was a black American. Most of the new land taken from reserves was in Mashonaland, where peasants were driven from their land into the reserves.

North-Western Rhodesia outside Barotseland was opened to white farm settlement in 1904 under its BSAC administrator Robert Coryndon. Farms were sold for as little as a shilling a hectare along the railway from Victoria Falls, which reached Broken Hill (Kabwe) in 1906 and Katanga in 1909. Many were bought by whites from the south, including Boer wagoners who settled around Lusaka station to sell maize and vegetables to the Broken Hill lead mine. But large areas of farm land did not find buyers, and the colonial capital at Kalomo, in white farming country, was moved to the new town of Livingstone next to the Victoria Falls in 1907.

5 German Conquest of South West Africa 1888-1907

German advance into the interior of South West Africa was delayed for over ten years by the strength of African states there. In 1888 Maherero renounced his previous treaty with Germany for a concession to a British syndicate from Kimberley. But the British then recognized German sovereignty over the whole of the Namibia area, including the Caprivi strip, in 1890. Maherero died in 1890, and was succeeded as king by his son Samuel Maherero. Meanwhile Hendrik Witbooi succeeded to his father's Nama chieftainship in 1888. He turned from bandit warfare with the Herero, to destroy the Orlam-Afrikaner nation once and for all in 1889. (Jan Jonker Afrikaner was shot dead by his own son as he laid down his rifle and walked towards Hendrik Witbooi in a truce.) Surviving Orlam-Afrikaners joined either the Nama or Herero nations.

By 1890 there was peace between Herero and Nama, but neither nation recognized the sovereignty of Germany. The new German chancellor Caprivi (1890-94) therefore determined 'at all costs' to impose sovereignty. For three years German troops attacked the Nama of Hendrik Witbooi with little success. Then in 1894 a new German commander, Theodor Leutwein, arrived in South West Africa with orders to set up a white settler colony in the interior by the cheapest means. Leutwein, who also became the colony's first governor (1898-1905), later explained his systematic policy of playing off one African group upon another — 'it was more difficult but also more serviceable to influence the natives to kill each other for us, than to expect streams of blood and streams of money from the Old Fatherland [i.e. Germany] for their suppression.'

German military conquest Leutwein first executed Andries Lambert of Gobabis for the death of a German trader, and then attacked Hendrik Witbooi. When Hendrik Witbooi escaped, Leutwein sent a demand for his surrender: 'In comparison with the German Emperor you are but a small chief. To submit yourself to him would not be a disgrace but an honour.' Hendrik Witbooi replied: 'God the Lord has established various kingdoms on the earth, and therefore I know and believe that it is no sin and no misdeed for me to wish to remain the independent Chief of my land and my people ... But you say that "Might is right" ... So I think I will shoot back, not in my name, not in my strength, but in the name of the Lord, and under His power.' Leutwein then attacked Hendrik Witbooi again, and Hendrik Witbooi made peace (1894).

Next Leutwein forced Samuel Maherero to agree to boundaries and cattle confiscations, and tried to stop the arms trade to Gobabis from Cape Colony across Bechuanaland. When Chief Kahimema of the Mbanderu around Gobabis and Nikodemus his Herero overlord came forward to negotiate after clashing with the Germans, they were shot as rebels.

African impoverishment Leutwein did not, however, agree with those Germans who wanted a 'war of extermination' to clear

Execution of Nikodemus, Herero chief, 1896
'There was no male Herero/Mbanderu to be seen, but
the women were rolling about on the ground and
covering their heads with sand and earth. From every
house, every hut, every garden, the long-drawn blood-
curdling lamentations accompanied the distinguished
chiefs on their last journey . . . The condemned men
were lifted from the cart. Proudly and with head
erect Kahimena walked to the tree and there he was
bound; Nikodemus, half-dead with fear, had to be
carried. The eyes of the two were then bound, and
the firing sections marched into their places. Present
— Fire! The volleys rolled like thunder through the
neighbouring mountains and two traitors had ceased
to live.' (A German soldier's account).

Africans from the land for small white
farmers and stock ranchers. Instead he wanted
gradual impoverishment, which would under-
mine the power of chiefs and push people
into cash employment as useful labour — on
large farms owned by well capitalized German
gentlemen.

Leutwein took advantage of the rinderpest
epidemic in 1897 to provoke quarrels between
African groups, and to take land for white settlement. Troops were recruited from Samuel
Maherero and Hendrik Witbooi to crush the
Swartbooi Nama, the only group to rebel
against rinderpest control measures. Then
after the rinderpest, land was removed from
the Herero and Nama on the pretext that,
with less cattle, Africans needed less land
(1898). German traders exploited the situation. They sold goods on credit to Africans

impoverished by the rinderpest, and then
demanded payment in the few cattle remaining with a debtor or his neighbours. A Herero
cattle owner later recalled: 'If we objected
and tried to resist, the police would be sent
for, and what with flogging and threats of
shooting, it was useless for our poor people to
resist. Once I got a bag of meal on credit and
later the trader came and took eight cows for
the debt and two more cows for what he
called credit [i.e. interest].'

Leutwein's *Credit Ordinance* of 1903 was
intended to stop these abuses by banning
traders from giving credit to Africans.
Leutwein saw credit as a danger in allowing
Africans to delay the need to earn cash by
outside labour. The ordinance caused a
scramble of traders trying to collect debts
before a deadline came into force in 1904. No
less than 106,000 claims were made on the
Herero in 1903-04, who therefore lost most
of their cattle and even some land to traders.
Traders 'took the ground for their farms and
claimed it as their private property . . . to
shoot our dogs if they trespassed on these
lands, and they confiscated any of our cattle
which might stray there.'

The Herero forsaw the loss of all their land
when wide belts were taken for white farms
along railways, from the coast to Windhoek
and to the Otavi copper mines in the north.
They decided to rise against German rule in
1904, when colonial troops were away in the
south disciplining the Bondelswarts group of
Nama. First Samuel Maherero contacted his
neighbours — Nama, Rehobother, and still
independent Ovambo — to join him against
the Germans. 'Rather let us die together,' he
wrote to Hendrik Witbooi as one Christian
monarch to another, 'and not die as a result
of ill-treatment, prisons . . . we are not fighting alone, we are fighting together.' But the
Rehobothers sent this letter to the Germans
instead of forwarding it to Hendrik Witbooi.
Samuel Maherero then told Leutwein: 'I did
not commence the war; it has been started by
the white people, particularly traders, with
rifles and in the prisons'. No English or Boers,
no German women and children, nor other
Africans, would be harmed. The Herero

would only attack German men.'

The Herero rising was unexpected by the Germans, but not unwelcome to Leutwein: 'Once the Herero are defeated and disarmed we will disarm the south. Destruction of the tribal organisations, the institution of locations and pass laws, will take place after the Herero have been defeated.'

German reinforcements were rushed from overseas under the command of General von Trotha. They attacked the Herero in the Waterberg mountains and defeated them. No prisoners were taken: all captured were shot. The remnants of the Herero nation fled westwards into the desert. 'Like a wounded beast the enemy was tracked down from one waterhole to the next,' ran a German account. Then von Trotha issued his notorious extermination order (1904):

'The Herero nation must now leave the country . . . Within the German frontier every Herero, with or without a rifle, with or without cattle, will be shot. I will not take over any more women and children, but I will either drive them back to your people or have them fired on. These are my words to the nation of the Hereros.

(signed) The Great General of the Mighty Emperor, von Trotha.'

When peace returned to Hereroland there were only 16,000 Herero left out of more than 60,000 before the war, and 2,000 of them, including Samuel Maherero, had fled to exile in Bechuanaland.

Nama rising Hendrik Witbooi, who had at first helped the Germans with troops against the Herero, then led his people against German rule. 'The account which I have to render to God the Father in Heaven is great indeed,' the eighty-year-old chief wrote to Leutwein. God had instructed Hendrik Witbooi — through a Kora prophet named Stuurman — to cancel his peace treaty of 1884 with the Germans. 'Therefore, do I depend on Him and have recourse to Him that He may dry our tears and in His own time liberate us . . . Furthermore I beg of Your Excellency do not call me a rebel.' After a long and bitter struggle, Hendrik Witbooi was killed in battle (1905). The Nama and Damara who followed him suffered the same fate as the Herero, losing their land and cattle.

The general state of war ended in 1907. Small reserves were marked off for the southern Nama and Damara. But the Herero remained as workers on white farms without a reserve until after German rule ended. In the north, the Portuguese begun to conquer the northern Ovambo and Nkhumbi during 1904-

Hendrik Witbooi (1840-1905) Son of a Nama chief at Gibeon, Hendrik Witbooi burned with a God-given sense of destiny. In 1880 he had been caught by the outbreak of the Nama-Herero war while on a visit inside Hereroland, and had rapidly made his escape on horseback. While riding for safety through the mountains he heard a voice say: 'It has come to pass — The road lies ahead — I lay on you a heavy burden.' He took this to be a message from God.

A chain gang of African prisoners in German South West Africa   Prisoners were chained together by the neck — the front and back men being padlocked — when they were marched to work.

07. The Germans then began to assert their power over the southern Ovambo by making treaties with them in 1908.

Nama and Herero people were affected by it. [Cambridge International School Certificate, 1979]

Questions

1 Discuss the events from 1881 onwards that led to the Jameson Raid. What were the effects of the raid on Anglo-Boer relations before 1899? [Cambridge International School Certificate, 1976]
2 Show the importance in the history of South Africa of *either* Paul Kruger *or* Cecil Rhodes. [Cambridge International School Certificate, 1977]
3 Why did it take so long for the Boers to be defeated in the South African War?
4 Discuss the role of Africans in the South African War.
5 Write an account of German colonization and administration of South West Africa (Namibia) and show how the

Activities

1 List the causes of the South African War. Discuss in the classroom which you consider to be the most important.
2 Imagine you are a Boer 'bitter-ender' fighting the British to the last. Describe your life as a guerrilla fighter.
3 Compare the experience of the South African War with that of the Difaqane for Africans living in the Orange Free State and Transvaal.

For references to Bibliography see p. 222.

Chapter 13

The Seeds of African Nationalism (c. 1895 – 1906)

African nationalism under colonial rule as both an elite (or 'petty-bourgeois') movement and as a mass (or 'proletarian') movement may be traced to origins in the late 19th and early 20th centuries. Workers on mines and farms came to identify themselves with *tribes* recognized by colonial authorities — usually a language group given the name of a pre-colonial military state. Workers from Natal, regardless of whether their families had ever been ruled by Cetshwayo, were known as — and came to know themselves as — Zulu. Tsonga and Chopi became Shangane; Pedi and others became Northern Sotho. Meanwhile the rulers of surviving African states promoted their own tribal-nationalism by reforming and educating themselves in colonial ways. At the same time, among workers and tribal rulers, and especially among Christian-educated people, there was a widening sense of *African* nationality. This early form of pan-Africanism, much inspired by contact with black Americans, was known as 'Ethiopianism' after the name (Ethiopia) usually given to Africa in the Christian Bible.

African nationalism was a reaction to the destruction of independent states and theft of land by imperialism. On the other hand it was a response to a paradox within imperialism, which promoted democratic ideas among a minority at the same time as imposing despotic rule on the majority. Christian-educated Africans in particular found themselves with democratic hopes frustrated by racial oppression. European missionaries responded by trying to reform Christian education away from producing clerks (needed by precolonial African states) towards 'industrial education' of semi-skilled artisans needed by the colonial economy.

Christian-educated Africans began to break away from European mission churches to found Ethiopianist churches and schools in the late 19th century. But this independent church movement, with its pan-African ideals, began to break up in the early 20th century. Numerous 'Zionist' churches under dynamic Christian leaders emerged to recruit the membership of the masses rather than of the educated elite. Most African nationalists thereafter remained within the established mission churches. But the Ethiopianist spirit of independence and pride in modernized African culture lived on in the political movement of African nationalism — the 'native congresses' that combined into one African National Congress.

1 Independent Church and School Movements

Churches and schools in African communities were colonized in the 1880s-90s by stricter mission control and a rush of immigrant white clergymen and teachers. This created a grievance for many experienced African clergymen, who had previously been in charge of church and school management and finance under only nominal mission control. These clergymen led their congregations out of the European missions to become independent churches, often supported by the local chief as the national church of the local

SOCIAL CHANGE IN THE 1890s

Students at Morija Training Institution, Basutoland, in the 1890s. Their principal, Rev. R.H. Dyke sits in the centre. Note that the students, probably a group of prefects, are in semi-military uniform. Morija, run by the Paris Evangelical Mission, competed with other elitist institutions — Lovedale run by Scottish presbyterians and Zonnebloem, near Capetown, run by the Anglican church. The institutions taught technical skills as well as academic classes to the new educated elite.

A Xhosa rural household in the Cape Colony in the 1890s. The photograph shows one adult man sucking a pipe, three adult women and nine children. Are all three women the man's wives? Why are two children standing apart? Note that older people are wearing Western clothing. These have been purchased with cash from earnings — from the sale of crops or labour.

'tribe'. African clergymen particularly in the Wesleyan (Methodist) and Congregational churches claimed it was their right, in the tradition of Protestantism, to form churches free from alien control. It is remarkable how often the immediate cause of breaking away was when European missionaries claimed capital funds or land obtained by the strenuous efforts of an African clergyman. As elsewhere, racial discrimination by whites against blacks was a way of stopping the rise of an African 'petty bourgeoisie'.

Earliest independent churches The first African church to break away from a European mission was a temporary schism in Basutoland, when the Hermon congregation near Mafeteng quarrelled with the Paris mission in 1872. The first major independent church, and the foundation of the Ethiopianist movement, was the Thembu National Church founded by Rev. Nehemiah Tile in 1884. Tile quarrelled with the Wesleyan mission when it tried to stop him from involvement in Thembu politics, opposing the rule of Cape magistrates in Tembuland. (He was arrested and imprisoned when Tembuland was annexed by the Cape Colony.) But Tile's influence spread to other black Wesleyan ministers elsewhere, notably on the Rand. His church became known as the 'Thembu Church of South Africa'.

A similar reaction to colonization led to the foundation of an independent national church for the Tlhaping of Mankurwane in British Bechuanaland in 1886, under the supervision of an independent African Congregational minister at Kimberley. The church was persuaded to rejoin the London mission in 1890. But a section of it then broke away in 1893 to assert the independence of the Tlhaping at Manthe from the rule of Mankurwane, and recruited another African minister from Kimberley.

Disputes within the Pedi ruling group led to the breakaway from the Berlin mission in 1892 of the Free Lutheran Bapedi Church — led by its former white missionary! This appears to have been an attempt by the missionary to bolster with a national church the regency of Kgolokwe (Geluk). Kgolokwe had been appointed by the SAR government during the infancy of Sekhukhune II, against the wishes of the Pedi majority represented in the old mission church.

Origin of the Ethiopian Church African preachers found ready congregations among migrant workers in the urban areas of Kimberley, Johannesburg and Pretoria. One such preacher was James Brander (or Kanyane Napo), who quarrelled with the Anglican mission over land he had obtained for a church in the northern Transvaal. He settled at Marabastad outside Pretoria in 1889 to found his own independent 'African Church'.

Meanwhile African Wesleyan ministers among migrant workers in the Transvaal, influenced by the example of Nehemiah Tile, quarrelled with white mission superiors. They marched out of a mission conference in 1892 under the leadership of Mangena Mokone, a powerful preacher, who declared: 'We are called Revs but we are worse than the boy working for the missionary.'

Mokone combined with Brander in one independent church for all Africans regardless of 'tribe' in 1892. They called it the *Ethiopian Church,* rather than the African Church — to fulfil the prophecy in the Bible: 'Ethiopia shall soon stretch out her hands unto God' (Psalm 68, verse 31). Marabastad alone soon

boasted twelve Ethiopian Church congregations. Johannesburg and Orange Free State independent Wesleyan congregations joined in 1893-94, under Revs. Jantjie Tantsi, Jacobus Xaba, and others.

Expansion of Ethiopianism Mokone persuaded the Thembu Church, now led by Jonas Goduka (since the death of Tile in 1892) and calling itself the African Native Church, to join the Ethiopian Church in 1895. At the same time Mokone began enquiries about the Ethiopian Church joining the African Methodist Episcopal Church (AMEC), the largest and most powerful black church in the United States of America. Mokone learnt about the AMEC from the letters of Charlotte Manye, a South African student at the AMEC's Wilberforce Institute in the USA. The AMEC replied by inviting the Ethiopian Church to send delegates for discussions at its headquarters in Philadelphia.

The Ethiopian Church elected Mokone, Xaba, and an ambitious new recruit to the Church named James Dwane. Dwane had joined in 1895 after quarrelling with the Wesleyan authorities in the eastern Cape Colony, who wanted to take away from him the funds he had earned on a preaching tour of England. Dwane set sail for Philadelphia in 1896, alone, because Mokone and Xaba had not yet succeeded in raising the money for their passages.

Dwane arrived back home as the AMEC-appointed supervisor of the Ethiopian Church. Mokone was reduced to 'presiding elder' of the Transvaal (1896). The Ethiopian Church flourished and grew as never before, incorporating more and more African congregations — including coloureds in Capetown — who broke away from white mission control. Unlike most mission churches, the Ethiopian Church did not demand literacy for membership. 'Ethiopianism' gave many Africans new hope in the face of white conquest, but it was rejected by some as a false hope. Tantsi records how difficult it was to convert an eighty-year-old man on the Kei river, who dismissed Ethiopianism as another Nongqause delusion. Tengo Jabavu attacked it in the very same terms in his *Imvo zaba-Ntshundu* newspaper.

Not all breakaway churches from European missions joined the Ethiopian Church in the 1890s, though they might still be seen as part of a wider 'Ethiopianist' movement. The Zulu Congregational Church, founded at Pieter-maritzburg in 1897, was a protest against the American Board (Congregationalist) missionary society handing over African congregations to the white settler Congregational Union of South Africa. The African Presbyterian Church, founded by Pambani Mzimba at Lovedale in 1898 probably shocked European missionaries more than any other schism. The Lovedale congregation was next to southern Africa's largest missionary and educational centre, and Mzimba was the senior African minister of the Free (Presbyterian) Church of Scotland. He had quarrelled with white colleagues about how to spend funds that he had collected on tour in Scotland. By 1903 his church had 6500 members and 22,000 followers, including former Methodists and Anglicans as well as Presbyterians and converted 'pagans'.

AMEC takes charge Bishop Henry McNeal Turner of the African Methodist Episcopal Church arrived in South Africa to admit the Ethiopian Church formally into the AMEC as its fourteenth episcopal district in 1898. Turner was already famous as the main spokesman of the 'Back to Africa' movement among black Americans. He first organized strong congregations in Capetown and then travelled north to Johannesburg, where he was greeted with song on the station platform by the McAdoo Jubilee Singers, a famous black American singing group on tour. He even visited president Kruger in Pretoria. Asked what he thought of Ethiopianism on another occasion, Kruger replied: 'Let the Kafirs preach to the Kafirs; why interfere with them?'

Turner preached African pride and confidence everywhere he went. AMEC membership expanded rapidly to 10,000 adults by the end of the year. Funds were raised by concerts at which members of the audience paid for popular songs to be repeated. Sixty-five AMEC ministers were ordained, under Dwane as acting vicar-bishop until a resident bishop could be brought from the United States. Nine sub-districts were organized in the two republics and Cape Colony. Turner was banned from entering Natal, Bechuanaland and Rhodesia, but African missionaries of the AMEC spread the word to Bechuanaland and Rhodesia, for which a Bulawayo sub-district was founded in 1899.

Meanwhile the Negro Baptist Convention, which had founded its first congregation for black American sailors at Capetown in 1894, extended a mission to Natal in 1899. The mission became known as the Cushite Church, 'Cush' being an alternative name to Ethiopia used for Africa in the Bible.

Dwane breaks away When Turner returned to the United States, he failed to persuade the AMEC to confirm the appointment of James Dwane as vicar-bishop for South Africa. Dwane reacted angrily by negotiating with Anglican missionaries to accept the Ethiopian Church as a new 'Order of Ethiopia', with him as its Anglican bishop. Dwane summoned a conference of Ethiopian Church delegates to the eastern Cape at the time the South African War broke out. With only two delegates from the Transvaal and Orange Free State present, he carried the Cape delegates with him. When the Transvaal heard of the matter and firmly rejected the breakaway, Dwane rejoined the AMEC. But he left once again in 1900 when the Anglicans founded an Order of Ethiopia for him. Only a minority in the eastern Cape followed Dwane into the Order of Ethiopia. (Dwane never became a bishop: he was not even ordained an Anglican minister for eleven years.) The majority remaining within the AMEC elected Tantsi as their new acting head. Then in 1900 Levi Coppin arrived from America as the first resident bishop.

Coppin arrived in Capetown and, after being greeted by the black American community, addressed a congregation of two to three thousand AMEC members. Coppin is said to have lifted his sixty-kilogram throne

AFRICAN METHODIST EPISCOPAL CHURCH c. 1900

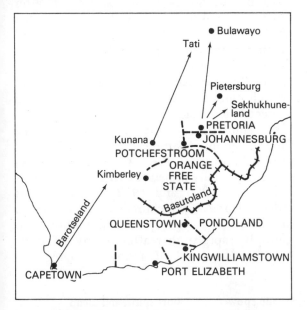

The AME Church under Bishop Turner in 1900 was divided between so-called Transvaal (including OFS and Basutoland) and South African (i.e. Cape Colony) Conferences, which were divided into districts marked here in capital letters — e.g. QUEENSTOWN. Each district was divided into circuits and stations, representing congregations of former Ethiopian Church or new AMEC congregations. Each district also sent out missions into its hinterland, and as far as Bulawayo and Basutoland. Pretoria district had 16 circuits and stations: Orange Free State had 18.

high above his head and shouted:

> 'With such strength I have come to lift the impoverished natives of Africa from their lowly state and to crush beneath my heel the so-called Christian who would keep his colored brother in darkness.'

Under Coppin's leadership the AMEC expanded its educational efforts rapidly. It planned to found educational institutes in Capetown, Johannesburg, Basutoland and Pondoland (though most of these plans did not materialize). It involved itself in the popular boom in African elementary education, which followed the South African War and had spread as far north as Barotseland. Numerous African students were sent to black colleges and universities in the United States. At least 150 such students studied there in the 1895-1905 decade, including doctors, lawyers and scientists, but not all returned home.

Ethiopianism splits up   The AMEC in South Africa, and therefore Ethiopianism as a united movement, was split by increasing dissentions in the 1904-07 period. In 1904 a scandal erupted within the AMEC over the funding of their main college, the Bethel Institute at Capetown. The principal of the college, a black American called Attaway, was accused of stealing or wasting funds, including £700 sent by Lewanika from Barotseland. Delegates from the Transvaal were particularly incensed that money collected in the Transvaal was being wasted in Capetown. Bishop Coppin stood by Attaway. The AMEC withdrew Coppin and Attaway, but Transvaal delegates

Mangena Mokone (1851-1936), founder of the Ethiopian Church 1892.

were soon in dispute again with the new black American bishop in 1905. This time the rebels, including Tantsi, were suspended. There was even open fighting among church members at Bloemfontein, and the colonial authorities took the opportunity to ban the AMEC from the Transvaal and Orange Free State in 1907.

Congregations of the AMEC began to break away and even refounded pre-Ethiopian independent churches. The old Thembu Church under Goduka broke away as the African Native Mission Church in 1904. The original African Church in Pretoria under Brander became the Ethiopian Catholic Church, reviving Brander's 'Catholic' origins of 'grandeur and solemnity' within the Anglican Church (1904). A large part of the Bloemfontein congregation broke away to form the Bechuana Methodist Church after objecting to AMEC services being conducted only in English (1905). The Tlhaping of Manthe in the northern Cape, who had joined the AMEC in 1898, broke free to become the Native Independent Congregational Church. Church movements in the Bechuanaland Protectorate declared their independence as 'free churches' – the Bangwaketse Free Church led by Mothowagae (1902-10), and the Bakhurutshe Free Church (1904-08) which eventually joined the Anglicans.

Between 1904 and 1912 the number of independent African churches in South Africa multiplied to a total of 76, and continued to multiply rapidly thereafter. Many of these churches consisted of a single congregation

Zionist baptism in the sea   Zionist churches emphasize the healing power of the holy spirit, and blend traditional and Christian religious practices. While the minister baptizes a member by total immersion in water (**left**), an assistant facing us (**right**) holds a cross and star of David made of palm leaf, to recall the original baptisms by Jesus in Israel. The stem of the cross is wrapped with traditional beads, and possibly a bell, while sea water is a traditional medicine in southern Africa. The thousands of Zionist churches can all be traced back to Zion City at Chicago, founded by a Scottish-American prophet in 1896.

under one minister or prophet. Most were not breakaways from the AMEC, but were inspired by two other American religious movements — 'Zionism' and 'Watch Tower'.

Zionist churches stressed the power of the Holy Spirit, especially for the healing of sickness. They originated with the Christian Catholic Church which baptized its first white and black converts in Johannesburg during 1904. The CCC had been founded by the prophet John Dowie in 1896 at Chicago in the United States, where he set up a holy settlement called Zion City. The CCC itself split into two churches at Zion City in 1906. The breakaway Apostolic Faith Mission took control of Johannesburg's Zionists. It took advantage of the 1907 Transvaal government ban on the AMEC to gather Ethiopianist congregations under its wing in the Zion Apostolic Church. Even Brander's Ethiopian Catholic Church added the words 'in Zion' to its title. But the Apostolic Faith Mission was not able to hold its members together for long. The blacks broke away to found 'Zionist' churches, while the whites founded 'Pentecostalist' churches.

Watch Tower The Watch Tower Bible and Tract Society was founded by the American prophet Charles Taze Russell in the 1890s. Russell denounced all churches and governments as the work of the devil, and prophesied the start of the *millennium* (end of the present world) in 1914-15 — which would see a 'world-wide revolution and overthrow of all law and order' by the masses, from which the kingdom of heaven on earth would emerge. The missionary Joseph Booth, who had previously tried to set up an African Christian Union in Natal (see below), was converted to Watch Tower and founded its African headquarters at Capetown in 1907. The society spread its revolutionary prophecies by literature sellers, roving as far north as Booth's old mission field of Nyasaland.

2 Early African National Political Movements

The earliest African political organizations along European lines were found among voters and potential voters in the eastern Cape Colony. Elijah Makiwane, a Presbyterian minister who had graduated from Lovedale, founded the Native Educational Association in 1879. That was followed by discussion groups at Port Elizabeth after 1882-83 — known variously as *Imbumba yama Afrika,* the South African Aborigines Association, or as the South African Native Political Association. They sought to unite Christian-educated Africans of all denominations, and claimed to be the true 'Afrikaner' Bond because they consisted of native Africans and not Boer settlers. The discussion groups were distinct from Jabavu's Native Electoral Association, which was founded in 1884 to support white candidates in Cape elections.

In Natal the radical white missionary Joseph Booth tried to organize Christian-educated Africans into a so-called African Christian Union in 1896. The union had the aim of setting up a cooperative development company, eventually to be owned by millions of black shareholders in Africa and America — to run plantations, mines and a shipping fleet between Natal and the United States. The union's manifesto concluded:

'To mould and guide the labour of Africa's millions into channels which shall develop the vast God-given wealth of Africa into the uplifting and common wealth of the people, rather than for the aggrandizement of a few already rich Europeans. Finally, to pursue steadily and unswervingly the policy AFRICA FOR THE AFRICAN*, and look for and hasten by prayer and united effort the forming of the AFRICAN CHRISTIAN NATION by God's power and in his own time and way.'

Booth was supported by Navuma Tembula, the first black South African to qualify

---

*The slogan, closely associated with Ethiopianism, originated with the plans of the American Martin Delany (1812-85) and the West African Edward Blyden (1832-1912) for the settlement of Americans of African descent back in Africa. It was first used by Delany in 1861.

Left: *Francis Zaccheus Santiago Peregrino (1851-1919), Ghana-born journalist, and former steel worker in Britain and the United States.*

Below left: *Henry Sylvester Williams (1869-1911), Trinidad born originator of the Pan-African movement.* Williams and Peregrino were representatives of the Pan-African Association, formed at the 1900 Pan-African Conference in London. Peregrino arrived at Capetown late in 1900, and published the *South African Spectator* there until his death. Williams, as Secretary of the Pan-African Association, arrived in Capetown in 1903, and practised as a lawyer until the following year when he returned to London. Both acted as advisers to African kings in the interior — Williams to Lerotholi and Peregrino to Lewanika, while the black American sea captain Harry Dean was envoy to Sigcawu (see below). In Capetown they became involved in coloured politics. Williams left the country after death threats; Peregrino stayed on as an electoral agent for white political parties.

Below right: *Sigcawu Mqikela, paramount chief or king of the eastern Mpondo (1887-1905)* Arrested in 1895 for resisting Cape rule of Pondoland. The Pan-Africanist Harry Dean encouraged Sigcawu with plans for a national college and a road through his country from Basutoland to the sea.

(overseas) as a university-trained medical doctor, and by Paul Msane later prominent in the 'native congress' movement. But the scheme collapsed because of Booth's paternalism. After twenty-six hours of continuous debate, a meeting of 120 educated Africans rejected the scheme because Booth refused to hand over control of the project to them. The last white man they could have trusted to look after African interests, they said, was Bishop Colenso, and he was dead.

In the western Cape Colony an Africanist political movement among coloured people

216

appears to have been stimulated by the settlement of black American sailors, mostly from whaling ships, who called themselves 'Africans' or 'Afric-Americans'. Bishop Turner of the AMEC made his first trip to Capetown in 1892 to visit the black American community. English-speaking coloured people at Capetown began to refer to themselves as *Africans* by the 1890s, just as Dutch-speaking people called themselves Afrikaners.

The black American community at Capetown was strengthened around 1900 by the arrival of delegates from the Pan-African Conference and the settlement of AMEC officials with Bishop Coppin. The Pan-African Conference in London had been attended by people of African descent from three continents. Strong attacks were made on 'the desire of the English capitalists to re-enslave the black man, especially in South Africa', and on Boer atrocities against Africans in the current war. Two delegates then sailed for Capetown — the Ghanaian-born journalist F.Z.S. Peregrino in 1900, and the Trinidadian lawyer Henry Sylvester Williams (secretary of the Pan-African Association) in 1901. Williams, Peregrino and others then took the message of pan-African pride and political awareness into the interior as far as Barotseland. But this early pan-Africanist influence declined with the breakup of the AMEC in South Africa after 1904.

Ethiopianism was the first national movement that linked Africans in the coastal colonies and interior republics, even before South Africa was united by British conquest. It promoted national consciousness, race consciousness through its AMEC links overseas, and even worker consciousness among black South Africans. White employers were worried about the effect of Ethiopianism on the labour market after the war, when employment was expanding and wages were considered too high by employers. The news editor of the *Rand Daily Mail* put the Ethiopianist position as: 'This is our country; these are our farms and mines, why are we not working them for overselves and for our benefit, instead of working them for the white people and giving them all the benefit?'

But Ethiopianism was a two-edged sword in producing white reaction which increased racial discrimination against educated Africans. Whites feared the 'black peril' (*swart gevaar*) of a pan-African rising against white rule, and saw Ethiopianist preachers as dangerous agitators. The Herero/Nama and Bambatha revolts increased such fears, clearly depicted in the novel *Prester John* written by one of Milner's 'kindergarten', John Buchan (1911). The 'black peril' cry was taken up by rural Boers who wanted to justify their being re-armed after defeat in the war, and by newspapers which sensationalized the sexual threat of black crime to white women.

Vigilance committees and native congresses
The threat of white mob violence over the 'black peril' may have stimulated the growth of African vigilance committees in Capetown, the Transkei and Transvaal, around 1903-04. The committees appear to have voiced the opinions of the African 'petty bourgeoisie' to local government authorities.

'Native congresses' — no doubt taking their title from Natal's Indian Congress — were larger meetings of educated Africans, founded in each colony after the war to represent African political opinion. The South African Native Congress, founded in 1902, re-named itself the Cape Native Congress when other congresses were formed for Natal, the Transvaal and Orange River Colony. The congresses gave evidence to Lagden's Native Affairs Commission enquiring into South Africa's 'native question' (1903-05). In the Transvaal the local congress united with the vigilance committee and a Basuto Committee (representing migrant workers) to give evidence to the commission. Congress members were also Ethiopianist church members: in the Orange Free State the 'native congress' was more or less governed by AMEC rules.

African-owned newspapers carried news and views of African political activities. (Unfortunately few copies have survived for historians to study.) Jabavu's well established *Imvo zabaNtshundu* was challenged in East London

217

Four men — a lawyer, a journalist, an educationalist, and a churchman — were the moving spirits behind the South African Native National Congress, founded in January 1912. Seme was elected treasurer, Plaatje secretary, Dube president, and Rubusana vice-president.

Left: *Pixley kaIsaka Seme (1880-1951)*   Lawyer, educated in New York and Oxford, and called to the bar in London. Seme delivered a prize-winning address when he graduated from Columbia University in New York in 1906, titled *The Regeneration of Africa.* 'The giant is awakening! From the four corners of the earth Africa's sons are marching to the future's golden door bearing the record of deeds of valor done . . . . . The brighter day is rising upon Africa. Already I seem to see her chains dissolve, her desert plains red with harvest, her Abyssinia and her Zululand the seats of science and religion, reflecting the glory of the rising sun from the spires of their churches and universities. Her Congo and her Gambia whitened with commerce, her crowded cities sending forth the hum of business, and all her sons employed in advancing the victories of peace — greater and more abiding than the spoils of war. Yes the regeneration of Africa belongs to this new and powerful period! The basic factor which assures their [Africans'] regeneration resides in the awakened race-consciousness.' 'Oh, for that historian,' wrote Seme, 'who, with the open pen of truth, will bring to Africa's claim the strength of written proof . . . '

Above left: *Walter Benson Rubusana (1858-1936)*   Rubusana was ordained a Congregationalist minister in 1884, and was awarded a degree by McKinley University in the USA for his thesis 'History of South Africa from a Native Standpoint', later being promoted to an honorary doctorate.

Above centre: *John Langalibalele Dube (1871-1946)*   American-educated educationalist. Founded the Ohlange Institute in Natal in 1889, following the ideas on industrial-education of the black American educationalist Booker T. Washington.

Above right: *Solomon Tshekisho Plaatje (1875-1932)*   Came to prominence as a court interpreter and agent between black and white at the siege of Mafeking. Then he became editor for seven years of the Mafeking newspaper *Koranta ea Becoana.*

by *Izwi laBantu* (People's Voice). *Izwi* was owned by Walter Rubusana, the leading black minister within the Congregational Church, and Meshack Pelem the 'red prophet' of Queenstown (1900). It supported Rhodes' Progressive Party in Cape elections, but also ran articles on African history and culture. Peregrino's *South African Spectator* in Capetown (1901) appealed to black or coloured African 'race pride'. Sol Plaatje's *Koranta ea*

Becoana (Bechuana Gazette) was published in both seTswana and English at Mafeking from 1901. Plaatje made a point of featuring 'white peril' stories of white assaults on blacks. John Dube's *Ilanga lase Natal*, founded at Dube's Ohlange Institute near Durban in 1906, protested so strongly at the ruthless crushing of the Bambatha rebellion that Dube was temporarily imprisoned.

Indian and coloured politics The Natal branch of the Indian Congress, under Mohandas Gandhi, became increasingly active after the South African War. The congress campaigned for Indian freedom from racial discrimination in Natal, and for the right of Indians to live and trade in the Transvaal (forbidden by the old republic). Gandhi developed the idea of 'passive resistance' (*satyagraha*) against unjust laws, e.g. to invite arrest by sitting in forbidden train compartments, so that the colonial authorities would break under the strain of continual disobedience. The first great *satyagraha* campaign was against pass-laws for Indians in the Transvaal in 1906–8.

The *African Political Organisation* (APO) was founded at Capetown in 1902 in the belief that the non-European people of the western Cape shared a common identity with Africans of the interior. Its leader from 1905 onwards, Dr Abdul Abdurahman (elected to Capetown city council in the previous year), never lost sight of issues concerning black Africans, but was most concerned with coloured African rights at Capetown and Kimberley.

3 Kingdoms As Protectorates Under Colonialism

The precolonial African states that survived as 'protectorates' under British colonialism had been key allies of the British before the South African War. But once British rule was fully established, the strategic importance of the protectorates — Barotseland, Bechuanaland, Basutoland and Swaziland — rapidly declined. The British began to regard them simply as labour reserves within the South African customs union (which included

Barotseland in 1905), which would eventually become part of the political union of South Africa. Protectorate rulers therefore emphasized their special treaty relationship with the British as protecting them from incorporation into other colonies, while the British denied that any such treaties were binding.

The paramount chiefs within the protectorates, former kings, were secured in power by colonial dependence upon them. They sought to use that power to modernize their states for their successors. They were therefore what some historians have called 'modernizing autocrats' — borrowing a term from earlier European history. Encouraged by Ethiopianist influences, they attempted to modernize their states by clerical and technical education, under royal patronage, of aristocratic children who would provide a future bureaucracy. In trying to prepare a smooth transition into the modern world, the protectorate rulers encouraged the growth of tribal-nationalism among young aristocrats.

BAROTSELAND Lewanika's 'modernizing autocracy' was at first based on collaboration with Paris missionaries and British South Africa Company officials. But by late 1902 disillusionment set in with both government and mission. Lewanika and most aristocrats had not converted to Christianity. The mission schools were closed to non-Christian children. 'What benefits do you bring us?' he asked the missionaries. 'What have I to do with a Bible which gives me neither rifles nor powder, sugar, tea nor coffee, nor artisans to work for me — none of the advantages I had hoped for?' The BSAC, on the other hand, did not respond to Lewanika's requests for training in cotton, rice and tobacco cultivation, cattle management and chicken farming, as well as for instruction in English and typing.

Education and Ethiopianism Lewanika turned to Willie Mokalapa, a Sotho teacher who had broken with the Paris mission. Mokalapa was ordained into the African Methodist Episcopal Church at Capetown in 1903, and returned to Barotseland as an AMEC missionary. Mokalapa's AMEC school attracted

SOUTHERN AFRICAN ROYALTY

1901 saw a unique occasion, when nearly all the royalty of southern Africa gathered at Capetown to greet British royalty on a visit to the Cape Colony. It was the first and last occasion on which formerly independent kings, chiefs and princes met together in such a large gathering. They were divided into 3 groups for the photographs on this page.

Only the chiefs in the bottom photograph have been identified — including Khama III (in top hat), Bathoen I (below him), and Lentswe (left of Khama), Isang (top left from Lentswe), Kgafela and Segale (standing at left and right extremes). The man right of Khama is probably Kealeboga. Readers who can identify other chiefs in the photographs are asked to write to the author (addressed to the local office of Macmillan).

aristocratic children away from the Paris mission. Plans were made for more advanced education and for the AMEC to organize road improvements, and a river service to Kazungula to carry agricultural exports. But the plans came to nothing: the £700 advanced to the AMEC disappeared in the scandal over building the Bethel Institute in Capetown.

A cat-and-mouse game ensued between the BSAC and Lewanika as the company put pressure on him to cut his Ethiopianist links. During 1904-05 the BSAC forced Lewanika to begin collecting colonial tax within Barotseland. This caused so much anger among indunas that the company brought in troops and a machine-gun to protect Lewanika from his people. Another blow to Lewanika's prestige in 1905 was the Italian arbitration of the disputed Rhodesia-Angola border, which simply drew a straight north-south line through western parts of the Lozi kingdom. Lewanika protested, but the BSAC's answer to such protests was: 'Do you want to be conquered?'

The AMEC venture finally collapsed in 1906. The BSAC stepped in to provide a Barotse National School for the sons of indunas. It then obliged Lewanika to sign a 'Proclamation of the Abolition of Slavery'. The proclamation was drawn up on the BSAC's behalf by the pan-Africanist journalist F.Z.S. Peregrino, who had travelled from Capetown to counteract the influence of the AMEC — with which he had quarrelled. The 'abolition of slavery' freed people from unpaid tribute labour maintaining the canals and dams of the upper Zambezi floodplain, so that they might be free to migrate southwards to sell their labour to the mines. Lewanika then turned to Peregrino and persuaded him to draw up a grand petition to the British government requesting the removal of BSAC rule.

BECHUANALAND The alliance of five major Tswana states and smaller chiefdoms, enclosed by the Bechuanaland Protectorate, was moved towards more effective confederation by having a colonial administration in common. Chamberlain and Milner appointed

Lerotholi, paramount chief of Basutoland (1891-1905), seated to the left of the British resident commissioner for Basutoland, Godfrey Lagden (1890-1901). Jonathan Molapo (lived 1844-1928) sits to the right of Lagden.

the dynamic Ralph Williams as resident commissioner in 1901 to organize the administration. Williams removed the BP police from BSAC control, reformed the law courts, and planned to move the capital from Mafeking outside the protectorate to Lobatse inside it. Williams however saw his main task as supporting the various chiefs against all challengers, on condition that each chief gave absolute loyalty to the British. The annual colonial tax was kept low (£1 against £2 in Basutoland) as a reward for service to the British in the war. But the Tawana paramount chief Sekgoma Letsholathebe was ruthlessly deposed, for ignoring German and Portuguese as well as British sovereignty in raiding the Mbukushu of the Okavango river (1906).

Khama III of the Ngwato was the most senior of the Tswana 'modernizing autocrats'. He had begun to organize a tribal bureaucracy in the 1890s, by appointing a well-educated relative in succession to a moSotho as his secretary. An independent school, free of missionary control, was founded for aristocratic children in 1902 after Khama moved his capital to Serowe. It was intended to use church buildings left at the former capital of (Old) Palapye for an independent college and technical institute. But the plans fell through with the economic decline of the Ngwato state in the first decade of the century. Out-

*Major chiefs of the southern Bechuanaland
Protectorate gather at Crocodile Pools (Ngotwane),
near Gaborone, in 1906.*
Sitting (Left): Linchwe of the Kgatla (ruled 1875-
1924), Sebele of the Kwena (1892-1911) — with
flywhisk, Bathoen of the Ngwaketse (1899-1910) —
with thin stick.
Standing: Richard Transfeldt (prosperous wood
trader, owner of Crocodile Pools), Segale Pilane
(brother of Linchwe), Jules Ellenberger (magistrate
at Gaborone, later resident commissioner 1923-27).

breaks of stock disease prevented cattle
exports, while drought destroyed crops. So
many local white traders approached bankruptcy that Khama bought up one major
company and went into partnership with
others in 1910. He saw this as an investment
that would ensure royal revenue in future for
his successors.

Independent tribal schools The first independent tribal school in Bechuanaland was
founded by chief Linchwe of the Kgatla at
Mochudi around 1900. It gave tuition to royal
children in English, a language neglected by
the Dutch reformed missionaries who had
accompanied the Kgatla from the Transvaal.
The mission gained control of the new school
in 1903 by continuing tuition in English. The
demand for secular tuition in English for

aristocratic children also accounts for the
foundation of independent tribal schools
among the Kwena at Molepolole and the
Ngwaketse at Kanye in 1903-04. The Kanye
school was run by the independent tribal-
national church of Mothowagae. The
Ngwaketse, Kwena and Ngwato independent
tribal schools were financed by an extra levy
of between two and five shillings, collected by
the tribal governments with colonial tax.

Fears of subversive Ethiopianist activity
moved the colonial and missionary authorities
to capture the independent schools movement. The chance came in 1910 when chief
Bathoen of the Ngwaketse finally broke with
Mothowagae. Colonial and missionary representatives took over supervision of all
schools in the reserve by joining the tribal
schools committee that administered the levy.
Similar tribal schools committees were set up
for the Kwena and Lete reserves, and later
spread elsewhere.

BASUTOLAND The defeat of Mashopa in
1898 made the paramount chief of Basutoland, Lerotholi I, safe from armed revolt. But
he also became 'anxious to strengthen the
position of his successor' by fixing laws of
government in a form of constitution. The
British occasionally consulted the king
through a national *Pitso* (general assembly)
open to all adult men. Lerotholi's predecessor
had suggested that the British should regularly
meet the king in a smaller national council,
nominated by him, which would assist him in
administration. The idea was rejected in 1891
by chiefs in the *Pitso*. But by the time of the
South African War Lerotholi felt strong
enough as a 'modernizing autocrat' to impose
such a new council on the nation. He consulted a black American lawyer employed by the
African Methodist Episcopal Church, Conrad
Rideout, on the form that this 'parliamentary
form of government' should take. The AMEC
also drew up plans for a major educational
centre in Basutoland. AMEC plans collapsed,
but the idea of a new national council was
encouraged by Milner and the new resident
commissioner Herbert Sloley (1902-16).

The Basutoland National Council (BNC)

was in effect an executive committee of the national *Pitso,* and consisted of chiefs dominated by the 'Sons of Moshoeshoe'. Its first action was to draw up a code of basic laws, known as the *Laws of Lerotholi* (1903), which laid down the rights of chiefs and people covering inheritance, land allocation, tribute labour, and the right to a fair trial. The Basutoland National Council was formally recognized by the colonial government in 1910. Letsie II (1905-13) won the right to nominate ninety-four members, while the colonial government could appoint six others.

Like the rest of southern Africa, Basutoland suffered drought and stock diseases during the 1903-09 period, which reduced agricultural production and restricted stock sales. Family cash reserves were used up on imported food and goods, while colonial tax took £2 annually from every adult man. The gradual reduction from prosperity to poverty can be seen in statistics of baSotho labour migration. The 25,000 migrants recorded in 1911 was less than the number estimated in 1892, but reached almost 50,000 by 1921.

SWAZILAND At the end of the South African War the British took control of Swaziland as a special reserve or protectorate within the Transvaal colony. In fact the terms of this protectorate were never spelt out. The British declared sovereignty over the area in 1903, subject to vaguely defined 'respect' for 'native laws'. The Swazi assumed that this meant the British were sovereign over external but not internal affairs. But in 1905 the British abolished the old SAR arrangement whereby the protecting power collected all concession revenue due to the royal government, in return for paying the king £12,000 a year. The British proceeded to revise all royal concessions without consulting the regents, and paid the royal government a mere £800 a year from then on.

Milner treated Swaziland as part of his policy of building up a strong English farming population in the Transvaal, to counterbalance its potentially rebellious Afrikaner population. Milner began a series of official enquiries into Swaziland concessions in 1904-05, which favoured English mining concessions over Afrikaner grazing concessions as owners of potential farm land. Meanwhile the Swazi regents petitioned for a protectorate separate from the Transvaal and directly under the British high commissioner.

The new Liberal government in Britain detached Swaziland from the Transvaal as a separate British colony in 1906, at the same time as the Transvaal became self-governing. The British intended to re-incorporate Swaziland into the Transvaal once it had become a viable 'white man's country' of English rather than Afrikaner white settlers. Meanwhile Swaziland was to be administered, like Basutoland and the Bechuanaland Protectorate, by a resident commissioner representing the British high commissioner. The three *High Commission Territories* or 'South African Protectorates' were thus established as a group, alongside the four self-governing colonies that later became the Union of South Africa.

Land partition British plans to divide Swaziland into white-owned and Swazi areas met determined opposition from the regents, headed by Labotsibeni and Malunge. The regents restated Mbandzeni's view that all concessions were leases, which would revert to the king without loss of sovereignty after a specified period of time or because of non-payment of rent. But the new resident commissioner Robert Coryndon (1907-16), hotfoot from setting up white settlement in North-Western Rhodesia, was determined to go ahead with British plans. The British recognized land concessions covering four-fifths of Swaziland, ignoring the rights and wrongs of how they had been granted, and converted them all from royal leases to absolute freehold. A third of each concession would be deducted as 'native reserve'. The remaining fifth of Swaziland would become Crown Land (i.e. colonial state land) reserved for future white purchase.

The regents protested that each concession should be allowed to run its course as specified in its original lease subject to payment of rent. Malunge sailed to London, but was fobbed off by the colonial minister with the false promise that Swazi could purchase Crown Land. Soon after Malunge returned to Swaziland the land partition was legalized by the *Swaziland Concessions Proclamation* of 1907.

Over the next year or two, demarcation between farms and 'native reserves' made it clear that the Swazi nation had lost over sixty per cent of the country, especially along main roads. Thirty-two small reserves were scattered among white farms. The regents called a *libandla* (general assembly) of the nation at the beginning of 1909 to express their anger. Labotsibeni told the British authorities, 'You are tearing my skirt — if Mbandini [Mbandzeni] sold land [rather than leased it], where did he think his children were going to live?' Malunge also ridiculed the idea that Mbandzeni had ever sold all rights to land: 'When I was in England I was living in a house which belonged to a white man and was paying rent. If I had remained in England would it have become mine?' Malunge therefore directly accused the British of racism: 'We only think it is being done because we are a different race. The land is ours.'

A few years later the nationalist Pixley Seme was looking for finance to bring the South African 'native congresses' together, and to found a nationalist newspaper. He found the strongest support among traditional rulers from Labotsibeni and Malunge.

Questions

1   What motives did clergymen and congregations have for breaking away from European missionary control? (Refer back to the introduction to Part II and to previous chapters.)
2   Discuss the roles of 'tribalism' and 'Africanism' in the Ethiopianist movement.
3   What was the extent of black American influence on early modern African nationalism?
4   Describe the career and show the importance of Khama III of Botswana. [Cambridge International School Certificate, 1976]

Activities

1   Write the sermon that an African clergyman might have preached to persuade his congregation to break away from a European missionary church.
2   Discuss in the classroom how much racism there was in early modern African nationalism to counteract the racism of European settlers. (See also the introduction to Part III.)

For Chapter 11 see Bibliography, pp. 337–42: B2 Booth; B6 Duminy & Guest; B18 Marks; B20 Matsebula; B21 Maylam; B22 Mazikana; B24 Minter; B32 Readers Digest; B43 Wood; D1 Beach; D13 Marks & Trapido; D18 Saunders; E1 Beach; E2–3 Beinart; E4 Beinart & Bundy; E9 Davidson; E11 Dreschler; E28 Ranger; E30 Rotberg; E41 Worger; E7 Bozzoli.

For Chapter 12 see references above for Chapter 11, and also Bibliography pp. 337–42: B4 Cameron; B5 Davenport; B24 Minter; B26 Muller; B42 Wilson & Thompson; E5 Bley; E7 Cammack; E8 Davenport; E10 Denoon; E12 First & Scott; E14 Jeal; E15 Jeeves; E17 Keegan; E18 Lau; E19 Longford; E21 Mendelsohn; E22 Nasson; E23 Newbury; E24 Pakenham; E25 Plaatje; E26 Porter; E27 Prins; E29 Rive; E32 Spies; E35–36 van Onselen; E37–38 Warwick; E40 Wheatcroft; F6 Bozzoli.

For Chapter 13 see Bibliography pp. 337–42: F38 Odendaal, also A7 Pampallis; A10 Sillington; B23 Mbeki; B32 Readers Digest; B41 Walker; D13 Marks & Trapido; D18 Saunders; E2–3 Beinart; E4 Beinart & Bundy; E26 Bundy; E25 Plaatje; E27 Prins; E36 van Onselen; E38 Warwick; E3 Bhana & Pachai; F4–5 Bonner; F6–8 Bozzoli; F9 Callicanos; F26 Kallaway & Pearson; F28 La Hausse; F34 Marks; F42 Plaatje; F45 Roux; F47 Simons & Simons; F55 Willan.

PART III

COLONIALISM AND INDEPENDENCE

Introduction

Most historians have seen the 20th century history of southern Africa as the struggle between European imperialism, settler nationalism and African nationalism for control of the colonial states. Some have seen the struggle mainly in racial or ethnic terms; others have seen it as between and within the social classes formed under colonial capitalism.

Imperialism and settler nationalism   Imperialism changed in nature as Western (i.e. European and American) capitalism developed in relation to the rest of the world economy. There was a shift from *national* (British, German, etc.) capitalism, which protected overseas markets by having colonies, to *multinational* capitalism usually with strong American links, which saw colonies as no longer necessary. Instead the multinational companies sought to ally themselves with the ruling class in independent states. Settler nationalism periodically challenged overseas capitalism during the 20th century. But on each occasion overseas capitalists eventually reached a new compromise with local-based capitalists and politicians by sharing control of colonial wealth.

African nationalism   The term 'nationalism' is usually distinguished from the patriotism of precolonial states, to refer to movements seeking a nation-state along capitalist or European lines. In that case we may recognize as 'nationalist' some movements usually dismissed as 'tribalist' in precolonial states or ethnic groups under colonialism. We may also distinguish *Africanist* and *socialist* traditions within the mainstream of African nationalism, leading to political parties seeking or taking political independence. Africanism flourished among Christian-educated Africans, even while colonialism was being imposed in the 1890s, preaching pride in African race and culture. Socialism, which preached class solidarity against capitalism, was boosted by the growth of an industrial working class that followed the First World War and revived during the Second World War.

Class formation   The rise of industrial capitalism in southern Africa divided people into new social classes, each with its role in producing and consuming the wealth of colonial society. Capitalists and skilled industrial workers at first came from overseas, but a local working class soon devoloped — though white workers attempted to keep separate from and superior to black workers as a 'labour aristocracy'. Many rural families became peasant farmers of crops for the new mines and towns -- until capitalist farmers took over production, and peasants were forced to become farm workers or were expelled to overcrowded tribal reserves. Few people succeeded in becoming capitalists owning any considerable property. But that was the dream of many whites and fewer Africans who moved into the lower parts of the 'middle class' as teachers, civil servants, highly skilled craftsman and small traders.

Racial segregation has been more fully developed in southern Africa than anywhere else in the world. The system of segregation in South Africa was set up by laws at the beginning of the 20th century. It was strengthened by new laws in the 1920s-30s, in the late 1940s and early 1950s (when it was first called *apartheid*), and again in the late 1950s and early 1960s. Why? Some historians argue that racial segregation began as a system of exploitation of black labour by foreign mining capitalists, and was strengthened by local agricultural capitalists and by manufacturing industry capitalists, who rose to power with Afrikaner nationalism. But we should also point out the part played by the white 'labour aristocracy' in promoting racial segregation, *and* that racial segregation was strengthened at each stage as a government reaction to stronger nationalist challenges from the rising African working class. The Africanist challenge of early years was to become increasingly socialist in later years.

Colonial society was legally segregated between whites and 'non-whites'. But colonial capitalism bound everyone together into a common economy — paying taxes, selling crops or labour, or managing and owning capital. However we must not assume that everyone in southern Africa was simply under the control of capitalism based on the Witwatersrand. People make their own history. The richness of southern African history is the great variety of responses and initiatives taken by individuals and groups of people in different parts of the region.

Keywords

national capitalism and *multinational* (or transnational) *capitalism; patriotism* and *nationalism; nation-state;* 'tribalism' and 'Africanism'; *socialism* and *class solidarity; working class,* 'middle class'; and 'labour aristocracy'; *segregation* and *apartheid;* 'non-whites' and 'tribal reserves'; *mining, agriculture,* and *manufacturing industry*.

Source-based Exercise

The real effect of the war was two-fold. In the first place it impoverished the landowner. His stock had disappeared, his buildings were demolished, and the whole orderly process of farming was disorganised, and required time, capital and industry before it could be set going again. Native labour was in many districts almost unobtainable, and was everywhere expensive, partly owing to the increased demand for labour in the mines, partly because of the large sums made by natives during the war.

The second effect of the war was that it swept into the towns from the country, in a destitute condition, a very large number of those [whites] who did not possess land of their own, and who had been previously sinking into poverty. . . . [some] people were left to their own resources with acquired habits of idleness and dependence upon others. Moreover diseases and pests have scourged the Transvaal . . . the bywoners — and many of the owners of small farms who have been unable to cope with the difficulties which beset them — have migrated to the towns, or are living as indigent squatters on their own lands.

The poor whites ['in shanties on the outskirts of towns'] manage to exist partly by doing casual work such as trolley or cab-driving, but more often by living on the money earned by their children as messengers, newspaper sellers, and in similar ways. . .' [Transvaal Colony, *Report of the Transvaal Indigency Commission 1906–8* Pretoria, 1908]

(a) What was a bywoner?
(b) How were 'large sums' made by Africans in 'the war'?
(c) Briefly, how was the 'problem' of African farm labour supply solved?
(d) Why did poor whites not do 'rough manual labour' like poor people elsewhere in the world?
(e) Briefly, how was the 'poor white problem' solved?

Chapter 14

The Rise of White Settler Power (1906 – 1922)

In the early decades of the 20th century a distinctive South African type of colonialism emerged, different from the types found in the rest of the continent. European settlers worked in new mines and towns, and managed farms on the healthy plateaux or coastal areas. They competed for employment and land with increasing numbers of skilled or semi-skilled Africans. But the settlers had the political advantage over Africans of being able to demand democratic rights enjoyed by other Europeans overseas.

White settler political power in South Africa grew hand in hand with capitalist farming and manufacturing industry. The Union governments of Botha and Smuts continued the imperial policy of encouraging agricultural production to meet the food needs of the mines. Botha and Smuts had been elected into power by Afrikaner farmers, and gave them government aid to become successful capitalist producers on a large scale. Botha and Smuts also came to terms with the gold mining capitalists, as they realized that government revenue was dependent on increasing profitable gold production. Meanwhile manufacturing capitalism emerged with the growth of industry to process food, drink and tobacco for consumption in South Africa.

The rapid growth of capitalism between about 1906 and 1922 was at the expense of workers' wages. The cost of living rose dramatically during and after the First World War, while employers sought to reduce their costs by cutting wages. A white worker earned over ten times more than a black worker. But white workers were more successful than black workers in fighting against wage reductions and for better working conditions. Two reasons may be given. Firstly, higher pay for a few more skilled workers might be less costly for employers than even a slightly better wage for the mass of workers. Secondly, white workers refused to combine with blacks as fellow workers, but insisted on a job 'colour-bar' instead. This bar would reserve all skilled and supervisory jobs for whites only, leaving unskilled jobs for blacks. Since most skilled jobs were already filled by whites, and all white men (with exceptions in Cape province) had the vote, white workers had the economic and political power to force a colour-bar on their employers.

The South African colonial system was based on migration of black labour to mines and white farms, to be returned to 'tribal' reserves when disabled or no longer needed. The average African family could not make a complete living either as peasants in the reserves or as workers in white areas. To survive, the family was forced to do both, and members of the family continuously migrated back and forth. Successful peasant producers in the reserves were usually headmen, with access to more land and capital. An increasing number of Africans also began to stay in towns with their families, including clerks and labourers. White politicians and employers attempted to keep black townspeople from combining in political or trade union movements. Tribalism was kept alive, or invented, by dividing blacks at work and at home along

227

White settlers — pioneer days are over and life becomes more comfortable. White household and servants at Mbabane, Swaziland, about 1910.

by its job colour-bar. But on the other hand it opened the way for Afrikaner nationalism to weaken imperial control; and the colour-bar pushed up the costs of skilled labour by restricting it to whites only.

1 Formation of the Union of South Africa (1907-09)

The question of forming a united South Africa was raised in July 1907 by the British high commissioner in South Africa, Lord Selborne. The 'Selborne Memorandum', published in that month, looked forward to the day when all British Africa south of the Zambezi, which had formed one customs union in 1903, would come together under one government.

language lines, often with tribal headmen appointed by employers.

The British government and imperial companies with interests in South Africa greeted the rise of white settler power with mixed feelings. On the one hand the granting of political power to the settlers kept them loyal to the imperial system by satisfying their local political ambitions. And settler rule pushed down the costs of plentiful unskilled labour

National Convention Representatives of the four settler-ruled colonies met in a 'National Convention' at Durban and Capetown, between October 1908 and February 1909, to plan the details of a united South Africa. The four colonies agreed to become provinces of one Union of South Africa, with their own provincial administrations and assemblies (parliaments), but subject to a strong Union government. The government was to consist

Colonial police — keepers of law and order, enforcers of tax collection. Bechuanaland Protectorate police at Kazungula on the Zambezi — where German, Rhodesian and Bechuanaland borders met.

of a national assembly, elected by white male citizens, and a senate representing the provinces. The Union administration was to be headed by a governor-general as the representative of the British king.

The white National Convention of 1908-09 failed to agree on three issues — a common 'native policy', a common system of education, and how to incorporate the other colonies of 'British South Africa' into the Union. The eventual constitution of the Union of South Africa left 'native policy' and education as they had been under the four colonies. All Africans came under the Native Affairs Department (NAD) of the Union administration, but the laws affecting them differed in the different provinces. 'Non-white' male voters in the Cape province kept their votes, but could not stand for election to the national assembly.

The British imperial government was quite aware of the fact that, by surrendering 'native policy' to the white settler governments, it was betraying the trust of the African population. Many Africans had expected that at least Cape 'native policy' would be applied to the rest of the Union. The imperial government therefore tried to sugar the pill of its betrayal by showing concern for the 'native territories' of Basutoland, Bechuanaland Protectorate and Swaziland.

Origin of the High Commission Territories
In July 1908 Lord Selborne proposed that Basutoland and Swaziland should be incorporated into the Union, because of their historical links with the Orange Free State and Transvaal. But Bechuanaland should not be incorporated until Southern Rhodesia, to which it was historically linked, joined the Union. However, the Colonial Office in London, aware of the argument that the chiefs of all three territories had been promised protection by the imperial government in the late 19th century, decided to treat Basutoland, Bechuanaland and Swaziland in the same way. The Colonial Office at first agreed that the three territories should become part of the Union, but should be under the governor-general as their 'high

commissioner' rather than the Union's Native Affairs Department. But protests from the territories were so strong that the Colonial Office revised its decision. The Swaziland regency had sent a delegation to London in 1907 to protest at land partition. The Bechuanaland chiefs, notably Linchwe of the Kgatla, sent petitions challenging the Selborne Memorandum. The Basutoland paramount chief Letsie II sent a delegation to London in 1909, and then threatened to join them.

The British government therefore decided not to incorporate the High Commission Territories into the Union for a period of up to five or six years. The Union would first have to satisfy missionary/humanitarian interests in Britain, who were backing the territories' protests, that its 'native policy' was satisfactory.

Black South African protests   Three African newspaper editors, Walter Rubusana, J. T. Jabavu, and John L. Dube, called a South African Native (National) Convention to counter the previous white National Convention. The new body met at Bloemfontein in March 1909 and called for a colour-blind franchise to include all adult males, and for an end to racial discrimination. The African Political Organisation (APO), meeting at Capetown in the following month, also attacked the proposed Union constitution as 'un-British in that it lies down a colour-line'. In June 1909 a combined African delegation, including Rubusana, Jabavu and Abdurahman of the APO, sailed for Britain under the leadership of the white liberal politician W.P. Schreiner. They found rival white delegations already had the ear of the British government, and few British politicians would support them. 'No longer must we look to our flabby friends in Great Britain,' concluded Abdurahman.

The South Africa Act was passed by the British parliament in 1909, and became effective as the constitution of the new Union of South Africa in 1910. The Act closely followed the recommendations of the National Convention of white settler delegates. But it

The Schreiner deputation in London, 1909 W.P. Schreiner, a liberal former Cape Colony prime minister, led a delegation of non-European representatives to petition against the South Africa Act passed by the British parliament in 1909, which set up the Union of South Africa. **Seated** (from left to right): John Tengo Jabavu (King Williamstown Native Association); Abdul Abdurahman (African Political Organisation), W.P. Schreiner; Walter B. Rubusana (South African Native Convention); Matt J. Fredericks (APO). **Standing**: T.M. Mapikela (Orange River Colony Native Congress); J. Gerrans (Mafeking trader representing Bechuanaland Protectorate chiefs); Daniel Dwanya (SANC); D.J. Lenders (APO). The South African Native Convention brought together representatives of black organizations, including Jabavu and Mapikela, as a counter to the all-white National Convention which had drawn up the new South African constitution. The African Political Organisation was a Cape-based, largely coloured, political party.

had two remarkable features. First there was a so called 'entrenched clause' maintaining the vote for non-white males in the Cape province. This could only be removed from the constitution by a two-thirds majority of senate and national assembly members sitting together. Secondly there was a schedule of twenty-five articles attached to the constitution to protect African rights in the High Commission Territories after they were incorporated into the Union of South Africa. When debating this schedule in the British parliament, the British government made an additional promise, which was to prove very important in later years. It promised to *consult* (though not to obtain agreement of) chiefs in the High Commission Territories before transfer to the Union.

2 The Botha Government and the Mining Industry (1910-14)

The first government of the Union of South

Africa was formed by the *South African Party* (SAP), under Louis Botha as prime minister and Jan Smuts as his deputy. The SAP brought together Afrikaner leaders like Botha and Smuts, who were prepared to collaborate with British imperialism, with former 'bitter-enders' like J. B. M. Hertzog fighting for Afrikaner cultural rights. The SAP was voted into power by Afrikaner farmers, and was supported by the *South African Labour Party* against other English-speaking parties in parliament. But the major part of government revenue came from taxing gold production and export. Botha therefore had to satisfy the mining capitalists who otherwise backed the opposition Unionist Party, as well as Afrikaner farmers and the white workers who voted for the Labour Party. He therefore did not attack the leading role of British capitalism in the economy, nor did he satisfy the ambitions of all Afrikaners, especially those impoverished by the 1899-1902 war. Hertzog quarrelled with Botha's attempts to recruit the support of English-speaking voters, and was expelled from the SAP in 1913. Hertzog founded his own *National Party* in 1914.

Gold mining The economic base of the Union of South Africa in this period rested firmly on gold mining. The Witwatersrand produced almost twenty-five per cent of the world's gold supply in 1899 and over fifty per cent of it in 1921. The money value of its gold production rose to £38.6 million by 1915. Meanwhile the profits of the industry rose greatly both because more gold was sold and because the costs of producing each ton were reduced. This reduction in costs was achieved largely because wages and recruitment costs for unskilled labour were reduced.

The mines stopped importing Chinese workers (see Chapter 12), as more African workers were driven to the mines by agricultural depression and the need to pay taxes and buy consumer goods.

WENELA & NRC The Witwatersrand Native Labour Association (WENELA) at first recruited workers for the gold and coal mines from as far north as Nyasaland. But the death rate of Africans who marched on foot across the Limpopo to the mines was particularly high, and the mines and white farms of Southern Rhodesia were crying out for black labour. So WENELA stopped recruiting workers from north of the 22nd parallel, including parts of Bechuanaland and Mozambique, from 1912-13 until 1933. Some workers avoided the ban by first working in the Messina copper mines of the northern Transvaal, after which they were recruited to the Rand as South Africans. At the same time the chamber of mines set up a new body called the Native Recruiting Corporation, also called 'Kwa-Teba' after the name of its head recruiter H. M. Taberer. The NRC recruited labour from the Union of South Africa, Basutoland, the Southern Bechuanaland Protectorate, and Swaziland.

White workers and the colour-bar One of the first laws passed by Botha's SAP government was the *Native Labour Regulation Act*, which made strikes by black workers in mines and industries a criminal offence punishable by imprisonment. The government also passed the *Mines and Works Act* of 1911, which enforced the job colour-bar against black workers in the Transvaal and Orange Free State, reserving all jobs classified as 'skilled' for whites.

Skilled workers in the mining industry had originally been Europeans imported from overseas, while Africans had come to the mines unskilled. But as the mines developed some African workers acquired skills, while unskilled white workers were recruited from within South Africa. Mining companies attempted to employ Africans in skilled jobs more cheaply than whites. White workers tried to maintain their higher wages by insisting that all whites be classified as 'skilled' — as supervisors of black workers if not as qualified craftsmen. When in 1907 the mines began to employ Africans and Chinese as operators of the new compressed air drills, the white miners went on strike. Africans and Chinese then proved that they could run a mine without the supervision of white miners. This made white miners all the more determined to maintain the job colour-bar. The Labour Party representing white workers therefore pressed the SAP government into the 1911 Mines and Works Act.

Though the SAP government of Botha and Smuts was prepared to favour white workers over black workers, it would not back them against the interests of the mining capitalists. The government refused to force the mining companies by law to improve white pay and working conditions. White workers on the Rand had taken up the demands of European and American workers overseas for a maximum eight-hour working day. The Labour Party failed to push an eight-hour day law through parliament and the white miners went on strike for reduced working hours in May 1913.

The 1913 Rand miners' strike began, like the previous 1907 strike, at Benoni and spread to Johannesburg, where there was widespread violence. The offices of *The Star* newspaper,

Police charge strikers' meeting on the Rand, 1914

owned by mining interests, were burned down. Twenty white demonstrators were shot dead by police guarding the Rand Club on Loveday Street, where mine owners met to eat and drink. Few black workers succeeded in striking. Most continued at work in the mines, or were locked into the compounds to stop them joining street demonstrations. The government of Botha and Smuts finally succeeded in ending the miners' strike by promising an enquiry into grievances. But the strike had spread to other industries on the Rand.

By the beginning of 1914 white socialists were planning a general strike of all industries on the Rand, to force the capitalists into conceding a kind of workers' control of industry. But the government sent in troops to arrest all white labour leaders. Nine revolutionary socialists were deported overseas, mostly back to Scotland; and the government passed laws giving the police powers to prohibit meetings and arrest suspects in trade unions.

3 The Rise of Capitalist ('Commercial') Farming

During the period after the South African War an increasingly large class of capitalist ('commercial') farmers emerged among white farm owners in South Africa. Poorer farm owners continued to make their living from share-cropping. Such land owners took a share, normally half, of the peasants' crops in return for allowing them to 'squat' on their farms. But aspiring capitalist farmers tried to clear peasants off their land and to replace them by workers who laboured on the owner's fields. Even where peasants were allowed to keep their own plots and to grow their own food, they had to labour on the farm owner's fields for part of the year, i.e. giving labour instead of crops or money as rent.

Capitalist farmers invested capital in improvements to the farm, such as fencing, dipping tanks, dams, silos, wells, etc. Such improvements produced more and better crops and livestock, and also increased the selling price of the land. As capitalists they tried to gain profits by reducing the costs and increasing the scale of production, and took risks in taking bank loans and in producing for unpredictable future markets.

Government aid to agriculture The steady growth of the gold mining industry created a large, regular demand for foodstuffs, especially maize, meat and wheat, to feed the labour force. Only large-scale farms could meet such demands. The SAP government therefore provided capital loans and better marketing, and prohibited farm squatters, to encourage the growth of capitalist production. White farmers who persisted in share-cropping were condemned as 'kaffir-farmers' because they 'farmed' blacks rather than directly farming the land. Some of these white 'kaffir-farmers' succeeded in becoming capitalist farmers. Others took government aid and bank loans until they were so deeply in debt that they had to sell their farms. Such people turned against the SAP government and gave their support to the National Party.

The Land Settlement Act of 1912 divided up land previously owned by the state or by large companies into new white farms. The Land and Agricultural Bank was set up in 1912 with capital provided by the state. The bank provided capital loans at low interest rates to white farmers who wished to buy more land or livestock, or to invest in farm improvements. Between 1910 and 1916 a further three thousand kilometres of railway branch lines were constructed so white farmers could market their increased production. Gold exports were carried by the railways at high freight rates and agricultural produce at low rates. The profits were used to pay for more railway construction.

1913 Natives Land Act The SAP government extended the 'native reserve' system of Natal and Cape Colony into the Transvaal and Orange Free State, and forced white farms to begin expelling black peasant squatters, by the *Natives Land Act* of 1913. This act, originally known as the Pass and Squatters Bill, followed the recommendations of the 1903-05 Lagden commission on South African 'native affairs'. It secured most of the Union's land area for white development by reserving only nine million hectares (about seven per cent of the Union) for so-called 'scheduled areas' of African tribal ownership. The Act allowed for the 'scheduled areas' of African tribal ownership to be increased. But it quashed the idea of Africans ever being allowed to own land as individuals in the reserves. Africans should not be economically independent, but should be workers on white farms or mines. The Act also laid down the regulation that Africans on white farms must be contracted to give at least ninety days' labour to the farm owner every year, or must

be expelled into the reserves. But it was left to provincial authorities to decide when and where to enforce this anti-squatter regulation.

Within weeks of the Natives Land Act being passed, the expulsion of peasant 'squatters' was ordered from white-owned farms in the Orange Free State. The plight of black peasants in the Free State, many of whom had been prosperous enough to live 'just like Dutchmen', was recorded by Sol Plaatje, the secretary of the South African Native National Congress, in his book *Native Life in South Africa*. The 1913 Act reserved only one small area in the Free State, around Thaba Nchu, for blacks. Most peasant families had to migrate into the reserves of Basutoland, the south-western Transvaal, and the northern Cape. Capitalist farming replaced share-cropping almost overnight in the Orange Free State (though share-cropping later resumed in a different form). In the Cape province Africans argued that the Natives Land Act was illegal discrimination against African voters, who had been guaranteed legal rights by the Union constitution. A judge ruled in favour of the Xhosa chief Kama who was challenging the Act, and the Act could not be enforced in the Cape province (1917). In the Transvaal the Natives Land Act stopped blacks in western districts who were buying 'white' farms. In the northern and eastern Transvaal the situation remained unclear for over twenty years, because farms and reserves had not previously been demarcated. Bushveld areas had been opened to cattle and crop farming by the 1896-97 rinderpest killing off wildlife and tsetse-fly. The 'native reserves' of the northern and eastern Transvaal were not laid out until 1936.

The 1913-16 Beaumont commission toured the countryside, enquiring into problems resulting from the Act. The commission recommended increasing the scheduled areas by eight million hectares, of which five million were in the Transvaal. But South African governments took no action on the matter until 1936.

Economic underdevelopment of the reserves The drought, famine and livestock diseases of

1903-09 made conditions worse in the black rural reserves. Crops were ruined and families had to buy food from local white traders. Cattle and sheep, which had sold well to towns and mines and white farms during and after the South African War, were seldom exported after about 1904. Livestock prices fell; the government restricted exports from reserves to prevent spreading livestock diseases; and white farms now supplied town and mine markets with livestock. As a result, numbers of cattle and sheep in black reserves doubled between the livestock censuses of 1904 and 1911, while their quality worsened because of drought and disease. Only the best livestock could be exported, instead of becoming breeding stock. Over-grazing turned good pastures into scrubland, while hastening erosion of hillsides and river courses.

People had become used to buying consumer goods, particularly clothing and utensils, from white-owned trading stores. Now as well as finding cash to pay taxes, travel and educational fees, they often had to buy food as well. Many got heavily into debt with traders and could only pay their debts by selling goods or labour to the traders. Traders often encouraged their customers to get into debt in order to buy the customers' goods or labour cheaply. In the Transkei traders were paid a fee by the gold mines for every migrant worker recruited. Families in continual debt were forced to send their men as migrant workers to pay off the debts. In Basutoland traders refused to give peasants cash for wool or wheat, giving them credit slips (known as 'good-fors') instead for goods to be bought from the same store. In this way wool and wheat were bought cheaply and imported goods were sold dearly.

Underdevelopment and labour migration Capitalist employers on mines and farms sought a large regular supply of cheap black labour. They welcomed the decline of peasant farming. The territories that had been most successful in peasant production, like the Ciskei, the Transkei and Basutoland, suffered most. These territories were crowded out with

people expelled from white farms by the 1892-1909 *Location Acts* in the Cape Colony and the 1913 Natives Land Act in the Orange Free State. In order to provide food for these immigrants and still produce a surplus of crops for sale, fertile soils were ploughed and planted so often that the soils became dry and powdery and were washed away by erosion.

The Ciskei and Transkei were the first black reserves to become 'underdeveloped' by capitalist agriculture and industry in the rest of South Africa. Previously prosperous farmlands in the reserves could no longer support the people living on them. Growing numbers of people were forced to migrate to labour on mines and white farms. The number of people leaving the Transkei to seek work doubled from about 50,000 in 1901 to almost 100,000 in 1912, of whom about thirty per cent in 1903 and sixty per cent in 1912 were working in the Rand mines. Such evidence of 'underdevelopment' came later to Basutoland. The figure of about 25,000 people in 1911 working outside Basutoland doubled by 1921 and rose to over 100,000 by 1936. Many people who went abroad stayed abroad.

Underdevelopment in Mozambique The largest number of workers in the Witwatersrand mines came from southern Mozambique. The Portuguese colonial authorities in Mozambique agreed to keep up a constant supply of labour to the mines. Usually about 50,000 workers were recruited every year to stay for two years, making a total of about 100,000 Mozambique workers in the mines at a time. From 1899 onwards, migration in southern and central Mozambique was strictly controlled by colonial law and police. Every African man and woman had to work — for the government, the *prazo* estates of the Zambezi valley, or as migrants to South Africa, Southern Rhodesia, Swaziland and the Portuguese island of São Thome in the Atlantic Ocean. Only children, old people, self-employed craftsmen, and chiefs, were exempt from this law. People were forced to work at gunpoint if necessary.

Peasant agriculture among the Tsonga and Chopi in southern Mozambique was left in the hands of women. These women peasants had to grow extra crops or give labour to government and settler farms, as well as to grow food to feed their families and to collect wild cashew nuts and oil-seeds to sell by the roadsides. The men workers, who went to South Africa for two years, were encouraged to spend their money quickly at home and then return to the mines. Heavy drinking of wine and cashew-nut liquor was common. These conditions led to serious social problems in family life among Tsonga and Chopi ('Shangane') both at home and abroad.

4 The First World War (1914-18)

When the British government declared war on Germany and Austria in August 1914, it did so on behalf of its empire, including the Union of South Africa. The Native National Congress stopped its protests against the Natives Land Act and declared its willingness to help provide African troops for the war. Offers of troops came from the chiefs of Basutoland, Bechuanaland — for service in South West Africa — Pondoland, Swaziland and Tembuland. Africans hoped that their loyalty to British imperialism would result in British support of their interests against the white settlers. But the Union government replied (November 2nd, 1914):

'the present war is one which has its origin among the white people of Europe and the Government are anxious to avoid the employment of its native citizens in warfare against whites.'

Within a few days of the outbreak of war there were clashes between Germans and British on the Caprivi Strip border between German South West Africa and Northern Rhodesia, and between gunboats on Lake Nyasa (Malawi). The Afrikaners of the Union were seriously divided about whether to fight for the British, remain neutral, or fight for the Germans. The Boer commando system had been revived by the *Defence Act* of 1912, which also banned blacks from being soldiers.

Afrikaner revolt   General Jacobus de la Rey, hero of the previous war and 'bitter-ender'

leader, was inspired by a Boer prophet to lead a Boer rising to throw off British imperialism and to revive republican independence. But de la Rey was accidentally shot dead by police in September in 1914, when his car crashed through a road block set up to catch a gang of criminals. The commando leader sent by Botha to the South West African border, Manie Maritz, then openly joined the Germans. Other Boer commandos tried to join Maritz by marching into the northern Cape province. Botha determined to crush them. The main rebel leader Christiaan de Wet was defeated in November 1914 and captured near the Molopo river. One other leader was defeated in battle, and then drowned while escaping across the flooded Vaal river. Another was captured by chief Seepapitso of the Ngwaketse while fleeing across Bechuanaland towards Maritz. Another managed to join Maritz, but surrendered to Botha in February 1915. Maritz himself fled north to exile in Angola — because he said he could not live in a land 'ruled by Englishmen, niggers and Jews'.

South West Africa   The British navy had captured Luderitz Bay in September 1914, and so cut off the Germans from coastal supplies. Botha therefore found German South West Africa an easy prey for conquest. Between April and July 1915 the German forces were defeated by South African forces, who refused help from coloured Afrikaners already living in South West Africa. South African forces from the south, and Portuguese forces from the north, then conquered the previously independent Ovambo and Nkhumbi states during 1915–17. The Kwanyama king Mandume, who led Ovambo resistance, was finally killed in 1917.

East African campaign   Victorious in German South West Africa, and no doubt looking to the future expansion of the Union, Smuts led South African forces into German East Africa (Tanganyika) in February 1916. Large numbers of British troops — mainly black soldiers from Kenya, Uganda and Nyasaland under white officers — were battling with a German army also consisting of black soldiers, under the brilliant command of General von Lettow-Vorbeck. The German forces fought in small guerrilla units, and East and West African troops rather than South Africans took the brunt of the fighting.

Smuts' army, which included Cape coloured as well as white South Africans, marched from Kenya to the south of Dar es Salaam at the end of 1916. Smuts then declared that von Lettow-Vorbeck's army was virtually defeated. Most South African troops went home, while Smuts went to London to become an imperial statesman. In fact von Lettow-Vorbeck was not defeated. In November 1917 he withdrew his army into northern Mozambique. Von Lettow-Vorbeck's army was the only German army undefeated in the First World War. When peace came in November 1918 the army was marching through Northern Rhodesia on its way to capture Katanga!

South African forces in France South African forces in South West Africa included 33,000 blacks as labourers, wagon drivers and servants. In East Africa there were 17,000 such blacks in the South African forces. But the best remembered are the 21,000 who served in the South African Native Labour Contingent in France during 1917-18. Despite the assistance given to recruitment by the South African Native National Congress (later ANC), blacks were reluctant to come forward for service in France. The governor-general thought blacks in the Union resented the refusal of the imperial government to stop the Natives Land Act. In Bechuanaland the chief Khama was willing to send money but not men to fight Britain's wars overseas.

White South Africans fought as part of the imperial army in France, winning honours at the battle of Delville Wood (1916). Black South Africans in France unloaded ships and trains or cut wood in forests. Strict orders were given by the South African government that Africans were to be segregated from other troops. They were locked in closed compounds at night, and prohibited from drinking liquor or from any friendship with

Europeans — 'as this is subversive to discipline and calculated to impair their efficiency as working units'. But segregation and discipline began to break down. During a riot against the compound system, thirteen men were shot dead by guards. The Union government feared this collapse of discipline, and withdrew the Native Labour Contingent from France some months before the war ended, despite imperial requests for 30,000 more men.

Over six hundred members of the Native Labour Contingent drowned when the ship *Mendi* sank in the freezing waters of the English-French Channel on February 21st, 1917. The memory of the disaster was kept alive by the Native National Congress's Mendi Memorial Club, as an event when black South Africans perished in the service of the world's freedom.

5 The Aftermath of War (1918-20)

Like the rest of the world, southern Africa was hard-hit by the disasters of influenza epidemic and economic depression in 1918-19. In some areas up to a quarter of the population died of the great 'Spanish influenza' epidemic. (However the effects of the epidemic have not yet been fully studied by historians.) The cost of living rose higher and higher. Black workers struck for more pay, and some Afrikaner nationalists still threatened revolt. The end of the war in November 1918 came as a great relief to Botha, who joined Smuts in Europe for the peace negotiations. Delegations from the National Party and the Native National Congress also went to Europe and unsuccessfully petitioned the British government. The National Party wanted less imperial power in South Africa; the Native National Congress wanted more.

Smuts as prime minister The South African Party government turned back to its pre-war policies of racial segregation and assistance to Afrikaner farming capitalists and English mining capitalists. Smuts became prime minister when Botha died in 1919. He relied on the support of the Unionist Party 'opposition' in parliament against Hertzog's National Party and against the Labour Party. The government used its police to crush numerous strikes by white and black workers. Parliamentary laws were passed to regulate the new manufacturing industry being set up in the Union. The *Native Affairs Act* of 1920 set up a permanent Native Affairs Commission, consisting entirely of white 'experts'. The law was intended to extend the 'native council' system of rule by chiefs from the Transkei to all the 'native reserves' of the Union.

Industrialization Gold mining was the driving force at the centre of the South African economy. When gold mining prospered so did the agriculture and industry that served it. Government revenue relied upon gold mining for direct taxation of profits and, more importantly, for indirect taxation of services provided to mining. Manufacturing industry grew up in South Africa to serve the mining industry with such goods as explosives and wire rope, and to process farming products such as tobacco, malt beer and canned fruit for the local market. Manufacturing industry was given a great boost by the First World War which cut off many European imports. Between 1911 and 1921 the value of goods manufactured in South Africa increased from £17 million to £79 million per year. New manufacturing industry was financed by overseas capital attracted by the gold industry, and to a lesser extent by local capital from the profits of trading.

Urbanization Johannesburg's black population grew from about 60,000 in 1904 to 102,000 in 1911. In 1911 the black population of the Rand industrial area was around 286,000.* But unlike the 180,000 whites living on the Rand, most of this black population was temporary. 190,000 migrant workers in the mines were due to return to rural reserves. The permanent black city residents

*All census figures of black urban population were probably under-estimates because 'illegal' residents without passes avoided being counted.

were a smaller unrecorded number. Their presence was recognized when the Johannesburg city authorities cleared black shanties in 1903-04 to set up the city's first 'urban location' for blacks, called Pimville, fifteen kilometres south of the city. The first great period of black urbanization along the Rand began during the First World War, when rural poverty and expansion of new manufacturing industries pushed and pulled Africans as well as Afrikaners to the city. By 1921 the total population of the Rand industrial area stood at 537,000, of whom three-fifths were black, including 173,000 black miners.

Town and city councils all over South Africa marked out urban locations for blacks during and after the First World War. High rents were charged – a Johannesburg township iron shed cost between £2 and £4 a month. Of the 217 town and city councils in 1916, 191 made more money from location rents than they spent on the locations.

Johannesburg laid out a new location called Western Native Township, next to the new city suburb of Sophiatown. Sophiatown was sold off in plots to richer Africans on freehold tenure. Plot owners in Sophiatown and in Alexandra, east of the city, subdivided their plots and rented them to people who built shanties. *Capetown,* as a rapidly growing centre of manufacturing, grew from 150,000 population in 1904 to over 200,000 by 1921. The African population of the city, almost entirely 'coloured' (of Khoisan and mixed descent), had expanded in the 1890s because of migration from the western Cape. By 1904 it was 65,000, rising to 90,000 by 1921. But only 15,000 blacks from the eastern and northern Cape were recorded in 1921. Officially these blacks were restricted by law to two small locations. But many lived as part of the coloured population in parts of the city such as District Six.

The growth of urban communities during wartime promoted the growth of African political activity and of African trade unions, which emerged around the end of the First World War. In 1917 the South African Native National Congress strongly protested against the Native Administration Bill, which would

237

have fixed the borders of the reserves proposed by the Natives Land Act and increased by the 1913-16 Beaumont commission. The bill was an unjust reward for African loyalty and service during the war. S.M. Makgatho, the Transvaal congress leader, threatened to lead a strike of African workers against the bill. The bill was eventually withdrawn by the government in 1918, and the 'final' segregation of land was left until 1936.

Miners on the Rand   Black pay and working conditions on the Rand continued to get worse, despite more efficient recruiting and management of labour. The average black pay (£28-29 p.a.) in 1911 was about a twelfth of the average white pay in the mines. By 1921 black pay was a fifteenth of white pay, although the figure returned to an eleventh in the 1920s-30s because white wages were reduced.

Death and injury rates in the mines were high. About four in every thousand miners were being killed in mine accidents every year at the beginning of the century. A total of 30,000 miners were killed in mine accidents in the half century up to 1950. There were also fatal diseases picked up in the mines. Twenty or thirty out of every thousand miners died of pneumonia every year, until WENELA medical laboratories developed an anti-pneumonia vaccine in the 1930s. Pneumonia was caused by exhaustion and damp clothing after working deep underground; only white miners were allowed to change into dry clothing at the pit head. Another disease, silicosis, took many years of dusty drilling to eat into a miner's lungs, but was finally fatal. When white miners realized this during the First World War, all drilling — previously a 'skilled' white job — became an 'unskilled' black job.

Africans were treated by the mines as 'muscle machines', whose life was cheap and who could easily be replaced. Only after 1911 was compensation given for injuries or death: the rates after 1914 were a maximum £20 for losing a leg and a maximum £50 for losing a life. By 1921, despite improvements, there were 637 deaths in accidents and 3,453 deaths from disease among black miners on the Rand in that year.

The Witwatersrand chamber of mines kept a black miner's wage low, as they explained around 1907, 'because we cannot afford a wage to make it possible for him to live in a urban area'. The black miner had to leave his family in the reserve because he could not support them on his wages in town. The miner's family in the reserve therefore carried the costs of the miner's welfare and his family's welfare, which should have been paid for by increased mine wages. Mining capitalism, which paid the black miner so little, was therefore subsidized by the subsistence agriculture of the reserves.

Post-war African worker strikes   The cost of living in South African cities doubled between 1910 and 1920, rising fast after 1917 and most rapidly in 1919. Workers responded by striking for more pay. White pay almost succeeded in keeping up with the rise in prices, while black wages fell behind. A black miner's wages in 1921 were worth 30 per cent less in real value (the amount of goods that could be bought with it), despite a rise in actual wages.

Members of the South African Native National Congress helped organize strikes and boycotts by black workers, like the strike of Johannesburg 'night-soil' (sewerage) bucket men in 1918. The women's section of the Native National Congress, under Charlotte Maxexe, fought against a new law that women must pay for passes to live in locations in the Orange Free State. Women went to prison rather than pay fines for not buying passes. This defiance succeeded. The government abolished the women's pass laws in 1920.

Selby Msimang and J. Mocher of the Orange Free State branch of the Native National Congress led strikers in Bloemfontein in 1919. Transvaal congress members like Makgatho, D.S. Letanka, Saul Msane and Bud Mbelle led African men in unsuccessful demonstrations in Pretoria and Johannesburg against the pass laws for men. White workers assisted the police in beating black demonstrators. Demonstrators sang 'Nkosi Sikelela' as African workers to go back to work. After nineteen black demonstrators had been killed by police, Selby Msimang went to settle the quarrel between Masabalala and Rubusana.

Socialism and the black trade unions The coming of the First World War had split the (all-white) South African Labour Party. Nationalist socialists supported Britain's fight with Germany. Internationalist socialists opposed the war, calling it a struggle between capitalists only, and not between the workers of the world. In 1915 the latter group under 'Comrade Bill' Andrews split from the Labour Party to form the International Socialist League. The ISL also began to realize that blacks and coloureds as well as whites in South Africa were workers of the world. Blacks and coloureds as well as whites could and should be organized as workers.

The first black trade unions were started by white socialists with experience of union organization. In 1917 the International Socialist League organized an Indian trade union in Natal, and an African trade union on the Rand called the Industrial Workers Union of Africa (IWA). The IWA was supported at first by members of both the Native National Congress and the (coloured) African Political Organization. It printed pamphlets in seSotho and isiZulu: 'Let there be no longer any talk of Basuto, Zulu or Shangaan. You are all labourers. Let Labour be your common bond. Deliver yourself from the chains of capitalism.' But the ISL attacked the position of the Native National Congress as 'bourgeois nationalism' and alienated black support. The IWA soon collapsed.

Founding of ICU In Capetown a non-revolutionary group of white socialists broke away from the South African Labour Party, to press for democratic and trade union rights for Africans in all four provinces. This group organized an African trade union in 1918, called the Industrial and Commercial Union (ICU). Its initial membership was mostly coloured dock workers, and its secretary was an educated immigrant worker from Nyasaland named Clements Kadalie.

Charlotte Maxexe (1874-1939) Born Charlotte Manye, at Ramakgopa in the northern Transvaal. She joined an African choir that toured Britain and the United States in the early 1890s. The choir broke up in Ohio State and she went to a local black college, Wilberforce University, run by the African Methodist Episcopal Church. A letter to her uncle Rev. M.M. Mokone in Pretoria resulted in his Ethiopian Church becoming part of the AMEC in 1896-98. She married a fellow South African student, Marshall Maxexe, and returned to teach in the northern Transvaal around 1903. She became the leading woman member of the South African Native Congress (later ANC), and founded its Women's League, which fought success-fully against the women's pass laws.

nationalists, and 'God Save the King' to show pro-British loyalties against the South African government. But the Native National Congress became split between older 'moderates' and younger 'militants'. When Samuel Masabalala led Port Elizabeth workers on strike in 1920, the city authorities brought in the veteran nationalist Walter Rubusana to persuade the

The ICU became important after it organized a strike at Capetown docks in December 1919, with the support of Cape branches of the IWA and of the Native National Congress. The strike failed to increase the workers' pay, but gained much publicity. Strikers refused to load ships with foodstuffs for export to Europe because workers in South Africa were starving.

During 1919 Selby Msimang contacted Clements Kadalie about organizing trade unions. In 1920 a meeting of fifty delegates was held at Bloemfontein to found a great union associated with the Native National Congress, to be called the Industrial and Commercial Workers Union (ICWU) and to include all black, coloured and Indian workers in southern Africa. Selby Msimang was elected president. But Kadalie returned home to Capetown annoyed at being left out of the leadership, and kept the ICU independent from the ICWU. From the same meeting Samuel Masabalala returned to Port Elizabeth to organize workers on strike.

During 1920 the South African government tried to deport Kadalie back to Nyasaland as a dangerous foreign agitator. But Kadalie appears to have bought a reprieve by declaring his support for Smuts in the general election! The ICU therefore broke its original link with white socialists. Later in 1921 the ICU took over the ICWU and became the largest black political organization in southern Africa, claiming to speak for all black workers.

6 The Smuts Government and the Rand Revolt (1920-22)

Smuts' government lost votes but regained power in the 1920 elections. The Unionist Party dissolved itself, after losing votes to the Labour Party, and its leading members joined Smuts' South African Party. The SAP was now clearly the party of the imperialists and capitalists, opposed to the National and Labour parties inside parliament and to nationalists and socialists, black and white, outside parliament. Temporary economic recovery in 1920 soon turned back into depression, strikes and widespread political discontent. Smuts' government stamped down on mass demonstrations with an iron heel. In 1920 the strike led by Samuel Masabalala resulted in the shooting of nineteen blacks at Port Elizabeth. In 1921 nearly two hundred members of the 'Israelite' religious sect were killed by machine-gun fire at Bulhoek near Queenstown. In 1922 the government killed a hundred Bondelswarts Nama, protesting against a tax on hunting dogs, by aerial bombing and machine guns in South-West Africa. After Smuts proclaimed his concern for mankind in moralistic terms, the South African poet Roy Campbell with bitter irony called him:
'The saint who fed the birds at Bondelswart And fattened up the vultures at Bulhoek.'

Growth of white socialism Between 1913 and 1922 there was a great growth of socialist ideas among white workers. Most white workers were now Afrikaners, originally poor whites from the countryside, rather than immigrant Europeans. The Labour Party representing white workers was therefore drawn increasingly towards Afrikaner nationalism. Right-wing white socialists in the Labour Party held to racist ideas of keeping blacks down as a despised slave class. This belief in socialism limited to a master race was further inspired by fascism in Italy and Germany. Left-wing white socialists, who formed the International Socialist League, held revolutionary ideas of a workers' state without colour discrimination. This belief was further inspired by the Russian revolution of 1917 and by communism in the Soviet Union. In 1921 the ISL became part of the *Communist Party of South Africa,* which had been formed in the previous year. The CPSA was a section of the Comintern (Communist-International), a world body set up by Lenin with head-quarters in the Soviet Union, which expected imminent revolution among workers all over the world. But in South Africa these distinctions between different types of socialism, and even between racism and communism, were often confused among white workers until the 1922 Rand revolt.

240

1922 RAND RISING
Photographs of the Newlands Red Commando in Johannesburg show clearly their slogan: 'Workers of the World Fight and UNITE for a White S.A.' (right). Many white workers held to this confusion of international and racial socialist ideas — which soon afterwards were being distinguished as 'communism' and 'fascism' respectively.

1922 Rand miners' revolt The support of the SAP for capitalism, backed by the use of force, led Smuts' government into violent confrontation with white socialists and Afrikaner nationalists during the 1922 Rand miners's strike.

The basic cause of the strike was the attempt by mining companies to reduce the cost of white labour. Profits had declined because of the falling price of gold on the world market. The world price of gold had dropped from 130 shillings per ounce at the beginning of 1920 to 95 shillings at the end of 1921. The Witwatersrand Chamber of Mines feared a further drop to 84 shillings, which would make twenty-four out of thirty-nine gold mines unprofitable. But the companies did not dare to reduce white wages for fear of legal action or a strike. So, with the permission of the Smuts government, in December 1921 the Chamber of Mines announced a raising of the level of the job colour-bar as agreed with the white trade unions in 1918. Blacks would take certain more skilled jobs, replacing expensive white labour with cheap black labour. It was this threat to the white 'labour aristocracy' that caused the white miners to strike. Strikes by white workers began in coal mines in January 1922, and soon spread to the gold mines.

The white workers formed their own armed commandos, and began to plot revolution for a white workers' republic on the Rand. White strikers also began to attack black workers who ignored the strike and continued to work. So on March 10th, Smuts sent in the army to break the strike. For five days there was a war along the Rand between striker commandos and the South African army, which used artillery, tanks, bombing aircraft and machine-guns. The last commandos surrendered at Fordsburg after heavy artillery shelling on March 14th. Two hundred and fourteen people died in the war, of whom thirty were black workers killed by angry white strikers.

State encouragement of Afrikaner farming Protected from overseas competition by the customs union, capitalist agriculture in South Africa grew rapidly in response to the demand for food from the mines and towns. The export market was less reliable. Up to 1915 the only agricultural exports from South Africa were wool to Europe, and maize and cattle to the new Katanga copper mines in the Belgian Congo. The First World War then opened up new exports in grain and fruit to Britain. However during the world depression of the early 1920s, with lower consumer demand and falling market prices, exports again declined. Depression, drought and locusts greatly reduced agricultural production in South Africa during 1920-23.

The South African Party government continued its aid to supporters among Afrikaner farmers, as well as to large, often foreign-owned, plantation companies in Natal or elsewhere. The government's Land and Agricultural Bank pressed farmers to come together as marketing co-operatives to seek loans. These marketing co-operatives fixed selling prices of a particular crop in a particular area, to stop competition from pushing prices down. The first big marketing co-operative in South Africa was the KWV (*Kooperatieve Wynbouwers Vereeniging*), the wine growers co-operative association founded at the Cape in 1917. The KWV took wine from its members for a guaranteed price, and then sold the wine in bulk to wine merchants. In 1922 the SAP government began to organize state marketing co-operatives, along the lines of the private KWV, by the *Co-operatives Act* of that year.

The 'poor white problem' The rise of capitalist farming pushed Afrikaner as well as African black squatters off the land on which they had lived. Afrikaner squatters, known as *bywoners,* were often the poor relatives who recognized the farm owner as their clan chief. Many had been self-employed as hunters or wagoners in the late 19th century, but had been deprived of their livelihood by the retreat of wildlife and the advance of the railways. Some had been farm owners who had been forced by poverty after the South African War to sell their land to black tenants or white neighbours. But the rising capitalist farmers employed few whites, so these 'poor whites' had to migrate to the towns to seek work. The 'poor white problem' was first identified by the Cape provincial parliament in 1906. By 1917, when capitalist farming was taking off in the Orange Free State and southern Transvaal, the problem was widespread and began to concern the Union government. But the SAP's attitude was simply that industrial development would open up employment in the towns. 'Poor white' grievances were ignored by the SAP, and became the basis of mass support for the National Party.

7 Settler Power Outside South Africa

White settlers elsewhere in southern and eastern Africa were inspired to seek greater power by events in the Union of South Africa – the achievement of self-rule in 1910, and of 'independence' in 1926-34. Local whites gained parliamentary rights with some power in the colonial government in every British colony except Basutoland. But British imperialism retained more white settler loyalty in other colonies than in South Africa. Their settlers were very small minorities dependent on imperial troops to defend them. British officials and police north of the Limpopo were commonly biased in favour of settlers against 'natives', but there were fewer laws to enforce racial discrimination against Africans than in the south.

The Union of South Africa looked to its neighbours for more land and resources. The incorporation of Basutoland and Bechuanaland would provide more 'native reserve' areas for the Union's black population. The incorporation of Swaziland and Southern Rhodesia would provide farming land for Afrikaner settlement. South African eyes also looked to Northern Rhodesia and even Katanga and Kenya. The Union developed its own sub-imperialist ambitions in Africa under the wing of British imperialism. Such sub-imperialism can be seen in the answer that Smuts gave to the question 'What is South Africa?' in 1911:

> *Smuts:* 'South Africa is a geographical expression which we advisedly do not define. It would surely cover any part of the continent south of the equator?'

The British South Africa Company The Union of South Africa looked forward to the incorporation of Southern Rhodesia after the royal charter of the BSA Company expired in 1914 (i.e. twenty-five years after 1889). That would also remove the British objection to the Union's incorporating the Bechuanaland Protectorate, and might even include North-Western Rhodesia along with Southern Rhodesia. But the BSA Company tried to resist Union incorporation by recruiting the support of English-speaking white settlers for the idea of 'British South Africa' against Afrikanerdom. It revived the memory of Cecil Rhodes and appointed his friend L.S. Jameson as its chairman in 1912. It amalgamated its two northern colonies into 'Northern Rhodesia', based on the white settler town of Livingstone in 1911. It also began to settle whites in its Bechuanaland farming blocks along the border with the Union from 1911-12.

White settlers in Southern Rhodesia were given a majority of the elected seats in the legislative council in 1911. Three years later the first settler-elected government took power under the anti-Afrikaner leader Charles

Coghlan as prime minister. The BSA Company then persuaded the British Government to extend its charter from 1914 to 1923. The company planned to use that period for intensive white settlement. The Coryndon Commission was set up in 1914-15 to prepare a land segregation plan for Southern Rhodesia, like those in Swaziland and South Africa. But the First World War interrupted such plans.

First South African bids for the High Commission Territories Botha laid claim to Swaziland and Bechuanaland on behalf of the Union in 1913. Jameson immediately made a counter-claim on behalf of the BSA Company to incorporate Bechuanaland into Southern Rhodesia. The queen-mother of Swaziland, Labotsibeni, felt her country was so much a part of South Africa already that she threw her support behind the South African Native National Congress and its struggle against the Natives Land Act of 1913. This contrasted with Bechuanaland where most chiefs considered themselves under direct imperial rule with no contacts with the Union. Only Linchwe of the Kgatla and Lekoko of the Rolong, both with territories stretching into the Union, had reason to accept the honorary vice-presidencies offered them by the South African Native National Congress.

Khama III, who refused the SANNC offer, attempted to give relative economic autonomy to his Ngwato state under colonialism in Bechuanaland. Between 1910 and 1916 his royal trading company took over much of the trade of his country and Ngamiland. The company provided a royal income, independent of the chief's share of colonial tax, from the profits of exporting livestock and importing consumer goods. But the company's success aroused the opposition of big business interests in South Africa and Rhodesia. In 1916 the British high commissioner in Pretoria forced the closure of Khama's company. All chiefs and headmen were forbidden to invest in trade in future. Khama ended his days embittered by colonial restrictions:

'I receive nothing of the good laws of England but oppression from the officials.'

Seepapitso of the Ngwaketse (ruled 1910-16) in Bechuanaland Seepapitso was the first of a new generation of progressive chiefs in Bechuanaland. Well-educated and versed in Western ways, they were highly literate bureaucrats who organized the development of schools, dams, boreholes and improved agricultural techniques. Seepapitso and his secretary, Peter Kgasa, codified laws and recorded court decisions, and suppressed the Bo-Mothowagae independent church which threatened the Ngwaketse state church under the London mission. In 1916 Seepapitso was assassinated dramatically in his kgotla by his younger brother Moyapitso – who had probably been incited by headmen annoyed with the chief for preventing them taking their share of taxes during tax collection.

Botha renewed his bid to bring Swaziland into the Union in 1919. This time he left out Bechuanaland to prevent a Rhodesian counter-claim. Besides, Khama was not yet dead, and the British colonial minister had said in 1913, 'so long as Khama is alive the bare suggestion of handing him over to the Union would bring the whole missionary world and others upon me at once.' Swaziland on the other hand, Botha argued, was a natural extension of the Transvaal; and the Union would prove its ability in Swaziland to rule the other two territories later. But the British would not consider incorporation of one 'High Commission Territory' by itself. Basutoland protested loudest against the possibility of being forced into the Union, as it was being crowded out with refugees from the effects of the Natives Land Act in the Orange Free State.

South West Africa under German and South African rule After the Herero and Nama risings, the German imperial administration of South West Africa was reformed to serve German capitalist interests more efficiently in mining and farming. Copper mines were opened at Otavi in 1906 and then at nearby Tsumeb. Diamond fields were opened at Luderitz Bay in 1908. Within the 'police zone' — the already conquered southern and central parts of South West Africa — all Africans (including Orlam and Nama) over the age of seven had to carry passes to prove their employment by whites. Unemployed Africans were arrested for vagrancy, and then were forced to work on white farms or road and railway construction. White employers as well as police had power to arrest Africans.

Little more than two million hectares of the almost fourteen million hectares in the 'police zone' were reserved for Africans. The rest was reserved as ranches and farms for German ex-soldier settlers or for large mining concessions. Mine labour came mainly from the Ovambo and Nkhumbi chiefdoms in the unconquered north. Chiefs there forced labourers to migrate because they needed cash to buy cloth, guns, liquor and beads. Previous income from selling slaves to Mossamedes on the Angolan coast had stopped, and rinderpest and drought had destroyed their wealth in cattle and crops.

After South West Africa had been captured by South African forces in the First World

GERMAN SOUTH WEST AFRICA

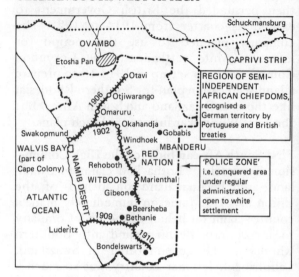

War, Smuts masterminded its semi-incorporation into the Union as a new type of colony — a 'C' class mandate under the League of Nations. (The League was a world body of British-French allies set up to preserve world peace and to divide up the German colonies in a new 'scramble'.) South African rule of South West Africa was justified in the League's moralistic language as 'a sacred trust of civilization' — to 'promote to the utmost the material and moral well-being and social progress of the inhabitants of the territory'. South Africa had to report annually to the League on such 'progress'.

Under South African rule the minimum age for Africans to carry a pass in the police zone was raised from seven to fourteen. Between 1920 and 1926 Afrikaners scrambled to take up farms and ranches in the territory, and the 'native reserves' within the police zone were reduced to less than one million hectares in 1921. British capital based in South Africa bought out German mining companies after the First World War. The Anglo-American Corporation of South Africa Ltd, headed by Ernest Oppenheimer, began its rise to wealth by taking over the Luderitz Bay diamond fields. It was to become the most important mining company in South Africa.

This semi-incorporation into the Union was not without violence. The Bondelswarts

(Gami-nun) group of Nama at Warmbad rose in protest in 1921 against a new dog tax (£1 for one dog, but £10 for five dogs), which threatened their livelihood as hunters and forced them to work on white farms instead. Smuts sent in South African troops and two aircraft, which machine-gunned and bombed the Bondelswarts into submission.

Southern Rhodesia self-government By 1922 the British South Africa Company was in economic difficulties, and had become reconciled to the Union of South Africa taking over its territory. The Union promised greater compensation for the loss of BSAC land rights than the British government. Smuts' government had also shown itself to be the friend of British capitalism in the Union. So the BSA Company pushed the voters of Southern Rhodesia into a referendum, to decide whether to become the Union's fifth province (1922). Smuts toured Southern Rhodesia to persuade the whites to vote 'yes', but let slip that he expected poor Afrikaners to take up farms there. Coghlan campaigned against joining the Union, playing on English fears of Afrikaners taking land and jobs. The results gave 9,000 'no' votes against 6,000 'yes' votes. Southern Rhodesia then became a self-governing British colony, under Coghlan as prime minister, when the extended BSA Company charter ended in 1923. But the new colony remained within the South African customs union (which it had joined in 1903) until 1935.

The white settlers of Southern Rhodesia developed their own ideas of sub-imperialism to the north. Southern Rhodesia had only been divided from Northern Rhodesia along the Zambezi by the fact that the Cape Roman-Dutch law system was enforced south of the Zambezi, while English common law was enforced north of the Zambezi. At the end of the First World War, Southern Rhodesia demanded unification with most of Northern Rhodesia, and suggested that Barotseland be united with Bechuanaland. Southern Rhodesia also wanted to take central Mozambique around Beira, in exchange for Portugal taking Tanganyika. But the imperial government made Northern Rhodesia a separate colony in 1924 when BSA Company rule ended there. The British planned to link Northern Rhodesia with their other colonies of Nyasaland and East Africa, rather than with settler-ruled Southern Rhodesia.

Questions

1   What were the main terms of the Union of South Africa Act, 1909? What problems did the Act solve and what did it leave unsolved? [Cambridge International School Certificate, 1977]
2   Why did the High Commission Territories and Southern Rhodesia not become part of the Union of South Africa in 1907-22?
3   What were the reasons for class warfare in the Rand strikes of 1913 and 1922? Were the strikes attempted revolutions?
4   Discuss the growth of capitalist farming and the decline of peasant farming in *either* (a) South Africa, *or* (b) Southern Rhodesia.

Activities

1   Discuss in the classroom why some Afrikaners rebelled against the South African government in 1914-15.
2   In 1922 Smuts brought in Afrikaner commandos from the countryside to help suppress white workers striking on the Rand. Imagine yourself to be a member of one of these commandos and explain your attitude towards crushing the strike.
3   Write an imaginary account of the conversation of an official of the Colonial Office in London with *either* (a) members of the South African Native National Congress protesting against the Union, *or* (b) chiefs and headmen from one of the three High Commission Territories not wanting to join the Union.

For references to Bibliography see p. 280.

Chapter 15

The Golden Age of Colonialism (1922–1939) I: South Africa and South West Africa

White South African socialism clashed with the interests of overseas capitalism in 1922. White socialists then combined with Afrikaner nationalists to defeat Smuts' government in 1924. The new National Party government under Hertzog gradually came to terms with the gold mining industry. By 1931 the overseas banks and mining houses had learnt to trust Hertzog as they had Smuts. But Hertzog also experimented with a form of 'national socialism' limited to whites only. The government invested state capital in basic industries, improved white workers' pay and conditions, and encouraged the growth of private capitalism among Afrikaner farmers and small businessmen.

Hertzog's government suppressed African nationalist movements and at the same time it increased police control of the black majority. The national economy grew rapidly after 1932. The state shared the profits of gold sales with overseas capitalists. Those profits were based on cheap black labour in mines, farms and industries. The South African colonial system of segregation between black and white grew, leaving blacks insecure as workers in urban locations but unable to survive as peasants in rural reserves. New laws reinforced the system, and labour migration extended it as far north as Tanganyika by the 1940s.

1 White Nationalism (1922-31)

Smuts *v* black workers   Between 1922 and

1924 the SAP government attempted to stop the development of a black urban working class. The 1922 *Apprenticeship Act* stopped all blacks and most coloureds from becoming apprentices to gain labour skills. In 1923 the government passed the *Native Urban Areas Act,* the urban equivalent of the Natives Land Act of 1913. The Act laid down the principle that the urban areas of South Africa were white property, and that blacks should only live there temporarily. They should be housed in locations owned by the town or city council, and should not own land in suburbs. Finally in 1924 the *Industrial Conciliation Act* excluded nearly all blacks and Indians, except those Cape voters exempted from the pass laws, from the definition of 'employees' who would be permitted to bargain with employers through a trade union.

African National Congress   The 1923 annual meeting of the South African Native National Congress, which protested against the Native Urban Areas Act, changed the name of the congress to the *African National Congress* (ANC)*. The congress had been weakened by the resignation from office of both John Dube and Pixley Seme in 1917 and by the failure of the 1919 delegation to Europe.

*The word African was preferred to 'native', which had been cheapened by colonialism to mean a person deprived of legal rights. The word 'Bantu' was used by some African intellectuals at this time, but never became popular. It was adopted as an official term by the South African government in the 1950s.

Under the presidency of Samuel Makgatho, younger members of the SANNC turned from politics into trade unionism. 1923 saw the last major political activity of the Congress for twenty years. A delegation was sent to Smuts to demand an end to segregation and equal rights for black and white. Smuts, like the British government previously, simply refused to take heed of the Congress. The ANC then declared its disillusionment with the British empire, and looked forward to South Africa as an independent republic. For that purpose it adopted a national anthem ('Nkosi Sikelela') and a national flag of green for the land, black for the people, and gold for the riches — possibly based on Marcus Garvey's flag for a united Africa.

'Beat Smuts' alliance   The violent suppression of the 1922 white miners' strike by Smuts' government brought together the South African Labour Party and the National Party of Hertzog into an allied opposition in parliament. Smuts, they said, was an agent of mining capitalism and of British imperialism. The communists too supported the 'Beat Smuts' campaign. Hertzog even asked black and coloured organizations for support in the 1924 general election, since the black vote was important in twelve Cape constituencies (including Transkei) and the coloured vote in the south-western Cape. Hertzog told the black trade unionist Clements Kadalie that sympathy 'between the white and black Africander' was essential for the nation's prosperity. He even gave Kadalie funds to persuade Cape Africans to vote against Smuts. But many African voters took the view that imperialism and capitalism combined in Smuts were better than a mixture of white socialism and racism.

The Pact government (1924-29)   Hertzog's National Party allied with the South African Labour Party and took power from Smuts in the 1924 general election to form the 'Pact' government. This government pushed forward a political programme of economic nationalism and further segregation between white and black. It continued to encourage capitalist farming but tried to include smaller-scale Afrikaner farmers of maize and cattle as well. The government protected cattle farmers in South Africa from the competition of Bechuanaland and Swaziland peasant producers by insisting on high minimum weights of cattle exported from those territories to South Africa. In Bechuanaland the new abattoir at Lobatse had to be closed down in 1926 because the Union refused to import its meat.

The Pact government extended the system of agricultural export levies begun by the previous government. Food sales in the customs union were taxed to subsidize the price of exports, so that exports were cheap enough to compete on the world market. Capitalist farmers producing for export could expand production almost indefinitely for prices guaranteed in advance. The state began to subsidize meat for export in 1923; wine (legalising the KWV monopoly), dairy products, and fruit in 1924-26; and later, in 1931, wheat and maize. Imported farm products on the other hand were heavily taxed. The state also assisted smaller white farmers who had difficulties in converting to capitalist production, since these smaller farmers were the backbone of support for the National Party. Land Bank loans were given to poorer farmers, who had previously been considered too risky, and more land was opened up to ownership by former *bywoners*.

In industry the Pact government began to experiment with state capitalism in combination with private capitalism. Manufacturing industry in South Africa was protected by high customs duties on imported goods. Between 1925 and 1929 the value of manufactured goods produced in South Africa increased by almost forty per cent, and opened up much new employment reserved for white workers. Advisers from Germany prepared plans for a national company called ISCOR (Iron & Steel Industrial Corporation), to build the first modern iron ore smelting and steel works on the continent of Africa. This would make South Africa independent of European imports of the iron and steel essential to all building, construction and machine making. Because overseas interests opposed economic self-sufficiency in South Africa, private capital refused to invest in such a company. So in 1931 the state took over ISCOR almost entirely, and used state capital derived from the gold boom to expand it rapidly during the 1930s.

Hertzog's segregation policies Hertzog outlined his political programme for increased segregation in a famous speech at Smithfield in the Orange Free State during 1925. Segregation, he said, would protect 'civilized labour' – a new term to include coloureds who shared Afrikaans culture as well as whites – from 'uncivilized labour', meaning the cheap labour of blacks. Blacks were only to be allowed into 'civilized' areas to perform unskilled labour, after which they must return to their reserves. Black reserves would be enlarged (from the seven per cent of the country scheduled in 1913), and blacks would be given chiefly councils and white representatives in parliament in return for losing their vote in the Cape.

Hertzog then presented these proposals to parliament in the form of draft laws, known as the 'Hertzog Bills'. The *Wage Act* of 1925 allowed the government to set minimum 'civilized' wages in any industry. Next the *Mines and Works Act* of 1926 pushed the job colour-bar down to a level where blacks could no longer have even semi-skilled jobs. Then the *Native Administration Act* of 1927 made all blacks outside the Cape subject to tribal law and chiefs appointed by the governor-general as 'supreme chief'. Hertzog failed to push through parliament a bill to remove the vote from Cape blacks. He also failed to make a final post-1913 land settlement, because the British would not hand over the High Commission Territories essential to this plan. Hertzog had to wait until 1936 to see his programme of segregation laws completed.

2 Black Trade Unionism (1921-31)

Economic nationalism increased the cost of living, as local produce replaced imported goods which had been cheaper. Both a 1926

government commission and a book called *The Anatomy of African Misery,* published in 1927, pointed out that high wages for the white 'aristocracy of labour' meant poverty for the black masses.

Industrial & Commercial Workers Union As the government's attack on African living standards became stronger, so too did African resistance. In fact black wages in South Africa improved more during 1921-25 than in any other period between 1900 and 1970, largely because of numerous small strikes. The ICU rose from strength to strength after 1923 when it extended its organization to all provinces of the Union. By 1926 its membership was perhaps 50,000, rising to maybe 100,000 in 1927 and even 200,000 in 1928. At one time or another there were branches in every town in the Union and in six other countries – Basutoland, Mozambique, South West Africa, Southern Rhodesia, Nyasaland, and Northern Rhodesia.

The ICU was never a single organized body. It was a collection of local branches, owing allegiance to the national council of the ICU and to Clements Kadalie as national secretary. The national council helped create new branches, but ICU finance and administration were too poorly organized to control their growth or keep them alive. When the ICU moved its headquarters from Capetown to Johannesburg in 1925, branches were dying out in the Cape province at the same time as new ones were starting in the north. This internal weakness in organization explains why the ICU collapsed under government attack in 1927-28, even while it was the greatest mass movement ever known in southern Africa.

Smuts' labour laws of 1922-24 denied blacks recognition and rights as workers. The ICU lost its right to bargain with employers as a trade union. The Hertzog Bills of 1924-27, which reduced all blacks to 'tribesmen', further threatened the ICU. And as the ICU grew larger, power struggles developed in its ranks between ambitious politicians and national organizers who sought to make the ICU an effective trade union. Many of these

Clements Kadalie (1896-1951), photographed at Witwatersrand University   Kadalie was born at Chifira on the shore of Lake Nyasa (Malawi). After school at Bandawe and Livingstonia, he became a clerk — first on a cotton plantation in Mozambique, then in Southern Rhodesia at Shamva and Falcon mines and Bulawayo, moving to relatives at Kimberley and Capetown in 1917. In Capetown he became a packer and delivery man, and met the white socialist A.F. Batty in 1918, who persuaded him to organize a trade union for African dock-workers in the port. Out of that union grew the Industrial and Commercial Workers Union of Africa (ICU)

Below: *A group of men and women who formed an ICU factory branch*   Note the woman, probably secretary or treasurer, who holds a register of branch members.

national organizers were African communists, including James La Guma from South West Africa, who was the ICU's secretary-general, Thomas Mbeki from Transkei, and Samuel Dunn from Zululand.

Kadalie became one of the most important politicians in South Africa, drawing crowds wherever he went to speak and making headlines in the newspapers. The ANC, under Mahabane as president (1924-27), was almost forgotten. The ANC's opposition to the Hertzog Bills appealed to 'Kings, Chiefs and leaders' — the only Africans possibly to benefit from the bills — instead of appealing to the masses like the ICU. But in 1926

Kadalie weakened the ICU by expelling its communist organizers. Kadalie, who was more an Africanist than a socialist, had been persuaded by white friends that the communists would sometime seize power from him. In 1927 Kadalie visited Geneva, Paris and London to make contact with social-democrat trade unionists in Europe, like those who had originally founded the ICU.

ICU disintegrates   Kadalie arrived back from Europe in 1927, determined to make the ICU into a British-type trade union and himself into a British-type trade union bureaucrat. But Kadalie was no longer in effective control

249

of the ICU. He clashed with George Champion, the second strongest leader of the ICU and Natal provincial secretary. In 1928 Champion declared the Natal branch to be independent of Kadalie as the *ICU yase Natal*. Many other local branch leaders then declared their independence. Kadalie brought in a British trade unionist, William Ballinger, to reorganize the ICU. But, as Kadalie later explained, 'I asked for an adviser, and received a dictator'. Ballinger ran the ICU's central office efficiently, but was completely ignorant of African politics. The ICU continued to disintegrate. During 1929 Kadalie himself broke away from the ICU, to form the 'Independent ICU' based in East London. The original branch under Ballinger soon ceased to operate!

Suppression of ICU by government Meanwhile the outbreak of strikes by breakaway branches of the ICU, or by black unions backed by the Communist Party, led to violence between white and black crowds and to police shootings during 1928-29. The 1929 general election brought back Hertzog's National Party without the Pact with the Labour Party. The new government · was determined to stamp out black revolution. The new minister of justice and police, Oswald Pirow, himself led police raids on blacks at Durban in 1929 – the first time tear gas was used against crowds in South Africa. In 1930 the National Party government passed the *Riotous Assemblies Act*, which permitted Pirow to banish Champion from Natal and after which the *ICU yase Natal* collapsed.

Communism and Black Nationalism The Pact government added a clause to the 1927 Native Administration Act, which made a criminal offence of promoting 'any feeling of hostility between Natives and Europeans'. This clause was particularly aimed at communists. The Communist Party of South Africa (CPSA) had been an all-white party, but no longer attracted white workers who had benefited from Pact government. Young white communists, like Eddie Roux, wanted to recruit black workers instead into the party.

After being expelled from the ICU, James La Guma visited Europe in 1927 and persuaded the Comintern in Moscow to revise the CPSA's attitude towards African nationalism. The CPSA could no longer expect to overthrow capitalism immediately by a white workers' revolution. It should collaborate with African nationalists to set up a 'black republic', in which whites would have minority rights, before attempting the greater task of overthrowing capitalism.

Many white communists in South Africa rejected the 'black republic' programme and left the CPSA. They were replaced by black members. For a short period the CPSA cooperated actively with the ANC. The ANC president, James Gumede (1927-30), though not a communist, had accompanied La Guma to Moscow in 1927, and had been very impressed by the Soviet Union. The CPSA set up a united front organization of all black nationalist groups, called the League of African Rights, and even contested the 1929 general election for the Transkei black vote.

3 The Gold Boom (1933-40)

Hertzog's second government of 1929-33 recruited further support by giving the vote to all previously voteless white adults. White women gained the vote in 1930, and those whites barred from voting under the old 'colour blind' franchise of the Cape, for being too poor or too uneducated, gained the vote in 1931. Hertzog then planned to revive his 'Native Bills', previously abandoned.

Gold crisis and boom Hertzog's political plans were interrupted by the great depression that hit the world economy in 1929-33.

The devaluation of other world currencies made South African exports too expensive to compete in the world market. Australia for example devalued by forty-five per cent, and therefore made its wool exports forty-five per cent cheaper. Reduced exports and drought combined to cut the value of South African agricultural production by almost half between 1928 and 1932. The value of South African and South West African diamond exports dropped from £16.5 million in 1928 to only £1.4 million in 1934, because of depression in the USA, the main market for diamonds.

Since the 1890s the world currencies had been valued against a fixed gold price, known as 'the gold standard'. The value of the British pound sterling in international exchange dropped so much during the great depression that Britain devalued by thirty per cent against the gold price. Hertzog refused to follow Britain in 'abandoning' the gold standard. For sixteen months Hertzog's government held on to the gold standard, proclaiming its economic independence from Britain. But capitalists started to withdraw their capital from South Africa, and to gamble in currency exchange. They realized the South African pound must follow sterling and devalue also. In the last few days of December 1932 over £2 million was withdrawn in panic from South African banks.

The abandonment of the gold standard led to unexpected immediate prosperity for the gold industry. Foreign capital poured in to increase the scale of gold mining. Between 1933 and 1939 no less than £80 million was pumped into expanding gold production, compared with £23 million in all the years from 1914 to 1932. Increased production, and an increase in the gold price (from over £4 per ounce in 1932 to over £7 in 1935), brought enormous profits for foreign and local investors. The value of gold production rose from £47 million in 1932 to £118 million in 1940. As much as a quarter of the value of production was profit. The profit from world gold sales by the Bank of England was given back to the Rand mining companies as an annual 'premium'; after 1933 the South African government taxed this 'premium'. By 1937 gold provided at least a quarter of government income, while state enterprises such as the railway also made profits from services to the industry.

Effects of the gold boom   The gold boom which began in 1933 affected the growth of the South African economy as a whole. The value of goods manufactured in South Africa doubled from £30.5 million in 1932 to £64 million in 1939. These were mostly canned food and drink, but also included metal goods and textiles. Private capital (mostly from overseas) was invested in new mines producing copper, manganese and chrome for export, and iron ore, coal and cement limestone for the local market.

State capital was pumped into the great new ISCOR works near Pretoria, which came into full production in 1934 and doubled its production between 1934 and 1939. High customs duties protected ISCOR from cheaper imports from overseas. The state railways agreed to use only ISCOR iron and steel. ESCOM, the state electricity supply corporation founded in 1922, expanded rapidly, using new coal-powered generating stations. Finally, in 1940, the government set up the Industrial Development Corporation (IDC) to use state investment to build up basic industries to produce goods previously imported from overseas, such as paper and chemicals.

The gold boom of the 1930s helped to solve the 'poor white' problem by giving jobs to poor whites. The government expanded white employment on the railways and in the police force, and in the Defence Force (army, navy and airforce) which was set up in 1934. Industrial schools were set up in 1937 to train poor white children to be skilled workers. The lowered job colour-bar made sure that white workers took semi-skilled, as well as skilled, employment in new manufacturing industries.

Witwatersrand urbanization   The boom in manufacturing as well as mining caused towns and cities to grow rapidly, especially along the Rand and around the major ports. The white population of the Rand rose from 233,000 in 1921 to 410,000 in 1936, while the black population rose even faster — from 304,000 to 620,000. Some of the growth of white population came from new immigrants from overseas. Immigrants from western Europe were attracted by the high wages and standard of living among whites in South Africa. Immigrants from eastern Europe were mostly Jews driven out by persecution at home. The South African government tried unsuccessfully to restrict immigration to skilled workers and western Europeans only.

During the 1930s an increasing number of black families settled in urban areas, as opposed to single men living and working there temporarily. The proportion of black men to black women in the urban areas reflects this change. In 1911 there had been about four men to every woman in towns. By 1936 the proportion had been reduced to about two men to every woman. (A normal settled population has about one male to every female.) Up to the early 1930s nearly all black servants in white households were men. But municipal authorities wanted to replace men by women as domestic workers, so that the men could be employed in heavy unskilled labour. To encourage this, municipal authorities built women's hostels in black townships. Orlando township was laid out by the Johannesburg authorities in the 1930s to accommodate a limited number of black

Shembe, Zulu prophet (1870-1935) He founded the Nazarite healing church in 1911, and became the greatest religious leader of the Zulu people. John L. Dube's biography of Shembe was published in 1937.

families. By the late 1930s Orlando was already becoming overcrowded.

Hertzog-Smuts Fusion government The 1932 political crisis over the gold standard brought out new political divisions and rivalries. Some Afrikaner nationalists moved closer to Smuts' South African Party, while most Labour Party members had withdrawn support from the Pact government in 1931. In 1933, therefore, Hertzog approached Smuts to form a govern-

Sophiatown, black suburb of Johannesburg, in the 1930s Demand for housing in this limited area for African purchase was so high that house plots sold for as much as half a hectare of land in neighbouring whites-only suburbs. Sophiatown landlords therefore packed as many tenants as possible on their plots to reap high rents. Note electricity poles and street lamp. Unlike locations, suburbs were provided with basic municipal services.

ment of national unity after the 1934 elections. Smuts agreed. In 1934 the SAP and the National Party joined together as the United South African National Party, soon known simply as the *United Party*. Hertzog became prime minister, with Smuts as his deputy in the 'Fusion' government (1934-39). But some people felt Hertzog and Smuts had betrayed their followers. Supporters of British imperialism, particularly in Natal, broke away from the SAP to form the *Dominion Party*. Afrikaner nationalists who refused to join the United Party formed the *Purified National Party* under D. F. Malan.

Hertzog in alliance with Smuts carried on his agricultural and segregation policies. But they also placed new emphasis on foreign capital to invest in mining and manufacturing.

The 1937 *Marketing Act* extended the system of marketing co-operatives, produce control boards and export subsidies, to every agricultural product except wine, which was already controlled by the KWV co-operative of wine producers. Meat, wheat, sugar, wool and mohair, fruit, dairy products, and even wattle bark, all had produce control boards. These boards paid producers fixed prices for their crops, and then sold them within South Africa at higher prices and overseas at lower prices. The boards rewarded producers whose crops were good enough for export with higher bonuses at the end of each year. This system of agricultural marketing benefited producers, but it raised the cost of living in South Africa higher than the world average. For example, in 1933 consumers paid £1.75 million more than the world price to the wheat control board for their bread. And not all producers benefited equally. The biggest and best capitalized farmers producing for export profited most. Small producers were forced to sell through co-operatives, but they had no representation on the control boards, and they did not receive bonuses.

Hertzog's 'Native Bills', first presented in 1925, were completed by two acts of parliament in 1936. The *Natives Representation Act* (1936) removed the 16,000 black voters in the Cape province from the common voters' roll, and placed them on a separate roll

to elect three white representatives to parliament. These blacks also lost the right to buy land. All other blacks were to be represented in parliament by four white senators, and by a new body to be called the Native Representative Council made up of twelve black representatives. Elections were to be through the local councils started in 1920, and through the general councils of the Transkei (1930) and Ciskei (1934), consisting of chiefs, headmen, and 'educated natives'.

The *Natives Trust and Land Act* of 1936 set up a new body called the South African Native Trust, under the Native Affairs Department. This trust would buy up to six million hectares of 'released' land for 'native reserves', in addition to the nine million hectares already 'scheduled' for blacks in 1913. Over

LAND PARTITION IN MARICO (TRANSVAAL)
Illustrating effects of Land Acts by the 1950s

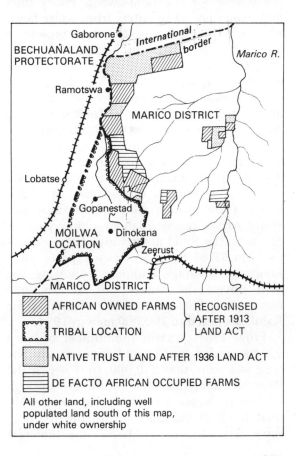

All other land, including well
populated land south of this map,
under white ownership

a million hectares of the 'released' land was state land, already marked out for white farms but not yet sold. The rest was under white ownership, and could be bought by tribal councils or black syndicates only through the Native Trust. Poll tax paid by people living on purchased 'released' land was to be three times higher than on 'scheduled' land. The Native Trust was to collect fees, rents and profits from all black-owned land to finance further land purchases. In effect the Trust became the bank of the Native Affairs Department. It also had the power to exchange small areas of black land surrounded by white land (known as 'black spots') for white land next to black areas.

The Natives Trust and Land Act enforced anti-squatter laws more harshly than before, to end share-cropping finally on white farms in areas like the eastern Transvaal. Black labour tenants on white farms had to work at least 180 days (rather than the previous 90) in every year for the farm-owner. Police fines and expulsions of squatters from white farms after 1936 helped cause the rapid growth of black urban population in the 1940s.

Economic expansion into Africa   The growth of the South African economy in the 1930s made the Union government look north into Africa for labour supplies and future markets. Oswald Pirow, a senior minister in the Fusion government, revived Smuts' dream of a South African sub-imperialism as far north as Kenya.

The *Mozambique Convention* of 1928, between the governments of Portugal and South Africa, renewed labour supply arrangements to the Rand in exchange for a guaranteed quota of South African exports using Lourenço Marques harbour. Following the gold boom, the number of Mozambique miners that Portugal agreed to send to the Rand was raised to 100,000 men in 1934.

From 1934 onwards the number of black miners needed by the gold mines at any one time was more than 250,000. In that year the Witwatersrand Chamber of Mines, through WENELA, began to recruit labour directly from north of the Limpopo for the first time since 1912-13. In 1936-37 the colonial

The first aircraft to land at Palapye Road airfield, Bechuanaland, on the new Cape-to-Cairo air route, 1920.   Airfields along the route were laid out in 1919.

governments of Nyasaland and Northern Rhodesia agreed to allow WENELA recruiting centres in southern Nyasaland and Barotseland. In Bechuanaland WENELA built roads from Francistown to the Okavango swamps to carry recruits by motor truck (1937-38). Finally, in the 1940s, WENELA recruiting was extended as far north as Tanganyika. These recruiting centres on British territory also recruited workers from neighbouring parts of Portuguese Mozambique and Angola. River barges and motor trucks took recruits to railheads at Blantyre, Livingstone and Francistown.

Pirow, known for his ruthlessness as minister of justice in the previous Pact government, was both minister of defence and minister of railways in the Fusion government. In 1934 he introduced a five-year plan for building up the Defence Force. He combined the military airforce with a new national airline run by the railways. South African Airways bought thirty-eight German aircraft which could be converted into heavy bombers in time of war.

Both in war and peace Pirow saw aircraft as the key to South Africa's expansion of power and commercial interests in Africa. South African Airways took over the Imperial (British) Airways route to Kenya through the Rhodesias and Tanganyika. Pirow also

SOUTH AFRICAN AIRWAYS ROUTES IN THE 1930s

Minister Oswald Pirow aggressively pushed SAA routes northwards into the Union's 'natural' sphere of influence in Africa south of the equator.

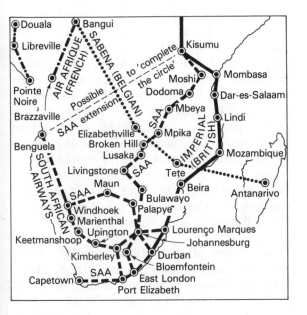

arranged SAA flights to Angola from South West Africa, and planned to extend them through the Belgian Congo to Kenya.

Relations with Nazi Germany Pirow wanted Africa south of the equator to become a South African zone independent of British, Portuguese and Belgian imperialism. He flew to Europe in 1938 to negotiate this with the Nazi leaders of Germany. Hitler was claiming back the old German colonies lost in the First World War. Pirow proposed that Germany should take back the Cameroons enlarged by neighbouring British, French and Belgian territory, while South Africa would keep South West Africa and take Tanganyika. Pirow's proposal failed, because Germany really wanted more territory in Europe not overseas territory. But Pirow returned from Europe very impressed by the discipline and racial pride of fascism in Germany, Italy, Portugal and Spain.

South West Africa The Nazi Party began secret recruitment of German settlers in

South West Africa in 1930. Although German settlers had been made British-South African citizens in 1924, they still felt threatened by large-scale settlement of Afrikaners in the 1920s and 1930s. In ten years after 1925, the South West African administration spent more money on two thousand Boer settlers (former 'thirstland trekkers') from Angola than on the territory's 282,000 Africans. The Herero in the 'police zone' were forced off land desired for Boer settlement in 1925 by aircraft dropping bombs nearby*.

When during the 1930s Afrikaners pressed for incorporation of South West Africa into the Union of South Africa, the strongest opposition came from German settlers. Nazism became open among German settlers between 1933 and 1939, who were anti-Afrikaner as well as anti-British. Only later after the defeat of Germany in the Second World War did German settler nationalism became reconciled with Afrikaner nationalism.

Political crisis over war with Germany When France, Britain, Australia and New Zealand declared war on Germany on September 3rd, 1939, the Fusion government split. Hertzog wished South Africa to remain neutral in the war to show its independence from British imperialism. Smuts wished South Africa to join the war against Germany, and talked of supporting democracy against dictatorship in Europe. Pirow sympathized with Germany, and may have considered war against Britain for control of Africa. But British imperialism still held the allegiance of the bureaucrats and businessmen who ran the country, and the officers in charge of its military forces. Smuts' view prevailed.

Hertzog was forced to resign. The governor-general as representative of the British king appointed Smuts as prime minister. Smuts declared war. The Fusion was at an end: the United Party government under Smuts was really the old SAP again. Smuts' government

*The Herero monarch, Samuel Maherero, and later his son Frederick, remained in exile in Bechuanaland. Samuel appointed Hosea Kutako as paramount chief of Hereroland (1920-70).

was faced by a parliamentary opposition of two National Parties. The old party under Hertzog and the new 'Purified' party under Malan eventually came together in the *Reunited National Party* (1940).

4 African and Afrikaner Nationalism in the Thirties

The 1930s saw changes within the forces of both African and Afrikaner nationalism. New segregation laws and tough police action in the late 1920s and early 1930s were followed by expanding employment but a strict job colour-bar. All of these factors helped to quiet the black labour militancy previously seen in the ICU.

ANC internal dissension The African National Congress expelled its president James Gumede for pro-communist sympathies in 1930, and replaced him by the veteran Pixley Seme. As Gumede said, the ANC was a bird that had chopped off its left wing, and could no longer fly. Seme as its president (1930-37) condemned mass action, such as boycotts and strikes, and called for the growth of an African trading class to give Africans power within the economy. During the early 1930s the ANC did not even hold annual meetings, and its newspaper *Abantu-Batho* was sold to a company selling patent medicines. The newspaper then closed down, whereupon its readers turned to the new *Bantu World* newspaper. The *Bantu World* (later called *The World*) was founded in 1932 by the white liberal Howard Pim and was edited by R.V. Selope Thema.

All-African Convention of 1935 The strongest African voice during the 1930s came from the All-African Convention. Five hundred delegates met in 1935 at Bloemfontein, chaired by A. B. Xuma, to protest against the Hertzog Bills. Hertzog persuaded the All-African Convention to accept his assurances that the new Native Representative Council, set up in 1936, would give all blacks genuine representation. John Dube, Thomas Mapikela, and Selope Thema were all elected to the NRC. Africans, even communists, waited to see if the body had any real powers.

The All-African Convention continued to function as a permanent body during the later 1930s, with D.D.T. Jabavu as president and James Moroka as treasurer. The ANC celebrated its twenty-fifth anniversary in 1937, and replaced Seme with Mahabane again as president. Both the Convention and the Congress condemned the Italian invasion of Ethiopia, in solidarity with other African states. But both organizations were out of touch with the masses of South Africa's rapidly growing cities. People rioted in the Vereeniging black townships against police brutality during 1937, but neither the Convention, the Congress, or the Representative Council took up their grievances.

Broederbond plans Afrikaner revival Many Afrikaner nationalists followed D. F. Malan into the Purified National Party in 1934, because Hertzog had 'betrayed' their principles. Malan found a political programme for his party in the organization called the *Broederbond* (the brotherhood), which he had joined in 1933.

The Broederbond had been founded in 1918 by a group of Afrikaner intellectuals, notably H. J. Klopper. It operated as a secret fraternity after 1922. It recruited members mainly among teachers and clerks, and swore them to secrecy about the membership and plans of the organization. Membership was restricted to white men of Afrikaans ancestry, who must already be members of one of the three Dutch reformed churches. At first the Broederbond aimed to promote Afrikaans language and culture, by members secretly assisting each other to gain top jobs in education and the churches. In 1929 the Broederbond founded a public 'front' body called the Federation of Afrikaans Cultural Organizations, known as FAK after its Afrikaans initials. FAK set up cultural organizations to rival 'English' cultural organizations such as the Boy Scouts, the Red Cross and the National Union of South African Students. It also promoted the 'Christian National Education' movement in Afrikaans education

1931 joint meeting of the ANC and APO in Bloemfontein, which prepared the way for the 1935 All-African Convention. D.D.T. Jabavu and Abdul Abdurahman chair the meeting (4th & 5th from left seated on platform). Other delegates included P.kaI.Seme, W.B. Rubusana, T.M. Mapikela, C. Kadalie, Z.R. Mahabane, S.M. Makgatho, S. Leshoai, and S. Mini.

DISSENSION IN COMMUNIST RANKS. The Communist Party of South Africa tore itself apart and reformed itself in the late 1920s and early 1930s. First it expelled its left-wingers, the Trotskyists who believe in world rather than national revolution. Then it expelled its right-wingers, who collaborated with social-democrats and 'bourgeois' nationalists. Then there was a struggle for power among CPSA leaders, who went to the Soviet Union for approval by the Communist International organization. A young African, Moses Kotane, won the contest with his plea for revived 'united fronts' with 'progressive' politicians and trade unionists — including Trotskyists, social-democrats, and African nationalists.

in every way possible.

A movement to build up Afrikaner capitalism grew up in the Cape, independent of the Broederbond which operated mainly in the Transvaal and Orange Free State. An insurance company known by its initials as SANLAM was founded in 1917, followed by an investment trust known as SANTAM. The first Afrikaner bank was founded in 1918. These financial institutions planned to attract the savings of Afrikaner farmers, workers and small traders, and to lend this money out as capital for enterprising Afrikaner businessmen. Among other businesses, Afrikaner nationalists founded the Nasionale Pers, a publishing company for spreading nationalist culture and education.

D. F. Malan and other leaders of the new Purified National Party joined the Broederbond in 1933-34. They transformed it into a political and economic planning group for the party. The Broederbond planned that Afrikaners selected by the Broederbond would gradually take over key positions in the state administration and judiciary, at that time held by English-speaking white South Africans.

In 1934 the Broederbond set up a co-operative trading company and then a co-operative bank (Volkskaas) in the Transvaal and Orange Free State with members sharing the profits. Also in 1934 the Broederbond pioneer H. J. Klopper set up a railway workers' union called Spoorbond. The union failed to recruit many workers, but its members' savings fund later became the Afrikaner building society called SAAMBOU. Meanwhile, the Broederbond began a long campaign, lasting from the mid-1930s until 1948, to take over the trade union of the strongest group of workers in South Africa, the white miners of the Rand.

Afrikaner capitalism or national-socialism?
Much of the growth of Afrikaner nationalism in the 1930s centred around the centenary celebrations of the 'Great Trek' (1935-38). The trek was re-enacted by wagons following the route of the Voortrekkers, ending outside Pretoria, where a monument and museum were built. Once this celebration of past culture was over, a great congress on the economic future of the Afrikaner people was held during 1939. Speakers such as Nicolas Diederichs argued that Afrikaner private capitalism must take control of the economy. A minority of Afrikaners, however, believed in a form of 'national-socialism' along the lines of Nazi Germany, with state control of private enterprise on behalf of the *volk* (race or nation). All Afrikaner nationalists agreed that Afrikaner economic independence could only be built by continuing the exploitation of black workers.

The Broederbond founded the Reddings-daadbond (reconstruction society) under Diederichs in 1939, to supervize the growth of Afrikaner private capitalism through business-men's groups. They persuaded the three Dutch Reformed Churches to do business with and to invest their savings only in Broederbond-approved companies and institutions.

Afrikaner nationalists who believed in 'national-socialism' found a home under Pirow in the Reunited National Party's 'New Order' group (1940), or in the *Ossewa-Brandwag*. The Ossewa-Brandwag ('ox wagon fire guards') was originally a cultural society that grew out of the Voortrekker celebrations. It developed its own military wing, which drilled in uniform like Nazi 'storm-troopers' in Germany, and strongly supported a German victory in the Second World War.

Questions

1 Why did African trade unionism grow so rapidly in the 1920s and decline in the 1930s?

2 Compare the segregation of land in the Union of South Africa up to 1936 with other countries in southern Africa. (Refer also to Chapter 16.)

3 How different from previous German rule was South African rule of South West Africa before 1939?

4 Why did some Afrikaner nationalists ally with the white labour movement against other Afrikaner nationalists who allied with mining capitalism?

Activities

1 How did South African governments between 1910 and 1939 come to terms with the interests of Afrikaner agri-culture and 'English' mining capitalists? Discuss this in the classroom.

2 Mark on a map the major economic developments within the Union of South Africa between 1902 and 1939.

3 You are a member of the ICU in Natal. Explain why you break away from the ICU under Kadalie and join the *ICU yase Natal* under Champion.

For references to Bibliography see p. 280.

Chapter 16

The Golden Age of Colonialism (1922–1939) II: The High Commission Territories and the Settler North

European imperialism between the two World Wars was determined to make African colonies into efficient and profitable ventures. In southern African states outside the Union of South Africa, the colonial powers relied heavily on white settlers to develop mining and agriculture, while discouraging settlers from the sort of nationalist ventures pursued in South Africa. African populations felt the full impact of colonialism, as peasants were evicted to make room for capitalist estates and workers were pressed into one contract after another of migrant labour. The first stirrings of a new African nationalism, claiming colonial borders as its own, could be heard in disturbed rural areas and new towns.

1 The High Commission Territories (1920-30)

As an essential part of his segregation plans, Hertzog tried unsuccessfully to persuade the British to transfer the High Commission Territories to the Union during 1924-27. The British ruled out immediate transfer, but encouraged Hertzog to believe in eventual incorporation. It removed the territories from the control of the Colonial Office in London to the new Dominions Office in charge of relations with the white dominions (1926). When the Hertzog Bills failed to pass through the South African parliament, the urgency of transfer faded between about 1927 and 1932.

The British dominions minister in the Conservative government of 1924-29, Leopold Amery, saw himself as a second Joseph Chamberlain. He determined to delay transfer of the High Commission Territories to the Union for about ten years. During this time they would be developed economically to become strong rather than weak provinces, so that after incorporation they would help pro-British politicians to gain power within the Union. He wanted to build prosperous pro-British white communities in Swaziland and Bechuanaland, and well-disciplined black communities in all three territories. Swaziland was given aid to construct roads under the 1929 *Colonial Development Act;* and Bechuanaland received a dynamic new resident commissioner, Charles Rey, to reform its inadequate administration.

But 1929 saw the defeat of the Conservative government by the Labour Party in Britain, and the beginning of the great depression. British government expenditure was drastically cut. The colonial and dominions minister in the Labour government of 1929-31, Sidney Webb the pioneer social-democrat, saw himself as the protector of the colonial masses from imperialist exploitation. Amery's development plans collapsed. However, the financial administration of Swaziland, Bechuanaland and Basutoland was improved by a commission headed by Alan Pim, whose Pim Reports on the territories were published in 1932-35.

Representative councils in the territories
Blacks out-numbered whites by forty to one in Swaziland, and by ninety to one in Bechuanaland, compared with about four blacks to every white in the Union of South

Sobhuza leads a second deputation to London in 1925 The king had sued leading white concession holders in Swaziland, in order to establish that they came under Swazi rather than British sovereignty. But the Privy Council in London ruled that British sovereignty, under the 1890 Foreign Jurisdiction Act, was not limited in any way by Swazi royal claims to land leased to whites by Sobhuza's grandfather Mbandzeni. The king sits in the centre. Pixley Seme of the ANC sits on the king's extreme left, with Sol Plaatje (hatless) by his shoulder.

Africa*. But both the British and South African governments regarded Swaziland almost as a 'white man's country', and regarded the whites of Bechuanaland as important. Both territories were given their own white parliaments, known as European Advisory Councils (EAC), in 1921, in return for settlers beginning to pay income tax.

In Bechuanaland a Native Advisory Council (NAC), consisting of chiefs and headmen, was set up in 1920. Unlike the EAC it could not discuss the whole government budget, but was limited to questions of 'native welfare'. Chief Isang of the Kgatla tried and failed to get the government to rename it the 'National Advisory Council' and to allow it to adopt the constitution of the South African Native National Congress as its own. Khama III boycotted the NAC as colonial interference with his rule, and also persuaded whites from his reserve to boycott the EAC. There were no

*This compares with twenty-one blacks to every white in Southern Rhodesia, and nearly one hundred blacks to every white in Northern Rhodesia. (Figures are rough approximations based on figures of the 1920s.)

Ngwato representatives in the Native Advisory Council until the 1930s. But the council kept alive the old idea of an alliance (or potential federation) between the precolonial states of boTswana.

In Swaziland there was no equivalent to the Native Advisory Council. The *Libandla* (general assembly), and its smaller executive committee known as the *Liqoqo*, became known as the 'Swazi National Council'. But the colonial government did not consult its opinions on 'native welfare', and it kept no written records.

In Basutoland, where there were more than three hundred blacks to every white, the Basutoland National Council had been recognized by the colonial authorities in 1910. It was allowed to discuss the whole colonial budget, as there were no white settlers besides a few traders. By the 1920s the National Council was under increasing attack from leading commoners as being unrepresentative of the whole nation. It was said to represent conservative chiefs and headmen, who exploited their people by enforcing the outdated Laws of Lerotholi. Commoners who broke the laws were fined. Chiefs and headmen lived off these fines as personal income, and did not share their new wealth with the people as their forefathers had done. The corruption of the courts by chiefs and headmen was satirized in a popular animal story and play, *Pitso ea Linonyana* (the parliament of birds) by Azariele Sekese, eventually published in 1928.

Progressive movements in the territories
Educated commoners in Basutoland found a voice through the Progressive Association (*Lekhotla la Tsoelopele*). This was founded in 1907 by Azariele Sekese and Simon Phamotse, both followers of Chief Jonathan Molapo. By the 1920s the association had a thousand members, the most famous of whom was the writer Thomas Mofolo*. The Progressive

*Mofolo's biography of Shaka was published in seSotho in 1926, in English in 1931, and in French in 1940, making him the most widely read southern African author of his day.

Isang, chief regent of the Kgatla (ruled 1921-29), photographed on October 14th, 1929, by the anthropologist Isaac Schapera. Isang was the leading democratic voice in Bechuanaland's Native Advisory Council. He called for equality with the European Advisory Council, greater economic powers, and for majority voting in its procedure.

Isang reacted strongly to South African attempts to take over the High Commission Territories, and criticized residence of their British High Commissioner in the Union. Within Bechuanaland he looked to the British to limit settler power and protect African rights. But his greatest passion was for education. In 1921 he founded a Bakgatla National School at Mochudi in the hope of its becoming a national college for all Bechuanaland. But his plans failed because of economic depression, colonial government parsimony, and his own removal from power in 1929. (Today the school building houses a museum.)

Disillusioned with Kgatla politics, he began to collaborate with the colonial government, and was eventually persuaded to back South African claims to the territory.

Association was given one official member in the National Council in 1919, but it continued to press for greater representation.

Basutoland had a larger educated community than Bechuanaland or Swaziland, and therefore a stronger 'progressive' movement. Protestant and Catholic missions competed for converts by providing education. The Basutoland government spent almost £50,000 each year on education by 1931, while the Bechuanaland government spent only £10,000 (including white pupils) and the Swaziland government less than £2,500 on black education. In Bechuanaland 'progressives' were scattered among the many tribes, often as chief's secretaries or as chiefs themselves. In Swaziland a Progressive Association was founded in 1929 by Benjamin Nxumalo, an African Methodist Episcopal teacher and an uncle to the king, who had accompanied Sobhuza to London in 1922-23. The Swaziland Progressive Association included foreign as well as Swazi teachers, but never exceeded a hundred members. It remained mainly a debating society, although it was given representation in the Libandla.

Josiel Lefela and Lekhotla la Bafo A more radical movement than the Progressive Association, called *Lekhotla la Bafo* (the people's council) was founded in Basutoland in 1919 by Josiel Lefela. Lefela was a commoner who had been a miner on the Rand and then became a small businessman, founding the village of Mapoteng as his home in 1919. Lefela is best described as a 'populist'. He believed in the rights of the common people, and looked back to the past when he believed the people had prospered under Moshoeshoe. He kept alive Sotho complaints over the loss of the 'conquered territory' to the Orange Free State. He refused to accept that the British had any right to rule Lesotho.

Lefela entered the Basutoland National Council as headman of Mapoteng. As a populist spokesman, at times he appeared to be a pan-Africanist, a traditionalist, and even a communist. During the 1920s the colonial government expelled him from the National Council as 'a public agitator', although they later reinstated him. He even wrote to the president of the USA saying that Marcus Garvey was 'doing well to rouse the Negroes of the world to build a Government of their own in Africa, their motherland'. He tried first to work through the African National Congress, and later through the Communist Party of South Africa. He invited James Gumede the ANC president to speak in Basutoland, and the CPSA newspaper published his views.

Simon Ratshosa and Sarwa slavery In Bechuanaland the early nationalist Simon Ratshosa may perhaps be described as an embittered progressive. When Sekgoma II of the Ngwato died in 1925, Simon Ratshosa attempted to set up a regency council of progressives to rule for the infant Seretse Khama. But Seretse's young uncle Tshekedi Khama was appointed as single regent instead, and Simon Ratshosa attempted to assassinate Tshekedi publicly after a quarrel in 1926. For this attempted murder he was imprisoned, and then banished. While in prison he started writing his political thoughts for eventual publication. Simon Ratshosa attacked chieftainship as 'cruel and repulsive' and the colonial government as an 'absolute farce'. He looked back with nostalgia to the great days of the old kings before colonialism. But he also looked forward to the rule of Bechuanaland by 'a party of enlightened natives' in a National Council. He also believed that black capitalism should be encouraged by allowing private ownership of land and property within tribal reserves.

Simon Ratshosa became most influential as a champion of the Sarwa people — former Khoisan hunters now working as herdsmen for Ngwato cattle-owners. He threatened to 'prove before a committee of experts', and to 'astound the whole civilized world' with the fact that slavery existed with British blessing in Bechuanaland. Fearing such publicity, the Dominions Office published a report on Sarwa labour conditions in 1932-33 which denied that there was slavery. The London Missionary Society published a similar report in 1935, and the League of Nations also published one written by a British colonial official in 1938.

2 European Colonies North of the Union

White settlers in the Rhodesias, and in the Belgian or Portuguese colonies, looked enviously at the Union of South Africa as the most 'developed' state in Africa. But British, Belgian and Portuguese colonial rulers justified their rule in Africa in terms acceptable to the League of Nations, talking of their 'sacred trust' of civilizing the indigenous peoples. Where white farm settlement failed, colonial development consisted of using local labour for large plantations, for forcible peasant production, or more often for export to development areas such as mines. Faced by world economic uncertainty in the 1920s-30s, colonial powers tried to make their colonies into efficient producers of cheaper raw materials such as copper, tobacco, and cotton.

Plans for a greater Rhodesia While Southern Rhodesia seemed destined to become part of South Africa, the British imperial authorities tried linking Northern Rhodesia and Nyasaland to East Africa. The white settlers of Kenya were pressing for an East African dominion based on Kenya. But the 1929 Hilton Young Report on East African federation decided that Northern Rhodesia and Nyasaland were too remote, without railway or good road communications with East Africa. The opening up of the Copperbelt mines, and the building of the Benguela railway from Katanga to the Angolan coast, even gave Northern Rhodesian whites grand ideas of their own future dominion called 'Zambezia'.

In fact the opening of the Copperbelt linked Northern Rhodesia to Southern Rhodesia even more firmly. The railways of the two colonies and of northern Bechuanaland had been amalgamated in 1927 under 'Rhodesia Railways'. White miners and farmers migrated north to the Copperbelt from Southern Rhodesia and South Africa. In 1934 the imperial authorities proposed a 'Greater Rhodesia' to include the two Rhodesias, Nyasaland, the northern half of Bechuanaland (the rest was to be given to South Africa), and possibly Tanganyika.

In 1935 Southern Rhodesia broke away from the common customs union with South Africa. The immediate cause of the break was South African restrictions on the import of meat, although the same restrictions were suffered in silence by Bechuanaland, Swaziland, and South West Africa. The general cause of the break was growing antagonism between English and Afrikaner white settler

Mozambique: the realities of forced cultivation and labour policies Women peasants, under the eye of a black policeman, queue for their cotton production to be weighed by a white official or trader. This is a photograph from the 1950s. Peasants tried to sabotage forced crop production quotas by placing stones in cotton bales, which ruined ginning machinery.

nationalists in southern Africa. Prime minister Huggins wanted Southern Rhodesia to be the basis of a separate Central African dominion, loyal to British imperialism like Australia or New Zealand. This finally put paid to the possibility of incorporating Southern Rhodesia into South Africa.

The way was. now clear for founding a Central African dominion. But the British government's Bledisloe Report of 1939 agreed with the argument of Africans in Northern Rhodesia and Nyasaland that amalgamation with Southern Rhodesia would mean that its racial segregation would be extended to the two northern colonies. That would be a betrayal of British 'trusteeship' for the welfare of their native populations.

Portuguese colonialism: theory and practice
Portugal had become a republic in 1910, after a revolution which ousted its last king. The republican government of 1910-26 slowly made liberal reforms in the colonies, giving them greater self-government. But the colonies

were seen as provinces of the mother-country. The Portuguese delegate to the League of Nations rejected the proposal that imperialism should prepare Africans for eventual independence from the mother-country. 'The ideal is the slow, unforced assimilation of weak or inferior communities [i.e. Africans] by strong or more highly developed communities [i.e. Europeans].'

The military government which seized power in Portugal during 1926 believed that the colonies must become as profitable to Portugal as possible. An economics professor called Antonio Salazar became finance minister within the military government in 1928. Salazar subsequently became the dictator of Portugal from 1932 to 1968. His *Estado Novo* ('new state'), modelled on the fascism of Mussolini in Italy, first disciplined the working class in Portugal and then turned to the colonies.

The old system of colonial exploitation, based on forced labour rather than capital investment, was intensified in Mozambique

263

and Angola. But Salazar's *Colonial Act,* published in 1930, justified Portuguese colonialism as 'altruism, self-denial, faith, and a historic responsibility of civilization'. The Portuguese colonial minister even declared: 'To colonize is, in the final analysis, to teach and educate.' Debates in Portuguese over colonialism were confused for many decades by such deceptive language, which found its way into both academic and popular literature.

4 The High Commission Territories (1930-40)

The economic boom, and the growing need for foreign labour in the Rand mines after 1933, strengthened the bid of the Fusion government in South Africa to incorporate the High Commission Territories. The terri-

tories were essential to Hertzog's 'native reserve' policy outlined in the 1936 Land Act, as additional land (or dumping-grounds) for surplus labour from the Union. The defiance of colonial rule by Tshekedi Khama in Bechuanaland during 1933 also showed that the territories might become a threat to white rule in South Africa, if they were not incorporated.

The Union's case was weakened by its own actions, and by outside political pressures on the British government. Hertzog claimed that the Union was no longer legally bound by the South Africa Act of 1909. This meant that the Union might ignore the schedule attached to the Act, designed to protect African rights in the territories when they were incorporated. The question of the High Commission Territories also became a rallying point for

---

SOUTHERN RHODESIA

1919	Ndebele 'home rule' movement, supported by South African Native National Congress, failed to persuade British to recognize monarchy in Matabeleland along the lines of Bechuanaland or Barotseland.
1923	Southern Rhodesia became a self-governing colony, ruled by a parliament elected by whites and very few 'civilized' blacks. Charles Coghlan as prime minister (1923-27).
1923	*Rhodesian Bantu Voters Association* founded by Abram Twala to organize black voters as in the Cape and Transkei. Martha Ngano, the most radical RBVA leader, took up peasant grievances against government-appointed chiefs.
1927	Industrial and Commercial Workers Union (ICU) from South Africa began organizing black workers in Bulawayo and Salisbury: 'We are workers suffering . . . . Why are you black people asleep?'
1930	*Land Apportionment Act* increased white-owned land from 13 to 20 million hectares. Half of the 3 million hectares reserved for African smallholders (as 'native purchase areas')

	were later declared unfit for farming. The Act helped finally replace black peasant farmers on the fertile highlands by white capitalist farmers. Capital and marketing aid were restricted to 'persons of European descent only'.
1933-53	Godfrey Huggins (later Lord Malvern) as prime minister of Southern Rhodesia. Huggins talked grandly of a 'two pyramid policy' of separate white and black development, but blacks at the top of their pyramid were to be barely equal to whites at the bottom of theirs.
1934	RBVA and other African welfare societies, after unsuccessful opposition to the Land Act, formed a *Southern Rhodesia African National Congress.* But welfare societies in Southern Rhodesia were often missionary controlled, and SRANC was not effective until the 1940s.
1934	*Industrial Conciliation Act* laid basis for white trade unions to negotiate with employers, but excluded Africans from category of 'workers' with such rights.

---

opponents of Afrikaner nationalism and of Hertzog's segregation plans. Pan-Africanists, liberals, socialists and even conservatives in Britain supported the cause of the territories in books, pamphlets and newspaper articles. Furthermore the government of Southern Rhodesia continued to claim at least half of Bechuanaland for itself.

The British government proposed a compromise to Hertzog in 1935. The Union would first prove its good intentions to the Africans of the territories by economic aid for their development. But African protest was so loud in the councils of the three protectorates that the plan was not revived until 1938-39. By that time Hertzog had reorganized the administration of the Union's own 'native territory' of the Transkei. He proposed that the Union would follow the Transkei model in administering the High Commission Territories. Protectorate and Union officials met to discuss economic cooperation, but the Second World War interrupted negotiations.

After thirty years of discussion, the High Commission Territories had still not been incorporated into the Union. Meanwhile Basutoland, Bechuanaland and Swaziland were left without sufficient funds or clear political aims, and steadily declined in economic and political importance.

BECHUANALAND: Tshekedi Khama challenges colonial rule

Charles Rey took up his post as resident commissioner in 1930, confident that Bechuanaland could follow Northern Rhodesia in its recent rise to prosperity. He left the post in 1937 bitterly denouncing the British government for blocking nearly all his plans for development.

Rey tried to press forward the re-opening of copper mining by the British South Africa Company in the Ngwato reserve. But Tshekedi Khama led Ngwato resistance to such a concession. The Ngwato feared that mining would lead to the loss of their land and water resources to white settlement. A second clash between Rey and Tshekedi came over reforms in tribal administration. The British government tried to introduce the system of administration known as 'indirect

Serowe show ground, 1933 Tshekedi (third from left in row of men) confronts British marine troops. Note the briefcase, stuffed with documents, at the foot of his secretary.

rule', previously developed in Nigeria and Tanganyika. This made chiefs responsible for local government, but restricted them by laws limiting their powers. Tshekedi objected that chiefs would lose their independence to become local officials of the colonial government: in fact 'indirect rule' for Bechuanaland would mean an increase in *direct* rule!

Tshekedi and the flogging incident   The most serious clash between Rey and Tshekedi was over the 'flogging incident' of 1933. Tshekedi tried a local white man in his court on a charge of assault, and the man was punished by a beating. When Rey heard about the 'flogging' of a white man in an African court, he interpreted it as an act of rebellion by Tshekedi. British sailors and marine soldiers were rushed up the railway from Capetown to Bechuanaland. South Africa offered troops and even a bombing aircraft to help. With armed troops facing the Ngwato crowds, Rey deposed Tshekedi from his post as chief regent.

Tshekedi made the British look rather foolish when he answered their military might with quiet legal arguments. The white man who had been 'flogged' claimed his punishment had been just, and declared himself a loyal subject of Tshekedi. Tshekedi was reinstated a mere three weeks after being deposed. 'Tshekedi has opened all our eyes,' one British newspaper remarked, to the 'possibility of the African becoming some day competent to govern some regions, at any rate, of his own country.'

Watermeyer judgement   In 1936 Tshekedi

and Bathoen II of the Ngwaketse took the high commissioner to court, in order to stop 'indirect rule' proclamations being enforced. They saw the proclamations as following Hertzog's 'native policy' in South Africa, and argued that the proclamations were illegal because of British agreements with Tswana kings in 1885 and 1895. In November 1936 the Dominions Office in London handed down judgement, through Judge Watermeyer of the Protectorate's special court. The Watermeyer judgement followed the doctrine of the Foreign Jurisdiction Act of 1890 that once British power was established anywhere abroad it could ignore all previous treaties or agreements.

Failure of development plans   Meanwhile the Bechuanaland economy suffered from prolonged drought, as well as depressed markets for peasant sale of cattle and dairy products. Because of poverty, less hut tax was collected in 1928 than in 1917, even though each man now had to pay 25 rather than 20 shillings. In 1933 the Government was forced to reduce the hut tax to 15 shillings per man. The number of men from Bechuanaland going to work in the Rand gold mines rose from 3,400 in 1926 to 15,500 in 1940. Thousands more went to work on farms and mines elsewhere in South Africa, or in Southern Rhodesia and South West Africa.

Bechuanaland cattle were exported to Northern Rhodesia's Copperbelt, Katanga, and even to the Italian troops invading Ethiopia. But the main market in South Africa was blocked by South African restrictions till 1941, though white farmers and police on the borders conducted a profitable smuggling trade.

The spread of foot-and-mouth disease from Ngamiland to eastern Bechuanaland was stopped by veterinary cordons, manned by police, to check cattle movements. But grander development projects pressed by the resident commissioner Charles Rey were dropped. These projects included irrigation from the Okavango swamps, a railway across the Kalahari to Windhoek, and copper mining in the Ngwato reserve.

BASUTOLAND: impoverishment and education   Peasant production suffered from the great drought, which reached its height in 1933-34, and from depressed prices for wheat and wool exports. Basutoland had to import food for its people in large quantities from South Africa. It exported high quality mountain wheat at low prices to South African bakeries, while it imported low quality maize at high prices. The value of exports began to drop in the 1920s, and continued to drop in the 1930s. In 1929 exports and imports were about equal in value at around £700,000. But exports dropped to less than half of that value by 1936, while imports remained the same. Poverty at home forced people to work abroad. The number of men and women from Basutoland working in the Union doubled between 1921 and 1936 to over a hundred thousand – no less than fifteen per cent of Basutoland's total population. Peasant production failed to recover in the 1930s-40s, despite colonial government attempts to stop soil erosion and blight.

The expansion of Western education in Basutoland slowed down between 1922 and 1936 because of the economic depression – which deprived parents of school fees, Christian missions of funds, and the colonial government of taxes. Besides five hundred elementary (lower primary) schools, the Protestant (Paris), Catholic and Anglican missions ran small teacher training colleges at their mission headquarters of Morija, Roma and Masite. Only Morija had middle (higher primary/junior secondary) school classes, until the government opened middle schools at Maseru, Mafeteng and Matsieng in 1929-31. The government also ran a national technical school at Maseru, founded by Lerotholi, on behalf of the Basutoland National Council. Higher education was only to be found outside Basutoland, notably at Fort Hare University College in the eastern Cape province.

Paris mission and Anglican finances barely survived the economic depression. But colonial government expenditure benefited from taxation of rising numbers of migrant workers. The Roman Catholics, on the other hand, began a crusade throughout Africa to educate and therefore 'capture' the African élite of the future for Catholicism. A middle school was founded at Roma in 1937, and higher education followed there, after the government had opened Basutoland's first high (senior secondary) school at Maseru in 1939. But widespread education added little to the development of Basutoland, as employment was so limited within the country. Instead it provided clerks; and semi-skilled or skilled workers, for industry in the Union of South Africa. In other words, education in Basutoland aided and subsidized industrial expansion in South Africa.

Indirect rule reforms In Basutoland, as in Bechuanaland, so-called 'indirect rule' reforms of local administration in the 1930s helped to strengthen direct rule by colonial officials over chiefs. The Basutoland National Council rejected 'indirect rule' proposals in 1930. But the British persuaded paramount chief Griffith (ruled 1913-39) to cooperate. The 'indirect rule' reforms would limit the number of chiefs claiming court powers over local areas, which challenged the power of both the British and the paramount chief. Indirect rule proclamations were finally issued in 1938. A total of 1,340 chiefs were officially recognized as 'native authorities' with the power to hold local courts. But an almost equal number of chiefs were not recognized, and therefore lost power. Bitter rivalries developed among recognized and unrecognized chiefs, and resentment of British rule increased.

SWAZILAND: beginnings of capitalist development

In Swaziland, by contrast, 'indirect rule' proclamations were not introduced until the 1940s. The 1930s appear to have been politically very quiet. The Swaziland colonial administration aimed to help white economic development by keeping law and order among the 'natives'. White farmers in the Transvaal sent a quarter of a million sheep each year for winter pasture on the Swaziland highveld. The lowveld was taken up by large white-owned ranches, which fattened cattle in the winter for the Rand meat market. In fact forty per cent of white land owners in Swaziland

actually lived in South Africa. White farmers in the middleveld, producing maize, cotton and tobacco, suffered from South African control of marketing in which they had no say. Small amounts of tin and gold were mined in the highveld for export.

Peasant farming revived in the later 1920s, only to fall back in the great drought of 1929-34. By the late 1930s there were 10,000 Swazi men working in the Rand mines every year, which compared with 12,000 from Bechuanaland and around 80,000 from Basutoland. Then in 1938 large scale mining began in Swaziland for the first time, at Havelock (Bulembu) mine near Piggs Peak. By 1940 Havelock mine produced almost £500,000 worth of asbestos annually. Unlike South African mines it employed skilled black miners, mostly of Nyasa origin, as well as unskilled Swazi who would otherwise have migrated to the Rand.

Growth of Christianity By the 1930s up to thirty small Christian missions had settled Swazi areas. Methodists, Anglicans, Lutherans and Baptists arrived before 1900. They were followed in the next twenty years by the AME Church, the (ex-pentecostal) Nazarene church, the first 'Zionists', the Roman Catholics, and the Seventh Day Adventists. Yet traditional religion clearly remained the national religion. Annual ceremonies, notably the *incwala,* were retained to link traditional religion with the health of the paramount chief and the welfare of the nation.

Royal schools were founded at Zombodze and Matsapha to avoid sending royal children to mission schools. By 1940 only two chiefs were Christians.

The Nazarenes, the Roman Catholics and the Zionists all began to grow rapidly in the 1930s. The Nazarene church founded the country's main hospital at Bremersdorp (Manzini) in 1927, from which medical services were spread over Swaziland hand-in-hand with preaching. The British colonial authorities, fearing that American missionaries would spread dangerous democratic ideas, insisted that the hospital's superintendent be British. The Roman Catholics meanwhile

1906	Union Miniere copper company, based in Belgium, took control of mining in Katanga (later Shaba).
1908	Belgian Congo founded, with Katanga as its southern province, out of previous Congo Free State.
1909	Railway from South Africa to Katanga completed through the Rhodesias. Katanga mines then used Rhodesian (Wankie) coal and coke, and imported food and labour from the south.
1928	Katanga divided into peasant food-producing zones and labour exporting zones to supply its mining-industrial area. Police and headmen enforced this system despite falling crop prices and mine wages during the 1930s. The system was made necessary by competition for food and labour by new Rhodesian mines, and because of the failure to develop local white settler farming.
1929-32	Rapid development of mining on Northern Rhodesia's Copperbelt by Anglo American Corporation (based in South Africa) and by Rhodesian

	Selection Trust (mostly American-owned), using labour from Nyasaland and Northern Rhodesia which formerly went to Katanga.
1930s	Copperbelt mining declined in the early 1930s with a decline in world copper price from £75 to £26 a ton, but recovered to £38 a ton by 1936, when the Copperbelt employed 15,000 black and 10,500 white miners.
1935	Black miners went on strike on the Copperbelt against increased tax. Six shot dead by police. Copperbelt miners were better paid than in Katanga (or Southern Rhodesian mines), but Katanga miners were better housed and fed by Union Minière, which owned and controlled mine townships.
1936	White miners on the Copperbelt formed their own *Mine Workers' Union*, after failing to form a branch of the South African union of that name.

increased their educational work and appointed their first bishop in Swaziland in 1939. Numerous small but popular Zionist churches came to Swaziland, often brought by Swazi workers turned preachers returning from the Rand. By the 1940s there were so many churches that the paramount chief proposed to combine them in a 'Swazi National Church'. But the plan failed because each church had its own leader resisting unity. A building for the national church was started at the royal capital of Lobamba in 1948, but was left unfinished for thirty years.

Questions

1   What were the effects on the rest of southern Africa of the gold and manu-facturing boom in the Union of South Africa during the 1930s-40s?
2   Give the terms of the Southern Rho-desian constitution of 1923 and describe the development of Southern Rhodesia

from 1923 to 1953. [Cambridge International School Certificate, 1978]
3   Account for the rise of 'progressives' in the tribal-national movements of Basuto-land, Bechuanaland and Swaziland.
4   Compare the social and economic impact on African people of copper mining on the Copperbelt/Katanga with that of gold mining on the Witwatersrand.

Activities

1   Discuss how different politics and society in Southern Rhodesia were from politics and society in the Union of South Africa in the 1922-48 period.
2   Invent a conversation between Josiel Lefela and Tshekedi Khama discussing their attitudes towards British rule.

For references to Bibliography see p. 280.

Chapter 17

Second World War and Aftermath (1940 – 1953) I: South Africa

The 1940s and early 1950s saw a new phase in the development of both European imperialism and African nationalism. Governments in Europe, pressed by war, needed to recruit the support of their own nationals and of the colonized peoples within their empires. Since the depression of the 1930s, colonies had become more and more important again as suppliers of cheap raw materials, of cheap labour for southern African mines, and as markets for manufactured goods. Wartime economic recovery and rapid urbanization encouraged the growth of African nationalism. Western-educated Africans began to lead mass political movements of townspeople with new hopes and country people with old grievances.

In South Africa, Afrikaner nationalists, who had themselves recently risen to power, wished to preserve their new wealth and privilege and reacted to this African nationalism with a new policy called *apartheid*.

1 United Party Government under Smuts (1940-48)

Smuts lost no time in committing his government to war against Germany, once Hertzog and his followers had resigned from the government. The Defence Force rapidly expanded in numbers of men and quantity of equipment. The new British prime minister of 1940, Winston Churchill, told the British empire that the war was a fight to the death between democracy and tyranny. Africans and Indians in South Africa joined whites, mostly English-speaking, in volunteering to fight for democracy. The Atlantic Charter, pressed by the American president Franklin Roosevelt on Churchill in 1941, proclaimed the natural right of all peoples to determine their own future and to resist aggressive imperialism. But the Smuts government did not extend the fight for democracy and freedom to its own population. In 1943 it took the first step towards fully segregating coloureds from whites and blacks by creating a separate Coloured Affairs Department, along the lines of the Native Affairs Department. In the same year, the Smuts government also moved to bar Indians from owning land or houses previously owned by whites.

South African troops in Africa and Europe By the end of 1940 the South African Defence Force had 137,000 men under arms. As in the First World War, black South Africans were forbidden to carry firearms. Instead they became servants, labourers and watchmen in a body that became known as the South African Native Military Corps. South African law defined the 'operational area' of the Defence Force as 'any part of South Africa'. Smuts interpreted this to mean anywhere in Africa. South African forces were therefore sent to Kenya in 1940, to help British East and West African forces attack the Italians in Somalia and Eritrea.

Smuts, it will be remembered, believed that East Africa was a natural extension of South Africa. He therefore insisted on defeating the Italians in East Africa, before South African forces could help the British against Germans and Italians in North Africa. After the last Italians had been defeated in Ethiopia during 1941, 160,000 South African troops were sent to Egypt. A German army advancing into Egypt captured many of them at Tobruk in Libya. After the Germans were turned back in 1942, South African forces (and troops from the Protectorates) joined the westward British advance along the North African coast. Also in 1942 South African forces seized the port of Diego Suarez in Madagascar from pro-German French forces, and occupied the island. Finally in 1943 they joined the invasion of Italy by American forces. (The United States had joined the war in 1942.) Smuts had to push a special act through parliament to enable South African forces to go 'overseas'. Altogether 335,000 South Africans served in the Defence Force during 1940-45, of whom over one third were black or coloured.

Afrikaner dissension over the war   The Second World War produced deep and bitter political divisions among Afrikaners. Many Afrikaners thought that Smuts and those Afrikaners who fought on the British side during the war were traitors. Smuts himself avoided such problems at home by spending more and more time touring overseas, establishing himself as a world statesman rather than as a national leader. A good example of his lack of contact with reality is the fact that he wrote the preamble to the charter of the United Nations Organisation, founded by the victorious allies in 1945. The preamble talks of 'faith in fundamental human rights, in the dignity and worth of the human person'. Smuts ignored the fact that such words could be applied to the oppressed majority of the South African population.

The Reunited National (or People's) Party wished to achieve a South African republic independent of British imperialism. Most Afrikaner nationalists adopted a wait-and-see attitude of neutrality towards the war. But large numbers wanted South Africa to be Germany's ally. Malan was elected leader of the Reunited National Party. Hertzog and

Pirow continued to challenge his leadership until mid-1941, and he took longer to overcome the challenge of Johannes van Rensburg of the Ossewa-Brandwag.

Pro-Nazi Afrikaner movements   Hertzog was defeated within the National Party over the issue of education and linguistic rights in the future independent republic. He wanted equal rights for Afrikaans and English. The rest of the National Party stood for purely Afrikaans ('Christian-national') education to the exclusion of English. Hertzog was forced to resign, and became leader of a new party called the *Afrikaner Party* in 1941. Before he died in 1942 he called for South Africa to follow Germany in achieving freedom by dictatorship rather than parliamentary democracy.

Pirow also declared himself a national-socialist. Later he claimed it was the national-socialism of Salazar in Portugal, rather than of Hitler in Germany. Pirow followed the lead of Otto du Plessis, a professor at Stellenbosch University, who had written:

'It is clear that the pre-war democracies will be superseded by a new order, not only in Europe but throughout the whole world . . . a disciplined system of government in which all power is concentrated in a Party or a leader, who is the personification of the whole nation, and who interprets through his will the view of life or ideology of the nation.'

Pirow organized his 'New Order' group within the Reunited National Party. He clashed with Malan, who believed Afrikaner nationalism needed racial parliamentary democracy rather than racial party dictatorship. Pirow was forced out of the National Party, and founded his own *New Order Party* in early 1942. The party strongly supported Germany, and stood for racial discrimination against Jews as well as against blacks. But all his sixteen members of parliament were defeated in the 1943 general elections, and the party disappeared.

The Ossewa-Brandwag claimed 300,000 members as a cultural group. Under its new leader Johannes van Rensburg, who was elected its commandant-general at the beginning of 1941, it became a revolutionary political force. Van Rensburg challenged Malan for control of the National Party. Smuts assisted Malan by ordering all civil servants to resign from the 'OB', but membership continued in secret. The 'OB' began a campaign of sabotage, planting bombs under main railway lines and electric pylons during the summer of 1941-42. The government arrested guerrilla members of the 'OB', including 350 policemen. Some 'OB' members were tried for acts of sabotage, but no Afrikaner was sentenced to death for treason during the whole of the Second World War. Other 'OB' members were detained in camps – including an ex-Stellenbosch student called Balthazar John Vorster and young Hendrik van den Berghe. The Ossewa-Brandwag declined as the hope of German victory died around 1943, and Malan's leadership of the National Party grew in strength.

Broederbond plans for nationalist victory
Leading members of the Broederbond gave increasingly strong support to Malan. Malan always remained strong in the Cape province, his political homeland. He gained support in the north from J.G. Strijdom (Strydom), leader of the Transvaal branch of the party, and from Hendrik Verwoerd the editor of *Die Transvaler* newspaper. Verwoerd however was also strongly sympathetic to 'OB'.

After the National Party failed to win the 1943 general elections, the Broederbond planned how to win the 1948 elections. The National Party dropped the cry for a republic, and started a newspaper in English to attract the right-wing English-speaking Dominion Party. The 'White Workers Protection League' was formed in 1945 to organize white workers in rapidly expanding manufacturing industries — especially women — against cheaper coloured or black labour. By 1947 the Broederbond's Reddingsdaabond under Nicolas Diederichs controlled fourteen major companies with an annual business turnover of over £400 million. The South African Bureau of Racial Affairs was founded in 1947 to formulate future racial policy. It discussed the form that racial segregation should take as part of National Party policy.

The South African economy boomed as never before during the Second World War. The expansion of the gold mining industry began in 1933, and reached a peak in 1941 at £121 million worth. By 1950 the expansion levelled off at £145 million. The government itself poured £650 million into the war effort. Most of this was spent in South Africa: Britain carried much of the cost of South African forces in North Africa. Foreign capital set up new industries to produce arms and ammunition in South Africa. Before the main ammunition factory at Pretoria exploded accidentally in early 1945, South Africa was producing almost half the rifle, pistol and machine-gun bullets used by the Western allies in the war. The South African ports were expanded to repair allied ships, as it was safer to sail around Africa than to use the Suez canal and risk being sunk in the Mediterranean. Britain set up training schools for airmen in South Africa and Southern Rhodesia.

All of this helped industries to grow. The reduction of imports from war-torn Europe helped still further. In 1940 ISCOR produced thirty-eight per cent of iron and steel used in South Africa: by 1945 it produced fifty-eight per cent. Both foreign and local private capital poured into industries processing food and drink and manufacturing textiles and clothing. More complicated engineering, electronics and chemical production also started. Building and construction work expanded rapidly to accommodate the new industries. The value of goods manufactured each year in South Africa rose from £64 million to £138 million during the war years.

The government attempted to guide the growth of manufacturing through the Industrial Development Corporation. The government also set up trade missions in Central and East Africa to encourage South African manufacturers to sell their goods there 'for Africa'. The South African consumer market by itself was too small to support a large amount of industry. The majority of South Africans workers, being black, were too poorly paid to be able to afford to buy many consumer goods.

The wartime manufacturing boom continued into the late 1940s. Though ISCOR increased production in 1945-50 from about 450,000 to 600,000 metric tonnes, it only supplied forty-eight per cent of iron and steel used in South Africa in 1950 against its fifty-eight per cent in 1945. By 1955 ISCOR was producing 1.3 million tonnes — seventy per cent of the iron and steel used in South Africa. Meanwhile the value of manufactured goods rose from £138 million to £482 million worth in 1945-55 (though the real value increase was less due to the decline in value of the pound sterling).

Urbanization   The new manufacturing industries in the towns needed more and more labour. The pass laws were relaxed to allow African workers to move to urban areas to take these new jobs between 1942 and 1945. The total population of the Rand towns, which had reached over a million by 1936, rose to over a million and a half in the 1940s. By 1951 the recorded population of Johannesburg by itself was 920,000 (half black, half white); Capetown was 630,000 (half coloured, a tenth black); Durban was 500,000 (one

Workers waiting outside government offices in the late 1940s   Increasingly strict and complex pass laws meant hours of queueing and waiting for yet another official stamp on pass documents. African workers were often at the mercy of an army of petty bureaucrats and policemen, and simple passes expanded into pass books requiring many stamps.

Accommodation for migrant workers in a brick factory.

third Asian, one third black); and Pretoria was 285,000 (more than half white).

Urban Africans developed their own culture and lifestyle, and began to demand political rights as full citizens of the Union of South Africa. White politicians, especially Afrikaner nationalists, reacted by calling for stricter pass laws and greater segregation between blacks and whites in the cities.

2 National Party Government under Malan (1948-53)

The National Party won the 1948 general election in South Africa by promising *apartheid* to the white electorate. *Apartheid* (literally, 'apartness') meant total separation between white and black in politics, education, and home territory. It aimed to preserve white supremacy or *baaskap* (boss-dom) for ever from the threat of black majority rule. In other words, *apartheid* was to tighten up the racial segregation already achieved in South Africa, at a time when segregation was being loosened or at least challenged elsewhere in Africa and Asia. The United Nations Organisation had begun to criticize South Africa under Smuts. Newly-independent India, supported by the Soviet Union, raised the question of discrimination against Indians and other non-whites in South Africa. UN members had also begun to criticize South Africa over its 'trusteeship' for South West Africa. Now in 1948 a government came to power in South Africa which said clearly that it believed in segregation, unlike Smuts who talked about human rights. The world therefore came to see what Afrikaners saw as the triumph of nationalism as the triumph of anti-black racism. Afrikaner nationalists therefore developed a grievance against the world for so misunderstanding them.

The first problem of Malan's National Party government was to increase its slender majority in parliament over the opposition parties. It achieved this in 1950 by bringing into parliament representatives, all members of the National Party, of the white population of South West Africa. It also recruited members of parliament from the Afrikaner Party — the followers of Hertzog, who had broken away from the National Party in 1941. It halted the plans of the previous government for mass immigration from Europe, particularly from Britain, in order to preserve the Afrikaner majority in the electorate. But Malan abandoned his previous idea of breaking away from the British Commonwealth to make South Africa a republic.

Apartheid laws 1949-52 Malan's *apartheid* political programme strengthened the segregation of the Hertzog Bills of the 1920s-30s, and converted previous customs of racial discrimination into laws backed by police powers of arrest and imprisonment. The United Party only resisted Malan's plans to exclude coloureds completely from national political power.

The first *apartheid* law was the *Prohibition of Mixed Marriages Act* of 1949. Marriage between blacks and whites had been banned in 1923: now the ban was extended to marriages between whites and coloureds or Indians. This was followed by the *Immorality Act* of 1950 which made illegal any form of sexual contact between whites and non-whites.

The most basic *apartheid* laws were passed in 1950. The *Population Registration Act* gave officials the power to classify every individual South African by race, i.e. as Native (later 'Bantu'), European ('White'), Indian ('Asian'), or Coloured (later split into three groups). The *Group Areas Act* in the same year gave officials the power to declare rural and urban residential areas for each race anywhere outside of the black reserves.

Other laws ensured that only essential black labour remained in towns, and that other blacks had to return to their rural reserves — the system known in South Africa as influx control. The *Prevention of Illegal Squatters Act* of 1951 gave officials the right to remove 'surplus natives' to emergency camps. Officials could remove blacks living without permission on white land, or blacks on black-owned land in areas declared white under the 1913 and 1936 Land Acts but not yet bought by whites.

By 1952 the National Party government had learnt to give more mild or liberal-sounding titles to its *apartheid* laws. The *Native Abolition of Passes Act* of 1952 in fact strengthened the old pass laws. Blacks had to carry so many different passes, giving them permission to do this or that, that the passes were now consolidated in a pass book ('reference book'). Every black outside the rural reserves had to carry this pass book all the time. Every change in the pass book had to be endorsed (i.e. approved and stamped) by an official of the Native Affairs Department. For the first time since 1920 all women as well as men would have to carry passes in certain areas.

The *Native Laws Amendment Act* of 1952 went back to Hertzog's policy of 1937 that blacks could be only temporary residents in 'white' towns. Blacks endorsed out of urban areas were deported to emergency camps, labour colonies on white farms, or to their rural reserves.

White political opposition The *Separate Representation of Voters Act* (1951) gave coloureds separate white representatives in parliament as a start towards removing their representation in national politics altogether. United Party opposition to the act was strengthened by a surge of post-war liberalism, particularly among ex-servicemen, after the war against fascism. The Torch Commando, an organization of white ex-servicemen and women closely linked with the still largely English-speaking army, marched in protest through the streets of Capetown. The Springbok Legion, a smaller and more radical group of ex-servicemen, also included coloured and black members. By 1953 there was talk of a military coup to prevent the National Party from being re-elected. But the all-white Torch Commando split up in disputes about whether or not to admit coloureds to its membership.

The Separate Representation of Voters Act was passed by a narrow majority of just over half the members of parliament, not by the two-thirds majority required for major amendments to the constitution. So the Act was challenged in the supreme court and declared illegal.

White supremacy and economic prosperity
The National Party under Malan entered the 1953 general elections determined to eliminate opposition both inside parliament and outside it, where black protest against *apartheid* was growing. *Apartheid* would in future follow guide lines laid down for 'native' administration and education by Hendrik Verwoerd and Werner Eiselen, two former Stellenbosch professors. Verwoerd had become minister of Native Affairs in 1950. Eiselen had chaired a 1949-51 commission on future black education policy. Verwoerd had already started planning territorial *apartheid* by appointing a commission, chaired by F.R. Tomlinson, on the 'social-economic development of the Native Areas within the Union of South Africa'.

Meanwhile Malan's government had reassured international capitalism about investing in South Africa. The National Party rejected 'national-socialism' and the nationalization of foreign capital. Instead it en-

---

SECTION 10 RIGHTS

The rights to stay in an urban area became known as 'Section 10 Rights', because they were laid out in Section 10 (1a-d) of the 1954 *Native Urban Areas Act*. Black people could only stay in an urban area for more than 12 hours if they:

(a) had been born there and had lived there ever since

(b) had worked there for ten years under one employer, or had lived there for fifteen years without breaking any law (including pass laws)

(c) were the child or wife of a man permitted to live in the urban area on the conditions of (a) or (b) above

(d) signed a contract to migrate from a rural reserve to a specific job for a limited period of time in an urban area — after which they must return home. (Families of such 'contract workers' were not allowed to live with them in an urban area.)

couraged foreign capital to invest in further new mining projects and more complex manufacturing, while Afrikaner private capital increased its role in banking, insurance, commerce and less complex manufacturing. The world economic boom of the early 1950s led to higher prices for gold and other minerals, and for exports such as fruit and wool. Production of metals apart from gold rose from £22 million worth in 1945 to over £100 million in 1955. New gold mines around Welkom in the Orange Free State were opened in 1951. From the late 1940s onwards, South Africa exported uranium for atomic fuel to the USA and Britain, as a very valuable by-product of gold mining. British preference for Commonwealth products over those from Europe also opened up the overseas market for fruit, especially 'Outspan' oranges from South Africa.

3 Revival of African Nationalism in South Africa

Between the 1930s and the 1950s the African population of South Africa was converted from a largely *peasant* population into a largely *worker* population. The censuses of 1921 and 1936 recorded about half the black population as peasants deriving their income from crops. The 1946 and 1951 censuses recorded the proportion of peasants as dropping to a fifth, and then to a tenth. (This may have been an exaggeration since women, who were more likely to be peasants than workers, were classified in the two earlier censuses but were not in the later censuses.) Urbanization also appears to have increased the rate of population growth. The 1921 and 1936 censuses claim to record almost the same total black population at around 4.75 million, while the 1951 census records 5.2 million.

Rand urban life The number of black workers employed in manufacturing industry on the Rand doubled soon after the Second World War, to over two hundred thousand. The expanding white middle class suburbs around Johannesburg opened up employment for black workers in building and maintenance, new shops and private houses. Women replaced men in poorly paid domestic work, living alone in white backyards or commuting from their families in the townships.

Townships on city outskirts became overcrowded with shanty houses using every available space. The police tried to discipline the new urban masses by constant raiding of houses for illegal home-brewed beer or other liquor. Some private houses became shebeens, typically run by women brewers known as 'aunties' or 'shebeen-queens'. As well as home-brewed beer, they might sell home-brewed liquor known as *skokjaan,* sometimes fatally poisonous. It was illegal for blacks to buy or drink bottled 'European' beer or liquor. The only legal drinking places were municipally-owned halls selling corn beer. The municipal authorities financed services to black townships, such as sanitation and education, from beer hall profits, thereby encouraging the police to enforce their monopoly on drinking.

Shebeens were often havens for gangsters and petty criminals, including the *tsotsi* street gangs of unemployed youth that appeared in the 1940s. But shebeens were the centre of township social life at night, and provided income for women brewers who were often supporting families without a husband. Police raids on shebeens were therefore bitterly resented, and sometimes started riots, such as the serious riot at Vereeniging in 1937.

Squatter movements Urban overcrowding on the Rand in the 1940s led to groups of people moving out of the municipal townships to settle in new shanty towns on neighbouring private land. The most successful of seven squatter movements was led by James 'Sofazonke' Mpanza, who marched his followers out of Orlando township early one morning in 1944 to settle on the open veld. The police failed to move the squatters, and the municipal authorities eventually recognized it as Moroka township – the centre of later Soweto. Other squatter movements were less successful. Black ex-servicemen, members of the Springbok Legion, founded a well-run shanty town outside Pimville named 'Tobruk'. The police destroyed it.

Segregation revived The relaxation of pass laws encouraged people to demonstrate for their complete abolition in 1944. But after the war, police control of the pass laws was tightened up. *Apartheid* after 1948 used pass laws to direct necessary labour to mines, industries and white farms, while 'surplus natives' were sent to rural reserves. Every African in an urban area had to carry his passes, or pass book after 1952, at all times to prove his right to be there. Pass books became known as '*dom*-passes' — *dom* being Afrikaans for stupid. A black person's greatest fear was that his pass book would be stamped as invalid, because of the whim of an individual policeman or Native Affairs Department official. *Apartheid* gave enormous personal powers to police and officials over the every-day lives of Africans. Only the richest or best educated Africans might challenge these powers by appealing to higher officials or law courts. The law courts became crowded out with pass offenders, each one tried and sentenced in a matter of minutes or even seconds. By 1952 over a quarter of a million blacks were convicted each year of breaking the pass and influx control laws. An equal number of both blacks and coloureds were convicted of breaking beer and liquor laws.

The 1940s, before segregation was again revived, were remembered as days of hope among the township masses. The war against fascism spread ideas of the struggle for eventual democracy. The speeches of the American president, and even the speeches of prime minister Smuts, encouraged this.

Pan-Africanist ideas spread from the 5th Pan-African Congress held in England (1945), while socialist ideas were popularized by the wartime alliance between South Africa and the Soviet Union. (The Soviet Union had diplomatic representation in South Africa from 1942 till 1954.) The growth of popular American culture during the war, seen and heard in magazines, records and films, influenced all sections of South African society. American music was combined with tradi-

tional and church melodies to create a new township music, based on the guitar, tea-chest bass, and penny whistle.

Black worker unions and strikes The Industrial Conciliation Act of 1924 had taken away from blacks the right to bargain with employers through a trade union. After the collapse of the ICU — a general trade union covering all crafts — the number of black trade unions for a particular craft had risen rapidly. Independent black, coloured and Indian unions were brought together in 1941 by the Council of Non-European Trade Unions. CNETU was founded at a conference called by Moses Kotane, the new secretary of the Communist Party of South Africa, but it was by no means a communist body.

Trade unions took advantage of wartime labour shortages to put pressure on employers by strikes and threats of strikes. African pay and working conditions improved significantly in every industry, except mining, during the war as a result of this increased pressure. Black wages in manufacturing rose in real (rather than currency-inflated) value by ten per cent in 1931-40, and by fifty per cent in 1940-46. By 1942 the number of small black strikes had become so serious that the government introduced a war emergency law making all black strikes illegal. This emergency law was difficult to enforce in industries short of labour, but was renewed every year until 1953. In that year the *Native Labour Settlement of Disputes Act* made black strikes permanently illegal.

Foundation of ANC Youth League Dr A. B. Xuma became president of the African National Congress at the end of 1940. He made the national executive stronger than the provincial branches for the first time, so that the policy decisions of annual national meetings would be carried out. The ANC adopted a new constitution in 1943, which eliminated its house of chiefs. It recruited growing numbers of black intellectuals, especially at Fort Hare, and planned to become a mass movement of up to a million members. The ANC looked forward to a democratic post-

Anton Lembede (1914-47) Son of a Natal farm-worker and a teacher mother. Lawyer in the office of Pixley Seme. Founder and inspirer of the ANC Youth League (1944). Lembede picked up the Africanist ideas of Seme in more socialist form. He looked forward to 'the era of African socialism' — meaning socialism based on African principles and not on foreign ideology. Africans had to throw off their 'worship and idolisation of white men' and rediscover their identity as Africans. Only Africans could lead Africans to freedom, 'because no foreigner can ever truly and genuinely represent the African spirit'. Lembede claimed: 'I am a peasant and I was born a peasant. I am one with the soil of Africa.'

war society in which all adult South Africans would have the vote. It published its proposed Bill of Rights for post-war South Africa in a pamphlet titled *Africans' Claims* (1943).

Younger members of the ANC had more militant ideas about black majority rule in a future democratic society. They formed the ANC Youth League under Anton Lembede at Johannesburg in 1944. Lembede's closest collaborator in the Youth League was Peter Mda. Founder members of the Youth League included Nelson Mandela, Walter Sisulu, Govan Mbeki, Oliver Tambo and Ntsu Mokhehle. Later members included Robert Sobukwe (chairman of the Fort Hare branch

in 1947), and Gatsa Buthelezi.

Pan-Africanism abroad The ANC Youth League at Fort Hare helped to spread Africanist ideas among graduates, who carred these ideas as far north as Uganda and Kenya. The ANC saw itself as part of the Pan-Africanist movement towards freedom for people of African ancestry in Africa, America and the Caribbean. But the South African government refused passports to delegates trying to attend the Pan-African Congress in 1945 — at which W.E.B. DuBois, Marcus Garvey's widow, George Padmore, Kwame Nkrumah, Jomo Kenyatta and Hastings Banda were all present. South Africa was represented only by two people already living in Britain. The Pan-African Congress condemned fascist policies in South Africa and demanded the vote for all men and women over twenty-one, universal free education, and full civil rights for everyone regardless of colour. Their resolution ended with the ANC slogan, *Mayibuye iAfrika*! ('Let Africa return'). A further resolution demanded freedom for Basutoland, Bechuanaland and Swaziland.

Other political movements The Communist Party at first opposed the Second World War as an imperialist war. But it changed its mind when the Soviet Union joined the war against Germany as a crusade against fascism (1941). From then on the party pushed forward a 'united front' policy of working with 'progressives' in black trade unions, and increasing numbers of whites and Indians joined it.

The All-African Convention under D. D. T. Jabavu was transformed into the Non-European Convention in 1943, and finally into the *Non-European Unity Movement*. Its membership was largely restricted to the western Cape, where it took over from the old APO as the main political movement among coloureds. Trotskyists took the lead in campaigning against the new Coloured Affairs Department in 1943, and subsequently dominated the Unity Movement. Meanwhile in the Transvaal, Paul Mosaka of the Native

Representative Council founded another alternative party to the ANC, called the *African Democratic Party* (1943), which became a home for black Trotskyists.

The South African Indian Congress, consisting of Natal and Transvaal branches, declined to join the Non-European Convention and instead was drawn into closer collaboration with the ANC. It was inspired by the success of Indian nationalism and the approach of independence in India itself. It vigorously resisted Smuts' attempt to impose further segregation on Indians during the war. But there was tension between Indians and Africans in Durban. Indians owned the small shops which often exploited African customers with high prices or strict credit. Such resentment sparked off violent riots at Cato Manor outside Durban in 1949, which left 284 people dead.

Trade unionists recruiting African factory workers during the lunch break.

4 1946 Mineworkers' Strike and 1952 Defiance Campaign

Black trade unions demanded, and usually obtained, a minimum wage of 40 shillings (£2) a week in manufacturing industry during 1942. But the gold mining industry presented a much greater challenge to trade union organizers. No fewer than 308,000 black workers were employed in 1943 at a wage of less than 14 shillings a week. (This compared with 12 shillings in 1942, 10 shillings in 1935, and 15 shillings back in 1890 when money was worth much more.) Workers spent around twelve hours underground every day for six days a week. They ate and slept in guarded compounds. Experienced gold miners left to find better work in manufacturing industry, but they were always replaced by more men. Improved labour recruitment brought men from as far north as Tanganyika, where increasing demand for cash drove people into migrant labour for more money than could be got from farming or employment locally.

The Native Representative Council, at its first meeting in 1937. Note that the eighteen 'natives' stand behind twelve whites. 'We have been asked to cooperate with a toy telephone,' said representative Paul Mosaka at a council debate of 1946. 'We have been speaking into an apparatus which cannot transmit sound and at the end of which there is nobody to receive the message.' Members then boycotted meetings of the council. The National Party government finally abolished the council in 1951.

The African Mine Workers Union (AMWU) was founded in 1941, with the black communist J. B. Marks as its secretary, by the Transvaal branch of the African National Congress. The AMWU gradually recruited mine workers by first recruiting mine clerks, who were free to enter and leave the labour compounds. By 1944 the union claimed 25,000 men.

The AMWU began to move towards strike action, after the mine owners refused to improve the pay and conditions of mine workers as recommended by a 1944 government commission. (The mining companies had made a record profit of £15.6 million in the previous year.) Black miners were made rebellious by cuts in their food rations, and the AMWU began to demand 60 shillings (£3) a week. Finally in August 1946 the union called the workers out on strike. 75,000 men responded, of whom nine were killed when the police violently crushed the strike by driving strikers down the mines.

Paul Mosaka thundered: 'You can do what you like, you can shoot us, arrest us, but you are not going to break our spirit . . . in the land of our birth, the land that is ours.' The Native Representative Council discussed the suppression of the miners' strike, and adopted Mosaka's motion condemning 'Fascism which is the antithesis and negation of the letter and spirit of the Atlantic Charter and the United Nations Charter'. When the government refused to respond, the council suspended itself in protest, after Mosaka had described it contemptuously as a 'toy telephone'.

ANC-SAIC doctors' pact The African National Congress responded to post-war tightening up of segregation by allying itself more closely with the South African Indian Congress. The SAIC was conducting a campaing of 'passive resistance' in Natal along Gandhian lines by mass boycotts, sit-down strikes, blocking roads with crowds, etc. The ANC president Dr Xuma made the so-called 'doctors' pact' with the SAIC leaders Dr Y. M. Dadoo and Dr G. M. Naicker, pledging ANC support for this passive resistance campaign in 1947.

Both Dadoo and Naicker were communists, and many people within ANC reacted strongly against collaboration with communists and non-Africans in the SAIC and elsewhere. The ANC Youth League voiced this reaction. Anton Lembede himself died suddenly in 1947, aged only 33. But his ideas were drawn up in the Youth League Manifesto of 1948.

The Youth League Manifesto declared that every African had a 'primary, inherent and inalienable right to Africa which is his continent and Motherland'. The manifesto agreed that non-African minorities should be allowed to live in Africa, but only in a 'people's free society where racial oppression and persecution will be outlawed'. There was to be an African form of socialism, based on co-operatives and redistribution of land to the people. Marxist socialism was attacked for rejecting 'the fundamental fact that we are not oppressed as a class, but as a people, as a Nation'.

Programme of Action How was the new society to be achieved? Mda, Mandela, Tambo, Sisulu and others drew up a Pro-

279

gramme of Action for the ANC, based on 'boycott, strike, civil disobedience'. Both the Programme of Action and the Youth League Manifesto were presented to the 1949 ANC annual conference. Xuma and the 'old guard' of the party opposed the two Youth League documents, but they were defeated. The documents were accepted as ANC policy. The Youth League succeeded in getting James Moroka elected as president of the ANC in place of Xuma, with Sisulu at his side as secretary of the party. Moroka was not a youth leaguer but an older man, previously a leader of the All-African Convention. But the 'old guard' of the ANC remained strong on the party's national executive. The youth leaguers ironically found they had to ally with Kotane and Marks, the communists on the executive, to push the party into militant action.

The Suppression of Communism Act The alliance of youth leaguers and communists helped to convert some previously anti-communist youth leaguers to sympathy with communism. The alliance also hastened a South African government crackdown on communism, in the belief that ANC militancy would die without communist 'agitators' behind it. Sisulu was already close to communists because of trade union work. But Mandela and Tambo were anti-communist, at first opposing ANC joining with communists to protest against the government's Unlawful Organisations Bill of 1950. But Kotane organized a successful May Day strike on the Rand, in which around seventy per cent of black workers stayed at home. This strike pushed militants like Mandela and Tambo into support of the communists against the bill. Younger youth leaguers like Joe Matthews and Duma Nokwe openly admired communism. But Mda, Sobukwe and others continued their distrust of communists as agents of a foreign ideology.

The Unlawful Organisations Bill was renamed the *Suppression of Communism Act* when it became law (1950). The Communist Party of South Africa quickly dissolved itself before the Act was passed, telling its members to join 'progressive' nationalist parties instead. The South African Communist Party was reformed 'underground' in 1953 by whites who had found no acceptable alternative white party to join, under the secret leadership of the Afrikaner lawyer Bram Fischer. The Suppression of Communism Act gave the minister of justice the right to name any person a 'communist', whether or not they thought themselves to be one, and then to ban them from attending meetings, joining organizations or travelling in any areas within South Africa. To put it simply, a 'communist' was anyone who wanted social, economic or political change in South Africa which could not come through the white parties inside the parliament.

Origins of the Defiance Campaign The ANC national executive decided to put the Programme of Action into operation during 1952, when whites would be celebrating the three hundredth anniversary of van Riebeeck's landing at the Cape. The ANC would organize a national campaign against the most oppressive *apartheid* laws — the pass laws; the 'native authorities' acts and livestock limitation acts, affecting blacks; the Separate Registration of Voters Act, affecting coloureds; the Group Areas Act, particularly affecting Indians; and the Suppression of Communism Act, affecting militants of all groups but particularly whites.

What became known as the 'Defiance Campaign' began on June 26th, 1952. It was a combined operation by the ANC and the South African Indian Congress in three stages. The first stage was the deliberate breaking of *apartheid* laws in the cities by trained volunteers. The second and third stages were to follow if the government did not repeal the most hated laws. The second stage was to extend protests by volunteers to other towns; the third stage was to be mass protests in town and countryside. Sisulu, the ANC's first full-time secretary, was the main organizer of the Defiance Campaign. Three ANC leaders in the Transvaal did not join the campaign — Mda, Sobukwe, and Potlhako Leballo. Instead they formed an 'Africanist Watchdog

Defiance Campaign demonstrators under arrest, entering a police van outside a South African Railways and Harbours Police charge office. Note the thumbs-up salute that became the symbol of the campaign.

Committee', to uphold the Youth League Manifesto against the increasing adoption of socialist ideas.

Between June 1952 and January 1953 over eight thousand volunteers were arrested after demonstrating peacefully in the cities. They defied pass laws and segregation by sitting in whites-only cafés, entering areas reserved for other races, and by burning their passes in public. They planned to be arrested, and to crowd out the prisons and law courts, so that the official machinery of *apartheid* would break under the strain. The campaign was strongest in Port Elizabeth and its black township, New Brighton, where about six thousand were arrested. In a matter of a few months the paid-up membership of the ANC rose from 7,000 to 100,000 across the country.

Effects of the Defiance Campaign The Defiance Campaign drew the attention of the world to the injustices suffered by Africans in South Africa. The United Nations set up a commission of enquiry into *apartheid*, and

Many early staffers on 'Drum', a weekly pictorial magazine for Africans published in Johannesburg, went on to fame as writers and photographers. **Left**: Todd Matshikiza, who wrote the music for *King Kong*, a musical stage play about township life that captured the spirit of the late 1950s. **Right**: Can Themba, short story writer about city and township life, whose stories were later anthologised as *The Will to Die*.

there was widespread admiration for the disciplined non-violence of African defiance. But when the campaign reached its peak in October and November 1952, police fired on African crowds, in Port Elizabeth, East London and Kimberley. Non-violent demonstrations turned into riots looting and destroying buildings and attacking white people.

Moroka wanted to call off the Defiance Campaign in the eastern Cape, and quarrelled with other members of the ANC national executive. ANC leaders were arrested under the Suppression of Communism Act, and were put under various banning orders which prevented them from attending public meetings, leaving their homes at night, etc. The National Party government passed a *Public Safety Act* and a *Criminal Law Amendment Act* (1953). These gave the minister of justice the right to declare a 'state of emergency' (i.e. full police powers without appeal to law courts) in any area and to punish defiance of any law heavily. Moroka was voted out as ANC president in 1953. He was replaced by Albert Luthuli, a respected Natal teacher and minor chief. The Defiance Campaign was called off before it could reach its planned second stage, and the ANC was left without clear plans for the future.

Questions

1   Show how the development of mining and other urban industries has affected the African peoples of the Republic of South Africa. [Cambridge International School Certificate, 1976] (Refer also to Chapter 19.)

2   What were the roots of the new form of Afrikaner nationalism that took power in 1948?

3   When and why did 'passive resistance' by African nationalists in South Africa fail after the Second World War?

4   How much was the development of African nationalism in South Africa affected by nationalism elsewhere in Africa between 1945 and 1959?

Activities

1   True to his own principles — or a 'sell-out' of Afrikaner nationalism? Discuss these two views of the career of Smuts.

2   Make population graphs of urban growth during the 20th century from what figures you can find in this and other books.

3   In March 1944 James 'Sofazonke' Mpanza led a group of people out of Orlando township into the open countryside to erect shanty housing. Imagine and describe the scene, including the reactions of municipal officials, over the first few days.

Chapter 14 references see Bibliography pp. 337–42: A2 Boyce; A3 Denoon & Nyeko; A4 Kallaway &c; A11 van Jaarsveld; B4 Cameron; B18 Marks; B26 Muller; B30 Palmer & Parsons; B32 Readers Digest; B36 Thompson; B42 Wilson & Thompson; B43 Wood; D13 Marks & Trapido; E5 Bley; E6 Bundy; E15 Jeeves; E17 Keegan; E20 Marks & Rathbone; E23 Newbury; E27 Prins; E35 van Onselen; E40 Wheatcroft; F5 Bonner; F6–7 Bozzoli; F9–10 Callicanos; F18 Edgar; F20 Grundlingh; F26 Kallaway & Pearson; F33 Macmillan; F35 Marks & Trapido; F53 Webster; F55 Willan; G5 Daniel & Stephen; G12 Machobane; G16 Palmer; G17 Phimister; G23–24 van Onselen.

Chapter 15 references as 14 above, and also Bibliography pp. 337–42: B7 Eriksen & Moorsom; B14/1 Konczacki; E2–3 Beinart; E4 Beinart & Bundy; F13 Coplan; F14 Couzens; F15 Crush &c; F15 Dubow; F22 Hirson; F24 Houghton; F25 Innes; F29 Lerumo; F30 Lipton; F32 Macmillan & Marks; F34 Marks; F37 Meli; F40 Packard; F44 Rich; F45 Roux; F46 Shava; F47 Simons & Simons; F48 Sundkler.

Chapter 16 references as 14 above, also pp. 337–42: B14/2 Koncacki; B39 Vail; G1 Booth; G3 Chanock; G4 Crowder; G7 Edgar; G8 Hyam; G11 Kuper; G13 Meebelo; G14 Morton & Ramsay; G19 Ranger; G21 Rey; G26 Wylie.

Chapter 17 references as 15 above, also pp. 337–42: B2 Bozzoli; F1 ANC; F2 Benson; F19 Gerhart; F27 Karis & Carter; F28 La Hausse; F39 O'Meara; F50 Vilakazi; F52 Walker; F54 Wilkins & Strydom.

Chapter 18
Second World War and Aftermath (1940–1953)
II: The Settler North, the High Commission Territories and South West Africa

The Second World War accelerated the growth of African nationalism and worker movements. African troops served in Asia and Europe, as well as in Africa, and brought back ideas of a wider world. Africans noted that the war was proclaimed as a struggle for freedom against tyranny, when they were themselves denied democratic rights. The war also stimulated rising production of raw materials, and even of manufactured goods, in the colonies. Towns expanded with new workers. Africans rose to more skilled positions, while the colonial power tried to push forward the war effort by avoiding industrial unrest.

1 Moves toward Central African Federation

Wartime growth of mining and manufacturing in the Rhodesias, and expansion of settler agriculture within Nyasaland, led to growth of both settler and African nationalism. There was rapid urbanization, particularly around Salisbury and on the Copperbelt. African trade unions pressing for better pay and conditions combined, sometimes uneasily, with African congresses seeking political rights.

NORTHERN RHODESIA The copper mining companies expanded production to over 200,000 tons by 1938, and during the Second World War Northern Rhodesia became the world's fourth largest copper producer. The war effort needed copper for brass shell and bullet casings, and for electrical wiring in trucks, tanks, ships, and aircraft. Every bomber aircraft had three kilometres of copper wire inside it. The number of African workers employed in the Copperbelt mines rose to over 36,000 by 1943, while the companies kept down the number of expensive white miners to around 3,000.

Origins of Northern Rhodesia African Congress
Northern Rhodesia contributed to the British war effort in men as well as copper. As well as migrating to the Copperbelt, over 50,000 men went annually from Northern Rhodesia to work in Southern Rhodesia and South Africa. 15,000 blacks and 800 local whites served in the Northern Rhodesian Regiment in East Africa and Burma. Peasants remaining on the land were rounded up to serve in an 'African Labour Corps', under military command, to work on white farms producing maize and wheat for the Copperbelt.

NYASALAND Tobacco production expanded on white estates in southern Nyasaland during the 1930s. African peasant 'squatters' were obliged to give labour-rent (*thangata*) on the estates, or were pushed into overcrowded tribal reserves. From about 1943 onwards there were rural riots in the southern province against threats of eviction. Meanwhile over 100,000 men migrated annually from the central and northern provinces to work abroad — mostly to Southern Rhodesia, but also to the Rand and the Copperbelt. Soldiers in the King's African Rifles fought for the British as far away as Burma.

SOUTHERN RHODESIA Mining and manufacturing industry grew rapidly during and after the Second World War. The value of manufacturing production rose from £5 million in 1939 to £31 million in 1949 (though real value increase was lower), and its number of employees trebled. Increasing numbers of Africans came to urban-industrial areas in the two main cities of Bulawayo and Salisbury, and in the towns between them, to work in industries or to service new white suburbs. The white population of Southern Rhodesia was swelled by immigration of skilled and semi-skilled workers from Britain and South Africa — rising from 55,000 in 1936 to 135,000 by 1951.

Bulawayo remained the main industrial centre until the early 1950s, as it serviced the railway between South Africa and the Copperbelt. But Salisbury overtook it in growth. It was the centre of a rich area of white farming and small mines, and was served by the convenient and growing port of Beira in Mozambique. The number of registered African workers in Salisbury took off from 46,000 in 1946 and rose continually, passing the 75,000 mark in 1951.

The idea of federation The white settlers of Southern Rhodesia, under prime minister Godfrey Huggins, clung to the notion of a great white dominion of Central Africa. Expressing his admiration for Smuts, Huggins even talked of a Union of Central Africa joining a Union of South Africa and other white states in a 'United States of Africa'. British imperial reluctance was gradually overcome by reaction to the Afrikaner nationalist victory in South Africa in 1948. A greater Rhodesia might secure British interests in southern Africa from Afrikaner nationalist take-over. Huggins was prepared to accept a federation of the three colonies, as the first stage towards eventual amalgamation. He recruited the support of Roy Welensky, leader of the white settlers in Northern Rhodesia. Huggins then called a white settlers' conference at Victoria Falls in 1949 — to which no Africans or British officials were invited — to make plans for federation.

African opposition in the northern colonies Federation, rather than immediate amalgamation, was an attempt to reassure Africans that Southern Rhodesian 'native policy' — meaning loss of land to white settlers — would not be extended northwards. But opposition to federation became the main issue behind the remarkable growth of Nyasaland and Northern Rhodesian black nationalism from the late 1940s. Congress leaders from the two colonies attacked the 1949 Victoria Falls proposals as 'the same old pill of amalgamation, coated with the sugar of federation to make it easier for the Africans and the Imperial Government to swallow'.

Mining companies back federation By 1950, however, the Labour Party government in Britain was turning a deaf ear to African opinion. It listened instead to the Copperbelt mining companies, which had come out in favour of federation. The Anglo-American Corporation and the Rhodesian Selection Trust (RST) wished to build up Salisbury as their business base — fearing the possibility of state take-over of large capitalist firms based in London or Johannesburg. The mining companies tried to sell the idea of federation to the Africans and to the British government as a great and noble experiment. *Partnership* between the races would open up a peaceful multi-racial future, in contrast to inevitable race conflict under *apartheid*.

Britain imposes federation A Conservative government was elected to power in Britain during 1951. It called a London conference of white delegates from Central Africa to draw up a federal constitution in 1952. The *Federation of Rhodesia and Nyasaland* came into being in August 1953, with Huggins as its prime minister.

African protests had failed to stop federation. In Nyasaland there were widespread riots in the southern province against white settler farms. In Northern Rhodesia African trade unionists on the Copperbelt broke ranks with African nationalists in Lusaka because of improved mine wages. When the Congress called for two days of 'national prayer' against federation, i.e. a national strike, the call was ignored by African mine workers. In Southern Rhodesia African nationalists were quietened by the promise of a new liberalism. The new prime minister Garfield Todd proposed to improve the labour laws and African education. The trade unionist and nationalist leader Joshua Nkomo stood for election to the new multi-racial federal parliament, but, unlike some African nationalists in the northern territories, failed to be elected.

The coming of Central African federation coincided with a world boom in export commodity prices, including copper and tobacco, which led to prosperous mining and white agriculture in the federation. African workers in the towns felt some benefit from the boom in improved wages and working conditions. But peasants in the countryside were threatened with eviction to make way for more productive farming of export crops. As a result, there was widespread peasant resistance to all forms of agricultural improvement by the colonial governments, while only a minority of productive peasants prospered. In southern Nyasaland this helped to split the nationalist movement. Some leaders of the anti-federation campaign led peasant resistance, while others supported government agricultural improvement.

2 BECHUANALAND:
The Ngwato Chieftainship (1940-53)

'Bechuana' troops in the World War Bechuanaland chiefs offered soldiers to fight for the British in the war and to crush any Boer rebellion in South Africa. But the chiefs refused to recruit men for the Native Military Corps of the Union's Defence Force. Between 1941 and 1943 ten thousand men were recruited instead into the African Pioneer Corps of the British army. They served in North Africa, in Italy, and as far north as Jugoslavia. They were divided into twenty-five companies along tribal lines, under the command of headmen as their sergeants and sergeant-

'Bechuana' and British military pioneers build a wooden bridge south of Castel del Rio in wartime Italy. High Commission Territories' troops also served as anti-aircraft gunners, smokescreen makers, camp guards and general labourers in Egypt, Libya, Tunisia, Jugoslavia and Syria. Troops from Nyasaland and Northern Rhodesia served in India and Burma.

majors, and colonial officials or settlers as their officers. The 'Bechuana' companies of the African Pioneer Corps were at first employed only as unarmed labourers. But in time they were trained as armed guards, anti-aircraft gunners, and as smokescreen-making units in battle. When the companies were disbanded in 1946, a thousand trained men joined in the short-lived High Commission Territories Corps in the Middle East. But the South African government protested against the training of 'armed natives' in neighbouring territories. The HCTC was disbanded in 1948, leaving the High Commission Territories without armies until after independence.

Indirect rule reforms A new resident commissioner, Charles Arden-Clarke (1937-42)*, persuaded Tshekedi Khama and Bathoen II to accept the 'indirect rule' reforms that they had previously resisted. They were persuaded that the reforms would merely improve the efficiency and financial control of the tribal administrations, which had been created by progressive chiefs over the previous fifty years. The 'indirect rule' proclamations began in 1938 by instituting tribal treasuries in each

*Later governor of the Gold Coast (1949-57), where he collaborated with Kwame Nkrumah in bringing the country to self-government and independence.

Chiefs as honorary whites (above) During the 1947 visit of British royalty to southern Africa, Bechuanaland chiefs Tshekedi (laughing), Molefi (near Tshekedi) and Bathoen II (with glasses), with their wives, were given the same food and service but were seated separately from whites (inside the marquee on the right).

Chiefs as bureaucrats (left) Tribal governments in the High Commission Territories carried the bulk of local administration. Bathoen II (ruled 1928-1969) pictured here in his tribal office at Kanye, 1955.

reserve. They were completed in 1943 when the powers of chiefs as 'native authorities' were defined, and chiefs' courts were recognized and their judgements recorded.

Tshekedi as strong ruler Encouraged by the colonial government, Tshekedi pushed ahead with development of the Ngwato reserve as soon as the war ended. He pushed his people by taxation and compulsory labour service, and by keeping headmen under strict control. The main resistance came from a Kalanga headman in the north of the Ngwato reserve, who eventually fled to exile in Southern Rhodesia. But a growing number of young educated Kalanga also began to press for Kalanga cultural and language rights within the Ngwato reserve and the Bechuanaland Protectorate.

Tshekedi Khama's greatest development project was the Bamangwato College, founded at Moeng in the Tswapong hills in 1947. It was intended to combine advanced agricultural and technical education with academic studies at secondary level. A compulsory cattle levy raised the sum of £100,000 which was spent on roads, buildings, and a dam, using compulsory labour from age-regiments.

Tshekedi-Seretse dispute Tshekedi, however,

was only a regent for his nephew Seretse Khama. Seretse went to England in 1945 for university education before returning to take up the chieftainship. In London he married an English woman, Ruth Williams, without previously consulting his uncle. Tshekedi tried to get the marriage dissolved. Seretse returned to explain his action in the town's *Kgotla*. At a first *Kgotla* meeting in November 1948, the Ngwato backed Tshekedi's view. By the time of a second *Kgotla,* young men had begun to speak up for Seretse's right to choose his own wife, as his uncle, his father and his grandfather had done before him. Seretse and Tshekedi exchanged bitter words in public, and Seretse flew back to his wife in London. He returned for a third *Kgotla* at Serowe in June 1949, when his succession to the chieftainship came into question rather than his marriage. The majority of people now turned against Tshekedi, accusing him of usurping the rightful chief. Seretse's right to the chieftainship and his marriage were now accepted. Tshekedi therefore resigned the regency and withdrew with his followers to the southern border of the reserve. Ruth Khama arrived from London and preparations were made to install Seretse as chief.

Both Seretse and Tshekedi Khama exiled
The British High Commissioner in Pretoria came under strong pressure from white settlers in South Africa and Southern Rhodesia to overrule the majority decision of the third *Kgotla*. The Union had just passed its Prohibition of Mixed Marriages Act, and Seretse Khama's marriage threatened the whole future of *apartheid* in separating black and white. Malan began to demand immediate incorporation of the High Commission Territories into the Union to stop the threat. Huggins in Southern Rhodesia added his voice to the protest. The British therefore tried to satisfy them by appointing a commission of enquiry at the end of 1949. Seretse was summoned to London by the British government in March 1950, and was told on arrival that he was banned from returning home. Tshekedi was also exiled from the Ngwato reserve. The Ngwato were left with-

out a chief. Seretse Khama sent his wife, still in Bechuanaland, a terse telegram summing up the situation:

TRIBE AND MYSELF TRICKED BY BRITISH GOVERNMENT AM BANNED FROM WHOLE PROTECTORATE LOVE SERETSE

For three years between 1950 and 1953 the Serowe district commissioner acted as the 'native authority,' i.e. paramount chief, of the Ngwato. The Ngwato boycotted meetings, in *Kgotla,* and booed their new 'chief'. Followers of Seretse and Tshekedi argued over the ownership of cattle. Old rivalries emerged between the headmen who sat on the tribal council ruling the reserve. Police from Southern Rhodesia, Basutoland and Swaziland were brought in to control the Ngwato. Serious riots broke out in Serowe (June 1952). Three policemen were killed, and five senior headmen were sentenced to three years imprisonment for incitement of the riots.

Tshekedi was allowed back into the Ngwato reserve towards the end of 1952. But the colonial authorities failed to persuade the Ngwato to elect another chief to replace Seretse. The chieftainship was declared vacant. Rasebolai Kgamane, a senior headmen and supporter of Tshekedi, was appointed acting 'native authority' in 1953, assisted by pro-Seretse, pro-Tshekedi, and neutral headmen. Seretse Khama remained in exile, living in London.

4 South West Africa and the United Nations (1939-54)

The League of Nations was always critical of South Africa for its administration of South West Africa. It was administered in the interests of its white settler population, rather than 'in the interests of the indigenous population' as required in the League of Nations mandate. The mandate system of the League of Nations then lapsed during the Second World War, and was replaced by the 'trusteeship' system of the United Nations in 1945.

Smuts made a determined effort to persuade the United Nations to allow the incorporation of South West Africa into the Union of South Africa as a new province. Chiefs and headmen were persuaded to sign documents petitioning for transfer of the territory to the Union. But the UN rejected this 'referendum'. Reports were received from Ovamboland and Okavango that chiefs had understood themselves to be petitioning for British rule to replace South African rule. The referendum also ignored hostile opinion among the Herero and Nama of the 'police zone'. The South African government replied to the UN's rejection by refusing to register South West Africa as a UN trusteeship territory. But' the South African Government declared itself bound to continue to observe 'the spirit of the Mandate', and submitted an annual report on conditions in the territory to the United Nations. By doing this it recognized the UN as the legal successor to the League of Nations.

Herero protest to the UN   Herero delegates attempted to reach the United Nations to petition for transfer of South West Africa to British or American rule. Smuts refused passports to the Herero delegates, claiming that he would represent their interests himself at the United Nations. Paramount chief Hosea Kutako of the Herero then contacted the chiefs of Bechuanaland, led by Tshekedi Khama, to present their view to the UN. The British stopped Tshekedi Khama from travelling to the United Nations in New York. So Tshekedi recruited a liberal English clergyman, Michael Scott, to record opinions in South West Africa and present them to the United Nations. Scott continued to present African opinion in South West Africa to the UN even after being banned from visiting the territory in 1947.

Effective annexation by South Africa   In 1948 the National Party government under Malan told the UN that the mandate over South West Africa had now lapsed. South Africa would no longer submit annual reports on the territory. South Africa began to treat South West Africa as its fifth province, by giving its white population representation in the South African parliament. The United Nations then challenged South Africa's

actions in the International Court of Justice. The court ruled (1950) that South Africa was still bound by the 1919 mandate, and must report to the UN as the League of Nations' successor. But South Africa refused to accept the court's ruling. In 1954 the African population of South West Africa was placed under the Union's Native Affairs Department.

Meanwhile South West Africa became increasingly important as an exporter of diamonds, copper and lead, fish, and karakul (black lamb) wool. The value of the territory's production and services (GDP) rose from £11 million in 1946 to £74 million in 1962. De Beers (part of the Anglo-American Corporation group) sifted sand for diamonds. The American-owned Tsumeb Corporation mined copper and lead in the north. West German capital began to move back into South West Africa. The territory proved increasingly valuable to South Africa as an earner of foreign exchange — needed for South Africa's imports of expensive Western electronic and chemical technology.

5 Swaziland and Lesotho in War and Peace (1940-53)

SWAZILAND was the only High Commission Territory in which a powerful white settler community existed side by side with a powerful African monarchy. But until the 1940s the Swaziland colonial administration was almost entirely concerned with white settler development, even borrowing from Basutoland to do so. The Second World War awakened British awareness of the importance of the African population in the colony. Swaziland would never become a 'white man's country' as many whites had expected. Monarchy and traditional allegiance would not simply die out under the impact of 'progress'. The Swazi were even resisting Western culture in clothing and religion.

The colonial authorities came to better terms with the previously suspicious or hostile leaders of the Swazi nation. But the authorities continued to think of Swaziland as divided between a 'modern' society, based on white

Young woman member of the Apostolic Sabbath Church of God – known as Vapostori or Vahosana in Southern Rhodesia, as Korsten Basket-makers in South Africa, and as 'Mazezelu' in Bechuanaland Founded by Shoniwa John Masowe in Mashonaland. in 1932, the Vapostori migrated to the Transvaal in 1943. After being expelled to Bechuanaland, they re-entered the Union and settled at Korsten near Port Elizabeth in 1947. Masowe insisted that all his followers become independent craftsmen: 'You are Israelites and should not work as slaves for non-Israelites.' Many became basket-makers and tin-smiths. Foreign born Vapostori were expelled from South Africa under the Group Areas Act in the later 1950s and early 1960s. They settled in Northern Rhodesia and Bechuanaland as well as in Southern Rhodesia, where the women are distinguished by their white dresses and headscarves.

enterprise and a 'traditional' society based on the monarchy. The 'traditional' society was encouraged to look after itself, while the 'modern' society was developed by the heaviest capital investment (per head of total population) of any British colony in Africa.

Swazi troops in the World War The Union Native Military Corps recruited Swazi to serve as labourers with South African forces overseas until 1941. Swazi troops then joined the African Pioneer Corps of the British army, alongside 'Basuto' and 'Bechuana' regiments in North Africa and the Middle East. Nearly four thousand Swazi were recruited. Some Swazi opposed help for the British war effort because of the land question, still a burning issue with both traditionalists and progressives. But the paramount chief argued that such help would remind Britain of its obligations to the Swazi, which Britain had neglected since the 1880s.

Land question and Lifa Fund In 1941 the paramount chief Sobhuza II and his *Libandla* (general assembly) renewed their efforts to regain land lost in 1907. The British responded in 1942-43 by buying up abandoned white farms for Swazi occupation, and by permitting Swazi as well as whites to purchase Crown Land (unsold state land). The paramount chief and *Libandla* organized the Lifa (i.e. 'inheritance') Fund, to buy back Crown or private land for the Swazi nation, using money from a levy in cash or cattle on all Swazi men. From 1946 onwards the British

Students at Fort Hare in the mid 1940s Seretse Khama (**left**), future president of the Republic of Botswana, and Charles Njonjo (**right**), future attorney-general of the Republic of Kenya. Fort Hare University College was founded in 1916 as an extension of Lovedale College.

sold Crown Land to individual Swazi owners, but after 1954 only to the Lifa Fund. Some Swazi, particularly commoner cattle owners, resented the Lifa Fund. They said it enriched chiefs with land, money and cattle, which were then kept by the chiefs' families or distributed to their favourites. But the Swazi nation increased its ownership of Swaziland from under 40 per cent to over 50 per cent of the country between the 1940s and 1960s.

'Indirect rule' reforms were imposed on Swaziland in 1950 after nine years of discussion. Proclamations based on the 1938 reforms in Basutoland were produced for discussion with the paramount chief and *Libandla*. But the *Native Administration Proclamation* of 1944 was withdrawn because of the paramount chief's protest. The proclamation had taken powers of appointing and dismissing chiefs from the paramount chief, and had given them to the resident commissioner. The 1950 *Native Administration (Consolidation) Proclamation* therefore gave these powers to the *Ngwenyama*-in-Libandla,* i.e. to the paramount chief and the *Libandla* together, subject to the resident commissioner's approval. Further proclamations of the same year gave the *Ngwenyama-in-Libandla* power to set up a Swazi National Treasury and courts of law. Since the *Libandla* met infrequently, and did not publish its proceedings, effective power was vested in the *Ngwenyama* and the 'standing committee' (*Liqoqo*) of the *Libandla* which met more frequently. The *Ngwenyama* of Swaziland emerged from 'indirect' rule' proclamations much stronger than the paramount chief of Basutoland or the chiefs of Bechuanaland.

In 1954 the *Ngwenyama-in-Libandla* strengthened his control over local chiefdoms within Swaziland by setting up *tinkudla,* meaning local centres of government. Each *nkudla* served as a meeting place for local members of *Libandla* (in theory all adult

men), under the chairmanship of a royal induna. The forty *tinkudla* across the country also became centres for social services, such as health clinics and schools.

Large-scale capitalist development Big business came to Swaziland in the late 1930s, when the Havelock asbestos mine was developed by a British mining firm, Turner & Newall. The mine became one of the five largest asbestos mines in the world, transporting its asbestos to Barberton in South Africa by a 21-kilometre overhead cableway. Further capital investment in Swaziland came from private South African capitalists, who bought up relatively cheap land from white settlers for large scale agricultural production. Johannesburg businessmen had bought ranches in the lowveld to supply the Rand market with winter-fed beef in the 1930s. Other businessmen began planting wood for eventual manufacture into boxwood and chipboard to be sold in South Africa. Forest planting began on the southern highveld in 1944. Peak Timbers around Piggs Peak was founded in 1947 on a much larger scale. Peak Timbers eventually covered 34,000 hectares of the northern highveld, and was then bought out by the Anglo-American Corporation.

The Colonial Development Corporation, a British state body, bought up 45,000 hectares of the central Swaziland highveld on either side of the Great Usutu valley. The land had previously been over-grazed and badly eroded by sheep brought from the Transvaal for winter grazing. Swazi peasants were evicted in 1948, and the area was cleared for planting the Usutu Forest, one of the largest man-made forests in Africa. The capital risk was high as it was fifteen years before the trees were ready for cropping. But the same conifer trees could take forty years to grow in colder climates, so potential profits were high.

BASUTOLAND Paramount chief Griffith Lerotholi of Basutoland died in 1939, after a reign of 26 years, leaving the succession in dispute between his two sons Seeiso and Bereng. Seeiso Griffith had been declared the

---

*Ngwenyama: traditional title, meaning 'the lion'. The term was acceptable to both the British, who refused to recognize any 'king' but their own, and to the Swazi who objected to 'paramount chief'.

heir in 1925, but his father had changed his mind and tried to make Bereng Griffith his heir instead. The disputed succession was settled by the Basutoland National Council, which declared Seeiso the paramount chief in 1939. Seeiso proved an energetic and progressive ruler, but died in the following year. The Basutoland National Council then decided to continue the family line of Seeiso against the counter-claims of Bereng Griffith. They appointed Seeiso's senior widow, Mantsebo, as regent for Bereng Seeiso (later Moshoeshoe II), Seeiso's infant son by another wife.

The regency of Mantsebo (1941-60) marks an important phase in Sotho political history. During that period constitutional monarchy emerged, subject to the control of chiefs and people.

The 'indirect rule' proclamations of 1938 took effect in the early 1940s. These further reduced the powers of minor chiefs. By 1946 only 122 local courts of justice in Basutoland were recognized, as compared with 1,300 recognized in 1938. The disputed succession to the paramountcy also enabled the Sons of Moshoeshoe (i.e. the greater chiefs descended from Moshoeshoe I), and educated progressives, to increase their political power in the Basutoland National Council. In 1944 the National Council demanded that the British should consult it equally with the regency. Both the regent and the high commissioner agreed to this. But the power of the major chiefs and the educated elite was checked in 1948, when nine district councils of smaller headmen were directly represented in the Basutoland National Council.

'Basuto' troops and Josiel Lefela Twenty thousand 'Basuto' served in the African Pioneer Corps during the Second World War, and many then joined the High Commission Territories Corps. One thousand died overseas. Josiel Lefela and his *Lekhotla la Bafo* opposed recruitment, because men were recruited as labourers and not given the dignity of being armed soldiers. Lefela and other *Lekhotla la Bafo* leaders were imprisoned for urging men not to serve in a white man's war. At the end of the war, Lefela was released and elected again to the Basutoland National Council, where he became the bitterest critic of the colonial administration.

Chieftainship and liretlo murders Lefela was imprisoned again in the late 1940s, for accusing the British of inventing evidence against various chiefs to convict them of *liretlo* ('medicine') murders. Such murders, previously rare, increased dramatically in the 1940s — three in 1941 and twenty by 1948, but declining thereafter. Chiefs who had lost political power, because of 'indirect rule' reforms or other causes, might turn to magic to regain it. The strongest medicine for such magic came from living human beings, like herdboys who disappeared in a storm. In 1949 Bereng Griffith himself was convicted and executed for *liretlo* murder.

Origins of Basutoland African Congress Despite Lefela's populism, which appealed to both traditionalism and radicalism, he never succeeded in making *Lekhotla la Bafo* a mass movement. Lefela was respected rather than followed by young radicals. One such radical was Ntsu Mokhehle, who joined *Lekhotla la Bafo* in 1942, and then became a member of the ANC Youth League when a student at Fort Hare in South Africa. On his return to Basutoland, he became president of the Basutoland Teachers' Association and in 1952 founded the *Basutoland African Congress,* which was closely modelled on the ANC of South Africa. James Moroka, as president of the ANC, opened the first annual meeting of the Basutoland African Congress; and Walter Sisulu as secretary of the ANC made frequent trips to Basutoland.

Questions

1   Why was the Federation of Rhodesia and Nyasaland (Central African Federation) formed? Why did it meet with so much opposition from African leaders? [Cambridge International School Certificate, 1979]

2 Did banishment from the Ngwato reserve make Botswana nationalists of both Tshekedi and Seretse Khama?

3 How successful was South Africa in incorporating South West Africa? (See also Chapter 19.)

4 Discuss the role of the 'Sons of Moshoeshoe' in the 20th century history of colonial Lesotho.

Activities

1 Discuss in the classroom why the Federation of Rhodesia and Nyasaland was set up despite African protests.

2 Imagine that you are living in one of the southern African colonies during the Second World War. How does the war affect you, and what do you think of it?

AFRICAN NATIONALISM IN CENTRAL AFRICA

1940   White miners' strike on the Copperbelt, winning a minimum wage of £60 a month, followed by African miners' strike demanding £12 a month. Seventeen African workers shot dead. Thereafter wages kept pace with wartime inflation of the cost of living.

1944   Nyasaland welfare societies (dating from 1912) met to form the *Nyasaland African Congress*, led by James Sangala with aid from K. T. Motsete of Bechuanaland and others.

1944   *Rhodesia Railways African Employees Association* (RRAEA) founded by Africans excluded from the powerful white railway union at Bulawayo and Livingstone. In 1945 RRAEA struck successfully for higher wages.

1945   5th Pan-African Congress held in Manchester, England, bringing together nationalist leaders of the next generation. Dr Hastings Kamuzu Banda of London represented the Nyasaland African Congress, which tried to persuade the ANC of South Africa to convene a 6th Congress in Africa.

1946   *Federation of African Societies of Northern Rhodesia* founded, led by Dauti Yamba — became the *Northern Rhodesia African Congress* in 1949.

1946   *Reformed Industrial and Commercial Workers Union* (RICU) founded — a revival of the old ICU for the expanding working class of Salisbury, led by Charles Mzingeli from Bulawayo.

1947   *African Voice Association* founded by Benjamin Burumbo to organize workers in Bulawayo, later extending to peasants. Around this time the old

Southern Rhodesia African National Congress was revived as a national association of nationalist groups and trade unions.

1948   *Northern Rhodesia African Mineworkers Union* (NRAMU) founded, led by Lawrence Katilungu, with aid from the British trades union congress.

1951   *Land Husbandry Act* of Southern Rhodesia, to give land rights to a few productive peasants and to oblige the majority to seek work in expanding urban-industrial areas. Opposition to the Act became the main focus of African nationalism in Southern Rhodesia during the early 1950s.

1951   *City Youth League* founded in Salisbury, led by George Nyandoro and James Chikerema, to attract political support from young workers flocking to town from rural areas.

1951-53   Alliance of Nyasaland, Northern Rhodesia and Southern Rhodesia African (National) Congresses against plans for federation of the three colonies. For the first time there were mass meetings which called for one-man-one-vote and majority rule. In Nyasaland leading chiefs joined Congress and were deposed by government. In Northern Rhodesia the African National Congress, under Harry Nkumbula, campaigned against racial discrimination by boycotting shops in Lusaka. In Southern Rhodesia an *All-African Convention* of nationalist parties and trade unions, formed to fight federation, dissolved when federation was imposed.

For references see p. 320.

Chapter 19
Apartheid and African Independence (1953–1968) I: South Africa – Union and Republic

The challenge of African nationalism was answered in South Africa by the *apartheid* programme of Afrikaner nationalists. *Apartheid* was intended to make white supremacy permanent. In response, African nationalism itself began to undergo changes in South Africa. Mass protests and passive resistance were met by even firmer police repression. African nationalism was forced underground, and turned towards plans for armed revolution.

1 Consolidation of Apartheid Laws (1953-59)

The National Party of South Africa won the 1953 general elections, with an increased majority of members of parliament. The government's firm action against the ANC's Defiance Campaign had won it much support from the white electorate. Its *apartheid* programme could now go ahead without effective parliamentary opposition. In 1954 the aged Malan was replaced as prime minister by J.G. Strijdom, the leader of the Transvaal branch of the National Party. Strijdom was a blunt and uncompromising supporter of the *apartheid* laws. These were pushed through parliament by his deputy Hendrik Verwoerd, the minister of Native Affairs (soon renamed Bantu Affairs).

The *Separate Representation of Voters bill,* to eliminate coloured voters from white constituencies, was reintroduced into parliament in 1954, three years after the supreme court

had declared it illegal. When it failed again to achieve a two-thirds majority of the two houses of parliament sitting together, Strijdom pushed through the *Senate Act* in 1955. The Senate Act allowed government to appoint more senators, to give it a certain two-thirds majority in parliament. The Separate Representation of Voters bill was then reintroduced for a third time, and passed with a two-thirds majority. Meanwhile Strijdom had appointed pro-government judges to the supreme court. When the law was challenged as unconstitutional, eleven out of twelve supreme court judges ruled in the government's favour. Finally, in 1958, the Senate Act was withdrawn because it had fulfilled its function.

Strijdom's great personal ambition was to make South Africa into a republic and to remove the last remains of British sovereignty by replacing the governor-general (representative of the British queen) by a state president. In 1957 Strijdom banned the flying of the British flag and the singing of 'God Save the Queen' on official occasions. But he died in 1958 before he achieved his final goal of a republic.

Apartheid laws, 1953-59 Between 1953 and 1959 Verwoerd continued to introduce the long and complex series of *apartheid* laws. As he had told the Senate in 1952, 'the various Acts, Bills and also public statements I have made all fit into a pattern, and together form a single constructive plan.'

Following the recommendations of the

Eiselen Report (1951), Verwoerd introduced a bill in 1953 to remove black education from missionary control to that of the Native Affairs Department. As he put it:

'I will reform it [black education] so that Natives will be taught from childhood to realize that equality with Europeans is not for them.'

Verwoerd attacked the liberalism of missionary education, which gave black children ideas of growing up to live in a world of equal rights between black and white. He later explained to the Senate that there was 'no place' for blacks outside the reserves 'above the level of certain forms of labour'. So, 'What is the use of teaching a Bantu child mathematics when he cannot use it in practice?' He added: 'Education must train and teach people in accordance with their opportunities in life.'

The *Bantu Education Act* (1953) was put into operation in April 1955. Only two major churches continued to run state-assisted missionary schools, the Dutch Reformed Church and the Swedish Lutheran mission. The other major churches refused to accept government conditions, including new Bantu Education syllabuses and other controls on teaching, in return for continued state financial aid. Some mission schools were sold or leased to the government. Some closed down. Others, particularly Catholic schools, tried to keep going on school fees and mission funds alone. Among famous mission schools, Adams College in Zululand closed down completely; Tiger Kloof in the northern Cape was leased to government, and was later re-founded as Moeding College in Bechuanaland; St Peter's at Rosettenville in Johannesburg became a whites-only school, but was re-founded as Waterford/Kahlamba in Swaziland.

Black schools no longer studied the same syllabuses as non-black schools, but followed new Bantu Education syllabuses based on officially recognized Bantu languages. English, which had been the most common medium of instruction, was stopped in primary schools and limited in secondary schools. The Bantu Affairs Department had to approve teachers, and also controlled the local school boards —

consisting of parents and officials — which managed the everyday running of schools.

Widespread boycotts by pupils and teachers developed the day that Bantu Education came into effect, 25th April 1955. Seven thousand pupils and one hundred and sixteen teachers were dismissed. The government later passed similar laws to control Indian and coloured education.

The *Extension of University Education Act* of 1957 closed undergraduate classes at white universities to non-whites. Instead, non-white 'tribal' university colleges were created to take University of South Africa degrees and diplomas. In addition to Fort Hare, which was now reserved for Xhosa, new colleges were opened at Turfloop (Tswana/Sotho), Durban-Westville (Indian), Capetown-Bellville (Coloured), and Ngoye (Zulu). After many protests, the Act came into force in 1959. Most lecturers at Fort Hare resigned, including its African vice-principal Z.K. Matthews. Within a few years, only one or two of the original lecturers remained. The five non-white colleges were in future staffed largely by Afrikaans-speaking white lecturers.

1956 ANC Bus Boycott Policeman checking the pass of a cyclist travelling from a Johannesburg township towards the city before dawn. Police harassed people who walked or cycled instead of taking a bus.

Population removals under apartheid Verwoerd was emphatic that 'South Africa is a white man's country and he must remain the master here', and that 'the urban Bantu are visitors in the white areas . . . for their own economic benefit'. Two laws of 1954 laid down Verwoerd's *apartheid* policy for both white farms and urban areas. The *Native Tenant and Land Amendment (Squatters) Act* made it clear that no adult blacks could live on white farms, even for rent, except as labourers, and must leave when no longer labouring. The *Natives Resettlement (Western Areas) Act* led to the removal of the shanty towns and black suburbs of western Johannesburg, and their replacement by the new location-city known as 'South Western Townships' — Soweto for short.

Between 1954 and 1956 blacks were removed from the Sophiatown suburb and the old Western Native Township, to be resettled in Soweto. Sophiatown became a white suburb called Triomf. Western Township (Martindale and Newclare) was reserved for coloureds. The move from Sophiatown was immortalised by its people in the popular song 'Meadowlands', named after the location in Soweto in which they were re-settled. Meanwhile black families from Alexandra, an eastern suburb of Johannesburg, were gradually re-settled in the Diepkloof location of Soweto. What remained of Alexandra was to consist of 'bachelor' hostels only.

Soweto was laid out as a large grid of unpaved roads around Orlando and Moroka. Small, almost identical, one-storey houses replaced shanties and spread in regular rows over rolling countryside as far as the eye could see. Like other townships there was no electricity for light or heating, and a heavy pall of coal smoke hung over it in the early morning and evening. Construction was financed by the Johannesburg city council from rents paid by Africans. But control of Soweto was put in the hands of the Bantu Affairs Department. Like other townships built or re-built in South Africa during the 1950s, Soweto was designed with bus routes and railways to serve the 'white' city with its labour force during the day. At night people returned home squeezed into buses and trains.

Verwoerd's vision of the apartheid future Verwoerd recognized that expanding industries in 'white areas' needed an expanding black labour force. But he predicted that black urban population would begin to fall in the late 1970s, by which time *apartheid* would have succeeded in developing the black rural reserves as alternative areas of employment. Verwoerd saw total separation between white and black societies as the final aim of *apartheid*. Black labour in white society was like 'donkeys, oxen and tractors', which could someday be replaced by other machinery.

Bantustans and the Tomlinson Report The Tomlinson Commission, set up in 1952, reported on the development of black reserves in 1955. The report was so long that only a summary was published. It concluded that the reserves, which provided a living for only one-fifth of South Africa's black population, could provide a living for one half of the black population if agriculture were properly developed — and for even more if all the extra land 'released' by the 1936 Land Act were added to the reserves. So the first priority in developing the reserves had to be agriculture. Productive tenant farmers should be encouraged to develop along capitalist lines, and the state should run plantations of sugar, timber, etc. The second priority of development was to be trade, mining and industry, to give jobs to black labour at present only employable in the 'white areas'. Outside private capital would finance plantations, mines and industries through a state development corporation, modelled on Britain's Colonial Development Corporation (already active in Swaziland).

The Tomlinson Report took the idea of developing the reserves' economic potential too far for the South African government's liking. The government rejected any economic independence for the reserves, limiting them to subsistence agriculture. The reserves would not be allowed to compete for capital or labour with the white areas. There therefore could be no capitalist class of black farmers based on individual tenure of land. White-owned private capital should not be invested in the reserves, but should stay within the white areas on the edge of black reserves — so-called 'border industries'. The government was in no hurry to set up the Bantu Development Corporation either. Tomlinson's plans for the government to spend £104 million on the reserves over the next ten years were shelved. But all the same the Tomlinson Report became the basis of Verwoerd's plans to develop what were known as 'Bantustans'.

Bantustans and the High Commission Territories The Tomlinson Report treated the British colonies of Basutoland, Bechuanaland and Swaziland as an essential part of its plans for the future. By including them as part of the Union, the thirteen per cent of South Africa which had been promised to blacks by the 1936 Land Act, would be increased to forty-five per cent. Between 1955 and 1959 the South African government shifted from demanding incorporation towards seeing the three protectorates, together with the Transkei, as model Bantustans.

The 1959 *Promotion of Bantu Self-Government Act* provided for the separating of eight Bantustans (or 'Bantu Homelands') from white South Africa as self-governing states. Every black person in South Africa was to become a citizen of one of these states. The 1959 law abolished white representatives for 'natives' sitting in parliament, because blacks were in future to have their own governments. There would be no black South African citizens. Instead there would be a South African commonwealth of Bantustans under South African leadership. As Verwoerd said, 'Britain never contended that her [Commonwealth] territories should be represented in her parliament' — and neither should South Africa.

2 Rural and Urban Resistance to Apartheid (1953-59)

The South African colonial system was based on rural reserves as labour pools for 'white' farms and industries, and as dumping-grounds for discarded black labour. Peasant production

collapsed to below subsistence level, except for a few fortunate farmers who were usually of chiefly origins. Rural families had to rely on migrant workers sending cash home. Over-cultivation of the soils, and over-stocking of unsaleable cattle on limited pastures, led to erosion and blight. One simple solution was to increase the area of the reserves to catch up with the growth of population. Another solution lay in changing the nature of the South African colonial system. But under *apartheid* the government was committed to both the old colonial system and to making the reserves viable as Bantustans.

To make the reserves viable, government tried to make them more efficient in agriculture and administration. The South African government began to enforce laws strictly to reduce the number of cattle, and to improve their quality by dipping them in anti-tick disinfectant — at the expense of their owners. To improve administration the government passed the *Native Authorities Act* in 1951 (replacing a law of 1927). The Act was enforced, together with other *apartheid* laws, in reserve after reserve, starting in the north and working southward. Between 1953 and 1959 the 324 'tribal authorities' outside the Transkei were organized in the reserves under sixteen 'regional authorities'. The Transkei already had twenty-six 'district authorities' under one 'territorial authority', i.e. the old *Bunga* (house of assembly). The 1959 Promotion of Bantu Self-Government Act gave similar 'territorial authorities' for the seven other Bantustans.

Like the earlier 'indirect rule' proclamations in the High Commission Territories, the Native Authorities Act was bitterly resisted, because it turned chiefs into junior civil servants who had to carry out government policies efficiently or be dismissed.

Peasant revolts in the Bantustans Rural protests against government tended to grow strongest at times of economic depression. During partial depressions there was less money coming from men in towns; during greater depression unemployed men returned to their rural homes. The 'peasant revolts' of

RURAL APARTHEID

Zulu authorities pay tribute to the Minister of Bantu Affairs, M.D.C. de Wet Nel, with the gift of an enormous leopardskin rug. The minister represented the governor-general, 'supreme chief' of all Bantu authorities. Paramount Chief (later King) Goodwill Zwelithini (in uniform) presents the rug; Gatsha Bukthelezi (dark glasses) stands behind.

rural South Africa around 1950 and 1956-60 came at times of partial depression between economic booms. The 'revolts' usually began as non-violent boycotts of government activities. Outbreaks of rural resistance occurred at the same time as urban resistance, though the ANC based in the towns had little hand in organizing these 'peasant revolts'.

One form of revolt was against loss of land to government agricultural schemes. Around 1950 the government took drastic action to prevent erosion in the over-crowded reserves of the Drakensberg, where it threatened to destroy the sponges from which major rivers flowed. The Qwaqwa (Kwa-Kwa) Sotho of the tiny Witziehoek reserve in the mountains tore down the new fences, which stopped their cattle from grazing on the sponges. The police were brought in: fourteen Qwaqwa were shot dead and two policemen killed. In 1956, again as part of the anti-erosion scheme, the Mamathola of the northern Drakensberg near Tzaneen were removed fifty kilometres to the lowveld, so that their old reserve could be planted with a forest. The Mamathola resisted and their chief was deposed.

Other 'revolts' were aimed at rural *apartheid* laws. In 1957 peasants in the Tswana areas of the south-western Transvaal protested against women being forced to buy pass books, under

the terms of the so-called Natives Abolition of Passes Act. The Act had already met strong resistance in the towns from the ANC Women's League. At Lichtenburg, four men in a bus queue were shot dead when they threw stones at police attacking women demonstrators with sticks. In the Hurutshe reserve, women boycotted pass book registration and burnt pass books that had been bought. Chief Abram Moiloa was deposed by government, and many families fled into neighbouring Bechuanaland to escape riot police.

In the Pedi reserve (Sekhukhuneland) of the eastern Transvaal there were violent riots in 1958 when government interfered in a chieftainship dispute. In Pondoland (eastern Transkei) a 'peasant revolt' between 1957 and 1960, which began with a chieftainship dispute under the Native Authorities Act, became general resistance against *apartheid* laws with ANC support. The revolt reached its climax after attacks on government collaborators ('stooges'). Riot police and aircraft attacked the rebel stronghold on Ngquza Hill. More than eleven Mpondo were killed in the battle (1960).

'BANTU AREAS ' AND 'REMOVALS'   Main Bantu reserve areas in the Tomlinson Report 1955, and subsequent population removals from white farms and 'black spots' in white areas.

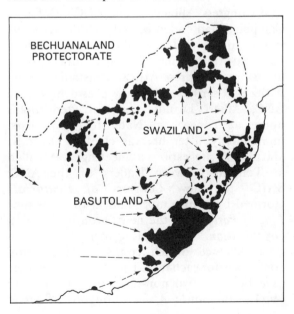

Congress of the People, held at Kliptown near Johannesburg in 1955 ANC members were joined by delegates from sympathetic coloured, Indian and white organizations. The meeting adopted a 'Freedom Charter', laying out plans for a future free South African state.

The Congress Alliance The ANC's Defiance Campaign had ended in early 1953, after the arrest of its leaders. The South African government determined to use police power in future to repress African resistance before it became serious. The new president of the ANC, Albert Luthuli, was restricted to his home at Tongaat in Natal for two years, immediately after he was elected. On Z.K. Matthews' suggestion a meeting was called at Tongaat between leaders of the ANC, SAIC, the new *Congress of Democrats* (formed by whites more radical than the new *Liberal Party*) and the new *Coloured People's Organization*. This meeting formed the Congress Alliance, which consisted of separate congresses for each race. The Congress Alliance gave birth to two non-racial organizations in 1954 — the *South African Congress of Trade Unions* and the *Federation of South African Women.*

Congress of the People and Freedom Charter The Congress Alliance convened a national convention of its members on 26th June 1955 on open ground outside Kliptown, just south of Johannesburg. This 'Congress of the People' was attended by nearly three thousand people of all races. It was chaired by the Congress of Democrats' president, a white Afrikaner, as he was the only Congress Alliance leader not banned by the police before the convention. It adopted a 'Freedom Charter' as the guidelines for a future non-racial South African constitution. The charter called for equal legal rights for all, based on the UN's Declaration of Human Rights. It added socialist goals, such as one that 'the mineral wealth beneath the soil, the banks and monopoly industry shall be transferred to the ownership of the people as a whole'.

Albert Luthuli (1898-1967) President of the ANC from 1952 until his death. Temporarily released from rural restriction in 1961 to fly overseas and receive the Nobel Peace Prize. In this photograph he is garlanded with flowers.

The Freedom Charter was written in English, seSotho and isiXhosa. Each congress party then had to approve it. Within the ANC the charter was opposed by the group calling itself the Africanist Watchdog Committee, formed by Sobukwe and Mda to keep alive the ideas of Lembede. They argued that the charter betrayed the principles of the Youth League Manifesto and Programme of Action, which sought a primarily African state based on black majority power. The Freedom Charter looked to a multi-national state, in which the non-black minorities would have equal rights with the black majority. The Africanists argued that the Freedom Charter would therefore perpetuate non-black domination of South African politics and culture.

ANC's Women's League 1956 saw an upsurge of the ANC Women's League, led by Lillian Ngoyi, against the requirement for women to carry pass books. Up to 20,000 women protested peacefully on the lawns outside the main government offices in Pretoria, singing 'Strijdom, you have struck a rock once you have touched a woman'.

Treason Trial of Congress leaders The rise of protest against *apartheid* laws led the South African government to arrest Congress Alliance leaders for plotting revolution against the state. The 'Treason Trial' began with the arrest of 156 men and women in December 1956, and ended when the last thirty were acquitted in March 1961. Oswald Pirow was brought out of retirement to head the prosecution. Bram Fischer (secret head of the SACP) joined the defence team of lawyers. Despite the huge amount of evidence acquired by police raids on Congress Alliance offices, the prosecution failed to prove its case against any of the accused. In August 1958, the remaining ninety-one accused were put on bail, and were required to attend the court every day from their homes rather than from jail. It was clear that the prosecution was incompetent. ANC protest campaigns began afresh, but differences between Charterists (supporters of the Freedom Charter) and

Leaders of the Pan-Africanist Congress in 1959
Right: Robert Mangaliso Sobukwe (1924-1978), the national president. **Left:** Potlako K. Leballo (1924 –), the national secretary.

Africanists became more acute.

Pan-Africanist Congress splits from ANC At the 1956 and 1957 annual meetings of the ANC the Africanists blocked ANC approval of the Freedom Charter. At the November 1958 annual meeting the Charterists pushed approval through. A hundred Africanists, led by Sobukwe, walked out of the ANC, although they still claimed that they were the true followers of ANC policy from 1912 up to the Congress Alliance. On 6th April 1959, the Pan-Africanist Congress (PAC) was founded, with Sobukwe as its president, Leballo as its secretary, and an executive composed of former ANC Youth Leaguers.

Sobukwe, like Lembede and Seme, called on Africans to draw courage from a glorious pre-colonial history — 'to free Africans from the [colonial] inferiority complex which keeps them in chains'. He also called on black South Africans to look north to the rest of the continent where European rule was in retreat. The PAC flag had a gold star on it, to symbolize newly independent Ghana shining on the rest of Africa.

Toivo Herman Ja Toivo, who helped found the South West African People's Organization in 1959 together with Sam Nujoma.

PAC grew rapidly, building upon the widespread grievance among Africans against *apartheid* laws. It recruited 25,000 members in its first four months. PAC particularly recruited migrant workers, who then took PAC ideas back to the rural areas. Sobukwe believed that 'the primary task of liberation' must be to bring political awareness to these illiterate or semi-literate masses.

3 Apartheid Extends to South West Africa (1954-68)

South Africa effectively ruled South West Africa as its fifth province, without United Nations recognition. South Africa had with-

drawn from the trusteeship committee of the UN. But it was persuaded to rejoin in 1957 for negotiations over South West Africa with Charles Arden-Clarke as UN negotiator. The negotiations failed and the UN returned to active condemnation of South African administration in 1959.

Resistance to South African rule Riots broke out in Windhoek in 1959 over the extension of urban *apartheid* to South West Africa. The Bantu Affairs Department destroyed the old location close to Windhoek. People were then resettled in a new location remote from the city, sub-divided into 'tribal' zones, called Katatura township. People protested against this move, and police opened fire on demonstrators, killing eleven before the bulldozers flattened homes.

Rising political consciousness resulted in the founding of the South West African People's Organization (SWAPO) in Capetown during 1959. Toivo Ja Toivo and Sam Nujoma organized migrant workers from South West Africa into SWAPO, which then spread back home. The South West African National Union (SWANU) was founded inside South West Africa in 1962, and a political party organized by the Herero tribal council under Clemens Kapuuo tried to extend itself to Ovamboland and Okavango in 1964. But all nationalist parties were limited by strict government controls between reserves. SWAPO remained strongest in the north, SWANU in the centre, and small tribal parties developed in the south.

Ethiopia and Liberia challenge South Africa The news of riots in South West Africa moved the second conference of independent African states, held at Addis Ababa in 1960, into action. Ethiopia and Liberia, as the only two African members of the former League of Nations apart from South Africa, challenged South Africa's right to administer South West Africa in the International Court of Justice. The case dragged on for eight years. Lawyers for Ethiopia, Liberia, and South Africa presented their arguments and evidence at great length before fifteen judges. Proceedings were eventually stopped in 1968, when a pro-South African judge sat as president of the court and ruled that Ethiopia and Liberia had no right to be there.

Apartheid plans for South West Africa Meanwhile the trusteeship committee of the United Nations tried several times to prevent the extension of *apartheid* to South West Africa. In 1964 the South African government published its Odendaal Report, which laid out a master-plan for rural *apartheid* in South West Africa along the lines of the Tomlinson Report in South Africa. The report recommended that eleven tribal reserves should be increased in area by fifty per cent, and should then become self-governing 'homelands'. (African reserves constituted twenty-five per cent of the territory, and white farms forty-eight per cent: the remaining areas were nature and mining reserves.)

Guerrilla war begins When the United Nations failed to find a solution, SWAPO began to plan an independent state to be called Namibia, and turned to guerrilla warfare in 1966. SWAPO guerrillas from Zambia clashed with South African forces in the Caprivi Strip during 1967-68. SWAPO leaders in Windhoek were arrested, though the party was not banned. Toivo Ja Toivo admitted to assisting the guerrilla struggle: 'I am a loyal Namibian . . . only when we are granted our independence will the struggle stop. Only when our human dignity is restored to us, as equals of the whites, will there be peace between us.' He was sentenced to twenty years in prison.

UN Council for Namibia In October 1966 the General Assembly of the United Nations passed a resolution ending South Africa's League of Nations mandate over South West Africa. The UN then appointed a Council for Namibia, as a sort of government-in-exile made up of UN officials. But leading Western members of the UN, who sat on the Security Council of the UN, at first refused to recognize the UN General Assembly's resolution. The Security Council later confirmed the

1966 General Assembly resolution in 1968. But the Western powers still did not support active de-colonization of Namibia.

4 The Victory of White Supremacy in South Africa (1960-68)

1960, 'the year of Africa', brought confrontation to the boil between African nationalism and white supremacy in South Africa. With African discontent rising in both urban and rural areas, the ANC and PAC competed with each other in militant but peaceful boycotts and deliberate breaking of unjust laws.

Verwoerd's plans for a republic and 'commonwealth' Hendrik Verwoerd had become prime minister on the death of J.G. Strijdom in 1958. He announced that South Africa would become a republic. He split the old Native Affairs Department into two — the Department of Bantu Administration and Development (BAD) and the Bantu Education Department (BED). The term *apartheid* was no longer used officially, but replaced by 'separate development'. The Promotion of Bantu Self-Government Act of 1959 then paved the way for the creation of 'independent' Bantustans and a South African-led 'commonwealth'.

The wind of change ANC and PAC were encouraged by *uhuru* (freedom) in other African states to press more strongly for freedom in South Africa. In January 1960 rioters, carrying on the protests of many months against liquor and beer laws, killed nine policemen in Cato Manor township outside Durban. In February the British prime minister, Harold Macmillan, warned white South Africa of the strength of this African nationalism in his 'wind of change' speech to the South African parliament in Capetown.

Pass laws protest: Sharpeville massacre The ANC announced plans for an anti-pass campaign to begin on March 31st. The PAC announced an anti-pass campaign to begin ten days earlier, March 21st. PAC told people

1. *March 21st:* PAC members begin to burn their pass books.

2. *Sharpeville township:* PAC demonstrators suround the police station, most standing round its main west gate (left).

1

3. Police reinforcements arrive and, fearing the fence will collapse under the weight of the crowd, start to fire on people at the west gate. This photograph, taken on the north side, shows people on other sides of the fence beginning to flee after the police, standing on armoured vehicles, had fired on the west gate.

4. Two policemen come out of the west gate to view the dead. The crowd has retreated down a road to the south. Official casualty figures were 67 dead, 186 wounded.

5. *March 30th:* Capetown PAC leader Philip Kgosana leads a march to demand release of detained Transvaal PAC leaders. He is arrested.

6. *April 9th:* Prime Minister Hendrik Verwoerd is shot twice in the head by a white farmer, when opening the Rand Easter Show. In this dramatic photograph, Verwoerd clasps his blood-stained hands to the temples where he has been shot. He survived the assassination attempt.

2

5

3

4

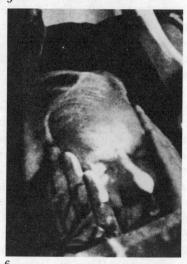

6

to gather outside police stations on that day, to burn their pass books and then to demand to be arrested. At Orlando the demonstration went according to plan, and Sobukwe and others were arrested. At Sharpeville township near Vereeniging, and at Langa and Nyanga townships outside Capetown, large crowds of up to ten thousand people gathered outside police stations. They had been told that the police might announce changes in the pass laws. At Sharpeville police opened fire, killing 69 people. At Langa and Nyanga police opened fire, killing five. That night rioters attacked and burnt down Bantu Administration buildings and Bantu Education schools in Langa.

International repercussions The Sharpeville massacre resulted in strong international condemnation, not only by the UN but by South Africa's western allies and the world's press. Multinational companies, which had invested large sums in South African mining and manufacturing, withdrew capital or refused to invest more, because they feared revolution in South Africa. It is estimated that in the year after Sharpeville £6 million worth of foreign capital was withdrawn every month from South Africa. By the end of 1960 this was hurting the economy, and the South African government was desperate to end the threat of revolution.

ANC and PAC banned ANC responded to the Sharpeville massacre by calling for a national day of mourning, meaning a stay-at-home strike on the day of the victims' funerals, March 28th. On the same day the government announced it would ban both ANC and PAC. ANC sent Oliver Tambo secretly abroad through Bechuanaland to head an ANC wing in exile. PAC sent out Peter Raboroko. On March 30th the government declared a temporary country-wide 'state of emergency', and began to arrest thousands of ANC and PAC members. There were mass protests in Durban and Capetown. In Capetown Philip Kgosana of the PAC led 30,000 people to see the minister of justice. When they arrived, Kgosana was arrested.

Verwoerd survives assassination attempt On April 8th the permanent ban on ANC and PAC as 'unlawful organizations' became effective. On April 9th Verwoerd was shot by an English-speaking white farmer.

When Verwoerd recovered six weeks later, he announced that 'separate development' would go ahead as the answer to communist-inspired revolution. To gain African approval, he promised to increase the responsibilities of Bantu Authorities in local government, and to abolish the prohibition on blacks buying wines and spirits. But he insisted that black wages could not be improved; wages must already be good, he claimed, to have attracted so many migrants from outside the Union. And, Verwoerd argued: 'Protection by a greatly increased police force within the Bantu residential area is essential.'

South Africa leaves the Commonwealth In October 1960 a referendum was held for the white electorate to decide if South Africa should become a republic. Fifty-two per cent voted 'Yes', against forty-seven per cent who voted 'No'. In March 1961 Verwoerd attended the Commonwealth prime ministers conference in London. He applied for South Africa to remain within the Commonwealth as a republic. India, Ghana and even Canada, protested so strongly that he withdrew the application. In effect South Africa had been expelled from the Commonwealth for its racist policies. On May 31st, 1961, South Africa became a republic outside the Commonwealth.

Police repression of African resistance In March 1961 the remains of the Congress Alliance (without the banned ANC) convened an All-In African Conference at Pietermaritzburg. They wanted to set up a new united political party to oppose the *apartheid* republic. But the conference was boycotted by Africanists (supporters of the banned PAC) and by Liberals and the *Progressive Party* that had split off from the United Party in 1959. The conference called for a general strike on May 31st, to be organized by Mandela, Sisulu and Kotane of the banned

ANC. But in May government declared a permanent country-wide 'state of emergency', and arrested up to 10,000 people.

The South African government decided to build a police force so powerful that it would smash any African resistance movement, before it had a chance to gain mass support. The Special Branch of the police was organized as a secret political police force, and trained by the French in the ruthless methods which they had used in Algeria. The police Gun Squad was strengthened to ensure that fire-arms did not cross the borders to reach blacks in rural or urban areas. All policemen were given extensive powers to arrest and detain suspects under the 'state of emergency', and later under new security laws.

ANC and PAC found military wings In June 1961 the internal and external wings of the ANC met secretly at Lobatse in Bechuanaland. The ANC organized itself into an underground political party, and into a military organiza-

tion called *Umkhonto we Sizwe* (spear of the nation). The high command of *Umkhonto,* under Nelson Mandela, worked from a large house in the northern Johannesburg suburb of Rivonia. From there they maintained contact with regional, area, and local groups. Recruits were sent overseas for guerrilla training. *Umkhonto* began to sabotage non-human targets, such as electric power-lines and bridges, from December 1961.

An underground movement called *Poqo** was formed out of PAC ranks while PAC leaders were still in jail. When Leballo was released from jail in 1961, he attempted to organize *Poqo* from Maseru in Basutoland. Recruits were sent abroad from guerrilla training, while *Poqo* led armed risings during 1962-63 in the Transkei and around Capetown, attacking both human and non-human targets.

*Meaning 'alone' or 'pure' as in *Um-Afrique Poqo:* 'Africa alone!'

Nelson Mandela (1918 –) and Walter Sisulu (1912 –) in the courtyard of Robben Island prison, 1966 Note the warder and other prisoners, with blocks of stone for chiselling, in the background. This was the last photo of Mandela available until 1990 when he was released.

The police station and shops in the centre of Paarl, near Capetown, were attacked with firearms and burnt down. In the Transkei the police claimed that *Poqo* had assassinated seventeen chiefs and headmen and had murdered white tourists. Late in 1963 the British colonial police in Basutoland raided Leballo's offices in Maseru, and handed over a PAC membership list to the South African police. Five thousand PAC members were detained and *Poqo*'s power was broken.

Rivonia trial of Congress leaders The South African police captured Mandela in August 1962. In July 1963, police discovered and raided the Rivonia headquarters, capturing seventeen of the remaining nineteen members of the *Umkhonto* high command. The 'Rivonia trial' lasted from December 1963 until June 1964. Police had discovered a plan for armed revolution at Rivonia, called 'Operation Mayebuye', which had been presented by the South African Communist Party to *Umkhonto* for discussion. The revolution would start with attacks on towns from the Transkei and near the Bechuanaland border. 'Operation Mayebuye' had not yet been adopted by *Umkhonto,* but two communists, the black John Marks and the white Joe Slovo, had already gone overseas to prepare for it.

Mandela, Sisulu, Mbeki and the other accused were sentenced to life imprisonment on Robben Island for sabotage. The *Umkhonto* high command was re-founded by Wilton Mkwayi (who had escaped arrest at Rivonia), in cooperation with the SACP under Fischer, who also led the defence team of lawyers at the Rivonia trial. The police discovered and arrested *Umkhonto*/SACP leaders in 1964. Mkwayi was sentenced to life imprisonment. Fischer escaped and reformed *Umkhonto*/SACP high command once again. But he was also arrested and imprisoned for life in 1965.

African Resistance Movement A third sabotage organization called the African Resistance Movement was formed by radical students and intellectuals in English-speaking white university cities. Seventy members, of whom six were coloured and the rest white, blew up electricity pylons and railway signal-boxes between 1961 and 1964. Police arrested its leaders in 1964. One member was executed for placing a bomb in Johannesburg railway station which killed a white woman.

House arrest and detentions By 1965 all revolutionary movements in South Africa had been suppressed by the security police, and by the strengthened powers of the ministry of justice and police. The security police was headed by Hendrik van der Berghe. His former colleague in the Ossewa-Brandwag, B.J. Vorster had become minister of justice and police in 1961. Over the next few years Vorster gained enormous powers under the new security laws. The minister banned over a hundred people from public life in 1962, and started 'house-arrest' to keep banned people at home all day and night. In 1963 the minister was given the right to detain any individual without trial, in solitary confinement for up to ninety days, without having to give reasons to the public for doing so. Over two hundred people were detained in 1963, and over eight hundred and fifty in 1964, under this law. In 1965 the period of detention was extended up to one hundred and eighty days. A special law was passed to keep the PAC leader Robert Sobukwe in prison indefinitely.

Economic recovery boom In 1961 the South African government imposed banking and currency controls to stop capital being taken out of the country. Export production was stepped up to bring in more foreign exchange. Then between 1965 and 1970 there was 'a massive and somewhat unexpected inflow of foreign capital', amounting to R1,566 million.* The South African economy grew at one of the fastest rates in the world. South Africa gained renewed confidence in its economic and political role in Africa. The economic boom meant fuller employment for

*R2 = £1 from 1962 when the Rand was adopted as South African currency until 1967 when the British pound was devalued to R1.68.

Africans, but the colour-bar prevented any significant rise in wages and kept Africans from becoming skilled workers. The South African government preferred to recruit skilled labour from abroad by bringing in white immigrants.

Assassination of Verwoerd In September 1966 Verwoerd was stabbed to death in the parliament building at Capetown. His murderer, Demetrio Tsafendas, was a Mozambican Greek immigrant to South Africa, of partial African ancestry, with a history of mental illness. When asked why he did it, Tsafendas replied: 'I don't know. I can't explain. It is complex, frustrations, you know.'

Apartheid's apparent triumph Vorster replaced Verwoerd as prime minister, promising to 'go further along the road which Dr Verwoerd followed'. Internally this meant the encouragement of Bantustans, notably the Transkei. Externally this meant improved relations with black African states, which had started when Verwoerd met the new prime minister of Basutoland, and continued with the opening of diplomatic relations by Vorster with Malawi in 1967. Attempts by the United Nations to end South African rule in South West Africa were rejected. Good business relations with the USA, West Germany, France and Japan were encouraged, as well as with Britain — the traditional home of multinational companies operating in South Africa.

Anti-*apartheid* movements at home and abroad were muted by South Africa's apparent peace and prosperity in the later 1960s. But there was no weakening of *apartheid* or police control in South Africa. Besides the police, the defence budget steadily increased — from R38.5 million in 1960 to R230 million in 1966 to R1,350 million in 1970. South African military forces were sent in strength to the Caprivi Strip and to the Zambezi border of (Southern) Rhodesia, where the first incursions of SWAPO, ZAPU and ANC's *Umkhonto* guerrillas occurred in 1967. Within South Africa itself virtually the only legal

public voices against *apartheid* came from within the Christian churches. But a new kind of voice was emerging through university student and religious organizations, a voice that would become known as 'black consciousness'. Its centre was the University of Natal's black medical school, under a student leader called Steve Biko.

Questions

1 Why did South Africa become a republic and leave the Commonwealth? [Cambridge International School Certificate, 1976]

2 What were the aims of the Promotion of Bantu Self-Government Act, 1959, and what has been done so far to carry them out? [Cambridge International School Certificate, 1977]

3 Give an account of the history of the African National Congress, 1912-61. What were its objectives? [Cambridge International School Certificate, 1978]

4 What were the contributions made to the cause of African nationalism in South Africa by two of the following: (a) Chief Albert Luthuli; (b) Robert Sobukwe; (c) Nelson Mandela; (d) Clements Kadalie? [Cambridge International School Certificate, 1980]

5 Discuss the growth of security laws and police power in South Africa between the 1930s and the 1960s.

Activities

1 Discuss in the classroom the effectiveness of new policies adopted by the African National Congress in 1956 and 1961.

2 An Afrikaner nationalist and an African nationalist, both from South Africa, meet in a bar in Basutoland in the early 1960s. They begin to exchange views. What do they say to each other?

3 Debate the principles of 'Bantu Education' as introduced by Drs Verwoerd and Eiselen.

For references see p. 320.

Chapter 20

Apartheid and African Independence (1953 – 1968) II:`Southern´ and`Central´Africa

Trends in the growth of African nationalism and European imperialism since the 1930s and 1940s bore fruit in the 1950s and 1960s. Nationalist movements grew strongest in urban-industrial areas, or where peasants had been deprived of land by capitalist farming. Nationalist demands for equal rights with settlers became demands for self-government and independence. Meanwhile overseas companies operating in Africa tended to become multinational, owned by capitalists based in many European countries and in the USA, whereas before they had been owned by capitalists in the imperial country only. Imperial rule over colonies eventually became politically and economically unacceptable to both colonized peoples and to the imperial powers in Europe. Portugal remained an exception – a poor country which clung to its comparatively rich colonies.

The pattern of decolonization was complicated in southern Africa, not only by Portugal but by large white settler populations. Whites in South Africa and Rhodesia had already won their own struggle for self-government in the 1920s and 1930s, and had made their own compromises with imperialism. Southern African countries where the British government retained power followed the path of independence taken by the rest of Africa, after a period of hesitation. In countries where white settlers were in power, governments attempted to divert African nationalism into new forms of 'tribalism' with localized and limited power. African nationalists turned to more revolutionary tactics as they were met by more efficient police repression.

1 The High Commission Territories

The High Commission Territories of Basutoland, Bechuanaland and Swaziland had little in common with each other in the 1950s, beyond being large labour reserves under British imperial rule serving the South African economy. Basutoland was the most populous and politically most active. As population outstripped agricultural production, Basutoland continued to decline in economic importance. But the large number of labour migrants kept the baSotho involved in the mainstream of South African politics. Bechuanaland remained, in the words of a journalist, the 'land without a future'. The Ngwato chieftainship dispute continued to attract world attention. But 'modern' economic activity consisted of little more than the regular passage of steam trains along the Rhodesia-South Africa railway. Swaziland on the other hand became a centre of activity by multinational companies, investing in agro-industry and mining. The monarchy dominated internal Swazi politics, which had little relation to the politics of white 'Swazilanders'.

The early 1960s saw rapid changes in all three territories. Britain suddenly began to prepare them for sovereign independence in the space of a few years. New conservative democratic forces challenged Pan-Africanist parties and won power in Basutoland and Bechuanaland, while in Swaziland all parties including white settlers eventually gave way to revived monarchism. The economic trends of the 1950s continued in Basutoland and Swaziland during the 1960s, but Bechuanaland was put on the road to economic development by cattle exports and mineral prospecting.

South Africa's plans to incorporate the three territories were effectively ended when it left the British Commonwealth in 1961. In 1963 the Republic of South Africa imposed strict border controls on previously unpatrolled frontiers. Verwoerd then appealed to traditionalist forces within the territories, to combine against the threat of democratic nationalism in a South African commonwealth. 'If South Africa were to be, or become, the guardian, the protector or the helper of these adjacent territories, instead of the United Kingdom,' — wrote Verwoerd — 'we could lead them far better and much more quickly to independence and economic prosperity than Great Britain can do.' Britain meanwhile failed to change the 1910 customs union agreement, which tied the territories to South Africa without giving them any say in South African economic policies. South Africa would not yield more than the 1.3 per cent of customs revenues allotted to the territories in 1910 — despite the growth of their economies, especially Swaziland's, since then. So in 1965-66 Britain redistributed the 1.3 per cent; Basutoland's share was halved, Swaziland's was tripled, and Bechuanaland's was slightly increased!

There was little coordination between the three High Commission Territories before 1961. They only cooperated in recruiting

Pius XII College in Basutoland became the University of Basutoland, Bechuanaland and Swaziland in 1963
The Catholic college had been offering University of South Africa degrees to South African, Rhodesian and Basutoland students. The new university, known as UBBS and later as UBLS, continued to accept students for a four year course after ordinary matriculation level entry, rather than the advanced level required in British West, East and Central African universities. UBBS soon faced its first troubles, as non-British or non-Catholic lecturers left and there was no hurry to replace them. Also, as a student magazine remarked, 'this federation imposed by British experts' might be a source of conflict between the three countries after their independence, because 'Lesotho, being the chief shareholder, by virtue of the grounds on which the University is built, will exert more power'.

colonial officials, most of whom came from the Union of South Africa. But South Africa's departure from the Commonwealth forced Britain to put the territories on the road to independence. The resident commissioners were instructed to eliminate racial discrimination in public places, and official commissions looked into the promotion of African civil servants and economic development for all three territories. South Africa also closed its educational facilities to citizens of the High Commission Territories. This forced Britain to coordinate educational and nursing standards, and to provide university education for the High Commission Territories. In 1962-63 a junior secondary examinations council was set up, and matriculation candidates sat for Cambridge overseas examinations in place of South African examinations. The new University of Basutoland, Bechuanaland and Swaziland opened its doors at Roma in Basutoland in January 1964.

2 The Path to Lesotho Independence (1953-66)

Basutoland's modern nationalist movement can be dated from the response of educated baSotho to the colonial government's Moore Report in 1954. The report failed to answer widespread criticism of incompetent local colonial officials, or to recommend that Basutoland (as Britain's second most educated African colony after Sierra Leone) should have an elected legislative council. The Basutoland National Council therefore unanimously rejected the Moore Report. The political future of the country became a matter of lively public debate. A political journal called *Mohlabani* carried the radical views of teachers, like the South Africans Zepheniah Mothopeng and Ezekiel Mphahlele, attacking racial discrimination. The veteran nationalist Josiel Lefela became so outspoken in the National Council that he was expelled from it, once again, in 1955. In spite of this, young militants flocked to join Ntsu Mokhehle's Basutoland African Congress rather than Lefela's *Lekhotla la Bafo*, though the two bodies did hold joint meetings with

their flags flying side by side.

Emergence of political parties Between 1955 and 1958 the Basutoland National Council and the British authorities continued to exchange constitutional proposals for an elected legislative council. The ranks of the Basutoland African Congress were swelled by popular awareness of events in South Africa and the rest of the continent. Two new political parties were formed, to fight forthcoming democratic elections for the proposed legislative council. Monarchists formed the *Marema-Tlou Party* to support Bereng Seeiso (later Moshoeshoe II) when he came of age as paramount chief. Supporters of the existing regency in the Basutoland National Council, including many small chiefs and some Sons of Moshoeshoe, formed the *Basutoland National Party* (BNP), headed by Leabua Jonathan. Meanwhile the Basutoland African Congress was renamed the *Basutoland Congress Party* (BCP). The BCP joined the Pan-African freedom movement led by Ghana. Mokhehle attended the All African People's Conference at Accra in 1958.

After 1959 elections, the Basutoland National Council became a legislative council in 1960. The chiefs and headmen of the previous Basutoland National Council took half of the eighty seats. The remaining half were elected from district councils; and the district councils were elected by all taxpayers — i.e. all adult men and some women. 'For the first time in South Africa's history,' a journalist remarked, 'and in the very heart of the country, an election took place in which a decisive degree of political power rested in the hands of a predominantly black electorate.' Most of the elected seats went to the BCP, but the BNP held most of the former National Council seats. Each of the three parties then nominated one member each to join British officials as government ministers in the executive council, which was answerable to the legislative council. Bereng Seeiso was declared paramount chief, and was hailed as the new Moshoeshoe who would head independent Lesotho.

Peasants and migrants The new government was faced by formidable economic problems. Population had outstripped production. Enough people emigrated to the Union in the 1940s to keep the population stable: both the 1936 and 1946 censuses recorded a population of 560,000. But the Union began to restrict migration from 1951 onwards, and the natural increase in population had to be accommodated within Basutoland. Malnutrition and infant death became widespread in the 1950s, according to a World Health Organization report of 1960. Labour migration to South Africa grew from 155,000 in 1956 to 200,000 in 1960, but wives and children now had to be left behind. Peasant production could supply the needs of only a few wealthier families who had access through chiefs to mountain land, where they pastured woolled sheep and reaped profits from high world wool prices. Co-operative movements, which shared responsibility for bank loans, attempted to improve peasant agriculture with new techniques. The seSotho novelist and thinker James Machobane began a peasant co-operative called *Mantsa-Tlala* ('eliminate famine'), to press his belief in using the potato for crop rotation. The BCP leader Mokhehle became president of the Basutoland Co-operative Banking Union, funded by a private British charity ('Oxfam').

Employment outside agriculture was limited to government service, missions and trading companies. Racial discrimination in these fields became a major target of BCP attacks, which condemned whites as ticks and parasites living on cheap black labour. An official commission confirmed that Africans were poorly paid and blocked from promotion in the civil service of all three High Commission Territories. But incompetent white officials were rarely removed. Instead they were transferred from job to job, or from territory to territory.

Catholics and communists Short-lived Catholic and communist parties were set up following the 1960 elections. The Catholic 'League of Thakatsa Mesa-Mohloane' was set up with money from Canadian and German anti-communists, to act as a pressure group on the Basutoland National Party. It was dissolved when the BNP broadened its appeal to include conservative Protestants and Indian traders previously supporting the Congress, in order to increase its popular vote in future elections. The 'Communist Party of Lesotho' was a pressure group on the Basutoland Congress Party, to counteract Mokhehle's alliance with the Africanists (and against the socialists) in the South African nationalist movement. Meanwhile the BCP also lost supporters to the progressive monarchist supporters of Moshoeshoe II.

Relations with South Africa Basutoland became the haven for numerous refugees fleeing from the repression of 1960-64 in South Africa. Some were chased, kidnapped or bombed by South African agents, who received tacit support from Basutoland's colonial police. South Africa tightened up its border controls, so that the number of baSotho workers dropped from 200,000 in 1960 to under 120,000 by 1966. But the BCP openly defied South African pressures. After the banning of ANC and PAC in South Africa (1960), the BCP saw itself as the natural leader of African nationalism south of the Limpopo. It allied itself with popular nationalist parties in Bechuanaland and Swaziland. The National Party of South Africa therefore attempted to develop contacts with traditionalists within the conservative parties of all three High Commission Territories, including the BNP, during 1964-65.

Dissention in the BCP The Basutoland Congress Party was at the peak of its influence when it helped to organize strikes by government workers and company workers at Maseru in 1961. But after this, both pro-Western and pro-communist trade union organizers began to challenge its influence in the labour movement. Finally in 1964 the BCP alienated supporters with traditionalist sympathies when it bitterly attacked chiefs in general, after learning of the friendly contacts of the South African ruling party with tradi-

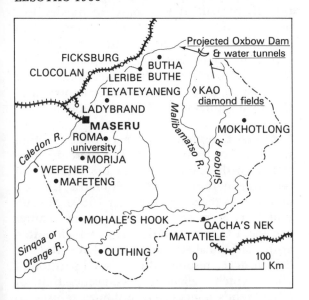

tionalists. Ten of the BCP's thirty national council members resigned from the BCP, just before new constitutional talks in London.

Self-government The political parties fought fiercely in the general election of 1965 based on universal adult franchise. Forged letters libelling opponents were passed around, and some party agents were even killed. The BNP made every effort to get women in rural areas, most of whom had not been able to vote in 1960, to vote, and appealed to their conservative family values. Out of sixty seats in the new parliament, the BNP won thirty-one and the BCP won twenty-five. Leabua Jonathan as BNP leader became prime minister.

Lesotho independence Tension remained high between the BCP and BNP during the period of self-government. British troops were flown in to help police the country. Parliamentary debates were extremely heated, because both parties were so fully represented yet only one held executive power. The prime minister accepted a large gift of grain from the South African prime minister to distribute as famine relief. The BNP claimed that friendly relations with South Africa were necessary to maintain 'the kingdom of the stomach'.

The BCP on its part now wanted to increase the powers of the monarchy, as a check on BNP control of the executive. But Lesotho reached independence on October 4th, 1966, as a kingdom in which parliament reigned supreme under the prime minister, over a constitutional monarchy without power.

3 The Path to Swaziland Independence (1953-68)

Multinational companies, based in Britain or South Africa, invested huge sums in Swaziland agro-industry and mining in the 1950s and 1960s. The main investor was Britain's Colonial Development Corporation, a state body founded in the 1940s to ensure the supply of raw materials from the colonies to Britain. The CDC provided basic capital and expertise to help large private companies to invest profitably in Swaziland, beginning with forestry, sugar and citrus production, and moving into mining and tourism.

A banned South African newspaper openly on sale in Maseru, 1959-60.

Mining recruits being signed up by an official of South Africa's Native Recruiting Corporation (1963). Migrant labour provided nearly three-quarters of Basutoland's national income.

The CDC's major investments in the Usutu Forest and the Mhlume and Big Bend sugar plantations came to fruition with the opening of milling industries in 1959. Massive investment in new roads and canals had been necessary. But the projects proved profitable for the CDC and its partners, partly because of the low cost of land and labour.

The largest single development projects were an iron ore mine at Ngwenya and a railway built across the width of Swaziland to serve the mine. The Anglo-American Corporation of South Africa (backed by the CDC) signed a contract in 1957 with Japanese steel firms, to supply twelve million tonnes of raw ore over three years. The open cast mine eventually opened in 1964 when the railway was completed. Specially built ships took the ore to Japan from Matola docks near Lourenço Marques. Critics of the scheme said that Swaziland would be left without any profits, but only a hole in the ground and a useless railway when the Japanese contract ended, because the mine was so lightly taxed by government and the railway was unsuitable for passengers. If the iron ore could have been smelted into pig iron within Swaziland, it would have provided local employment and fetched a much higher price in Japan.

The opening up of large capitalist production in Swaziland was matched by development of roads, electricity generation, and air services in central Swaziland. The colonial capital of Mbabane began to expand with the growth of commerce. Plans were laid by the CDC for a casino and tourist complex near the royal capital in the Ezulwini valley.

Nationalist response The colonial administration gave its full support to these developments, with scant regard to the interests of the Swazi nation headed by Sobhuza II. Swazi nationalism revived in the later 1950s. Mbandzeni's concessions seventy years earlier became a burning political issue which united both traditionalists and progressives. But the British never responded to a Swazi petition of 1956 which called for reconsideration of Mbandzeni's concessions. Sobhuza refused to negotiate with the Ngwenya mining company, until Britain recognized that the mineral rights belonged to the Swazi nation. As a result the colonial administration allowed the company to pay a mere £200 in annual rent to the Swazi nation for the use of its land. But, with the sudden prospect of independence ahead in the early 1960s, the CDC considered it wise to come to terms with Sobhuza II. It made the Swazi royal government a share-holder in its forestry and sugar companies.

Settlers and the Ngwenyama Economic development increased the number and strength of white settlers, who proudly called themselves 'Swazilanders'. Like whites elsewhere in southern Africa, their fears of African nationalism came to a head in 1960. The European Advisory Council, led by Carl Todd, called for the formation of a legislative council – combining the EAC and the royal government with equal power – in order to block a one-man-one-vote constitution. Sobhuza, speaking as the *Ngwenyama* (king), agreed to the power-sharing proposal. He added: 'If only we could be able to extricate Africa from this idea of one man, one vote, I'm sure we would have achieved our objective.' The *Ngwenyama* then stood aside from constitutional negotiations as a monarch above politics.

Political parties emerged to represent different interests in the constitutional negotiations of 1960-63. First the old Swaziland Progressive Association transformed itself into the *Swaziland Progressive Party,* which called for a democratic constitution rather than the power-sharing proposal. Its head, J.J. Nquku, was expelled from the constitutional committee for obstructive behaviour. The SPP then boycotted further negotiations, and became a militant African nationalist party. In 1962 the SPP split into three rival factions — the largest was led by Dr Ambrose Zwane, which renamed itself the *Ngwane National Liberatory Congress* (NNLC) in 1963. Zwane, and his youth wing leader Dumisa Dlamini (a nephew of the *Ngwenyama*), began to organize mass support by promoting trade unionism among workers employed by multinational companies. After pulp mill workers forced their company to recognize their union by a strike, forestry and railway construction workers struck for better pay and conditions in 1962. Meanwhile another African nationalist party, the *Swaziland Democratic Party,* was formed with support from progressive white businessmen. It pressed for a 'non-racial, stable, democratic government endowed with checks and balances guaranteeing freedom of opposition and criticism'.

Constitutional negotiations ended in failure in early 1963, when the alliance between Swazi traditionalists and white settlers broke down. They disagreed as to whether the *Ngwenyama* or a parliament should control land and mineral rights. The African nationalist parties refused to compromise over a one-man-one-vote constitution, so the British imposed a compromise constitution. One third of legislative council members would be royal representatives, one third would be whites, and one third would be elected on universal franchise. Elections were planned for mid-1964.

1963 strikes The NNLC then helped organize a series of major strikes, with support from the SDP. Sugar workers at Big Bend, who earned less than R10 (£5) a month, struck for R30 a month. Mine workers at Havelock (Bulembu) struck for R2 a day, and police used teargas for the first time in Swaziland to disperse NNLC demonstrations in support. Meanwhile the SDP organized protests by domestic workers in Mbabane against wages of R4 to R11 a month. Matters came to a head when police arrested Havelock strike leaders in June. The NNLC brought out Mbabane workers, sugar workers and lowveld ranch workers in a general strike in sympathy.

British troops were flown in from Kenya (via Bechuanaland) to break the Havelock and Big Bend strikes. They sealed off the areas, and detained those workers who refused to return to work. Dumisa Dlamini was sentenced to five months in prison. Traditionalists had opposed the strikes and welcomed the crushing of disorder by the British. But when British troops stayed in Swaziland for four years, their social behaviour caused much resentment among Swazi traditionalists.

Electioneering and referendum While most white Swazilanders gave their support to Carl Todd's pro-South African *United Swaziland Association,* the British wanted the Swaziland Democratic Party to take power. The SDP, led by the cousins Sishayi and Allen Nxumalo, had broken their alliance with the NNLC. The SDP was now seen as combining liberal democracy with security for British investments in Swaziland. It called for parliament to be sovereign over a constitutional monarchy, with the slogan 'Sobhuza II for Democracy and Progress'.

The *Ngwenyama* and *Libandla* (traditional assembly), however, were determined to stop the one-man-one-vote elections. They organized a national referendum to reject the new constitution at the beginning of 1964. Only 162 votes were cast against the *Ngwenyama,* out of almost 125,000 votes in the referendum. But the resident commissioner, Brian Marwick, refused to alter the constitution and lectured Sobhuza on the inevitable decline of monarchy under democracy. So in April 1964 the *Ngwenyama* and *Libandla,* after consultations with South African legal advisers, formed *Imbokodvo* — described as a national cultural movement rather than as a political party — to fight the elections.

Swaziland independence *Imbokodvo* took all elected seats with eight-five per cent of the total votes in the 1964 election. The United Swaziland Association and *Imbokodvo* shared political power in the legislative council. *Imbokodvo* then absorbed the SDP and other small parties, together with individuals from NNLC, and it became a more broadly nationalist movement. It no longer saw a one-man-one-vote constitution as a threat, but rather as an opportunity to escape from too close an alliance with white Swazilanders and with South Africa. In April 1967 elections, *Imbokodvo* won all twenty-four seats in parliament, although one fifth of all voters had voted for NNLC. In the same month Swaziland became a self-governing state, and the *Ngwenyama* was declared King. Finally on September 6th, 1968, the Kingdom of Swaziland regained its independence — keeping its English name, rather than reverting to its siSwati name 'kaNgwane'.

Swaziland was the only pre-colonial monarchy in southern Africa to survive the colonial period, by stubbornly refusing to accept any constitution or loss of sovereignty imposed by the colonial power.*

SWAZILAND 1968

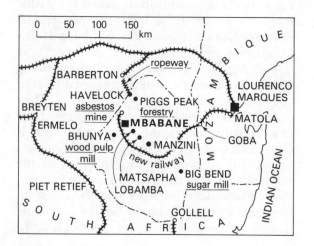

His Majesty Sobhuza II (Ngwenyama and King of Swaziland) and His Excellency Sir Francis Loyd (Her Majesty's Commissioner) in their traditional dress.

4 The Path to Botswana Independence (1953-66)

The economic prospects of the Bechuanaland Protectorate appeared dim in the early 1950s. Cattle were exported in small numbers by train to South Africa and on the hoof to Northern Rhodesia, swimming across the Zambezi. The only significant mining was the small Monarch gold mine at Francistown. Plans to bring water from the Okavango swamps to the Kalahari, first put forward by Professor E.H.L. Schwarz in 1920, were shown to be impractical by a South African government report in 1945. A large ranching scheme proposed by the Colonial Development Corporation for northern Bechuanaland was abandoned because much of the pasture was poisonous to cattle. But the CDC did succeed in setting up an abattoir at Lobatse in 1954, which exported chilled beef to South

*Economic development in Swaziland by 1968 was dominated by large agro-industrial and mining schemes, owned by multinational companies and Britain's Commonwealth (former Colonial) Development Corporation. The only obvious failure in such developments was the attempt to grow pineapples in the Malkerns valley. The scheme began as a co-operative of white farmers; the CDC stepped in with capital in 1959, and finally in 1969 the scheme was taken over by an American-based multinational company, Libby's. Meanwhile the railway linked goods traffic to a Mozambique port for overseas shipping, while new roads linked Swaziland more closely to South Africa from which it drew its imports.

Africa, Northern Rhodesia and the Belgian Congo. Many of the cattle slaughtered came from white settler ranches, but an increasing number came from wealthier African families in the reserves.

Tshekedi Khama Banishment from the Ngwato reserve, and exile in the Kwena reserve (1950-52), turned Tshekedi into a Botswana nationalist. As a Kwena representative in the African Advisory Council, he pressed for a revival of the old alliance of Tswana states in the form of a 'tribal federation', and for a legislative council as the first step towards self-government. He attacked South Africa for renewing its claim to the High Commission Territories in 1954. He accused the British of delaying constitutional advance in the territories in order to please the South African government. He became honorary president of the Africa Bureau in London, a small group of liberals putting pressure on the British government. In pamphlets and press articles published in 1955-56, Tshekedi called for political evolution in Bechuanaland through tribal federation towards non-tribal national unity, and for closer economic links with the Rhodesias as an alternative to South Africa.

Mining development Chiefs like Tshekedi had long resisted mineral prospecting in their reserves, for fear that mining would mean permanent loss of land to companies and white settlers. But by the mid-1950s they saw that mining could become an economic basis for self-government rather than for white settlement. Bathoen II reopened the Moshaneng asbestos mine in the Ngwaketse reserve, under a small South African mining firm. Tshekedi approached the Rhodesian Selection Trust, on the Copperbelt in Northern Rhodesia, about copper prospects in the Ngwato reserve.

Khama reconciliation The Ngwato people in *Kgotla* refused to discuss any mining concession to RST without both Seretse and Tshekedi Khama being present. This pushed the British into inviting Seretse back from

exile in England. Seretse and Tshekedi were fully reconciled with each other, and became private citizens without any claim to the Ngwato chieftainship. The Ngwato then elected Seretse Khama as vice-chairman and Tshekedi Khama as secretary to the tribal council (1956), though the British did not allow Tshekedi to take up his post for another two years. Under Seretse Khama's leadership the Ngwato tribal council became a dynamic local government, and the model for reform of tribal councils elsewhere. The Ngwato council reached provisional agreement with RST on a mineral concession in 1957 and final agreement in 1959.

Constitutional advance Younger members of the reformed tribal councils looked to Seretse Khama as their national leader. Botswana nationalism was also stimulated by reaction to events in South Africa. Tshekedi Khama gave refuge in his village to Hurutshe refugees under chief Abram Moiloa, who had fled from police raids enforcing *apartheid* in the western Transvaal. Tshekedi died in 1959, after adding his signature to the Ngwato-RST

Tshekedi Khama (left) welcomes Seretse Khama back to Africa after years of exile. Scene at Francistown airport, 1956, with the local provincial commissioner between them. They had been reconciled in London shortly before.

concession on his sickbed in a London hospital. Seretse Khama continued to call for a legislative council, with the support of progressive white businessmen. A veteran Ngwato nationalist and playwright, L.D. Raditladi, formed a political party known as the Bechuanaland Protectorate *Federal Party* (or *Liberal Party*), to campaign for a self-governing state based on tribal federation and multi-racialism (1959). But the party was ill-organized and short-lived. Finally, after Macmillan's 'wind of change' speech, the British agreed to a legislative council to be elected from tribal councillors and settler representatives in 1961.

Political parties Events in South Africa and the Rhodesias, and a stream of refugees from South Africa during 1960-64, helped to raise mass political consciousness in towns along the railway. The *Bechuanaland People's Party* (inspired by the Convention People's Party of Ghana) was founded in Francistown at the end of 1960 under K.T. Motsete, the Ngwato educationalist who had helped found the Nyasaland African Congress in 1944. The BPP appealed to urban workers and students by attacking colonialism, capitalism, racialism and tribalism, and by demanding independence for Botswana. A mass demonstration in Francistown was quelled by police with teargas. After this, however, the BPP split into several factions. An Africanist faction, under Philip Matante, first expelled a smaller socialist faction under Motsamai Mpho (1962), and later expelled Motsete. Matante, a former Johannesburg preacher, maintained contact with South Africa's PAC and Basutoland's BCP. Mpho, a former ANC Treason Trialist in South Africa, eventually renamed his faction the *Botswana Independence Party* (1964) and made his Ngamiland home area into his base.

Members of the legislative council, led by Seretse Khama with the assistance of Quett Masire (a journalist and progressive farmer from Kanye), replied to the challenge of the BPP at the beginning of 1962 by forming the *Bechuanaland Democratic Party*. The BDP looked beyond tribal federation to a unified state. It attracted the younger democrats of the reformed tribal councils, and recruited successful educated Africans (including non-Tswana such as Kalanga) and progressive white businessmen. Several of its members were chosen as executive council members by the colonial authorities. One of them, chief Bathoen II, had joined the BDP as a matter of course, but became increasingly unhappy about BDP plans to curtail 'tribalism' and the power of chiefs.

The British moved the Bechuanaland Protectorate towards independence on the BDP's timetable, which called for full self-government in 1965. Plans were laid to remove the capital from Mafeking to a completely new city at Gaborone by that date. For the first time the colonial authorities tried to assert control of the Tati district and the railway strip over the companies that owned them. Bechuanaland became a full colony, no longer subject to the high commissioner based in South Africa. The word 'Protectorate' was dropped from its title. All laws discriminating against Africans on grounds of race were removed or revised.

White settler reaction White traders with business interests in the African reserves usually supported the BDP. The white traders of Mafeking even proposed that their town should be ceded by South Africa to Bechuanaland, to keep it as the commercial capital after independence. But most white settlers were farmers along the borders with Southern Rhodesia and South Africa. Tati whites talked of a unilateral declaration of independence to join Southern Rhodesia. They were discouraged by a British military base at Francistown, which had been set up to supply troops by air to Swaziland and Basutoland, and was kept to guard a British radio station broadcasting against Rhodesian UDI in 1965.

Botswana independence Despite BDP plans to assert the sovereignty of a national parliament over regional chieftainships, the BDP was backed by tribal councils in seven of the eight reserves. In the first one-man-one-vote elections of 1965, the BDP won twenty-eight

BOTSWANA 1966   Populated agricultural and fishing areas shaded.

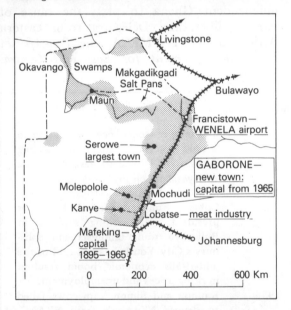

THE BECHUANALAND PROTECTORATE BECOMES THE REPUBLIC OF BOTSWANA.

Economic development at the time of independence.   There was no significant mining, besides a small amount of asbestos, and no metalled roads except the main streets of Lobatse, Francistown and Gaborone. The new city of Gaborone replaced Mafeking as capital in 1965. It contained the first secondary school built by the colonial government, and a small technical college. Lobatse was the only industrial centre, with a large abattoir. Francistown housed the 'Wenela' airport (above) flying mine labourers to and from Nyasaland and Ngamiland, as well as Northern Rhodesia until 1964. Miners were sent by train between Francistown and the Rand. Wenela could claim to be Africa's largest passenger airline in numbers of men flown every year. The most pressing issue for Botswana at independence was the continuing drought.

of the thirty-one parliamentary seats. The BPP of Matante won the three remaining seats, among the workers of Francistown and Tati, and in the Kgatla capital of Mochudi. Then on September 30th, 1966, Bechuanaland became the independent Republic of Botswana. A hymn by K.T. Motsete became its national anthem. Sir Seretse Khama, knighted by the British, became the republic's executive president. (South Africa meanwhile announced that the 1949 ban on his entering that country had been lifted.) With parlia-

317

mentary sovereignty and independence established, the Botswana government and multinational mining companies got down to preparing mining plans as the basis for economic development.

5 Central African Federation (1953-63)

Southern Rhodesia, Northern Rhodesia and Nyasaland retained their own laws and governments under federation. But they surrendered to the federal government their control of foreign relations and defence, customs and currency, railways and airports, electricity and broadcasting, and white education. The federal budget grew fat on taxing copper production, and planned to spend £70 million on prestige projects in 1954-57, including the world's largest dam, an airline, and a university. Salisbury as the federal capital became a boom town of tall buildings, including the headquarters of the copper companies. Northerners complained that Salisbury and Southern Rhodesia were *bamba zonke* ('taking everything') in development funds under federation.

Multi-racial partnership 'Trusteeship' by Britain for the African population north of the Zambezi was replaced by the federal policy of multi-racial 'partnership'. Godfrey Huggins, federal prime minister between 1953 and 1956, quite openly described this 'partnership' in terms of white supremacy, as the partnership of 'the rider and the horse'. When African nationalists in Northern Rhodesia and Nyasaland continued to campaign for federation to be abolished, a visiting British minister told them: 'It is good for you and you must accept it' (1957).

Pan-Africanist influence The economic boom of early federation days had died down by 1957. Rising prices and unemployment sparked off new militancy in the congresses of all three colonies. The militants were then brought together and given new spirit by the All-African People's Conference of 1958, convened by president Nkrumah of newly-independent Ghana to press the cause of African liberation. Delegates from eastern Africa formed PAFMECA, the *Pan-African Freedom Movement for East and Central*

AFRICAN NATIONALISM IN CENTRAL AFRICA 1953-58

1953-58	Garfield Todd as prime minister of Southern Rhodesia, with liberal ideal of partnership with growing educated class of Africans.
1955	Militant NRANC activity in rural area resulted in brief imprisonment of Nkumbula and Kenneth Kaunda.
1956	'Rolling Strikes' on Copperbelt — a series of small strikes by NRAMWU conflicted with new NRANC policy of moderation to gain government respect. 'Is it true that we have been toiling and going to imperialist prisons because we want respect from the white nincompoops?' objected one young NRANC leader.
1957	Young militants Henry Chipembere, Kanyama Chiume and others take over the Nyasaland African Congress, and call Dr Banda back from 42 years abroad. As NAC president Banda

demands independence and an end to 'stupid so-called Federation', adding 'Very soon I hope to have the whole of Nyasaland on fire' (1958).

1957	Southern Rhodesia African National Congress under Joshua Nkomo as president, with strong support of Bulawayo trade unionists and Salisbury's City Youth League. End of the mid-1950s economic boom resulted in rising prices and unemployment.
1958	Kaunda and Simon Kapwepwe failed to depose Nkumbula from NRANC, and formed their own Zambia African National Congress. (Zambia, a shortened version of 'Zambezia'.)
1958-62	Edgar Whitehead as prime minister of Southern Rhodesia: the promise of liberalism had proved empty, and African nationalism was reinvigorated.

Africa, chaired by Tom Mboya of Kenya, which looked forward to eventual federation of their countries. Banda, Nkomo, Nkumbula and Kaunda arrived home in Central Africa from Ghana confident of eventual victory. 'To hell with Federation!' was Dr Banda's slogan. 'Zambia may be banned, public meetings may be banned, but the spirit of Zambia will march on until independence is obtained,' said Kaunda.

Central Africa emergency Riots began in Nyasaland in February 1959. Fifty Africans were shot dead by troops. The Nyasaland African Congress was banned. Dr Banda and a thousand others were arrested in March. Nyasaland leaders met with 'Zambia' and Southern Rhodesia African National Congress leaders, and discontent seethed throughout the federation. The colonial authorities react-

---

CONGO CRISIS

1958	Patrice Lumumba arrived back in the Belgian Congo from the All-African People's Conference. Riots against Belgian colonialism ensued.
1960	*June 30th:* Belgium conceded independence to the Congo under Lumumba as prime minister.
	July 10th: Belgium invaded to crush Congo soldiers' mutiny against their Belgian officers. Simultaneously Katanga was declared an independent republic under Moise Tshombe, an educated traditional ruler backed by the Union Minière and Belgian troops.
	August: United Nations troops expelled Belgian troops from Katanga.
	September: Lumumba deposed by his army commander, Joseph Mobutu. A few months later Lumumba was murdered.
1961	*December:* Katanga rejoined to Congo Republic, but UN troops continued to occupy the province until 1964. (The name Republic of *Zaïre* was adopted in 1971, when Katanga was also named *Shaba*.)

RHODESIA 1963-68

1963	*Zimbabwe African National Union* (ZANU) founded after quarrel with Nkomo's leadership of ZAPU (banned in September 1962) from exile in Tanganyika. ZANU led by Ndabaningi Sithole with Leopold Takawira, Herbert Chitepo, Robert Mugabe, etc. Nkomo supporters, including Nyandoro and Chikerema, reacted by founding *People's Caretaker Council* as legal branch of ZAPU inside the country.
1964	Both ZAPU and ZANU vigorously suppressed by new security laws, police raids, banning and detention without trial.
1965	*Unilateral declaration of independence* (UDI) under prime minister Ian Smith — the country's name was shortened to *Rhodesia.* Followed by United Nations sanctions forbidding international trade with Rhodesia in early 1966.
1966	First attack by ZANU guerrillas on white farm near Chinoyi (Sinoia); and incursion by ZAPU guerrillas, together with SWAPO and ANC, near Victoria Falls.
1966-68	British and Rhodesian prime ministers met on board naval ships *Tiger* and *Fearless,* but talks failed to resolve their independence dispute.

---

ed by arresting fifty ZANC and five hundred SRANC leaders, and Southern Rhodesia adopted new security laws along South African lines.

The banned NAC reappeared as the *Malawi Congress Party* and the banned ZANC reappeared as the *United National Independence Party* (UNIP) in September 1959. SRANC reappeared as the *National Democratic Party* in January 1960.

British policy change The Central African emergency forced Britain to reconsider its

African policies. Prime minister Harold Macmillan toured Africa to announce that Britain recognized 'the wind of change'. Dr Banda was released in April 1960 and the path was laid towards Malawi independence. But the federal government of prime minister Roy Welensky (1956-63) and the copper companies began a counter-offensive against African nationalism. White settlers in the Rhodesias and South Africa pointed to the Congo crisis of 1960-61 to claim that chaos must follow from African independence.

The Malawi Congress Party was swept into power by elections in Nyasaland in August 1961. The British delayed giving in to African nationalists in Northern Rhodesia because of Welensky's protests. But mass protests and sabotage in rural areas (known as 'Cha Cha Cha'), which threatened to spread into the Copperbelt, persuaded the copper companies to come to terms with African nationalism. Elections in October 1962 resulted in a UNIP-NRANC coalition government.

Southern Rhodesia Serious urban riots in 1960, inspired by events both north and south of the country, resulted in ever stronger police controls by the *United Federal Party* government under Edgar Whitehead. The UFP and the British government devised a new constitution to include African 'middle class' voters on an 'A' roll of white electors, with the majority of poorer Africans on a 'B' roll

to elect only fifteen members of a sixty-five-member parliament. The National Democratic Party held its own referendum which overwhelmingly rejected the constitution. The NDP was then banned (November 1961) and re-emerged only a week later as the *Zimbabwe African People's Union* (ZAPU).

Serious urban unrest continued in Southern Rhodesia, with ZAPU youth leaders to the fore. ZAPU led a boycott by qualified African voters of the December 1962 elections. The 'multi-racial' UFP was swept out of power by the white racist *Rhodesia Front* which represented white farmers and urban artisans, rather than big business as the UFP had done.

End of federation By the end of 1962, anti-federal parties had taken power in all three colonies of the federation. The British government bowed before the strongest local forces. Independence was promised to Nyasaland when Dr Banda became its prime minister in January 1963, and negotiations for independence began in Southern and Northern Rhodesia. The Federation of Rhodesia and Nyasaland was formally dissolved on the last day of December 1963. The bulk of federal property, including most of the armed forces, reverted to Southern Rhodesia.

6 Confrontation Across the Zambezi (1963-68)

Nyasaland became the independent Republic of Malawi, under the presidency of Dr Banda, on July 6th, 1964. Northern Rhodesia became the independent Republic of Zambia, under a UNIP government led by president Kaunda, on October 24th, 1964. Southern Rhodesia, under prime minister Ian Smith (1964-79), declared its own independence without British consent on November 11th, 1965.

The Labour government in Britain (elected in late 1964) refused to stop Rhodesia's unilateral declaration of independence with military force. Instead, it relied on international sanctions on trade to reduce the Rhodesian economy to surrender point. But Rhodesia had the full economic support,

GUERRILLA WAR IN THE 1960s

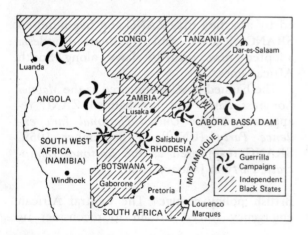

Africans in central Salisbury hear the news of UDI on a radio, while Rhodesian police look on.

including oil supplies, of the Republic of South Africa and of the Portuguese rulers of Mozambique. Multinational American, British, Dutch, French, German and Japanese corporations continued to trade with Rhodesia through their South African or Mozambican subsidiary companies. Meanwhile, the Rhodesian government maintained its suppression of African nationalist politics within the country, and ZAPU and ZANU abroad realized that they could only win power by armed struggle.

After failing to persuade the Rhodesian 'rebels' to return to the spirit of the 1961-62 constitution, Britain abandoned direct political interests in Africa with the independence of Swaziland in 1968. Rhodesian UDI had in effect been accepted by the Western powers as a necessary part of regional political stability for more vital economic interests in South Africa. In 1969 the Smith government recognized this by cutting its last constitutional links with the British crown, declaring Rhodesia a republic, and adopting a new *apartheid*-type constitution.

Guerrilla war along the Zambezi Even as white power triumphed in South Africa and Rhodesia during the later 1960s, a new phase of African national struggle was beginning. 1966-68 saw the first clashes between African nationalist guerrillas and Rhodesian/South African troops. Small actions by ZANU, ZAPU, ANC (SA) and SWAPO guerrillas at Sinoia (Chinoyi) and around the Victoria

Falls, paved the way for intensive guerrilla war south of the Zambezi five years later. But the main thrust of that warfare was to come from the Mozambique Liberation Front (FRELIMO) fighting its way south from the Tanzania border.

Questions

1 Describe the steps leading to independence of *one* of the following: (a) Botswana; (b) Lesotho; (c) Swaziland. [Cambridge International School Certificate, 1978]

2 Discuss the role of trade unionism in African nationalism in Northern Rhodesia, Southern Rhodesia, and Swaziland.

3 Why did nationalist movements in Mozambique and Zimbabwe turn to guerrilla warfare?

4 Discuss the reactions of Western powers to events in southern Africa during the 1960s.

Activities

1 What did the three High Commission Territories ever have in common? Discuss this in the classroom.

2 You are a white South African journalist writing in the early 1960s. Discuss the effect that the Congo Crisis of 1960-61 would have on the attitudes of whites in southern Africa.

3 How much has southern Africa changed since the late 1960s?

Chapter 18 references as 16 above (p. 280), also Bibliography pp. 337–42: B11 Grotpeter; B12 Haliburton; B25 Morton &c; B31 Rasmussen; G1 Bhebe; G14 Morton & Ramsay.

Chapter 19 references as 17 above (p. 280), also pp. 337–42: B34 Saunders; F16 de Gruchy; F23 Hooper; F36 Meer; F41 Patel; F43 Platsky & Walker; F49 Themba; F56 Wilson; H1 Barber & Barrat; H3 Boonzaier & Sharp; H3 Carter & O'Mara; H15 Lodge.

Chapter 20 references as 18 above, also pp. 337–42: G6 Dingake; G15 Nyagumbo; G18 Picard; G20 Ranger; G26 Wood; H1 Barber & Barratt; H6 Davies; H24 Nkomo; H25 Picard.

Chapter 21

The Struggle Continued (1968–1992)

By the end of the 1960s, a world economic boom with high prices for exports – especially minerals – gave increasing economic strength and political confidence to South Africa and Rhodesia, and also to Zambia. Even the predominantly agricultural economies of the Portuguese colonies, Angola and Mozambique, as well as Tanzania to the north, were relatively prosperous.

The confident new governments of Tanzania and Zambia gave residence and support to African nationalist refugees, political parties and guerrilla movements from the Portuguese colonies, from Rhodesia and South Africa. But by the end of the 1960s these refugee movements were proving to be increasingly ineffective. The governments of South Africa, Rhodesia and the Portuguese colonies were pushing ahead with schemes to increase the power and wealth of their white minorities, and to further control and restrict the rights of their black majorities.

South Africa had long seen itself as the core of a Southern African region. By the end of the 1960s it was trying to push back the advance of black nationalism from the rest of Africa, by further developing the ideals of *apartheid*. The ruling party talked in terms of 'separate development' and cooperation between new nations in Africa – with White South Africa as the senior nation in the lead.

1 Peak of Apartheid 1967–72

The size of the South African economy doubled between 1960 and 1970; the gross domestic product (GDP) grew at an average of 8.9 per cent a year. Combining repression of its majority population at home and attraction for foreign capital from abroad, South Africa appeared to be a prosperous and politically stable state. Its government saw *apartheid* as a successful model of 'social engineering', with the aim of reforming the whole of South African society along racially segregated lines. But the term *apartheid* was no longer officially used, because of its bad odour in international circles. The alternative term 'separate development' was used instead.

Pragmatic adaption of apartheid Prime minister Verwoerd had begun to adapt *apartheid* to the realities of African nationalism by the 1959 Promotion of Bantu Self-Government Act, which provided for separate nation-states subordinate to the South African government. The aim was to give Africans a vent for their nationalist energies, and a framework for separate economic development to provide alternative employment for educated and semi-skilled Africans. All blacks in 'white areas' would become foreigners, with only temporary residence for unskilled labour. At the same time it was recognized that White South Africa must be dependent on the influx of cheap migrant black labour for at least twenty years.

After 1964 the government tightened up 'influx control', to try to limit black residence in white areas to migrant workers only. The Bantu Labour Act and subsequent laws resulted in 1.2 million people being expelled ('endorsed out' in bureaucratic language) from white areas into black homelands between 1960 and 1972. The Bantu Labour Regulation Act of 1968 tried to ensure that Africans never left a black 'homeland' without first getting a work permit for a specific job in a white area.

Bantustans   After Transkei in 1963, no other Bantustan was given a form of self-government until 1972. From 1963-64 the aim was for Bantustans to eventually follow the lines of Lesotho and Swaziland, as independent black states clustered around the economic and political core of White South Africa. The Bantu Homelands Development Corporation was set up in 1965, to finance basic infrastructure for territorial independence.

The Physical Planning Act of 1967 gave incentives to capitalists to set up 'border industries' in white areas on the edges of black homelands. The idea of 'border industries' was first proposed by the government in 1960,

to employ semi-skilled workers from the homelands as daily commuter migrants.

Urban Africans   The 1971 Bantu Affairs Administration Act can be seen as the climax of *apartheid* — but also the seed of its final destruction. The act tried to speed up the removal of black urban dwellers from 'white' cities, by taking away the administration of black townships from white city councils, and placing them directly under the Bantu affairs department.

In future all township infrastructure and services would be financed by direct taxation of township dwellers — rather than by the cities in which blacks continued to labour and pay indirect taxation. Thus Soweto was removed from Johannesburg's responsibility and placed under a West Rand Administration Board (WRAB). The result was that township infrastructure and services began to deteriorate, at a time when more prosperous times increased demand for them.

South Africa's 'Outward Policy' bearing fruit.   President Banda of Malawi stands with South Africa's external affairs minister Hilgaard Muller, flanked by presidential guards, at Pretoria in August 1971. Banda combined the traditional Western symbols of a doctor and politician (suit, tie and homburg hat) with African symbols — the fly-whisk of a traditional doctor and the stick of a colonial chief.

Reinforcing the police-state   The succession of B. J. Vorster as prime minister in 1967 further reinforced the role of the security police in South Africa. Some scholars say that South Africa underwent a 'creeping coup' because of the increasing power of the security forces — first police and then military — between the 1960s and 1989.

The Bureau of State Security (BOSS) was set up in 1968–9 by Vorster's friend and police chief, Hendrik van den Berghe. It operated secretly, with secret funds provided by government, both inside and outside South Africa.

Peak of the economic boom   Britain had long been the largest foreign investor in South Africa; the Johannesburg stock exchange was closely tied to the London one until 1961. But during 1965–72, 2.8 billion Rand of new foreign investment capital poured into South Africa — 1.5 billion of it from West Germany alone, and much from France and Japan, as well as the USA. British and American investors kept ahead by re-investing the profits of the industries they already owned. But trade with Britain declined from 33 to 26 per cent of South African exports, and from 30 to 21 per cent of imports, in the period 1965–72. Meanwhile, in the same period, exports and imports between from South Africa and the rest of Africa almost tripled —though most of this trade was with Rhodesia.

South African capitalists, particularly Afrikaners, had bought up stocks in older industries and in gold mining at rock-bottom prices during the economic recession at the beginning of the 1960s. So foreign capital later in the 1960s went into the main growth sectors of the South African economy — manufacturing, especially motor vehicles and 'high-tech' electronic goods, and into production of rare minerals other than gold. By the end of the 1960s the economic boom was seen in widespread and very profitable speculation on the Johannesburg stock exchange, which enriched the new Afrikaner upper-middle class of businessmen and professionals.

Capitalist objections to apartheid   Big business people — notably the Anglo American Corporation, South Africa's main gold producing and industrial group — argued that *apartheid* held back the economic development of South Africa. Job reservation made white workers expensive and kept out cheaper black workers. This held back profits and industrial expansion. Lower wages would increase the number of black workers who could be employed, while increased education would improve their skills. Manufacturing industries would gain from a consumer market of increasing size and sophistication.

VERLIGTE AND VERKRAMPTE

The movement to develop Afrikaner private capitalism, boosted in 1939 (p. 256), was very successful. A second economic congress of Afrikaner nationalists, held in 1950, proclaimed: 'the poor white problem no longer exists and Afrikanerdom is now established in the most important strategic points in urban commerce.'

The Afrikaner insurance group Sanlam began to invest widely in industry, and the Volkskas bank flourished because of the high agricultural prices of the 1950s. When foreign capital fled from South Africa in the early 1960s immediately after the Sharpeville massacre, Afrikaner capitalists rushed to buy local industries while shares were cheap. Anglo American Corporation of South Africa seized the opportunity to collaborate with Afrikaner capitalists, and helped the Sanlam group to found the General Mining (GenMin) Corporation in 1963, which became the second largest mining group after AAC. For the first time, 'national capital' rather than foreign capital was apparently in charge of the South African economy.

The economic boom of later 1960s led to the growth of a large and prosperous class of Afrikaner business people and professionals. Their voices became stronger in the Broederbond and the National Party. After Vorster replaced Verwoerd as prime minister in late 1966, there was much talk of the *verligte* ('enlightened) among Afrikaner leaders, with liberal economic ideas, being opposed by the *verkrampte* ('narrow-minded'). When *verkrampte* leaders were expelled from the Broederbond and National Party in 1969, they formed a new party — the Hestigte National Party (HNP), upholding the old ideals of *apartheid*.

By the end of the 1960s, some *verligte* ('enlightened') Afrikaner leaders had begun to appreciate such liberal economic ideas. But they looked at first to new black markets outside White South Africa, rather than to economic reforms inside the country.

2 Africa and South Africa 1964–73

In 1963–64 Verwoerd developed the idea of a commonwealth of independent states in southern Africa under South Africa's leadership. Lesotho, Swaziland Botswana were invited to join; and were offered South African aid in 1965 through the new Bantu Homelands Development Corporation. Relations proved closest with the new government of Lesotho under prime minister Leabua Jonathan, who displayed open friendship and negotiated with both Verwoerd and Vorster.

Rhodesia   Relations with the white settler regime in Rhodesia were at first complicated by traditional rivalries between Afrikaans and English-speaking whites. But Rhodesia's legal break with Britain in 1965 gave South Africa the opportunity to become Rhodesia's new protecting power, and major trading partner. South African exports grew from less than a quarter of Rhodesia's imports in 1964 to over half by 1967. From 1967 South Africa sent police military units and helicopters to Rhodesia to fight African nationalist guerrillas, and continued to supply military aid to Rhodesia for a further twelve years.

South African aid   From 1965, and especially from 1969 onwards, South Africa provided state development loans for industrial development in the Portuguese southern African colonies and Malawi. The great Cahora Bassa dam on the Zambezi in Mozambique, and the smaller Cunene dam in Angola, were the centres of ambitious new plans for Portuguese white settlement in Africa as well as for electricity supply to South Africa and South West Africa. South African investment in Malawi, particularly for a new capital city at Lilongwe, and 'technical assistance' providing white South African personnel, were

aimed at detaching Malawi from alliance with neighbouring Tanzania and Zambia.

Dialogue   President Kamuzu Banda had offered to open full diplomatic relations with South Africa in 1964. The South African government refused because that would mean a black person as an ambassador in Pretoria.

In 1967, however, 'dialogue' began in correspondence between Banda and Vorster, the new South African prime minister. They discussed their differences over racial policy, and Banda sent one of his white officials as the first Malawi envoy resident in Pretoria. Finally, in 1971, Banda made a well-publicized state visit to Pretoria as the honoured guest of the South African government. Even President Kaunda of Zambia sent a secret envoy to Pretoria in 1967, beginning a dialogue by private correspondence.

Outward policy   *Verligte* Afrikaners among Vorster's officials and in BOSS pushed for South Africa to adopt a new 'outward policy', based on good relations with Black Africa. This was not only good for trade with Africa but also for foreign relations with Western powers, to disarm anti-*apartheid* movements there calling for boycotts of South African goods and sporting links.

The 'outward policy' was announced in early 1969. South Africa's ultimate aim was a 'constellation of states', within the economic orbit of South Africa and under its political influence.

Zambia and Botswana   Zambia was seen as the great prize to be won for South Africa's constellation. But Zambia was taking its own initiative in encouraging Botswana to show its political independence as a non-racial democratic state in opposition to *apartheid*. In late 1969 this was made clear by Botswana at the United Nations and overseas.

South Africa responded in 1970 by trying to stop the building of a direct road from Botswana to Zambia crossing the Zambezi 'freedom ferry' at Kazungula. Zambia used its chairmanship of the Non-Aligned Movement to arouse world opinion against South Africa.

Lesotho and Swaziland coups   In 1970 Leabua Jonathan's government in Lesotho stopped elections when it became clear that the opposition BCP would win a majority of seats. This 'constitutional coup' was supported by South Africa. Similarly in 1973 South Africa supported the 'constitutional coup' of King Sobhuza in Swaziland, when he abolished parliament to stop the growth of opposition parties. South Africa now had a 'constellation' of autocratic allies in Africa – Malawi, Lesotho and Swaziland, plus settler Rhodesia and the Portuguese colonies.

Rhodesia declared itself a republic in 1970, but only South Africa recognized its independence. Prime minister Smith tried to get international recognition from Britain by declaring: 'Our Africans are the happiest Africans in the world.' But an official British commission, headed by Lord Pearce, toured the country in 1972 and found that this was not so. African opinion had been organized by a new party called the African National Council, under Bishop Abel Muzorewa.

3 Guerrilla wars 1966-72

Guerrilla wars were begun by African liberation movements in Angola in 1961 and Mozambique in 1964. By the mid-1960s large areas of central Angola were under the control of the worker-based MPLA (Popular Movement for Liberation of Angola), and the peasant-based FNLA (National Front for Liberation of Angola) led by Holden Roberto and UNITA (National Union for Total Independence of Angola) led by Jonas Savimbi. Meanwhile Mozambique's Liberation Front, FRELIMO, controlled most of the northern province of Cabo Delgado and was moving into Niassa province.

The success of anti-Portuguese guerrillas encouraged other African nationalist parties exiled in Tanzania and Zambia also to send guerrillas southwards. ZANU guerrillas attacked a white farm in Rhodesia in early 1966. In September that year, guerrilla troops from ZAPU, SWAPO and the South African ANC crossed the Zambezi into the Caprivi Strip and north-western Rhodesia. After pitched battles in the Hwange game reserve in 1967-68, South Africa sent reinforcements to Rhodesia. By the end of 1968 guerrilla incursions had ceased.

FRELIMO in Mozambique   Meanwhile FRELIMO had problems. Older nationalists were satisfied with the liberation of Cabo Delgado. Younger nationalists wanted to push the war southwards. Portuguese secret agents encouraged disputes within the party; and Mondlane was assassinated at Dar es Salaam in 1969.

Soldiers led by Samora Machel, with the support of Marxist intellectuals like Marcelino dos Santos, took control of FRELIMO to carry on Mondlane's policies. By 1971-72 FRELIMO was controlling most of Tete province in central Mozambique. Their main target was Cabora (Cahora) Bassa, an enormous dam on the Zambezi, being built to supply hydro-electric power to South Africa and as the centre of new white farm settlement.

Frelimo officer and captured Portuguese troops. As the war neared its end in 1974 the victorious Frelimo forces were transforming themselves into a more conventional army, taking many prisoners and expecting to take over government of the whole country.

FRELIMO success in Tete province opened up routes for ZANU guerrillas to enter north-eastern Rhodesia in December 1972. The success of FRELIMO, and of MPLA in Angola, also encouraged the growth of Marxist ideas of worker-peasant revolution in Zimbabwe's ZANU and ZAPU and South Africa's ANC. The ANC had voted to become a non-racial movement in 1969, and now included non-African radicals in its ranks as also did FRELIMO and MPLA.

4 End of the Economic Boom 1971–73

South Africa saw a great growth of port cities and of manufacturing industries around ports or on the Rand. New factories, financed by foreign capital and depending on imported components, such as car-assembly plants, also demanded increasing numbers of lower-paid workers with basic technical skills. The boom years therefore saw the growth of a black urban working class, despite government attempts to restrict it with *apartheid* laws.

Black workers began to feel their new power within the economy, and to take industrial action to improve wages and working conditions.

Strikes began among Walvis Bay dock-workers and spread to Durban dock-workers in 1971. During 1972–73 there was a wave of strikes by workers in manufacturing industries around Durban. These 'wildcat' strikes were without coordination or identifiable leaders, as trade unionism was illegal for Africans. Indian workers in Durban, however, revived the Natal Indian Congress from 1971 onwards.

Recession and unrest Recession of the world economy began in 1971, and became acute in 1973 when oil-producing countries in the Middle East trebled the world price of oil and petrol. There was a great rise in the cost of fuel and manufactured goods imported into Africa, and a continuing fall in the value of crops and metals exported from Africa. This affected Zambia most severely, as it depended too much on exporting copper, which dropped to only a quarter of its pre-

vious world price between the 1970s and the 1980s.

In South Africa as elsewhere the recession of the early 1970s resulted in inflation of the cost of living, and in government and company attempts to stop or reverse the rise in workers' wages. The wave of strikes in South Africa died down after police shot dead twelve striking gold miners at Carletonville (Western Deep) mines south-west of Johannesburg in September 1973.

Gold and diamonds However, there were two export commodities whose value rose faster than the rising cost of imports in the 1970s – gold and diamonds. This explains the survival of the South African economy, and the enormous growth of the Botswana economy, during the 1970s and for much of the 1980s – while other African economies stagnated. Gold and diamonds gave increased revenue to governments, and to certain companies, notably the Anglo American Corporation group – and paid for the import of essential technology including machinery and computers.

Black wages The struggle for improved wages and working conditions therefore continued in South Africa. African wages increased by 60 per cent in manufacturing during the 1970s. Wages also doubled from very low levels on white farms, and increased fourfold on the gold mines. For the first time since the 1890s African workers had the bargaining power to get a larger share of the national cake in South Africa.

5 Liberation of Portuguese Africa 1974–76

Increased military expenditure against African guerrillas, combined with the world economic recession, broke the back of the Portuguese imperial economy in 1973–74. Radical army officers overthrew the fascist government in Lisbon in a military coup of April 1974. Within six months there were cease-fires with the liberation movements in Mozambique and Angola.

Front-Line States Presidents Kaunda of Zambia, Nyerere of Tanzania and Khama of Botswana responded by forming an alliance known as the 'Front-Line States' in October 1974 — looking forward to independent Mozambique and Angola joining them. They proposed to avoid further bloodshed in southern Africa by *detente* (relaxation of crisis between states) with South Africa in return for the liberation of first Zimbabwe and then Namibia.

Detente Kaunda negotiated with Vorster. Vorster persuaded Smith of Rhodesia to release from prison ZAPU leader Joshua Nkomo and ZANU leaders Ndabaningi Sithole and Robert Mugabe.

Bishop Muzorewa led Zimbabwe nationalist negotiations with Smith. Talks finally broke down in August 1975, after Kaunda and Vorster called a meeting on board a train on the railway bridge at Victoria Falls.

Mozambique and Angola Though FRELIMO had not conquered southern and coastal areas, it had strong support among workers in the capital city as well as among peasants in liberated areas. Despite white settler protests and threatened revolt, Portugal recognized Mozambique as an independent state under a FRELIMO government in June 1975. Large numbers of whites, about 80,000 out of 100,000, including essential technicians, then left to re-settle in Portugal or South Africa.

In Angola, however, there were three liberation movements and they went to war with each other in August 1975. The Portuguese eventually chose to hand over power in November 1975 to MPLA, the Marxist party which controlled the capital city of Luanda and the oil-rich province of Cabinda (north of the Congo/Zaire river), and had the support of workers in the main towns on the railways. Angola had had twice Mozambique's number of white settlers: almost nine out of ten fled.

South-West Africa The liberation of Angola made South Africa fearful for the future of South-West Africa. It had been placed under

The beginning of demonstrations at Turfloop, 1971, as well-dressed male students boycott lectures. The University of the North was the jewel in the crown of Bantustan apartheid, founded by the apartheid ideologue Dr. Eiselen to produce a respectable middle class educated in 'Bantu' ways. But students, inspired by ideas of black consciousness, began to reject that role. Their ideas were voiced by their leader Abram Tiro, who was forced to flee to Botswana where he was assassinated by a parcel bomb in 1974.

direct South African rule in 1969 — with its own Bantustans, as if it were the fifth province of South Africa. By 1975 the most populated Bantustan, Ovamboland, on the northern frontier, was having elections for a ruling council. But already SWAPO, in alliance with Angolan guerrillas, was preparing guerrilla bases just over the frontier.

SADF invasion of Angola The South African army or Defence Force (SADF) crossed into southern Angola in July 1975. In October the SADF invaded almost as far north as Luanda itself, in support of UNITA and FNLA in their war on MPLA.

Angola, like the Congo fifteen years earlier, became embroiled in the 'Cold War' between East and West.

MPLA called in well-equipped troops with aircraft and powerful artillery from Cuba, the Soviet ally most hated by the USA. But the USA decided not to support the South African invasion of Angola, because MPLA had accepted an American company pumping out oil from the MPLA-controlled Cabinda province.

Other countries began to follow Portugal in recognizing MPLA as the legitimate government of Angola. Humilitated and annoyed, South Africa had to withdraw its army from Angola in January 1976.

6 Soweto uprising and aftermath 1976-79

FRELIMO's victory over Portuguese colonialism and the independence of Mozambique inspired demonstrations of support by black university students in South Africa. The 'defeat' of White South Africa by MPLA in Angola in January 1976 gave further fuel to 'black consciousness' among youths in schools as well as colleges.

Industrial policy The South African government had responded ambiguously to the growth of black urban-industrial employment in the late 1960s and early 1970s. On the one hand by sticking to *verkrampte* rules of restricting urban residence and endorsing out 'surplus' people to rural homelands. On the other hand by adopting *verligte* policies to 'capture' the new black working class by conceding some measures of responsibility in industrial relations and urban affairs.

Township administration We have seen (in section 1 above) how the South African government introduced final *apartheid* laws in 1964-71. Between 1960 and 1983 at least 3.5 million Africans were endorsed out to Bantustans. The ban on African trade unions also remained, though the government encouraged works-councils for black workers, which had no power to strike.

The new township administration boards, created by the Bantu Affairs Administration Act of 1971, were staffed and run by central government officials. What people actually saw in 1972-73 was white Afrikaners coming in to take control of the townships. The new boards proved instantly unpopular for taking vigorous action to collect rents and to clear out 'squatters' (illegal residents).

Black education *Verligte* demands for a more skilled black work force were met by increasing the number of blacks in secondary schools almost fivefold between 1965 and 1975, from 66,600 to 319,000.

By 1975-76 the ill-equipped urban black secondary schools were bursting with students. But the curriculum remained under the control of the *verkrampte* 'Bantu education' ministers who insisted that the use of Afrikaans be made compulsory in some lessons at black secondary schools.

Anniversaries of the Soweto uprising of June 16th, 1976, kept alive the spirit of youth protest. This photograph of students, dancing and singing freedom songs in White City, Soweto, was taken in 1982. A new spirit of confidence and confrontation had been born in 1976.

Soweto uprising   Soweto schools rebelled on June 16th, 1976, the day that Afrikaans was to be enforced. A hundred and seventy school children were shot dead in the first week, and at least six hundred by the end of the year. Thousands of students fled into exile in the rest of Africa.

The uprising took the world by surprise. It spread rapidly from Soweto to students in other city townships and even into Bantustan centres. It was partly a rebellion by youth against age. Youths destroyed the beer-halls and shebeens which had kept their parents in a stupor of subjection to *apartheid*.

The Soweto rising was also the first great outburst of the new 'black consciousness' that defined blacks as the people oppressed by whites — a class rather than a race, including 'coloureds' and Indians as well as Africans. The old Africanism and socialism of the ANC and PAC were rejected.

Government response   The South African government tried to 'capture' black consciousness with promises of community councils and house purchase schemes for black workers in the townships, and by pushing the independence of Bantustans to employ middle class blacks as administrators, professionals and business people. 'Petty *apartheid*' was ended in expensive hotels, so that black business people could eat and stay there.

Transkei in the eastern Cape province became 'independent' in October 1976, recognized only by South Africa. Bophuthatswana, scattered in many pieces west and south-west of Pretoria, followed in 1977. The government also considered ways (suggested by the Theron report of 1976) in which coloured people could be induced from black consciousness towards identity as brown Afrikaners.

Death of Steve Biko   When the uprising had barely subsided after a year, the government decided to chop off the heads of the black consciousness movement. Steve Biko, restricted and harassed since 1973, was killed in prison by police in September 1977. Numerous black consciousness organizations and

newspapers were then banned, and other leaders restricted, in October 1977.

South Africa's justice minister, Jimmy Kruger, openly triumphed at Biko's death. Prime minister Vorster was equally blunt: 'the whites will rule, let there be no mistake.'

'Total strategy'   The defence minister, P. W. Botha, like Verwoerd before him, saw overseas communists behind every form of opposition to *apartheid* — from black consciousness to church theology and international sports boycotts. The answer, he argued in 1977, must be 'total strategy' to attack all opponents of *apartheid* in every possible way — including legal reforms that would take away the grievances of black urban dwellers being exploited by 'communists.'

Botha reforms   P. W. Botha succeeded Vorster as prime minister in 1978, after a corruption scandal about government information funds ('Infogate' or 'Muldergate') that implicated Vorster and his BOSS secret police chief van den Berghe.

The new prime minister pushed ahead with planning a new constitution. In 1979, two commissions reported on legal reforms. The Wiehahn report recommended the recognition of black trade unions in industrial relations, and an end to the job colour bar. The Riekert report recommended leasehold tenure to encourage people to buy township houses, and that pass laws be scrapped for non-Bantustan citizens.

7 Zimbabwe and Namibia towards freedom 1976–80

The advances of Zimbabwe and Namibia towards internationally recognized independence were closely linked, in the eyes of both the Front-Line States and South Africa, after Mozambique and Angola gained independence.

Turnhalle negotiations in Namibia   Having failed to depose MPLA from power in Luanda, South Africa continued to back UNITA to keep southern Angola cleared of SWAPO guerrilla camps. Within South-West Africa the

South African government went ahead with constitutional development based on eleven separate ethnic administrations.

Constitutional talks, held at Windhoek's old gymnasium hall or Turnhalle, began in 1975. The Turnhalle talks produced a complex constitution in 1977, based on three 'tiers' of administration – local, ethnic, and national – with power concentrated in the eleven ethnic administrations. Economic prospects for the country looked good, with the opening of uranium mining at Rossing in 1978. Meanwhile the SADF was brought in to occupy the northern Bantustans of South West Africa, including the Caprivi Strip, on the border with Angola and Zambia: there were 45,000 soldiers there by the end of 1977.

South Africa tried and failed to get the approval of the United Nations for South-West Africa/Namibia's constitutional development. But the United Nations insisted on peace with SWAPO and free non-ethnic elections, in September 1978 (Security Council resolution 435). So South Africa went ahead with ethnic-based elections on the Turnhalle constitution for a national assembly. The majority of seats were won by a party representing the eleven ethnic administrations, calling itself the Democratic Turnhalle Alliance (DTA).

Second Chimurenga in Zimbabwe   The new FRELIMO government of Mozambique gave ZANU bases along Rhodesia's eastern frontier in 1975. The 'Second Chimurenga' or civil war resumed in January 1976 with the incursion of ZANU guerrillas from three Mozambique provinces. Thousands of school children now crossed over to join ZANU; the Rhodesian army attacked ZANU camps and killed hundreds of them. Rhodesia also set up a guerrilla force, known as MNR or RENAMO (National Resistance Movement), to harass and attack FRELIMO inside Mozambique.

Zimbabwe's Patriotic Front   Further peace negotiations with the Rhodesian government, at Geneva in Switzerland, arranged by the USA, failed in October 1976. ZANU and ZAPU formed a coalition known as the Patriotic Front (PF). The war became more

Black and white Rhodesian soldiers on patrol. Black soldiers – recruited from the towns, heavily armed, and given good pay and conditions – became essential for the defence of White Rhodesia. Such soldiers are often called *askaris*. The Rhodesians also used black and white 'pseudo' special forces pretending to be African nationalist guerrillas, in order to commit atrocities in their name and thus discredit them. Such ideas were taken to South Africa by Rhodesian troops who joined the SADF in 1979-80.

intense, reaching a peak in 1979. By then ZANU had up to 15,000 guerrillas in rural areas as far west as Matabeleland. ZAPU had about 2,000 guerrillas inside Zimbabwe and 15,000 conventional troops, with guns and vehicles, ready to cross the Zambezi from Zambia.

In 1977–78 prime minister Smith's government was forced to recruit and to begin sharing power with African allies inside the country. Despite the assistance of South African troops, the conscription of all non-black males and recruitment of urban black males, the Rhodesian army was not big or strong enough to fight guerrilla incursions.

Zimbabwe-Rhodesia's internal settlement   In March 1978 Smith signed an 'internal settlement' with the two main African politicians inside Rhodesia – Muzorewa and Sithole – and with the chairman of Rhodesia's council of African chiefs. The war became even more bitter, with ZAPU attacks on Rhodesian aircraft and Rhodesian air-raids on ZAPU camps in central Zambia. Muzorewa and Sithole became 'warlords' with their own private armies acting as auxiliaries to the Rhodesian army.

The suffering spread to the Front-Line States, which were being frequently raided by Rhodesian forces, and to South Africa, whose economy suffered from heavy financial support to Rhodesia. South Africa pushed Rhodesia to follow the pattern of South-West Africa/Namibia in adopting a multiracial constitution that would guarantee white power and property. In June 1979, multiracial elections were held, and Muzorewa was declared prime minister of 'Zimbabwe-Rhodesia'.

Zimbabwe independent negotiations   Zimbabwe-Rhodesia tried to get Britain, as the old colonial power, to recognize its independence. But Kaunda, Nyerere and Khama used a Commonwealth leaders conference, held at Lusaka in August 1979, to persuade Britain to sponsor new talks between all parties to negotiate real independence.

These talks were held at Lancaster House in London in September–December 1979. All parties eventually agreed on peace and a new constitution. In February 1980 elections were held under Commonwealth supervision. ZANU (PF) won a majority of seats and invited ZAPU (PF) to join it in government. On April 18th, 1980, Zimbabwe became an independent republic with Mugabe as prime minister.

Consequences of Zimbabwe independence. The victory of guerrilla movements in Zimbabwe was a great shock to Smith and Muzorewa, and to the South African and British governments, who assumed that simple peasants would only vote for conservative leaders.

In South Africa, it strengthened those who favoured 'winning hearts and minds' by force. The military budget was increased, and the power of the SADF increased at home and abroad.

Fearing that SWAPO might repeat the success of ZANU in free elections, the South African government pressed ahead with its Turnhalle constitution in South-West Africa/Namibia. In June 1980, it installed a council of ministers in Windhoek drawn from the DTA party, chaired by the white settler leader Dirk Mudge.

The Front-Line States   (Zambia, Tanzania, Botswana, Mozambique, Angola), on the other hand, invited newly independent Zimbabwe to join them – seeing South Africa as the next target for liberation. They also looked to the future by forming a Southern African Development Coordination Conference (SADCC), in 1979–80. SADCC was joined by Lesotho, Malawi and Swaziland in 1980.

SADCC was the Front-Line States' answer to South Africa's regional strategy. It tried to coordinate the industrial and agricultural production policies of each state, and to develop trade routes to world markets avoiding South Africa. It operated mainly through regular annual meetings, and though direct correspondence between departments in each state, but also had a small secretariat based in Gaborone.

8 Constellation and destabilization, 1980–84

South African government restrictions placed on the black consciousness movement in 1977 opened the way for better organized movements to recruit black South Africans.

Worker consciousness   Inside South Africa, new organizations mapped out pathways for the future in 1978–79. AZAPO (Azanian People's Organization), founded in 1978, saw itself as promoting worker consciousness as much as black consciousness. FOSATU (Federation of SA Trade Unions) brought together black trade unions seeking recognition under the 1979 Industrial Relations Act. COSAS (Congress of South African Students) helped move student and community politics towards ANC ideals.

Inkatha   There was also Inkatha yeNkululeko ye Sizwe, a Zulu royalist movement of the 1920s revived in 1974 – along the lines of the ruling Imbokodvo party in Swaziland. Led by

Gatsha Buthelezi of the KwaZulu administration, it had quarrelled with the black consciousness movement by 1978, and with the ANC by 1980. But Inkatha was as yet largely confined to Natal rural areas.

Exile movements Outside South Africa, fleeing South African students were increasingly recruited by exile nationalist parties. PAC in exile, however, was torn by disputes and murders, especially in 1978 after its founder Sobukwe died inside South Africa. PAC did not recover until 1981, when John Pokela — recently released from Robben Island — became its leader. ANC, on the other hand, based in Lusaka with guerrilla training elsewhere in Africa, was organized to take in the new recruits.

ANC revival Between 1978 and 1980 ANC worked out its strategy for South African liberation. The main task was to build up mass political support among community groups and workers in urban areas. Actual 'cells' of ANC members in South Africa probably remained few and small. MK(Umkhonto) guerrillas were also to be infiltrated to attack strategic targets — to show ANC power rather than to seriously disrupt the state.

The year 1980 proved vital for the ANC. The 25th anniversary of the Freedom Charter on June 26th was used as a rallying cry in the townships, and Zimbabwe independence made communications southwards from Zambia much easier. Zimbabwe's liberation inspired schools boycotts and nationwide protests in the townships. MK guerrillas caused a sensation by setting fire to part of SASOL's massive oil-from-coal plant, in the Vaal triangle south of Johannesburg, in June 1980.

MK supply routes into South Africa were set up through neighbouring states. SA security services tried to block these routes by assassination (usually by parcel bombs) of key ANC members in Zimbabwe, Mozambique, Swaziland and Angola.

SA constellation of states As part of its 'total strategy', South Africa wanted to surround itself with a constellation of weak friendly states — beginning with independent Bantustans or TBVC states (Transkei 1976, Bophutatswana 1977, Venda 1979 and Ciskei 1981), South-West Africa/Namibia, and Zimbabwe–Rhodesia. But this plan was seriously undermined in 1980 by the independence of Zimbabwe and the formation of SADCC.

South Africa resorted to economic and military pressures on its neighbours to join its Constellation of Southern African States (CONSAS). It tried by every means to control the region's oil and petrol supplies, and to stop its neighbours using Mozambique's ports and railways instead of South Africa's. It used its control of the customs union to try and make Botswana, Lesotho and Swaziland accept the TBVC states as equal members.

South Africa offered its neighbours the chance of signing security pacts, which would allow the SADF or SA police to cross borders in search of 'terrorists'. The alternative was 'destabilization'.

Destabilization was part of South Africa's 'total strategy'. It meant military attacks by the SADF or SADF-supported guerrillas on railway and road traffic, and state services such as schools and health-posts in the Front-Line States — in order to disrupt their economies, and to reduce their political power and prestige in the eyes of their people. Destabilization was intended to make SADCC countries politically as well as economically dependent on South Africa.

South Africa's first political goal was to block ANC routes through Mozambique to Swaziland and Lesotho, from which MK guerrillas entered South Africa. In Mozambique, South Africa took over support of MNR anti-FRELIMO guerrillas from Rhodesia after Zimbabwe's independence. Possibly encouraged by a more anti-communist president assuming power in the USA, Ronald Reagan, the SADF raided ANC houses at Matola near Maputo in January 1981.

With SADF aid, MNR expanded in 1981–2, attacking and killing rural people in central and southern Mozambique — as well as the railways that linked Zimbabwe and other SADCC states with coastal ports.

Swaziland pact A secret security pact was signed with Swaziland in early 1982 — in return for Natal coastal land, which was never handed over by South Africa because of Inkatha protests. SA and MK forces continued to skirmish inside Swaziland for a number of years.

Lesotho refused to sign a security pact. The SADF gave support to relatively ineffective anti-government guerrillas of the Basotho Congress Party. Then, at the end of 1982, the SADF raided Maseru in search of ANC supporters, killing 42 people. Ten days later MK guerrillas damaged South Africa's nuclear power station at Koeberg, near Cape Town.

In May 1983, MK guerrillas blew up an airforce and secret police building in central Pretoria — the last act of really spectacular sabotage by MK. A few days later 58 people were killed by a SADF air attack on Maputo.

Angola and Namibia 'linkage' In Angola, the SADF raided northwards in support of UNITA, against MPLA and Cuban forces from 1981 onwards, and occupied part of southern Angola in 1983. The SADF had the military advantage of its airforce being in control of Angola's skies.

In South-West Africa/Namibia the DTA government collapsed because of administrative inefficiency and corruption in 1983, and was replaced once again by direct South African rule. A new 'transitional' multi-party government was installed in 1985. Meanwhile South Africa prolonged negotiations with the United Nations, the Front-Line States and the Western 'contact group' (USA, Germany, France, Britain and Canada) — by insisting on 'linkage' between SADF withdrawal from Namibia and withdrawal of Cuban forces from Angola.

Zimbabwe destabilization The SADF sponsored the growth of anti-government guerrilla forces in Zimbabwe. The SADF had taken many white and black ex-Rhodesian troops into its own special forces in 1980. In 1981–82 the ZANU headquarters in Harare, and all its new jet fighters, were blown up by ex-Rhodesians.

In 1982 ZANU and ZAPU quarrels became public, and Nkomo was sacked from the government. So-called 'Super-ZAPU' guerrillas, with SADF support, attacked government supporters in Matabeleland during 1983–88.

The success of South African destabilization was seen between 1982 and 1985, when inland SADCC states were forced to divert their imports and exports through South African ports — as other ports were blocked by war. Mozambique had always depended on this traffic with the interior, and the effects on its economy were catastrophic.

Nkomati accord By 1983 the FRELIMO government sought aid from Western countries to stop serious and widespread MNR disruption of Mozambique's economy. The USA pushed FRELIMO towards a security pact with South Africa — 'hugging the hyaena' the ANC leader Oliver Tambo called it. The pact, known as the Nkomati accord, was signed in March 1984 — but it did not stop the SADF raiding Maputo once again in May.

March, 1984: Presidents Machel and Botha salute at the Nkomati Accord.

9 The turning of the tide, 1984-88

Prime minister P. W. Botha was carried along into reforms by South Africa's economic recovery based on a 1978-81 gold boom. Following the Wiehahn and Riekert commissions, laws were made for the 'orderly' control of African workers and township dwellers outside the Bantustans. In 1982 right-wingers broke away from the National Party in protest and founded a Conservative Party.

Presidential rule   P. W. Botha turned to constitutional reform, to increase his power and militarize the state. He would become a powerful state president, advised by state councils, but in effect ruling through committees of SADF and security police chiefs. Parliament was to be reduced in power to a 'tri-cameral' (three-house) structure, with separate houses for whites, Indians, and 'coloureds'.

'Civics' and foundation of UDF   Civic associations ('civics'), as well as trade unions, grew rapidly among black township dwellers in the early 1980s. Civics and other organizations – both 'coloured' and Indian – began to combine in protest against the proposed new constitution. Black consciousness groups held a National Forum in protest.

'Chartist' groups, who adopted the Freedom Charter of the ANC, founded a United Democratic Front (UDF) in August 1983. UDF was organized as South Africa's first mass political party since 1960 – at national, regional and local levels. The UDF promoted a 'culture' of resistance' using slogans on tee-shirts as well as posters, and rock music concerts as well as protest meetings.

The new republican constitution, under P. W. Botha as president, came into force in September–October 1984. Protests by civics and trade unions led to riots in the townships of the Vaal-triangle around Vereeniging, notably Sebokeng but also Sharpeville. In response, the SADF began military occupation of the townships, starting with the invasion of Sebokeng by 7,000 soldiers. The ANC now turned from 'armed propaganda' by MK to 'arming the people'.

'Ungovernability'   Between October 1984 and about August 1987 there was a period of 'ungovernability' in the black townships of South African cities – taking its name from the ANC call to 'Render South Africa ungovernable'. The SA police and SADF tried to regain control through shootings and arrests, but every funeral became another protest demonstration with more shootings leading to new funerals.

Pupils boycotted classes; householders refused to pay rent to township councils; workers stayed away from work on days of mourning. Civics – organized down to the level of street committees – even began to take over the functions of local government, such as street cleaning. Protests spread to all provinces, and were particularly widespread in the eastern Cape, where police shot 19 people dead in the Langa township of Uitenhage on Sharpeville Day 1985. Youthful supporters of the civics known as 'comrades', with MK support, began to punish and sometimes to assassinate councillors and some businessmen seen as collaborators with *apartheid*.

Attack on Gaborone   The South African government hit back in mid-1985. The most effective eastern Cape leader of the UDF, Matthew Goniwe, was assassinated in June 1985. In the same month the SADF crossed into Botswana – the main MK route to the western Cape and the Transvaal – and killed 14 people in an almost random attack on Gaborone suburbs.

This attack on a 'free enterprise' African democracy, which Westerners saw as a model for southern Africa, promoted drastic revaluation of Western support for South Africa. American banks and companies began to withdraw investment from South Africa, and the US Congress pushed President Reagan into trade sanctions on South Africa. Other foreign banks refused South Africa more credit and SA Rand currency dropped fast in foreign exchange value during 1985. Gold had also dropped drastically in US dollar value since 1980.

P. W. Botha promised more reforms, but big businessmen in South Africa realized that this was empty talk. In September 1985 Anglo American Corporation and others began talking with the ANC in Lusaka face-to-face about the future of South Africa.

State of emergency   Meanwhile a state of emergency — meaning direct police and military control — was declared over the townships in July 1985. Civic and UDF leaders at all levels were detained without trial — 7,000 by December. The police also gave support to vigilante groups to make war on the 'comrades'. At KTC compound outside Cape Town, vigilantes known as *witdoeke* (white headscarves) expelled 70,000 squatters by violence. Battles over eviction between squatters and *witdoeke* spread to Cape Town's Crossroads compound in 1986.

This 'black-on-black violence' was used by government to justify the state of emergency to the world. Newspapers and television were only allowed to carry government reports of any violence after December 1986.

Trade unions continued to campaign for workers' rights, but also became more involved in political activities. In 1985 FOSATU was joined by Charterist unions, including the dynamic new National Union of Mineworkers (NUM), and was re-named COSATU (Congress of South African Trade Unions). Then in 1986 a United Workers Union (UWUSA) was founded by Inkatha, with South African government support, to rival COSATU.

Destabilization of Lesotho reached a peak in January 1986, when the South African government blocked food supplies across the border into Maseru. Prime minister Jonathan agreed to pass an internal security law to stop MK activities in Lesotho, and was then deposed in a military coup by the head of the Lesotho army, General Justin Lekhanya. In October that year, Lesotho signed an agreement for a great long-term dam and hydroelectric project to supply water from its northern highlands to the Republic of South Africa.

Peace negotiations fail   The Commonwealth sent an 'eminent persons group' to South Africa in early 1986 to start peace negotiations between the government and the ANC. The state of emergency was lifted in March 1986, in time for a more peaceful Sharpeville Day. May Day was celebrated by one and half million workers taking a holiday. But the State Security Council soon overruled the diplomatic efforts of cabinet ministers.

Renewed emergency   In May 1986, simultaneous SADF air raids were launched on three Commonwealth capitals — Gaborone, Harare and Lusaka — and negotiations with the Commonwealth were broken off. But the Broederbond at least had been converted to the idea of negotiation, and cabinet ministers began to talk to Nelson Mandela in jail.

A strengthened state-of-emergency was re-imposed across South Africa in July 1986. By the end of the year 23,000 people, including 9,000 child 'comrades', had been detained without trial in police cells. Black-on-black violence in the townships resumed with a vengeance.

Renewed destabilization   New pressures, including threats of invasion, were put on South Africa's neighbours to stop MK infiltration. Mindful of the Lesotho coup, Botswana agreed to pass an SA-model internal security law; and security checks were placed on all its major roads to search for MK weapons.

Mozambique   SADF support for MNR had been stepped up secretly at the end of 1984. The SADF disagreed with SA official foreign policy towards the FRELIMO government. It wanted MNR to exploit the increasing unpopularity in rural areas of FRELIMO seen as the party of bureaucrats and town-dwellers.

South African relations with Mozambique reached an all-time low when President Machel died in a plane crash on the South African border in October 1986. The pilot was probably confused by South African radio beacons. Was this confusion deliberate?

By 1987–88 almost a million people had fled abroad from MNR banditry in Mozambique, half of them to Malawi. A US government report noted widespread atrocities, including murder and mutilation, against rural families in Mozambique.

Comrades and warlords   By August 1987, after arrests of MK guerrillas in the western Cape, the revolt against government control in the townships had been crushed — but civil war continued between 'comrades' and police-supported vigilantes.

Battles between police-allied Inkatha 'warlords' from KwaZulu and UDF-allied civics started in Pietermaritzburg townships in 1985–87, and spread to Durban. On the Witwatersrand there was continuing strife between male hostel-dwellers, newly arrived from rural KwaZulu, and families in surrounding township areas.

Trade union action   Arrests and detentions continued until the UDF itself was banned in February 1988. Trade unions, however, remained unbroken. The NUM showed its strength by a well-organized three-week strike of gold miners on the Witwatersrand in 1987. That same year also saw a bitter strike by black railway workers — including destruction of railway property and bloody police repression.

Bantustan coups   Political instability spread to the Bantustans. The Transkei government of the Mantanzima brothers was overthrown in a military coup of December 1987. A coup in Bophutatswana was quickly crushed by the SADF in February 1988. But the SADF did not interfere in successful military coups in Ciskei and Venda in 1990.

10 Period of negotiation, 1988–92

Negotiations between the South African government and the ANC in exile began in August 1987, after a group of sixty leading Afrikaners had met ANC leaders in West Africa at Dakar in July. But P. W. Botha refused to discuss the need for a new constitution and re-incorporation of the Bantustans, and refused to talk to communists on the ANC side.

Talks between South Africa and Angola and Cuba — sponsored by the USA and USSR — began in May 1988. (The USSR, led by the reformer Mikhail Gorbachev since 1985, was at the same time withdrawing its own troops from Afghanistan in Asia.)

Battle of Cuito Cuanavale   While negotiations continued, the war in Angola intensified. Cuban and Angolan troops recaptured south-western Angola. The turning point came in November 1988, when South African troops were repulsed in a three-day battle in south-eastern Angola at Cuito Cuanavale — an airbase which the SADF had been besieging for a year.

South Africa had lost command of the skies to modern Angolan aircraft. SADF aircraft were out-dated and poorly equipped, because of French and American sanctions stopping military supplies to South Africa.

Angola/Namibia Accords   In December 1988 a ceasefire was signed by Angola, Cuba and South Africa. The advance of Namibia towards independence, along lines approved by the United Nations, was guaranteed by the phased withdrawal of Cuban troops from Angola.

From Botha to de Klerk   The retreat of the SADF from Angola, and his refusal to push ahead with reforms, led to the downfall of P. W. Botha in South Africa. He was replaced by F. W. de Klerk, first as head of the National Party in February 1989 and then as president in August–September. De Klerk, unlike Botha, was prepared to bend in negotiations with the ANC for a New South Africa. Before Botha finally retired, he met Mandela in July, but refused to be friendly.

Mass defiance campaign   Meanwhile, with the UDF restricted, anti-*apartheid* groups and COSATU were organized into a so-called Mass Democratic Movement (MDM). The MDM turned back to pre-1960 tactics of 'moral force', in the city centres rather than in the townships, starting a new defiance

The commanding height, Church Square, Pretoria, September 1987. Protestors against police brutality mount the Paul Kruger statue, the symbol of Afrikanerdom in the centre of the capital. Such legal protest in so 'sacred' a place had previously been inconceivable.

campaign against unjust laws in August 1989. The campaign began successfully: black patients demanding to enter white city hospitals were admitted.

The churches took a leading part in the MDM defiance campaign. Both Protestant and Catholic churches had senior black clergy by the early 1980s. Desmond Tutu, the 1984 Nobel peace prize winner, had become Anglican archbishop of Cape Town in 1986. He appealed for peace at numerous township funerals, and led demonstration marches of churchmen to parliament and presidential buildings in Cape Town. Increasing numbers of clergy agreed with the 1985 Kairos declaration by radical church leaders — that God was on the side of the poor and oppressed, and against an evil state.

Namibia independence   Battles between SWAPO guerrillas and the SADF in northern Namibia reached their peak in April 1989. But Cuban withdrawal from Angola, and a new president in South Africa, ensured that arrangements for Namibia's independence went ahead. November elections resulted in a SWAPO majority, and a DTA minority in the new national assembly. Both parties compromised on a new multi-party constitution.

On 21 March 1990, Namibia became an independent republic, with a SWAPO government and Sam Nujoma as president.

Release of Mandela   In October 1989 the South African government released eight ANC leaders, including Walter Sisulu and Govan Mbeki, from a lifetime in jail. The world's most famous prisoner, Nelson Mandela, was released after 27 years imprisonment on 11 February 1990.

Negotiations for a New South Africa   The ANC, PAC, SA communist party, UDF and COSATU were unbanned on 2 February 1990. Full negotiations between the South African government and the ANC, now led by Mandela, began in May 1990. In June the state of emergency was lifted. In August the ANC agreed to a ceasefire (the 'Pretoria minute') after thirty years.

During 1991 the basic *apartheid* laws relating to racial classification, rural land and urban residence were repealed. The UDF incorporated itself into the ANC. Constitutional negotiations began at CODESA (Convention for a Democratic South Africa) in December, at which all parties — except Inkatha and Bophutatswana — agreed on 'a democratic, non-racial, non-sexist country with justice for all'.

CODESA negotiations faltered in May 1992, when the ruling National Party and ANC disagreed on a new constitution. The National Party was trying to create structures and alliances which would keep it in power after one-person-one-vote elections. The ANC meanwhile insisted that the government was encouraging black-on-black violence in order to discredit the ANC in the townships. Negotiations broke down after the massacre by Inkatha-supporters of 43 township dwellers at Boipatong next to Sharpeville on 17 June 1992.

Regional prospects   Peace returned to most southern Africa states as South Africa began negotiating with its African nationalists and

ANC demonstration in the Vaal Triangle, Vereeniging, 1989. Police or SADF troops have segregated the demonstrators from Saturday morning shoppers with coils of razor-wire. These coils could be laid over hundreds of metres from drums on the back of moving trucks in a matter of seconds. The demonstrators are jogging along, singing or chanting and doing the *toyi-toyi* dance. Many of them are wearing tee-shirts with ANC slogans on them. Such tee-shirts and posters could be printed in small workshops, and were important in spreading the new 'civic' ideas of the 1980s.

ceased directly attacking its neighbours in 1989. But destabilization by anti-government guerrillas continued in Angola and Mozambique into 1992. During on-off peace negotiations between MPLA and UNITA, and FRELIMO and MNR, the rural economies of Angola and Mozambique were beset by drought and starvation.

Faltering economies   The region as a whole suffered from world economic depression and widespread drought by the early 1990s. Earlier economic growth slowed down and even reversed.

South Africa's economy had failed to keep pace with rising population, or with other new industrial countries in Asia and Latin America. Over the previous quarter century, the South African economy had grown at more or less the same pace as other southern African countries such as Zimbabwe and Tanzania. Only Angola and Botswana, because of oil and diamonds respectively, had

grown much faster — while Swaziland and Namibia, and particularly Zambia, had lagged behind the South African rate. Mozambique had developed until about 1980, then rapidly declined. Economists argued that all southern African economies, including South Africa, had been destabilized by mismanagement as well as by *apartheid* and war, recession and debt.

The wealth ('real' gross domestic product) of all SADCC countries together was estimated at about $80 billion in 1989, matched against South Africa's $175 billion. But SADCC had more than 80 million people to feed, reducing its wealth per person to some of the lowest levels in the world. South Africa had less than 40 million to feed, but its wealth was very unevenly distributed between the rich minority and the poor majority of the population.

Political developments   Economic unrest over worker unemployment resulted in strikes in Swaziland in 1989, and a second military coup in Lesotho in 1990 and riots in 1991. In Zambia, Kaunda was defeated by the trade unionist-led Movement for Multi-Party Democracy (MMD) in elections of 1991. New opposition movements for multi-party democracy also developed in Zimbabwe and, illegally, in Malawi.

Revolutionary socialist ideas became unfashionable with the rapid decline and eventual 1991 break-up of the Soviet Union. FRELIMO in Mozambique ceased to be a Marxist–Leninist party in 1989. But ideas of democratic socialism persisted among black workers in the more industrialized economy of South Africa.

Meanwhile, in 1992 there were initiatives for economic recovery and political stability through regional cooperation, SADCC renamed itself the Southern African Development Community (SADC), looking forward to a free trade area including South Africa.

Questions

1 '*Apartheid* created South African economic growth, and *apartheid* killed it'. Discuss.

2 How was southern Africa 'destabilized' in the 1980s? What were the causes of destabilization?

3 What events changed the political face of southern Africa in 1989–90? How effective have changes been since then?

Activities

1 Make and keep up to date a weekly 'wall newspaper' of news and pictures from other southern African countries apart from your own. (Take clippings from newspapers and magazines, or reports of radio news; organize them with your own headings and/or editorial comment; and attach them to a board or wall with pins or tape.)

2 Keep a diary of current events (with handwritten notes from press, radio or tv) in one particular southern African country). [Different countries may be assigned to groups within a class.]

3 Debate how much history explains current events, and how much it does not explain.

For references see Bibliography pp. 337–42 — n.b. H1–H36 listed under 'South and Southern Africa since 1968'; J1–4, J9, J15, J18, J20, J24–27 under 'Journals'; also: B2 Bozzoli & Delius; B3 Bundy; B4 Cameron; B5 Davenport; B7 Eriksen & Moorsom; B12 Haliburton; B14 Konczacki; B23 Mbeki; B25 Morton &c; B32 Readers Digest; B34 Saunders; B43 Wood; F16 de Gruchy; F43 Platsky & Walker; F57 Wolpe; G2 Burdette; G12 Lan; G18 Picard; G20 Ranger.

Bibliography of Major Sources and Further Reading

[Books in print and for sale, or recently enough published to be available in good libraries]

GENERAL

School and College Textbooks

A1   BHEBE, N. & NGCONGCO, L. (eds.), *Junior Certificate History of Southern Africa, Books 1 & 2* (Oxford: Heinemann International, 1979–81)

A2   BOYCE, A. N., *The Modern World and South Africa*, Stds 8 & 9 (Manzini: Macmillan Boleswa, 1990)

A3   DENOON, D. & NYEKO, B. *Southern Africa since 1800* London: Longman, 1984 edn. & New York: Praeger, &c.

A4   KALLAWAY, P., etc. *History Alive, Standards 9 & 10* Pietermaritzburg: Shuter   & Shooter, 1986 & 1987

A5   MBUMBA, N. & NOISSER, N. H. *Namibia in History, Junior Secondary History Book* Bremen: CAS Centre for African Studies & London: Zed, 1988

A6   OMER-COOPER, J. D. *A History of Southern Africa* London: James Currey & Cape Town: David Philip, 1987

A7   PAMPALLIS, J. *Foundations of a New South Africa* London: Zed & Cape Town: Longman Maskew Miller, 1991

A8   PARSONS, N. *Focus on History Book 3, a [Senior] Secondary Course for Zimbabwe* Harare: College Press, 1991

A9   PROCTOR, A. & I. PHIMISTER *People and Power: an O-Level Textbook for Zimbabwe, Book One* Harare: Academic Books, 1991

A10   SHILLINGTON, K. *History of Southern Africa* London: Longman, 1987

A11   van JAARSVELD, F. A. *New Illustrated History* Johannesburg: Perskor, 1975 edn.

A12   WITZ, I., *Write Your Own History* Johannesburg: Ravan/SACHED, 1988

Other General Histories

B1   BOOTH, A. R. *Swaziland: Tradition and Change in a Southern African Kingdom* Boulder: Westview & Aldershot: Gower, 1983

B2   BOZZOLI, B. & P. DELIUS (eds.) *History from South Africa* New York: Radical History Review (46/7)/MARHO, 1990

B3   BUNDY, C. *Re-Making the Past: New Perspectives in South African History* Cape Town: U. Cape Town DAE & EMS, 1986

B4   CAMERON, T. (ed.) *A (New) Illustrated History of South Africa* Johannesburg: Jonathan   Ball, 1991 edn.

B5   DAVENPORT, T. R. H. *South Africa: a Modern History* Cambridge: Cambridge   U.P. & Toronto: U. Toronto Press, 4th edn. 1991

B6   DUMINY, A. & B. GUEST (eds.) *Natal and Zululand from Earliest Times to 1910, a New History* Pietermaritzburg: Shuter & Shooter & U. Natal Press, 1989

B7   ERIKSEN,   T. L. & R. MOORSOM *The Political Economy of Namibia: an Annotated Bibliography* Uppsala & Oslo: Scandinavian Institute of African Studies & Lusaka: United Nations, 1990 edn.

B8   FORMAN,   S. & A. ODENDAAL, (eds.) *A Trumpet from the Housetops: the Selected Writings of Lionel Forman* London: Zed & Cape Town: David Philip, 1992

B9   FREDERICKSON, G. M. *White Supremacy: a Comparative Study in American and South African History* New York & Oxford: Oxford U.P., 1981

B10   GREENBERG, S. *Race and State in Capitalist Development: (South Africa in) Comparative Perspectives* New Haven: Yale U.P. & Johannesburg: Ravan, 1980

B11   J. J. GROTPETER *Historical   Dictionary   of   Swaziland* Metuchen, NJ: Scarecrow, 1975

B12   G. HALIBURTON *Historical Dictionary of Lesotho* Metuchen, NJ: Scarecrow, 1977

B13   JAMES, W. G. & M. SIMONS (eds.) *The Angry Divide: Social and Economic History of the Western Cape* Cape Town: David Philip, 1989

B14   KONCZACKI, Z. A., &c. (eds.) *Studies in the Economic History of Southern Africa Vol. 1: Front-Line States; Vol. 2: South Africa, Lesotho and Swaziland* London: Frank Cass, 1990–91

B15   KRUGER, H. *The Making of a Nation* Johannesburg: Macmillan, 1972

B16   LAMAR, H. & L. M. THOMPSON (eds.) *The Frontier in History: North America and Southern Africa Compared* New

Haven: Yale U.P., 1981

B17 LYE, W. F. & C. MURRAY *Transformations on the Highveld: the Tswana and Southern Sotho* Cape Town: David Philip, New York: Barnes & Noble, & London: James Currey: 1985

B18 MARKS, S. 'South Africa' in *Encyclopaedia Britannica* Chicago: 1993 edn.

B19 MARKS, S., &c. Chapters in R. Oliver (ed.) *Cambridge History of Africa*, 1971–85. 8 vols.

B20 MATSEBULA, J. S. M. *A History of Swaziland* Cape Town: Longman, 1976 edn.

B21 MAYLAM, P. *The History of the African People of South Africa: From the Early Iron Age to the 1970s* Cape Town: David Philip, 1987; New York: St Martin's Press & London: Routledge, 1987

B22 MAZIKANA, P. C., &c. *Zimbabwe Epic* Harare: National Archives, 1982

B23 MBEKI, G. *The Struggle for Liberation in South Africa: a Short History* Cape Town: David Philip, 1992

B24 MINTER, W. *King Solomon's Mines Revisited: Western Interests and the Burdened History of Southern Africa* New York: Basic Books, 1986

B25 MORTON, F., &c. *Historical Dictionary of Botswana, New Edition* Metuchen, N.J: Scarecrow, 1989

B26 MULLER, C. F. J. (ed.) *Five Hundred Years: a History of South Africa* Pretoria: Human & Rousseau, 1975 edn.

B27 NATIONAL EDUCATION CRISIS COMMITTEE *What is History? A New Approach to History for Students, Workers and Communities* Johannesburg: Skotaville, 1987

B28 *New Nation New History*, vols. 1– Johannesburg: New Nation, 1989–

B29 NXUMALO, J. M. *The National Question in the Writing of South African History* Milton Keynes: Open U. DPP Working Paper, 1992

B30 PALMER, R. & N. PARSONS (eds.) *The Roots of Rural Poverty in Central and Southern Africa* London: Heinemann & Berkeley: U. California Press, 1977 & London: James Currey, 1989

B31 RASMUSSEN, R. K. *Historical Dictionary of Zimbabwe/Rhodesia* Metuchen: Scarecrow, 1979

B32 READERS DIGEST *Illustrated History of South Africa: the Real Story* New York, Montreal & Cape Town: Readers Digest, 1988

B33 ROBERTS, A. D. *A History of Zambia* London: Heinemann, 1976

B34 SAUNDERS, C. C. *Historical Dictionary of South Africa* Metuchen: Scarecrow, 1983

B35 SAUNDERS, C. C. *The Making of the South African Past: Major Historians on Race and Class* Cape Town: David Philip & New York: Barnes & Noble, 1988

B36 THOMPSON, L. M. *A History of South Africa* New Haven & London: Yale U.P., 1990

B37 TLOU, T. & A. CAMPBELL *History of Botswana* Gaborone: Macmillan, 1984

B38 TSOTSI, W. M. *From Chattel to Wage Slavery: a New Approach to South African History* Maseru: Lesotho Printing, 1981

B39 VAIL, L. (ed.) *The Creation of Tribalism in Southern Africa* Berkeley: U. California Press, London: James Currey, & Cape Town: David Philip, 1989

B40 van JAARSVELD, F. A. *The Afrikaner's Interpretation of South African History* Cape Town: Simondium, 1964

B41 WALKER, C. (ed.) *Women and Gender in South Africa to 1945* London: James Currey, Bloomington: Indiana U.P. & Cape Town: David Philip, 1990

B42 WILSON, M. & L. M. THOMPSON (eds.) *The Oxford History of South Africa, Vols. 1 & 2* Oxford: Clarendon Press & Cape Town: Oxford U.P., 1969–71

B43 WOOD, B. (ed.) *Namibia 1884 1984: Readings on Namibia's History and Society* London: Namibia Support Committee & Lusaka: United Nations, 1988

PART I: THE PEOPLING OF SOUTHERN AFRICA

C1 AXELSON, E. *Portuguese in South-East Africa 1488–1600* Cape Town: Struik, 1973

C2 BEACH, D. N. *The Shona & Zimbabwe 900–1850: an Outline of Shona History* London: Heinemann & Gweru: Mambo Press, 1980

C3 DENBOW, J. & J. DENBOW *Uncovering Botswana's Past* Gaborone: National Museum, 1989

C4 ELPHICK, R. *Kraal and Castle: Khoikhoi and the Founding of White South Africa* New Haven: Yale U.P., 1977

C5 ELPHICK, R. & H. GILIOMEE (eds.) *The Shaping of South African Society, 1652–1840* [Cape Colony] Cape Town: Longman, 1989 edn.

C6 GARLAKE, P. S. *Great Zimbabwe Described and Explained* Harare: Zimbabwe Publishing House, 1982

C7 GARLAKE, P. S. *Life at Great Zimbabwe* Gweru: Mambo Press, 1982

C8 GARLAKE, P. S. *Early Zimbabwe from the Matopos to Inyanga* Gweru: Mambo Press, 1983

C9 HALL, M. *The Changing Past: Farmers, Kings and Traders in Southern Africa, 200–1860* Cape Town: David Philip, Chicago: Chicago U.P. & London: James Currey, 1987

C10 HAMILTON, C. (ed.) *The Mfecane Aftermath: towards a New Paradigm in South African History* Johannesburg: Witwatersrand U.P., Berkeley: U. California Press & London: James Currey, 1993

C11 HUMPHREYS, A. J. B. *Searching for the Past; the Methods and Techniques of Archaeology* Cape Town; David Philip, 1986

C12 INSKEEP, R. R. *The Peopling of Southern Africa* Cape Town: David Philip & London: Rex Collings, 1979

C13 JOHNSON, R. T. & T. MAGGS *Major Rock Paintings of Southern Africa* Cape Town: David Philip & Indiana U.P., 1986

C14 LEWIS-WILLIAMS, D. *Discovering Southern African Rock Art* Cape Town: David Philip, 1990

C15 MAGGS, T. M. O'C. *Iron Age Communities of the Southern Highveld* Pietermaritzburg: Natal Museum, 1976

C16 MALHERBE, C., &c. (Shuter's History Reference Library) 1 *These Small People (Hunter-Gatherers)*; 2 *Men of Men (Herders)*; 3 *Always Working (Slaves)*; 4 *Changing the Land (Early Farmers)*; 5 *Struggle for the Land (19th Century Farmers)* Pietermaritzburg: Shuter & Shooter, 1983-90

C17 MASON, R. J. *Origin of the African People of the Johannesburg Area* Johannesburg: Skotaville, 1987

C18 MASON, R. J. *Origins of Black People of Johannesburg and the Southern Western Central Transvaal AD 350-1880* Johannesburg: U. Witwatersrand, Archaeology Research Unit, 1986

C19 MILLER, J. C. *Way of Death: Merchant Capitalism & the Angolan Slave Trade 1730-1830* Madison: U. Wisconsin Press & London: James Currey, 1989

C20 MUDENGE, S. J. G. *A Political History of Munhumutapa c. 1400-1902* Harare: Zimbabwe Publishing House, London: James Currey & Portsmouth, N. H.: Heinemann, 1989

C21 OMER-COOPER, J. D. *The Zulu Aftermath: a Nineteenth Century Revolution in Bantu Africa* Ibadan & London: Longman, 1966

C22 PEIRES, J. (ed.) *Before and After Shaka: Papers in Nguni History* Grahamstown: Rhodes U., 1983

C23 PHILLIPSON, D. W. *The Later Prehistory of Eastern and Southern Africa* London: Heinemann, 1977

C24 PLATTJE, S. T. *Mhudi (An Epic of South African Native Life a Hundred Years Ago)* Alice, Cape: Lovedale Press, 1930; Johannesburg: Quagga Press, 1975; Longman: Heinemann & Washington: Three Continents, 1978

C25 RANDLES, W. G. I. *The Empire of Monomotapa, from the Fifteenth to the Nineteenth Century* Gweru: Mambo, 1979 (French edn. 1975)

C26 ROSS, R. *Cape of Storms: Slavery and Resistance in South Africa* London: Routledge, 1983

C27 SAUNDERS, C. & R. DERRICOURT (eds.) *Beyond the Cape Frontier: Studies in the History of the Transkei and Ciskei* Cape Town: Longman, 1974

C28 SUTTON, J. *A Thousand Years of East Africa* Nairobi: British Institute in Eastern Africa, 1990

C29 THOMPSON, L. M. (ed.) *African Societies in Southern Africa: Historical Studies* Berkeley: U. California Press & London: Heinemann, 1969

C30 van WAARDEN, C. (ed.) *Kalanga Retrospect and Prospect* Gaborone: Botswana Society 1991

C31 WILMSEN, E. N. *Land Filled with Flies: a Political Economy of the Kalahari* Chicago: U. Chicago Press, 1989

C32 WORDEN, N. *Slavery in Dutch South Africa* Cambridge: Cambridge U.P., 1985

C33 WOODHOUSE, B. *The Bushman Art of Southern Africa* London: Macdonald, 1979

PART II: CONQUEST AND RESISTANCE

Before the Scramble

D1 BEACH, D. N. *Zimbabwe before 1900* Gweru: Mambo Press, 1984

D2 BERGH, J. S. & A. P. BERGH *Tribes and Kingdoms* Cape Town: Don Nelson, 1984

D3 BONNER, P. *Kings, Commoners and Concessionaires: the Evolution and Dissolution of the Nineteenth-Century Swazi State* Cambridge: Cambridge U.P. & Johannesburg: Ravan, 1983

D4 COMAROFF, J. & J. COMAROFF *Of Revelation and Revolution: Christianity, Colonialism and Consciousness in South Africa, Volume One* [S. Tswana] Chicago: U. Chicago Press, 1991

D5 DELIUS, P. *The Land Belongs to Us: the Pedi Policy, the*

Boers and the British in Nineteenth Century Transvaal Johannesburg: Ravan Press, 1983

D6 GRAY, S. *Southern African Literature, an Introduction* [19th century] London: Rex Collings & Cape Town: David Philip, 1979

D7 GUY, J. *The Heretic: a Study of the Life of John William Colenso 1814-1883* Johannesburg: Ravan & Pietermaritzburg: U. Natal Press, 1983

D8 HERD, N. *The Bent Pine (The Trial of Chief Langalibalele)* Johannesburg: Ravan, 1976

D9 HODGSON, J. *Princess Emma* [Sandile's daughter] Craighall, Cape: Ad Donker, 1987

D10 LANGWORTHY, H. W. *Zambia Before 1890* London: Longman, 1972

D11 LAU, B. *Namibia in Jonker Afrikaner's Time* Windhoek: National Archives, 1987

D12 MAJEKE, N. [D. Taylor] *The Role of the Missionaries in Conquest* Cape Town: Unity Movement, 1952 & Cumberwood: APDUSA, 1986

D13 MARKS, S. & A. ATMORE (eds.) *Economy and Society in Pre-Industrial South Africa* London & New York: Longman, 1980

D14 PEIRES, J. B. *The House of Phalo: a History of the Xhosa People in the Days of their Independence* Johannesburg: Ravan, 1981

D15 PEIRES, J. B. *The Dead Will Arise: Nongqawuse and the Great Xhosa Cattle Killing of 1856-7* Johannesburg: Ravan, London: James Currey & Bloomington: Indiana U.P., 1989

D16 ROSS, A. *John Philip (1775-1851): Missions, Race and Politics in South Africa* Aberdeen: U. Aberdeen Press, 1986

D17 SANDERS, P. B. *Moshoeshoe, Chief of the Sotho* London: Heinemann, 1975

D18 SAUNDERS, C. C. *Black Leaders in Southern African History* London: Heinemann, 1979

D19 THOMPSON, I. M. *Survival in Two Worlds: Moshoeshoe of Lesotho 1786-1870* London: Oxford U.P., 1975

D20 VENTER, C. *The Great*

Trek Cape Town: Don Nelson, 1983

The Scramble

E1   BEACH, D. N. *War and Politics in Zimbabwe 1840–1900* Gweru: Mambo Press, 1986

E2   BEINART, W. *The Political Economy of Pondoland 1860–1930* Cambridge: Cambridge U.P. & Johannesburg: Ravan, 1982

E3   BEINART, W., &c. (eds.) *Putting a Plough to the Ground: Accumulation and Dispossession in Rural South Africa 1850–1930* Johannesburg: Ravan, 1986

E4   BEINART, W. & C. BUNDY, *Hidden Struggles in Rural South Africa: Politics and Popular Movement in the Transkei & Eastern Cape* Johannesburg: Ravan, London: James Currey & Berkeley: U. California Press, 1987

E5   BLEY, H. *South-West Africa Under German Rule 1894–1914* London: Heinemann & Evanston: Northwestern U.P., 1971 (German edn. 1968)

E6   BUNDY, C. *The Rise and Fall of the South African Peasantry* London: Heinemann & Berkeley: U. California P., 1979; London: James Currey & Cape Town: David Philip, 1988

E7   CAMMACK, D. *The Rand at War 1899–1902* Berkeley: U. California Press, London: James Currey & Pietermaritzburg: U. Natal Press, 1990

E8   DAVENPORT, T. R. H. *The Afrikaner Bond, the History of a South African Political Party, 1880–1911* Cape Town: Oxford U.P., 1966

E9   DAVIDSON, A. *Cecil Rhodes and His Time* Moscow: Progress Publishers, 1988 (Russian edn. 1984)

E10   DENOON, D. J. N. *A Grand Illusion: the Failure of Imperial Policy in the Transvaal during the Period of Reconstruction, 1900–1905* London: Longman, 1973

E11   DRESCHLER, H. *Let Us Die Fighting: the Struggle of the Herero and Nama against German Imperialism (1884–1915)* London: Zed, 1980 (German edn. 1966)

E12   FIRST, R. & A. SCOTT *Olive Schreiner: a Biography* London: Women's Press, 1989

E13   GUY, J. *The Destruction of the Zulu Kingdom: the Civil War in Zululand, 1879–1884* London: Longman, 1979 & Johannesburg: Ravan, 1982

E14   JEAL, T. *Baden-Powell* London: Pimlico, 1989

E15   JEEVES, A. H. *Migrant Labour in South Africa's Mining Economy: the Struggle for the Gold Mines' Labour Supply 1890–1920* Kingston: McGill-Queen's U. P. & Johannesburg: Witwatersrand U.P., 1985

E16   KEEGAN, T. *Rural Transformations in Industrializing South Africa: the Southern Highveld to 1914* Johannesburg: Ravan, 1986

E17   KEEGAN, T. *Facing the Storm: Portraits of Black Lives in Rural South Africa* [OFS & S. Transvaal] Cape Town: David Philip, 1988

E18   LAU, B. (ed.) *The Hendrik Witbooi Papers* [1884–1905] Windhoek: National Archives, 1990

E19   LONGFORD, E. (E. Pakenham) *Jameson's Raid (The Prelude to the Boer War)* London: Weidenfeld, 1960 & Granada Panther, 1982

E20   MARKS, S. & R. RATHBONE (eds.) *Industrialisation and Social Change in South Africa: African Class Formation, Culture and Consciousness 1870–1930* London: Longman, 1982

E21   MENDELSOHN, R. *Sammy Marks, The Uncrowned King of the Transvaal* Cape Town: David Philip & Athens, Ohio: Ohio U.P., 1991

E22   NASSON, B. *Abraham Esau's War: a Black South African's War in the Cape, 1899–1902* Cambridge: Cambridge U.P. & Cape Town: David Philip, 1991

E23   NEWBURY, C. *The Diamond Ring: Business, Politics and Precious Stones in South Africa 1867–1947* Oxford: Clarendon Press, 1989

E24   PAKENHAM, T. *The Boer War* London: Wiedenfeld, 1979

E25   PLAATJE, S. *Mafeking Diary: a Black Man's View of a White Man's War* London: James Currey, Johannesburg: Southern Books & Athens, Ohio: Ohio U.P., 1990 new edn.

E26   PORTER, A. N. *The Origins of the South African War: Joseph Chamberlain and the Diplomacy of Imperialism 1895–99* Manchester: Manchester U.P., 1980

E27   PRINS, G. *The Hidden Hippopotamus: the Early Colonial Experience in Western Zambia* Cambridge: Cambridge U.P., 1980

E28   RANGER, T. O. *Revolt in Southern Rhodesia 1896–7: a Study in African Resistance* London: Heinemann, 1967

E29   RIVE, R. (ed.) *Olive Schreiner: Letters 1871–1899* Cape Town: David Philip & Oxford: Oxford U.P., 1987

E30   ROTBERG, R. *The Founder: Cecil Rhodes and the Pursuit of Power* New York: Oxford U.P., 1988

E31   SCHREUDER, D. M. *Gladstone and Kruger: Liberal Government and Colonial 'Home Rule' 1880–85* London: Routledge & Toronto: U. Toronto Press, 1969

E32   SPIES, S. B. *Methods of Barbarism? Roberts and Kitchener and Civilians in the Boer Republics: January 1900–May 1902* Cape Town: Human & Rousseau, 1977

E33   TURRELL, R. V. *Capital and Labour on the Kimberley Diamond Fields 1871–1890* Cambridge: Cambridge U.P., 1987

E34   van JAARSVELD, F. A. *The Awakening of Afrikaner Nationalism, 1868–1881* Johannesburg: Human & Rousseau; Atlantic Highlands, NJ: Humanities, 1961

E35   van ONSELEN, C. (Studies in the Social and Economic History of the Witwatersrand 1886–1914): 1 *New Babylon*; 2 *New Nineveh* London: Longman, 1982

E36   van ONSELEN, C. *The Small Matter of a Horse: the Life of 'Nongoloza' Mathebula 1867–1948* Johannesburg: Ravan, 1984

E37   WARWICK, P. (ed.) *The South African War* London: Longman, 1980

E38   WARWICK, P. *Black People and the South African War 1899–1902* Cambridge: Cambridge U.P.

& Johannesburg: Ravan, 1983

E39   WELSH, D. *The Roots of Segregation, Native Policy in Natal (1835-1910)* Cape Town: Oxford U.P., 1971

E40   WHEATCROFT, G. *The Randlords: South Africa's Robber Barons and the Mines that Forged a Nation* New York: Simon & Shuster, 1985

E41   *South Africa's City of Diamonds: Mine Workers and Monopoly Capitalism in Kimberley, 1867-1895* New Haven: Yale U. P., 1987

PART III: COLONIALISM AND INDEPENDENCE

South Africa

F1   AFRICAN NATIONAL CONGRESS *Unity in Action, a Photographic History of the African National Congress South Africa 1912-1982* London: ANC, 1982

F2   BENSON, M. *A Far Cry: the Making of a South African* [autobiography] New York & London: Viking-Penguin, 1989

F3   BHANA, S. & B. A. PACHAI *Documentary History of Indian South Africa* Stanford: Hoover Press & Cape Town: David Philip, 1984

F4   BONNER, P. *Working Papers in Southern African Studies, Volume 2* Johannesburg: Ravan, 1981

F5   BONNER, P., &c. (eds.) *Holding their Ground: Class, Locality and Culture in 19th and 20th Century South Africa* Johannesburg: Ravan & Witwatersrand U.P., 1989

F6   BOZZOLI, B. (ed.) *Town and Countryside in the Transvaal: Capitalist Penetration and Popular Response* Johannesburg: Ravan, 1983

F7   BOZZOLI, B. (ed.) *Class, Community and Conflict: South African Perspectives* Johannesburg: Ravan, 1987

F8   BOZZOLI, B. & M. NKOTSOE *Women of Phokeng: Consciousness, Life Strategy and Migrancy in South Africa, 1900-83* Johannesburg: Ravan, London: James Currey & Portsmouth, NH: Heinemann, 1991

F9   CALLICANOS, L. *Gold and Workers [on the Rand] 1886-1924* Johannesburg: Ravan Press, 1981

F10   CALLICANOS, L. *Working Life 1886-1940: Factories, Townships and Popular Culture on the Rand* Johannesburg: Ravan, 1987

F11   CLAYTON, C. (ed.) *Women and Writing in South Africa: a Critical Anthology* Johannesburg: Heinemann, 1989

F12   CLINGMAN, S. (ed.) *Regions and Repertoires: Topics in South African Politics and Culture* Johannesburg: Ravan, 1991

F13   COPLAN, D. R. *In Township Tonight!: South Africa's City Black Music and Theatre* London: Longman & Johannesburg: Ravan, 1985

F14   COUZENS, T. *The New African: a Study of the Life and Work of H.I.E. Dhlomo* Johannesburg: Ravan, 1985

F15   CRUSH, J., &c. *South Africa's Labor Empire: A History of Black Migrancy to the Gold Mines* Bridgport Conn: Westview Press & Cape Town: David Philip, 1991

F16   de GRUCHY, *The Church Struggle in South Africa* New York: Eerdmans & Cape Town: David Philip, 1986

F17   DUBOW, S. *Racial Segregation and the Origins of Segregation in South Africa 1919-36* [SA Native Administration] Basingstoke: Macmillan, 1989

F18   EDGAR, R. *Because They Chose the Plan of God: the Story of the Bulhoek Massacre* Johannesburg: Ravan, 1988

F19   GERHART, G. M. *Black Power in South Africa: the Evolution of an Ideology* Berkeley: U. California Press, 1978

F20   GRUNDLINGH, A. *Fighting Their Own War: South African Blacks and the First World War* Johannesburg: Ravan, 1987

F21   HINDSON, D. C. (ed.) *Working Papers in Southern African Studies, Vol. 3* Johannesburg: Ravan, 1983

F22   HIRSON, Baruch *Yours for the Union: Class and Community in South Africa, 1930-1947* London: Zed & Johannesburg: Witwatersrand U.P., 1989

F23   HOOPER, C. *Brief Authority* London: Faber, 1960 & Cape Town: David Philip, 1989

F24   HOUGHTON, D. H. *The South African Economy* Cape Town: Oxford U.P., 1973 edn.

F25   INNES, D. *Anglo American and the Rise of Modern South Africa* New York: Monthly Review, London: James Currey & Johannesburg: Ravan, 1984

F26   KALLAWAY, P. & P. PEARSON *Johannesburg: Images and Continuities, a History of Working Class Life through Pictures 1885-1935* Johannesburg: Ravan, 1986

F27   KARIS, T. & G. CARTER (eds.) *From Protest to Challenge: a Documentary History of African Politics in South Africa 1882-1964* Stanford: Hoover Institution, 1972-72. 4 vols.

F28   La HAUSSE, P. *Brewers, Beerhalls and Boycotts: a History of Liquor in South Africa* Johannesburg: Ravan, 1988

F29   LERUMO, A. [M. Harmel] *Fifty Fighting Years: the Communist Party of South Africa 1921-1971* London: Inkululeko, 1971

F30   LIPTON, M. *Capitalism and Apartheid: South Africa, 1910-1986* London: Wildwood House & Cape Town: John Philip

F31   LODGE, T. (ed.) *Resistance and Ideology in Settler Societies* Johannesburg: Ravan, 1986

F32   MACMILLAN, H. & S. MARKS (ed.) *Africa and Empire: W. M. Macmillan, Historian and Social Critic* London: Temple Smith, 1989

F33   MACMILLAN, W. M. *The South African Agrarian Problem and its Historical Development* Pretoria: State Library, 1974 reprint of 1919 edn.

F34   MARKS, S. *The Ambiguities of Dependence in South Africa: Class, Nationalism, and the State in Twentieth Century Natal* [Solomon, J.L. Dube, Champion & G. Buthelezi] Johannesburg: Ravan, 1986

F35   MARKS, S. & S. TRAPIDO

(eds.) *The Politics of Race, Class & Nationalism in Twentieth Century South Africa* London & New York: Longman, 1987

F36　MEER, F. *Higher than Hope: Mandela, The Biography* Durban: Madiba, 1989

F37　MELI, F. *South Africa Belongs to Us: a History of the ANC* Harare: Zimbabwe Publishing House, London: James Currey & Bloomington: Indiana U.P., 1989

F38　ODENDAAL, A. *Vukani Bantu! The Beginnings of Black Protest Politics in South Africa to 1912* Cape Town: David Philip & New York: Barnes & Noble, 1984

F39　O'MEARA, D. *Volkskapitalisme: Class, Capital and Ideology in the Development of Afrikaner Nationalism, 1934-1948* Johannesburg: Ravan, 1983

F40　PACKARD, R. M. *White Plague, Black Labor: Tuberculosis & the Political Economy of Health & Disease in South Africa* [1912-70] Berkeley: U. California Press 1989: London: James Currey & Pietermaritzburg: U. Natal Press, 1990

F41　PATEL, E. (ed.) *The World of Nat Nakasa* Johannesburg: Ravan/Bateleur, 1975

F42　PLAATJE, S. T. *Native Life in South Africa before and since the European War and the Boer Rebellion* London, P. S. King, New York: the Crisis & Kimberley: Tsala ea Batho, 1916; Johannesburg: Ravan, 1982

F43　PLATSKY, L. & C. WALKER *The Surplus People: Forced Removals in South Africa* Johannesburg: Ravan, 1985

F44　RICH, P. B. *White Power and the Liberal Conscience: Racial Segregation and South African Liberalism 1921-60* Manchester: Manchester U.P., & Johannesburg: Ravan, 1984

F45　ROUX, E. *Time Longer than Rope: a History of the Black Man's Struggle for Freedom in South Africa* Madison: U. Wisconsin Press, 1966

F46　SHAVA, P. V. *A People's Voice: Black South African Writing in the Twentieth Century* London: Zed, 1989

F47　SIMONS, J. & R. SIMONS *Class and Colour in South Africa 1850-1950* London: Penguin, 1969 & International Defence & Aid, 1983

F48　SUNDKLER, B. G. M. *Bantu Prophets in South Africa* London: Oxford U.P., 1961 edn.

F49　THEMBA, C. *The Will to Die* [township short stories] London: Heinemann & Cape Town: David Philip, 1982 reprint

F50　VILAKAZI, A., etc. *Shembe: the Revitalization of African Society* Johannesburg: Skotaville, 1986

F51　WALKER, C. *Women and Gender in Southern Africa to 1945* New York: Monthly Review, 1982, Cape Town: David Philip & London: James Currey, 1990

F52　WALKER, C. (ed.) *Women and Resistance in South Africa* London: Onyx Press, 1982

F53　WEBSTER, E. (ed.) *Essays in Southern African Labour History* Johannesburg: Ravan, 1978

F54　WILKINS, I. & STRYDOM, H. *Broederbond: the Super-Afrikaners* London: Paddington, 1979

F55　WILLAN, B. *Sol Plaatje, South African Nationalist 1876-1932* London: Heinemann, Johannesburg: Ravan & Berkeley: U. California Press, 1984; London: James Currey, 1990

F56　WILSON, F. *Migrant Labour (in South Africa)* Johannesburg: Spro-Cas, 1972

F57　WOLPE, H. *Race, Class and the Apartheid State* London: James Currey/Unesco, 1988

Rest of Southern Africa

G1　BHEBE, N. M. B. *B. Burombo: African Politics in Zimbabwe 1947-1958* Harare: College Press, 1989

G2　BURDETTE, M. M. *Zambia Between Two Worlds* Boulder: Westview Press & London: Avebury, 1988

G3　CHANOCK, M. (*Unconsummated Union:*) *Britain, South Africa and Rhodesia, 1900-45* Manchester: Manchester U.P. 1977

G4　CROWDER, M. *The Flogging of Phinehas McIntosh: a Tale of Colonial Folly and Injustice,* *Bechuanaland, 1933* New Haven & London: Yale U.P., 1988

G5　DANIEL, J. & M. F. STEPHEN (eds.) *Historical Perspectives on the Political Economy of Swaziland* Kwaluseni: U. Swaziland SSRU, 1986

G6　DINGAKE, M. *My Fight Against Apartheid* [Botswana/S.A. autobiography] London: Kliptown Books, 1987

G7　EDGAR, R. (ed.) *Prophets with Honour:a Documentary History of Lekhotla la Bafo* Johannesburg: Ravan, n.d. [c. 1987]

G8　HYAM, R. *The Failure of South African Expansion 1908-1948* London: Macmillan, 1972

G9　KATJAVIVI, P. *A History of Resistance in Namibia* London: James Currey/Unesco, 1988

G10　KUPER, H. *Sobhuza II, Ngwenyama and King of Swaziland* London: Duckworth, 1978

G11　LAN, D. *Guns and Rain: Guerrillas and Spirit Mediums in Zimbabwe* London: James Currey, Harare: Zimbabwe Publishing House & Berkeley: U. California Press, 1985

G12　MACHOBANE, L. B. B. *J. Government and Change in Colonial Lesotho* Manzini: Macmillan, 1990

G13　MEEBELO, H. S. *Reaction to Colonialism: a Prelude to the Politics of Independence in Northern Zambia 1893-1939* Manchester: Manchester U.P., 1971

G14　MORTON, F. & J. RAMSAY (eds.) *The Birth of Botswana: a History of the Bechuanaland Protectorate from 1910 to 1966* Gaborone: Longman, 1987

G15　NYAGUMBO, M. G. *With the People: an Autobiography from the Zimbabwe Struggle* London: Allison & Busby, 1980

G16　PALMER, R. H. *Land and Racial Domination in Rhodesia* [1890-1936] London: Heinemann, 1977

G17　PHIMISTER, I. *An Economic and Social History of Zimbabwe 1890-1948: Capital Accumulation and Class Struggle* London: Longman, 1988

G18　PICARD, L. A. *The Politics of Development in Botswana: a*

Model for Success? Boulder & London: Lynne Riener, 1987

G19   RANGER, T. O. *The African Voice in Southern Rhodesia 1898-1930* London: Heinemann, 1970

G20   RANGER, T. O. *Voices from the Rocks [Matabeleland]* London: James Currey, 1993

G21   REY, C. F. *Monarch of All I Survey: Bechuanaland Diaries 1929-37* Gaborone: Botswana Society & London: James Currey, 1988

G22   TORDOFF, W. (ed.) *Politics in Zambia* Manchester: Manchester U.P., 1974

G23   van ONSELEN, C. *Chibaro: African Mine Labour in Southern Rhodesia 1900-1933* London: Pluto, 1976

G24   van ONSELEN, C. & I. R. PHIMISTER *Studies in the History of African Mine Labour in Colonial Zimbabwe* Gweru: Mambo Press, 1978

G25   WOOD, J. R. T. *The Welensky Papers: a History of the Federation of Rhodesia and Nyasaland* Durban: Graham Publishing, 1983

G26   WYLIE, D. *A Little God, The Twilight of Patriarchy in a Southern African Chiefdom [Tshekedi Khama]* New Haven & London: Yale U.P., 1990

SOUTH AND SOUTHERN AFRICA SINCE 1968

H1   BARBER, J. & J. BARRAT *South Africa's Foreign Policy: the Search for Status and Security 1945-1988* Cambridge: Cambridge U.P., 1990

H2   BOONZAIER, E. & J. SHARP (eds.) *South African Keywords: the Uses and Abuses of Political Concepts* Cape Town: David Philip, 1988

H3   CARTER, G. & P. O' MEARA (eds.) *Southern Africa: the Continuing Crisis* London: Macmillan, 1979 &c.

H4   CHAN, S. *Exporting Apartheid: Foreign Policies in Southern Africa 1978-1988* London: Macmillan, 1980

H5   COCK, J. & I. NATHAN (ed.) *War and Society: the Mili-* *tarization of South Africa* Cape Town: David Philip, 1989

H6   DAVIES, R. H. &c. *The Kingdom of Swaziland: a Profile* London: Zed Press, 1987

H7   de WAAL, V. *Zimbabwe, the Politics of Reconciliation* London: Hurst & Cape Town: David Philip, 1990

H8   Du BOULAY, *Tutu: Voice of the Voiceless* London: Penguin, 1988

H9   FREDERIKSE, J. *None but Ourselves: Masses vs. Media in the Making of Zimbabwe* Harare: Zimbabwe Publishing House, New York: Viking Penguin, London: James Currey & Johannesburg: Ravan, 1982

H10   FREDERIKSE, J. *South Africa: A Different Kind of War, from Soweto to Pretoria* Johannesburg: Ravan, 1986

H11   HANLON, J. *Beggar your Neighbours: Apartheid Power in Southern Africa* London: James Currey, Bloomington: Indiana U.P. & Cape Town: David Philip, 1986

H12   HOLM, J. & P. MOLUTSI (eds.) *Democracy in Botswana* Gaborone: Macmillan, 1989

H13   JOHNSON, P. & D. MARTIN *Destructive Engagement: Southern Africa at War* Harare: Zimbabwe Publishing House, 1986

H14   LIBBY, R. T. *The Politics of Economic Power in Southern Africa* Princeton: Princeton U.P., 1987

H15   LODGE, T. *Black Politics in South Africa since 1945* London: Longman, 1983

H16   LODGE, T. &c. *All Here and Now: Black Politics in South Africa in the 1980s* New York: Ford Foundation & Cape Town: David Philip, 1992

H17   LONSDALE, J. (ed.) *South Africa in Question* London: James Currey & Portsmouth, N.H.: Heinemann, 1988

H18   MAGUBANE, B. M. *The Political Economy of Race and Class in South Africa* New York: Monthly Review, 1979

H19   MARTIN, D. & P. JOHNSON *The Struggle for Zimbabwe: the Chimurenga War* Harare: Zimbabwe Publishing House, 1981

H20   MARTIN, D. & P. JOHNSON *The Chitepo Assassination* Harare: Zimbabwe Publishing House, 1985

H21   MBEKI, G. *Learning from Robben Island* London: James Currey, Cape Town: David Philip & Athens, Ohio: Ohio U.P., 1991

H22   MEREDITH, M. *The Past is Another Country: Rhodesia U.D.I. to Zimbabwe* London: Andre Deutsch, 1979

H23   MOORCROFT, P. & P. McLAUGHLIN *Chimurenge! The War in Rhodesia 1965-80* Johannesburg: Sygma/Collins, 1982

H24   NKOMO, J. *Nkomo: the Story of My Life* London: Methuen, 1984

H25   PICARD, L. A. (ed.) *The Evolution of Modern Botswana: Politics and Rural Development of Development in Southern Africa* Lincoln: U. Nebraska Press & London: Rex Collings, 1985

H26   PITYANA, B. &c. *Bounds of Possibility: the Legacy of Steve Biko and Black Consciousness* London: Zed & Cape Town: David Philip, 1991

H27   RANGER, T. O. *Peasant Consciousness and Guerrilla War in Zimbabwe* London: James Currey, Harare: Zimbabwe Publishing House & Berkeley: U. California Press, 1985

H28   SACHS, A. *The Soft Vengeance of a Freedom Fighter* Cape Town: David Philip & London: Grafton, 1990

H29   SAMPSON, A. *Black and Gold: Tycoons, Revolutionaries and Apartheid* London: Hodder & Stoughton, 1987

H30   SMITH, D. & C. SIMPSON *Mugabe* Salisbury: Pioneer Head, 1981

H31   SOUTH AFRICAN HISTORY ARCHIVE, Poster Book Collective *Images of Defiance: South African Resistance Posters of the 1980s* Johannesburg: Ravan, 1992

H32   SOUTHALL, R. *South Africa's Transkei: the Political Economy of an 'Independent' Bantustan* London: Heinemann, 1982

H33   STADLER, A. *The Political Economy of Modern South Africa*

Cape Town: David Philip & London: Croom Helm, 1987

H34 STONEMAN, C. & I. CLIFFE *Zimbabwe Politics, Economics and Society* London & New York: Pinter, 1989

H35 STREEK, B. & R. WICK-STEED *Render unto Kaiser: a Transkei Dossier* Johannesburg: Ravan, 1982

H36 THOMPSON, C. B. *Challenge to Imperialism: the Frontline States in the Liberation of Zimbabwe* Harare: Zimbabwe Publishing House, 1985

Journals

J1 *Africa Contemporary Record* London: Rex Collings, annual

J2 *Africa Perspective* Johannesburg: Witwatersrand U., semi-annual

J3 *Africa South, the News-Magazine of Southern Africa* Harare & Johannesburg, monthly

J4 *African Affairs* London: Royal African Society, x4 a year

J5 *African Archaeological Review* Cambridge: Cambridge U.P., annual

J6 *African Economic History* Madison: U. Wisconsin, African Studies Program, annual

J7 *Africana Notes and News* Johannesburg: Public Library, x2 a year

J8 *Azania* [Archaeological Journal] Nairobi: British Institute in Eastern Africa, annual

J9 *Botswana Notes and Records* Gaborone: Botswana Society, annual

J10 *The Digging Stick (Newsletter)* Vlaeberg, Cape: SA Archaeological Society, x2 a year

J11 *History in Africa* Madison: U. Wisconsin, African Studies Program, annual

J12 *History in Zambia* Lusaka: U. Zambia, Dept. History, semi-annual

J13 *International Journal of African Historical Studies* Boston: U. Boston, African Studies Center, x4 a year

J14 *Journal of African History* Cambridge: Cambridge U.P., x4 a year

J15 *Journal of Contemporary African Studies* Pretoria: Afrika Instituut & Grahamstown: Rhodes U., x2 a year

J16 *Journal of Imperial & Commonwealth History* London, x2 a year

J17 *Journal of Natal and Zulu History* Durban: U. Natal, Dept. History, annual

J18 *Journal of Southern African Studies* Oxford: Oxford U.P., x4 a year

J19 *Mohlomi, Journal of South-ern African History* Roma: National U. of Lesotho, semi-annual

J20 *Social Dynamics* Rondelosch, Cape: U. Cape Town, x2 a year

J21 *Societies of Southern Africa in the 19th and 20th Centuries* London: U. London, Institute of Commonwealth Studies, annual

J22 *South African Archaeological Bulletin* Claremont, Cape: SA Archaeological Society, x2 a year

J23 *South African Historical Journal* Pretoria: Unisa, Dept. History, x2 a year

J24 *Southern Africa, Political & Economic Monthly* Harare: SAPES Trust, monthly

J25 *Southern African Economist* Harare: SADCC Press, x6 a year

J26 *Southern African Review of Books* Bellville: U. Western Cape, x3 a year

J27 *Survey of Race Relations in South Africa* Johannesburg: SA Institute of Race Relations, annual

J28 *Transafrican Journal of History* Nairobi: Gideon Were, annual

J29 *Zimbabwe History* Harare: U. Zimbabwe, Dept. Hist. semi-annual

Index